/ D. Watkins

D1744012

THE
LAWYER'S REMEMBRANCER
1977

THE

LAWYER'S REMEMBRANCER

Revised and Edited for the Year

1977

By

G. R. N. CUSWORTH, M.A.

LONDON

BUTTERWORTHS

1976

Dies Memorandi, etc.

LAW SITTINGS, 1977

Hilary Sittings begin Jan. 11 and end April 6; *Easter Sittings* begin April 19 and end June 3; *Trinity Sittings* begin June 14 and end July 31; *Michaelmas Sittings* begin Oct. 1 and end Dec. 21.

UNIVERSITY FULL TERMS, 1977

OXFORD: Hilary Term, Jan 16 to March 12; Trinity Term, April 24 to June 18; Michaelmas Term, Oct. 9 to Dec. 3.

CAMBRIDGE: Lent Term, Jan. 11 to March 11; Easter Term, April 19 to June 10; Michaelmas Term, Oct. 4 to Dec. 2.

FASTS, FESTIVALS, &c., 1977

Epiphany	..	..	.. Jan. 6	Spring Bank Holiday .. June 6
Ash Wednesday	..		.. Feb. 23	Silver Jubilee Bank Holiday June 7
St. David's Day	..		.. Mar. 1	Queen's Official Birthday .. June 14
St. Patrick's Day	..		.. Mar. 17	Summer Bank Holiday .. Aug. 29
Good Friday	..		.. Apr. 8	Remembrance Sunday .. Nov. 13
Easter Day	..		.. Apr. 10	St. Andrew's Day .. Nov. 30
Easter Monday	..		.. Apr. 11	First Sunday in Advent .. Nov. 27
Queen's Birthday	..		.. April 21	Christmas Day (Sun.) .. Dec. 25
St. George's Day	..		.. April 23	Boxing Day (Mon.) .. Dec. 26
Ascension Day	..		.. May 19	Sundays after Trinity .. xxiv
Whit Sunday	..		.. May 29	

Quarter Days: March 25, June 24, Sept. 29, Dec. 25.

Half Quarter Days: Feb. 8, May 9, Aug. 11, Nov. 11.

Scots Terms: Candlemas, Feb. 2; Whitsunday, May 15; Lammas, Aug. 1; Martinmas, Nov. 11. Scots Removal Terms: May 28 and Nov. 28.

MISCELLANEA

Summer Time: in Great Britain and Northern Ireland, one hour in advance of G.M.T. will be kept from Mar. 20th (0200 hrs.) to Oct. 23rd (0200 hrs.) G.M.T.

Brewster Sessions: (the general annual licensing meeting) must be held within the first fourteen days of February (Licensing Act, 1964, Sched. I para. 7).

Solicitors' Certificates: expire Oct. 31 and must be renewed by Dec. 31.

Close Times: Grouse—Dec. 11 to Aug. 1, Partridge—Feb. 2 to Aug. 31, Pheasant —Feb. 2 to Sept. 30. It is also unlawful to kill these birds on a Sunday or Christmas Day.

Calendar for 1977

	JANUARY						FEBRUARY						MARCH				
Sun.	. 2	9	16	23	30	. .	6	13	20	27	. .	6	13	20	27
Mon.	. **3**	10	17	24	31	. .	7	14	21	28	. .	7	14	21	28
Tues.	. 4	11	18	25	..	. 1	8	15	22	..	. 1	8	15	22	29
Wed.	. 5	12	19	26	..	. 2	9	16	23	..	. 2	9	16	23	30
Thu.	. 6	13	20	27	..	. 3	10	17	24	..	. 3	10	17	24	31
Fri.	. 7	14	21	28	..	. 4	11	18	25	..	. 4	**11**	18	25	..
Sat.	1 8	15	22	29	..	. 5	12	19	26	..	. 5	12	19	26	..

	APRIL					MAY						JUNE				
Sun.	. .	3	10	17	24	. 1	8	15	22	29	. .	5	12	19	26
Mon.	. .	4	**11**	18	25	. 2	9	16	23	**30**	. .	**6**	13	20	27
Tues.	. .	5	12	19	26	. 3	10	17	24	31	. .	**7**	14	21	28
Wed.	. .	6	13	20	27	. 4	11	18	25	..	. 1	8	15	22	29
Thu.	. .	7	14	21	28	. 5	12	19	26	..	. 2	9	16	23	30
Fri.	. 1	**8**	15	22	29	. 6	13	20	27	..	. 3	10	17	24	..
Sat.	. 2	9	16	23	30	. 7	14	21	28	..	. 4	11	18	25	..

	JULY					AUGUST					SEPTEMBER				
Sun.	. 3	10	17	24	31	. .	7	14	21	28	. .	4	11	18	25
Mon.	. 4	11	18	25	..	. 1	8	15	22	**29**	. .	5	12	19	26
Tues.	. 5	12	19	26	..	. 2	9	16	23	30	. .	6	13	20	27
Wed.	. 6	13	20	27		. 3	10	17	24	31	. .	7	14	21	28
Thu.	. 7	14	21	28	..	. 4	11	18	25	..	. 1	8	15	22	29
Fri.	1 8	15	22	29	..	. 5	12	19	26	..	. 2	9	16	23	30
Sat.	2 9	16	23	30	..	. 6	13	20	27	..	. 3	10	17	24	..

	OCTOBER					NOVEMBER					DECEMBER				
Sun.	. 2	9	16	23	30	. .	6	13	20	27	. .	4	11	18	**25**
Mon.	. 3	10	17	24	31	. .	7	14	21	28	. .	5	12	19	**26**
Tues.	. 4	11	18	25	..	. 1	8 .	15	22	29	. .	6	13	20	**27**
Wed.	. 5	12	19	26	..	. 2	9	16	23	30	. .	7	14	21	28
Thu.	. 6	13	20	27	..	. 3	10	17	24	..	. 1	8	15	22	29
Fri.	. 7	14	21	28	..	. 4	11	18	25	..	. 2	9	16	23	30
Sat.	1 8	15	22	29	..	. 5	12	19	26	..	. 3	10	17	24	31

Note.—Good Friday, Christmas Day and Bank Holidays are indicated by **heavy type**

Calendars for Last Year and Next Year

1976

	JANUARY	FEBRUARY	MARCH	APRIL
S	. . 4 11 18 25	. 1 8 15 22 29	. . 7 14 21 28	. . 4 11 18 25
M	. . 5 12 19 26	. 2 9 16 23 . .	. 1 8 15 22 29	. . 5 12 19 26
T	. . 6 13 20 27	. 3 10 17 24 . .	. 2 9 16 23 30	. . 6 13 20 27
W	. . 7 14 21 28	. 4 11 18 25 . .	. 3 10 17 24 31	. . 7 14 21 28
T	. 1 8 15 22 29	. 5 12 19 26 . .	. 4 11 18 25 . .	. 1 8 15 22 29
F	. 2 9 16 23 30	. 6 13 20 27 . .	. 5 12 19 26 . .	. 2 9 16 23 30
S	. 3 10 17 24 31	. 7 14 21 28 . .	. 6 13 20 27 . .	. 3 10 17 24 . .

	MAY	JUNE	JULY	AUGUST
S	. 2 9 16 23 30	. . 6 13 20 27	. . 4 11 18 25	. 1 8 15 22 29
M	. 3 10 17 24 31	. . 7 14 21 28	. . 5 12 19 26	. 2 9 16 23 30
T	. 4 11 18 25 . .	. 1 8 15 22 29	. . 6 13 20 27	. 3 10 17 24 31
W	. 5 12 19 26 . .	. 2 9 16 23 30	. . 7 14 21 28	. 4 11 18 25 . .
T	. 6 13 20 27 . .	. 3 10 17 24 . .	. 1 8 15 22 29	. 5 12 19 26 . .
F	. 7 14 21 28 . .	. 4 11 18 25 . .	. 2 9 16 23 30	. 6 13 20 27 . .
S	1 8 15 22 29 . .	. 5 12 19 26 . .	. 3 10 17 24 31	. 7 14 21 28 . .

	SEPTEMBER	OCTOBER	NOVEMBER	DECEMBER
S	. . 5 12 19 26	. 3 10 17 24 31	. . 7 14 21 28	. . 5 12 19 26
M	. . 6 13 20 27	. 4 11 18 25 . .	. 1 8 15 22 29	. . 6 13 20 27
T	. . 7 14 21 28	. 5 12 19 26 . .	. 2 9 16 23 30	. . 7 14 21 28
W	. 1 8 15 22 29	. 6 13 20 27 . .	. 3 10 17 24 . .	. 1 8 15 22 29
T	. 2 9 16 23 30	. 7 14 21 28 . .	. 4 11 18 25 . .	. 2 9 16 23 30
F	. 3 10 17 24 . .	1 8 15 22 29 . .	. 5 12 19 26 . .	. 3 10 17 24 31
S	. 4 11 18 25 . .	2 9 16 23 30 . .	. 6 13 20 27 . .	. 4 11 18 25 . .

1978

	JANUARY	FEBRUARY	MARCH	APRIL
S	. 1 8 15 22 29	. . 5 12 19 26	. . 5 12 19 26	. 2 9 16 23 30
M	. 2 9 16 23 30	. . 6 13 20 27	. . 6 13 20 27	. 3 10 17 24 . .
T	. 3 10 17 24 31	. . 7 14 21 28	. . 7 14 21 28	. 4 11 18 25 . .
W	. 4 11 18 25 . .	. 1 8 15 22 . .	. 1 8 15 22 29	. 5 12 19 26 . .
T	. 5 12 19 26 . .	. 2 9 16 23 . .	. 2 9 16 23 30	. 6 13 20 27 . .
F	. 6 13 20 27 . .	. 3 10 17 24 . .	. 3 10 17 24 31	. 7 14 21 28 . .
S	. 7 14 21 28 . .	. 4 11 18 25 . .	. 4 11 18 25 . .	1 8 15 22 29 . .

	MAY	JUNE	JULY	AUGUST
S	. . 7 14 21 28	. . 4 11 18 25	. 2 9 16 23 30	. . 6 13 20 27
M	. 1 8 15 22 29	. . 5 12 19 26	. 3 10 17 24 31	. . 7 14 21 28
T	. 2 9 16 23 30	. . 6 13 20 27	. 4 11 18 25 . .	. 1 8 15 22 29
W	. 3 10 17 24 31	. . 7 14 21 28	. 5 12 19 26 . .	. 2 9 16 23 30
T	. 4 11 18 25 . .	. 1 8 15 22 29	. 6 13 20 27 . .	. 3 10 17 24 31
F	. 5 12 19 26 . .	. 2 9 16 23 30	. 7 14 21 28 . .	. 4 11 18 25 . .
S	. 6 13 20 27 . .	. 3 10 17 24 . .	1 8 15 22 29 . .	. 5 12 19 26 . .

	SEPTEMBER	OCTOBER	NOVEMBER	DECEMBER
S	. 3 10 17 24 . .	. 1 8 15 22 29	. . 5 12 19 26	. 3 10 17 24 31
M	. 4 11 18 25 . .	. 2 9 16 23 30	. . 6 13 20 27	. 4 11 18 25 . .
T	. 5 12 19 26 . .	. 3 10 17 24 31	. . 7 14 21 28	. 5 12 19 26 . .
W	. 6 13 20 27 . .	. 4 11 18 25 . .	. 1 8 15 22 29	. 6 13 20 27 . .
T	. 7 14 21 28 . .	. 5 12 19 26 . .	. 2 9 16 23 30	. 7 14 21 28 . .
F	1 8 15 22 29 . .	. 6 13 20 27 . .	. 3 10 17 24 . .	1 8 15 22 29 . .
S	2 9 16 23 30 . .	. 7 14 21 28 . .	. 4 11 18 25 . .	2 9 16 23 30 . .

Sunrise and Sunset at London

Day am pm	Day am pm	Day am pm	Day am pm	Day am pm
JAN. 2 0806-1603	9 0804-1612	16 0759-1622	23 0752-1634	30 0742-1646
FEB. 6 0731-1659	13 0719-1712	20 0705-1725	27 0651-1737	
MAR. 6 0635-1749	13 0620-1802	20 0704-1914	27 0648-1925	
APR. 3 0632-1937	10 0616-1949	17 0601-2000	24 0547-2012	
MAY 1 0533-2024	8 0520-2035	15 0509-2046	22 0500-2056	29 0452-2105
JUNE 5 0446-2112	12 0443-2118	19 0443-2121	26 0445-2122	
JULY 3 0449-2120	10 0455-2116	17 0503-2110	24 0512-2101	31 0522-2051
AUG. 7 0533-2039	14 0544-2025	21 0555-2011	28 0606-1956	
SEPT. 4 0618-1941	11 0629-1925	18 0640-1909	25 0651-1853	
OCT. 2 0703-1837	9 0714-1821	16 0726-1806	23 0638-1651	30 0650-1638
NOV. 6 0703-1625	13 0715-1614	20 0727-1605	27 0738-1558	
DEC. 4 0748-1554	11 0756-1552	18 0802-1552	25 0806-1556	

N.B. These times are in G.M.T., except between 0200 on Mar. 20 and 0200 on Oct. 23, when the times are in B.S.T. (1 hour in advance of G.M.T.)

Phases of the Moon 1977

	New Moon				First Quarter				Full Moon				Last Quarter	
	D	H	M		D	H	M		D	H	M		D	H	M
								JAN.	5	12	10	JAN.	12	19	55
JAN.	19	14	11	JAN.	27	05	11	FEB.	4	03	56	FEB.	11	04	07
FEB.	18	03	37	FEB.	26	02	50	MAR.	5	17	13	MAR.	12	11	35
MAR.	19	18	33	MAR.	27	22	27	APR.	4	04	09	APR.	10	19	15
APR.	18	10	35	APR.	26	14	42	MAY	3	13	03	MAY	10	04	08
MAY	18	02	51	MAY	26	03	20	JUNE	1	20	31	JUNE	8	15	07
JUNE	16	18	23	JUNE	24	12	44	JULY	1	03	24	JULY	8	04	39
JULY	16	08	37	JULY	23	19	38	JULY	30	10	52	AUG.	6	20	40
AUG.	14	21	31	AUG.	22	01	04	AUG.	28	20	10	SEPT.	5	14	33
SEPT.	13	09	23	SEPT.	20	06	18	SEPT.	27	08	17	OCT.	5	09	21
OCT.	12	20	31	OCT.	19	12	46	OCT.	26	23	35	NOV.	4	03	58
NOV.	11	07	09	NOV.	17	21	52	NOV.	25	17	31	DEC.	3	21	16
DEC.	10	17	33	DEC.	17	10	37	DEC.	25	12	49				

The figures printed above are reproduced, with permission, from data supplied by H.M. Nautical Almanac Office, for the Science Research Council.

General Holidays, 1976–1981

Year	Easter Monday	Spring Bank Holiday	Summer Bank Holiday	Chr. Day	Year	Easter Monday	Spring Bank Holiday	Summer Bank Holiday	Chr. Day
1976	Apr. 19	May 31	Aug. 30	Sat.	1979	Apr. 16	May 28	Aug. 27	Tu.
1977	Apr. 11	June 6–7	Aug. 29	Sun	1980	Apr. 6	May 26	Aug. 25	Th.
1978	Mar. 27	May 29	Aug. 28	Mon	1981	Apr. 20	May 25	Aug. 31	Fri.

Note. The dates of Spring and Summer Bank Holidays in England and Wales are fixed by the Banking and Financial Dealings Act 1971.

Postal Information

LETTER POST

Not over	First Class	Second Class
60 g (2.1 oz.)	8½	6½
100 g (3.5 oz.)	11½	9
150 g (5.3 oz.)	15	11
200 g (7.1 oz.)	18½	14
250 g (8.8 oz.)	22	17
300 g (10.6 oz.)	25½	20
350 g (12.3 oz.)	29	23
400 g (14.1 oz.)	32½	26
450 g (15.9 oz.)	36	29
500 g (1.1 lb.)	39½	32
750 g (1.7 lb.)	57	47
1000 g. (2.2 lb.)	74½	Not admissible over 750 g.

Each extra 250 g (8·8 oz) 17½p

Rebates. For information about rebates on postings of over 4250 second class items ask at any Head Post Office.

Articles for the Blind. Certain articles for the blind, listed in the Post Office Guide, may be sent free of postage up to a maximum weight of 7 kg.

Certificate of Posting. 1p.

Search Fee. For correspondence addressed to the person making the request (except Poste Restante items) 10p.

PARCEL POST

Not over	Ordinary Parcels	Local Parcels
1 kg. (2.2 lb.)	55	45
2 kg. (4.4 lb.)	70	60
3 kg. (6.6 lb.)	85	75
4 kg. (8.8 lb.)	100	90
5 kg. (11.0 lb.)	110	99
6 kg. (13.2 lb.)	120	109
7 kg. (15.4 lb.)	130	119
8 kg. (17.6 lb.)	140	129
9 kg. (19.8 lb.)	150	139
10 kg. (22.0 lb.)	160	149

Local Parcels. Are those which have in their address the same post town as that of the office of posting. The local rate does not apply within the London postal districts.

Compensation Fee (CF) Parcels

For compensation up to	Fee (in addition to postage)
£10	7p
£50	12p
£100 maximum	20p

Although the Post Office is not legally liable, compensation within the above limits will nevertheless be paid for loss or damage in the post providing all the relevant conditions, including adequate packing, have been met.

Certificate of Posting. For non CF Parcels 1p each (maximum 10p).

Search Fee. For parcels addressed to the person making the request (except Poste Restante items) 10p.

CASH ON DELIVERY

Money collected by the Post Office from the addressee on behalf of the sender of a parcel or registered packet.
Trade charge not over £50 Fee 40p COD items may not be sent by the Second Class Service.

REGISTRATION & RECORDED DELIVERY

Registration First Class Letter Post Only

For compensation up to	Fee (in addition to postage)
£200	45p
£400	50p
£600	55p

Registration is not a safeguard against damage and compensation for this can only be paid if the contents have been adequately packed.

Recorded Delivery. Fee (in addition to first or second class postage) 18p. This service provides a record of posting and delivery, and is especially suitable for documents.

It must not be used for jewellery or money. The fee covers compensation up to £2 maximum. Compensation cannot be paid if the packet contains money or other inadmissible articles.

Advice of Delivery (for registration and recorded delivery services)

requested at time of posting   10p
requested after time of posting   20p

Enquiry Fee.   20p (for enquiry about the loss or non-delivery of a registered or recorded delivery packet, unless the advice of delivery fee has already been paid).

POSTAL & MONEY ORDER

Postal Orders

Value	Fee on each Order
Up to £1	7p
£2 to £10	9p
(in £1 steps)	

Inland Telegraph Money Orders

Value	Fee on each Order
Up to £100 (maximum)	£2.00 (plus Telegraph charges)

EXPRESS POST

Express Messenger all the way. Per mile or part of a mile for single packet 50p; for each additional packet after the first, irrespective of distance 3p. If a taxi or other conveyance has to be used, or other costs have to be incurred, these will be charged at actual cost.

Express Messenger from Delivery Office at Addressee's Request. Per mile or part of a mile for single packet 50p; for every 10 packets or less after the first 2½p. If a taxi or other conveyance has to be used, or other costs have to be incurred, these will be charged at actual cost. This service is available for both First and Second Class letters and packets.

Railex. Conveyance of packets by Post Office messenger to a railway station for despatch by the first available train, and for its delivery by Post Office messenger from station of destination. Charge per packet £4. (Maximum weight is 450 g if posted in Northern Ireland; 60 g elsewhere.)

Special Delivery at Sender's Request. Delivery of packet by Post Office messenger after arrival at the office of delivery, provided it arrives at a time when messengers are available and also provided that this will ensure earlier delivery than by normal postal treatment. In addition to full postage (weekdays) 60p; (where service is provided on Sundays) £1.50. Special delivery packets are sent from the office of posting to the office of delivery in ordinary mails. If a quicker delivery is wanted one of the express services should be used. Not available in Second Class Service. The fee will be refunded on application should the packet receive normal postal treatment.

Miscellaneous Licences

Dog Licence. For dogs over 6 months old (12 months in the case of a hound not yet used for hunting), 37½p. Exemptions for sheep dogs and blind persons' dogs. Issued through P.O. Licences, expire on last day of month preceding month of issue in following year.

Driver's Licence. £5.00 until age of 70. Provisional Licence £1 for 1 year. Obtainable from County Council or County Borough Council Offices. Application form from P.O.

Game Licences. **1.** (Red) To kill game August 1–July 31, £6. **2.** (Green) To kill game August 1–October 31, £4. **3.** (Blue) To kill game November 1–July 31, £4. **4.** Occasional Licence (valid 14 days), £2. **5.** Gamekeeper's Licence £4. Application Form (137G in England and Wales, and 137 in Scotland) must be handed in to P.O. **6.** Game Dealer's Licence, July 2–July 1, £4. Requires grant from Local Authority. Issued through P.O.

Guns. A certificate must be obtained from the local Chief of Police: Shotgun certificate, £2.00, renewal, £1.50. Firearms certificate, £7.00, renewal £4.50. Firearms Dealer's Certificate £20, annual re-registration, £10.

Marriage Licences. Marriages other than Church of England, £8. 1 clear day's notice. Apply local Civil Registrar. Church of England. **1.** Banns read three consecutive weeks before marriage in parishes of bride and groom, £2.00. Certificate of proof of banns having been read £1.50. Marriage Certificate, 50. **2.** Bishop's or Common Licence, £6.50. 15 clear days notice. Apply surrogate. **3.** Archbishop of Canterbury's Licence, £25. Enables marriage to take place in any Church of England church in England and Wales.

Motor Car Licences (Private). £40 p.a., £14.65 for 4 months. (Some small cars excepted).

Radio and Television Receiving Annual Licences. Sound, domestic or car radio; nil. Monochrome T.V. £8, blind persons, £6.75. Colour T.V. £18, blind persons £16.75. Apply P.O. Homes for the aged: 5p per annum for each old person licensed. Apply in writing to local Television Licence Office.

Indices of Prices and Wages; Change in Value of Pound

	PRICES			
	1974 January	1975 January	1976 January	1976 April
General Index of Retail Prices	100.0	119.9	147.9	153.5

	WAGES			
				March
Index of Average Earnings of all employees	100.0	128.8	155.4	160.1

VALUE OF POUND

The Table below shows the sum of money which, in 1920, had internal purchasing power equal to that of £100 in the year in question. *E.g.*, it will be seen that £21 in 1920 had equivalent internal purchasing power to £100 in 1975.

	£		£		£
1920 ..	.. 100	1937 ..	.. 161	1961 ..	.. 54
1921 ..	.. 110	1938 ..	.. 159	1962 ..	.. 52
1922 ..	.. 136	1946 ..	.. 94	1963 ..	.. 51
1923 ..	.. 143	1947 ..	.. 88	1964 ..	.. 50
1924 ..	.. 142	1948 ..	.. 82	1965 ..	.. 47
1925 ..	.. 141	1949 ..	.. 80	1966 ..	.. 46
1926 ..	.. 145	1950 ..	.. 78	1967 ..	.. 44
1927 ..	.. 148	1951 ..	.. 71	1968 ..	.. 42
1928 ..	.. 150	1952 ..	.. 67	1969 ..	.. 40
1929 ..	.. 152	1953 ..	.. 66	1970 ..	.. 38
1930 ..	.. 157	1954 ..	.. 65	1971 ..	.. 35
1931 ..	.. 169	1955 ..	.. 63	1972 ..	.. 32
1932 ..	.. 173	1956 ..	.. 60	1973 ..	.. 30
1933 ..	.. 178	1957 ..	.. 58	1974 ..	.. 26
1934 ..	.. 176	1958 ..	.. 57	1975 ..	.. 21
1935 ..	.. 174	1959 ..	.. 56		
1936 ..	.. 169	1960 ..	.. 56		

Judicial Committee of the Privy Council

OFFICE:—Downing Street, S.W.1

The Judicial Committee of the Privy Council consists of the Lord Chancellor. Lord President, ex-Lords President, the Lords of Appeal in Ordinary, the Lords Justices of the Court of Appeal, and such other members of the Privy Council as shall from time to time hold or have held "High Judicial Office" within the meaning of the Appellate Jurisdiction Acts 1876 and 1887. By virtue of the Judicial Committee Amendment Act 1895 as amended by the Appellate Jurisdiction Act 1908 certain Judges from the Commonwealth are members.

Registrar of the Privy Council:—E. R. MILLS

The Courts of Justice

HOUSE OF LORDS.—The Lords entitled to hear appeals are The Lord High Chancellor, the Lords of Appeal in Ordinary, and Peers who have held high judicial office.

JUDICIAL COMMITTEE OF THE PRIVY COUNCIL.—This consists of The Lord Chancellor, Lord President, ex-Lords President, the Lords of Appeal in Ordinary, the Lords Justices of the Court of Appeal, and such other members of the Privy Council as shall from time to time hold, or have held, high judicial office within the meaning of the Appellate Jurisdiction Acts, 1876 and 1887. *See also* Administration of Justice Act, 1928, s. 13, and Appellate Jurisdiction Act, 1929.

THE SUPREME COURT OF JUDICATURE is divided into the Court of Appeal and the High Court of Justice.

COURT OF APPEAL: *Ex-officio Judges.* The Lord High Chancellor (President), the Lord Chief Justice, the Master of the Rolls, and the President of the Family Division. *Ordinary Judges:* The Master of the Rolls, and not less than 8 or more than 16 Lords Justices.

HIGH COURT OF JUSTICE.

Chancery Division. Judges: The Lord High Chancellor, the Vice-Chancellor and not less than five Justices.

Queen's Bench Division. Judges: The Lord Chief Justice and not less than 17 Justices.
Commercial Court.
Admiralty Court.

Family Division. The Lord Chancellor will nominate High Court Judges to sit in these courts.

The Judges and Lords of Appeal

Lord High Chancellor.
  Rt. Hon. Lord Elwyn-Jones (1974)

Lords of Appeal in Ordinary.
  Wilberforce (1964)
  Diplock (1968)
  Dilhorne (1969)
  Simon (1971)
  Kilbrandon (1971)
  Salmon (1972)
  Edmund-Davies (1974)
  Fraser (1975)
  Russell (1975)

Lord Chief Justice of England.
  Rt. Hon. Lord Widgery (1971).

Master of the Rolls.
  Rt. Hon. Lord Denning (1962) (*Judge Q.B.D.*, 1944, *L.J.*, 1948 *Ld. of Appeal in Ord.*, 1957).

President of the Family Division.
  Rt. Hon. Sir George Baker.

Lords Justices
  John Megaw (*Judge Q.B.D.*, 1961 *L.J.*, 1969).
  Denys Burton Buckley (*Judge Ch.D.*, 1960, *L.J.*, 1970).
  David Arnold Scott Cairns (*Judge P.D.A.*, 1960, *L.J.*, 1971).

Edward Blanshard Stamp (*Judge Ch.D.*, 1964, *L.J.*, 1971).
John Frederick Eustace Stephenson (*Judge Q.B.D.*, 1962, *L.J.*, 1971).
Alan Stewart Orr (*Judge P.D.A.*, 1965, *L.J.*, 1971).
Eustace Wentworth Roskill (*Judge Q.B.D.*, 1962, *L.J.*, 1971).
Frederick Horace Lawton (*Judge Q.B.D.*, 1961, *L.J.*, 1972).
Leslie George Scarman (*Judge F.D.*, 1961, *L.J.*, 1973).
Roger Fray Greenwood Ormrod (*Judge F.D.*, 1961, *L.J.*, 1974).
Patrick Reginald Evelyn Browne (*Judge Q.B.D.*, 1965, *L.J.*, 1974).
Geoffrey Dawson Lane (*Judge Q.B.D.*, 1966, *L.J.*, 1974).
Reginald William Goff (*Judge Ch.D.*, 1965, *L.J.*, 1975).
Nigel Cyprian Bridge (*Judge Q.B.D.*, 1968, *L.J.*, 1975).
Sebag Shaw (*Judge Q.B.D.*, 1968, *L.J.*, 1975).
George Stanley Waller (*Judge Q.B.D.* 1965, *L.J.*, 1976).

Clerks to Lords Justices. Room 135A, East Wing, Royal Courts of Justice, Strand, W.C.2.

Justices, Chancery Division.
 Robert Edgar Megarry *Vice-Chancellor* (1976).
 John Patrick Graham (1969).
 Peter Harry Batson Woodroffe Foster (1969).
 John Norman Keates Whitford (1969).
 John Anson Brightman (1970).
 Ernest Irvine Goulding (1971).
 Sydney William Templeman (1972).
 Raymond Henry Walton (1973).
 Peter Raymond Oliver (1974).
 Michael John Fox (1975).
 Christopher John Slade (1976).

Justices, Queen's Bench Division
 Aubrey Melford Steed Stevenson (1957).
 Gerald Alfred Thesiger (1958).
 Basil Edward Nield (1960).
 Bernard Joseph Maxwell MacKenna (1961).
 Alan Abraham Mocatta (1961).
 John Thompson (1961).
 Helenus Partick Joseph Milmo (1964).
 Joseph Donaldson Cantley (1965).
 Hugh Eames Park (1965).
 Ralph Vincent Cusack (1966).
 Stephen Chapman (1966).
 John Ramsay Willis (1966).
 Graham Russell Swanwick (1966).
 Patrick McCarthy O'Connor (1966).
 John Francis Donaldson (1966).
 John Robertson Dunn Crichton (1967).
 Samuel Burgess Ridgway Cooke (1967).
 Bernard Caulfield (1968).
 Hilary Gwynne Talbot (1968).
 Edward Walter Eveleigh (1968).
 William Lloyd Mars-Jones (1969).
 Ralph Kilner Brown (1969).

Philip Wien (1970).
Peter Henry Rowley Bristow (1970).
Hugh Harry Valentine Forbes (1970).
Desmond James Conrad Ackner (1971).
William Hugh Griffiths (1971).
Robert Hugh Mais (1971).
Neil Lawson (1971).
David Powell Croom-Johnson (1971).
Tasker Watkins (1971).
John Raymond Phillips (1971).
Leslie Kenneth Edward Boreham (1972).
John Douglas May (1972).
Michael Robert Emmanuel Kerr (1972).
Alfred William Michael Davies (1973).
John Dexter Stocker (1973).
Kenneth George Illtyd Jones (1974).
Peter Richard Pain (1975).
Kenneth Graham Jupp (1976).
John Francis Scott Cobb (1976).
Robert Lionel Archibald Goff (1976).
Gordon Slynn (1976).

Justices, Family Division
 Charles William Stanley Rees (1962).
 Reginald Withers Payne (1962).
 Neville Major Ginner Faulks (1963).
 James Rousaleyn Cumming-Bruce (1964).
 John Brinsmead Latey (1965).
 Elizabeth Kathleen Lane (1965).
 Henry Vivian Brandon (1966).
 Robin Horace Walford Dunn (1969).
 William Arthur Bagnall (1970).
 Alfred Kenneth Hollings (1971).
 John Lewis Arnold.
 Charles Trevor Reece (1973).
 Francis Brooks Purchas (1974).
 Haydn Tudor Evans (1974).
 Rose Heilbron (1974).
 Stephen Brown (1975).

Presiding Judges

South Eastern Circuit
 The Rt. Hon. the Lord Chief Justice of England.
 The Hon. Mr. Justice Eveleigh.
 The Hon. Mr. Justice Stocker, M.C.

Midland & Oxford Circuit
 The Hon. Mr. Justice Swanwick, M.B.E.
 The Hon. Mr. Justice May.

North Eastern Circuit
 The Hon. Mr. Justice Boreham.
 The Hon. Mr. Justice Cobb.

Northern Circuit
 The Hon. Mr. Justice Hollings, M.C.
 The Hon. Mr. Justice Caulfield.

Wales & Chester Circuit
 The Hon. Mr. Justice Watkins, V.C.
 The Hon. Mr. Justice Wier.

Western Circuit
 The Hon. Mr. Justice Dunn, M.C.
 The Hon. Mr. Justice Ackner.

THE CIRCUITS

MIDLAND AND OXFORD. Cambridge-shire (that part of the county which was formerly the county of Hunting-don and Peterborough; remainder in the South Eastern Circuit); Derbyshire (the Petty Sessional Division of Glossop to commit to centres in the Northern Circuit. The Petty Sessional Division of High Peak to have discretion to commit to centres in The Midland & Oxford Circuit or to centres in the Northern Circuit, Hereford and Worcester; Humberside (that part of the county which was formerly in Lincolnshire, including the former County Borough of Grimsby; remainder in the North Eastern Circuit. The Petty Sess-ional Division ,of Epworth and Gode to commit to centres in the North Eastern Circuit); Leicester-shire; Lincolnshire; Northampton-shire; Nottinghamshire; Oxfordshire; (The Petty Sessional Division of Henly to commit to Reading in the South Eastern Circuit); Salop; Staffordshire; Warwickshire; West Midlands.

NORTH EASTERN. Cleveland, Durham, N. Humberside (the whole county with the exception of that part which was formerly in Lincolnshire and which remains in the Midland and Oxford circuit); Northumberland; North Yorkshire; South Yorkshire; Tyne and Wear; West Yorkshire.

NORTHERN. Cumbria, Greater Man-chester, Lancashire, Merseyside.

SOUTH EASTERN. Bedfordshire, Berk-shire, Buckinghamshire (Class 1, 2 and 3 cases from the Petty Sessional Divisions of Fenny Stratford, New-port Pagnell and Stony Stratford to be committed to Northampton), Cambridgeshire (the whole county except that part which was formerly the county of Huntingdon and Peterborough and which remains in the Midland and Oxford circuit), East Sussex, Essex, Greater London, Hertfordshire, Kent, Norfolk, Suf-folk, Surrey, West Sussex.

WALES AND CHESTER. Cheshire (except those parts shown in the Northern circuit), Clwyd, Dyfed, Gwent, Gwynedd, Mid-Glamorgan, Powys, South Glamorgan, West Glamorgan.

WESTERN. Avon, Cornwall, Devon, Dorset, Gloucestershire, Hampshire, Isle of Wight, Somerset, Wiltshire.

Circuit Judges

Abdela, T.D., Q.C. (SE)
Allardice (M & O)
Anwyl-Davies, Q.C. (SE)
Argyle, M.C., Q.C. (SE)
Arthur, DFC (N)
Babington (SE)
Bailey (N)
Baker (SE)
Barr (SE)
Bax, Q.C. (SE)
Beaumont, M.B.E. (NE)
Beezley (SE)
Bennett, Q.C. (NE)
Best (W)
Bingham, T.D., Q.C. (N)
Blackett-Ord, Vice-Chancellor of the County Palatine of Lancaster (N)

Blaker, Q.C. (W)
Blomefield (SE)
Bolland (SE)
Booth (N)
Booth, Q.C. (N)
Braithwaite (SE)
Brodrick, Q.C. (W)
Buckee, D.S.O. (SE)
Bulger (W)
Burrell, Q.C. (W & C)
Bush (M & O)
Buzzard (SE)
Callman (SE)
Campbell, Q.C. (SE)
Sir Harold Cassel, Bart., T.D., Q.C. (SE)
Cassels, T.D. (SE)
Chapman, Q.C. (NE)
Chetwynd-Talbot (M & O)
Chope (W)
Clapham (SE)
Leo Clark, Q.C. (M & O)

Clarke, Q.C. (SE)
Clarke (W)
Clover, T.D., Q.C. (SE)
Cohen, Myrella, Q.C. (NE)
Her Honour Judge Patricia Coles, Q.C. (SE)
Collinson (N)
Coplestone-Boughey (SE)
Corcoran (SE)
Corley (SE)
Cotton (NE)
Counsell (SE)
Cox (W)
Crocker (SE)
Cunliffe, Christopher (SE)
Curtis (N)
Curtis-Raleigh (SE)
da Cunha (N)

David, Q.C., D.L. (W & C)
Davies, Q.C. (N)
Davison (M & O)
Dean, Q.C. (NE)
Joseph Dean (SE)
Dewar (SE)
Dewhurst (N)
Dow (SE)
Dunboyne, Lord (SE)
Edie (SE)
Edmondson (N)
Elder-Jones (W)
Ellis (M & O)
Ellison, V.R.D. (SE)
Evans, Meurig (W & C)
Everett, Q.C. (SE)
Fay, Q.C. (SE)
Fife, M.C., T.D. (SE)
Figgis (SE)
Finestein, Q.C. (SE)
Bernard Finlay, Q.C. (SE)
John Finlay, Q.C. (SE)
FitzHugh, Q.C. (N)
Forrest (W)
Forrest, Haddow, Q.C. (SE)
Forrester-Paton, Q.C. (NE)
Francis (W & C)
Franks (N)
Freeman (SE)
Friend (SE)
Gage (M & O)
Garrard (M & O)
Gerrard (N)
Gibbens (SE)
Gibbens, Brian, Q.C. (SE)
Gill (NE)
Gillis, Q.C. (SE)
Goodall, M.C. (W)
Gosnay (NE)
Gower, Q.C. (SE)
Grant, D.S.O., Q.C. (SE)
Grant, Brian (SE)
Green (M & O)
Greenwood (SE)
Grieves, Q.C. (SE)
Griffith-Jones, M.C., Common Serjeant (SE)
Griffiths, Q.C. (W & C)
Graham Hall (SE)
Hall (NE)
Hammerton (SE)
Harrison-Hall (M & O)

Hartley (NE)
Hayman (SE)
Head (SE)
Heald (M & O)
Heron (M & O)
Hickman (SE)
Hill-Smith, V.R.D. (SE)
Hill Starforth, Q.C. (W)
Hinchliffe, Q.C. (N)
Hines, Q.C. (SE)
Hobson (SE)
Holdsworth, Q.C. (SE)
Honig (SE)
Hughes (SE)
Hughes, Morgan (W & C)
Hurwitz (NE)
Hutchinson (M & O)
Irvine (M & O)
Jalland (N)
James, Ewart (W)
Johnson (NE)
Jones (N)
Jones, Geoffrey (M & O)
Karmel, Q.C. (SE)
Kee (SE)
Kellock, Q.C. (M & O)
Kershaw (W)
Henry Kershaw (N)
King (W)
King-Hamilton, Q.C. (SE)
Kingham (SE)
Laughton-Scott, Q.C. (SE)
Lauriston, Q.C. (NE)
Lavington, M.B.E. (W)
Lawson, Q.C. (SE)
Lawton (N)
Layton (SE)
Lea, Christopher, M.C. (SE)
Lee, D.S.C., Q.C. (W)
Lee, John (M & O)
Leech (N)
Leonard (SE)
Lermon, Q.C. (SE)
Leslie (SE)
Lewis, Bernard (SE)
Lewis, Daly (M & O)
Lewis, Sir Ian (W)
Lewisohn (SE)
Lipfriend (SE)
Llewellyn (SE)
Llewellyn, Seys (W & C)
Lloyd (M & O)

Lloyd-Jones, V.R.D. (W & C)
Lonsdale (SE)
Lovegrove, Q.C. (SE)
Her Honour Judge Lowry (SE)
Lyall Wilkes (NE)
Lymbery, Q.C. (SE)
Sir Rudolph Lyons, The Recorder of Liverpool (N)
McCreery, Q.C. (W)
Macdonald (W)
McDonnell, O.B.E. (SE)
Macgregor (M & O)
McIntyre, Q.C. (SE)
McKinnon, Q.C. (SE)
McLellan (W)
MacManus, T.D., Q.C. (SE)
Macnair (SE)
Main, Q.C. (W)
Marnan, M.B.E., Q.C. (SE)
Martin, Q.C. (SE)
Mason, Q.C. (SE)
Mendl (SE)
Milner (NE)
Miskin, Q.C., The Recorder of London (SE)
Monier-Williams (SE)
Morgan, Hopkin, Q.C. (W & C)
Morris, Gwyn, Q.C. (SE)
Morris, Sir William, The Recorder of Manchester (N)
Morton, T.D. (SE)
Moylan (SE)
Murchie (SE)
Mynett, Q.C. (M & O)
Nance (N)
Nevin, T.D. (NE)
Noakes (SE)
Northcote (M & O)
Norwood (SE)
Oddie (SE)
Olson (SE)
Openshaw, D.L. (N)
Parnall (SE)
Paterson (N)
Pears (NE)
Peck (SE)
Pennant (W)
Perks, M.C., T.D., (SE)
Perret (M & O)
Petre (SE)
Phelan (SE)

Pickering (SE)
Pigot, Q.C. (N)
Pitchford (W & C)
Polson, Q.C. (W)
Potter (SE)
Powell (W & C)
Prestt, Q.C. (N)
Price, Stanley, Q.C. (NE)
Randolph (NE)
Ranking (SE)
Rees, Geraint (SE)
Richards, Bertrand (SE)
Richards, Norman, O.B.E., Q.C. (SE)
ap Robert (W & C)
Pickles (NE)
Ross, Q.C. (M & O)
Rowland (SE)
Rubin (SE)
Russell (W)
Rutter (W & C)
Ruttle (SE)
Salmon, Q.C. (SE)
Scarlett (SE)
Scott, Q.C. (NE)
Sellers, V.R.D. (SE)

Sharp, M.B.E., Q.C., D.L. (NE)
Sheldon (W)
Sime, M.B.E., Q.C. (M & O)
Skinner, Q.C. (M & O)
Slack, Granville (SE)
Sleeman (M & O)
Smith, Q.C. (NE)
Smith, Dennis (SE)
Smith, Mark (SE)
Smithies (W)
Solomon (SE)
Stabb, Q.C. (SE)
Stansfield (N)
Stephen (NE)
David Stinson (SE)
Stock, Q.C. (W)
Stockdale (SE)
Stockdale, Eric (SE)
Streeter (SE)
Stroyan, Q.C. (NE)
Stucley, D.S.C. (SE)
Suddards (NE)
Sumner, O.B.E., Q.C. (SE)
Sunderland, D.L. (M & O)

Sutcliffe, Q.C. (SE)
Taylor, Q.C. (M & O)
Thomas, M.B.E. (SE)
Toyn (M & O)
Trapnell (SE)
Turner (SE)
Verney, T.D. (SE)
Vick (SE)
Vowden, Q.C. (W)
Wakley, M.B.E. (SE)
Walker (NE)
Wallis-Jones (W & C)
Ward (SE)
West-Russell (SE)
White (SE)
Wickham (M & O)
Wild (SE)
Willcock, Q.C. (W)
Williams (SE)
Willis, T.D. (SE)
Willis, Brooke (M & O)
Wingate, Q.C. (SE)
Wood (N)
Woods (M & O)
Woolley (W & C)
Youds (SE)
Zigmond (N)

Recorders

F. J. Aglionby
J. D. Alliott, Q.C.
B. J. Appleby, Q.C.
J. F. A. Archer, Q.C.
P. Ashworth, Q.C.
T. G. F. Atkinson
P. Back, Q.C.
G. Baker, Q.C.
J. B. Baker, Q.C.
P. M. Baker, Q.C.
D. A. Barker, Q.C.
D. Barker
J. M. A. Barker
R. O Barlow
A. R. Barrowclough, Q.C.
P. M. Beard
C. O. M. Bedingfield, T.D., Q.C.
A. R. A. Beldam, Q.C.
A. W. Bell
P. Bennett, Q.C.
R. H. Bernstein, D.F.C., Q.C.
J. C. Beveridge
T. H. Bingham, Q.C.

G. J. Black, D.S.O., D.F.C.
I. J. Black, Q.C.
F. A. Blennerhassett, Q.C.
J. C. C. Blofeld, Q.C.
J. F. Blythe, T.D.
Miss J. W. Bracewell
J. N. W. Bridges-Adams
S. E. Brodie, Q.C.
D. D. Brown, Q.C.
J. W. A. Butler-Sloss
N. McL. Butter, Q.C.
A. C. Caffin
D. C. Calcutt, Q.C.
G. A. Carman, Q.C.
B. R. O. Carter
P. Chadd, Q.C.
M. L. M. Chavasse, Q.C.
B. W. Chedlow, Q.C.
J. D. Clarke
D. J. Clarkson, Q.C.
J. L. Clay, T.D.
C. M. Clothier, Q.C.

J. N. Coffey
G. J. K. Coles
J. M. Collins, Q.C.
J. P. Comyn, Q.C.
R. K. Cooke, O.B.E.
Miss M. D. Cosgrave
A. G. W. Coulthard
D. M. Cowley, Q.C.
A. E. Cox
B. R. E. Cox, Q.C.
P. J. Cox, D.S.C., Q.C.
J. Crabtree
P. J. Crawford, Q.C.
C. J. Crespi
M. A. L. Cripps, C.B.E., D.S.O., T.D., Q.C.
F. P. Crowder, Q.C., M.P.
R. H. Curtis
G. W. Davey
I. T. R. Davidson
Sir Alan T. Davies, Q.C.
L. J. Davies, Q.C.
W. L. M. Davies, Q.C.
C. F. Dehn, Q.C.
W. E. Denny, Q.C.

A. C. H. de Piro, Q.C.
T. M. Dillon, Q.C.
J. M. Dodson
F. M. Drake, D.F.C., Q.C.
D. P. Draycott, Q.C.
G. A. Draycott
J. M. Drinkwater, Q.C.
B. R. Duckworth
M. Dyer
T. M. Eastham, Q.C.
J. B. S. Edwards
Q. T. Edwards, Q.C.
A. H. M. Evans, Q.C.
J. F. Evans, Q.C.
J. K. Q. Evans
T. M. Evans, Q.C.
A. B. Ewbank, Q.C.
G. N. Eyre, Q.C.
P. Fallon, Q.C.
D. H. Farquharson, Q.C.
B. A. Farrer
P. R. Faulks, M.C.
M. H. Feeny
J. D. A. Fennell, Q.C.
D. B. B. Fenwick
T. G. Field-Fisher, T.D., Q.C.
W. A. B. Forbes, Q.C.
J. R. B. Fox-Andrews, Q.C.
C. J. S. French, Q.C.
A. N. Fricker
R. H. K. Frisby, Q.C.
B. J. F. Galpin
E. L. Gardner, Q.C., M.P.
P. N. Garland, Q.C.
L. Gassman
M. Gibbon, Q.C.
R. B. Gibson, Q.C.
W. J. Glover, Q.C.
P. W. Goldstone
R. N. Gooderson
K. F. Goodfellow, Q.C
M. B. Goodman
J. K. Gore
J. P. Gorman, Q.C.
H. G. A. Gosling
Lord Grantchester, Q.C.
G. Gray, Q.C.
R. I. Gray, Q.C.
W. P. Grieve, Q.C., M.P.
I. O. Griffiths, Q.C.
J. C. Griffiths, Q.C.
L. Griffiths
H. Hague
J. A. S. Hall, D.F.C., Q.C.

Sir Lincoln Hallinan
A. W. Hamilton, Q.C.
G. M. Hamilton, T.D.
R. G. Hamilton
J. A. T. Hanlon
R. J. Hardy
Miss R. Hare, Q.C.
R. D. Harman, Q.C.
J. P. Harris, D.S.C., Q.C.
C. S. Harvey, M.B.E., T.D.
R. J. S. Harvey, Q.C.
C. L. Hawser, Q.C.
J. B. R. Hazen, Q.C.
D. Herrod, Q.C.
H. Hewitt
B. J. Higgs, Q.C.
W. D. T. Hodgson, Q.C.
D. A. Hollis, V.R.D., Q.C.
H. E. Hooson, Q.C., M.P.
A. C. W. Hordern
R. Houlker, Q.C.
W. McL. Howard, Q.C.
D. W. Howells
J. Hugill, Q.C.
D. S. Hunter, Q.C.
W. G. Humphries
A. E. Hutchinson
M. Hutchison, Q.C.
G. B. Hutton
B. A. Hytner, Q.C.
C. F. Ingle
J. H. Inskip, Q.C.
N. F. Irvine, Q.C.
F. C. Irwin, Q.C.
R. Ives
J. Jeffs, Q.C.
A. C. Jolly
E. S. Jones
I. H. Morris Jones, Q.C.
T. G. Jones
E. F. Jowitt, Q.C.
D. Karmel, C.B.E., Q.C.
D. N. Keating, Q.C.
R. D. L. Kelly, M.C.
M. E. I. Kempster, Q.C.
I. A. Kennedy, Q.C.
P. J. M. Kennedy, Q.C.
R. I. Kidwell, Q.C.
H. L. Lachs
G. F. B. Laughland
R. B. Lauriston
L. D. Lawton, Q.C.

C. N. Lees
A. P. Leggatt, Q.C.
H. J. Leonard, Q.C.
J. G. Le Quesne, Q.C.
J. M. Lever
S. Levine
E. ap G. Lewis, Q.C.
Miss G. M. Lewis
T. E. I. Lewis-Bowen
A. L. J. Lincoln, Q.C.
F. Ashe Lincoln, Q.C.
V. J. Lissack
I. P. Llewellyn Jones
J. Lloyd-Eley, Q.C.
J. H. Lord
R. J. Lowry, Q.C.
E. Lyons, Q.C., M.P.
J. R. V. McAulay
A. J. D. McCowan, Q.C.
I. C. R. McCullough, Q.C.
A. C. Macdonald
G. A. MacDonald
D. B. McNeill, Q.C.
W. A. MacPherson, T.D., Q.C.
J. G. Marriage, Q.C.
M. J. W. Marsh, M.C., T.D.
P. W. Medd, O.B.E., Q.C.
K. S. W. Mellor, Q.C.
J. C. K. Mercer
A. L. Mildon, Q.C.
Sir Joseph Molony, K.C.V.O., Q.C.
D. G. Morgan
L. J. J. Morgan
W. G. O. Morgan, Q.C. M.P.
M. Morland, Q.C.
A. J. H. Morrison
J. B. Mortimer, Q.C.
H. C. Muscroft
M. J. Mustill, Q.C.
A. L. Myerson, Q.C.
A. S. Myerson, Q.C.
B. T. Neill, Q.C.
F. P. Neill, Q.C.
E. G. Neville
J. H. R. Newey, Q.C.
R. M. H. Noble
M. P. Nolan, Q.C.
J. S. Oakes
E. M. Ogden, Q.C.
H. H. Ognall, Q.C.
B. R. Oliver
D. A. Orde
P. H. Otton, Q.C.

J. A. D. Owen, Q.C.
P. L. W. Owen, T.D., Q.C.
Miss H. E. Paling
R. H. S. Palmer
M. C. Parker, Q.C.
T. I. Payne
The Hon. R. B. Holroyd Pearce, Q.C.
I. Percival, Q.C., M.P.
R. A. Percy
Prof. A. Phillips, O.B.E.
D. A. Phillips
O. B. Popplewell, Q.C.
F. M. Potter
F. H. Potts, Q.C.
H. C. Pownall
M. J. Pratt, Q.C.
A. J. Price, Q.C.
E. J. Prosser
A. Rankin, Q.C.
A. D. Rawley
L. F. Read, Q.C.
H. C. Rigby, D.F.C.
Sir Ivo Rigby
H. E. P. Roberts, Q.C.
J. Harvey Robson
J. W. Rogers
J. O. Roch, Q.C.
G. H. Rooke, T.D.
R. G. Rougier, Q.C.
T. P. Russell, Q.C.
P. J. McNamara Ryan
D. M. Savill, Q.C.
H. M. Self, Q.C.
B. C. Sheen, Q.C.
M. D. Sherrard, Q.C.
L. S. Shields, Q.C.
G. J. Shindler, Q.C.
A. Simpson

J. K. E. Slack, T.D.
P. M. J. Slot
F. B. Smedley
M. Stuart Smith, Q.C.
D. A. L. Smout, Q.C.
Miss J. M. Southworth, Q.C.
G. C. H. Spafford
J. A. C. Spokes, Q.C.
R. O. C. Stable, Q.C.
S. A. Stamler, Q.C.
C. S. T. J. T. Staughton, Q.C.
J. Stephenson
N. F. Stogdon
C. S. Stuart-White
J. G. St. G. Syms, Q.C.
H. C. Taylor
J. B. Taylor, M.B.E., T.D.
K. J. Taylor
P. M. Taylor, Q.C.
E. S. Temple, M.B.E., Q.C.
K. J. Tetley
D. O. Thomas, Q.C.
J. Thomas, Q.C., M.P.
The Rt. Hon. P. Thomas, Q.C., M.P.
R. N. Thomas, Q.C.
S. B. Thomas, Q.C.
R. N. Titheridge, Q.C.
H. J. M. Tucker, Q.C.
R. H. Tucker, Q.C.
M. J. Turner, Q.C.
A. R. Tyrell, Q.C.
M. T. B. Underhill, Q.C.
A. R. Vandermeer
A. O. R. Vick
D. C. Waddington, Q.C.

D. St. J. R. Wagstaff
A. F. Waley, V.R.D., Q.C.
M. Walker
P. H. C. Walker
B. Walsh
M. B. Ward
R. L. Ward, Q.C.
J. R. Warde
R. G. Waterhouse, Q.C.
V. B. Watts
C. D. G. P. Waud
P. A. Webster
P. E. Webster, Q.C.
P. Weitzmann, Q.C.
W. T. Wells, Q.C.
M. C. B. West, Q.C.
C. H. Whitby, Q.C.
G. G. A. Whitehead, D.F.C.
F. Whitworth, Q.C.
Lord Wigoder, Q.C.
G. W. Willett
D. B. Williams, T.D., Q.C.
H. G. Williams
Sir Thomas Williams, Q.C.
J. G. Wilmers, Q.C.
J. K. Wood, M.C., Q.C.
J. Woodcock, T.D.
H. K. Woolf
G. H. Wootton
N. G. Wootton
G. N. Worthington
J. M. Wright, Q.C.
O. Wrightson
R. Wyeth
R. M. Yorke, Q.C.
C. G. Young

Officers of the Supreme Court, &c

All addresses Royal Courts of Justice, Strand, London W.C.2A 2LL unless otherwise indicated.

OFFICIAL REFEREES*

His Honour *Judge* Norman Richards, O.B.E., Q.C., Room 744, His Honour *Judge* William Stabb, Q.C., Room 721, His Honour *Judge* Edgar Fay, Q.C., Room 740.

* Under s. 16 and Sched. 2 to Courts Act 1971, Official Referees are Circuit Judges.

QUEEN'S BENCH DIVISION

Senior Master and Queen's Remembrancer: I. H. Jacob, Q.C.; *Masters:* J. Ritchie M.B.E., M.A., J. B. Elton, B.A., J. R. Bickford Smith, M.A., I. S. Warren, B.A.C., W. S. Lubbock, S. J. Waldman and P. B. Creightmore. *Queen's Coroner and Attorney and Master of the Crown Office, Registrar of Criminal Appeals and Registrar of Courts-Martial Appeals:* D. R. Thompson, C.B.

Assistant Master attached to the Crown Office, Assistant Registrar of Criminal Appeals and Assistant Registrar of Courts-Martial Appeals: W. H. Greenwood. *Assistant Registrar of Criminal Appeals:* M. W. Palmer.

Assistant Solicitor: P. J. Morrish.

CENTRAL OFFICE OF THE SUPREME COURT (East Wing)

Chief Clerk: J. F. Mason, Room 106.
Chief Clerk to the Queen's Bench Judge in Chambers: N. Sims, Room 93.
Action Department (Writs and appearances etc., Judgments and Executions).
  A–K Miss U. Beeny, Room 119
  L–Z P. Emery, Room 129
Summonses (including Judge in Chambers)
  A–Z C. Hicks, Room 130
Orders
  A–Z C. Hicks, Room 130
  Appeals and Applications to Q.B. Judges in Chambers A–Z Room 128.
Filing Department—Chief Clerk: C. Harman, Room 86.
Masters' Secretary's Department and Queen's Remembrancer's Department —Head Clerk and Secretary to the Masters: F. W. Simpson, Room 118.
Criminal Appeal Office and Courts-Martial Appeals Office—Head Clerk A. F. P. Ottway, Room 239.
Crown Office and Associates Department (Centre Block): *Clerk of the Lists:* C. King, Room 420; *Crown Office— Head Clerk:* F. Hearn, Room 479. *Chief Associate:* B. M. Spicer, M.B.E., Room 481.
Admiralty Registry and Marshal's Office: Room 733, West Wing, Royal Courts of Justice, Strand, W.C.2.
Registrar: J. P. H. Rochford.
Marshal: P. V. Gray.

CHANCERY DIVISION (East Wing)

Chief Master: R. E. Ball, M.B.E.
Chief Clerk and Secretary: W. E. Loveday, Room 175.
Registrar of Revenue Appeals: F. Glenister, Room 170.
Group A: Chambers of Megarry, Brightman, Templeman, Oliver and Slade, JJ.—Masters: (A to F) Cholmondeley Clarke; (G to N) Ball, M.B.E.; (O to Z) E. R. Heward.
Group B: Chambers of Foster, Goulding, Walton and Fox, JJ.—

Masters (A to F) Taylor; (G to N) Dyson; (O to Z) R. Chamberlain, T.D.
Chief Registrar: C. M. Kidd.
Registrars: P. Halliday, H. J. Wilson, D. G. Leach, M. S. Edwards and H. W. Nichols and A. J. Hancock.
Petition and Entry Seat: Room 161.
Appeal and Cause Clerks: Room 136.

COMPANIES COURT

Registrar: G. F. Dearbergh.
Chief Clerk: A. A. Clipstone.
General Office: Thomas More Building, Room 312.

BANKRUPTCY

Thomas More Building

Chief Registrar: G. M. Parbury.
Registrars: R. H. Hunt.
  A. J. Wheaton.
Principal Clerk: H. Chaffey.

TAXING OFFICE (Centre Block)

Chief Master: G. J. Graham-Green, T.D.
Masters: L. H. Razzall; E. J. T. Matthews, T.D.; F. T. Horne; M. A. Clews; F. G. Berkeley; A. J. Wright and C. R. N. Martyn.
Chief Clerk: D. Hutchings, Room 295.
Rota Clerk: Room 294.

FAMILY DIVISION

Principal Registry: Somerset House, Strand, WC2R 1LP, Tel. 01-405 7641.
Senior Registrar: R. L. Bayne-Powell
Registrars: W. D. S. Caird; D. R. Le B. Holloway, LL.B.; L. I. Stranger-Jones; C. Kenworthy; B. Garland, Mrs. A. E. O. Butler-Sloss; B. P. Tickle; C. F. Turner, LL.B.; T. G. Guest; D. H. Colgate; D. Morris.
Secretary: R. B. Rowe, Room 76.
Establishment Officer: Miss J. J. Learmonth, LL.B.
Taxing Officers: R. S. G. Norman, G. A. Wood, W. I. Martyn, LL.B., G. A. Goodwin, E. W. Morris.
Probate Department: Principal: B. W. Campbell, Room 72; *Enquiries:* A–F. Room 74, Ext. 3385; G–O, Room 83, Ext. 3507; P–Z, Room 98, Ext. 3375, Personal Application Dept., Tel. 01-836 7366, Room 111, 1st Floor,

South West Wing, Bush House, Strand, WC2B 4QR.

Contentious Department — Principal Clerk: L. T. Hyder.

Clerk of the Rules: West Green Building, Royal Courts of Justice, Strand, WC2A 2LL, W. G. Mason, LL.B., Room 772.

COURT OF PROTECTION
25 Store Street, W.C.1E 7BP

Master: J. A. Armstrong, O.B.E., T.D., M.A.

Deputy Master: P. W. E. Currie, M.C.

Assistant Masters: A. M. Creasy, E. R. Taylor, LL.B. (Hons.), R. Farrance, G. R. Isard, I.S.O., LL.B.

Chief Clerk: J. A. Johnston.

DEPARTMENT OF OFFICIAL RECEIVERS
IN BANKRUPTCY
Thomas More Building

Senior Official Receiver: J. B. Clemetson.

Official Receivers: A–K, D. A. Thorne; L–Z, J. Tye.

Assistant Official Receivers: A–K Division: G. C. Churcher, A. G. Davonport, D. E. Dolman; L–Z Division:

B. Lyons, T. J. White, K. V. Whiting.

DEPARTMENT OF OFFICIAL RECEIVERS
—COMPANIES

Atlantic House, Holborn Viaduct, London, EC1N 2HD.

Senior Official Receiver: J. B. Clemetson.

Official Receivers: N. Saddler, L. R. Bates, H. W. J. Christmas.

Assistant Official Receivers: E. W. Ebsworth; G. B. Gillvray; G. C. Enderby; J. R. Donnison, P. R. Joyce and T. B.Thompson.

DEPARTMENT OF THE OFFICIAL
SOLICITOR
48–49 Chancery Lane, WC2A 1JR

Official Solicitor: N. H. Turner.

Assistant Official Solicitor: T. W. Swift.

Assistant Solicitor: R. S. Dhondy.

Chief Clerk: J. A. P. Morris, Room 105.

Receivership Divisions—Principal: J. A. Dawson, Room 208.

Litigation Division—Principal: B. C. Harris, Room G2.

Income Tax Division—Principal: R. F. Dunn.

Circuit Administration

MIDLAND AND OXFORD CIRCUIT

Circuit Administrator's Office: 15th Floor, 2 Newton Street, Birmingham, B4 7LU. Tel.: 021-233 1234.

Circuit Administrator: C. W. Pratley.

NORTHERN CIRCUIT:

Circuit Administrator's Office: 2nd Floor, Aldine House, New Bailey Street, Salford, M3 5EU. Tel: 061-832 9571.

Circuit Administrator: C. R. Seaton.

SOUTH EASTERN CIRCUIT:

Circuit Administrator's Office: 4th Floor, Thanet House, 231/2 Strand, London, WC2R 1DA. Tel: 01-353 8060.

Circuit Administrator: Peter D. Robinson.

NORTH EASTERN CIRCUIT:

Circuit Administrator's Office: 4th Floor, National Westminster House, 29 Bond Street, Leeds, LS1 5BQ. Tel: 0532 41841.

Circuit Administrator: T. A. Whittington.

WESTERN:

Circuit Administrator's Office: Bridge House, Clifton Down, Bristol BS8 4BN. Tel: 0272 32231.

Circuit Administrator: I. E. Ashworth.

WALES AND CHESTER:

Circuit Administrator's Office: 3rd Floor, Churchill House, Churchill Way, Cardiff, CF1 4HH. Tel: 0222 396925.

Circuit Administrator: A. Howe.

Law Officers and other Officials

Attorney-General. Rt. Hon. Samuel Charles Silkin, Q.C., M.P.

Solicitor-General. Peter Kingsby Archer.

Legal Secretary to the Law Officers (Law Officers' Dept., Royal Courts of Justice, W.C.2). W. C. Beckett, LL.B. Tel: 01-405 7641.

Conveyancing Counsel of the Court, Room 160, East Wing, Royal Courts of Justice, W.C.2: V. G. H. Hallett, J. Monckton, and P. W. E. Taylor.

Examiners of the Court, Room 160, East Wing, Royal Courts of Justice, W.C.2; M. F. Meridith-Hardy, K. S. Lewis, M. E. M. Brooke, R. Walker and M. R. M. Nunns.

Official Solicitor, Norman Henry Turner, 48/49 Chancery Lane, London, W.C.2A 1JR.

Director of Public Prosecutions. 4/12 Queen Anne's Gate, S.W.1. Sir Norman Skelhorn, K.B.E., Q.C.

Deputy Director. M. J. Jardine.

Assist. Directors. J. M. Evelyn; P. R. Barnes; O. Nugent.

Solicitors to the Treasury and Queen's Proctor, B. Hall, C.B., K.C., T.D., 3 Central Buildings, Matthew Parker Street, S.W.1 (mail); 35 Old Queen Street, S.W.1 (callers).

Solicitor, Department of Trade and Industry: 66–74 Victoria Street, S.W.1. Sir Gerard Ryder, C.B.

Board of Inland Revenue: Somerset House, W.C.2. *Solicitor:* E. G. R. Moses.

Lord Chancellor's Department: House of Lords, S.W.1: *Permanent Secretary,* Sir Denis Dobson, K.C.B., O.B.E., Q.C., *Deputy Secretaries:* A. D. M. Oulton; J. W. Bourne, C.B.

Charity Commissioners. Office: 14 Ryder. Street, St. James's, S.W.1. *Chief Commissioner:* T. C. Green, C.B.

Chief Registrar Friendly Societies and Industrial Assurance Commissioner: K. Brading, C.B., M.B.E. (Office, 17 North Audley Street, W.1).

Criminal Injuries Compensation Board: 10–12 Russell Square (4th Floor), W.C.1. *Secretary:* D. H. Harrison.

Companies' Registration Office: Crown Way, Maindy, Cardiff CS4 3UZ.

Patent Office and Industrial Property Department (Head Office: 25 Southampton Buildings, W.C.2). *Comptroller-General:* E. Armitage.

Solicitor for Customs and Excise: King's Beam House, Mark Lane, E.C.3. G. Krikorian.

Judge-Advocate-General of the Forces F. H. Dean, 6 Spring Gardens, Cockspur Street, S.W.1.

Judge Advocate of the Fleet: W. H. Howard, Q.C., 3 Kings Bench Walk, E.C.4.

Land Registry: (Lincolns' Inn Fields, W.C.2), *Chief Registrar:* R. B. Roper.

Lands Tribunal: 5 Chancery Lane, London, W.C.2. *President:* Sir Douglas G. H. Frank, Q.C. *Registrar:* O. L. Mott.

Law Commission, Conquest House, St. John St., Theobald's Road, W.C.1. *Secretary:* J. M. Cartwright Sharp.

Ministry of Agriculture, Fisheries and Food and Ministry of Land and Natural Resources, 55 Whitehall, S.W.1. *Solicitor and Legal Adviser:* G. F. Aronson.

Department of the Environment, 2 Marsham St., S.W.1. *Solicitor:* K. A. T. Davey, C.B.

Department of Health and Social Security: Alexander Fleming House, Elephant and Castle, S.E.1. *Solicitor:* M. W. M. Osmond.

Parliamentary and Health Commissioner, Church House, Great Smith Street, S.W.1. Sir Alan Marre.

Office of Fair Trading, Restrictive Trading Agreements: Legal Director, M. J. Ware (Office, Chancery House, Chancery Lane, W.C.2).

Transport Tribunal: President, G. D. Squibb, Q.C., Watergate House, 15 York Buildings, Adelphi, W.C.2.

Greater London Council, County Hall, S.E.1: *Solicitor and Parliamentary Officer:* H. S. W. Wilson.

Public Trustee: A. A. Creamer, D.S.C., (Offices, 24 Kingsway, W.C.2).

Rating of Government Property Dept.: Jameson House, 69 Notting Hill Gate, W.11. *Treasury Valuer*, W. W. Brown.

Stamp Duty Adjudication Offices: The Controller of Stamps (Adjudication Section), West Block, Barrington Road, Worthing, Sussex.

Statute Law Committee: House of Lords, S.W.1. *Secretary*, J. M. Davies. *Statutory Publications Office*, Queen Anne's Chambers, 41 Tothill Street, S.W.1.

Commissioner of National Insurance: 6 Grosvenor Gardens, S.W.1. Sir Robert Gore Micklethwait, Q.C.

Public Record Office: Chancery Lane, W.C.2; *Keeper of Public Records:* Jeffery Raymond Ede.

Central Industrial Arbitration Committee: 1 Abbey Gardens, Great College Street, S.W.1. *Chairman:* Professor J. C. Wood. *Secretary:* D. C. J. Bolt. Tel: 01-930 4571.

Council on Tribunals, 6 Spring Gardens, S.W.1. *Secretary:* W. S. Carter, C.M.G., C.V.O. *Scottish Committee:* 22 Melville Street, Edinburgh, 3. *Chairman:* R. K. Will, W.S. *Secretary:* I. K. Kennedy.

County Courts in and near London

Mayor's and City of London Court: Guildhall Buildings, E.C.2.

Barnet: Kingmaker House, 19/21 Station Road, New Barnet.

Bloomsbury and Marylebone: 7 Marylebone Road N.W.1.

Bow: 96 Romford Road, Stratford, E.15 4EG.

Brentford: Alexandra Road, High Street, Brentford, Middx. TW8 0JJ, (¾ m. S.W. of Brentford Sta.).

Bromley (*Lent*): Court House, College Road, BR1 3PX.

Clerkenwell: 33 Duncan Terrace, Islington, N1 8AN (¼ m. N.E. of "Angel").

Croydon: The Law Courts, Barclay Road, CR9 1RE.

Edmonton: Court House, Fore Street. Upper Edmonton, N18 2TN (¾ m, N. of White Hart Lane Station (Silver Street nearest Station)).

Ilford: Buckingham Road, Ilford, Essex, IG1 1TP.

Epsom: The Parade, Epsom, Surrey (¼ m. from Epsom Station).

Gravesend: 25 Pelham Road, Gravesend, Kent, DA11 0HY.

Kingston: St. James Road, Kingston-upon-Thames, KT1 2AD.

Lambeth: Cleaver Street, Kennington Road, SE11 4DZ.

Shoreditch: 19 Leonard Street, EC2A 4AL (off City Road—near Old Street).

Southwark: Swan Street, Trinity Street, SE1 1DG.

Staines: The Law Courts, Knowle Green, Staines, TW18 1XH.

Uxbridge: 114 High Street, Uxbridge.

Wandsworth: 76–78 Upper Richmond Road, London SW15 (nearest station East Putney).

Watford: King Street, WD1 8BS (near High Street Station).

West London: 43 North End Road, W.14 (200 yds. N. of West Kensington Sta.).

Westminster: 82 St. Martin's Lane, WC2N 4AG.

Willesden: 9 Acton Lane, Harlesden, N.W.10.

Woolwich: The Court House, Powis Street, SE18 6JW.

Courts, Registries, &c., in and near London

Admiralty Registry. Royal Courts of Justice, W.C.2.

Aliens Registration Office. 10 Lambs Conduit Street, W.C.1.

Bankruptcy Court and Official Receivers. Thomas More Building, Royal Courts of Justice, W.C.2..

Business Names, Registrar of. Companies House, 55–71 City Road, E.C.1.

Central Criminal Court, Old Bailey, E.C.4. *Judges:* The Lord Mayor, Lord Chancellor, Lord Chief Justice, Judges of Q.B.D. Division of High Court of Justice, Aldermen of London, Recorder of London, Common Serjeant.

Charity Commission. 14 Ryder Street, St. James's, S.W.1.

Church Commissioners. 1 Millbank, S.W.1.

City Magistrates' Courts. Mansion House, E.C.4 and Guildhall, E.C.2.

Civil Service Department. Whitehall, S.W.1.

Companies Court. Thomas More Building, Royal Courts of Justice, W.C.2. *Official Receivers,* Atlantic House, Holborn Viaduct, EC1N 2HD.

Companies Registration Office, Crown Way, Maindy, Cardiff CS4 3UZ.

Court of Protection, 25 Stone Street, W.C.1.

Criminal Appeal Office and *Courts-Martial Appeals Office,* Room 708. Royal Courts of Justice, W.C.2.

Crown Agents for Overseas Governments and Administrations. 4 Millbank, S.W.1.

Customs and Excise. King's Beam House, Mark Lane, E.C.3.

Development Commission. 11 Cowley Street, S.W.1.

Estate Duty Office. Minford House, Rockley Road, W.14.

General Register Office. Somerset House, W.C.2.

Government Actuary's Department. Steel House, Tothill Street, S.W.1.

House of Lords, Palace Westminster S.W.1.

Judicial Committee of the Privy Council. Downing Street, S.W.1.

Land Registry. Lincoln's Inn Fields, W.C.2.

Lands Tribunal. 5 Chancery Lane, London W.C.2.

London Crown Courts.
   Inner London. Sessions House, Newington Causeway, S.E.1.
   Woodford. 177–191 High Road, South Woodford, E.18.
   Croydon. Law Courts, Barclay Road, Croydon.
   Surbiton. Sessions House, 17 Ewell Road, Surbiton.
   Middlesex. Guildhall, Westminster, S.W.1.
   Kingston upon Thames. County Hall, Penrhyn Road, Kingston.

London Court of Arbitration. London Chamber of Commerce, 69 Cannon Street, E.C.4.

Lord Chamberlain's Office. St. James's Palace, S.W.1.

Mayor's and City of London Court. Guildhall Buildings, Basinghall Street, E.C.2. *Registrar:* A. M. Myers.

Parliamentary Counsel. Parliament Square House, Parliament Street, S.W.1.

Patent Office and Industrial Property Department. 25 Southampton Buildings, Chancery Lane, W.C.2.

Principal Probate Registry. Somerset House, W.C.2; Personal Application Dept., First Floor, South West Wing, Bush House, Strand, W.C.2.

Principal Registry of the Family Division. Somerset House, London, W.C.2.

Public Record Office. Chancery Lane, W.C.2.

Public Trustee Office. Kingsway, W.C.2.

Public Works Loan Board. Roydex House, Aldermanbury Square, E.C.2.

Rating of Government Property Department. Jameson House, 69 Notting Hill Gate, W.11.

Registry of County Court Judgments. 140 Gower Street, London W.C.1.

Restrictive Practices Court. The Royal Courts of Justice, Strand, W.C.2.

Secondary's Court. Guildhall, E.C.2.

Sheriff's Court, County of London. c/o 13-15 Arundel Street, W.C.2.

Stamp Office. Bush House, South-west Wing, W.C.2. *Adjudication Section,* West Block, Barrington Road, Worthing, Sussex.

Statute Law Committee. House of Lords S.W.1.

Transport Tribunal. Watergate House, 15 York Buildings, Adelphi, W.C.2.

Treasury Solicitor's Department and H.M. Procurator-General. 3 Central Buildings, Matthew Parker Street, S.W.1 (mail); 35 Old Queen Street, S.W.1. (callers).

Metropolitan Stipendiary Magistrates

COURTS		
Bow Street, W.C.2		
Camberwell Green (D'Eynsford Road, S.E.5)		
Clerkenwell (King's Cross Road, W.C.1)		
Marlborough Street, W.1		
Greenwich (Blackheath Rd., S.E.10)⎫ Woolwich (Market St., S.E.18) ⎬		
Horseferry Road, S.W.1		
Highbury Corner, Holloway Road, N.7.		
Marylebone (181 Marylebone Road, N.W.1)		
South Western (Lavender Hill, S.W.11)		
Thames (Aylward St., Stepney, E.1)		
Tower Bridge (Tooley St., S.E.1)		
West London (Southcombe Street, West Kensington, W.14)		
Wells Street (59/65 Wells St., Oxford St., WIA 3AE)		

MAGISTRATES		
Chief Metropolitan		
Magistrate		*Appointed*
K. J. P. Barraclough, C.B.E., T.D.		1954
Magistrates		
St. J. B. V. Harmsworth		1961
N. M. McElligott		1961

E. C. S. Russell..	..	.. 1961
N. F. M. Robinson	..	.. 1962
J. D. Purcell ..	..	.. 1963
C. R. Beddington	..	.. 1963
T. Springer	..	.. 1963
C. Besley	..	.. 1964
M. J. Guymer ..	..	.. 1967
K. D. E. H. Harington	..	.. 1967
R. R. Rawden-Smith	..	.. 1967
E. L. Bradley	..	.. 1967
E. J. R. Crowther	..	.. 1968
D. Prys Jones ..	..	.. 1969
A. W. Clark	..	.. 1970
I. G. McLean	..	.. 1970
D. A. Hopkin	..	.. 1970
R. K. Cooke	..	.. 1970
E. J. Branson ..	..	.. 1971
D. Fairbairn	..	.. 1971
P. W. Goldstone	..	.. 1971
W. E. C. Robins	..	.. 1971
M. L. R. Romer	..	.. 1972
Mrs. A. M. Frisby	..	.. 1972
R. J. A. Romain	..	.. 1972
P. D. Fanner ..	..	.. 1972
E. G. MacDermott	..	.. 1972
J. W. Cheeseman	..	.. 1972
R. D. Bartle ..	..	.. 1972
K. J. H. Nichols	..	.. 1972
J. H. Jobling ..	..	.. 1973
R. H. Lownie ..	..	.. 1974
C. J. I. Bourke ..	..	.. 1974
R. Knox Mawer	..	.. 1975
P. G. N. Badge ..	..	.. 1975
B. J. Canham ..	..	.. 1975
G. L. J. Noel ..	..	.. 1975
H. J. Cook	..	.. 1975
Sir Ivo Rigby ..	..	.. 1976
D. Barr ..	..	.. 1976

Juvenile Courts

Juvenile courts for the Inner London Area and the City of London have been established under the Children and Young Persons Acts, 1963 and the Administration of Justice Act, 1964.

At present, the courts sit as follows:

Hackney Juvenile Court, 1 Digswell Street, N. 7. Monday and Thursday at 10 a.m.

Camden Juvenile Court, 163a Seymour Place, W.1. Tuesday at 10 a.m.

Wandsworth Juvenile Court, 217 Balham High Rd., S.W.17. Tuesday at 10 a.m.

Southwark South Juvenile Court, 4 Kimpton Road, Camberwell Green, S.E.5. Wednesday at 10 a.m.

Southwark North Juvenile Court, 4 Kimpton Road, Camberwell Green, S.E.5. Friday at 10 a.m.

Chelsea and Kensington Juvenile Court, 163a Seymour Place, W.1. Monday at 10 a.m.

Lambeth West Juvenile Court, 217 Balham High Road, S.W.12. Monday at 10 a.m.

Lambeth East Juvenile Court, 217 Balham High Road, S.W.12. Wednesday at 10 a.m.

Lambeth South Juvenile Court, 217 Balham High Road, S.W.12. Friday at 10 a.m.

Westminster Juvenile Court, 163a Seymour Place, W.1. Wednesday at 10 a.m.

Hammersmith Juvenile Court, 163a Seymour Place, W.1. Thursday at 10 a.m.

Lewisham North Juvenile Court, 4 Kimpton Road, Camberwell Green, S.E.5. Tuesday at 10 a.m.

Lewisham South Juvenile Court, 7 Blackheath Road, S.E.10. Thursday at 10 a.m.

Tower Hamlets Juvenile Court, 58b Bow Road, E.3. Tuesday and Thursday at 10 a.m.

Greenwich Juvenile Court, 7 Blackheath Road, S.E.10. Friday at 10 a.m.

Islington Juvenile Court, 1 Digswell Street, N. 7. Friday at 10 a.m.

In case of need a Juvenile Court may be held in a magistrate's room at Bow Street Magistrates' Court.

The Senior Chief Clerk of the Inner London Juvenile Courts has an office at 185 Marylebone Road, NW1 5QG, to which all communications should be sent. Telephone: 01-262-3211.

Stipendiary Magistrates

Birmingham	J. F. Milward
Cardiff	H. W. J. ap Robert
Greater Manchester	J. N. Coffey
	C. T. Latham, O.B.E.
Kingston-upon-Hull	I. R. Boyd
Leeds	F. D. L. Loy
Liverpool	Leslie M. Pugh
Merthyr Tydfil	D. P. Rowland
Mid Glamorgan	D. A. Phillips
Pontypridd	P. G. D. Sixsmith
Salford City	Leslie Walsh
South Glamorgan	Sir Lincoln Hallinan
South Yorkshire	J. A. Henham
Wolverhampton	H. W. M. Coley

High Sheriffs and Under-Sheriffs, 1976–77

HIGH SHERIFF'S SHRIEVALTY (to whom writ directed)	BAILIWICK OF UNDER-SHERIFF (with whom writ lodged)	UNDER-SHERIFF
		ENGLAND
Greater London	Greater London	A. K. L. Black, 13–15 Arundel St., Strand WC2R 3EA.
City of London	City of London	R. M. Snagge, M.B.E., T.D., M.A., Central Criminal Court, Warwick Square, Warwick Lane, EC4 M7BS.

Metropolitan Counties

HIGH SHERIFF'S SHRIEVALTY	BAILIWICK OF UNDER-SHERIFF	UNDER-SHERIFF
Greater Manchester	Lancashire	J. W. Wilson, 6 Chapel St., Preston, PR1 8AN.
	Cheshire	H. L. Birch, White Friars, Chester, CH1 1XS.
	Yorkshire	B. C. R. Dodsworth and W. H. C. Cobb, Duncombe Place, York. YO1 2DY.
Merseyside	Lancashire	J. W. Wilson, 6 Chapel St., Preston, PR1 8AN.
	Cheshire	H. L. Birch, White Friars, Chester, CH1 1XS.
South Yorkshire	Yorkshire	B. C. R. Dodsworth and W. H. C. Cobb, Duncombe Place, York, YO1 2DY.
	Hallamshire	"
	Nottinghamshire	A. K. Dickins, Leeds House, 14 Clumber St., Nottingham, NG1 3DS.
Tyne and Wear	City of Newcastle-upon-Tyne	H. A. Potts, Cross House, Westgate Rd., Newcastle-upon-Tyne, NE99 1SB.
	Northumberland	R. M. Wilson, Cross House, Westgate Rd., Newcastle-upon-Tyne, NE99 1SB.
	Durham	E. Luxmoore, 5 North Bailey, Durham, DH1 3EY.
West Midlands	Staffordshire	E. M. Huntbach, 17 Martin St., Stafford.
	Worcestershire	C. L. Whatley, 16 The Tything, Worcester, WR1 1HG.
	Warwickshire	H. K. Blenkinsop, D.L., 1 New St., Warwick, CV34 4RX.
West Yorkshire	Yorkshire	B. C. R. Dodsworth and W. H. C. Cobb, Duncombe Place, York, YO1 2DY.

HIGH SHERIFF'S SHRIEVALTY (to whom writ directed)	BAILIWICK OF UNDER-SHERIFF (with whom writ lodged)	UNDER-SHERIFF
Non-Metropolitan Counties		
Avon	Somersetshire	T. H. R. Poole, T.D., The Parade, South Petherton, TA13 5DG.
	City of Bristol	J. G. Grenfell, Netherton House, 23–29 Marsh St., Bristol, BS1 4AQ.
	Gloucestershire	A. A. Scott, T.D., 4 College Green, Gloucester, GL1 2LU.
Bedfordshire	Bedfordshire	W. G. Park, 14A Mill St., Bedford.
Berkshire	Berkshire	P. M. Blandy, M.B.E., 1 Friar St., Reading, RG1 1DA.
	Buckinghamshire	J. O. Jones, O.B.E., T.D., 14 Bourbon St., Aylesbury, HP22 RS.
Buckinghamshire	Buckinghamshire	,,
Cambridgeshire	Cambridgeshire & Isle of Ely	M. A. Robinson, M.A., LL.B., 39 Parkside, Cambridge, CB1 1PN.
	Huntingdon & Peterborough	,,
Cheshire	City of Chester	R. M. Miln, St. Werburgh Chambers, Chester, CH1 2EP.
	Lancashire	J. W. Wilson, 6 Chapel St., Preston, PR1 8AN.
	Cheshire	H. L. Birch, Friars, White Friars, Chester, CH1 1XS.
Cleveland	Durham	E. Luxmoore, 5 North Bailey, Durham, DH1 3EY.
	Yorkshire	B. C. R. Dodsworth and W. H. C. Cobb, Duncombe Place, York, YO1 2DY
Cornwall	Cornwall	J. W. M. Graham, 5 High Cross St., St. Austell, PL25 4AB.
Cumbria	Lancashire	J. W. Wilson, 6 Chapel St., Preston, PR1 8AN.
	Cumberland	M. Carter, 21 Castle St., Carlisle, CA3 8SZ.
	Westmorland	R. C. Peltzer, M.B.E., T.D., P.O. Box 27, Exchange Chambers, 106 Highgate, Kendal.
	Yorkshire	B. C. R. Dodsworth and W. H. C. Cobb, Duncombe Place, York, YO1 2DY.
Derbyshire	Derbyshire	J. R. S. Grimwood-Taylor, 35 St. Mary's Gate, Derby, DE1 3JU.
	Cheshire	H. L. Birch, Friars, White Friars, Chester, CH1 1XS.
Devon	City of Exeter	M. Noel Ford, T.D., D.L., 8 Cathedral Close, Exeter, EX1 1EZ.
	Devonshire	
Dorset	Hampshire	R. S. L. Bowker, O.B.E., 31 Southgate St., Winchester, SO23 9EE.
	Southampton Town	A. A. Woodford, 20 Havelock Road, Southampton, SO9 5TT.
	Borough of Poole	J. M. Wallace, 5 Parkstone Rd., Poole, BH15 2NL.

HIGH SHERIFF'S SHRIEVALTY (to whom writ directed)	BAILIWICK OF UNDER-SHERIFF (with whom writ lodged)	UNDER-SHERIFF
Durham	Durham	E. Luxmoore, 5 North Bailey, Durham, DH1 3EY.
	Yorkshire	B. C. R. Dodsworth and W. H. C. Cobb, Duncombe Place, York, YO1 2DY.
East Sussex	Sussex	E. J. Colley, 86 High St., Lewes, BN7 1XR.
Essex	Essex	T. C. Gepp, T.D., DL., 66 Duke St., Chelmsford, CM1 1JR.
Gloucestershire	City of Gloucester	R. A. Eggleton, 43 Brunswick Rd., Gloucester, GL1 1JS.
	Gloucestershire	A. A. Scott, T.D., 4 College Green, Gloucester, GL1 2LU.
Hampshire	Hampshire	R. S. L. Bowker, O.B.E., 31 Southgate St., Winchester, SO23 9EE.
	Southampton Town	A. A. Woodford, 20 Havelock Rd., Southampton, SO9 5TT.
Hereford and Worcester	City of Worcester	A. G. Duncan, 16 The Tything, Worcester, WR1 1HG.
	Herefordshire	P. Gwynne James, 5 St. Peter St., Hereford, HR1 2LB.
	Worcestershire	C. L. Whatley, 16 The Tything, Worcester, WR1 1HG.
Hertfordshire	Hertfordshire	C. J. N. Longmore, 24 Castle St., Hertford, SG14 1HP.
Humberside	Lincolnshire	P. S. Scorer, Stonebow, Lincoln, LN1 2DA.
	City of Kingston-upon-Hull	T. H. Farrell, T.D., P.O. Box 77, Cogan House, Bowlalley Lane, Hull, HU1 1YJ.
	Yorkshire	B. C. R. Dodsworth and W. H. C. Cobb, Duncombe Place, York, YO1 2DY.
Isle of Wight	Hampshire	R. S. L. Bowker, O.B.E., 31 Southgate St., Winchester.
Kent	City of Canterbury	K. P. Barrett, 70/72 King St., Maidstone, Kent, ME14 1BH.
	Kent	,,
Lancashire	Lancashire	J. W. Wilson, 6 Chapel St., Preston, PR1 8AN.
	Yorkshire	B. C. R. Dodsworth and W. H. C. Cobb, Duncombe Place, York, YO1 2DY.
Leicestershire	Leicestershire	J. M. Symington, 10 New St., Leicester, LE1 5ND.
	Rutlandshire	R. E. Browne, 1 Barn Hill, Stamford, Lincs.
Lincolnshire	City of Lincoln	P. S. Scorer, Stonebow, Lincoln, LN1 2DA.
	Lincolnshire	,,
Norfolk	City of Norwich	E. A. Rutherford, Paston House, 13 Princes St., Norwich.
	Norfolk	F. J. C. Thwaites, 3–7 Redwell St., Norwich, NR2 4TJ.
	Suffolk	H. B. Walrond, 88 Guildhall St., Bury St. Edmunds, IP33 1PT

HIGH SHERIFF'S SHRIEVALTY (to whom writ directed)	BAILIWICK OF UNDER-SHERIFF (with whom writ lodged)	UNDER-SHERIFF
North Yorkshire	City of York	K. W. H. Bloor, 1 St. Saviourgate, York, YO1 2NQ.
	Yorkshire	B. C. R. Dodsworth and W. H. C. Cobb, Duncombe Place, York, YO1 2DY.
Northamptonshire	Northamptonshire	I. G. Barnett, 7 Spencer Parade, Northampton, NN1 5AB.
Northumberland	Northumberland	H. A. Potts, Cross House, West-gate Rd., Newcastle-upon-Tyne, NE99 1SB.
	Berwick-upon-Tweed	J. R. Reay, 9 Church St., Berwick-upon-Tweed, TD15 1EF.
Nottinghamshire	City of Nottingham	Col. G. A. Wharton, C.B.E., T.D., D.L., 100 Friar Lane, Nottingham, NG1 6EH.
	Nottinghamshire	A. K. Dickins, Leeds House, 14 Clumber St., Nottingham, NG1 3DS.
Oxfordshire	Oxfordshire	A. T. F. Vallance, St. Georges Mansions, George St., Oxford, OX1 2AR.
	Berkshire	P. M. Blandy, M.B.E., 1 Friar St., Reading, RG1 1DA.
Salop	Shropshire	J. Newell, 4 College Hill, Shrewsbury
Somerset	Somersetshire	T. H. R. Poole, T.D., The Parade, South Petherton, TA13 5DG.
Staffordshire	Staffordshire	E. M. Huntbach, 17 Martin St., Stafford.
	City of Lichfield	A. D. Chapman, 18 Bore St., Lichfield, Staffs, WS13 6LW.
Suffolk	Suffolk	H. B. Walrond, 88 Guildhall St., Bury St. Edmunds, 1P33 1PT.
Surrey	Surrey	D. G. Longden, St. Martin's House, 140 Tottenham Court Rd., London, W1P 9LN.
Warwickshire	Warwickshire	H. G. Blenkinsop, D.L., 1 New St., Warwick, CV34 4RX.
West Sussex	Sussex	E. J. Colley, 86 High St., Lewes, BN7 1XR.
	Surrey	D. G. Longden, St. Martin's House, 140 Tottenham Court Rd., London, W1P 9LN.
Wiltshire	Wiltshire	F. H. Alsop, St. Mary's St., Chippenham, Wilts, SN15 3JL.

WALES

Clwyd	Flintshire	H. P. Gough, 95 High St., Mold, Clwyd, CH7 1BJ.
	Denbighshire Merionethshire	J. M. L. Meredith, Bridge St., Dolgellau, Gwynedd.
Dyfed	Cardiganshire	I. M. Evans, 50 Great Darkgate St., Aberystwyth, Dyfed. SW23 1DP.
	Carmarthenshire	H. Richards, 8 Thomas St., Llanelli, Dyfed. SA15 3JD.
	Town of Carmarthen	W. G. H. James, Gwynne House, 6 Quay St., Carmarthen, Dyfed. SA31 3JX.

HIGH SHERIFF'S SHRIEVALTY (to whom writ directed)	BAILIWICK OF UNDER-SHERIFF (with whom writ lodged)	UNDER-SHERIFF
Dyfed	Pembrokeshire	H. P. Williams, 4 Bridge St., Haverfordwest, Dyfed. SA61 2AG
	Town of Haverfordwest	Roger H. Smith, 33 Hill Lane, Haverfordwest, Dyfed, SA61 1PS.
Gwent	Monmouthshire	E. G. Evans, Victoria Chambers, 11 Clytha Park Rd., Newport, Gwent, NPT 4TS.
	Breconshire	H. W. J. Llewellyn, M.C., 4 The Bulwark, Brecon, Powys.
Gwynedd	Anglesey	M. J. S. Preece, Wellfield Offices, Bangor, Gwynedd, LL57 1EE
	Caernarvonshire	R. H. Ellis-Davis, 9 Segontium Terrace, Caernarvon, Gwynedd.
	Merionethshire	J. M. L. Meredith, Bridge St., Dolgellau, Gwynedd.
	Denbighshire	H. P. Gough, 95 High St., Mold, Clwyd, CH7 1BJ.
Mid-Glamorgan	Glamorganshire	F. H. Gaskell, 29 Park Place, Cardiff, CF1 3QD.
	Breconshire	H. W. J. Llewellyn, M.C., 4 The Bulwark, Brecon, Powys.
	Monmouthshire	E. G. Evans, Victoria Chambers, 11 Clytha Park Rd., Newport, Gwent, NPT 4TS.
Powys	Montgomeryshire	R. J. H. Cooke, Sheriff's Office, 11 Berriew St., Welshpool, Powys.
	Radnorshire	P. B. Morris, Oxford Chambers, Temple St., Llandrindod Wells, Powys.
	Breconshire	H. W. J. Llewellyn, M.C., 4 The Bulwark, Brecon, Powys.
South Glamorgan	Glamorganshire	F. H. Gaskell, 29 Park Place, Cardiff, CF1 3QD.
	Monmouthshire	E. G. Evans, Victoria Chambers, 11 Clytha Park Rd., Newport, Gwent, NPT 4TS.
West Glamorgan	Glamorganshire Districts of Swansea and Llew Valley	Col. F. d'A. Wilson, M.C., E.R.D., D.L., Calvert House, Calvert Terrace, Swansea, SA1 6AP.
	Districts of Afan and Neath	F. H. Gaskell, 29 Park Place, Cardiff, CF1 3QD.

SHERIFFS' AGENTS' OFFICES

London (Greater). Burchell & Ruston, 13–15 Arundel St., W.C.2.
Surrey. Joynson-Hicks & Co., St. Martin's House, 140 Tottenham Court Rd., W1P 9LN.
East Sussex. Burchell & Ruston, 13–15 Arundel St., W.C.2.
West Sussex (Surrey). Joynson-Hicks & Co., St. Martin's House, 140 Tottenham Court Rd., W1P 9LN.
        (Sussex). Burchell & Ruston, 13–15 Arundel St., W.C.2.
Herts. Burchell & Ruston, 13–15 Arundel St., W.C.2.
Essex. Iliffe & Edwards, 5 John St., WC1N 2HP.
Kent. Joynson-Hicks & Co., c/o Murray Coombs & Co., Jesse, Chambers, 88/90 Chancery Lane, W.C.2.

Some Government Departments

Name of Department	*Address and Telephone Number*
AGRICULTURE, FISHERIES AND FOOD, MINISTRY OF	3 & 10 Whitehall Place, S.W.1. *Tel:* 01-839 7711, and Great Westminster House, Horseferry Road, S.W.1. *Tel:* 01-834 8511
CUSTOMS & EXCISE, BOARD OF	King's Beam House, 39–41 Mark Lane, EC3R 7HE. *Tel:* 01-626 1515
EDUCATION AND SCIENCE, DEPARTMENT OF	York Road, S.E.1. *Tel:* 01-928 9222
EMPLOYMENT, DEPARTMENT OF	8 St. James' Square, S.W.1 *Tel:* 01-214 6000
ENVIRONMENT, DEPARTMENT OF THE	2 Marsham Street, London, S.W.1. *Tel:* 01-212 3434
FOREIGN AND COMMONWEALTH OFFICE	Downing Street, S.W.1. *Tel:* 01-930 8440
HEALTH AND SOCIAL SECURITY, DEPARTMENT OF	Alexander Fleming House, Elephant and Castle, London, S.E.1. *Tel:* 01-407 5522
INDUSTRY, DEPARTMENT OF	1 Victoria Street, London, S.W.1. *Tel:* 01-215 7877
HOME OFFICE	Whitehall, S.W.1. *Tel:* 01-930 8100
INLAND REVENUE, BOARD OF	Somerset House, W.C.2. *Tel:* 01-438 6622
LORD CHANCELLOR'S DEPARTMENT	House of Lords, London, S.W.1. *Tel:* 01-219 3000
TRADE, DEPARTMENT OF,	1 Victoria Street, London, S.W.1. *Tel:* 01-222 7877
TREASURY	St. George Street, London, S.W.1. *Tel:* 01-930 1234

Crown Proceedings

LIST OF AUTHORISED GOVERNMENT DEPARTMENTS

The following is the list of authorised Government departments with names and addresses for service on the person, who is, or is acting for the purposes of the Crown Proceedings Act 1947 as, the solicitor for such departments (see ss. 17 and 18 of the 1947 Act).

Authorised Government Departments	*Solicitors and Addresses for Service*
Administrator of Bulgarian Property	
Administrator of German Enemy Property	
Administrator of Hungarian Property	
Administrator of Italian Property	
Administrator of Japanese Property	
Administrator of Roumanian Property	
Board of Trade	
Civil Service Department	
Crown Estate Commissioners	
Custodian of Enemy Property for England	
Ministry of Defence	
Department of Education and Science	The Treasury Solicitor,
Department of Energy	3 Central Buildings,
Department of the Environment	Matthew Parker Street,
Export Credit Guarantees Department	Westminster,
Director General of Fair Trading	London, SW1H 9NN
Registry of Friendly Societies	
Home Office	
Department of Industry	
Department for National Savings	
Northern Ireland Office	
Department of Prices and Consumer Protection	
Public Works Loan Board	
Registrar General	
HM Stationery Office	
Department of Trade	
HM Treasury	
Welsh Office	
Ministry of Agriculture Fisheries and Food	The Solicitor to the Ministry of Agriculture Fisheries and Food,
Forestry Commission	55 Whitehall,
Intervention Board for Agricultural Produce	London, SW1A 2EY
Commissioners of Customs and Excise	The Solicitor for the Customs and Excise, King's Beam House, Mark Lane, London, EC3R 7HE
Department of Employment	The Solicitor for the Department of Employment, 32 St James's Square, London, SW1Y 4JR
Department of Health and Social Security	The Solicitor to the Department of Health and Social Security, State House, High Holborn, London WC1R 4TB
Commissioners of Inland Revenue	The Solicitor of Inland Revenue, Somerset House, London WC2R 1LB

Officers of Legal Societies

Senate of the Inns of Court and of the Bar.—Secretary, Vice-Admiral Sir Arthur Mackenzie Power, K.C.B., M.B.E. 11 South Square, Gray's Inn, London WC1R 5EU. Tel.: 01-242-0082.

Council of Legal Education.—Dean, C. A. Morrison, M.A., 4 Gray's Inn Place, W.C.1. Tel.: 01-405 4665.

Law Society. — Secretary - General, J. L. Bowron, Law Society's Hall, 113 Chancery Lane, W.C.2. Offices, Bell Yard, W.C.2. Tel.: 01-242 1222.

City of London Solicitors' Company.—Clerk, E. C. Robbins, Grindall Honse, 25 Newgate Street, E.C.1. Tel.: 01-606 6677.

Institute of Legal Executives.—Director-General, L. W. Chapman, Ilex House, Barrhil Road, London, S.W.2. Tel.: 01-671 0161/4.

The Senate of the Inns of Court and the Bar, 1976–1977

OFFICERS OF THE COUNCIL

President ..	..	..	..	..	The Rt. Hon. Lord Justice Scarman, C.B.E.
Chairman ..	..	..	..	..	Peter Webster, Q.C.
Vice-Chairman ..	..	..	..	David McNeill, Q.C.
Treasurer ..	..	..	..	..	Hubert Monroe, Q.C.

EX OFFICIO MEMBERS

The Rt. Hon. the Attorney-General, Q.C., M.P.
The Solicitor-General, Q.C., M.P.
The Chairman of the Council of Legal Education

INN REPRESENTATIVES

Nominated Representatives

Hall Representatives

Lincoln's Inn

The Hon. Mr. Justice Foster
Mervyn Davies, M.C., T.D., Q.C.
His Hon. Judge Gillis
Roger Parker, Q.C.
The Rt. Hon. Sir David Renton, K.B.E., Q.C.
John Bradburn

Gerald Godfrey Q.C.
John Knox
P. J. Talbot

Inner Temple

The Hon. Mr. Justice Nield
His Hon. Judge Leonard
His. Hon. Judge Stabb
Michael Browne, Q.C.
J. H. Inskip, Q.C.
John Wilmers, Q.C.

W. A. Macpherson, Q.C.
C. S. T. J. T. Staughton, Q.C.
His Hon. Judge Stroyan

Middle Temple

The Rt. Hon. Sir George Baker, O.B.E.
The Hon. Mr. Justice Bristow
The Hon. Mr. Justice Templeman, M.B.E.
John Davies, Q.C.
Douglas Falconer, M.B.E., Q.C.
Hubert Monroe, Q.C.

Robert Alexander, Q.C.
Donald J. Nicholls, Q.C.
Derek Wheatley

Gray's Inn
The Hon. Mr. Justice Cusack
Maurice Bathurst, C.M.G., C.B.E., Q.C.
Leonard Caplan, Q.C.
P. J. Cox, Q.C.
The Rt. Hon. Lord Justice Megaw,
   C.B.E., T.D.
Professor C. J. Hamson, Q.C.

Lionel Read, Q.C.
Michael Underhill, Q.C.
Miss C. Dickson-Wright

BAR REPRESENTATIVES

A. R. Barraclough, Q.C.
John Blofeld, Q.C.
C. M. Clothier, Q.C.
Quentin Edwards, Q.C.
John Griffiths, Q.C.
David Hirst, Q.C.
Andrew Leggatt, Q.C.
David McNeill, Q.C.
Michael Miller, Q.C.
Michael Nolan, Q.C.
J. M. Price, Q.C.
Rt. Hon. Sir Peter Rawlinson, Q.C.,
   M.P.
Charles Whitby, Q.C.
Michael Wright, Q.C.

Sheila Anderson
Ian Barby
Peter Cowell
John B. Deby
Michael Dingle
Michael Edwards
Richard Ellis
Nigel Fricker
R. M. K. Gray
Graeme Hamilton
T. C. Hetherington, C.B.E.
J. A. Hornsby
Brian Kealy
J. D. Keir
Christopher McCall
Ann Mallalieu
John Nutting
Nicholas Purnell
C. H. Ramsden
Alan Rawley
Kenneth Richardson
N. A. L. Rudd
F. B. Smedley
David Webster

ADDITIONAL MEMBERS

Bar
Richard Du Cann, Q.C.
Joseph Jackson, Q.C.
A. R. H. Urquhart
Bruce Pitt
John Leonard, Q.C.

Benchers
The Hon. Mr. Justice Arnold
John Vinelott, Q.C.
Peter Webster, Q.C.
Michael Wheeler, Q.C.
Lord Justice Stephenson, P.C.
The Hon. Mr. Justice Goff

Circuit Judges
His Hon. Judge Braithwaite
His Hon. Judge Sunderland
His Hon. Judge Trapnell
Alternates
   His Hon. Judge Lyons
   His Hon. Judge Gill
   His Hon. Judge Willis

Additional Member
Master I. H. Jacob, Q.C.

HONORIS CAUSA

The Rt. Hon. Lord Pearce
The Rt. Hon. Lord Justice Roskill

The Law Society Council, 1976–77

President: Mr. D. Napley
Vice-President: Mr. R. K. Denby
Secretary-General: Mr. J. L. Bowron

Members who have passed the chair:
Sir Desmond Heap

Sir Martin Edwards
Sir Edward Singleton
Sir Edmund Liggins

Other members in alphabetical order:

Mr. Anderson
Mr. Barratt
Mr. Bickforth Smith
Mr. Billington
Mr. Bolton
Mr. Bradbeer
Mr. Brooks
Mr. Brown
Mr. Carter-Ruck
Mr. Clarke
Mr. A. H. Cole
Mr. Cooper
Mr. Cox
Mr. G. R. Davies
Mr. E. L. Davies
Professor A. L. Diamond
Mr. B. E. Edwards
Mr. Evans
Mr. Foord
Mr. Franks
Mr. Gaskell
Mr. Gerrard
Mr. Gordon
Mr. Grimwood-Taylor
Mr. Hewetson
Mr. H. Hewitt
Mr. J. A. Holland
Mr. Hoole
Mr. Hyde
Mr. Jackson
Mr. Jefferson
Mr. Johnson-Gilbert

Mr. King
Mr. Leslie
Mr. Loup
Mr. MacDonald
Mr. D. A. Marshall
Mr. R. B. F. Marshall
Mr. Matthissen
Mr. Montgomery Campbell
Mr. Morgan
Mr. Mosley
Mr. O'Brien
Mr. Palmer
Mr. Porter
Mr. Prestige
Mr. Purton
Mr. Race
Mr. Roberts
Mr. Rutherford
Mr. Smith
Mr. Stebbings
Mr. Stevens
Sir James Swaffield
Mr. Taylor
Mr. Tunnicliffe
Mr. Verdui
Mr. Ward
Mr. Webb
Mr. Wegg-Prosser
Mr. Wickerson
Mr. Williams
Mr. Woodcock
Mr. Young

The Institute of Legal Executives, 1976–77

PRESIDENT
D. T. Jones, B.E.M.
VICE PRESIDENT
C. Egan
DIRECTOR GENERAL
L. W. Chapman, M.B.E.

PAST PRESIDENTS

G. W. Bunt
D. W. Benjamin
Mr. C. A. Broom
Mr. L. Parr

Mr. F. J. Pellman
Mr. H. Bradburn
Mr. R. W. J. Hubbard, M.B.E.
Mr. C. R. Baines

OTHER COUNCIL MEMBERS

Mr. B. N. Dennison
Mr. N. F. Dyer
Mr. L. C. Gladman
Mr. H. A. Shaw
Mr. C. A. Neal
Mr. N. Robson
Mr. G. D. Leaker
Mr. J. A. Schofield
Mr. P. R Stevens
Mr. L. I. Raven-Hill
Mr W. R. Mullins
Mr. R. P. Brackstone
Mr. B. Chester
Mr. R. E. Cannon

Mr. G. R. Scrowston
Mr. H. R. Turner
Mr. R. W. Duval
Mr. J. L. Bell
Mr. G. F. Ballard
Mr. J. A. Corcoran
Mr. K. L. Hayes
Mr. R. H. Gill
Miss J. M. Arram
Mrs. V. Ashworth
Mr. J. W. Astell
Mr. N. F. Bradshaw
Mr. D. Pearson
Mr. D. O. Spain

Legal Aid and Advice

LAW SOCIETY AREA SECRETARIES AND AREA HEADQUARTERS

AREA No. 2
P. P. Danson, Esq., The Law Society, No. 2 (South Eastern) Legal Aid Area, Area Headquarters, 9–12 Middle Street, Brighton, BN1 1AS. *Tel.*: 0273 27003.

AREA No. 3
J. C. Hodgson, Esq., T.D., The Law Society, No. 3 (Southern) Legal Aid Area, Area Headquarters, Crown Ho., 10 Crown Street, Reading, RG1 3SJ. *Tel.*: 0734-586883.

AREA No. 4
G. E. C. Dougherty, Esq., The Law Society, No. 4 (South Western) Legal Aid Area, Area Headquarters, 98 Pembroke Road, Bristol, BS8 3EH. *Tel.*: 0272 38784.

AREA No. 5
J. M. Gregory Jones, Esq., The Law Society, No. 5 (South Wales) Legal Aid Area, Area Headquarters, Arlbee House, Greyfriars Place, Cardiff, CF1 3JP. *Tel.*: 0222 37971.

AREA No. 6
D. A. Banks, Esq., LL.B., The Law Society, No. 6 (West Midland) Legal Aid Area, Area Headquarters, Lloyd House, 2 Colmore Circus, Birmingham, B4 6DJ. *Tel.*: 021-236 3106.

AREA No. 7
D. K. Berry, Esq., LL.B. The Law Society, No. 7 (North Western) Legal Aid Area, Area Headquarters, Pall Mall Court, 69 King Street, Manchester, M60 9AX. *Tel.*: 061-832 7112.

AREA No. 8
W. W. Williams, Esq., The Law Society, No. 8 (Northern) Legal Aid Area, Area Headquarters, 18 Newgate Shopping Centre, Newcastle upon Tyne, NE1 5RU. *Tel.*: 0632 23461.

AREA No. 9
A. Beal, Esq., The Law Society, No. 9 (North Eastern) Legal Aid Area, Area Headquarters, City House, New Station Street, Leeds, LS1 4JS. *Tel.*: 0532 42851.

AREA No. 10
T. C. Blagg, Esq., The Law Society, No. 10 (East Midland) Legal Aid Area, Area Headquarters, 5 Friar Lane, Nottingham, NG1 6BW. *Tel.*: 0602 42341.

AREA No. 11
E. Knott, Esq., The Law Society, No. 11 (Eastern) Legal Aid Area, Area Headquarters, Leda House, Station Road, Cambridge, CB1 2JT. *Tel.*: 0223 66511.

AREA No. 12
R. Rutherford Edwards, Esq., The Law Society, No. 12 (Chester and North Wales) Legal Aid Area, Area Headquarters, North West House, City Road, Chester, CH1 3AL. *Tel.*: 0244 23591.

AREA No. 13
J. G. N. Grafton, Esq., The Law Society, No. 13 (London East) Legal Aid Area, Area Headquarters, 29/37 Red Lion Street, London, WC1R 4PP. *Tel*: 01-405 6991.

AREA No. 14
C. H. Ruffhead, Esq., The Law Society, No. 14 (London West) Legal Aid Area, Area Headquarters, 29/37 Red Lion Street, London, WC1R 4PP. *Tel.*: 01-405 6991.

AREA No. 15
J. Middlehurst, Esq., The Law Society, No. 15 (Merseyside) Local Aid Area, Area Headquarters, Moor House, James Street, Liverpool, L27SA. *Tel.*: 051-236 8371.

LOCAL COMMITTEES WITH ADDRESSES OF LOCAL SECRETARIES

AREA No. 2 (SOUTH EASTERN)
Sussex
Mrs. J. M. Williams, The Law Society, No. 2 (South Eastern) Legal Aid Area, Local Office, 9/12 Middle Street, Brighton, BN1 1AS. *Tel.*: 0273 27003.
Kent
R. T. Watson, Esq., The Law Society, No. 2 (South Eastern) Legal Aid Area, Local Office, 6 Gardiner Street, Gillingham, Kent. *Tel.*: 0634 53781.
Surrey
G. L. Hawthorn, Esq., The Law Society, No. 2 (South Eastern) Legal Aid Area, Local Office, 59 High Street, Kingston on Thames, KT1 1LX. *Tel.*: 01-546 7244.

AREA No. 3 (SOUTHERN)
Thames Valley
R. W. Parry, Esq., LL.B., The Law Society, No. 3 (Southern) Legal Aid Area, Local Office, Crown House, 10 Crown Street, Reading, RG1 2SJ. *Tel.*: 0734 50698.

Southern Counties
J. R. Woolford, Esq., The Law Society, No. 3 (Southern) Legal Aid Area, Local Office, Brunswick House, 8–13 Brunswick Place, Southampton SO9 3JF. *Tel.*: 0703 27537.

AREA No. 4 (SOUTH WESTERN)
Bristol and Western Counties
F. Woollam, Esq., The Law Society, No. 4 (South Western) Legal Aid Area, Local Office, 16 Arlington Villas (off Lower Pembroke Road), Bristol, BS8 2EQ. *Tel.*: 0272 36824.

Plymouth and South Western Counties
G. J. Shyrane, Esq., M.A., Oxon., The Law Society, No. 4 (South Western) Legal Aid Area, Local Office, Mayflower House, 178 Armada Way, Plymouth, Devon, PL1 1LE. *Tel.*: 0752 63076.

AREA No. 5 (SOUTH WALES)
Cardiff and Pontypridd
R. J. Bromley, Esq., The Law Society, No. 5 (South Wales) Legal Aid Area, Local Office, Arlbee House, Greyfriars Place, Cardiff, CF1 3JP. *Tel.*: 0222 37971.
Swansea, Mid and West Wales
E. L. Jones, Esq., The Law Society No. 5 (South Wales) Legal Aid Area, Local Office, Mansel House, Mansel Street, Swansea, SA1 5UA. *Tel.*: 0792 50611.

AREA No. 6 (WEST MIDLAND)
Birmingham and Coventry
R. F. Kent, Esq., The Law Society, No. 6 (West Midland) Legal Aid Area, Local Office, Commercial Union House, Martineau Square, Birmingham B2 4UD. *Tel.*: 021 236 7576.
Staffordshire and Shropshire
T. Lindley, Esq., The Law Society, No. 6 (West Midland) Legal Aid Area, Local Office, Norwich Union House, 40 Trinity Street, Hanley, Stoke-on-Trent, ST1 5LS. *Tel.*: 0782 23734.

AREA No. 7 (NORTH WESTERN)
Manchester and Stockport
East Lancashire
A. Wynn Jones, Esq., The Law Society, No. 7 (North Western) Legal Aid Area, Local Office, Faulkner House, Faulkner Street, Manchester, M1 4DU. *Tel.*: 061-236 9811.
West Lancashire and Westmorland
A. R. Uwins, Esq., The Law Society, No. 7 (North Western) Legal Aid Area, Local Office, Unicentre, Lords Walk, Preston, PR1 3LB. *Tel.*: 0772 55042.

AREA No. 8 (NORTHERN)
Cumberland, Northumberland and North Durham
South Durham and North Yorkshire
D. Stather, Esq., The Law Society, No. 8 (Northern) Legal Aid Area,

Local Office, 18 Newgate Shopping Centre, Newcastle upon Tyne, NE1 5RU. *Tel.*: 0632 23461/4.

AREA No. 9 (NORTH EASTERN)
West Yorkshire
Miss J. M. Stocks, LL.B., and P. O. Chippindale, Esq., The Law Society, No. 9 (North Eastern) Legal Aid Area, Local Office, City House, New Station Street, Leeds 1, LS1 4JS. *Tel.*: 0532 42851.
North Humberside
B. E. Croston, Esq., The Law Society, No. 9 (North Eastern) Legal Aid Area, Local Office, Eagle Star House, 1 Market Place, Hull, HU1 1RF. *Tel.*: 0842 25391.
South Yorkshire
G. B. Hooper, Esq., The Law Society, No. 9 (North Eastern) Legal Aid Area, Local Office, Chesham House, 3 Charter Row, Sheffield, S1 1RF. *Tel.*: 0742 23303 and 79815.

AREA No. 10 (EAST MIDLAND)
Leicester, Northampton
J. R. Stewart-Peter, Esq., The Law Society, No. 10 (East Midland) Legal Aid Area, Local Office, 10 Salisbury Road, Leicester, LE1 7QT. *Tel.*: 0533 26547.
Lincolnshire
M. J. Mitchell, Esq., The Law Society, No. 10 (East Midland) Legal Aid Area, Local Office, 1st Floor, Aquis House, 18/28 Clasketgate, Lincoln, LN2 1ED. *Tel.*: 0522 31431.
Derby, Nottingham
C. F. Butler, Esq., The Law Society, No. 10 (East Midland) Legal Aid Area, Local Office, 3rd Floor, Commercial Union House, 40 Friar Lane, Nottingham, NG1 6DQ. *Tel.*: 0602 40327.

AREA No. 11 (EASTERN)
West Anglian
T. J. Cockerill, Esq., The Law Society, No. 11 (Eastern) Legal Aid Area, Local Office, Kett House, Station Road, Cambridge CB1 2JT. *Tel.*: 0223 66511.
Essex
S. N. Hales, Esq., The Law Society, No. 11 (Eastern) Legal Aid Area,

Local Office, Fairfax House, North Station Road, Colchester, CO1 1QJ. *Tel.*: 0206 5003.
Norfolk and Suffolk
C. M. Stevens, The Law Society, No. 11 (Eastern) Legal Aid Area, Local Office, Prudential House, 19 Bank Plain, Norwich, NOR OIJ. *Tel.*: 0603 20418/20031/20844.

AREA No. 12 (CHESTER AND NORTH WALES)
Gwynedd, Clwyd, and Powis
Chester and District
East Cheshire
J. B. Dodd, Esq., The Law Society, No. 12 (Chester and North Wales) Legal Aid Area, Local Office, North West House, City Road, Chester, CH1 3AL. *Tel.*: 0244 23591.

AREA No. 13 (LONDON EAST)
London East
The City of London
The London Boroughs of: Barking, Camden, Enfield, Greenwich, Hackney, Haringey, Islington, Lewisham, Newham, Redbridge, Tower Hamlets, Waltham Forest
F. W. P. Lupton, Esq., The Law Society, No. 13 (London East) Legal Aid Area, Local Office, 29/37 Red Lion Street, London, WC1R 4PP. *Tel.*: 01-405 6991.

AREA No. 14 (LONDON WEST)
London West
The London Boroughs of Barnet, Brent, Ealing, Hammersmith, Harrow, Hillingdon, Hounslow, Kensington & Chelsea, Lambeth, Southwark, Wandsworth, Westminster
G. Francis Woods, Esq., The Law Society, No. 14 (London West) Legal Aid Area, Local Office, 29/37 Red Lion Street, London, WC1R 4PP. *Tel.*: 01-405 6991.

AREA No. 15 (MERSEYSIDE)
Liverpool
Mrs. M. T. Flanagan, LL.B. The Law Society, No. 15 (Merseyside) Legal Aid Area, Local Office, Moor House, James Street, Liverpool, L2 7SA. *Tel.*: 051-236 8371.

The College of Law

GOVERNORS: W. J. Brown (Chairman), J. D. Clarke, Sir Arthur Driver, Sir Martin Edwards, Lord Goodman, C.H., J. G. Gordon, C. R. Hewetson, A. H. Hoole, C. A. B. Leslie, Sir Godfrey Morley, S. J. Mosley, J. C. Palmer, J. C. Stebbings, J. H. Walford, R. V. B. Webb, Sir Charles Whishaw, J. A. E. Young.

BOARD OF MANAGEMENT: E. R. Dew (Chairman), R. A. Donell, (Deputy Chairman), R. Lowe, I. G. Carvell, L. R. H. Griffiths, L. P. K. Brindley, R. G. Holbrook, N. Henderson, M. J. T. Godfrey, B. I. Caulfield.

READERS: P. G. Chiswell, C. K. Liddle, R. F. Snow.

PRINCIPAL LECTURERS: S. J. Henry, E. A. Keay.

SENIOR LECTURERS: P. C. Assheton, R. A. Bullock, A. Cooklin, Mrs. P. A. Cooper, P. R. Dean, R. P. Gregory, R. H. Halberstadt, Miss C. G. Harmer, R. H. E. Heath, J. P. Ibbett, Miss H. W. Jackson, D. R. Jones, K. M. Kershaw, Mrs. M. Rutherford, Miss P. M. H. Sarton, J. Treleaven, Mrs. J. A. Treleaven, C. J. Whitehouse, R. E. Williams.

LECTURERS: C. J. H. Ashby, J. Barlow, G. A. Beecher, C. C. H. Bell, Mrs. S. L. Bramley, P. K. W. Burbidge, P. Butt, G. G. Cocker, Miss K. E. Colclough, I. J. Cross, P. Dukes, T. R. Earis, V. Fairclough, C. H. Fielding, P. A. Gausden, A. D. C. Giddins, G. H. Gypps, A. G. Harvey, Mrs. H. R. Higgs, R. N. Hill, K. G. Jones, Miss L. Jones, A. P. Lampier, M. A. Lane, P. J. Mott, Miss V. J. Patrick, Mrs. C. Pedley, M. C. Petley, D. M. Pettitt, R. J. Philpot, A. Rasheed, R. E. Riddett, P. E. E. Rumbelow, Mrs. F. J. Silverman, C. L. Smith, R. T. Steele, A. D. Thomas, T. P. Timson, B. M. Titman, R. T. Tuddenham.

COLLEGE SECRETARY: L. A. Tipson.

ASSISTANT SECRETARY: A. G. Bensley.

ADDRESSES: Braboeuf Manor, St. Catherine's, Guildford GU3 1HA [0483-76711]; 33–35 Lancaster-gate, London W2 3LU [(01)723-3212]; 27 Chancery Lane, London WC2A 1NL [(01)242-3757]; Christleton Hall Chester CH3 7AB [0244-35577].

The Council of Legal Education

DEAN: Charles A. Morrison, M.A.

SUB-DEAN: E. Tenenbaum, M.A., B.C.L.

PERMANENT READER: Mrs. N. E. Michaels, LL.B., Ph.D.

READER IN COMMON LAW: Professor A. G. Guest, M.A.

READER IN PUBLIC INTERNATIONAL LAW: I. Brownlie, M.A., D.Phil.

READERS AND LECTURERS: *Contract*—M. P. Furmston, M.A., B.C.L. *Tort*—Professor A. G. Guest, M.A. *Criminal Law*—Mrs. N. E. Michaels, LL.B., Ph.D. *Law of Land*—P. Baker, Q.C., M.A., B.C.L.; E. H. Burn, M.A., B.C.L. *Constitutional and Administrative Law*—D. J. Bentley, M.A., B.C.L. *Legal System and Legal History*—J. H. Baker, LL.B., Ph.D.; *Equity and Trusts*—Mrs. J. L. Barbour, M.A.; J. A. Hopkins, M.A., LL.B. *Company Law*—C. I. Howells, M.A., LL.B. *General Paper I: (Common Law)*—P. Cresswell, B.A., LL.B.; Professor A. G. Guest, M.A.; Mrs. N. E. Michaels, LL.B., Ph.D.; S. R. Silber, LL.B. *General Paper II: (Equity & Trust Breach of Contract)*—L. Hoffman, M.A., B.C.L.; J. A. Hopkins, M.A., LL.B. *Procedure (Civil and Criminal) and Evidence*—P. B. Carter, M.A., B.C.L.; D. N. Barnard, B.A.; His Honour Judge I. B. Fife, M.C., T.D.; P. W. Murphy, M.A. *Revenue Law*—D. J. Hayton, LL.B.; Mr. H. H. Monroe, Q.C.; I. A. Saunders, B.A. *Family Law*—Mrs. N. E. Michaels, LL.B., Ph.D. *Landlord and Tenant*—J. S. Colyer, M.A.; Miss L. Megarry, B.A., LL.B. *Practical Conveyancing*—P. J. Millett, M.A., Q.C. *Hire Purchase and Sale of Goods*—J. L. Yelland, M.A., B.C.L. *Local Government and*

Planning—K. Davies, M.A., LL.B.; V. W. E. Moore, LL.M. *Conflict of Laws*—P. B. Carter, M.A., B.C.L., J.P. *Public International Law*— I. Brownlie, M.A., D.Phil. *Law of International Trade*—Professor P. S. Atiyah, M.A.; Mrs. H. M. Fox, M.A., J.P.

The Society of Public Teachers of Law

1976–77

Hon. Treasurer: Professor L. Neville Brown, The University, Birmingham.

Hon. Secretary, Professor P. B. Fairest, The University, Hull HU6 7RX

Hon. Senior Editor of the Journal of the Society: J. A. Jolowicz, M.A., Trinity College, Cambridge.

Hon. Assistant Editor: Professor J. F. Garner, LL.D. (Lond.), Solicitor, Professor of Public Law, The University, Nottingham.

(Journal: to be obtained from Butterworth & Co. (Publishers) Ltd.)

List of Lord Chancellors, Chief Justices and Masters of the Rolls since 1750

LORD CHANCELLORS

1736–56, Hardwicke; 1757–66, Henley (Northington); 1765–70, Camden; 1770–71, Yorke; 1771–78, Apsley (Bathurst); 1778–92, Thurlow; 1793–1801, Loughborough (Rosslyn); 1801–6, Eldon; 1806–7, Erskine; 1807–27, Eldon; 1827–30, Lyndhurst; 1830–4, Brougham; 1834–5, Lyndhurst; 1836–41, Cottenham; 1841–6, Lyndhurst; 1846–50, Cottenham; 1850–2, Truro; 1852, St. Leonards; 1852–8, Cranworth; 1858–9, Chelmsford; 1859–61, Campbell; 1861–5, Westbury; 1865–6, Cranworth; 1866–8, Chelmsford; 1868, Cairns; 1868–72, Hatherley; 1872–4, Selborne; 1874–80, Cairns; 1880–5, Selborne; 1885–6, Halsbury; 1886, Herschell; 1886–92, Halsbury; 1892–5, Herschell; 1895–1905, Halsbury; 1905–12, Loreburn; 1912–15, Haldane; 1915–16, Buckmaster; 1916–19, Finlay; 1919–22, Birkenhead; 1922–24, Cave; 1924, Haldane; 1924–28, Cave; 1928, Hailsham; 1929–35, Sankey; 1935–38, Hailsham; 1938–39, Maugham; 1939, Caldecote; 1940–45, Simon; 1945–51, Jowitt; 1951–54, Simonds; 1954–62, Kilmuir; 1962–64, Dilhorne; 1964–1970, Gardiner; 1970–74, Hailsham; 1974–, Elwyn-Jones.

CHIEF JUSTICES (OF ENGLAND)

1737–54, Lee; 1754–56, Ryder; 1756–88, Mansfield; 1788–1802, Kenyon; 1802–18, Ellenborough; 1818–32, Tenterden; 1832–50, Denman; 1850–59, Campbell; 1859–80, Cockburn; 1880–94, Coleridge; 1894–1900, Russell; 1900–13, Alverstone; 1913–21, Reading; 1921–22, Trevethin; 1922–40, Hewart; 1940–46, Caldecote; 1946–58, Goddard; 1958–71, Parker; 1971–, Widgery.

(*Common Pleas*).—1737–72, Willes; 1762–65, Pratt; 1765–66, Camden; 1766–71, Wilmot; 1771–80, De Grey; 1780, Wedderburn; 1780–93, Loughborough; 1793–99, Eyre; 1799–1801, Eldon; 1801–4, Alvanley; 1804–14, Mansfield; 1814–18, Gibbs; 1818–24, Dallas; 1824, Gifford; 1824–29, Best; 1829–46, Tindal; 1846–50, Wilde; 1850–56 Jervis; 1856–59, Cockburn; 1859–66, Erle; 1866–73, Bovill; 1873–75, Coleridge.

MASTERS OF THE ROLLS

1750–54, Sir John Strange; 1754–64, Sir Thomas Clarke; 1764–84, Sir Thomas Sewell; 1784–88, Sir Lloyd Kenyon; 1788–1801, Sir R. P. Arden; 1801–18, Sir Wm. Grant; 1818–24, Sir Thos. Plumer; 1824–26, Lord Gifford; 1826–27, Sir John Copley; 1827–34, Sir John Leach; 1834–36, Sir Chas. Pepys; 1836–51, Lord Langdale; 1851–73, Sir John (Lord) Romilly; 1873–83, Sir Geo. Jessel; 1883–97, Sir W. Balliol Brett (Lord Esher); 1897–1900, Sir Nath. Lindley; 1900, Lord Alverstowe; 1900–1, Sir Archd. Smith; 1901–06, Sir Richd. Henn Collins; 1907–18, Lord Cozens-Hardy; 1918–19, Lord Swinfen; 1919–23, Lord Sterndale; 1923–35, Lord Hanworth; 1935–37, Lord Wright; 1937–49, Lord Greene; 1949–62, Lord Evershed; 1962–, Lord Denning.

Table of Legal Precedence

Lord High Chancellor; Lords of Appeal; Lord Chief Justice; Master of the Rolls; President of Family Division; Lords Justices of the Court of Appeal, according to seniority; Judges of the High Court according to seniority; Judge of the Arches Court; the Attorney General; the Solicitor General; Circuit Judges; Queen's Counsel; Doctors of Civil Law; Doctors of Law; Barristers; Solicitors.

Principal Acts of 1975–6

Acts passed between 7th August 1975 and 1st August 1976

1975

Criminal Jurisdiction (c. 59)

Inheritance (Provision for Family and Dependants) (c. 63)

Sex Discrimination (c. 65)

Employment Protection (c. 71)

Children (c. 72)

Community Land (c. 77)

1976

Development Land Tax (c. 24)

Table of Regnal Years

Noted up to 11 Eliz. II*

George III Oct. 25, 1760		George III (cont.)		William IV June 26, 1830		Victoria (cont.)		Edw. VII Jan.20, 1901		Edw. VIII Jan. 20, 1936	
Year of Reign	Year of our Lord	Year of Reign	Year of our Lord	Year of Reign	Year of our Lord	Year of Reign	Year of Our Lord	Year of Reign	Year of Our Lord	Year of Reign	Year of Our Lord
1	1760	42	1801	1	1830	31&32	1868	1	1901		1936
2	1761	43	1802	1&2	1831	32&33	1869	2	1902	George VI	Dec. 11, 1936
3	1762	44	1803	2&3	1832	33&34	1870	3	1903		
4	1763	45	1804	3&4	1833	34&35	1871	4	1904	1	1937
5	1764	46	1805	4&5	1834	35&36	1872	5	1905	1&2	1938
6	1765	47	1806	5&6	1835	36&37	1873	6	1906	2&3	1939
7	1766	48	1807	6&7	1836	37&38	1874	7	1907	3&4	1940
8	1767	49	1808	7&8	1837	38&39	1875	8	1908	4&5	1941
9	1768	50	1809	Victoria	June 20, 1837	39&40	1876	9	1909	5&6	1942
10	1769	51	1810			40&41	1877	10	1910	6&7	1943
11	1770	52	1811	1&2	1837-38	41&42	1878	George V	May 6, 1910	7&8	1944
12	1771	53	1812	2&3	1839	42&43	1879			8&9	1945
13	1772	54	1813	3&4	1840	43&44	1880	1	1910	9	1945
14	1773	55	1814	4&5	1841	44&45	1881	1&2	1911	9&10	1946
15	1774	56	1815	5&6	1842	45&46	1882	2&3	1912	10&11	1947
16	1775	57	1816	6&7	1843	46&47	1883	3&4	1913	11&12	1948
17	1776	58	1817	7&8	1844	47&48	1884	4&5	1914	12, 13, 14	1949
18	1777	59	1818	8&9	1845	48&49	1885	5&6	1915	14	1950
19	1778	60	1819	9&10	1846	49&50	1886	6&7	1916	14&15	1951
20	1779			10&11	1847	50&51	1887	7&8	1917	15&16	1952
21	1780			11&12	1848	51&52	1888	8&9	1918	Eilzabeth II	Feb. 6, 1952
22	1781	George IV	Jan.29,1820	12&13	1849	52&53	1889	9&10	1919		
23	1782			13&14	1850	53&54	1890	10&11	1920	1	1952
24	1783	1	1820	14&15	1851	54&55	1891	11&12	1921	1&2	1953
25	1784	2	1821	15&16	1852	55&56	1892	12&13	1922	2&3	1954
26	1785	3	1822	16&17	1853	56&57	1893	13&14	1923	3&4	1955
27	1786	4	1823	17&18	1854	57&58	1894	14&15	1924	4&5	1956
28	1787	5	1824	18&19	1855	58&59	1895	15&16	1925	5&6	1957
29	1788	6	1825	19&20	1856	59&60	1896	16&17	1926	6&7	1958
30	1789	7	1826	20&21	1857	60&61	1897	17&18	1927	7&8	1959
31	1790	8	1827	21&22	1858	61&62	1898	18&19	1928	8&9	1960
32	1791	9	1828	22&23	1859	62&63	1899	19&20	1929	9&10	1961
33	1792	10	1829	23&24	1860	63&64	1900	20&21	1930	10&11	1962
34	1793	11	1830	24&25	1861			21&22	1931	11	1962
35	1794			25&26	1862			22&23	1932		
36	1795			26&27	1863			23&24	1933		
37	1796			27&28	1864			24&25	1934		
38	1797			28&29	1865			25&26	1935		
39	1798			29&30	1866			26	1936		
40	1799			30&31	1867						
41	1800										

* From 1963 Statutes are described by their calendar year and chapter number e.g., 1964 c.12.

Law Reic Abbreviations

This Table shows the abbreviations commonly used in the citation of the principal series of English law reports. For a complete Table including Scottish, Irish and overseas reports see Volume 1 of the English and Empire Digest.

A. C. ..	..	Law Reports, Appeal Case, 1891– (current)
A. T. C.	..	Annotated Tax Cases, 1922– (current)
Ad. & El.	..	Adolphus and Ellis's Reports, 12 vols., 1834–1842
Aleyn..	..	Aleyn's Reports, 1 vol., 1646–1649
All E. R.	..	All England Law Reports, 1936– (current)
All E. R. Rep.		All England Law Reports Reprint, 36 vols., 1558–1935
App. Cas.	..	Law Reports, Appeal Cases, 15 vols., 1875–1890
Asp. M. L. C.	..	Aspinall's Maritime Law Cases, 1870–1943
Atk. ..	..	Atkyn's Reports, 3 vols., 1736–1754
B. & Ad.	..	Barnewall and Adolphus' Reports, 5 vols., 1830–1834
B. & Ald.	..	Barnewall and Alderson's Reports, 5 vols., 1817–1822
B. & C.	..	Barnewall and Cresswell's Reports, 10 vols., 1822–1830
B. & C. R.	..	Reports of Bankruptcy and Companies Winding up Cases 1918– (current)
B. & S.	..	Best and Smith's Reports, 10 vols., 1861–1870
B. T. R. L. R.		Brewing Trade Review Law Reports, 22 vols., 1913–1957
B. W. C. C. ..		Butterworths' Workmen's Compensation Cases, 41 vols. 1908–1950
Beav..	..	Beavan's Reports, 36 vols., 1838–1866
Bing. ..	..	Bingham's Reports, 10 vols., 1822–1834
Bli. ..	..	Bligh's Reports, 4 vols., 1819–1821
Bli. N. S.	..	Bligh's Reports, New Series, 11 vols., 1827–1837
Bos. & P. ..	..	Bosanquet and Puller's Reports, 3 vols., 1796–1804
Bos. & P. N. R.		Bosanquet and Puller's New Reports, 2 vols., 1804–1807
Br. T. Rev. ..		Brewing Trade Review, 1958– (current)
Bro. C. C. ..		W. Brown's Chancery Reports, 4 vols., 1778–1794
Bulst..	..	Bulstrode's Reports, 3 parts in 1 vol., 1610–1626
Burr. ..	..	Burrow's Reports, 5 vols., 1756–1772
Burrell	..	Burrell's Reports, 1 vol., 1648–1840
C. & P.	..	Carrington and Payne's Reports, 9 vols., 1823–1841
C. B. ..	..	Common Bench Reports, 18 vols., 1845–1856
C. B. N. S. ..		Common Bench Reports, New Series, 20 vols., 1856–1865
C. L. R.	..	Common Law Reports, 3 vols., 1853–1855
C. L. Y.	..	Current Law Yearbook, 1947–(current)
C.M.L.R.	..	Common Market Law Reports, 1962—(current)
C. P. D.	..	Law Reports, Common Pleas Division, 5 vols., 1875–1880
Camp.	..	Campbell's Reports, 4 vols., 1807–1816
Car. & Kir. ..		Carrington and Kirwan's Reports, 3 vols., 1843–1853
Car. & M. ..		Carrington and Marshman's Reports, 1 vol., 1841–1842
Ch. ..	..	Law Reports, Chancery Division, 1891– (current)
Ch. App.	..	Law Reports, Chancery Appeals, 10 vols., 1865–1875
Ch. D.	..	Law Reports, Chancery Division, 45 vols., 1875–1890
Chit. ..	..	Chitty's Practice Reports, 2 vols., 1770–1822
Cl. & Fin.	..	Clark and Finnelly's Reports, 12 vols., 1831–1846
Co. Rep.	..	Coke's Reports, 13 parts, 1572–1616
Com. Cas.	..	Commercial Cases, 1895– (current)
Cowp..	..	Cowper's Reports, 2 vols., 1774–1778

Cox C. C.	..	E. W. Cox's Criminal Law Cases, 31 vols., 1843-1945
Cr. & J.	..	Crompton and Jervis's Reports, 2 vols., 1830-1832
Cr. & M.	..	Crompton and Meeson's Reports, 2 vols., 1832-1834
Cr. App. Rep.		Cohen's Criminal Appeal Reports, 1908- (current)
Cr. & Ph.	..	Craig and Philips' Reports, 1 vol., 1840-1841
Cr. M. & R.	..	Crompton, Meeson, and Roscoe's Reports, 2 vols., 1834-1835
Crim. L. R.	..	Criminal Law Review, 1954- (current)
Cro. Car.	..	Croke's Reports *temp.* Charles I, 1 vol., 1625-1641
Cro. Eliz.	..	Croke's Reports *temp.* Elizabeth, 1 vol., 1582-1603
Cro. Jac.	..	Croke's Reports *temp.* James I, 1 vol., 1603-1625.
Dears. & B.	..	Dearsly and Bell's Crown Cases Reserved, 1 vol., 1856-1858
Dears. C. C.	..	Dearsly's Crown Cases Reserved, 1 vol., 1852-1856
De G...	..	De Gex's Reports, 2 vols., 1844-1848
De G. & J.	..	De Gex and Jones's Reports, 4 vols., 1857-1859
De G. & Sm...		De Gex and Smale's Reports, 5 vols., 1846-1852
De G. F. & J.	..	De Gex, Fisher and Jones's Reports, 4 vols., 1859-1862
De G. J. & Sm.		De Gex, Jones, and Smith's Reports, 4 vols., 1862-1865
De G. M. & G.		De Gex, Macnaghten and Gordon's Reports, 8 vols., 1851-1857
Dods...	..	Dodson's Reports, 2 vols., 1811-1822
Doug. K. B.	..	Douglas' Reports, King's Bench, 4 vols., 1778-1785
Dow.	..	Dow's Reports, 6 vols., 1812-1818
Dow. & Cl.	..	Dow and Clark's Reports, 2 vols., 1827-1832
Dow. & L.	..	Dowling and Lowndes' Practice Reports, 7 vols., 1843-1849
Dow. & Ry. M. C.		Dowling and Ryland's Magistrates' Cases, 4 vols., 1822-1827
Dow. & Ry. N. P.	..	Dowling and Ryland's Reports, Nisi Prius, 1 part, 1822-1823
Dowl...	..	Dowling's Practice Reports, 9 vols., 1830-1841
Dowl. N. S.	..	Dowling's Practice Reports, New Series, 2 vols., 1841-1843
Drew...	..	Drewry's Reports, 4 vols., 1852-1859
Drew. & Sm.		Drewry and Smale's Reports, 2 vols., 1859-1865
Dyer	..	Dyer's Reports, 3 vols., 1513-1581
E. & B.	..	Ellis and Blackburn's Reports, 8 vols., 1852-1858
E. & E.	..	Ellis and Ellis's Reports, 3 vols., 1858-1861
E. B. & E.	..	Ellis, Blackburn and Ellis's Reports, 1 vol., 1858-1860
E.C.R.	..	Reports of cases before the Court of Justice of the European Communities
E. R.	..	English Reports, 176 vols., 1220-1865
East	..	East's Reports, 16 vols., 1800-1812
Esp.	..	Espinasse's Reports, 6 vols., 1793-1810
Ex. C. R.	..	Exchequer Court Reports, 1875-1922
Ex. D.	..	Law Reports, Exchequer Division, 5 vols., 1875-1880
Exch...	..	Exchequer Reports, 11 vols., 1847-1856
Exch. C. R.	..	Exchequer Court Reports, 1923- (current)
F. & F.	..	Foster and Finlason's Reports, 4 vols., 1856-1867
Fam.	..	Law Reports, Family Division, 1972- (current)
Fost.	..	Foster's Crown Cases, 1 vol., 1708-1760
Gal. & Dav.	..	Gale and Davison's Reports, 3 vols., 1841-1843
H. & C.	..	Hurlstone and Coltman's Reports, 4 vols., 1862-1866
H. & N.	..	Hurlstone and Norman's Reports, 7 vols., 1856-1862
H. & Tw.	..	Hall and Twell's Reports, 2 vols., 1846-1850

H. & W.	.. ..	Hurlstone and Walmsley's Reports, 1 vol., 1840–1841
H. L. Cas.	..	Clark's Reports, House of Lords, 11 vols., 1847–1866
Hag. Adm.	..	Haggard's Reports, Admiralty, 3 vols., 1822–1838
Hag. Con.	..	Haggard's Consistorial Reports, 2 vols., 1789–1821
Hag. Ecc.	..	Haggard's Ecclesiastical Reports, 4 vols., 1827–1833
Hare...	..	Hare's Reports, 11 vols., 1841–1853
Hob. ..	..	Hobart's Reports, 1 vol., 1613–1625
Holt, M. B.	..	Sir John Holt's Reports, King's Bench, 1 vol., 1688–1710
I. T. R.	..	Reports of Decisions of the Industrial Tribunals, 1966– (current)
J. P. ..	..	Justice of the Peace Reports, 1837– (current)
J. P. Jo.	..	Justice of the Peace and Local Government Review
Jur. ..	..	Jurist Reports, 18 vols., 1837–1854
Jur. N. S.	..	Jurist Reports, New Series, 12 vols., 1855–1867
K. & J.	..	Kay and Johnson's Reports, 4 vols., 1853–1858
K. B.. .	..	Law Reports, King's Bench Division, 1901–1952
Kel.	..	Sir John Kelyng's Reports, 1 vol., 1662–1707
Kel. W.	..	W. Kelynge's Reports, 1 vol., 1730–1734
L. G. R.	..	Local Government Reports, 1902– (current)
L. J. Adm.	..	Law Journal, Admiralty, 1865–1875
L. J. Bcy.	..	Law Journal, Bankruptcy, 1832–1880
L. J. C. C. R.	..	Law Journal (County Courts Reporter), 1912–1947
L. J. C. P.	..	Law Journal, Common Pleas, 1831–1875
L. J. Ch.	..	Law Journal, Chancery, 1831–1946
L. J. Eccl.	..	Law Journal, Ecclesiastical Cases, 1866–1875
L. J. Ex.	..	Law Journal, Exchequer, 1831–1875
L. J. Ex. Eq.	..	Law Journal, Exchequer in Equity, 1835–1841
L. J. K. B. or Q. B.		Law Journal, King's Bench or Queen's Bench, 1831–1946
L. J. M. C.	..	Law Journal, Magistrates' Cases, 1831–1896
L. J. N. C.	..	Law Journal, Notes of Cases, 1866–1892
L. J. O. S.	..	Law Journal, Old Series, 10 vols., 1822–1831
L. J. P.	..	Law Journal, Probate, Divorce and Admiralty, 1865–1946
L. J. P. & M.		Law Journal, Probate and Matrimonial Cases, 1858–1859, 1866–1875
L. J. P. C.	..	Law Journal, Privy Council, 1865–1946
L. J. P. M. & A.		Law Journal, Probate, Matrimonial and Admiralty, 1860–1865
L. J. R.	..	Law Journal Reports, 1947–1949
L. R. A. & E.		Law Reports, Admiralty and Ecclesiastical Cases, 4 vols., 1865–1875
L. R. C. C. R.		Law Reports, Crown Cases Reserved, 2 vols., 1865–1875
L. R. C. P.	..	Law Reports, Common Pleas, 10 vols., 1865–1875
L. R. Eq.	..	Law Reports, Equity Cases, 20 vols., 1865–1875
L. R. Exch.	..	Law Reports, Exchequer, 10 vols., 1865–1875
L. R. H. L.	..	Law Reports, English and Irish Appeals and Peerage Claims, 7 vols., 1866–1875
L. R. P. & D.		Law Reports, Probate and Divorce, 3 vols., 1865–1875
L. R. P. C.	..	Law Reports, Privy Council, 6 vols., 1865–1875
L. R. Q. B.	..	Law Reports, Queen's Bench, 10 vols., 1865–1875
L. R. R. P.	..	Law Reports, Restrictive Practices, 1957– (current)
L. R. Sc. & Div.		Law Reports, Scottish and Divorce Appeals (House of Lords), 2 vols., 1866–1875
L. T. ..	..	Law Times Reports, 1859–1947
L. T. O. S.	..	Law Times Reports, Old Series, 34 vols., 1843–1860

Ld. Raym.	.. ..	Lord Raymond's Reports, 3 vols., 1694–1732
Le & Ca.	.. ..	Leigh and Cave's Crown Cases Reserved, 1 vol., 1861–1865
Leach..	.. ..	Leach's Crown Cases, 2 vols., 1730–1814
Lev.	.. ..	Levinz's Reports, 3 vols., 1660–1696
Lew. C. C.	.. ..	Lewin's Crown Cases (Northern Circuit), 2 vols., 1822–1838
Litt.	.. ..	Littleton's Reports, 1 vol., 1627–1631
Lloyd L. R. or (from 1951) Lloyd's Rep.		Lloyd's List Law Reports, 1919– (current)
Lofft ..	.. ..	Lofft's Reports, 1 vol., 1772–1774
Lush..	.. ..	Lushington's Reports, 1 vol., 1859–1862
M. & S.	.. ..	Maule and Selwyn's Reports, 6 vols., 1813–1817
M. & W.	.. ..	Meeson and Welsby's Reports, 16 vols., 1836–1847
Mac. & G.	.. ..	Macnaghten and Gordon's Reports, 3 vols., 1849–1852
Man. & G.	.. ..	Manning and Granger's Reports, 7 vols., 1840–1845
Man. & Ry. K. B.	..	Manning and Ryland's Reports, King's Bench, 5 vols., 1827–1830
Man. & Ry. M. C.	..	Manning and Ryland's Magistrates' Cases, 3 vols., 1827–1830
Mar. L. C.	.. ..	Maritime Law Reports (Crockford), 3 vols., 1860–1871
Mer.	.. ..	Merivale's Reports, 3 vols., 1815–1817
Mod. Rep.	.. ..	Modern Reports, 12 vols., 1669–1755
Moo. & P.	.. ..	Moore and Payne's Reports, 5 vols., 1827–1831
Moo. & S.	.. ..	Moore and Scott's Reports, 4 vols., 1831–1834
Moo. P. C. C.	..	Moore's Privy Council Cases, 15 vols., 1836–1863
Mood. & M.	.. ..	Moody and Malkin's Reports, 1 vol., 1826–1830
Mood. & R.	.. ..	Moody and Robinson's Reports, 2 vols., 1830–1844
Mood. C. C.	.. ..	Moody's Crown Cases Reserved, 2 vols., 1824–1844
Moore, C. P. ..	..	J. B. Moore's Reports, Common Pleas, 12 vols., 1817–1827
My. & Cr.	.. ..	Mylne and Craig's Reports, 5 vols., 1835–1841
My. & K.	.. ..	Mylne and Keen's Reports, 3 vols., 1832–1835
Nev. & M. K. B.	..	Nevile and Manning's Reports, King's Bench, 6 vols., 1832–1836
Nev. & M. M. C.	..	Nevile and Manning's Magistrates' Cases, 3 vols., 1832–1836
Nev. & P. K. B.	..	Nevile and Perry's Reports, King's Bench, 3 vols., 1836–1838
Nev. & P. M. C.	..	Nevile and Perry's Magistrates' Cases, 1 vol., 1836–1837
New Mag. Cas.	..	New Magistrates' Cases, 5 vols., 1844–1850
New Pract. Cas.	..	New Practice Cases, 3 vols., 1844–1848
New Rep.	.. ..	New Reports, 6 vols., 1862–1865
New Sess. Cas.	..	New Sessions Magistrates' Cases, 4 vols., 1844–1851
O. Bridg.	.. ..	Sir Orlando Bridgman's Reports, 1 vol., 1660–1666
O'M. & H.	.. ..	O'Malley and Hardcastle's Election Cases, 1869–1934
Owen ..	.. ..	Owen's Reports, 1 vol., 1557–1614
P.	.. ..	Law Reports, Probate, Divorce and Admiralty Division 1891–1971
P. & C. R.	.. ..	Planning and Compensation Reports, 1949– (current)
P. D. ..	.. ..	Law Reports, Probate, Divorce and Admiralty Division 15 vols., 1875–1890
P. Wms.	.. ..	Peere Williams' Reports, 3 vols., 1695–1735
Peake..	.. ..	Peake's Reports, 1 vol., 1790–1794
Peake, Add. Cas.	..	Peake's Additional Cases, 1 vol., 1795–1812
Per. & Dav. ..	..	Perry and Davison's Reports, 4 vols., 1838–1841
Ph.	.. ..	Phillips' Reports, 2 vols., 1841–1849

Phillim.	..	..	J. Phillimore's Ecclesiastical Reports, 3 vols., 1809–1821
Plowd.	..	..	Plowden's Reports, 2 vols., 1550–1580, and Plowden's Queries Vol. 1
Poll. ..	..	..	Pollexfen's Reports, 1 vol., 1670–1682
Poph. ..	..	..	Popham's Reports, 1 vol., 1591–1627
Price ..	..	..	Price's Reports, 13 vols., 1814–1824
Q. B. ..	..	..	Queen's Bench Reports (Adolphus and Ellis, New Series), 18 vols., 1841–1852
Q. B. ..	..	..	Law Reports, Queen's Bench Division, 1891–1901; 1953– (current)
Q. B. D.	..	..	Law Reports, Queen's Bench Division, 25 vols., 1875–1890
R. ..	..	..	The Reports, 15 vols., 1893–1895
R. A. ..	..	..	Rating Appeals, 1965– (current)
R. & I. T.	..		Rating and Income Tax Reports, 1947–1960
R. P. C.	..	..	Reports of Patent Cases, 1884– (current)
R. R. C.	..	..	Ryde's Rating Cases, 1956– (current)
R. V. R.	..	..	Rating and Valuation Reports, 1961– (current)
Rep. Ch.	..	..	Reports in Chancery, 3 vols., 1615–1710
Roll. Abr.	..	..	Rolle's Abridgment of the Common Law, 2 vols.
Roll. Rep.	..	..	Rolle's Reports, 2 vols., 1614–1625
Russ. ..	..	..	Russell's Reports, 5 vols., 1824–1829
Russ. & M.	..	..	Russell and Mylne's Reports, 2 vols., 1829–1833
Russ. & Ry.	..	..	Russell and Ryan's Crown Cases Reserved, 1 vol., 1800–1823
Ry. & Can. Cas.			Railway and Canal Cases, 7 vols., 1835–1854
Ry. & Can. Tr. Cas.			Railway and Canal Traffic Cases, 1855–1950
S.T.C.	..	..	Simon's Tax Cases, 1973—(current)
Saund.	..	..	Saunders's Reports, 2 vols., 1666–1672
Sav. ..	..	..	Savile's Reports, 1 vol., 1580–1591
Scott ..	..	..	Scott's Reports, 8 vols., 1834–1840
Scott, N. R.	..	..	Scott's New Reports, 8 vols., 1840–1845
Sea. & Sm.	..	..	Searle and Smith's Reports, 1 vol., 1859–1860
Sel. Cas. Ch.	..	..	Select Cases in Chancery, 1 vol., 1685–1698
Sess. Cas. K. B.			Sessions Settlement Cases, King's Bench, 2 vols., 1710–1747
Sid. ..	..	..	Siderfin's Reports, 2 vols., 1657–1670
Sim. ..	..	..	Simons' Reports, 17 vols., 1826–1852
Sim. & St.	..	..	Simons and Stuart's Reports, 2 vols., 1822–1852
Sm. & G.	..	..	Smale and Giffard's Reports, 3 vols., 1852–1857
Smith, L. C.	..	..	Smith's Leading Cases, 2 vols.
Sol. Jo.	..	..	Solicitors' Journal, 1856– (current)
Stark.	..	..	Starkie's Reports, 3 vols., 1814–1823
State Tr.	..	..	State Trials, 34 vols., 1163–1820
State Tr. N. S.	..	..	State Trials, New Series, 8 vols., 1820–1858
Stra. ..	..	..	Strange's Reports, 2 vols., 1716–1747
Sty. ..	..	..	Style's Reports, 1 vol., 1646–1655
Sw. ..	..	..	Swabey's Report, 1 vol., 1855–1859
Sw. & Tr.	..	..	Swabey and Tristram's Reports, 4 vols., 1858–1865
T. L. R.	..	..	Times Law Reports, 71 vols., 1884–1952
T. R. ..	..	..	Taxation Reports, 1939– (current)
T. Raym.	..	..	Sir T. Raymond's Reports, 1 vol., 1660–1683
Taunt.	..	..	Taunton's Reports, 8 vols., 1807–1819
Tax Cas. (or T. C.)	..		Tax Cases, 1875– (current)
Term Rep.	..	..	Term Reports (Durnford and East), 8 vols., 1785–1800
Traf. Cas.	..	..	Traffic Cases, 1951 (vol. 30)– (current)

Tyr. ..	..	..	Tyrwhitt's Reports, 5 vols., 1830–1835
Tyr. & Gr.	..		Tyrwhitt and Granger's Reports, 1 vol., 1835–1836
Vaugh.	..	..	Vaughan's Reports, 1 vol., 1666–1673
Vent. ..	..	..	Ventris' Reports, 2 vols., 1668–1691
Ves. ..	..	..	Vesey Junior's Reports, 19 vols., 1789–1817
Ves. & B.	..	..	Vesey and Beames's Reports, 3 vols., 1812–1814
Ves. Sen.	..	..	Vesey Senior's Reports, 2 vols., 1747–1756
W. C. C.	..	..	Workmen's Compensation Cases (Minton-Senhouse), 9 vols., 1898–1907
W. C. & I. R.			Workmen's Compensation and Insurance Reports, 22 vols., 1912–1933
W. L. R.	..	..	Weekly Law Reports, 1953– (current)
W. N...	..	..	Law Reports, Weekly Notes, 87 vols., 1866–1952
W. R...	..	..	Weekly Reporter, 54 vols., 1852–1906
Willes..	..	..	Willes' Reports, 1 vol., 1737–1758
Wm. Bl.	..	..	William Blackstone's Reports, 2 vols., 1746–1779
Wm. Rob.	..	..	William Robinson's Reports, 3 vols., 1838–1850
Wms. Saund.	..		Williams' Notes to Saunders' Reports, 2 vols.
Yelv. ..	..	..	Yelverton's Reports, 1 vol., 1602–1613

Architects' Fees

The Royal Institute of British Architects Conditions of Engagement currently in force are those first published on May 1 1971, revised January 1976.

The complete edition of the RIBA 1971 Conditions of Engagement is obtainable from RIBA Bookshop, 66 Portland Place, London, W1N 4AD, price 30p (45p including postage) each.

Printed below in full are Parts 2 and 3 which describe the most frequently required services.

PART 2: NORMAL SERVICES

2.00 *This part describes the services normally provided by an architect for a building project. The fees for Work Stages C to H are generally charged on a percentage basis as described in Part 3 of these Conditions. Stage C begins where the architect's brief has been determined in sufficient detail. Fees otherwise, including work in Stages A and B to determine the architect's brief, are charged additionally on a time basis as described in Part 5 of these Conditions. Initial consultations may be given free of charge.*

2.1 *Work Stages*

2.10 Work Stages charged on a *time* basis:

A **Inception**
Receiving an initial statement of requirements, outlining possible courses of action, and advising on the need for a quantity surveyor and consultants. Determining the brief in sufficient detail for subsequent Stages to begin.

B **Feasibility studies**
Undertaking a preliminary technical appraisal of a project sufficient to enable the client to decide whether and in what form to proceed, and making town planning inquiries or application for outline town planning approval. Such an appraisal may include an approximation of the cost of meeting the client's requirements, a statement on the need for consultants, an outline timetable and a suggested contract procedure.

2.11 Work Stages normally charged on a *percentage* basis:

C **Outline proposals**
Analysing the client's requirements and where necessary instructing the quantity surveyor and consultants. Preparing, describing and illustrating outline proposals, including an approximation of the cost of meeting them.

Informing the client of any major decisions which are needed and receiving any amended instructions.

D Scheme Design

Preparing in collaboration with the quantity surveyor, and consultants if appropriate, a scheme design consisting of drawings, and outline specification sufficient to indicate spatial arrangements, materials and appearance. Presenting a report on the scheme, the estimated cost and timetable for the project, for the client's approval.

E F G Detailed design, production drawings, specification and bills of quantities

Completing a detailed design, incorporating any design work done by consultants, nominated subcontractors and suppliers. Carrying out cost checks as necessary. Obtaining quotations and other information from nominated subcontractors and suppliers. Preparing production drawings and specification of materials and workmanship required. Supplying information necessary for the preparation of bills of quantities, if any.

H Tender action to completion

Obtaining and advising on tenders and preparing and advising on the contract and the appointment of the contractor. Supplying information to the contractor, arranging for him to take possession of the site and examining his programme. Making periodic visits to the site as described in Clause 1.33; issuing certificates and other administrative duties under the contract. Accepting the building on behalf of the client, providing scale drawings showing the main lines of drainage and obtaining drawings of other services as executed, and giving initial guidance on maintenance.

2.2 *Development studies*
To be charged on a time basis
2.20 Services where a client's initial statement of requirements in Stage A requires a special service (such

as operational research) before consideration of the brief and development of outline proposals as described in Stage C can begin.

2.3 *Development plans*
To be charged on a time basis
2.30 Preparing development plans for any large building or complex of buildings which will be carried out in phases over a number of years.
2.31 Preparing a layout only, or preparing a layout for a greater area than that which is to be developed immediately.

2.4 *Sites and buildings*
To be charged on a time basis
2.40 Advising on the selection and suitability of sites, conducting negotiations concerned with sites or buildings, making measured surveys taking levels and preparing plans of sites and buildings or existing buildings.
2.41 Making inspections, preparing reports or giving general advice on the condition of premises.
2.42 Work in connection with soil investigations.

2.5 *Constructional research*
To be charged on a time basis
2.50 Research where the development of a scheme in Stage D involves special constructional research, including the design, construction or testing of prototype buildings or models.

2.6 *Negotiations*
To be charged on a time basis
2.60 Exceptional negotiations such as those arising from applications for Town Planning, Building Byelaw, Building Act or Building Regulations approvals.
2.61 Providing information, making all applications other than those covered by the Normal Services, such as those including applications for licences, negotiations in connection with party walls and grant aids.
2.62 Submission to the Royal Fine Art Commission and town planning appeals.

2.7 *Special drawings*
To be charged on a time basis
2.70 Preparing any special drawings, models or technical informa-

tion specially for the use of the client, or for Town Planning, Byelaw and Building Regulations approvals; for negotiations with ground landlords, adjoining owners, public authorities, licensing authorities, mortgagors and others.

2.8 *Furnishings and works of art*
  To be charged on a time basis
  2.80 Advising on the selection and suitability of loose furniture, fittings and soft furnishings, on the commissioning or selection of works of art, obtaining tenders and supervising their installation.

2.9 *Approvals in the Normal Services*
  2.90 Except in Scotland, Stages C to E F G of the Normal Services include the duty of making and negotiating applications for Town Planning consents, Building Byelaw, Building Act and Building Regulations approvals, as appropriate. All work in connection with these applications will not necessarily be included in any particular Stage.
  2.91 In Scotland, the Normal Services cover the duty of preparing drawings and technical information necessary for submission of applications for licences, Town Planning and Building (Scotland) Act approvals as appropriate. The actual completion of the application and its presentation to the appropriate Court is not part of the architect's responsibility.

PART 3: FEES FOR THE NORMAL SERVICES
3.00 *This part describes how the percentage fees for the Normal Services are calculated and may be varied, and when they and other charges are due. Percentage fees are based on the total construction cost of the works and on the issue of the final certificate shall be re-calculated on the actual total construction cost.*

3.1 *Total construction cost*
  3.10 The total construction cost shall be the cost, as certified by the architect, of all works (including site works) executed under his direction, subject to the following conditions:
    3.101 The total construction cost shall include the cost of all work

designed or supervised by consultants which the architect is responsible for directing and co-ordinating in accordance with Clause 1.22, irrespective of whether such work is carried out under separate building contracts for which the architect may not be responsible. The architect shall be informed of the cost of any such separate contracts.
  3.102 The total construction cost shall not include nominated sub-contractor's design fees for work on which consultants would otherwise have been employed. Where such fees are not known, the architect shall estimate a reduction from the total construction cost.
  3.103 For the purpose of calculating the appropriate fees, the total construction cost shall include the actual or estimated cost of any work executed which is excluded from the contract but otherwise designed by the architect.
  3.104 The total construction cost shall include the cost of built-in furniture and equipment. Where the cost of any special equipment is excluded from the total construction cost, the architect shall charge for work in connection with such items on a time basis.
  3.105 Where appropriate the cost of old materials used in the work shall be calculated as if they were new.
  3.106 Where any material, labour or carriage are supplied by a client who is not the builder, the cost shall be estimated by the architect as if they were supplied by the builder and included in the total cost.
  3.107 Where the client is the builder, a statement of the ascertained gross cost of the works may be used in calculating the total construction cost of the works. In the absence of such a statement, the architect's own estimate shall be used. In both a statement of the ascertained gross and an architect's estimate there shall be included an allowance for the builder's profit and overheads.

3.11 The fee for any part of the work omitted on the client's instruction shall be calculated in accordance with Section 3.5 of these Conditions.

3.2 *New works*

3.20 Fees for new works generally are shown in Table 1, *post*.

3.3 *Works to existing buildings*

3.30 Higher percentages are chargeable for works to existing buildings and are shown in Table 2, *post*.

3.31 The percentage in Table 2 will not necessarily be sufficient for alterations to all buildings, especially those of historic importance, and higher fees may be appropriate.

3.32 Where extensions to existing buildings are substantially independent, fees may be as for new works, but the fee for those sections of works which marry existing buildings to the new shall be charged separately at the fee in Table 2 applicable to an independent commission of similar value.

3.4 *Repetition*

3.40 Where a building is repeated for the same client fees for the superstructure excluding all work below the top of ground floor slabs may be reduced as follows:

3.401 On all except the first three of any houses of the same design.

3.402 On all except the first, i.e. the prototype, of any other buildings to the same design.

3.41 Where a single building incorporates a number of identical compartments such as floors in multi-storey or complete structural bays in single-storey buildings, fees may be reduced on all identical compartments in excess of 10 provided that the building does not otherwise attract fee reductions and that it is completed in a single contract.

3.42 Reductions shall not be made for repeated individual dwelling units in multi-storey housing schemes but such schemes may qualify for fee reductions under Sub-clause 3.402 or Clause 3.41.

3.43 Reductions in accordance with Clauses 3.40 and 3.41 shall be made by waiving the fee for either Stages D and E F G of the Normal Services where a complete design

can be re-used without modification other than the handing of plans, or for Stage E F G where a complete design can be re-used with only minor modification.

3.44 The handing of a plan shall not constitute a modification.

3.45 The total construction cost of the works shall be taken first and the fee for normal or partial services calculated thereon. The appropriate reduction shall then be applied to the cost of the repeated superstructures or sections and the result deducted from the full fee.

3.46 Screen walls and outbuildings and garages shall be excluded from the construction cost of works on which fees are waived unless they are included in the type drawings and specifications.

3.47 The fees for work in Stage H of the Normal Services shall not be reduced for repetitive works or repeated buildings, and any additional work arising out of repetition shall be charged on a time basis.

3.5 *Partial services*

3.50 Where for any reason the architect provides only part of the Normal Services described in Part 2 of these Conditions he shall be entitled to commensurate remuneration, and his fees and charges shall be calculated as follows:

3.501 Where an architect completes the work described in any of Stages C to E F G he shall be entitled to the appropriate proportion of the full percentage fee for the service in accordance with Table 3.

3.502 Where an architect is commissioned to undertake only the work described in Stage H, whether in whole or part, fees shall be on a time basis.

3.503 Where an architect originally engaged to provide the Normal Services does part only of the work described in Stage H, he shall be entitled to not less than the percentage fee otherwise due to him under Clause 3.61.

3.504 Where an architect provides part only of the services described in Stages C to E F G, fees for service in any Stage which is incomplete shall ce on a time basis, except by prior written agreement in accordance with Clause 3.51.

3.505 Where an architect has previously completed the work described in Stages C to EFG on a commission which has been abandoned under the terms of Part 7 of these Conditions and the commission is resumed within two years fees for the work in Stage H shall be on a percentage basis. Where the commission is resumed after two years Sub-Clause 3.502 will apply.

3.51 Where work done by a client results in the omission of part of Stages C to H described in Part 2 of these Conditions or a sponsored constructional method is used, a commensurate reduction in fees may be made by prior written agreement, provided each such agreement specifies in sufficient detail the work to be done by the client which would otherwise have formed part of the Stages provided by the architect, and is either made in accordance with the RIBA Memorandum on the application of this Clause or is approved by the RIBA.

3.52 All percentage fees for partial service shall be based on the architect's current estimate of the total construction cost of the work. Such estimates may be based on an accepted tender or, subject to Clause 3.53, on the lowest of unaccepted tenders.

3.53 Where partial service is provided in respect of works for which the executed cost is not known and no tender has been accepted, percentage fees shall be based either on the architect's estimated total construction cost or the most recent cost limit agreed with the client, whichever is the lower.

3.6 *Mode and time of payment*

3.60 On completion of each Stage of Stages C to H of the Normal Services described in Part 2 of these Conditions, the appropriate proportion of the full percentage fee calculated on the current estimated construction cost of the works, plus any other fee and out of pocket expenses which have accrued, shall be due for payment.

3.61 Notwithstanding Clause 3.60, fees in respect of Stages E F G and H shall be due for payment in instalments proportionate to the drawings and other work completed or value of the works certified from time to time.

3.62 Alternatively, the architect and client may arrange for interim payment of fees and charges during all Stages of the work, including payment during Stage H by instalment other than those related to the value of the works certified from time to time.

3.63 On the issue of the final certificate the final instalment of all fees and other charges shall be then due for payment.

PERCENTAGE FEES FOR THE NORMAL SERVICES

Minimum charges are laid down in Table 1 and 2 so that a fee shall not be less than the fee for works having a lower construction cost.

TABLE I: NEW WORKS

Total construction cost	Minimum % rate	Minimum charges for work stages completed up to and including:			
		H	E F G	D	C
Up to £2,500	10.0	—	—	—	—
£2,500–£8,000	8.5	£250	£187.50	£87.50	£37.50
£8,000–£14,000	7.5	£680	£510.00	£238.00	£102.00
£14,000–£25,000	6.5	£1,050	£787.50	£367.50	£157.50
£25,000–£750,000	6.0	£1,625	£1,218.75	£568.75	£243.75
*£750,000–£1,750,000	5.75	£45,000	£33,750.00	£15,750.00	£6,750.00
*£1.750,000 and over	5.5	£100,625	£75,468.75	£35,218.75	£15,093.75

* Does not apply to certain hospitals, see Clause 1-81 or to works for which the fee is reduced for repetition as provided in section 3·4. In those cases the minimum fee for works having a total construction cost of £25,000 and over shall be 6.0%.

TABLE 2: WORKS TO EXISTING BUILDINGS

Total construction cost	Minimum % rate	Minimum charges for work stages completed up to and including:				
		H	E F G	D	C	
Up to £2,500	13.0	—	—	—	—	
£2,500–£8,000	12.5	£325	£243.75	£113.75	£48.75	
£8,000–£14,000	12.0	£1,000	£750.00	£350.00	£150.00	
£14,000–£25,000	11.0	£1,680	£1,260.00	£588.00	£252.00	
£25,000 and over	10.0	£2,750	£2,062.50	£962.50	£412.50	

TABLE 3: APPORTIONMENT OF FEES BETWEEN STAGES OF SERVICE

On completion of each Stage of the Normal Services described in Part 2 of these Conditions, the following proportions of the cumulative fee shown in Tables 1 and 2 are payable:

Work Stage		Proportion of fee	Cumulative total
C	(Outline proposals)	15%	15%
D	(Scheme design)	20%	35%
E F G	(Detail design)	40%	75%
H	(Tender action)	25%	100%

Auctioneers' and Estate Agents' Fees

By courtesy of the Royal Institution of Chartered Surveyors, the following summary is given of parts of their *Scales of Professional Charges*, as amended from Feb. 15, 1971. For fuller information references should be made to the Institution's Scales. In this summary the Scales are given the same numbers as those they carry in the official print.

VALUATIONS.—Where one valuer acts between parties, the charge shall be scale and a half, divisible between the parties.

1. VALUATION OF FREEHOLD OR LEASEHOLD PROPERTIES
   (a) *Freehold Property:* 1 per cent on the first £1,500; 0.5 per cent on the next £11,000; and 0.25 per cent on the residue of the valuation of the freehold. (Minimum fee £10.)
   (b) *Leasehold Property:* 1 per cent on the first £1,500; 0.5 per cent on the next £11,000; and 0.25 per cent on the residue of the valuation of the leasehold. And in addition 7.5 per cent on the first £300; 4.5 per cent on the next £700; 3.0 per cent on the next £1,500; and 2.0 per cent on the residue of the annual rent

payable under the lease. (Minimum fee £10.) Where the necessary instructions are held, for the separate assessment of goodwill in addition to the other assets of a business, 5.0 per cent on the first £1,000 and 2.5 per cent on the residue of such valuation.

3. VALUATION FOR PROBATE AND ESTATE DUTY
   (a) *Freehold Property:* See Scale 1 (a) above; *Leasehold Property:* See Scale 1 (b) above.

4. VALUATION FOR RATING PURPOSES, INCLUDING NEGOTIATIONS WITH THE VALUATION OFFICER
   (a) *Where single properties are valued, whether for ratepayers or otherwise:* 7.5 per cent on the first £300; 4.5 per cent on the next £700; 3.0 per cent on the next £1,500; and 2.0 per cent on the residue of the net annual value of the property. (Minimum fee £10.)
   (b) *In addition:* (i) For each attendance before a local valuation court: A fee by arrangement according to the circumstances, including the professional status and qualifications of the surveyor.

Note to Scales 10, 16 and 19 below:

Since the coming into effect of the Restriction on Agreements (Estate Agents) Order 1970 at 20th November 1970 these scales no longer apply to the acquisition and disposal of unfurnished dwellings.

10. SALES OF FREEHOLD PROPERTY OR GROUND LEASES (as defined in the published scale) AND SALES OF LEASEHOLD PROPERTY where the rent (exclusive of any payment in respect of rates, heat, light, water, service or other incidental charges) is less than one-fifth of the net annual value for rating purposes.

For effecting a sale on terms authorised by the vendor: (a) *By Private Treaty* (including the preparation of particulars), Negotiating a sale by private contract or introducing a purchaser. (b) *By Auction or Tender* (including the preparation of particulars and advising on reserves):—5 per cent on the first £500; 2.5 per cent on the next £4,500; and 1.5 per cent on the residue. (Minimum fee £10.)

In addition, whether on a sale by private treaty, auction or tender:—

(i) On payments for goodwill:—5 per cent on the first £1,000; and 2.5 per cent on the residue of the payment made for the goodwill.

(ii) On payments for chattels:—5 per cent (to include inventory and valuation, if required) on any payment, or payments, made for chattels, fixtures, fittings, furniture, plant and machinery, trade stocks, book debts and other movable effects, timber and timber-like trees, and tenant right.

In cases where two agents are co-operating at the request of the owner, the commission shall be at the rate of scale and a half.

Sale before Auction. Between date of acceptance of instructions and date of auction, same scale as auction.

Non-Sale. A fee, which is a matter of arrangement, is payable.

Sale after Auction. In the event of the property being sold within 90 days after the auction, same scale as auction, any non-sale fee merging into the commission then payable.

Division of an Estate into Lots. Where this involves substantial additional work, an extra fee may be charged.

11. ON SALES OF FURNITURE, TRADE STOCKS AND CHATTELS ON THE VENDOR'S PREMISES.—7.5% on the amount realised.

16. DISPOSAL OF LEASEHOLD PROPERTY.—*On disposal of all Leases (other than leases to which Scales 10 and 16 (b)* ("*Assignment of Building Agreements or Building Leases at a Premium*" apply) the same commission as for a letting (see *e.g.* Scale 19). *In addition* a commission of 5% on the first £1,000, and 2.5% on the residue of the premium or any consideration which is equivalent thereto; *and in addition* on payments for goodwill and for chattels etc. the same commissions as those set out in Scale 10, *ante.*

19. ON LETTING UNFURNISHED PREMISES.—*In cases where there is a premium or equivalent consideration and the rent (exclusive of services, etc.) is less than one-fifth of the net annual value for rating purposes:*—the same commission as is payable under Scale 10 for the sale of leasehold property. *In all other cases:* (i) Lettings for a term certain of 12 months or more, 10% on 1 year's rent; (ii) periodic tenancies subsisting for 12 months or more, fee by arrangement (max. 10% on 1 year's rent); (iii) periodic tenancies subsisting for less than 12 months, 10% on rent payable under the letting. In addition, a commission on the premium, consideration and/or goodwill of 5% on the first £1,000 and 2.5% thereafter.

Building Societies Surveyors' Fees

The Building Societies Association recommend survey fees, agreed in consultation with the Royal Institution of Chartered Surveyors and the Incorporated Society of Valuers and Auctioneers, which most societies follow:

Inspection Fees

Valuation of Property	*Survey fee*
Not exceeding £2,000	£5 (minimum chargeable)
Exceeding £2,000 but not exceeding £15,000	£5 plus £1 per £500 or part thereof in excess of £2,000
Exceeding £15,000 but not exceeding £30,000	£31 plus £1 per £1,000 or part thereof in excess of £15,000
Exceeding £30,000 but not exceeding £40,000	£46 plus £1 per £2,000 or part thereof in excess of £30,000

Where the valuation exceeds £40,000 the fee to be settled by negotiation between the society and the surveyor.

These fees apply to properties within a radius of five miles of the surveyor's office and must accompany the mortgage application. For distances beyond five miles, a small additional fee may be charged for travelling expenses.

Valuers' Fees

For work under the Lands Clauses Consolidation Act or other Acts for the Compulsory Acquisition of property—

(a) *To the Valuer who prepares the case (including negotiation for a settlement where required): the scale set out below.*

(b) *To any additional Valuer who qualifies to give evidence: three-quarters of the scale set out below.*

Amount	£	Amount	£	Amount	£	Amount	£
£100	10.50	£2,400	52.50	£5,400	84.00	£8,400	115.50
200	14.70	2,600	54.60	5,600	86.10	8,600	117.60
300	18.90	2,800	56.70	5,800	88.20	8,800	119.70
400	23.10	3,000	58.80	6,000	90.30	9,000	121.80
500	27.30	3,200	60.90	6,200	92.40	9,200	123.90
600	29.40	3,400	63.00	6,400	94.50	9,400	126.00
700	31.50	3,600	65.10	6,600	96.60	9,600	128.10
800	33.60	3,800	67.20	6,800	98.70	9,800	130.20
900	35.70	4,000	69.30	7,000	100.80	10,000	132.30
1,000	37.80	4,200	71.40	7,200	102.90	11,000	142.80
1,200	39.90	4,400	73.50	7,400	105.00	12,000	153.30
1,400	42.00	4,600	75.60	7,600	107.10	14,000	174.30
1,600	44.10	4,800	77.70	7,800	109.20	16,000	195.30
1,800	46.20	5,000	79.80	8,000	111.30	18,000	216.30
2,000	48.30	5,200	81.90	8,200	113.40	20,000	237.30
2,200	50.40						

Beyond this 1.05 per cent. on the remainder

(Minimum Fee £7.50)

Stock Exchange Information

TABLE FOR THE CALCULATION OF YIELDS ON UNITS OF £1

Price	@ 5%	@ 6%	@ 7%	@ 7½%	@ 8%	@ 9%	@ 10%
£	£	£	£	£	£	£	£
0.50	10.00	12.00	14.00	15.00	16.00	18.00	20.00
0.60	8.33½	10.00	11.66½	12.50	13.34	15.00	16.66½
0.70	7.14	8.57	10.00	10.71½	11.42½	12.86	14.28½
0.75	6.66½	8.00	9.33½	10.00	10.66½	12.00	13.33½
0.80	6.25	7.50	8.75	9.37½	10.00	11.25	12.50
0.90	5.55½	6.66½	7.78	8.33½	8.89	10.00	11.11
1.00	5.00	6.00	7.00	7.50	8.00	9.00	10.00
1.10	4.55	5.45½	6.36	6.81½	7.27	8.18½	9.09
1.20	4.16½	5.00	5.83½	6.25	6.66½	7.50	8.33½
1.25	4.00	4.80	5.60	6.00	6.40	7.20	8.00
1.30	3.85	4.61½	5.38½	5.77	6.15½	6.92½	7.69
1.40	3.57	4.29	5.00	5.36	5.61	6.43	7.14
1.50	3.33½	4.00	4.66½	5.00	5.33½	6.00	6.66½
1.60	2.12½	3.75	4.37½	4.69	5.00	5.62½	6.25
1.70	2.94	3.53	4.11½	4.41	4.71	5.29½	5.88½
1.75	2.86	3.43	4.00	4.29	4.57	5.14	5.71
1.80	2.78	3.33½	3.89	4.16½	4.44½	5.00	5.55½
1.90	2.63½	3.16	3.68½	3.94½	4.21	4.74	5.26
2.00	2.50	3.00	3.50	3.75	4.00	4.50	5.00

Illustration of use: If £1 shares carry a dividend of 6% and can be bought for 70p each, the yield on cost is £8.57.

Weights and Measures

Acre. 4 roods or 10 square chains or 4840 sq. yds.; a piece of land rather less than 70 yds. square.

Ampere. Unit of measurement of electrical current, see *Electrical Units*, post.

Are. 100 square metres = 119.6 sq yds.

Avoirdupois weight. The ordinary weight. 16 drams = 1 ounce; 16 oz. = 1 lb.; 28 lb. = 1 quarter; 4 quarters, or 112 lb. = 1 hundredweight (cwt.); 20 hundredweight = 1 ton.

Barrel (of beer), 36 gallons; (of butter), 224 lbs.; of flour), 196 lbs.; (of soap), 256 lbs.

Bottle (of wine) holds about one-sixth of a gallon, (26⅔ fl. oz.).

Butt (of ale) 108 gallons or 2 hogsheads; of wine 126 gals. = 1 pipe or 2 h.hds.

Cable's length. 120 fathoms or 720 ft.

Carat. ⅕ gramme; 3 grains or 205.5 milligrammes. The fineness of gold is determined by the quantity of pure gold in 24 carats. The standard for coin is 22 carats of pure gold to two of alloy (copper); gold jewellery is commonly made of 18, 15, or 9 carat gold, i.e. metal consisting of 18 (15 or 9) carats of pure gold to 6 (9 or 15) of alloy.

Cental. 100 lb.

Centigramme. 1-100th of a gramme. It = .154 grains.

Centilitre. 1-100th of a litre = .0176 pint.

Centimetre. 1-100th of a metre. It = .393 (or 2-5ths) of an inch. 10 centimetres = 4 inches nearly.

Chain. 22 yds. or 20.1 metres.

Chaldron. 36 bushels.

Coomb. 4 bushels; 10 to a load or wey.

Cubic measure. 1728 cu. in. = 1 cu. ft.; 27 cu. ft. = 1 cu. yard. Cf. "Foot", "Yard", "Litre".

Dekagramme. 10 grammes = 0.35 oz.

Dekalitre. 10 litres = 2 gals. 1.6 pints.

Dekametre. 10 metres = 10 yds. 33.7 inches.

Decigramme. 1-10th of a gramme = 1.54 grain.

Decilitre. 1-10th of a litre = about a wineglassful.

Decimetre. 1-10th of a metre = 3.937 (nearly 4) inches.

Dram (avd.). One sixteenth of an oz. or 27.3 grains.

Dyne. Unit of force; that force which, acting on matter weighing a gramme for one second generates a velocity of one centimetre a second.

Fathom. 6 ft.; of timber, 216 cu. ft.

Firkin. 9 galls.

Flagon. 2 galls.

Folio. 72 words.

Foot. 12 inches = 30.479 centimetres, 3 to a yard.

Foot (square). 144 sq. inches = 9.29 sq. decimetres. 9 sq ft. = 1 sq. yd.

Foot (cubic). 1,728 cu. inches = 28.3153 cu. decimetres. 27 cu. ft. = 1 cu. yard. A cu. ft. of water weighs 1,000 oz. av. nearly.

Foot pound. A unit in measuring work. It represents 1 lb. raised through a height of 1 foot.

Furlong. 220 yds = 201.165 metres, 8 to a mile.

Gallon. 4 quarts or 8 pints. The gallon contains 10 lb. of distilled water weighed in air of specific density = 4.546 litres. In the United States the old Winchester gallon of 231 cu. in. is the basis.

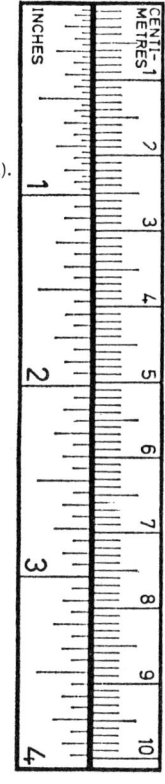

Gill. One-fourth of a pint: 5 fluid ounces.

Grain = .0648 grammes, 7,000 grains go to 1 lb.

Gramme. One thousandth of a kilogramme, the metric unit of weight = 15.432 grains.

Hand (horse measure). 4 inches.

Hectare. 100 ares = 10,000 sq. metres = 2.47 acres. The usual unit for measuring land in France.

Hectolitre (100 litres). 22 gallons. The common measure for grain; 2¾ imperial bushels (nearly).

Hogshead. 52½ gallons.

Horse-power. The power required to raise 33,000 lb. one foot high in one minute. An electrical H.P. = 746 Watts.

Hundredweight (cwt.). 112 lb = 50.7 kilogrammes; 20 to a ton. In America often 1 cwt means 100 lb.

Imperial units of mass or weight. See *Avoirdupois weight, Central and Grain,* supra. Ounce troy, 480 grains.

Inch. 1-12th of a foot = 25.4 millimetres.

Kilderkin. 18 gallons.

Kilogramme (1,000 grammes) = 2,2046 lb. av. Roughly 10 kilos = 22 lb. and 1,015 = 1 ton.

Kilogrammetre. Unit of work. It is equal to the work performed raising a kilogram through a metre of space, and = 7.233 foot pounds.

Kilometre (1,000 metres) = .6214 mile, or about 1,094 yards. Roughly 8 kilometres = 5 miles, and 100 kils. = 62½ miles.

Knot. A speed of one nautical mile an hour.

League. 3 miles.

Line. One-twelfth of an inch.

Litre. The metrical unit of capacity: = 1 cubic decimetre = 1.76 pint, or 0.22 gal. Roughly a litre is 1¾ pint; 4½ make a gallon, A litre of water weighs a kilogramme.

Load (of bricks), contains 500; (of corn) 10 coombs or 40 bushels; (of hay, &c.), 36 trusses.

Metre. The metrical unit of length = 39.3708 inches. Technically defined in relation to wavelength of the radiation of the krypton-86 atom. Roughly, a yard and a tenth; 3 metres = 10 ft. 11 metres = 12 yards.

Mile (Eng. Stat.). 1,760 yards, or 8 furlongs or 80 chains. A mile = 5,280 ft = 1,609.315 metres.

Mile (square). 640 acres = 1,609.3 sq. metres.

Mile (Nautical or Geographical), is 800 ft. more than a Stat. mile.

Millimetre. 1-1,000th of a metre = .039 inch. 25 to an inch.

Myriametre. 10,000 metres = 6.214 miles.

Ohm, the unit of measurement of electrical resistance; see *Electrical Units, post.*

Ounce (avoir.). 16 drams or 437½ grains = 28.35 grams. 16 to 1 lb. av.

Ounce (fluid). 20 to a pint.

Ounce (troy). 480 grains.

Pin (of beer): 4½ gallons.

Pint. Half a quart or 1-8th of a gal. = .568 litre. A pint of water weighs 1¼ lb.

Pound (imperial). 16 ounces or 7,000 grains = 0.453 592 37 kilogramme.

Quart. 2 pints = 1.135 litre. 4 to a gallon. A quart of water weighs 2½ lb.

Quarter (weight). 28 lb. 4 to 1 cwt.

Quarter (of corn). 8 bushels or 2 coombs.

Quintal. 100 kilogrammes.

Quire (of paper). 24 sheets. A quire of "outsides" is 20 sheets.

Ream (of paper). 480 sheets or 20 quires; but printing papers are often of 500 sheets, and a "perfect" ream of printing paper is 516 sheets.

Rood. 2½ sq. chains or 1,210 sq. yds. 4 to an acre.

Runlet. 18 gallons.

Sack of potatoes, 168 lb.; of flour, 280 lb.; of coal, 224 lb.

Square Measure. 144 sq. inches = 1 sq. foot. 9 sq. ft. = 1 sq. yard; 4 roods = 1 acre; 640 acres = 1 sq. mile.

Standard of Timber. 165 cu. ft.

Stere. A cubic metre.

Stone (ordinary). 14 lb.

Strike. 2 bushels.

Therm. 100,000 British Thermal Units. A British Thermal Unit is the amount of heat required to raise 1 lb. of water 1 degree Fahr. in temperature.

Tierce. 42 gall. *Tod* (of wool). 28 lb.

Ton. 20 cwt. or 2,240 lb. = 1,016.05 kilogrammes. Metric ton = 1,000 kilogrammes.

Ton register (of ships). 100 cu. ft.

Truss of straw, 36 lb.; of old hay, 56 lb.; of new hay, 60 lb.

Tun. 2 pipes, or 252 gallons.

Verst (Russian). 3,500 ft. (abt. ¾ mile).

Volt, the unit of measurement of

difference of electrical potential, see *Electrical Units, post.*

Watt, the unit of measurement of electrical power, see *Electrical Units, post.*

Wey or *Load* (of corn). 5 quarters, or 40 bushels.

Yard. 3 ft. or 36 inches = .9144 metre.

Yard (square). 9 sq. ft. or 1,296 sq. in. = .836 sq metre.

Yard (cubic). 27 cu. ft. = .7646 cu. metre.

CIRCLE.—*Circumference* = Diam. × 22 ÷ 7; or diam. × 3.1416. *Area* = radius squared × 3.1416. SPHERE, *Solidity of* = cube of diam. × .5236.

ELECTRICAL UNITS.—The *Volt* is the unit of electromotive force (E.M.F.); and is rather less than the E.M.F. of one Daniell's cell; it is the difference of electrical potential between two points of a conducting wire carrying a constant current of 1 ampere when the power dissipated between these two points is equal to 1 watt. The *Farad* is the B.A. unit of electrostatic capacity. The *Coulomb* is the unit of quantity of electricity; it is that quantity which is contained in one farad when electrified to the potentiality of one volt. The *Ampère* is the unit of current; it is the constant current which, if maintained in two straight parallel conduits of infinite length and of negligible circular sections and placed 1 metre apart in vacuum, will produce between the conductors a force equal to 2 × 10⁻⁷ M.K.S. units of force per metre of length. The *Ohm* is the unit of resistance; the legal ohm is the electrical resistance between two points of a conductor when a constant difference of potential of 1 volt applied between the two points produces in the conductor a current of 1 ampere, the conductor not being the seat of any electromotive force. The *Watt* is the unit of power or activity; it is the power which gives rise to the production of energy of 1 joule per second. The *Joule* is the unit of electrical energy; it is the work done in one second by a current of one ampère flowing through a resistance of one ohm; equal to 10 million ergs. The *Horse-power* (electrical) is 746 watts. The *Board of Trade Unit* is 1.34 horse-power hours = 10 ampères at 100 volts per hour. A *Meg-ohm* is a million ohms. A *Micro-farad* is a millionth of a farad.

PHYSIOLOGICAL.—The normal temperature of the human body is 98.4 F. (37 C). The normal pulse of a man of 35 is 70 to 75 to the minute; in youth and extreme age it is quicker.

THERMOMETER.—9 deg. Fahrenheit = 5 deg. Centigrade, or 4 deg. Réamur. Hence 1 deg. C. = 1.8 deg. F. Water freezes at 32 F, 0 C, 0 R, and boils at 212 F, 100 C, 80 R. 10 C = "50" F.; 15 C = "59" F; 20 C = "68" F.; 25 C = "77" F.

Abbreviations of Commercial Terms

@—At.
100 A1—First Class at Lloyd's.
a.a.r.—Against all risks.
A/C—Account current.
a/c—Account.
a/d—After date.
A/o—Account of.
A/S—Account sales. After sight.
B/E—Bill of exchange.
B/L—Bill of lading.
B/P—Bills to be paid.
B/R—Bills payment of which is to be received.
B/S—Bill of sale.
c. & f.—Cost and freight.
c.i.f.—Cost, insurance, freight.
c/o—Care of.
C.O.D.—Cash on delivery.
C/P—Charter-party.
cp. or cf.—Compare.
cr.—Creditor.
c/s—Cases.
cum. div.—Including dividend.
D/d—Days after date.
Dft.—Draft (Bill of exchange).
div.—Dividend.
do.—Ditto.
dr.—Debtor.
D/s—Days after sight.
d.w—Deadweight.
Dy—Delivery.
E. & O.E.—Errors and omissions excepted.
e.g.—For example (*exempli gratia*).
ex div.—Without dividend.
f.a.a.—Free of all average.
f.a.q.—Fair average quality.
F.G.A.—Foreign general average.
f.o.b.—Free on board (expense of putting on board included).
f.o.r.—Free on rail.
fo.—Folio.
f.o.w.—First open water (Baltic).
f.p.a.—Free of particular average.
ib.—In the same place.
id.—The same.
i.e.—That is.
Inv.—Invoice.

I.O.U.—I owe you.
J.A.—Joint account.
L/C—Letter of credit.
L.S.—Place of seal (*locus sigilli*).
Ltd.—Limited.
M/C—Metalling clause (mar. insurance).
M/d—Months after date.
M/s—Months after sight.
MSS.—Manuscripts.
N/a—No advice.
n/a—Non-acceptance.
N.B.—Take note (*Nota bene*).
N.E.—No effects.
N/f.—No funds.
n/s.—Not sufficient (banking).
o/a—On account.
o/d—On demand.
%—Per cent.
o/s—out of stock.
o/p—Out of print.
P/N—Promissory note.
P.O.—Postal order.
P.P.O.—Post Office order
p.p., p. pro., and per pro.—*Per procurationem.* (By proxy.)
pro. tem.—For the time being (*pro tempore*).
P.S.—Postscript.
q.v.—Which see (*quod vide*).
R. and Rs.—Rupee and Rupees.
R/D—Refer to drawer.
R.O.—*Rendu ouvert* (Telegraphic).
R.P.—*Réponse payé* (Reply paid).
$—Dollars.
S/N—Shipping note.
S.P.—Supra protest.
S.S.—Steamship.
t.l.o.—Total loss only.
t.t.—Telegraphic transfer.
U.K.—United Kingdom.
uw.—Underwriter.
v.—Against (*versus*).
via.—By way of.
viz.—Namely.
x.c.—Ex coupon.
x.d.—Ex dividend.
x.new—Ex right to new shares.

Administration of Estates

EXECUTORS AND ADMINISTRATORS

(*See Halsbury's Laws of England* (3rd Edn.), vol. 16, p. 115, et seq.)

An executor derives his title from the will, and may act as such before obtaining probate, whereas an administrator derives his title entirely from the grant though the Courts have adopted the doctrine that upon the grant being made the title of the administrator relates back to the date of death. This doctrine does not, however, regularise proceedings commenced by an administrator, in his capacity as such, before the grant (*Hilton* v. *Sutton Steam Laundries*, [1945] 2 All E.R. 425) or operate to disturb interests validly acquired in the interval (*Long (Fred) and Son, Ltd.* v. *Burgess,* [1949] 2 All E. R. 484, C.A.).

No one is obliged to serve as an executor, but if he takes up the administration he must prove the will and act until the Court releases him. A purported renunciation before grant in order to purchase part of the estate is void if the executor has already acted as executor: *Holder* v. *Holder*, [1968] 1 All E. R. 665, C.A. A corporation may be executor. Where an executor delays to act, he may be compelled by the Court to accept or refuse within a reasonable time.

Should a minor (i.e. a person under 18: Family Law Reform Act 1969, s. 1) be sole executor, his guardian or other person appointed by the Family Division may act until he attains his majority. If an executor has been appointed merely for a limited period his powers will cease upon the expiration of such period.

An executor cannot transfer his executorship, but the executor of a sole or last surviving executor becomes by devolution executor of the original will.

Generally as to the practice as to grants of representation to the estates of persons domiciled abroad, see the Non-Contentious Probate Rules, 1954, r. 29 as amended by s. 1 1967 No. 748 (and as to Rhodesian grants see Practice Direction dated 7 April 1970, [1970] 1 All E. R. 1248; [1970] 1 W.L.R. 687; whilst the notes relating to Commonwealth and Colonial grants are varied by Administration of Estates Act 1971, s. 11). As to the recognition within one part of the U.K. of grants made in another part, see Administration of Estates Act 1971, ss. 1-7.

As from 1 January 1972, an administration bond will no longer be required as a condition of the grant of letters of administration: Administration of Estates Act 1971, s. 8. Instead, the Court *may* require one or more sureties to give a guarantee. The circumstances in which this will be done, and the form the guarantee should take, are set out in the Non-Contentious Probate (Amendment) Rules 1971, s. 1, 1971, No. 1977.

Upon a death, the deceased person's land (which includes leaseholds, see Administration of Estates Act, 1925, s. 3 (1)) devolves, notwithstanding any testamentary disposition, to and becomes vested in the personal representatives subject to their executorial rights and duties, and after the conclusion of those duties, as trustees for the persons beneficially entitled thereto (*see* Administration of Estates Act 1925, Pt. I.) Where an executor is also a trustee, the legal estate in land will not vest in him in the latter capacity until he executes a written assent (*Re King's Will Trusts, Assheton* v. *Boyne*, [1964] 1 All E.R. 833), and the same principle would apply to an executor who is also beneficially entitled.

Since 1897 all the deceased's property not held in joint tenancy has devolved on the personal representative, though since 1925 a testator may appoint special personal representatives of settled land continuing to be settled after his death or such personal representatives may be deemed to be appointed (*see* Administration of Estates Act, 1925, s. 22). As to where there is such continuing settled land, see *Williams on Title*, 4th Edn.

The first duty of an executor or administrator is to provide for the burial of the deceased person; he may also at once pay or discharge debts due or owing, and sue or be sued on behalf of the estate, subject to probate. In particular, he will have to consider the liability of the estate to Capital Transfer Tax (*see* CAPITAL TRANSFER

TAX, post). Before finally distributing the estate collected by him, he should advertise for claims to be sent in by a certain date.

The Lord Chancellor's Office in consultation with the Law Society, has arranged with the editors of *The Times*, the *Daily Telegraph* and the *Guardian* that advertisements by personal representatives under s. 27 of the Trustee Act, 1925 may be inserted in the form of a schedule under a common heading. This results in the saving of space and of expense to personal representatives by avoiding the repetition in each advertisement of formal words.

The following are examples of the way in which advertisements should be submitted:—

> ROSEMARY LESLEY JOHNSON, 14 Park Road, Sale, Manchester, died 13th September, 1958; particulars to Smith, Jones & Tankerton, Solicitors, 21 Hobart Place, London, W.1. before December 31st, 1958.

> RAYMOND DANIEL DOBSON, Red Farm, Sandy Lane, Bicknoller, Somerset, died 26th September, 1958; particulars to Knowles & Crayson, Solicitors, 22 Johnson Road, Taunton, Somerset, before the 31st December, 1958.

Solicitors and others responsible for the entry of advertisements in the above-mentioned newspapers should ensure that they adhere as nearly as possible to the form of words of which the above are examples: otherwise the editor of the newspaper concerned will return the advertisements for re-wording.

Advertisements for other newspapers which are printed under separate headings should follow the wording of s. 27 of the Trustee Act, 1925, so as to invite claims to share beneficially as well as claims by creditors (see *Re Aldhous, Noble* v. *Treasury Solicitor,* [1955] 2 All E.R. 80, and see *Law Society's Gazette,* July, 1955, p. 307, for an amended form of words, drafted in consequence of this case, which now introduces advertisements in tabulated form in *The Times,* etc.).

There is no rule of law requiring all debts to be paid within a year. Circumstances inevitably vary and the

duty of executors is to pay with due diligence.

An executor *de son tort* is one who intermeddles with the property of a deceased person, without having been appointed an executor, or without having obtained a grant of administration; such a person has none of the privileges and more than the usual liabilities of an ordinary executor, *e.g.* he may be sued by a creditor or a legatee, while if a creditor himself he will not be permitted to pay himself out of the estate. Such acts, however, as are necessary to preserve the estate or to provide for the burial of the deceased may be safely done by a stranger.

Property vested in trustees subject to trusts is held by them in joint tenancy and upon the death of any one vests in the survivor or survivors but, of course, still subject to the trusts. If there is a sole trustee or a sole surviving trustee, then on his death the trust property vests in his personal representatives despite any provision in the trustee's will or in the instrument creating the trust (Administration of Estates Act, 1925, ss. 1 (2), (3)). These personal representatives may either carry on the trust (Trustee Act, 1925, s. 18 (2)) or appoint new trustees in their place (Trustee Act, 1925, s. 36); but, if there is a person nominated by the trust instrument to appoint new trustees, then an appointment by him will oust the personal representatives. It would appear, however, that one personal representative acting in a trust could not give a receipt for capital money unless such personal representative happened to be a trust corporation (Trustee Act, 1925, s. 18 (3)).

Property vested by way of mortgage in any person solely also devolves upon his personal representatives. They are entitled to receive and give a good discharge for the mortgage money and can exercise the statutory power of sale.

Joint representatives are regarded in the light of an individual person. Accordingly one of several executors can give a good discharge for a debt due to the estate and can settle an account with a person accountable to the estate. But the Bank of England and other corporations commonly provide by their regulations that all the proving executors must join in a transfer, and it must be remembered that the rule does not apply with regard to land which comes to the executors either upon trust for sale or under the Property Acts replacing the Land Transfer Act of 1897; all the executors who accept probate must join in a conveyance of the testator's land including leaseholds and all interests in land in possession reversion and remainder.

Personal representatives have what has been called a paramount title to all property of the deceased not vested in him for an interest terminating on his death, and, although they can in theory only sell such property in due course of administration, anyone dealing with them is not concerned with the reasons for the seal or with the application of the purchase money: *Bonney* v. *Ridgard*, [1784] 1 Cox Eq. Cas. 145 and see the statement by Lord Mansfield, C.J., in *Whale* v. *Booth*, [1784] 4 Term Rep. 625 set out in *English & Empire Digest* Repl. Edn.,

Vol. 24, p. 618. They are also entitled to possession of the property against anyone entitled on the intestacy, see *Williams* v. *Holland*, [1965] 2 All E.R. 157.

Apart from their powers under the Land Transfer Act of 1897, and the Administration of Estates Act, 1925, Part 1, personal representatives have power to convey for all their deceased's estate and interest therein any land in respect of which there was subsisting at the testator's death an enforceable contract for sale, but the conveyance is not to affect the beneficial rights of any person claiming under any testamentary disposition, or as persons entitled on intestacy. It should be noted that, where any such sale is completed by means of an assent in favour of the purchaser, such assent attracts *ad valorem* duty (*G.H.R. Co.* v. *I. R. Commissioners*, [1943] 1 All E.R. 424).

FAMILY PROVISION

This subject is governed by the Inheritance (Provision for Family and Dependants) Act 1975 which came into force on 1st April 1976. The Act constitutes a new comprehensive code relating to family provision from the estates of deceased persons. It thus repeals all the existing relevant legislation and re-enacts those portions of that legislation in respect of which no change is made. The new provisions are based on the familiar approach of the Inheritance (Family Provision) Act 1938 of enabling the court to make discretionary provision for a class of dependants for whom the deceased has not made reasonable provision on his death.

Where the court is of opinion that the disposition of the deceased's estate made by his will and/or the law of intestate succession is not such as to make reasonable provision for any of the "dependants" listed below, it may order reasonable provision to be made. The dependants who may apply are (s. 1 (1)):

    (a) the wife or husband of the deceased; the reference to a wife or husband includes a reference to a person who in good faith entered into a void

marriage with the deceased unless either—

the marriage of the deceased and that person was dissolved or annulled during the lifetime of the deceased and the dissolution or annulment is recognised by the law of England and Wales, or

that person has during the lifetime of the deceased entered into a later marriage (s. 25 (4)).

    (b) a former wife or former husband of the deceased who has not remarried; "former wife" or "former husband" means a person whose marriage with the deceased was during the deceased's lifetime dissolved or annulled by a decree of divorce or of nullity of marriage made under the Matrimonial Causes Act 1973 (s. 25 (1)).

The reference to remarriage or to a person who has remarried includes a reference to a marriage which is by law void or voidable or to a person who has entered into such a marriage, as the case may be, and a marriage is to be treated for the purposes of the Act as a remarriage, in relation to any party thereto, notwithstanding that the previous marriage of that party was void or voidable (s. 25 (5)).

(c) a child of the deceased, which includes an illegitimate child and a child en ventre sa mere at the death of the deceased (s. 25 (1)).

(d) any person (not being a child of the deceased) who, in the case of any marriage to which the deceased was at any time a party, was treated by the deceased as a child of the family in relation to that marriage;

(e) any person (not being a person included in the foregoing paragraphs of this subsection) who immediately before the death of the deceased was being maintained, either wholly or partly, by the deceased.

Where an application is made for an order under the Act the court may, if it is satisfied that the disposition of the deceased's estate effected by his will or the law relating to intestacy, or the combination of his will and that law, is not such as to make reasonable financial provision for the applicant, make any one or more of the following orders (s. 2 (1)):

(a) an order for the making to the applicant out of the net estate of the deceased of such periodical payments and for such term as may be specified in the order. The payments may be of such an amount specified in the order or equal to the whole of the income of the net estate or of such portion thereof as may be so specified or equal to the whole of the income of such part of the net estate as the court may direct to be set aside or appropriated for the making out of the income thereof the payments (s. 2 (2)).

(b) an order for the payment to the applicant out of that estate of a lump sum of such amount as may be so specified;

(c) an order for the transfer to the applicant of such property comprised in that estate as may be so specified;

(d) an order for the settlement for benefit of the applicant of such property comprised in that estate as may be so specified;

(e) an order for the acquisition out of property comprised in that estate of such property as may be so specified and for the transfer of the property so acquired to the applicant or for the settlement thereof for his benefit;

(f) an order varying any antenuptial settlement (including such a settlement made by will) made on the parties to a marriage to which the deceased was one of the parties, the variation being for the benefit of the surviving party to that marriage, or any child of that marriage, or any person who was treated by the deceased as a child of the family in relation to that marriage.

In considering whether to make an order or not, the court will have regard to the financial resources and financial needs which the applicant and the beneficiaries under the estate, have, or are likely to have. The size and nature of the net estate of the deceased will also be an important factor. When considering applications from spouses and former spouses the court will consider the age of the applicant and the duration of the marriage and the contribution made by the applicant to the welfare of the family (s. 3 (1)).

An application for an order under the Act must be made within six months from the date on which representation with respect to the estate of the deceased is first taken out, except with permission of the court (s. 4). The court has power to make an interim order where it appears that the applicant is in immediate need of financial assistance, but it is not yet possible to determine what order (if any) should be made under that section; and that property forming part of the net estate of the deceased is or can be made available to meet the need of the applicant (s. 5).

The Act contains several provisions which will have the effect of counter-acting avoidance and evasion devices. Thus the meaning of "net estate" is extended to include certain property subject to general powers of appointment (s. 25 (1)), property in co-ownership (s. 9), and property made the subject of nominations and *donationes mortis causa* (s. 8). The court is given power to review dispositions made by the deceased during his lifetime with the intention of defeating a claim for family provision (s. 10). Likewise the court is empowered to review contracts to leave property by will where the deceased entered into such a contract with the intention of defeating a claim for family provision (s. 11), thereby reversing the recent Privy Council decision in *Schaefer* v. *Schuhmann*, [1972] A.C. 572; [1972] 1 All E. R. 621.

Application must normally be made in the High Court but where the value of the deceased's net estate does not exceed £5,000 the application may be made in the County Court (s. 22 (1)).

INTESTACY

I.—WHERE DEATH OF INTESTATE OCCURRED BEFORE 1st JANUARY, 1926

(a) REAL ESTATE

(See Halsbury's Laws of England (3rd Edn.), vol. 16, pp. 422–432)

(b) PERSONAL ESTATE

(See Halsbury's Laws af England (3rd Edn.), vol. 16, pp. 414–422)

II.—WHERE DEATH OF INTESTATE OCCURRED BETWEEN 1st JANUARY, 1926 AND 31ST DECEMBER, 1952.

REAL AND PERSONAL ESTATE

(See Halsbury's Laws of England (3rd Edn.), vol. 16, pp. 410–412)

III.—WHERE INTESTATE DIED ON OR AFTER 1st JANUARY, 1953

REAL AND PERSONAL ESTATE

By s. 33 (1) of the Administration of Estates Act 1925, the real estate of an intestate is to be held by his personal representative upon trust for sale, and his personal estate upon trust for conversion, with power of postponement. Personal chattels (*i.e.* furniture, plate, etc.) are not to be sold unless necessary. The section contains directions as to the administration of the assets.

S. 46 as amended as respects persons dying on or after 1st January, 1953, by the Intestates' Estates Act, 1952, deals with the succession to the *real and personal* estate of an intestate, and provides that his residuary estate (*i.e.* the estate remaining after payment of funeral and testamentary expenses and debts, etc., under s. 33) is to be distributed as follows:—

(1) If the deceased leaves a husband or wife, he or she takes

(a) the personal chattels absolutely

(b) if the intestate leaves issue £5,000 (increased as from July 1st, 1972 to £15,000, see Family Provision Act 1966) free of death duties and costs, with interest at 4%; and if the intestate leaves no issue £20,000 (increased as from July 1st, 1972 to £40,000) free of death duties with interest at 4%. Although the Act states that the residuary estate shall "stand charged with" these sums, such charge is not registrable under the Land Charges Act, 1972;

(c) if the intestate leaves issue, the income of half the residue for life;

(d) if the intestate leaves no issue, but leaves one or both parents or brothers or sisters of the whole blood or their issue half the residue absolutely, the other half devolving on the parent(s) of the intestate absolutely or if neither survive being held on the statutory trusts for the brothers and sisters of the whole blood; or

(e) if the intestate leaves no issue and no parent or brother or sister of the whole blood and no issue of such brother or sister the whole residue absolutely.

(2) If the intestate leaves issue then, subject to the interest under (1) (a) (b) and (c) above of the husband or wife if surviving, the residue is to be held on "statutory trusts" for the intestate's issue. These trusts are (s. 47 (1) (i)) for all children of the intestate, living at his death, who attain 21 or marry under that age, in equal shares; and for the issue living at the intestate's death (who attain 21 or marry) of any child of the intestate who predeceases him leaving issue living at his death, such issue to take *per stirpes*. In the case of deaths occurring on or after 1 January 1970 the age of 18 is substituted for the age of 21: Family Law Reform Act, 1969, s. 5(2).

(3) If the intestate leaves both parents but no husband or wife and no issue, then the residuary estate belongs to the father and mother in equal shares absolutely, whilst, if he leaves one parent, he or she takes the whole (s. 46 (1) (iii) and (iv)).

(4) If the intestate leaves no husband or wife and no issue or parent, then, subject to (1), the residue is (s. 46 (1) (v)), held for the following persons and in the following order:—

(a) On "statutory trusts" for the brothers and sisters of the whole blood;

(b) On "statutory trusts" for the brothers and sisters of the half blood;

(c) The grandparents of the intestate in equal shares;

(d) On "statutory trusts" for the uncles and aunts (whole blood) of the intestate;

(e) On "statutory trusts" for the uncles and aunts (half blood) of the intestate.

"Statutory trusts" here mean (s. 47 (3)) trusts corresponding to the statutory trusts for issue (with an exception) including, of course, the issue of a brother or sister, etc., who predeceased the intestate.

In default of any person taking as above the residuary estate goes as *bona vacantia* to the Crown (s. 46 (1) (vi)).

A surviving husband or wife can require redemption of any life interest to which he or she is entitled under (1) (c) above (s. 47 A).

These rules also apply where part only of a testator's property is disposed of by his will. Benefits under such a will need not be brought into account (s. 49) except by a surviving husband or wife against the sum of £5,000 (or £15,000) or £20,000 (or £40,000) (as the case may be—see above) and interest thereon to which he or she is entitled under (1) (b) above and by issue. Personal chattels specifically bequeathed to the husband or wife need not be brought into hotchpot.

Persons formally adopted are treated for the purpose of the devolution of property, as children of the adopters; see ss. 16 and 17 of the Adoption Act 1958.

In the case of the deaths on or after 1 January 1970 the Family Law Reform Act 1969, s. 14, provides that an intestate's illegitimate child and his issue are to be entitled in the same way as if he was legitimate. For the meaning of "illegitimate child" see s. 14(8). In the case of deaths on or after 1st August, 1970, a spouse who is judicially separated from the intestate has no claim on the estate: Matrimonial Causes Act 1973, s. 18 (2).

PROBATE AND ADMINISTRATION MATTERS

CAVEATS

By entry of a caveat any person asserting an interest in the estate of a deceased person may prevent the sealing of a grant in such estate without notice to himself. The procedure is by simple entry—either at the Principal or at any district probate registry —in a book kept at such registry or by sending the necessary particulars by post to the registry. If entered by a solicitor on behalf of a caveator the name of the latter must appear in the caveat. Fee for entry £2. Ordinarily a caveat remains in force for six months from entry and may be renewed, but within that period the caveator may withdraw the caveat or it may be warned at the instance of any person interested. The person warning must state his interest, and the warning will also require the caveator to give particulars of any contrary interest he may have in the estate of the deceased. The warning (which can only issue from the Principal Registry—fee £2) must be served on the caveator who, should he then withdraw, must notify forthwith the person warning of the withdrawal. Unless the caveator enters an appearance to the warning—in which case the matter may become a contentious one, the applicant, on proof of service of the warning and that he has not been served with any summons by the caveator, will be entitled to proceed with his application for a grant.

If the caveator enters an appearance to warning, no grant can issue without an order.

OBTAINING PROBATE

To obtain a grant of probate the following documents are required:—

1.—*Inland Revenue Account* made by the executor or executors applying, and containing full particulars of all the real and personal estate of the deceased and of the debts and funeral expenses.

2.—*Oath of Executors.* A short printed form proving the death and exhibiting the testamentary documents lodged for proof. The Oath must state where the deceased died domiciled: if outside England and Wales, the country or the particular State or Province should be sworn, e.g. "deceased died domiciled in the Republic of Ireland *or* in the State of New York *or* in the Province of Quebec". Where the deceased died domiciled in England and Wales the grant covers the estate in the whole of the United Kingdom: otherwise the grant covers the estate in England and Wales only.

3.—*Renunciation* by any executor who does not wish to act. When an executor appointed by the will does not prove and does not renounce, power to prove subsequently will be reserved to him.

4.—*Engrossments.* Where the Will is unsuitable for photography or there is any alteration, addition or other matter which is not admitted to probate, it is necessary to lodge a copy made in accordance with the directions of the District Probate Registrar or the Clerk of the Probate Department at the Principal Registry and this is photographed instead of the Will.

5.—Where necessary an *affidavit of due execution* or other evidence to establish validity of the will should also be lodged; or an affidavit to set up an "alias" of the Testator; or as to identity of the Executor.

6.—The documents, with the appropriate fee (see *post*) may be lodged at, or sent by post to, the Principal Registry or any District Probate Registry or Sub-Registry. These are situate at Bangor (Gwynedd), Birmingham, Bodmin, Brighton, Bristol, Carlisle, Carmarthen, Chester, Exeter, Gloucester, Hull, Ipswich, Lancaster, Leeds, Leicester, Lincoln, Liverpool, Llandaff, Maidstone, Manchester, Middlesbrough, Newcastle upon Tyne, Norwich, Nottingham, Oxford, Peterborough, Sheffield, Stoke on Trent, Winchester and York.

OBTAINING ADMINISTRATION WITH OR WITHOUT WILL

To obtain a grant the following are necessary:—

1.—*Inland Revenue Account* which is to be made by the proposed administrator in similar form to that mentioned in the previous column.

2.—*Oath of proposed Administrator* as to death, and character in which the applicant applies. If deceased died domiciled out of England and Wales a Registrar's order under Rule 29 will be necessary. As to the estate covered by the grant, see the previous section.

3.—In certain cases (see Non-Contentious Probate Rules 1954, rule 38), a guarantee by sureties that they will make good, within any limit imposed by the Court (normally up to the gross value of the estate) any loss suffered in consequence of a breach by the administrator of his duties. No stamp duty is chargeable on the guarantee.

In cases where a grant of *Administration with Will annexed* is sought a special form of "Oath with Will annexed" is required and the same considerations as to *proof of validity* (and *engrossment*) *of Will* or as to *alias* of deceased or *identity* of applicant apply as in a probate application. An engrossment of the Will should therefore be supplied in those cases where it would be necessary if the application were for a grant of probate.

COURT FEES PAYABLE

In addition to Capital Transfer Tax (see p. 85) certain *fees* are payable under the Supreme Court (Non-Contentious Probate) Fees Order 1975.

On application for a grant relating to an estate which is exempt from estate duty or capital transfer tax, or for a grant limited to settled land or trust property, or for a duplicate grant, or for a second or subsequent grant in the same estate or for re-sealing a colonial grant, the fee is £2.

In all other cases, whether for probate or letters of administration with or without the will, the court fee is assessed on the net value of the real and personal estate as follows:—

If the value of the net real and personal estate passing under the grant is stated in the Inland Revenue Account to be:—

Not more than

£				£
1,000	..	..	..	No fee
3,000	..	..	..	5
5,000	..	..	..	10
10,000	..	..	..	20
15,000	..	..	..	30
20,000	..	..	..	40
25,000	..	..	..	50
30,000	..	..	..	60
35,000	..	..	..	70
40,000	..	..	..	80
45,000	..	..	..	90
50,000	..	..	..	100
55,000	..	..	..	110
60,000	..	..	..	120
65,000	..	..	..	130
70,000	..	..	..	140
75,000	..	..	..	150
80,000	..	..	..	160
85,000	..	..	..	170
90,000	..	..	..	180
95,000	..	..	..	190
100,000	..	..	..	200

And for every additional £100,000 or any part thereof, a further additional fee of .. £50

Personal Applications only.—On application for a grant of probate or letters of administration by a personal applicant, or for resealing such a grant if the application is prepared in the registry there is a departmental fee in addition to the court fee, as follows:—

If the net real and personal estate is of the value of

(a) Not more than

£				£
500	..	..	..	1
1,000	..	..	..	2
5,000	..	..	..	5

(b) More than £5,000, for each £1,000 or fractional part of £1,000 1

SEARCH FOR GRANTS AND COPIES

Records are kept at the Principal Registry of the Family Division at Somerset House, London, WC2R 1LP of all grants of Probate and Letters of Administration issued from the Principal Registry and District Probate Registries. These records together with copies of the wills and codicils applicable thereto are open to public inspection. No fee is payable for a personal search made by the applicant, but a fee of 25p is charged for the inspection of an original will or any other document. Where application is made by post to the Principal Registry for a copy of a will or grant, a postal handling fee of 50p (payable in advance) is chargeable. Application may also be made at the Principal Registry for a "standing search" in an estate, on payment of a fee of £1, where a grant of representation has issued not more than twelve months prior to the application or is likely to issue within the following six months.

The charge for a plain or office copy of any document is 25p per page. The basic fee for an officially sealed and certified copy of any document is £1, with a further and additional fee of 25p payable for each page after the first. Copies can be obtained from either the Principal Registry or the District Probate Registry at which the grant was made.

NON-CONTENTIOUS PROBATE COSTS

Rules 1 and 2 of the Rules of The Supreme Court (Non-Contentious Probate Costs), 1956, as construed in accordance with the Solicitors Act 1974, s. 89 (4), read as follows:—

"*Rule* 1. For work done in respect of business to which these Rules apply a solicitor shall be entitled to charge and be paid such sum as may be fair and reasonable having regard to all the circumstances of the case and in particular to:—

(1) the complexity of the matter or the difficulty or novelty of the questions raised;

(2) the skill, labour, specialised knowledge and responsibility involved on the part of the solicitor,

(3) the number and importance of the documents prepared or perused, without regard to length;

(4) the place where and circumstances in which the business or any part thereof is transacted;

(5) the time expended by the solicitor;

(6) the nature and value of the property involved;

(7) the importance of the matter to the client:

Provided that:—

(a) without prejudice to the provisions of sections [70, 71 and 72 of the Solicitors' Act, 1974], (which relate to taxation of costs) the client may require the solicitor to obtain a certificate from The Law Society certifying that the sum charged is fair and reasonable or, if it is not, what is a fair and reasonable sum, and the sum so certified (if less than that charged) shall, in the absence of taxation under the said Act be the sum payable.

(b) before the solicitor brings proceedings to recover costs in respect of business to which these Rules apply, he must, unless the costs have been taxed under the Solicitor's Act [1974], have drawn the attention of the client in writing—

(i) to his right under paragraph (a) of this proviso to require the solicitor to obtain a certificate from The Law Society, and

(ii) to the provisions of the [Solicitors' Act, 1974] with regard to taxation of costs;

(c) the client shall not be entitled to require the solicitor to obtain a certificate from The Law Society under paragraph (a) of this proviso after the bill has been taxed under the Solicitors' Act [1974], or has been paid;

(d) on any taxation of a bill in respect of business to which these Rules apply it shall be the duty of the solicitor to satisfy the Taxing Master as to the fairness and reasonableness of his charge; and

(e) if the Taxing Master allows less than one half of the amount charged, he shall bring the facts of the case to the attention of The Law Society."

[NOTE.—This rule follows exactly the same lines as Schedule II to the Solicitors' Remuneration Act, General Orders, 1883, as replaced by the Solicitors' Remuneration Order, 1953.

By way of a guide to solicitors as to the charges to be made under this Rule in respect of obtaining grants of representation and for administering the estate where the work, etc. involved under the seven factors set out above is neither abnormally large or difficult nor abnormally small or easy, The Law Society has suggested charges on the following lines:— Where the Gross Estate (not including aggregate property) is £2,000 and up to £10,000 then the suggested Solicitors' charges are 3 per cent on gross value; on the next £40,000, 2½ per cent on gross value; on the next £50,000, 2 per cent; on the next £150,000, 1 per cent; and on the next £250,000, ½ per cent (see *Law Society's Gazette*, vol. 68, p. 133).]

Rule 2. These Rules apply to all non-contentious or common form probate business for which instructions are accepted on or after the date on which these Rules come into operation.

Affiliation

SEE MAGISTRATES' COURTS

Arbitration and Compulsory References

(See Halsbury's Laws of England (4th Edn.) Vol. 2, p. 263 et seq.)

THE ARBITRATION ACT 1950

The Arbitration Act 1950, consolidates the Arbitration Acts 1889 to 1934. S. 25 has been amended by the Administration of Justice Act 1970, s. 4(4) and Sch. 3, para. 11. The following are the more important sections of that Act:—

Sect. 1.   The authority of an arbitrator or umpire appointed by or by virtue of an arbitration agreement shall, unless a contrary intention is expressed in the agreement, be irrevocable except by leave of the High Court or a judge thereof.

Sect. 2.   (1) An arbitration agreement shall not be discharged by the death of any party thereto, either as respects the deceased or any other party, but shall in such an event be enforceable by or against the personal representative of the deceased.

(2) The authority of an arbitrator shall not be revoked by the death of any party by whom he was appointed.

(3) Nothing in this section shall be taken to affect the operation of any enactment or rule of law by virtue of which any right of action is extinguished by the death of a person.

Sect. 3.   (1) Where it is provided by a term in a contract to which a bankrupt is a party that any differences arising thereout or in connection therewith shall be referred to arbitration, the said term shall, if the trustee in bankruptcy adopts the contract, be enforceable by or against him so far as relates to any such differences.

(2) Where a person who has been adjudged bankrupt had, before the commencement of the bankruptcy, become a party to an arbitration agreement, and any matter to which the agreement applies requires to be determined in connection with or for the purposes of the bankruptcy proceedings, then, if the case is one to which subsection (1) of this section does not apply, any other party to the agreement or, with the consent of the committee of inspection, the trustee in bankruptcy, may apply to the court having jurisdiction in the bankruptcy proceedings for an order directing that the matter in question shall be referred to arbitration in accordance with the agreement, and that court may, if it is of opinion that, having regard to all the circumstances of the case, the matter ought to be determined by arbitration, make an order accordingly.

Sect. 4.   (1) If any party to an arbitration agreement, or any person claiming through or under him, commences any legal proceedings in any court against any other party to the agreement, or any person claiming through or under him, in respect of any matter agreed to be referred, any party to those legal proceedings may at any time after appearance, and before delivering any pleadings or taking any other steps in the proceedings, apply to that court to stay the proceedings, and that court or a judge thereof, if satisfied that there is no sufficient reason why the matter should not be referred in accordance with the agreement, and that the applicant was, at the time when the proceedings were commenced, and still remains, ready and willing to do all things necessary to the proper conduct of the arbitration, may make an order staying the proceedings.

Sect. 5.   Where relief by way of interpleader is granted and it appears to the High Court that the claims in question are matters to which an arbitration agreement, to which the claimants are parties, applies, the High Court may direct the issue between the claimants to be determined in accordance with the agreement.

Sect. 6.   Unless a contrary intention is expressed therein, every arbitration agreement shall, if no other mode of reference is provided, be deemed to include a provision that the reference shall be to a single arbitrator.

Sect. 7.   Where an arbitration agreement provides that the reference shall be to two arbitrators, one to be appointed by each party, then, unless a contrary intention is expressed therein—

(a) if either of the appointed arbitrators refuses to act, or is incapable of acting, or dies, the party who appointed him may appoint a new arbitrator in his place;

(b) if, on such a reference, one party fails to appoint an arbitrator, either originally, or by way of substitution as aforesaid, for seven clear days after the other party, having appointed his arbitrator, has served the party making default with notice to make the appointment, the party who has appointed an arbitrator may appoint that arbitrator to act as sole arbitrator in the reference and his award shall be binding on both parties as if he had been appointed by consent:

Provided that the High Court or a judge thereof may set aside any appointment made in pursuance of this section.

Sect. 8. (1) Unless a contrary intention is expressed therein, every arbitration agreement shall, where the reference is to two arbitrators, be deemed to include a provision that the two arbitrators shall appoint an umpire immediately after they are themselves appointed.

(2) Unless a contrary intention is expressed therein, every arbitration agreement shall, where such a provision is applicable to the reference, be deemed to include a provision that if the arbitrators have delivered to any party to the arbitration agreement, or to the umpire, a notice in writing stating that they cannot agree, the umpire may forthwith enter on the reference in lieu of the arbitrators.

(3) At any time after the appointment of an umpire, however appointed, the High Court may, on the application of any party to the reference and notwithstanding anything to the contrary in the arbitration agreement, order that the umpire shall enter upon the reference in lieu of the arbitrators and as if he were a sole arbitrator.

Sect. 9. (1) Where an arbitration agreement provides that the reference shall be to three arbitrators, one to be appointed by each party and the third to be appointed by the two appointed by the parties, the agreement shall have effect as if it provided for the appointment of an umpire, and not

for the appointment of a third arbitrator, by the two arbitrators appointed by the parties.

(2) Where an arbitration agreement provides that the reference shall be to three arbitrators to be appointed otherwise than as mentioned in subsection (1) of this section, the award of any two of the arbitrators shall be binding.

Sect. 10. In any of the following cases:—

(a) where an arbitration agreement provides that the reference shall be to a single arbitrator, and all the parties do not, after differences have arisen, concur in the appointment of an arbitrator;

(b) if an appointed arbitrator refuses to act, or is incapable of acting, or dies, and the arbitration agreement does not show that it was intended that the vacancy should not be supplied and the parties do not supply the vacancy;

(c) where the parties or two arbitrators are at liberty to appoint an umpire or third arbitrator and do not appoint him, or where two arbitrators are required to appoint an umpire and do not appoint him;

(d) where an appointed umpire or third arbitrator refuses to act, or is incapable of acting, or dies, and the arbitration agreement does not show that it was intended that the vacancy should not be supplied, and the parties or arbitrators do not supply the vacancy;

any party may serve the other parties or the arbitrators as the case may be, with a written notice to appoint or, as the case may be, concur in appointing, an arbitrator, umpire or third arbitrator, and if the appointment is not made within seven clear days after the service of the notice, the High Court or a judge thereof may, on application by the party who gave the notice, appoint an arbitrator, umpire or third arbitrator who shall have the like powers to act in the reference and make an award as if he had been appointed by consent of all parties.

Sect. 11. Where an arbitration agreement provides that the reference shall be to an official referee, any official referee to whom application is made shall, subject to any order of the High

Court, or a judge thereof as to transfer or otherwise, hear and determine the matters agreed to be referred.

Sect. 13. (1) Subject to the provisions of subsection (2) of section twenty-two of this Act, and anything to the contrary in the arbitration agreement, an arbitrator or umpire shall have power to make an award at any time.

(2) The time, if any, limited for making an award, whether under this Act or otherwise, may from time to time be enlarged by order of the High Court or a judge thereof, whether that time has expired or not.

(3) The High Court may, on the application of any party to a reference, remove an arbitrator or umpire who fails to use all reasonable dispatch in entering on and proceeding with the reference and making an award, and an arbitrator or umpire who is removed by the High Court under this subsection shall not be entitled to receive any remuneration in respect of his services.

For the purposes of this subsection, the expression "proceeding with a reference" includes, in a case where two arbitrators are unable to agree, giving notice of that fact to the parties and to the umpire.

Sect. 14. Unless a contrary intention is expressed therein, every arbitration agreement shall, where such a provision is applicable to the reference, be deemed to contain a provision that the arbitrator or umpire may, if he thinks fit, make an interim award, and any reference in this Part of this Act to an award includes a reference to an interim award.

Sect. 15. Unless a contrary intention is expressed therein, every arbitration agreement shall, where such a provision is applicable to the reference, be deemed to contain a provision that the arbitrator or umpire shall have the same power as the High Court to order specific performance of any contract other than a contract relating to land or any interest in land.

Sect. 20. A sum directed to be paid by an award shall, unless the award otherwise directs. carry interest as from the date of the award and at the same rate as a judgment debt.

Sect. 21. (1) An arbitrator or umpire may, and shall if so directed by the High Court, state—

(a) any question of law arising in the course of the reference; or
(b) an award or any part of an award, in the form of a special case for the decision of the High Court.

(2) A special case with respect to an interim award or with respect to a question of law arising in the course of a reference may be stated, or may be directed by the High Court to be stated, notwithstanding that proceedings under the reference are still pending.

(3) A decision of the High Court under this section shall be deemed to be a judgment of the Court within the meaning of section twenty-seven of the Supreme Court of Judicature (Consolidation) Act, 1925 ... but no appeal shall lie from the decision of the High Court on any case stated under paragraph (a) of subsection (1) of this section without the leave of the High Court or of the Court of Appeal.

Sect. 23. (1) Where an arbitrator or umpire has misconducted himself or the proceedings, the High Court may remove him.

(2) Where an arbitrator or umpire has misconducted himself or the proceedings, or an arbitration or award has been improperly procured, the High Court may set the award aside.

Sect. 24. (1) Where an agreement between any parties provides that disputes which may arise in the future between them shall be referred to an arbitrator named or designated in the agreement, and after a dispute has arisen any party applies, on the ground that the arbitrator so named or designated is not or may not be impartial, for leave to revoke the authority of the arbitrator or for an injunction to restrain any other party or the arbitrator from proceeding with the arbitration, it shall not be a ground for refusing the application that the said party at the time when he made the agreement knew, or ought to have known, that the arbitrator, by reason of his relation towards any other party to the agreement or of his connection with the subject referred, might not be capable of impartiality.

(2) Where an agreement between any parties provides that disputes which may arise in the future between them

shall be referred to arbitration, and a dispute which so arises involves the question whether any such party has been guilty of fraud, the High Court shall, so far as may be necessary to enable that question to be determined by the High Court, have power to order that the agreement shall cease to have effect and power to give leave to revoke the authority of any arbitrator or umpire appointed by or by virtue of the agreement.

(3) In any case where by virtue of this section the High Court has power to order that an arbitration agreement shall cease to have effect or to give leave to revoke the authority of an arbitrator or umpire, the High Court may refuse to stay any action brought in breach of the agreement.

Sect. 25. (1) Where an arbitrator (not being a sole arbitrator), or two or more arbitrators (not being all the arbitrators), or an umpire who has not entered on the reference is or are removed by the High Court [or the Court of Appeal], the High Court [or the Court of Appeal, as the case may be] may, on the application of any party to the arbitration agreement, appoint a person or persons to act as arbitrator or arbitrators or umpire in place of the person or persons so removed.

(2) Where the authority of an arbitrator or arbitrators or umpire is revoked by leave of the High Court, [or the Court of Appeal], or a sole arbitrator or all the arbitrators or an umpire who has entered on the reference is or are removed by the High Court [or the Court of Appeal] the High Court [or the Court of Appeal, as the case may be] may, on the application of any party to the arbitration agreement, either—

(a) appoint a person to act as sole arbitrator in place of the person or persons removed; or
(b) order that the arbitration agreement shall cease to have effect with respect to the dispute referred.

(3) A person appointed under this section by the High Court [or the Court of Appeal] as an arbitrator or umpire shall have the like power to act

in the reference and to make an award as if he had been appointed in accordance with the terms of the arbitration agreement.

(4) Where it is provided (whether by means of a provision in the arbitration agreement or otherwise) that an award under an arbitration agreement shall be a condition precedent to the bringing of an action with respect to any matter to which the agreement applies, the High Court [or the Court of Appeal], if it orders (whether under this section or under any other enactment) that the agreement shall cease to have effect as regards any particular dispute, may further order that the provision making an award a condition precedent to the bringing of an action shall also cease to have effect as regards that dispute.

Sect. 26. An award on an arbitration agreement may, by leave of the High Court or a judge thereof, be enforced in the same manner as a judgment or order to the same effect, and where leave is so given, judgment may be entered in terms of the award.

Sect. 27. Where the terms of an agreement to refer future disputes to arbitration provide that any claims to which the agreement applies shall be barred unless notice to appoint an arbitrator is given or an arbitrator is appointed or some other step to commence arbitration proceedings is taken within a time fixed by the agreement, and a dispute arises to which the agreement applies, the High Court, if it is of opinion that in the circumstances of the case undue hardship would otherwise be caused, and notwithstanding that the time so fixed has expired, may, on such terms, if any, as the justice of the case may require, but without prejudice to the provisions of any enactment limiting the time for the commencement of arbitration proceedings, extend the time for such period as it thinks proper.

Sect. 28. Any order made under this Part of this Act may be made on such terms as to costs or otherwise as the authority making the order thinks just.

Sects. 35–43. These sections relate to the enforcement of certain foreign awards.

COMPULSORY REFERENCES

These are regulated by s. 15 of the Administration of Justice Act, 1956, and R.S.C., O. 36. By s. 25 (1) of the Courts Act 1971, "official referees' business" covers cases in which jurisdiction or powers of the High Court or a judge of the High Court may be exercised by official referees (to whom references were made under s. 15 of the Act of 1956) and the functions of an official referee are now discharged by a Circuit Judge. The most common type of reference is the reference of the whole cause or matter and it can be made on the application of any party and if the court considers in the circumstances that it is desirable (O. 36, r. 1). The reference of a question or issue of fact for report or inquiry can be made upon application of the parties (O. 36, r. 1 (or under O. 36, r. 2). No reference can be made from a criminal proceeding by the Crown. In cases where Her Majesty or the Duke of Cornwall is a party no reference of the cause or matter or any issue or question of fact can be made without the consent of Her Majesty or the Duke of Cornwall (O. 36, r. 10).

PROCEEDINGS BEFORE REFEREES

O. 36, rules 1 and 2 are as follows:—

1. If, in any cause or matter in the Chancery Division or Queen's Bench Division other than a criminal proceeding by the Crown, the court considers, upon application by any party, that having regard to the nature of the case it is desirable (whether on grounds of expedition, economy or convenience or otherwise) in the interests of one or more of the parties, the court may, subject to any right to a trial with a jury, order that the cause or matter, or any question or issue of fact arising therein, shall be tried before an official referee, with or without assessors.

2. In any cause or matter in the Chancery Division or Queen's Bench Division other than a criminal proceeding by the Crown the court may, subject to any right to a trial with a jury, refer to an official referee for inquiry and report any question or issue of fact arising therein; and, unless the court otherwise orders, the further consideration of the cause or matter shall stand adjourned until the receipt of the official referee's report.

The powers conferred by rr. 1, 2 on the court or a judge may be exercised by the Court of Appeal (See O. 59, r. 10 (1)).

When the reference may be made.— Either at the trial or at any other time, *e.g.* on a summons for directions or to refer.

A Master can make the order. (See O. 73, r. 3).

To what Referee.—An order referring business to an official referee under rr. 1, 2 and 3 must not specify any particular referee (O. 36, r. 5 (1)).

Any application under s. 11 of the Arbitration Act, 1950 (see p. 71, *ante*), to an official referee shall be made to the referee to whom the reference has been allocated by the senior official referee, or to any other official referee to whom the reference has been transferred (O. 36, r. 5 (2)).

Proceedings on the Order.—The order of reference being drawn up, it is produced to the rota clerk to the senior official referee, who allocates it to one of the official referees and indorses it with the name of the referee who is to have the case (O. 36, r. 5 (3)). Allocation is by rotation (O. 36, r. 5 (4)).

By O. 36, r. 6 (1), where under r. 5 any business is referred to an official referee it must forthwith be entered with the clerk of the official referee to whom it is so referred. By O. 36, r. 6 (2), within fourteen days of the entry of any business under r. 6, application for directions shall be made to the official referee in question by the party by whom the order or agreement referring the business was produced to the rota clerk in persuance of r. 5. If that party does not make any application for directions, any other interested party may do so or may apply to the official referee (*a*) in the case of any cause or matter referred for trial, for an order to strike out the pleadings of the party in default, or where the party is default is the plaintiff or has made a counterclaim, an order to dismiss the action or counterclaim, or (b) in the case of any question or issue referred for trial or for inquiry and report, to have the matter referred back to the court (O. 36, r. 6 (3)). Upon application for an order to strike out the pleadings of the party in default or to dismiss an action or counterclaim, the official referee may make the order on such terms as may be just or deal with the application as if it were an application for directions (O. 36, r. 6 (4)).

Transfer of business.—By O. 36, r. 7, (1), if the Lord Chancellor or the Lord Chief Justice thinks it expedient, he may order the transfer of any business from any official referee to any other official referee. By O. 36, r. 7 (2), any official referee is given power to order the transfer of any business from himself to any other official referee who consents to the transfer.

Interlocutory applications may, in the absence of the official referee to whom any business is assigned or with his consent, be made to any other official referee (O. 36, r. 7 (3)).

The Trial or other proceedings may be held where the referee thinks most convenient (O. 36, r. 4 (3)). Subject to any directions contained in the order referring any business to an official referee, every trial and all other proceedings before an official referee shall, as nearly as circumstances admit, be conducted in the like manner as proceedings before a judge (O. 36, r. 4 (1) (b)). The official referee shall, as nearly as circumstances admit, have all the powers (including committal and discretion as to costs) and duties and the same jurisdiction as a judge (O. 36, r. 4 (1) (a)).

An Appeal lies to the Court of Appeal from a decision of an official referee on a point of law and from a decision on a question of fact relevant to a charge of fraud or breach of professional duty. An appeal also lies under s. 13 of the Administration of Justice Act, 1960, from an order or committal made by an official referee or from his refusal to make such an order. Save on the above grounds no other decision or order or judgment made by an official referee may be called in question by appeal (O. 58, r. 5).

The Report by the official referee under O. 36, r. 2, is to be made to the court, and notice must be served on each party to the reference. It may submit any question arising therein for the decision of the court or it may make a special statement of facts from which the court may draw such inferences as it thinks fit. The court may adopt the report in whole or in part, vary it or require an explanation from the official referee. The court may also remit the whole or any part of the question or issue originally referred to the referee to him or any other referee for further consideration, or may decide the question or issue originally referred to the referee on the evidence taken before him, with or without additional evidence (O. 36, r. 3 (1)–(3)).

On the hearing by the court of the further consideration of the cause or matter, an application to vary the report or remit the whole or any part of the question or issue originally referred may be made after giving not less than four days' notice; any other application relating to the report may be made on that hearing without notice (O. 36, r. 3 (4)).

Where on a reference under r. 2 the court orders that further consideration of the cause or matter in question shall not stand adjourned until receipt of the report, the order may contain directions with respect to the proceedings on the receipt of the report and the above provisions shall have effect subject to any such directions (O. 36, r. 3 (5)).

The provisions of O. 36, r. 3, apply to and are exercisable by the Court of Appeal (O. 59, r. 10 (1)).

Referee's Fees.—£15.00 is the court fee payable on a reference to an official referee (Supreme Court Fees Order, 1970, item 20).

Special Referees.—With the consent of the parties an order under O. 36, r. 1, may direct that the trial of the cause or matter, or any question or issue of fact arising therein, shall be before a Master or special referee instead of an official referee (O. 36, rr. 8, 9). By *ibid.*, Masters and special referees have all the powers of official referees except that Masters and special referees cannot sit with assessors and have no powers of committal, and that Masters do not have the discretion concerning the place of trials or proceedings, which is given to official referees by O. 36, r. 4 (3), and special referees do not have the powers as to claims relating to or connected with the original subject-matter of the cause by a party thereto against any other person which are given to official referees by O. 36, r. 4 (2).

A reference under O. 36, r. 2, may be made to a special referee instead of an official referee and rr. 2 and 3 of O. 36 shall have effect accordingly (O. 36, r. 8 (2)).

Bankruptcy

PRACTICE NOTES

(See Halsbury's Laws of England (4th Edn.) Vol. 3, p. 131 et seq.)

BANKRUPTCY NOTICE

Only a creditor who has an unfettered final judgment or order for money may issue a bankruptcy notice (Bankruptcy Act, 1914, s. 1 (g)). The court requires—(i) a formal request to issue signed by the judgment creditor or his solicitor; (ii) evidence of the judgment or order (i.e. office copy of High Court judgment or order, certificate in case of county court); (iii) three copies of the proposed notice which should follow the wording of the judgment, as deviations may invalidate it and a petition founded on it will fail *in limine* (see *Re a Debtor* (No. 21 of 1950), [1950] 2 All E.R. 1129; *Re a Debtor* (No. 41 of 1951) *Ex p. Debtor* v. *Hunter*, [1952] 1 All E.R. 107); (iv) a fee of £1 impressed on one of the notices. Two copies of the notice are sealed and returned to the applicant.

Service.—A sealed copy of the notice should be personally served on the debtor, but an order for substituted service may be obtained on satisfactory proof of inability to effect personal service.

The debtor has, where service is effected in England, 3 days inclusive of the day of service in which to apply to the Court to set aside the notice. The application must be supported by affidavit. From the Registrar's decision an appeal lies to the Divisional Court or, in London, to the C.A. Failure to comply with the terms of a bankruptcy notice is an act of bankruptcy.

BANKRUPTCY PETITION

A bankruptcy petition is presented to the County Court having jurisdiction for the district in which the debtor has resided or carried on business for the longest period during the 6 months immediately preceding the presentation thereof, but if the district is the London bankruptcy district or if the debtor is not resident in England or if the petitioning creditor is unable to ascertain the debtor's residence the petition must be presented to the High Court (Bankruptcy Act, 1914, s. 98).

The petition may be presented either by the debtor himself or by one or more creditors together, provided the debt or debts amount to £50. The *Fees* payable are £6 by way of stamp on the petition if presented by the creditor and £5 if presented by the debtor, and a deposit of £7.50 (creditor's petition) or £5 (debtor's petition) with the official receiver or County Court Registrar.

CREDITOR'S PETITION.

—When a creditor or creditors present the petition three copies of the petition are required together with an affidavit verifying the petition. On the presentation of the papers an appointment for the hearing is given, and notice thereof should be endorsed on the forms of petition, two copies of which are sealed and returned to the applicant, one copy for service and one to be exhibited to the affidavit of service.

Service.—A sealed copy of the petition should be personally served on the debtor; an order for substituted service may however be obtained on satisfactory proof of inability to effect personal service. As 8 days must elapse between the service and the hearing of the petition, the appointment for the hearing should be changed where necessary.

Hearing.—A debtor who intends to oppose the petition must file a notice of such intention with particulars, and send a copy thereof to the petitioning creditor or his solicitor not later than 3 days before the hearing. At the hearing before a Receiving Order will be made, proof is required of (i) the debt; (ii) service of the petition; and (iii) except where the act of bankruptcy is non-compliance with the creditor's bankruptcy notice or a declaration of inability to pay, an act of bankruptcy. This is done by separate affidavits. Where the petitioning creditor is a moneylender his affidavit proving the debt must incorporate a statement showing in detail the particulars required by the Moneylenders' Act, 1927, s. 9 (2).

SEARCHES IN BANKRUPTCY are made at Victory House, Kingsway, London, WC2B 6EX.

RULES. The Bankruptcy Rules, 1952, S.I. 1952 No. 2113, as amended.

FEES. See the Bankruptcy Fees Order, 1970, S.I. 1970, No. 2007, as amended.

SOLICITORS' REMUNERATION in bankruptcy matters is allowed in accordance with the scale laid down in Rules of 1967, S.I. 1967 No. 371. Items not included in the Bankruptcy scale may be allowed under R.S.C., Order 62, Appendix 2 and see *Butterworth's Costs*, Vol. 1.

DEEDS OF ARRANGEMENT

Under the Deeds of Arrangement Act, 1914, all writings whereby an insolvent makes any terms with his creditors, or any of them exceeding two, are deeds of arrangement. All such deeds must be registered at the Department of Trade and Industry (Bankruptcy Department), Gavrelle House, 2 Bunhill Row, London, E.C.1, within 7 clear days after the first execution thereof by the debtor, or any creditor. Where the deed is executed out of England it must be registered within 7 days after the time when it would in the ordinary course of post arrive in England, if posted within a week after execution thereof. The time for registration may be extended by a Judge of the High Court on an affidavit as to the facts that the omission to register was accidental, or due to inadvertence.

Registration is effected by producing (either personally or by an agent) (i) the deed of assignment, upon which a certificate of filing is endorsed, and filing (ii) such number of copies as the registrar may deem necessary, which where the debtor's residence is outside the London Bankruptcy District will usually be two, (iii) an affidavit by the attesting witness of the execution of the deed, to which affidavit the copy deed is to be an exhibit, (iv) an affidavit by the debtor stating the total amount of his property and liabilities included under the deed, the total amount of the composition (if any), and the names and addresses of the creditors.

Fees Payable: Filing Fees (*See* the Deeds of Arrangement Fees Order, 1973 No. 1993). Where the total amount of the property included under the deed does not exceed £1,000, £3; between £2,000 and £2,500, £5; between £2,500 and £5000, £8; over £5000, £10; in all other cases, £4. For filing each affidavit, 25p; for certificate of filing endorsed on original deed, 50p; for searching the register, 25p.

A deed for creditors generally is void unless within 21 days after its registration, or an extended time, it is assented to in writing by the majority in number and value of the creditors. The trustee must within 28 days of registration of the deed file a statutory declaration that the assent has been given, and within 7 days thereafter he must give the security required by the Act, to the registrar of the bankruptcy court of the district in which the debtor resides or carries on business, unless exonerated by a majority of the creditors in which case a statutory declaration is filed. A certificate of the giving of the security is to be filed with the Department of Trade.

The deed should, if any land is comprised therein, also be registered at the Land Registry, in the case of unregistered land as a Land Charge in the debtor's name and in the case of registered land by caution on the title, otherwise the deed will be void as against a purchaser for value of such land (Land Registration Act, 1925 and Land Charges Act, 1925, *see Encyclopaedia of Forms and Precedents*, 4th Edn., Vol. 17, pp. 112, 113).

On the appointment of a new trustee of the deed he must forthwith give notice to the Registrar of the court.

Bills of Sale Practice

(See Halsbury's Laws of England (4th Edn.), vol. 4, p. 235, et seq.)

Every bill of sale must be registered at the Filing Department of the Central Office within 7 clear days after the making thereof, or if executed out of England within the same period after the time when it would in the ordinary course of post arrive in England, if posted immediately after the execution thereof. When the time for registering expires on a Sunday, or other day on which the Department is closed, registration may validly be made on the next following day on which it is open. The time for registration may be extended by a Judge or Master on his being satisfied by affidavit (fee, £1) as to the circumstances that the omission to register was accidental or due to inadvertence.

Registration is effected by producing and filing at the department, (i) the bill of sale; (ii) if in the London District a true copy thereof and if elsewhere two or more copies thereof, as the circumstances may require (see Bills of Sale Act (1878) Amendment Act, 1882, s. 11, as amended by the Supreme Court of Judicature (Consolidation) Act, 1925, s. 23); and (iii) an affidavit in the required form by the attesting witness, to which affidavit the copy bill of sale is an exhibit.

Fees payable: On filing any document other than a fiat of satisfaction, £2.

The registration remains effective for 5 years only, at the expiration of which time the bill of sale, if still in force, requires re-registration which is carried out by filing at the department an affidavit in the prescribed form. *Fee* on filing the affidavit, £1. No registration is necessary on the transfer or assignment of a bill of sale.

On payment of the money secured by, or the discharge of a bill of sale, a *memorandum of satisfaction* may, by order of the registrar of the department be written upon the registered copy of the bill of sale. Leave is obtained by leaving a consent, signed by the grantee or his assignee, and attested by a solicitor, who verifies such signature by an affidavit, with a Master of the Supreme Court for his *fiat*. The fee for the *fiat* is £1.

The registers of bills of sale are open to public inspection. *Fee* £1 for one name, 50p for each additional name; copies may be obtained, the fee being calculated according to page size.

Business Names, Registration of

The principal rules are contained in S.I. 1949 No. 2441, as amended by S.I. 1969 No. 1330.

Names Required to be Registered

1. Every firm having a place of business in the United Kingdom and carrying on business under a name which does not consist of the true surnames of all the partners (whether individuals or corporations) without any addition other than the true Christian names of individual partners or initials of such Christian names (Application Form R.B.N.1A; fee £1).

2. Every individual having a place of business in the United Kingdom and carrying on business under a name which does not consist of his true surname without any addition thereto other than his true Christian names or the initials thereof. In the case of a peer or a person usually known by a British title different from his surname the title by which he is known is deemed to be his surname. The registration of the surname and the initial only of one of several Christian names is not sufficient to secure exemption under this paragraph (*Brown* v. *Thomas and Burrows* (1922), 39 T.L.R. 132). (Application Form R.B.N.1; fee £1.)

3. Every individual or firm having a place of business in the United Kingdom, who, or a member of which, has either before or after the passing of the Registration of Business Names

Act, 1916, changed his name, except in the case of a woman in consequence of marriage. Registration is not required under this paragraph if the change has taken place before the person who has changed his name attained the age of eighteen years or if not less than twenty years have elapsed since it took place (Companies Act, 1947, s. 116 (4) (b)). The exemption in case of a woman does not extend to a case where the woman carried on business under her true surname and changed her name on marriage but failed to change the name of her business to her new name *Seymour* v. *Chernikeef*, [1946] K.B. 434. (Form of Request for amendment of particulars arising out of the exceptions —individual R.B.N.7; firm R.B.N.7A; and Request for Removal from Regi - ter in such circumstances—individual R.B.N.8; Form R.B.N.8A; no fee).

4. Every Company as defined in the Companies Act, 1948 (*i.e.* this includes certain corporations not incorporated under the Companies Acts) carrying on business under a name which does not consist of its corporate name without any addition (Application Form R.B.N.1B or 1C; fee £1).

Exceptions
(*a*) Where the addition (*i.e.* to the true surname or surnames) merely indicates that the business is carried on in succession to a former owner of the business, that addition does not of itself render registration necessary.
(*b*) Where two or more individual partners have the same surname, the addition of an "s" at the end of that surname does not of itself render registration necessary.
(*c*) Where the business is carried on by a trustee in bankruptcy or a receiver or manager appointed by any court, registration is not necessary.
(*d*) The purchase or acquisition of property by two or more persons as joint tenants or tenants in common is not of itself to be deemed carrying on a business whether or not the owners share any profits arising from the sale thereof.

Registration by Nominees, etc.
Where a firm, individual or corporation having a place of business within the United Kingdom carries on the business wholly or mainly as nominee or trustee of or for another person, or other persons, or another corporation, or acts as general agents for any foreign firm, the first mentioned firm, individual or corporation must register under the 1916 Act and give certain additional particulars relating to the business for which it is nominee, trustee or general agent. (Statement of additional particulars, individual—Form R.B.N.2; firm or company—Form R.B.N.2A; fee of £1 if not filed at the same time as application form.)

Time for Registration
1. Within fourteen days after the firm or person commences business, or the business in respect of which registration is required, as the case may be.

2. Where registration is required in consequence of a change of name, within fourteen days after the date of such change.

3. Whenever a change of particulars is made or occurs in respect of a firm or person, particulars of such change must be registered within fourteen days after such change or such longer period as the Department of Trade and Industry may allow (Statement of change of particulars, individual—Form R.B.N.3; firm—Form R.B.N.3A; corporation—Form R.B.N.3B; fee 25p).

Choice of Name
The Registrar has power to refuse to register a name as a business name if (a) the name contains the word "British" or any other word which in the Registrar's opinion is misleading or (b) the name is undesirable. Any person aggrieved by the Registrar's decision may appeal to the Secretary of State for Trade and Industry, whose decision is final. Such an appeal must be made within twenty-one days of the notice of the Registrar's decision, by delivering or sending by post to the Registrar notice of appeal in Form R.B.N.6 (no fee) accompanied by a statement of the grounds of appeal and of the appellant's case in support and copies of the notice, statement and case must also be sent or delivered to the Assistant Secretary, Insurance and Companies Department of the Department of Trade and Industry.

Removal of Name from Register

1. When a firm or individual registered under the Act ceases to carry on business, it is the duty of the persons who were partners at the time it ceased to carry on business or of the individual, or if he is dead of his personal representative, to give notice within three months of ceasing business—failure to do so incurs a liability on summary conviction to a fine not exceeding £20 (Notice of cessation of business, Form R.B.N.4; no fee).

2. The Registrar has power, where he has reasonable cause to believe that a firm or individual has ceased to carry on business, to send a notice to the firm or individual, and if it is unanswered within one month or if an answer is received confirming that the business has ceased to be carried on, to himself remove the name from the register.

Enforcement of Provisions

The penalty for failing without reasonable excuse to furnish a statement of particulars or any change of particulars is a fine on summary conviction not exceeding £5 for every day the default continues and in the case of a firm this can be imposed on every partner. In addition default also renders the rights of the defaulter under or arising out of any contract made or entered into by or on behalf of the defaulter in relation to the business unenforceable by action or other legal proceeding either in the business name or otherwise. The defaulter may, however, apply to the High Court for relief against this disability or if the proceedings were commenced in the county court the county court may grant relief.

The Secretary of State for Trade and Industry also has power to require any person to furnish particulars to enable the Secretary of State to ascertain whether or not he or the firm of which he is a partner should be registered under the Act (or changes ought to be registered) and if any person so required fails to supply such particulars or furnishes false particulars he is liable on summary conviction to imprisonment not exceeding three months or to a fine not exceeding £20 or to both. False statements made in the particulars also attract the same penalties.

Searches

The file of documents may be inspected (fee 5p) at the Registrar's office (Companies House, Pembroke House, 40–56 City Road, E.C.1) and copies and extracts are obtainable.

Business Letters, etc.

All trade catalogues, trade circulars showcards and business letters in which the business name appears must include in legible characters, in the case of an individual, his Christian name or initials and surname, any former Christian name or surname and his nationality if not British, and in the case of a firm, similar particulars of all the partners or if a corporation is a partner the corporate name. Default incurs on summary conviction for each offence a fine not exceeding £5.

Capital Gains Tax

SEE TAXATION, p. 341, *post*

Capital Transfer Tax

See Foster, Capital Taxes Enclyclopaedia. References are to Finance Act 1975 unless indicated.

The capital transfer tax applies to transfers (including certain deemed transfers) in three main areas *i.e.* lifetime gifts, transfers on death, and transfers relating to settled property.

Basis of the tax.—The tax is chargeable, subject to certain exemptions, on the gifts and other gratuitous transfers of value made during a person's lifetime and on the property he leaves on his death. Broadly speaking, the tax applies to any lifetime transfer in which there is an element of gift; or, to put that another way, it does not apply to a transfer if it was made without donative intent and at arm's length (s. 20(4)). The amount chargeable to tax on a lifetime gift is measured by the donor's loss as a result of his making the transfer (ss. 19(1) and 20(2)).

The tax applies to lifetime transfers made after 26 March 1974: and to transfers on deaths on or after 13 March 1975. Estate duty continues to be chargeable in respect of earlier deaths.

Property chargeable.—The donor's loss is in general measured by the diminution in the value of his "estate" and the "estate" also forms the measure of the charges on death. For persons domiciled in the United Kingdom the "estate" includes all their property, wherever situated; and for persons not so domiciled it is only their property situated in the United Kingdom (s. 24(2)).

Subject to this, a person's "estate" includes everything to which he is entitled or which he can dispose of as he thinks fit (with exceptions in the field of settled property) (s. 23).

There is provision in particular cases for treating as domiciled in the United Kingdom persons who would not be so domiciled under the general law.

Method of charge.—The new tax is chargeable in respect of a person's lifetime transfers as they occur and on a cumulative basis. The final stage of cumulation will be the inclusion of the property passing on an assumed transfer of the whole of the deceased's estate immediately before the death (s. 22(1)). The rates of the tax are given in Section 37 and, like the estate duty rates, are progressively higher on successive slices of the person's cumulative total of chargeable transfers. There is a lower scale of rates for lifetime transfers than for transfer on death. If the transferor dies within 3 years after making the gift the difference between tax on the lifetime and death scales becomes payable with a restriction if the value of the gift (other than a chattel) has fallen. Tax on the death scale may also become payable if the transferor dies within a year of making gifts to charities or political parties.

A donee who makes transfers back to a donor is free of CTT up to the amount he received. The donor can claim cancellation of the original transfer, with a reduction of 4 per cent for each whole year which has elapsed, and receive repayment of CTT on the amount cancelled which is deducted from his accumulations for subsequent transfers. Transfers which are set aside as voidable (e.g. on bankruptcy) are treated as void *ab initio*.

Transfers reported late, after CTT on a later transfer has been agreed, are generally treated as made when discovered.

On death (and as for estate duty), tax is charged on the value of the deceased's estate and the tax comes out of that estate. On a lifetime gift the amount to be charged is calculated on a similar footing. If the tax will be borne by the donor and only the balance handed to the donee, the amount chargeable to tax will include the tax (and can be found by "grossing up" the net). If the tax on a lifetime transfer is borne by the donee the benefit he obtains is that much the smaller; the amount chargeable is correspondingly smaller because it is taken *without* addition for the tax (s. 27(6) and Sch. 10, para. 1(1) and (2)). Either way it is the total loss to the transferor which is chargeable. The amount of the "loss to the donor" is however taken as excluding any expenses incidental to the transfer which are borne by him (Sch. 10, para. 6) and any liability to capital gains tax which he incurs in respect of the gift (Sch. 10, para. 1 (2)).

Loans of money or property for less than a proper consideration, with certain exclusions, are chargeable each 5 April on the annual value plus the lender's expenses.

Valuation.—The basis of valuation to be used for the capital transfer tax largely follows that used for estate duty, *i.e.* the value of an asset is to be taken at what it would fetch if sold in the open market at the relevant time (s. 38). If the value of an asset retained by the transferor is affected by a transfer, two valuations will need to be made on this basis to determine the value of his "estate" before and after the transfer. Changes in value by reason of the death are taken into account so that *e.g.*, a *life* policy is included at its maturity value (Sch. 10, para. 9). There is a special rule for valuation of transferred life assurance policies (Sch. 10, para. 11).

In valuing shares owned by a man or his wife there are aggregated shares owned by each of them and shares settled by either of them before 27 March 1974 on discretionary or similar trusts or given by either of them to a charity etc. (Sch. 10, para. 7), (together with any shares to which either of them is treated as beneficially entitled under para. 3 of Sch. 5). These related property provisions apply to any property where aggregation increases the overall value, but not if property sold at lower price within 3 years of a death after 6 April 1976.

Liabilities of the transferor are taken into account in arriving at his net total "estate" (as provided in Sch. 10, paras. 1 to 3).

The estate duty provisions providing relief where quoted shares are sold at a loss within twelve months of a death are continued by Part II of Schedule 10.

Similar relief is given where land is sold at a loss of at least £1,000 and at least 5% within two years of a death after 6 April 1976.

Abolition of estate duty.—Estate duty no longer applies for deaths occurring after 12 March 1975 (s. 49 (1)).

There is some carry over of the seven year period for "gifts-intervivos" from the estate duty into the new tax. A gift made before 27 March 1974 by a donor who dies within seven years of making the gift (four years in Northern Ireland) is charged to the capital transfer tax on the death—as it would have been chargeable under the estate duty (s. 22(5)). The estate duty "tapering" arrangements (for gifts made some years before the death) will apply.

Exemptions.—S. 29 and Sch. 6 provide for the main exemptions from the new tax. Each exemption applies independently of other exemptions—for example a gift to one donee of £300 (not exempted as part of the donor's normal expenditure out of income) is exempt as to £100 below and the balance of £200 is exempt to the extent that the £1,000 has not been absorbed by other gifts.

Husband and wife.—Transfers between husband and wife in life and on death are generally exempt (Sch. 6, para. 1).

General exemptions.—

(*a*) Transfers made by a person in any one tax year are exempt up to a value of £2,000 *plus* the amount (if any) by which the transfers set against this exemption in the previous year fell short of £2,000 (Sch. 6, para. 2). It was £1,000 up to 1975–76. Thus if no gifts are made in years 1 and 2 the amount allowable in year 3 is £4,000. And if, say, £300 is set against this exemption in year 1 and £800 in year 2 the amount allowable in year 3 is £2,000 + (£2,000 − £800) = £3,200 (not £3,900). Before 6 April 1975, the estate duty "small gifts" relief is adapted to apply if it gives a more favourable result to a donor (paragraph 3).

(b) Outright gifts to any one person in any one tax year are exempt up to a value of £100 (Sch. 6, para. 4).

(c) Transfers made out of a person's income after tax, as part of his normal expenditure and leaving him sufficient to maintain his usual standard of living, are exempt (Sch. 6, para. 5).

(d) Transfers made in consideration of a marriage are exempt up to £2,500 (£5,000 if the donor is a parent of either party to the marriage) if the donor is a party to the marriage or is his or lineal ancestor; and up to £1,000 if the donor is anyone else (Sch. 6, paras. 6 and 7).

(These four exemptions apply only to lifetime transfers, and not to property passing on death or to transfers of settled property. (Sch. 6, para. 8).)

Dispositions that are not transfers of value.—

(a) Lifetime dispositions for the maintenance of a former spouse or of a child undergoing full-time education or training or of a dependent relative, subject to certain conditions (s. 46).

(b) Dispositions allowable in computing income.

(c) Dispositions on trust for benefit of employees.

(d) Waivers of remuneration.

(e) Waivers of dividends.

Excluded property.—Various categories of property are taken outside the ambit of the charge as "excluded" property. No account is to be taken of a disposal of excluded property in measuring the diminution in the value of a person's estate (s. 20(3)) and it is left out of an estate for the purpose of the charge on death (s. 22(1)). The main category of excluded property is property situated abroad belonging to a person not domiciled or treated as domiciled in the United Kingdom (s. 24(2)).

Charities and Political Parties.—Transfers to charities or political parties made a year or more before death are exempt without limit. Subject to certain conditions set out in para. 15 of Sch. 6, transfers to charities or political parties on or within a year before death are exempt up to a cumulative sum of £100,000 for charities and £100,000 for political parties for any one transferor (Sch. 6, paras. 10 and 11). Where this sum is exceeded tax is charged on the excess in the normal way.

National Heritage—Works of Art, Historic Houses etc.—The existing estate duty exemption for property going to certain bodies concerned with the preservation of the National Heritage is continued for capital transfer tax and applies to transfers both in life and on death. There is also complete exemption for transfers to local authorities, Government Departments and to universities and university colleges in the United Kingdom (Sch. 6, para. 12).

The existing estate duty exemption for works of art and other objects of a qualifying standard which remain in private hands is continued and extended to cover historic houses and their contents and land of scenic, historic or scientific interest, but so as to apply only to transfers on death. The exemption is conditional as under estate duty, on the giving of certain undertakings—*e.g.*, not to send the object out of the country—and is lost on a sale of the object or a breach of the undertaking (ss. 31–34).

From 7 April 1976 a claim can be made for conditional exemption from CTT for works of art and historic buildings which are of importance to the national heritage. This gives exemption, subject to conditions, for lifetime gifts of heritage property, in addition to transfers on death. It also extends the exemption to cover heritage property held on discretionary trusts.

Miscellaneous.— Certain special situations which enjoyed relief from estate duty are also relieved from capital transfer tax (by Sch. 7). They include transfers of certain Government securities by persons neither domiciled nor ordinarily resident within the United Kingdom; national savings in the ownership of persons domiciled in the Channel Islands or the Isle of Man; and transfers occurring on certain deaths of members of the armed forces.

Arrangements for relief from double

tax where transfers are charged by overseas countries are contained in Sch. 7.

S. 30 provides for relief when a transferee dies within 4 years of a transfer in his favour or of paying tax on a gift inter vivos. A proportion (varying from 80 per cent. if he dies within a year to 20 per cent. if he dies within 4 years) of the tax paid on the gift he received is deducted from the tax payable on his estate.

Relief in respect of agricultural property of "working farmers".—There are special arrangements for relief in respect of agricultural property transferred, whether in life or on death, by full time working farmers, *i.e.* those who qualify under the provisions of Sch. 8 of which the following is a summary.

Relief is available:

(*a*) If the transferor qualifies as a "working farmer", *i.e.*, as a person wholly or mainly engaged in agriculture as a farmer or farm worker (or as a student) in 5 of the 7 preceding years. (If more than three-quarters of the earned income in those years is obtained from those activities the qualification is automatic.)

(*b*) In respect of land including farmhouses and buildings occupied for farming by the transferor for at least two years before the transfer.

(*c*) By reducing the agricultural market value of the property by one half.

(*d*) Subject to overriding limits (which apply to each transferor on a cumulative basis of £¼m by value or 1,000 acres whichever provides the larger relief. Rough grazing land is counted at one-sixth of its actual area.

The relief extends to controlling shareholdings in farming companies.

Payment of tax by instalments.—The arrangements for the optional payment of estate duty in 8 yearly or 16 half yearly instalments are continued in respect of capital transfer tax chargeable on death. They apply, much as before, to land, to certain holdings of shares in companies, and to the net business assets of unincorporated businesses. These arrangements are extended to lifetime transfers where the person benefiting from the transfer bears the tax or, in the case of settled property where the property is retained in settlement. The whole of the tax becomes immediately payable, as it was under estate duty, if the relevant assets are sold (Sch. 4, para. 13).

Relief for business assets.—On all transfers after 6 April 1976 the value transferred is reduced by 30% if attributable to—

(*a*) a sole proprietor's business or a partner's interest in a partnership;

(*b*) a holding of unquoted shares giving (either by itself or in conjunction with the related property rules) control of the company; or

(*c*) land, buildings, plant or machinery owned by a controlling shareholder or partner and used wholly or mainly in the business of the company or partnership.

Investment and property dealing concerns, and those holding investments, including let land, are excluded from the relief.

The transferor must have owned the relevant business property for at least 2 years (or, where it replaced an earlier business, one or other business for a total of at least 2 years out of the 5 years preceding the transfer).

Assets not strictly required for current or future business use are excluded from the value of the property qualifying for relief.

In general, the relief applies to farms as to any other business property, apart from agricultural land qualifying for the 50% reduction.

In addition, tax may be paid by instalments in respect of business assets and shares in companies (excluding certain investment and dealing companies) (Sch. 4, para. 16). It applies in respect of land and buildings only if they are held as business assets and is limited to the first £¼m of such assets. For such tax, interest will be chargeable on each instalment separately and then only from the date on which the instalment is due. Thus if eight annual instalments are paid each on or before its separate due date then no interest at all will be payable.

Woodlands.—S. 36 and Sch. 9 permit the exclusion of growing timber from the charge on death. But tax will be charged by reference to that death if, before the woodland passes on another death, the timber is sold or given away, other than to the owner's spouse. The tax will be charged on the proceeds of sale (or value of the timber at the time of gift). To find the appropriate rate of tax, the sale proceeds (or value) will be added to the value of the estate at death and the value of any previous disposals of timber. The relief is subject to certain conditions, broadly that the deceased has owned the woodlands for 5 years (unless he acquired it by gift or inheritance) and that the woodland is subject to a Forestry Commission Dedication Scheme.

Persons liable.—The primary liability to pay the tax lies on the donor, or where the transfer affects settled property, the trustees. If tax is not paid by the due date, it can be recovered from the donee or other persons who come into possession of the property transferred (S. 25). Ss. 26 and 27 give details of exceptions from, and limitations of, liability to pay the tax.

A right of recovery of tax from a donor's spouse is provided, but the sum recoverable is limited to the value of property transferred, after 26 March 1974, by the donor to his or her spouse (S. 25(8)) further restricted if the property (other than chattels) has fallen in value.

Administration.— The administration provisions for the new tax are contained in Sch. 4. Their main features are as follows:

(*a*) Chargeable transfers are to be reported to the Inland Revenue within twelve months from the end of the month of transfer (Sch. 4, para. 2).

(*b*) Provision is made for the Board of Inland Revenue to obtain any necessary information (para. 5); for the formal determination of liabilities (para. 6); and for appeals (paras. 7 to 10) which are to lie mainly to the Special Commissioners.

(*c*) interest on unpaid tax will begin to run from the time at which the tax is due. The due date is, in the case of a transfer on death, 6 months after the end of the month in which the death occurs. For lifetime transfers it is six months after the end of the month in which the transfer is made or, in the case of transfers between 5 April and 1 October, the 30 April in the following year. Interest will be paid on repayments of overpaid tax, running from the date when the overpayment was made. The rates of interest are six per cent. for transfers on death and nine per cent. for other transfers (para. 19).

(*d*) Penalties are provided for failure to notify chargeability or otherwise to comply with statutory requirements, and for incorrect returns and statements (paras. 28 to 31).

(*e*) Arrangements for ensuring that tax chargeable on death is paid before probate is granted are continued (para. 38).

SETTLED PROPERTY

Treatment when property is settled.— When a settlement is made the charge is on the same basis as for outright gifts and for bequests on death. Where the person settles property on himself there is no charge when the settlement is made. Similarly when a person settles property on his or her spouse there is no charge on the making of the settlement unless the spouse is not domiciled in the United Kingdom.

Transfer of settled property.—The application of the charging provisions to property in a settlement depends on whether or not there is for the time being an interest in possession which carries the right to receive the income or otherwise enjoy the settled property.

In either case the scope of liability depends on the domicile of the settlor when the settlement was made. The charge applies to property wherever it is situated if the settlor was domiciled in the United Kingdom when he made the settlement or (except in the case of property settled before 10 December 1974) was treated, under S. 45, as so domiciled. Where the settlor was not so domiciled, or treated as domiciled, only property within the United Kingdom is within the scope of the tax (Sch. 5, para. 2).

Settlements where there is an interest in possession.—

(a) Chargeable events

An individual having an interest in possession is treated as the owner for the time being of the settled property. Accordingly there is a charge to tax when the right to the enjoyment of the property changes hands, whether in life or on death, and whether the interest terminates or is transferred by an act of the life tenant (*e.g.*, when it is assigned). However there is no charge where a person becomes absolutely entitled to property in which he had an interest in possession. Nor is there a charge when property reverts to the settlor in his lifetime or devolves on the settlor's spouse or, up to two years, widow(er) who is domiciled and resident in the United Kingdom. Where an interest in possession is disposed of for a payment in money or money's worth, deduction of the amount of the payment is allowed in arriving at the chargeable value (Sch. 5, para. 4(4)).

(b) The rate of tax

Where the interest in possession of a beneficiary comes to an end or is disposed of in his lifetime the rate of tax charged on the settled property is determined by the beneficiary's cumulative total at that time, and the beneficiary's cumulative total is increased by the chargeable value of the settled property. Where the beneficiary's interest in possession comes to an end on his death the chargeable value forms part of his final cumulation and is charged to tax at the same rate as other property then liable. The tax is primarily payable by the trustees out of the settled property.

(c) Relief for successive charges on interests in possession

There is relief from the full charge if two tax charges on settled property in which an interest in possession subsists occur within only a short interval between them. The chargeable value is abated by 80 per cent., 60 per cent., 40 per cent. or 20 per cent. on the later occasion of charge where the interval is not more than 1, 2, 3 or 4 years respectively (Sch. 5, para. 5).

(d) Reversionary interests

Reversionary interests in settled property are generally exempt, but this exemption does not usually apply if the reversion has been previously purchased or belongs to the settlor or his spouse (Ss. 23(3) and 24(3)).

Discretionary trusts

The term discretionary trust is used here, for convenience, to refer to trusts where and to the extent that no interest in possession subsists in the settled property.

(a) Chargeable events

Tax is charged on distributions of capital out of the settled property to beneficiaries (Sch. 5, para. 6). In addition there will be a periodic charge at 10-year intervals (Sch. 5, para. 12).

(b) Rate of charge on distributions of capital

In general the rate of tax charged on distributions up to the amount of the original settled capital is the rate, on the lifetime scale, that would have been charged on a gift of that amount by the settlor at the time when he made the settlement (Sch. 5, para. 7(2)). Distributions in excess of the original settled capital fall into the higher rate bands as further gifts by the settlor would have done (Sch. 5, para. 7(3)). If however property was already settled at 27 March 1974 distributions out of that property are charged on the progressive scale as if they were the only series of gifts made by an individual (Sch. 5, para. 8).

(c) The periodic charge

The periodic charge will in most cases fall on every tenth anniversary of the date on which the property was settled, starting with anniversaries on or after 1 April 1980. The charge will be 30 per cent. of the tax that would be chargeable if the whole capital held on discretionary trusts were distributed, subject to proportional abatements for any property so held only for nine or fewer years out of the preceding ten (Sch. 5, para. 12(1) and (4)). Credit is given for the periodic charge on the occasion of a capital distribution made out of the property within the next 20 years (Sch. 5, para. 13). If the trustees of the settlement are not resident in the United Kingdom there is an annual charge, starting in 1976, of 3 per cent. of the full tax and this will be allowed as a credit against the 10 year periodic charge and other capital distributions (Sch. 5, para. 12(2) and (3)).

(d) Transitional relief on capital distributions
In most cases the rate of tax on capital distributions made before 1 April 1980 out of settlements made before 27 March 1974 is to be a percentage of the rate that would normally be charged. The percentage varies from 10 per cent. for distributions before 1 April 1976 to 20 per cent. for distributions after 31 March 1979 (Sch. 5, paragraph 14).

Exemptions and reliefs from the charges on discretionary trusts

(a) Accumulation and maintenance settlements
Where a settlement provides for the maintenance, education or benefit of one or more beneficiaries up to an age not exceeding 25, the periodic charge will not apply and distributions to those beneficiaries are exempt from the usual distribution charge (Sch. 5, para. 15).

(b) Superannuation schemes
Property held on approved superannuation schemes is in general exempt from the charges on settled property (Sch. 5, para. 16).

(c) Employee and newspaper trusts
Subject to certain conditions, relief is given to trusts for employees and U.K. newspaper publishing companies (Sch. 5, paras. 17, 17A).

(d) Protective trusts
Tax is not charged when the principal beneficiary's interest in possession is terminated, nor is it charged on a distribution payment to him (Sch. 5, para. 18).

(e) Mentally disabled persons
Relief is given to trusts for the benefit of such persons (Sch. 5, para. 19).

(f) Charitable trusts
Property held for charitable purposes only is, similarly, exempt from the charges on discretionary trusts (Sch. 5, para. 20).

(g) Compensation funds
The discretionary trust provisions do not apply to funds held to provide compensation for losses incurred through the default of persons carrying on a trade or profession (Sch. 5, para. 21).

Death

A deed of family arrangement executed within two years of a death has effect from the date of death. A disclaimer of a legacy within that period attracts no charge. An election by a surviving spouse to redeem his or her life interest in a residuary estate is not a transfer of value (s. 47).
A beneficiary's interest in a deceased person's estate is backdated to the death even though unascertained during the administration period (Sch. 5, para. 22).
Where a beneficiary becomes entitled on surviving by up to 6 months, the vesting at the end of the period (or earlier death) is backdated to the death (Sch. 5, para. 22A).

CLOSE COMPANIES

If a close company (or non-resident equivalent) makes a transfer of value it is apportioned to the participators (but not to preference shareholders if their value is only slightly affected).
Tax is charged as if each participator has transferred that amount, less the extent (if any) to which the transfer increased his estate. The £2,000 annual exemption may apply.
Liability for the tax is on the company or, if unpaid, on the participator.
Where 5 per cent. or less is apportioned to a participator he is not liable for tax and his accumulations are not affected (s. 39).

Companies

(See Halsbury's Laws of England (4th Edn.) Vol. 7, and for the Exchange Control Act, 1947, and the Borrowing (Control and Guarantees) Act, 1946, see 22 Halsbury's Statutes (3rd Edn.), 890)

[In these notes references to the Companies Act 1948, are indicated by the sign "§" followed by the number of the section. References to other statutes are given in full. Forms prescribed by the Companies (Forms) Order, 1949 S.I. 1949, No. 382) are referred to as D. of T. forms.]

(1) INCORPORATION

Before lodging documents leading to incorporation, it is advisable to ascertain from the Registrar of Companies that the proposed name for the new company is available. This may be done by letter to the Companies Registration Office, Crown Way, Maindy, Cardiff, or to Companies House, Pembroke House, 40–56 City Road, London, E.C.1. The following documents must be lodged with the Registrar for examination:—(i) *Memorandum and Articles of Association*, signed in the case of a *public* company by at least seven persons and, in the case of a *private* company by at least two persons. While the Memorandum need not be printed, the Articles must be printed and it is usual to print both the Memorandum and Articles as one document; the Registrar will accept Articles prepared by type-lithographic process and certified by a law stationer as having been so produced. A company adopting Table A in its entirety need not register Articles with the Memorandum; (ii) *Statutory Declaration of Compliance* (D. of T. Form 41) with the provisions of the Companies Act, 1948 made by the solicitor engaged in the formation of the new company or a person named in the Articles as a director or secretary. Where the company is to be a *public* company the following are also required:—(iii) *Consents to act as Directors* (D. of T. Form 42); (iv) *List of Persons consenting to be Directors* (D. of T. Form 43); and where the proposed directors have not signed the Memorandum for their qualification shares (if any); (v) *Undertaking by Directors to pay for Qualification Shares.*

NOTE.—*Notice of Situation of Registered Office* (D. of T. Form 4) and *Particulars of Directors and Secretaries* (D. of T. Form 9) may be lodged at the same time as the other documents leading to incorporation, or may be filed in the case of the Notice of Situation within 14 days after incorporation and in the case of the Particulars within 14 days of the appointment of the first directors.

After the above-mentioned documents have been examined by the Registrar, the applicant must pay the fees under Sched. 3 to the Companies Act 1967 and the capital duty (if any) (see p. 333, *post*) when he will be given a date on which the Certificate of Incorporation will be ready for collection.

(2) SEARCHES

Separate files for each company registered are kept at the Companies' Registration Office, 55–71 City Road, E.C.1. The file is open to the inspection of any person upon payment of a search fee of 5p. Photographic copies of any document on the file may be bespoken.

(3) PROSPECTUS AND ISSUE OF SHARES

A dated copy of every prospectus, signed by all the directors named in it, and having certain endorsements or attachments, must be filed with the Registrar before issue (§§ 37, 41). No form of application for shares may be issued to the public unless accompanied by a prospectus (§ 38), unless the shares are of a class already dealt in on a recognised Stock Exchange. Every document offering to the public for subscription or purchase shares or debentures of a company is a prospectus (§ 45) and every published prospectus must contain the whole of the matters set out in Schedule IV to the Act, *unless* the shares are to be offered to the public and application is made to a recognised Stock Exchange for permission to deal in them and that Stock Exchange has granted a certificate of exemption permitting the publication of a prospectus showing only the particulars and information required on an application for permission to deal (§ 39). The minimum subscription of capital required must be set out in the prospectus showing under separate heads: (i) the purchase price of property to be provided out of the issue, (ii) preliminary expenses, (iii) repayments of any loans for the above two purposes, (iv) working capital. Material contracts and directors' interests must be disclosed. The issue of shares can be restricted by the Control of Borrowing Order, 1958, S.I. 1958, No. 1208 (as amended), made under the Borrowing (Control and Guarantees) Act, 1946. By the Control of Borrowing (Amendment) Order 1967. S.I. 1967, No. 69, the consent of the Treasury is no longer required for certain exempted transactions including the issue of non-sterling securities by or on behalf of persons resident outside the U.K. The general exemption is subject to conditions whereby the approval of the Bank of England is required of the terms of issue of any securities mentioned in paras. 1 to 5 of Part II of Schedule I to the Trustee Investments Act 1961 and of the timing of issues of sterling securities of £1m. or more.

(4) ALLOTMENT OF SHARES
No allotment of shares is permitted unless the minimum subscription is subscribed and sums payable on application (not less than 5%) paid in cash within 40 days after the issue of the prospectus (§ 47). No allotment may be made in pursuance of a prospectus issued to the public until the beginning of the third day after the date of issue (§ 50). Special provision is made as to allotments in pursuance of a prospectus stating that permission to deal on a recognised Stock Exchange will be applied for (§ 51). Within one month after any allotment a company must make a return to the Registrar (D. of T. Form 45), showing (i) the number of shares allotted, (ii) the names and addresses of the allottees, (iii) the amounts paid in cash, (iv) the number of shares, allotted otherwise than wholly for cash. Where shares are allotted otherwise than for cash, the original stamped contract constituting the title of the allottees, or, where there is no written contract, particulars of the verbal contract in the prescribed form (D. of T. Form 52), duly stamped with the same duty as would have been payable if the contract had been reduced to writing must be filed (§ 52). The issue of shares to non-residents is restricted by s. 8 of the Exchange Control Act, 1947.

(5) UNDERWRITING COMMISSION
(i) Must be authorized by the Articles, (ii) may not exceed 10%, (iii) must be disclosed in the prospectus, statement in lieu of prospectus or in the prescribed form. Where the prescribed form (D. of T. Form 58) is used, it must be filed before the commission is paid (§ 53). Companies are allowed to pay customary brokerage or commission to brokers employed on an issue of shares (§ 53).

(6) REDEEMABLE PREFERENCE SHARES AND SHARES ISSUED AT A DISCOUNT
Special provisions are contained in § 58 permitting the issue of redeemable preference shares under conditions, and in § 57 providing for an application to the Court to sanction the issue of shares at a discount.

(7) SHARE WARRANTS AND BEARER BONDS
No document of title to securities which is transferable by delivery may be issued, and no document of title to securities may be altered so as to make it so transferable without Treasury consent (Exchange Control Act, 1947, s. 10).

(8) REGISTRATION OF CHARGES
Charges on the property of a company of the types mentioned in § 95 must be registered with the Registrar within 21 days after creation. Where a company acquires property subject to a charge, the charge must be registered within 21 days after the property is completely acquired (§ 97). The Court has power to extend the time for registration where registration has been omitted by inadvertence or owing to other sufficient cause (§ 101). Every company must keep a register of charges on its property (§ 104) open to the inspection of any creditor or shareholder without fee and of any member of the public on payment of a fee not

exceeding 5p (§ 105). No fee is payable on registration with the Registrar. Forms for registration are D. of T. Forms 47, 47A, 47B and 48.

(9) COMMENCEMENT OF BUSINESS

The conditions imposed by § 109 to be complied with before a public company can obtain a certificate entitling it to commence business or to exercise its borrowing powers are (i) the allotment of shares amounting in nominal value to the minimum subscription; (ii) the taking and payment for their qualification shares by the directors; (iii) the filing of a declaration of compliance by the secretary or a director (D. of T. Form 44 or 44A); (iv) the filing of a statement in lieu of prospectus when no prospectus has been issued (Form in Schedule V to the Act). Further conditions are imposed where the prospectus states that permission to deal on a recognised Stock Exchange will be applied for. Private companies and companies not having a share capital may commence business immediately upon incorporation.

(10) STATUTORY BOOKS

The books required to be kept under the Act are: (a) Register of members (§ 110); (b) Dominion register, where necessary (§ 119); (c) Index of members where necessary (§ 111); (d) Register of debenture holders (§ 86); (e) Register of charges (§ 104); (f) Register of directors and secretaries (§ 200); (g) Register of directors' interests (Companies Act 1967, s. 29); (h) Minute book (§ 145); (i) Books of account (§ 147); (j) Register of information furnished to company as to substantial interests in share capital carrying unrestricted voting rights (Companies Act 1967, s. 34). The statutory books must all be kept at the registered office, except that (i) the register of members and register of debentures may be kept at a branch office or office of registrars; (ii) a duplicate of a Dominion register must be kept with the register of members, and (iii) Books of account may be kept elsewhere as the directors think fit, but if held outside Great Britain, returns to Great Britain showing the position must be made at intervals of not more than six months. Notice must be given to the Registrar of the situation of (a) register of members, (b) register of debenture holders, (c) register of

directors' interests (unless they have always been kept at the registered office) and (d) the Dominion register. The register of interests in shares must be kept with the register of directors' interests.

(11) TRANSFER OF SHARES

Restrictions on the transfer of shares by or to non-residents are imposed by s. 9 of the Exchange Control Act 1947.

Company registrars are responsible for seeing that no transfers are registered which involve a contravention of the restrictions.

(12) ANNUAL RETURN

Every company must make an annual return to the Registrar (made up as at the fourteenth day after each annual general meeting) within 42 days after such meeting (form set out in the 6th Schedule, Part I, to the Act, or, in case of a company not having a share capital D. of T. Form No. 7). The Annual Return must be accompanied by a certified copy of the last audited balance sheet, accounts and other attached documents, directors' and auditors' reports and (if necessary) translations (§§ 124, 125, 126 and 127). A private company must also complete certificates that it has not issued any invitation to the public to subscribe for its shares or debentures (§ 128) and, where the number of members exceeds fifty, that such excess consists of persons falling within the exemption contained in § 28 (1) (b).

(13) MEETINGS

The statutory meeting of a company limited by shares or by guarantee and having a share capital (other than a private company) must be held within a period of not less than one month nor more than 3 months from the date when the company was entitled to commence business. The statutory report must be sent to every member 14 days at least before the day on which the meeting is to be held, and a properly certified copy thereof must be filed forthwith (§ 130).

Once in every calendar year and not more than 15 months after the holding of the last preceding annual general meeting (or in the case of the first meeting within 18 months of incorporation) *an annual general meeting* of every company must be held (§ 131).

At least 21 days' notice must be given and the notice must specify that the meeting is the annual general meeting, and that members are entitled to appoint proxies, who need not be members (§§ 131, 133, 136).

Extraordinary general meetings may be convened at any time on 21 days' notice where a special resolution is to be passed and 14 days' notice for other purposes, but an unlimited company may give 7 days' notice only, except for the passing of a special resolution (§§ 132, 133, 141). See also § 142 as to giving special notice in certain circumstances.

(14) RESOLUTIONS

(1) *Extraordinary resolution* is a resolution passed by a 3/4ths majority of such members as, being entitled so to do, vote in person or (where proxies are allowed) by proxy, at a general meeting of which due notice has been given that the resolution would be proposed as an extraordinary resolution.

(2) *Special resolution* is one passed by a similar majority at a general meeting of which 21 days' notice has been given that the resolution would be proposed as a special resolution (§ 141).

(3) *Ordinary resolutions* require a simple majority only.

A certified copy of every special or extraordinary resolution must within 15 days of its passing be filed with the Registrar of Companies. A copy of every special or extraordinary resolution must be annexed to all copies of the Articles (§ 143).

(15) ACCOUNTS

There is a statutory duty upon companies to keep proper books of account (§ 147), and a profit and loss account and balance sheet must be laid before a general meeting once in every year made up to within not more than 9 months before the meeting (companies trading abroad 12 months) (§ 148). The accounts must comply with specified requirements as to contents and form (§ 149 and see ss. 3 to 12 of the Companies Act 1967). Loans to directors, directors' remuneration and remuneration of employees earning more than £10,000 a year must be set out in the accounts (§§ 196 and 197 and see ss. 6, 7 and 8 of the Companies Act

1967). Members of the Company are entitled to copies of the balance sheet without fee (§ 158). Special provisions are made as to the accounts of holding companies and their subsidiaries (§§ 150–154 and see ss. 3, 4 and 5 of the Companies Act 1967).

(16) DIRECTORS' REPORT

There must be attached to every balance sheet laid before a company in general meeting a report by the directors as to the state of the company's affairs, the dividend recommended to be paid and the amount to be carried to reserve (§ 157). The directors' report must also cover such subjects as contributions for political or charitable purposes, particulars of exports, changes of fixed assets, issues of shares, particulars of contracts, etc., in which directors have an interest, information as to turnover and information as to the number of employees and their wages (Companies Act 1967, ss. 16, 17, 18, 19).

(17) ALTERATIONS TO MEMORANDUM OR ARTICLES

In addition to the requirement under s. 5 of the 1948 Act that an amended copy of the Memorandum be delivered to the Registrar of Companies after an alteration of objects, s. 9 of the European Communities Act 1972 provides that whenever any alteration is made in a company's Memorandum or Articles a printed copy of the Memorandum or Articles as altered must be sent to the Registrar not later than 15 days after the alteration comes into force. [N.B. The Registrar will accept a printed copy of the Memorandum and Articles with pasted-over typewritten clauses, etc. or inserted pages as necessary.]

(18) BUSINESS LETTERS AND ORDER FORMS

Under s. 9 of the European Communities Act 1972, all note-paper and order forms must show (a) the company's registered number and the place of registration, i.e. England or Scotland or alternatively London or Edinburgh, (b) the address of its registered office and (c) if exempt from using the word "limited" in its title, a statement that it is, in fact, limited. If any mention is made on the stationery of the company's share capital, it must be to its paid-up share capital.

As to the inclusion of the company's name and names of the directors on business letters, etc., see ss. 108 and 201 of the 1948 Act.

(19) WINDING-UP

(i) *Compulsory.* Certain County Courts have concurrent jurisdiction with the High Court where the paid-up capital does not exceed £10,000. Grounds for compulsory winding-up are set out in § 222 and § 223 gives a statutory definition (not exclusive) of inability to pay debts. Compulsory winding-up dates from the presentation of petition except where preceded by voluntary winding-up, in which case it dates from the resolution (§ 229). Within 14 days of the order a statement of affairs must be submitted to the Official Receiver, verified by affidavit of one or more directors and the secretary or such other persons mentioned in § 235 as may be directed to verify.

(ii) *Voluntary.* A resolution for voluntary liquidation must be advertised within 14 days in the *Gazette* (§ 279). Unless a "declaration of solvency" is made, a meeting of creditors must be summoned by notice and advertisement for the same day or the day after the company's meeting (§ 293).

Declaration of solvency, if made, must be made by a majority of the directors, but it has no effect unless (a) it is made within the five weeks immediately preceding the passing of the resolution to wind up and is delivered to the Registrar for registration before that date, and (b) it embodies a statement of the assets and liabilities as at the latest practicable date before the making of the declaration (§ 283).

(20) FRAUDULENT TRADING

See § 332 under which, if the Court finds that business has been carried on with intent to defraud creditors, the directors may be made personally liable for debts or part of the debts of the company.

(21) RECONSTRUCTION

On reconstruction or sale to a new company under § 287, see that s. 55 of Finance Act, 1927, is complied with, in order to obtain relief from capital duty and stamp duty.

(22) SHARE HAWKING

The Prevention of Fraud (Investments) Act, 1958 as amended by the Protection of Depositors Act 1963, prohibits personal offering of shares etc., from house to house and restricts written offers (*cf.* also S.I. 1960 No. 1216). The following Orders made under earlier legislation remain in force: S.R. & O. 1944, No. 119 (application for licences); S.R. & O. 1944, No. 540 (form of undertaking which may be accepted in lieu of deposit); S.R. & O. 1944, No. 541 (method of making deposits). Enquiries as to this Act should be addressed to the Assistant Secretary, Companies Division, Department of Trade, Sanctuary Buildings, 16–20 Great Smith Street, London, S.W.1.

Compulsory References

SEE ARBITRATION

Conveyancing

SEE REAL PROPERTY

Copyright

The Law relating to copyright in the United Kingdom and Northern Ireland is now almost entirely contained in the Copyright Act, 1956 ("the Act") which repealed the Copyright Act, 1911 with the exception of ss. 15, 34 and 37 thereof. These sections deal with Libraries which are entitled to delivery of copies of books. The Act came into force on the 1st June, 1957 (s. 54 (2) and S.I. 1957 No. 863). It applies to all copyright, subject in respect of works in which copyright already subsists, to the transitional provisions contained in the Seventh Schedule, Part VII of which only applies to works in which copyright subsisted before July 1st, 1912. The Act has been amended by the Design Copyright Act, 1968 and the Copyright (Amendment) Act, 1971.

The Act defines separately the various matters in which copyright can subsist, how that copyright is infringed and the period for which it extends. Copyright means the exclusive right to do and to authorise other persons to do the acts referred to in the section dealing with the matters referred to (s. 1). The Act uses the expression: "a qualified person". In the case of an individual this means a British Subject, a British protected person or a citizen of the Irish Republic or a person who is domiciled or resident in the United Kingdom or in another country to which the appropriate provision of the Act extends. In the case of a body corporate it means a body incorporated under the laws of the United Kingdom or of another country to which the provision extends (s. 1 (5)). Part V of the Act provides for the extension of the Act wholly or in part to other parts of Her Majesty's Dominions and to foreign countries thereby enabling the United Kingdom to ratify the Brussels Convention (Cmd. 7815) on the 26th October, 1957 and the Universal Copyright Convention (Cmd. 8912) on the 27th June, 1957. A number of Orders have now been made extending the Act wholly or in part to different territories.

In the case of literary, dramatic and musical works copyright subsists in every such original work which is unpublished and of which the author was a qualified person when the work was made. Copyright is also acquired by an unqualified person when publication first takes place in this country.

Where an original literary, dramatic or musical work has been published copyright subsists for 50 years from the end of the calendar year in which the author dies and if it has not been published or any of the other acts specified in s. 2 have not been done copyright subsists for 50 years from the end of the calendar year in which publication takes place or such other act is done. Copyright in a literary, dramatic or musical work is infringed by reproducing or publishing the work, performing it in public, broadcasting the work, causing it to be transmitted over a diffusion service or making any adaptation thereof. S. 6 exempts from infringement matters defined as fair dealing in a literary, dramatic or musical work, reproduction for purposes of judicial proceedings or reports thereof, inclusion of passages thereof in collections for the use of schools, and reading or recitation of extracts other than for broadcasting. In all cases a sufficient acknowledgment identifying the author must be made. This section also contains provisions whereby Broadcast Authorities can make reproductions in the form of a record or film for their own purposes which must be destroyed within 28 days. Section 7 makes provision for the supply of copies by libraries subject to regulations to be made by the Department of Trade. See S.I. 1957 Nos. 865 and 868. Section 8 exempts from infringement records of a musical work if a similar record has already been made and a royalty of 6¼% of the retail selling price is paid. S.I. 1957 No. 866 contains regulations made under this section.

Copyright in artistic works (s. 3) subsists in paintings, sculptures, drawings, engravings and photographs irrespective of artistic quality, works of architecture and other works of artistic craftsmanship. It subsists in unpublished works where the author was a qualified person when the work was made and subsists in published works where published as defined in the Section. The period of copyright is 50 years from the end of the calendar year in which the author died but in the case of an engraving which has not been published before the death of the author it subsists for 50 years from the end of the calendar year in which it is first published. Copyright in photographs extends for 50 years from the end of the calendar year in which the photograph is first published. It is an infringement of copyright in an artistic work to reproduce it in any material form, to publish the work, to include it in a television broadcast or to cause a television programme which includes the work to be transmitted to subscribers to a diffusion service.

Importation and certain other dealings in literary, dramatic, musical and artistic works are declared to be infringement of copyright (s. 5).

In general copyright in literary, dramatic, musical and artistic works vests in the author but where such a work is made in the course of the author's employment with a newspaper or other periodical for the purpose of publication therein the proprietor is entitled to the copyright in respect of publication in newspapers and periodicals but not otherwise. Where a person commissions a photograph or portrait or an engraving for valuable consideration the person commissioning the work is entitled to the copyright. In any other case and subject to any specific agreement a copyright in a work made in the course of the author's employment under a contract of service is the property of the employer. Section 9 contains provisions whereby fair dealing with an artistic work for purposes of research or private study shall not constitute an infringement.

The provisions of the Copyright Act, 1911 whereby compulsory licences may be granted and whereby in certain circumstances a work may be reproduced on payment of royalty are not repeated but existing rights are maintained by the transitional provisions.

Until the passing of the Design Copyright Act 1968 copyright was lost where any article the subject thereof was reproduced industrially to the extent of 50 articles and protection was only possible under the Registered Designs Act 1949. By an amendment made by the Design Copyright Act 1968 to s. 10. of the Copyright Act 1956 copyright protection extends to such articles even if mass produced but for 15 years only and the copyright covers the articles in two or three dimensions.

Anonymous and pseudonymous works are dealt with in the Second Schedule to the Act and works of joint authorship in the Third Schedule (s. 11).

Copyright is created in sound recordings, cinematograph films, as such and in television and sound broadcasts. In the case of sound recordings copyright vests in the maker if a qualified person, or in any person commissioning the making of the recording for value. The period is 50 years from the end of the calendar year in which the recording is first published (s. 12).

Infringement consists in making a record embodying the recording, causing the recording to be heard in public or broadcasting the recording. The section provides that certain acts shall not be infringement. These include playing a recording in a Hotel or Boarding House where a special charge is not made and at a Club or other organisation not conducted for profit and having charitable, educational, or social welfare purposes where no charge is made. Where a sound broadcast or television broadcast is made by the B.B.C. or I.T.A. a person who by the reception of the broadcast causes the sound recording to be heard in public does not thereby infringe the copyright in that sound recording (s. 40 (1)). Copyright in a film vests in the maker and extends for 50 years from the end of the calendar year in which the film is registered under the Cinematograph Films Act, 1938 or if not registrable for 50 years from the end of the calendar year in which it was first published. Copyright is infringed by copying the film, causing it to be heard in public, broadcasting it, and causing it to be transmitted to subscribers to a diffusion service (s. 13). Where a television broadcast or sound broadcast is made by the B.B.C. or I.T.A. and the broadcast is an authorised broadcast a person who by reception of the broadcast causes a film to be seen or heard in public is not an infringer (s. 40 (2)). Copyright in the television and sound broadcasts of the B.B.C. and I.T.A. extends for 50 years from the end of the year in which the broadcast is made. Special provisions relating to these copyrights and the acts by which they are infringed are set out in s. 14 and see also s. 40 (3). Copyright extending for 25 years from the date of first publication is also created in published editions of works for a period of 25 years from the end of the year in which the edition is first published. Copyright vests in the publisher (s. 15). Further provisions regarding these new copyrights are contained in s. 16.

Infringements are dealt with in sections 17–20 and include provisions which save an innocent infringer from damages but in certain circumstances permit punitive damages to be awarded. An exclusive Licensee has the right to take proceedings for infringement. Certain matters are offences which can be summarily dealt with (s. 21).

Notice may be given to the Customs to prevent importation of published literary, dramatic or musical works (s. 22 and S.I. 1957 No. 875).

Ss. 24–30 and the Fourth Schedule establish a Performing Right Tribunal which is given power to determine disputes between licensing bodies (B.B.C., I.T.A., The Performing Rights Society, Phonographic Performances Limited and any other licensing body as defined) and persons requiring Licences in respect of copyright in a literary, dramatic or musical work or in a sound recording or a television broadcast and where a licensing scheme set up by any such body is brought into question. The tribunal has jurisdiction to confirm or vary a licence scheme or to determine a dispute on the application of a person requiring a licence either in accordance with a licence scheme or in a case not covered by a licence scheme. Provision is made for questions of law to be referred to the Court. Rules regarding procedure before the Tribunal are contained in S.I. 1965 No. 1506 which has revoked and consolidated the Rules of 1957, 1959 and 1960. See also R.S.C., Orders 56 and 93, rr. 10 and 14.

Assignments of copyright must be in writing (s. 36), and an Agreement in writing to assign future copyright vests the copyright in the Assignee when the copyright comes into existence (s. 37). A bequest of the manuscript of a literary, dramatic, musical or artistic work passes the copyright therein in the absence of an expression of contrary intention where the work was not published before the death of the testator (s. 38).

For Crown copyright and public records see ss. 39 and 42. Certain uses of copyright material for education are saved from infringement (s. 41). A right of action is established in favour of a person whose name is used without his consent under and in the circumstances provided in s. 43. The definitions in the interpretation sections 48 and 49 are important. The Dramatic and Musical Performers Protection Act, 1958 consolidates the provisions of the Dramatic and Musical Performers Protection Act, 1925 and those provisions of the Copyright Act 1956 which amend it. The provisions are mainly penal. See also the Performers Protection Act, 1963.

Corporation Tax

SEE TAXATION, p. 341, *post*

County Court Proceedings

GENERAL NOTES

See The County Court Practice, and McCleary's County Court Precedents, 4th Edn (2 vols.)

NOTE.—The general jurisdiction of the County Courts and procedure therein are governed by the County Courts Act, 1959 and the County Court Rules, 1936. These rules as amended (last amendment, April 1976) are shortly described under appropriate subheads below, except as to transfer from the High Court (for which see p. 160, *post*).

Jurisdiction in actions relating to land (s. 48) was raised to a rateable value of £1,000 by the Administration of Justice Act, 1973.

Appeals from the County Court lie to the Court of Appeal (1959 Act, s. 108). See *post*, p. 106.

Special jurisdiction is given to the County Courts under a variety of Acts in relation to which reference should be made to Part 2 of *The County Court Practice*.

The County Court Funds Rules 1975, provide machinery by which moneys and funds in Court are administered.

The County Court Fees Order 1975 sets out the fees payable in respect of proceedings in the County Court. See p. 131, *post*.

Legal Aid. The Legal Aid Acts and Regulations apply and are set out in *The County Court Practice* so far as applicable.

Rent Act. This Act is not included in *The County Court Practice* but reference may be made to *Hill and Redman's Landlord and Tenant*, 15th Edn.

Matrimonial Causes. Jurisdiction in undefended matrimonial causes is conferred on specially designated Divorce County Courts by the Matrimonial Causes Act 1967. The Matrimonial Causes Rules 1973 are dealt with on pp. 266 *et seq.*, *post*.

GENERAL JURISDICTION

Contract or Tort: limit £1000, but by agreement unlimited (ss. 39–42).

Recovery of land and title: limit £1000 net annual value for rating (ss. 39, 48, 51). Where a mortgage includes a dwellinghouse and no part of the land is in Greater London Jurisdiction up to this limit is exclusive unless the action is also for foreclosure or sale (Administration of Justice Act 1970, s. 37). Unlimited jurisdiction in cases within Rent Act

(1968 Act, s. 105), or by agreement, s. 42.

Equity: General limit £5,000. By agreement unlimited except proceedings under Variation of Trusts Act 1958, s. 1 (ss. 52, 53).

Admiralty (certain courts only): limit £3,500 salvage, £1,000 otherwise, but by agreement unlimited (ss. 55, 56).

Probate: limit £1,000 (ss. 62, 64).

Bankruptcy (certain courts only: unlimited (Bankruptcy Act, 1914, s. 98).

Administration order: where a debtor's whole liabilities do not exceed £1000 (ss. 148–156).

Counterclaims: Unlimited jurisdiction. Either party may apply to transfer to the High Court within 8 days of receipt or filing of counterclaim if counterclaim is beyond the jurisdiction of the county Court (s. 65(1); R.S.C. Ord. 107, r. 2).

Proceedings by and against the Crown are dealt with in O. 46, r. 13 and governed by the Crown Proceedings Act, 1947, and Taxes Management Act 1970, s. 66(1).

VENUE

General rule. Proceedings may be brought either (a) in the court for the district in which one or other of the defendants reside or carries on business or (b) in that for the district in which the cause of action wholly or in part arose (O. 2 r. 1(1)). An assignee must sue in a court in which the assignor could have sued (O. 2, r. 1(2)).

Hire-purchase and instalment contracts. Proceedings may be brought in the court for the district in which one or other of the defendants resides or carries on business or (where recovery of the goods is not sought) in that for the district in which one or other of the defendants resided or carried on business when the contract was made (O. 2, r. 1(3)) or (where recovery of the goods is claimed) in that for the district in which one or other of the defendants resided or carried on business at the date of the last payment made under the agreement (Hire-Purchase Act 1965, s. 49).

Recovery of possession of land or enforcement of a mortgage. Proceedings must be brought in the court for the district in which the land is situate (O. 2, r. 2).

Originating applications. Proceedings may be brought in the court for the district in which one or other of the respondents resides or carries on business or in which the subject matter is situate or, if there is no respondent, in that for the district in which one of the applicants resides or carries on business (O. 2, r. 13).

Proceedings against the Crown. Unless otherwise provided proceedings by action must be brought in the court for the district in which the cause of action arose and by originating application in that for the district in which the subject matter is situate. In case of doubt as to the right court proceedings may be brought in that for the district in which one of the plaintiffs resides or carries on business (O. 46, r. 13(2)).

COMMENCEMENT OF PROCEEDINGS

Proceedings to obtain relief against any person or to compel any person to do or abstain from doing any act must be brought by action (O. 6, r. 1). Actions (other than Admiralty actions) may be commenced by ordinary or default summons. All other proceedings are called matters and except where some special originating process is required, such as a petition, matters may be commenced by originating application (O. 6, r. 4).

A default action must be brought in respect of any debt or liquidated demand (which includes cost of repair to a vehicle arising out of an accident on land as a result of negligence (O. 49, r. 5(1)) except an action (a) against a person under disability (b) by a moneylender or mortgagee, (c) for more than unpaid instalments under a hire-purchase agreement or (d) to recover interest after the commencement of the action (O. 6, r. 2 (1)). Any other action is an ordinary action. No return day is fixed in a default action but in an ordinary action (other than for recovery of land) the return day is, unless otherwise ordered, an appointment for a pre-trial review.

A request in the appropriate form for the issue of the summons together with the plaint fee and particulars of claim and copies for service in each defendant must be filed at the Court office.

PARTICULARS OF CLAIM

Particulars are regulated by O. 7 and must specify the cause of action and the claims made (r. 1). Where a solicitor is acting he must sign them and state his address for service (r. 10) and when settled by counsel they must he signed by him (O. 48, r. 12). Where an account is claimed the particulars must so state and the amount claimed subject thereto. If no amount is stated the plaintiff is deemed to claim £1000 (r. 2).

There are specific requirements as to what must be stated in the particulars in the following actions: recovery of possession of land (r. 3); administration proceedings (r. 5); claims by money lenders (r. 6); claims by mortgagees (r. 7); hire-purchase (r. 7A). Where there is more than one cause of action the grounds of each cause must be separately stated (r. 8).

Summary proceedings for possession of land occupied solely by a person or persons (not being tenants holding over) who are in occupation without his consent or that of his predecessor (i.e. squatters) may be brought by originating application in Form 398. The plaintiff is not required to identify every person in occupation. An affidavit must be filed in support. Unless otherwise ordered the hearing date must be not less than 7 clear days after service (O. 26, rr. 1–7).

A rent action may be brought to recover arrears of rent from a tenant or former tenant who is still in occupation of the land. The request must contain a statement that the plaintiff requires a summons in Form 10. The summons must be served not less than 7 clear days before the return day and may be effected by post. In most of other respects a rent action is treated as an ordinary action (O. 26 rr. 8–11).

SECURITY FOR COSTS

Where the proposed plaintiff does not reside in England or Wales he must give security for costs, but the registrar may, on ex parte application, dispense with security if he thinks it reasonable to do so (O. 3, r. 1).

A dependant who neither resides nor carries on business within 20 miles of the Court may apply for security for his costs, on filing an affidavit setting out the grounds of his defence (O. 13, r. 7).

Security is usually by deposit of money in Court or on a personal undertaking by the solicitor (O. 48, r. 16).

SERVICE

An ordinary or default summons may be served by the plaintiff or by the Court (O. 8). Service by a party must be personal and an affidavit of service (Form 35) must be filed within 3 days of service (O. 8, r. 2). An ordinary summons must be served not less than 21 days before the return day (O. 8, r. 8(4)). Where the certificate for postal service on the form of request is given service of an ordinary or default summons is effected by the Court (O. 8, r. 8(2)). A solicitor may endorse on the copy summons to be retained by the plaintiff a memorandum signed and dated accepting service on behalf of a defendant and giving an address for service (O. 8, r. 11).

Where partners are sued in the firm name service is good if the summons is delivered to a partner personally or, at the principal place of the partnership business in the district of the court, to any person having or appearing to have control or management of the business (O. 8, r. 14). For service of a summons for recovery of land on a representative of the defendant or by fixing it to the property, see O. 8, r. 24. A representative means the husband or wife of the defendant or anyone who in the opinion of the court is, or is held out to be authorised to reside in, carry on business at, or manage the property for the defendant or receive the rent (r. 24(5)). Where no other mode of service is prescribed a document may be served by post (O. 8, r. 39). For service out of the jurisdiction see O. 8, r. 40 et seq.

Where an ordinary summons has not been served successive summonses may be issued on filing an amended request. A successive summons cannot be issued after 12 months from the date of issue of the original summons, unless application to extend the time is made within the currency of the last proceeding period (O. 8, r. 32). A default summons must be served within 12 months but the time may be extended for successive periods upon application made within the currency of the last proceeding period (O. 8, r. 35).

PAYMENT INTO COURT

Payment within 14 days of service. If the claim is for money only and the whole amount and costs on the summons are paid the action is stayed.

If less than the amount claimed is paid with the costs that would have been appropriate to that amount, which the plaintiff accepts, he must within 7 days after receipt of notice of payment but not less than 2 days before the return day give notice of acceptance to the registrar and the defendant and the action will be stayed. If the action is for a liquidated demand no further costs are payable unless otherwise ordered. In other cases the plaintiff must within the time for giving notice of acceptance give notice to the registrar and to the defendant that he requires taxed costs (O. 11, r. 7).

Payment in full more than 14 days after Service or without costs. The action is stayed and the defendant is not liable for costs after receipt by the plaintiff of notice of payment.

If the plaintiff requires additional costs he may within 14 days after receipt of notice of payment lodge a bill for taxation (O. 11, r. 8).

Payment—accepted in other cases. The plaintiff must within 7 days after receipt of notice of payment or before the hearing (if notice is received less than 7 days before the return day) give notice of acceptance, and the action will be stayed. He may then tax his costs incurred before receipt of notice of payment (O. 11, r. 9).

Late acceptance. Notice of acceptance may be given at any time before the hearing, but the plaintiff may be ordered to pay the defendant's costs reasonably incurred since the date of payment in O. 11, r. 11). An order for payment out must be obtained, but this may be done by post if the defendant's consent is filed.

DEFENCES AND ADMISSIONS

A form of admission, defence and counterclaim is appended to all ordinary and default summonses: if the defendant does not use this form, a copy of the defence, etc. must be filed for each plaintiff. An admission or defence must be filed within 14 days of service (C.C.R., O. 9, rr. 1–5; O. 10, rr. 1–4); but it may be filed afterwards at any time before judgment, subject to the risk of further costs.

If an admission is delivered in a default action and the offer is not accepted, a day for disposal is fixed (O. 10, r. 4). If a defence is filed, the registrar fixes a day for a pre-trial review or if he thinks fit a day for the hearing of the action (O. 10, r. 3).

As to Third Party Procedure see O. 12.

FURTHER PARTICULARS OF CLAIM

A defendant may file notice for further particulars of the particulars of claim and deliver a copy to the plaintiff within 8 days after service of the summons. Particulars must be filed and delivered in 5 days. In default the claim may be struck out or proceedings stayed (O. 7, r. 9). For further particulars of defence see O. 9, r. 4(6), O. 10, r. 9.

TRANSFER

The court may transfer proceedings to another court if satisfied that they can be more conveniently or fairly tried there (O. 16, r. 1(1)). A defendant who does not reside in the district of the court can apply ex parte in writing without fee for the action to be transferred to the district in which he resides or carries on business (O. 16, r. 1(2)). Proceedings commenced in the wrong court may be transferred, retained or struck out (O. 16, r. 4). Usually the plaint fee will be returned so that proceedings may be taken in the right court.

INTERLOCUTORY APPLICATIONS

Parties should apply for any particular directions at the pre-trial review and if an application which might have been made at the review is made subsequently the applicant must pay the costs unless the court is satisfied that there was sufficient reason for not having done so (O. 21, r. 3).

Any application may be made either ex parte or on written notice. Notice must be filed at the court office and a copy served on the other party not less than one clear day before the hearing. No affidavit is necessary but the court may call for evidence (O. 13, r. 1).

Interlocutory applications are normally heard by the registrar but the judge must hear applications for:— service out of jurisdiction (O. 8, rr. 41–50) appointment of guardian ad litem where no application has been made on defendant's behalf (O. 5, r. 13), interim injunction (O. 13, r. 8) appointment of receiver (O. 30, r. 1).

INTERIM INJUNCTION

Application may be made to the judge whether or not a claim for an injunction was included in the particulars of claim. Application may be ex parte on affidavit in cases of urgency otherwise it must be on notice. If made before issue of proceedings the affidavit must show that the court has jurisdiction to hear the action and the injunction will only be issued on terms providing for the issue of proceedings (O. 13, r. 8). A draft order must be prepared beforehand and settled by the registrar (O. 13, r. 13) except in cases of urgency.

AMENDMENT

The court may at any time amend any defects and errors in the proceedings and add, strike out or substitute any person as plaintiff or defendant and all such amendments as may be necessary to determine the real question between the parties must be made if duly applied for. No person may be added as a plaintiff without his written consent or, in the case of a person under disability, that of his next friend or other person acting on his behalf (O. 15, r. 1). Any amendment may be made at any stage by the court of its own motion or on application at the trial, or before the trial on notice (O. 15, r. 3).

Amended particulars of claim or amended defence or counter claim may be filed at any time before the return day without any order and any party may increase the amount of his claim or counterclaim on payment of the difference between the fees paid and those payable on the larger amount, but the court may on the return day disallow the amendment or allow it on terms (O. 15, r. 4). Note that the return day is usually the pre-trial review.

POSTAL PROVISIONS

Any act that can be done by attendance at the Court office may be done by post, provided that the requisite documents are sent by prepaid post with a postal or money order for the fee and a stamped addressed envelope. This does not affect the duty of a party to appear in proceedings before judge or registrar in court or chambers (O. 48, r. 24). By the Recorded Delivery Service Act, 1962, recorded delivery service may be used where registered post is required by statute.

PRE-TRIAL REVIEW

A pre-trial review is fixed in ordinary actions (other than possession actions) and in defended default actions unless the court otherwise directs (O. 6, r. 3; O. 10, r. 3). If no pre-trial review has been fixed the registrar may nevertheless give notice to the parties for directions (O. 21, r. 10). At the review the registrar gives directions for the just expeditious and economical disposal of the action and may exercise any power available to him on an interlocutory application and may do so on his own motion (O. 21, rr. 1, 2, 4).

If the defendant appears but has not filed a defence he may be ordered to do so with judgment in default (O. 9, r. 4(8); O. 21, r. 4; O. 24, r. 10). If the defendant admits the claim the registrar may enter judgment and make any necessary instalment order (O. 20, r. 6).

If the defendant does not appear the registrar may strike out any defence and enter an interlocutory judgment for damages to be assessed unless the plaintiff is ready to prove damage either personally or by affidavit (O. 13, r. 6; O. 21, rr. 5, 7, 8; O. 23, r. 2(3); O. 24, r. 10).

If the plaintiff neither attends nor files evidence on affidavit the action is struck out (O. 23, r. 2).

At the conclusion of the review the date of trial is fixed (O. 21, r. 9) or the action is adjourned for the hearing to be fixed at a later date.

DISCONTINUANCE

A plaintiff wishing to withdraw or discontinue must give notice to the court, or to the other party in Form 58, though a letter will usually suffice. On receipt of the notice the other party may lodge a bill of costs for taxation and if it is not paid within 14 days of taxation judgment may be entered. If the action is not wholly discontinued execution for the costs may not issue without leave (O. 18).

Registrar's Powers of Trial and Reference

The power of a registrar, by leave of the judge, to try cases where no objection is raised by any of the parties extends to any case in which either the sum claimed or amount involved does not exceed £100, but where consent is actually given it extends to any action or matter (O. 23, r. 1). The judge (or the registrar by consent) may refer to the Registrar or a referee with consent any proceeding, and without consent any proceedings involving accounts or prolonged examination of documents or scientific or local investigation, or any question in any proceedings (s. 93; O. 19, rr. 2, 3). The judge may also refer to the registrar any application under s. 17 of the Married Women's Property Act, 1882 (O. 46, r. 11).

Any judgment or final order of a registrar, and any execution thereon (except when made by consent), may, on notice served within 6 days stating the grounds of appeal, be set aside by the judge who may give such judgment or make such order as to a new trial or otherwise as he may think just (O. 37, r. 5).

The reference to a registrar for inquiry and report is governed by O. 19, and an order may be made on application by any party in accordance with the Rules as to interlocutory applications, or at the hearing on application or by the judge of his own motion. For the conduct of the reference see r. 2 (3).

On consideration of the report or any further report, if any, the judge may give such judgment and make such order in the action or matter as may be just, without prejudice to any right of appeal.

Arbitration

The court may on the application of a party order any proceedings to be referred to arbitration in such manner and on such terms as the court thinks just and reasonable, but where a charge of fraud against a party is in issue an order cannot be made without

the consent of that party (s. 92; O. 19, r. 1). The application may be dealt with by the registrar, but where the amount involved exceeds his jurisdiction any party may, before it is heard, request the registrar in writing to refer the application to the judge. Reference to an arbitrator other than the judge or registrar can only be ordered by consent and the judge is to act only with his consent. Application may be made in the particulars of claim or defence or by application on notice or at the pre-trial review. Where the amount involved does not exceed £100 the registrar may deal with the application without attendance, but the party who did not apply for the order may apply to vary or rescind it.

The terms of the reference may exclude strict rules of evidence, restrict liability for solicitors' costs, provide for hearing in private and allow the arbitrator to obtain reports and assistance from experts. The procedure is intended to assit litigants in person but may help to reduce costs in other cases, e.g. by enabling parties to be represented by legal executives.

The award is entered as the judgment of the court (s. 92(3)). The right of appeal is probably limited to error in law in the face of the award or misconduct by the arbitrator (see *Meyer* v. *Leanse*, [1958] 3 All E.R. 213). Application to set aside an award must be made within 6 days from receipt of the copy judgment (O. 37, r. 7).

New Trial

Provisions as to new trial are made under s. 98, by O. 37, rr. 1, 2, 5. For grounds and practice, see *Guest* v. *Ibbotson* (1922), 126 L.T. 738, C.A. The County Court judge can grant a new trial in any case in which the High Court could (*Astor* v. *Barrett*, [1920] 36 T.L.R. 888, C.A.). The application must be made forthwith, or at the first court held after the expiration of 12 clear days, upon 6 clear days' notice in writing stating the grounds. The notice is no stay unless the judge so orders (*Kelly* v. *White*, [1920] W.N. 220).

Setting Aside Proceedings

The practice is regulated by O. 37. Application to set aside a judgment or order must be to the judge if made by him or on appeal from a judgment or final order of the registrar, but in all other cases to the registrar. Non-compliance with the rules does not nullify the proceedings but they may be set aside or the Court may allow such amendments as it thinks fit (r. 4(1)). An application to set aside proceedings for irregularity must be made on notice in writing stating the objections relied on within "a reasonable time" and before any fresh step is taken (r. 4 (2)). (3) Where process has been served by post the court may set aside judgment of its own motion if satisfied that it did not come to the defendant's notice in time (O. 37, r. 6).

ADJOURNED ACTION

After an action or matter has been adjourned generally it will be struck out after 12 months on 14 days' notice if there is no application to fix a date for hearing (O. 13, r. 4 (4)).

APPEALS

An appeal from a County Court lies to the Court of Appeal, s. 108. R.S.C. O. 59, r. 19 provides for these appeals. Subject to which, the relevant rules on appeal from the High Court apply.

Ss. 108–114 deal with such appeals. An appeal lies without leave:—

(i) In actions of contract or tort, where the claim exceeds £20, on a point of law and where it exceeds £200 also on a question of fact.

(ii) In equity matters, on a point of law, also in garnishee proceedings.

(iii) Where there is a claim for an injunction on a point of law or a question of fact.

(iv) In all actions for recovery of land or where title to a hereditament is in question, on a point of law and if the net annual value for rating exceeds £500 also on a question of fact.

(v) On a counterclaim exceeding £20, on a point of law, or where this is or relates to a claim in which there would lie an appeal on a question of fact such appeal would also line on fact.

(vi) In replevin, where the value exceeds £20, on a point of law.

(vii) In interpleader proceedings where the value exceeds £20,

on a point of law and where it exceeds £200 also on a question of fact.

(viii) In probate proceedings on a point of law and if the value of the estate exceeds £500 also on a question of fact.

(ix) In Admiralty proceedings, the position is as under (i) (contract and tort), *supra*.

(x) On punishment for contempt of court.

(xi) On a question of law against a compulsory winding-up order.

An appeal lies only with leave of the judge in (i), (v), (vi), (vii) and (ix) above where the value of the claim does not exceed £20 in which case the appeal can only be on a point of law. An appeal lies from an interlocutory as well as a final order. If an application for a new trial on the ground of misdirection is refused an appeal will lie from such refusal.

The judge must if requested at the hearing take a note of the question of law and of the facts in evidence in relation thereto, and of his decision thereon (s. 112). Omission to ask this is not a bar to an appeal, and the court may hear such appeal upon other evidence of what occurred. The judge, having been requested to take a note, must supply any party, at such party's expense, with a signed copy whether notice of appeal be served or not (s. 112). Otherwise the judge's notes are his own property and he cannot be asked to furnish copies unless notice of appeal has been served on the registrar. Where this has been done it is the duty of the appellant to ask the judge for a signed copy of his notes. If a note is not produced, the court may determine the appeal on any other evidence or statement deemed sufficient (R.S.C., O. 59, r. 19 (4)). If the judge's notes are defective on vital points shorthand notes may be used, or counsel's notes, or the solicitor's affidavit. It is the duty of counsel to take a note of the judgment. If counsel's notes are to be used in appeal they should be submitted to the judge for his prior approval. An appellant cannot raise a point not taken in the County Court but a respondent can take any point whether raised below or not.

Notice of appeal must be served on the C.C. registrar and all parties directly affected, within the following periods from the date of the judgment or order appealed from; 14 days in appeals from interlocutory orders, 21 days in appeals from bankruptcy and winding-up orders or decisions, 6 weeks in other cases (R.S.C., O. 59, rr. 19; 4). The appellant must apply for the appeal to be set down within 7 days of service of the notice, or within such further time as may be allowed (R.S.C., O. 59, r. 5). The Court of Appeal has power to extend the time for appealing (R.S.C., O. 3, r. 5) and it may also be extended by the court below on an application made before the time has expired (R.S.C., O. 59, r. 15).

Papers for the use of the Court of Appeal. It is the duty of the solicitor for the appellant to see that the papers necessary for the use of the Court of Appeal reach the Lords Justices' Clerks' Room No. 321, Royal Courts of Justice, at least one week before the appeal is likely to be in the Daily Cause List for hearing.

Three copies of each paper are required, save in Admiralty cases where four copies must be supplied, or (if the Appeal Court is to sit with assessors) six copies.

Where an office copy is supplied, whether by the appellant's solicitor or (on bespoke by the appellant's solicitor) by the proper officer of the court, only two other copies (or in Admiralty cases three or five as the case may be) need be supplied.

The papers to be supplied are as follows:—

The notice of appeal.
The order appealed from.
The pleadings, if any, and (in Admiralty cases) the preliminary act, if any.
Copies of the judge's note.
List of exhibits.
Such affidavits (if any) as are relevant.
A copy of such exhibits and correspondence as are relevant.

These papers must be put together in three sets, numbered, and indexed. Failure to lodge the necessary papers in due time will entail personal liability on the solicitor to pay costs thrown

away. The costs of furnishing unnecessary papers will be disallowed on taxation.

In the case of lengthy documents where parts only of the document are relevant it will suffice to lodge one complete copy of the document and three copies of the relevant clauses.

[Practice Note. May, 1941]

ENFORCEMENT OF JUDGMENTS

Examination of judgment debtor (O. 25, r. 2).—Application is made ex parte to the court in which the debtor resides or carries on business in Form 149 for the debtor or in the case of a company any named officer thereof to be examined as to means. If the judgment was obtained in a different court application should be made by letter to transfer the proceedings (O. 25, r. 48). The registrar may give the debtor an opportunity to file an affidavit or statement as to means without attending for examination. The order must be served personally and conduct money tendered. If the debtor does not attend the order may be enforced by attachment.

Execution against goods (O. 25, rr. 13–32).—A warrant may issue when the debtor is in default. In the case of an instalment order the warrant may be for the whole amount or for any part thereof not less than £10 or one monthly or four weekly instalments whichever is the greater. Leave is required after 2 years from the date of judgment or some payment into court thereunder or where an attachment of earnings order is in force.

Where judgment is against a firm leave is required before a warrant can be issued against any partner personally who was not individually served with the summons or who has not admitted in the action that he was a partner or been adjudged liable as a partner. He must be personally served with 3 clear days notice of the application (r. 18).

An unexecuted warrant remains in force for one year but may be renewed by leave before expiry. Application may be by letter.

Costs of a warrant not recovered in execution may not be included in a new order or in an attachment of earnings order (rr. 65, 86 (2)).

If the bailiff is requested to withdraw

from possession the execution is abandoned but if the request indicates that it is by arrangement with the debtor the warrant is marked as suspended and may be re-issued (r. 25).

Interpleader proceedings (ss. 135, 136; O. 28, rr. 1–15).—Any claim to goods levied upon must be made in writing and the registrar sends notice to the execution creditor. If the creditor does not give notice admitting the claim within 4 days the registrar issues an interpleader summons.

This must be served 14 days before the return day and the claimant must within 8 days of service file 2 copies of particulars of goods alleged to be his and the grounds of his claim. His full name, address and occupation must be stated. Unless the claimant deposits the value of the goods or gives security the bailiff must sell them but the registrar may postpone the sale until the claim has been decided (s. 135; Administration of Justice Act 1965, s. 22 (3)). The claim is heard by the judge.

Attachment of Earnings (Attachment of Earnings Act 1971; O. 25, rr. 77–94).—Each court keeps an index of debtors residing within its district against whom attachment orders have been made and any judgment creditor may request a search to be made. A county court may make an attachment of earnings order to secure payments under (1) a High Court or County Court maintenance order, (2) a judgment debt of £5 or more or the balance outstanding under a judgment for not less than £5 or (3) under an administration order. Application is made in Form 402 and the name and address of the employer need not be stated if not known. If the registrar feels able to make an order without attendance by the parties he may notify the proposed order to them. The order will then be made if neither party requests a hearing date within the time specified. The hearing takes place in chambers and if the judgment creditor does not wish to attend he may file an affidavit or a request for the court to deal with the application in his absence. For the meaning of attachable earnings, see s. 24.

Judgment summons.—A judgment summons can be issued only in respect of maintenance payments and certain Crown debts such as income tax and national insurance contributions. The appropriate Court for the issue of a judgment summons is the Court of the district in which the debtor resides or carries on business (O. 25, r. 23).

Garnishee proceedings (O. 27).—Proceedings may be taken in any court in which the judgment debtor could have sued the garnishee. An affidavit in Form 205 (obtainable from the Court) must be filed with a certificate of judgment if the court is not that in which judgment was given. The garnishee summons must be served personally not less than 14 days before the return day and thereupon binds money owing to the judgment debtor to the extent of the judgment debt and costs on the summons. The garnishee may within 8 days of service pay into Court the amount due to the judgment debtor to the extent of the judgment debt and costs. Upon receipt of notice of payment the judgment creditor may within 7 days give notice of acceptance to the court and the garnishee, and the proceedings will be staged. Late notice of acceptance may render the judgment creditor liable for the garnishee's costs incurred after payment in. Upon production of consent by the judgment debtor the money may be paid out before the return day.

Charging orders: (a) LAND (s. 141; O. 25, r. 7). Application is made on notice setting out the facts to the judge (see interlocutory applications). A charging order may not be made in respect of land held by joint tenants unless judgment in the proceedings has been obtained against them all (*Irani Finance Ltd.* v. *Singh*, [1970] 3 All E.R. 199; *National Westminster Bank* v. *Allen*, [1971] 3 All E. R. 201). An order to discharge a charging order should provide for vacation of registration of the charge. The charge is enforceable as an equitable charge under hand either by sale by the court or by appointment of a receiver. Proceedings must be taken in the Court that made the order (O. 2, r. 2). (b) SECURITIES (O. 25, r. 6A). Application is made on notice setting out the facts to the judge (see interlocutory applications). No proceedings may be taken to enforce the charge for 6 months after the date of the order. Proceedings must be taken in the Court that made the order (O. 2, r. 2A). A fresh action will probably be required.

Appointment of receiver (s. 142; O. 30).—Application is made in notice to the judge (see interlocutory applications). An affidavit in support should be filed. In deciding whether to make the appointment the judge must have regard to the amount owing and the amount likely to be obtained by the receiver and the probable cost of his appointment (r. 11). Where the debt and costs do not exceed £50 the applicant may be directed to be answerable for the receiver in lieu of security (r. 12 (b)).

COSTS IN CASES TRANSFERRED FROM THE HIGH COURT

Costs in transferred actions are governed by ss. 47, 76 and O. 47.

The costs prior to the transfer depend on what is recovered in the action, unless (i) the order of transfer otherwise directs or (ii) unless the County Court judge makes a special order under the provisions of s. 76 (*Hawkins* v. *Miln*, [1921] 3 K.B. 633).

The costs after the transfer are in the discretion of the County Court judge (s. 76). See also O. 47, r. 9.

COSTS IN ORDINARY COUNTY COURT ACTIONS

The regulation of costs is by virtue of s. 102 contained in O. 47, which is here set out in full:—

ORDER 47. COSTS

PART I. GENERAL

1. *Discretion.*—Subject to the provisions of any Act or Rule, the costs of proceedings in a county court shall be in the discretion of the court:

Provided that nothing in this Rule shall deprive an executor, administrator, trustee, or mortgagee who has not unreasonably instituted or carried on or resisted any proceedings, of any right to costs out of a particular estate or fund to which he would be entitled according to the rules acted upon in the Chancery Division of the High Court.

2. *Litigant in person.*—(1) Where in any proceedings any costs of a litigant in person are ordered to be paid by any other party or in any other way, then, subject to the following paragraphs of this Rule, there may be allowed to the litigant in person such costs as would have been allowed if the work and disbursements to which the costs relate had been done or made by a solicitor on his behalf and the provisions of these Rules shall apply with the necessary modifications to the costs of a litigant in person as they apply to solicitors' charges and disbursements.

(2) Nothing in Rule 36 of this Order or Appendix D shall apply where the plaintiff is a litigant in person.

(3) In relation to the costs of a litigant in person, Rule 37(2) of this Order shall have effect—

  (a) where the costs are on scale 1, 2 or 3, as if for the words "may, if the solicitor for the party in whose favour the award was made so desires" there were substituted the words "shall, unless the court otherwise orders", and

  (b) where the costs are on scale 4, as if the words "the solicitor for" were omitted.

(4) Where the costs of a litigant in person are taxed or assessed without taxation—

  (a) he shall not be allowed more than £2 an hour in respect of the time reasonably spent by him on doing any work to which the costs relate if in the opinion of the court he has not suffered any pecuniary loss in doing the work, and

  (b) the amount allowed in respect of any work done by the litigant in person shall not in any case exceed two-thirds of the sum which in the opinion of the court would have been allowed in respect of that work if the litigant had been represented by a solicitor.

(5) Where the costs of a litigant in person are assessed under Appendix E, or where on the taxation of the costs of a litigant in person he is allowed a charge for attending court to conduct his own case, then, notwithstanding anything in Rule 29 of this Order, he shall not be entitled to a witness allowance in addition.

(6) Nothing in this Rule shall apply to a solicitor to whom Rule 26 is applicable.

3. *Taxing Officer.*—The registrar shall be the taxing officer of the court fo which he is registrar.

4. *Enforcement.*—An order for the payment of costs may be enforced in like manner as any other order of a county court for the payment of money.

Part II. As to Scale

5. *Scales of Costs.*—(1) For the regulation of solicitors' charges and disbursements otherwise than under Rule 37 of this Order there shall be a Lower Scale and four Higher Scales, namely Scale 1, Scale 2 Scale 3 and Scale 4.

(2) The Higher Scales, which shall be those set out in Appendix B, shall have effect subject to and in accordance with the Rules of this Order and the directions contained in the Scales.

(3) The Scale of Costs applicable to a sum of money only shall be as follows:—

Sum of Money	Scale applicable
Exceeding £5 and not exceeding £20	Lower Scale
Exceeding £20 and not exceeding £50	Scale 1
Exceeding £50 and not exceeding £200	Scale 2
Exceeding £200 and not exceeding £500	Scale 3
Exceeding £500	Scale 4

(4) Where the sum of money does not exceed £100, no solicitors' charges shall be allowed unless—

(a) a certificate is granted under Rule 13 of this Order;

(b) the sum exceeds £5, in which case there may be allowed—

(i) in respect of the charges of the plaintiff's solicitor, the costs stated on the summons;

(ii) the costs of enforcing any judgment or order;

(iii) such costs as are certified by the court to have been incurred through the unreasonable conduct of the opposite party in relation to the proceedings or the claim therein;

(c) a claim is made in the proceedings for damages for personal injuries exceeding £5.

(5) In addition to the disbursements shown in the Higher Scales the appropriate court fees shall be allowable.

6. *Recovery of money.*—(1) Subject to Rules 7, 8, 9 and 13 of this Order, the Scale of costs in an action for the recovery of a sum of money only shall be determined—

(a) as regards the costs of the plaintiff, by the amount recovered; and

(b) as regards the costs of the defendant, by the amount claimed; and

(c) as regards costs payable to a third party, by the amount claimed against him; and

(d) as regards costs payable by a third party, by the amount recovered against him.

(2) This Rule shall not apply to actions under the equity jurisdiction of the court or to Admiralty actions or actions in which the title to hereditaments comes in question.

7. *Counterclaim.*—(1) Subject to the next succeeding paragraph, Rule 6 of this Order shall apply to a counterclaim as it applies to a claim.

(2) Where in one action a claim for a sum of money only and a counterclaim for a sum of money only are tried—

(a) if the plaintiff is awarded costs on both claim and counterclaim the costs shall be on the Scale applicable to the amount which he recovers on the claim, but if such amount is less than the counterclaim, the costs subsequent to the filing of the counterclaim shall be on the Scale applicable to the amount of the counterclaim; and

(b) if the defendant is awarded costs on both claim and counterclaim, the costs shall be on the Scale applicable to the amount which he recovers on the counterclaim or the amount of the plaintiff's claim, whichever is the larger, but the costs prior to the filing of the counterclaim shall be on the Scale applicable to the amount of the claim:

Provided that the costs of work done solely in connection with the claim shall be on the Scale applicable to the claim and the costs of work done solely in connection with the counterclaim shall be on the Scale applicable to the counterclaim.

8. *Where money paid into court.*—(1) Where money in court is accepted in satisfaction of the cause of action in respect of which it was paid, and another cause of action remains to be tried, then the costs subsequent to the date of the payment into court shall, unless the registrar when taxing or fixing and allowing the costs otherwise directs, be determined by the amount recovered or claimed in respect of the cause of action remaining to be tried.

(2) Where money is paid into court and the plaintiff does not accept it in satisfaction of his claim or of the cause or causes of action in respect of which it was paid, the costs incurred after the date of the payment into court shall be on the scale which would have been applicable if no money had been paid into court, or on such lower scale as the court, or the registrar when taxing or fixing and allowing costs, may determine having regard to any saving of expense effected by reason of the payment into court.

(3) Paragraph (2) of this Rule shall apply where money is paid to the plaintiff in satisfaction or on account of the plaintiff's claim as it applies where money is paid into court.

(4) Nothing in this Rule shall limit the discretion of the judge as to Scale in a case to which Rule 15 of this Order applies.

9. *Action transferred from High Court.*—(1) Where proceedings have been transferred from the High Court to a county court and the amount remaining in dispute at the date on which the registrar receives the documents referred to in Section 77 of the Act is less than the amount originally claimed, the costs incurred after that date shall be taxed on the Scale, and subject to the Rules applicable to the costs of an action commenced in a county court to recover the amount so remaining in dispute.

(2) Nothing in this Rule shall limit the discretion of the judge as to Scale in a case to which Rule 15 of this Order applies.

10, 11.   [*Revoked*].

12.   *Garnishee proceedings.*—Subject to Rules 13 and 36 of this Order, the Scale of Costs in garnishee proceedings shall be determined—

(a) as regards the costs of the judgment creditor, by the amount recovered against the garnishee; and

(b) as regards the costs of the garnishee or the judgment debtor, by the amount claimed by the judgment creditor.

13.   *Difficult questions of law or fact.*—In any proceedings in which the judge certifies that a difficult question of law, or a question of fact of exceptional complexity is involved, he may award costs on such scale as he thinks fit.

14.   *Companies Act.*—The costs of proceedings under the Companies Act, 1948, other than proceedings which are regulated by the Companies (Winding-up) Rules, 1949, shall be on the Scale of costs applicable to similar proceedings in the High Court.

15.   *Other proceedings.*—(1) In any proceedings to which Rules 6, 7, 12, 14 and 36 of this Order do not apply, the judge may award costs on such Scale as he thinks fit.

Provided that, where notice of discontinuance has been given in respect of the proceedings, the registrar shall have power on taxation to determine the scale on which costs shall be taxed under Rule 2 of Order 18.

(2) Where any party desires to make an application to the judge to determine the scale on which costs are to be taxed, Rule 21(4) of this Order shall apply to the application as it applies to an application under paragraph (1), (2) or (3) of the last-mentioned Rule.

16.   *Discretionary increases.* — All charges or disbursements which are

discretionary shall, unless otherwise provided, be allowed at the discretion of the registrar, who, in the exercise of such discretion, shall take into consideration the other charges and disbursements to the solicitor and counsel, if any, in respect of the work to which the fee or allowance applies, the nature and importance of the action or matter, the amount involved, the interest of the parties, the general conduct and costs of the proceedings and all other circumstances.

PART III. ITEMS OF COSTS

17. *Allowance or disallowance of items by judge.*—Where the costs of any action or matter are on one of the Higher Scales, the judge may direct the registrar to allow or disallow on taxation any item in the Scale.

18. *Value added tax.*—In addition to the amount of costs allowed to a party on taxation in respect of the supply of goods or services on which value added tax is chargeable there may be allowed as a disbursement a sum equivalent to value added tax at the appropriate rate on that amount in so far as the tax is not deductible as input tax by that party.

19. *Counsel in interlocutory application.*—Where costs are on one of the Higher Scales, no fee for counsel shall be allowed on taxation in respect of an interlocutory application, unless the judge or registrar certifies that the application is fit for counsel.

20. *Counsel where claim admitted or not disputed.*—Unless the judge otherwise orders, no fee for counsel with brief shall be allowed in an action for the recovery of a sum of money only—(*a*) where the defendant has admitted the whole or part of the claim within the time limited by O. 9, r. 1 (1) or O. 10, r. 1 and the plaintiff recovers judgment for a sum not exceeding the amount admitted; or (*b*) where no defence has been delivered and the defendant does not appear at the hearing or resist the claim.

21. *Certificate for increased charges and fees.*—(1) Where the costs of any proceedings are on Scale 2, 3 or 4, the judge may certify that the proceedings are fit for the employment of more counsel than one.
(2) Where the costs of any proceedings are on one of the Higher Scales and the judge is satisfied from the nature of the case or the conduct of the proceedings that the costs which may be allowed may be inadequate in the circumstances, he may direct that the registrar on taxation shall not be bound by the amounts appearing in the Scale in respect of the items specified in the next succeeding paragraph.
(3) Where a direction has been given under the last preceding paragraph, the registrar may, if he thinks fit, allow on taxation such larger sums as he thinks reasonable in respect of all or any of the following items, namely: items 1, 2, 5, 6, 7, 8, 18, 26, 29 and 30.
(4) An application for a certificate pursuant to the foregoing paragraphs of this Rule may be made at the hearing or on notice which shall be served on the party sought to be made liable within 14 days of the making of the order awarding costs or within 14 days of the receipt of notice of payment into court; or of notice of discontinuance:
Provided that where an application which could have been made at the hearing is subsequently made, the judge may refuse the application on the ground that it ought to have been made at the hearing.
(5) Where the costs of any proceedings are on Scale 3 or 4 and no direction has been given by the judge that this paragraph shall not apply, the registrar may, if satisfied as to the matters mentioned in paragraph (2), exercise the powers conferred on him by paragraph (3) notwithstanding that no direction has been given by the judge under paragraph (2)

22. *Plans in collision actions.*—In an action of whatever nature, arising out of an accident on land due to a collision or apprehended collision, no plan of the place where the accident happened, other than a sketch plan, shall be receivable in evidence unless, at or before the trial, the court authorises the reception thereof or the parties consent.

23. *Where no provision in Scale.*—Where costs are taxed on one of the Higher Scales in a matter for which no provision is made in the Scale, reasonable costs may be allowed on taxation not exceeding those fixed by the Scale for proceedings of a similar nature.

24. *Scale items only allowable.*—Subject to Rules 18 and 23 of this Order no item shall be allowed on taxation between party and party which is not contained in the Scales.

25. *Apportionment of costs.*—Where judgment is given with costs against two or more defendants separately, the registrar may, subject to any direction of the judge, apportion any item of costs between the defendants as he thinks fit.

26. *Solicitor in person.*—Where a practising solicitor who is a party to the proceedings acts in person and is awarded costs, he shall be entitled on taxation to the same costs as if he had employed a solicitor, except in respect of items which the fact of his acting in person renders unnecessary.

27. *Where counsel disallowed.*—Where a party appearing by counsel is awarded costs, but the costs of employing counsel are not allowed, he may be allowed such costs as he might have been allowed if he had appeared by a solicitor and not by counsel.

28. *Sale of real property.*—Where any real property is directed to be sold, the ordinary conveyancing charges shall be allowed.

Part IV

Allowances to Witnesses & Parties

29. *Compensation for loss of time.*—(1) Subject to paragraph (2) where on the hearing of an action or matter a party to the proceeding or any other person attends the court as a witness of fact, or as a witness producing a document, there may be allowed in respect of his attendance such sum as the judge or registrar thinks reasonable, not exceeding the sum prescribed in Column 2 of Appendix C for a person of the class to which he belongs:

Provided that the sum allowed shall not, unless the court otherwise orders, exceed the sum prescribed in Col. 1 of Appendix C where—

(a) a witness or party has lost no wages, earnings, or other income in attending court; or

(b) the period during which the witness has been away from home or in respect of which he

has lost wages, earnings or other income by reason of his attendance does not exceed 4 hours.

(2) Where the costs are on Scale 3 or 4, the registrar on taxing or fixing and allowing the costs may, if satisfied that the sum specified in Appendix C may be inadequate in the circumstances, allow such larger sum as he thinks reasonable, notwithstanding that, in the case of a sum prescribed in column 1, no order has been made under the proviso to paragraph (1).

30. *Expert witnesses.*—(1) Where a person attends the court as an expert witness, or attends as a witness of fact and, being called upon to do so, gives in evidence his opinion as an expert, a fee may be allowed in respect of his attendance and in addition, if the judge or registrar thinks fit, a fee for qualifying to give evidence:

Provided that no fee as an expert witness may be allowed in respect of a person attending the court only to prove the correctness of a plan, drawing, chart, photograph, or model.

(2) Subject to paragraph (5) the fee for qualifying to give evidence shall be such sum as the registrar thinks reasonable, not being more than £10, and the fee for attending the court shall be such sum as the registrar thinks reasonable, not being more than £20 nor less than the sum appearing in Appendix C as compensation for loss of time for a person of the class to which the expert witness belongs.

(3) The judge or registrar may, if he thinks fit, allow the fee for qualifying to give evidence, notwithstanding that the witness does not attend the trial.

(4) Subject to paragraph (5) where a report in writing has been obtained from an expert witness who is not entitled to a qualifying fee the registrar may if he thinks such a report was reasonably necessary allow a fee of not exceeding £10 therefor.

(5) If in any particular case—

(a) the judge certifies that the fee for qualifying to give evidence or for a report in writing or for attending court ought not to be limited as aforesaid, or

(b) the costs of the proceedings are on Scale 3 or 4 and the registrar considers that any of the fees mentioned in sub-paragraph (a) ought not to be limited as aforesaid but no certificate

has been given under sub-paragraph (a) and no direction has been
given by the judge that this sub-
paragraph shall not apply.

The fee to be allowed on taxation
shall be such larger sum as the registrar thinks fit.

(6) Rule 21(4) of this Order shall apply
to an application for a certificate under
paragraph (5) of this Rule as it applies
to an application for a certificate under
that Rule.

31. *Travelling and hotel expenses.*—
There may be allowed in respect of a
witness or party who has attended the
hearing, in addition to any sum allowed
under Rule 29 or Rule 30 of this Order,
any expenses which the witness or
party has actually and reasonably incurred in travelling to and from the
court or in staying in an hotel.

32. *Attendance in more than one
action.*—Where a witness or party
attends the court in respect of two or
more actions or matters, the sum which
might be allowed to him under Rule
29 or Rule 31 of this Order in respect of
one action or matter may be apportioned between the several actions or
matters.

33. *Witness not called.*—Allowances
may be made to a witness whether he
was called or not, if his attendance was
necessary.

34. *Seaman detained.*—A seaman
necessarily detained on shore for the
purpose of an action or matter may be
allowed such sum as the registrar thinks
reasonable in respect of such detention.

34A. *Interpreters.*—Where on the
hearing of an action or matter a person
attends the court for the purpose of
interpreting evidence, there may be
allowed in respect of his attendance
such sum as might be allowed if he had
attended the court as a witness of fact
or, if the judge or registrar thinks fit,
such sum as might be allowed if he had
attended the court as an expert witness.

PART V. TAXATION AND REVIEW

35. *When taxation required.*—In
every action or matter in which one
party is liable to pay any costs incurred
by any other party, then except as
provided in the next two succeeding
Rules of this Order, the costs shall be
taxed.

36. *Fixed costs.*—(1) Appendix D to
these Rules shall have effect for the
purpose of showing the total amount
which, in the several cases to which
Appendix D applies, shall be allowed to
the solicitor for the plaintiff without
taxation, unless the judge or registrar
otherwise directs.

(2) In a case to which Appendix D
does not apply no amount shall be
entered on the summons for the charges
of the solicitor for the plaintiff, but
the words "to be taxed" shall be
inserted.

37. *Allowance without taxation.*—
(1) Where costs are on the Lower
Scale, they shall be fixed and allowed
without taxation and any reference in
these Rules to taxation shall, in relation to such costs, be treated as a
reference to fixing and allowing them
under this paragraph.

(2) Where in a case to which Appendix D does not apply, costs are awarded
on one of the Higher Scales, the costs
may, if the solicitor for the party in
whose favour the award has been made
so desires, be assessed without taxation.

(3) Where costs are assessed without
taxation pursuant to paragraph (1) or
(2) the court may allow such sum as
it thinks reasonable, within the limits
of the sums appearing in Appendix E
opposite the Scale applicable to the
proceedings, with such additions, if
any, as may be authorised by the said
Appendix or paragraph (6) of this Rule.

(4) Costs awarded in respect of an
application and not included in the
general costs of the action may be fixed
and allowed without taxation, unless
the court otherwise orders.

(5) Where the sum to be paid by one
party to another party in respect of the
costs of an action or matter has been
agreed between them, the court may
direct payment of that sum in lieu of
taxed costs.

(6) Where costs assessed or fixed and
allowed without taxation under paragraph (1), (2) or (4) of this Rule or
paragraph (4) (b) of the next following
Rule, Rule 18 of this Order shall apply
as it applies on taxation.

38. *Taxation between party and
party.*—(1) Where a party desires his
costs to be taxed, he shall within 14
days of the making of the order for
costs lodge a bill of costs in the court

office with all necessary vouchers and papers, and obtain an appointment for taxation and serve on the other party a copy of the bill of costs, and give him not less than 3 clear days' notice of the appointment.

(2) In a bill of costs the solicitor's charges shall be entered in a separate column from the disbursements.

(3) Where a party to an action or matter entitled to costs lodges a bill and obtains an appointment for taxation in a case where the costs might under these Rules be fixed and allowed without taxation, the registrar may disallow the costs of and incident to the preparation of the bill and the taxation of the costs.

(4) Where a party to an action or matter entitled to costs fails to comply with the requirements of paragraph (1) of this Rule within the time limited thereby or in any way delays or impedes the taxation, the registrar may—

    (a) disallow the costs of and incident to the preparation of the bill and the taxation of the costs; and

    (b) fix and allow such sum as he thinks reasonable for that party's costs of the action or matter, and tax and allow the costs of the other party (if any).

39. *Set-off costs.*—In any case in which a party entitled to receive costs is also liable to pay costs, the registrar may—

    (a) tax the costs which that party is liable to pay, and adjust them by way of deduction or set-off and direct payment of any balance; or

    (b) delay the allowance of the costs which he is entitled to receive, until he has paid the costs which he is liable to pay.

40. *Taxation between solicitor and client.*—(1) In this Rule references to a taxation of costs as between solicitor and client include references to—

    (a) taxation of a solicitor's bill to his own client, and

    (b) taxation on the common fund basis, that is to say, taxation as between solicitor and client where the costs are to be paid out of a common fund in which the client and others are interested.

(2) Where an order has been made for the taxation of costs as between solicitor and client, the solicitor shall lodge his bill within 14 days of the making of the order and Rule 38(4) of this Order (except paragraph (b)) shall apply as if for the reference therein to paragraph (1) of that Rule there were substituted a reference to this paragraph.

(3) On receipt of the bill the registrar shall fix a time and place for proceeding with the taxation and shall give to the applicant and any other party entitled to be heard on the taxation not less than 3 clear days' notice of the time and place so fixed.

(4) Subject to paragraphs (5) and (6) of this Rule, the costs as between solicitor and client in an action for the recovery of a sum of money only may be taxed on the scale applicable to the amount claimed.

(5) Rules 8 and 9 of this Order shall apply with the necessary modifications to the determination of the costs as they apply to the determination of costs as between party and party.

(6) Where there is a claim for a sum of money only and a counterclaim for a sum of money only, the costs of and subsequent to the filing of the counterclaim may be taxed on the scale applicable to the claim or that applicable to the counterclaim, whichever is the higher:

Provided that the costs of work done solely in connection with the claim shall not be on a scale higher than that applicable to the claim and the costs of work done solely in connection with the counterclaim shall not be on a scale higher than that applicable to the counterclaim.

(7) In garnishee proceedings the costs as between solicitor and client may be taxed on the scale applicable to the amount claimed by the judgment creditor.

(8) The judge by whom any order is made for the taxation of costs as between solicitor and client may, after affording to the solicitor an opportunity of making any representations that he desires to make—

    (a) determine the scale on which the costs are to be taxed under the preceding paragraphs of this Rule, and

    (b) exercise any discretion, whether as to scale or any other matter, give any direction and grant any certificate that the judge could have exercised, given or granted in relation to costs as between party and party.

(9) On a taxation of costs as between solicitor and client the registrar shall not be bound to follow any determination of the judge or registrar in relation to the costs as between party and party and accordingly, subject to any determination made under paragraph (8), the registrar may—

(a) exercise any of the powers conferred on the judge by that paragraph;

(b) allow items disallowed as between party and party, and

(c) allow a higher sum in respect of any item than the sum allowed as between party and party, not exceeding the maximum sum prescribed for that item in the scale on which the costs are being taxed.

(10) The costs of a taxation under the Solicitors Act 1974 shall be dealt with by the registrar in accordance with the provisions of that Act and shall be added to or deducted from the amount certified to be due.

41. *Taxation of costs awarded by tribunal.*—(1) An application for the taxation of any costs, fees or expenses which by or under any Act or statutory instrument other than the County Court Rules fall to be taxed by a county court shall be made by originating application.

(2) The applicant shall lodge with his originating application a bill of the costs, fees or expenses to be taxed and annex a copy of the bill to every copy of the originating application for service.

(3) The application may be made to the registrar and the Rules relating to originating applications shall apply as if the taxation were the hearing of the application.

(4) On the completion of the taxation or, in the case of a review by the judge, after the review the registrar shall send to every party a certificate of the result of the taxation.

(5) Nothing in this Rule shall apply to an application for the taxation of a returning officer's charges under section 20 of the Representation of the People Act, 1949.

42. *Review of taxation.*—(1) Any party dissatisfied with the taxation of any costs by the registrar may apply to the registrar to reconsider the taxation.

(2) The application may be made on the day of taxation and if not so made

(a) the application shall be made on notice; and

(b) the notice shall be filed in the court office within two days of the taxation and unless otherwise ordered by the court shall operate as a stay of execution in respect of the costs until the application has been heard; and

(c) the notice shall specify the items in respect of which the application is made and the grounds for the objections.

(3) On the hearing of the application the registrar shall reconsider his taxation on the objections and shall if requested by either party state in writing the reasons for his decision thereon.

(4) Any party who is dissatisfied with the registrar's decision to allow or disallow any item in whole or in part, or with the amount allowed by the registrar on his reconsideration of a taxation may apply for a review of the taxation by the judge.

(5) The application may be made on the day on which the registrar has reconsidered the taxation and if not so made sub-paragraphs (a) (b) and (c) of paragraph (2) of this Rule shall apply with the necessary modifications.

(6) If the judge sees fit to exercise in relation to the application his power to appoint assessors under section 91 of the Act without any application being made by any party to the proceedings, he shall appoint not less than two assessors, of whom one shall be a registrar, and Order 31, Rules 7 and 9, shall apply as if the assessors had been summoned on the application of a party.

(7) On the hearing of the application the judge may make such order as may be just.

PART VI. MISCELLANEOUS

43. *Costs out of fund.*—The judge may order any costs properly incurred by any party suing or sued in a fiduciary or representative character to be paid out of any fund in court available for the purpose.

44. *Costs not payable out of estate.*— The costs occasioned by any unsuccessful claim or unsuccessful resistance to any claim to any property shall not be paid out of the estate unless the judge otherwise directs.

45. *Costs of inquiries.*—The costs of inquiries to ascertain the persons entitled to any legacy, money, or share, or otherwise incurred in relation thereto, shall be paid out of such legacy, money, or share, unless the judge otherwise directs.

46. *Distribution not to be delayed.*— Where some of the persons entitled to a distributive share of a fund are ascertained, and difficulty or delay has occurred or is likely to occur in ascertaining the persons entitled to the other shares, the judge may order or allow immediate payment of their shares to the persons ascertained without reserving any part of those shares to answer the subsequent costs of ascertaining the persons entitled to the other shares; and in all such cases such order may be made for ascertaining and payment of the costs incurred down to and including such payment as the judge thinks reasonable.

47. *Taxation of costs payable out of estate.*—If on the taxation of a bill of costs payable out of a fund or estate (real or personal) the amount of the solicitor's charges and disbursements contained in the bill is reduced by a sixth part, no costs of and incident to the preparation of the bill and the taxation of the costs shall be allowed to the solicitor lodging the bill for taxation.

48. *Notice of taxation of costs payable out of fund.*—Where costs are directed to be taxed and paid out of any fund or property, the registrar may require the solicitor to deliver free of charge to any person for whom he has acted in the proceedings, a copy of the bill accompanied by any statement which the registrar may direct and notice of the day and hour appointed for the taxation of the bill.

49. *Bases of taxation.*—Subject to the provisions of this Order and to section 74 (3) of the Solicitors Act 1974, Order 62, Rules 28, 29 and 31, of the Rules of the Supreme Court shall apply, with the necessary modifications, to the taxation of costs in the county court as they apply to the taxation of costs in the High Court.

50. *Personal liability of solicitor for costs.*—(1) Subject to the following provisions of this Rule, where in any proceedings costs are incurred improperly or without reasonable cause or are wasted by undue delay or by any other misconduct or default, the judge may make against any solicitor whom he considers to be responsible (whether personally or through a servant or agent) and order—

(a) disallowing the costs as between the solicitor and his client, and

(b) directing the solicitor to repay to his client costs which the client has been ordered to pay to other parties to the proceedings; or

(c) directing the solicitor personally to indemnify such other parties against costs payable by them.

(2) No order under this Rule shall be made against a solicitor unless he has been given a reasonable opportunity to appear before the judge and show cause why the order should not be made, except where any proceeding in court or in chambers cannot conveniently proceed, and fails or is adjourned without useful progress being made—

(a) because of the failure of the solicitor to attend in person or by a proper representative; or

(b) because of the failure of the solicitor to deliver any document for the use of the court which ought to have been delivered or to be prepared with any proper evidence or account or otherwise to proceed.

(3) Before making an order under this Rule the judge may, if he thinks fit, refer the matter (save in the cases excepted from paragraph (2)) to the registrar for inquiry and report and direct the solicitor in the first place to show cause before the registrar.

(4) The judge may direct that notice of any proceedings or order against a solicitor under this Rule shall be given to his client in such manner as may be specified in the direction.

SCALES OF COUNTY COURT COSTS
APPENDIX B
HIGHER SCALES OF COSTS
Solicitors' Charges

Item No.		Scale 1 £	Scale 2 £	Scale 3 £	Scale 4 £
	Particulars of claim, &c.				
1*	Preparing particulars of claim or originating application, petition, or request for entry of appeal to a county court, or particulars of counterclaim, or third-party notice; preparing defence (to claim or counter-claim), answer, or reply if ordered; preparing preliminary act or pleading in admiralty action..	0.50 to 2.00	0.50 to 3.00	1.00 to 6.00	2.00 to 8.00

Note 1.—This item includes copies and is only to be allowed where the document is signed by the solicitor or his clerk duly authorised in that behalf.

Note 2.—Where the document is settled by counsel, items 2 (*a*) and 3 are allowable and not this item.

	Preparation of documents				
2*	(*a*) Preparing instructions to counsel to settle any pleading or other document or to advise on evidence or to advise on merits where counsel's fee is allowed under item 30	0.50 to 1.00	0.50 to 2.00	1.50 to 3.00	1.50 to 6.00
	(*b*) Preparing any necessary document not otherwise provided for and all necessary copies thereof ..				
	per brief or A3 ISO page ..	0.80	0.80	0.80	0.80
	per foolscap or A4 ISO page ..	0.50	0.50	0.50	0.50
	(in each case proportionately for less)				

Note.—Item 2 (*b*) is not be allowed for preparing a praecipe or a notice of acceptance or non-acceptance of an admission and proposal as to time of payment.

Copies

3 For copies of documents (including brief) not otherwise provided for, which the registrar considers necessary—

Item No.		Scale 1 £	Scale 2 £	Scale 3 £	Scale 4 £
(a) Typed per copy—					
per quarto or A5 ISO page	..	0.15	0.15	0.15	0.15
per foolscap or A4 ISO page	..	0.25	0.25	0.25	0.25
per draft page	.. ..	0.30	0.30	0.30	0.30
per brief or A3 ISO page	..	0.40	0.40	0.40	0.40
(in each case proportionately for less)					
(b) Photographic, printed or carbon copies—					
per quarto or A5 ISO page	..	0.07	0.07	0.07	0.07
per foolscap or A4 ISO page	..	0.10	0.10	0.10	0.10
per draft page	.. ..	0.15	0.15	0.15	0.15
per brief or A3 ISO page	..	0.20	0.20	0.20	0.20
(for printed or carbon copies only, in each case proportionately for less)					

Perusing

		Scale 1 £	Scale 2 £	Scale 3 £	Scale 4 £
4 Any document not otherwise provided for, which the registrar is satisfied justifies a charge for perusal	.. ..	0.25	0.25	0.25	0.25
And per folio beyond 5..	..	0.05	0.05	0.05	0.05

Preparing for trial

		Scale 1 £	Scale 2 £	Scale 3 £	Scale 4 £
5* Preparing for trial or hearing of action or matter..	.. ..	3.00 to 16.00	5.00 to 45.00	Such sum as is fair and reasonable in all the circumstances *not exceeding* £80.00	Such sum as is fair and reasonable in all the circumstances *not exceeding* £165.00

Note.—This item is intended to cover any work, not otherwise provided for, done in preparing for a trial or hearing, including—

(a) taking instructions to sue, defend, counterclaim or appeal, or for preliminary act, pleading or bail in admiralty action:

(b) taking instructions for preparing any document to which item 2(b) applies;

(c) considering the facts, evidence and law;

(d) preparing notes of facts or argument;

(e) attending on and corresponding with client;

(f) interviewing and corresponding with witnesses and potential witnesses and taking proofs of their evidence;

(g) preparing and serving notices to produce and admit documents and to admit facts;

(h) perusing pleadings, affidavits and other relevant documents;

(i) making necessary searches;

	Scale 1 £	Scale 2 £	Scale 3 £	Scale 4 £
Item No.				

(j) inspecting any property or place material to the proceedings;

(k) where counsel is instructed, instructions for and drawing brief;

(l) where the action or matter does not proceed to trial or hearing, work done in connection with the negotiation of a settlement;

(m) the general care and conduct of the proceedings; and

(n) the exceptional cost, if any, of conducting county court business in the area in which the solicitor practises, due to the small volume of such business in that area.

Attendances

6* At court on trial of action or matter for each day or part of a day—

	Scale 1 £	Scale 2 £	Scale 3 £	Scale 4 £
(a) without counsel	2.00 to 10.00	3.00 to 20.00	5.00 to 35.00	5.00 to 45.00
(b) with counsel	1.00 to 4.00	2.00 to 6.00	3.00 to 8.00	3.00 to 12.00

Note.—An attendance on the examination of a witness under Order 20, Rule 18 (1), is to be treated as an attendance to which this item relates.

7* At court where trial is adjourned for want of time or upon payment of the costs of the day—

	Scale 1 £	Scale 2 £	Scale 3 £	Scale 4 £
(a) without counsel	2.00 to 4.00	2.00 to 6.00	3.00 to 10.00	5.00 to 20.00
(b) with counsel	1.00 to 2.00	1.50 to 4.00	1.50 to 6.00	1.50 to 8.00

8* At court or in chambers on any application to judge or registrar in the course of or relating to the proceedings, including instructions, notice and service, and brief where counsel is instructed—

	Scale 1 £	Scale 2 £	Scale 3 £	Scale 4 £
(a) without counsel	1.00 to 3.00	1.00 to 8.00	1.50 to 12.00	3.00 to 18.00
(b) with counsel	1.00 to 2.00	1.00 to 3.00	2.00 to 6.00	3.00 to 7.00

Note.—Interpleader and garnishee proceedings are to be treated as an application to which this item refers.

Item No.		Scale 1 £	Scale 2 £	Scale 3 £	Scale 4 £
	Note to items 5, 6, 7 *and* 8.—These items apply to an arbitration, inquiry or reference, but item 5 may only be allowed once in the same proceedings. If the reference or inquiry was directed at the trial and the reference or inquiry began on the same day, item 6 may only be allowed once in respect of that day.				
9	To lodge papers when proceedings transferred to county court, including preparation of all necessary documents	2.00	2.00	2.00	2.50
10	On examination of witness under Order 14, Rule 1(10), or Order 25, Rule 2, for each hour or part thereof—				
	(a) without counsel	1.50	2.00	3.00	3.00 to 5.00
	(b) with counsel..	1.00	1.50	2.00	3.00
11	Where in consequence of anything done by the opposite party during the proceedings, attendance on the client is necessary to advise or receive instructions, for each attendance not otherwise provided for	1.00	1.00	1.00 to 2.00	2.00 to 4.00
12	(a) To obtain or give any necessary and proper consent or admission	1.00	1.00	1.00	1.50
	(b) Upon the opposite party, for each attendance not otherwise provided for	1.00	1.00	1.00	1.50
	(c) To arrange for attendance of a witness without subpœna	0.50	0.50	0.50	1.00
	(d) On counsel in conference where counsel's fee allowed under item 28 (to include appointing conference), for each half hour or part thereof	1.00	1.50	1.50	2.00
	Note to items 11 *and* 12 (a) *and* (b).—If the attendance is by telephone half of the charge is to be allowed.				
	Note to item 12 (c).—Only one charge is to be allowed where only one attendance is necessary to arrange for more than one witness.				

Item No.		Scale 1 £	Scale 2 £	Scale 3 £	Scale 4 £
13	At court to hear a deferred judgment or on further consideration pursuant to Order 29, Rules 18 and 19, or on entry of judgment on an award or report—				
	(a) without counsel	1.00 to 3.00	1.00 to 6.00	2.00 to 8.00	3.00 to 10.00
	(b) with counsel..	1.00 to 2.00	1.00 to 3.00	2.00 to 4.00	2.00 to 7.00
14	At court, on hearing of judgment summons if costs allowed under Order 25, Rule 66 (1), and for each attendance where the hearing is not concluded on the day on which it is commenced—				
	(a) without counsel	2.00	2.00	2.00	3.00
	(b) with counsel..	1.00	1.00	1.00	2.00
	Note.—This item includes attending to enter and service (unless allowed under Order 25, Rule 66 (2)).				
15	On deponent being sworn to an affidavit	0.50	0.50	0.50	0.75
	Note 1.—This charge may be allowed where the solicitor or his clerk is the deponent.				
	Note 2.—This charge is not to be allowed in respect of an affidavit of service or an affidavit under Order 20, Rule 5 (2).				
16	To delivery any document pursuant to any County Court Rule	0.50	0.50	0.50	0.75
17	Any attendance at the court office not otherwise provided for, which the registrar is satisfied justifies a charge	0.50	0.50	0.50	0.75
	Service				
18*	Of any document required to be served personally, other than a judgment summons unless allowed under Order 25, Rule 66 (2), including copy	0.50 to 1.00	0.50 to 1.00	1.00 to 2.00	1.00 to 4.00
19	(a) Of any document authorised to be served by post, including copy .. (b) For preparing a certificate resulting in postal service of an ordinary or default summons	0.25	0.25	0.25	0.25
	Notes to items 18 and 19 *Note 1.*—Where any two or more documents to be served on the				

Item No.		Scale 1 £	Scale 2 £	Scale 3 £	Scale 4 £
	same party have been or could have been served together, one charge only for service is to be allowed.				
	Note 2.—Where two or more parties have been or could have beenserve d together, one charge only for service is to be allowed.				
	Note 3.—Where two or more defendants were served at the same address, only one charge is to be allowed under item 19 (*b*).				
	Note 4.—These items are not to be allowed where item 20 (*a*) is applicable.				
20	Substituted service—				
	(*a*) if service by solicitor, to include attendances, making appointments to serve summons, preparing and attending to swear and file affidavits and to obtain order, and the fees paid for oaths ..	2.00	2.00 to 3.00	2.00 to 5.00	3.50 to 5.00
	(*b*) if service by bailiff, for attendances to request steps to be taken and to obtain order	1.00	1.00	1.00	1.50
21	Of process out of England and Wales, to include drawing, copying, attending to swear and file all affidavits and to obtain order, and the fees paid for oaths, such sum as the registrar thinks reasonable	—	—	—	—
	Letters, &c.				
22	Letter before action	0.50	0.50	0.50	0.50
23	Letters in lieu of attendances which could properly be allowed under items 11, 12, 16 and 17..	0.50	0.50	0.50	0.75
24	Circular letters	0.25	0.25	0.25	0.25
	Taxation of costs				
25	(*a*) For taxation of the costs of the action or matter, to include preparing bill, all necessary copies and notice, service, obtaining appointment to tax and attending taxation	2.00	3.00 to 6.00	3.00 to 10.00	3.00 to 14.00

Item No.	Scale 1 £	Scale 2 £	Scale 3 £	Scale 4 £
(b) For any other taxation, to include preparing bill, all necessary copies and notice, service, obtaining appointment to tax and attending taxation	1.00	1.00 to 2.00	2.00 to 3.00	2.00 to 5.00

Fees to Counsel

	Scale 1 £	Scale 2 £	Scale 3 £	Scale 4 £
26* With brief on trial or hearing ..	3.00 to 10.00	4.00 to 25.00	9.00 to 35.00	9.00 to 60.00
27 Where there is no local bar in the court town or within 25 miles thereof, if in the opinion of the registrar the maximum fee allowable with the brief is insufficient, a further fee may be allowed, not exceeding for each day on which the trial or hearing takes place..	3.00	3.00	4.00	4.00

Note 1.—For the purpose of this item there shall be deemed to be a local bar only in such places as may from time to time be specified in a certificate of the General Council of the Bar given to the Lord Chancellor.

Note 2.—This item is not to be allowed in any court within 25 miles of Charing Cross.

	Scale 1 £	Scale 2 £	Scale 3 £	Scale 4 £
28 On conference in chambers or elsewhere, if the fee was marked on the brief when delivered, or in the opinion of the registrar the conference was necessary, for each half hour or part thereof	2.50	2.50	2.50	3.50
and for leading counsel if case certified for more counsel than one	—	3.50	3.50	5.00
29* (a) Where trial or hearing of action is not concluded on day which it is commenced or is adjourned for want of time or on payment of the costs of the day, for each day or part of day on which it is continued .. .. (b) With brief on examination of witness under Order 20, Rule 18 (1), for each day or part of day .. .. (c) With brief on further consideration pursuant to Order 29, Rules 18 and 19, or to hear a deferred judgment; with brief on application in the	3.00 to 5.00	3.00 to 13.00	3.00 to 18.00	3.00 to 35.00

Item No.		Scale 1 £	Scale 2 £	Scale 3 £	Scale 4 £
	course of or relating to proceedings; with brief on examination of witness under Order 14, Rule 1 (10), or Order 25, Rule 2; with brief on hearing of judgment summons	3.00 to 5.00	3.00 to 10.00	3.00 to 14.00	3.00 to 17.00
30* (a)	For settling any document which in the opinion of the registrar is proper to be settled by counsel	3.00	3.00 to 5.00	3.00 to 6.00	4.00 to 8.00
(b)	For advising in writing on any question in the proceedings on which in the opinion of the registrar it was proper to obtain counsel's advice, including advising on evidence, advising on merits before action brought or defence filed and advising on quantum or on proposal and terms of settlement.. ..	3.00	3.00 to 5.00	3.00 to 6.00	4.00 to 8.00

Notes to items 26, 27, 28, 29 and 30.

Note 1.—The note to items 5, 6, 7 and 8 applies to fees to counsel as it applies to preparing trial, attending court or attending in chambers.

Note 2.—Fees to counsel are not to be allowed unless the payment of them is vouched by the signature of counsel.

Plans, Photographs, &c.

| 31 | For plans, drawings, charts, photographs or models for use at the trial, which in the opinion of the registrar it was reasonable to obtain, the sum actually and reasonably paid .. .. .. | — | — | — | — |

Miscellaneous

32 (a) For obtaining any documentary evidence or police reports or statements from the police which in the opinion of the registrar it was reasonably necessary to obtain for the purpose of the action or matter,

(b) for an advertisement in pursuance of an order for substituted service by advertisement, and

Item No.		Scale 1 £	Scale 2 £	Scale 3 £	Scale 4 £
	(c) for making any search in the companies register, the business names register or any public register which in the opinion of the registrar it was reasonably necessary to make for the purpose of the action or matter, the sum actually and reasonably paid	—	—	—	—
33	For oaths, sum paid, unless included in another item	—	—	—	—
34	(a) For postages, carriage and transmission of documents a sum *not exceeding*	2.00	3.00	4.00	5.00
	(b) For telegrams and telephone calls, the sum actually and reasonably paid	—	—	—	—
35	Where the solicitor does not carry on business within two miles of the place of trial of an action or matter, the place of hearing of an application to which item 8 relates, the place of inspection of documents or the place where a taxation is carried out—				
	(a) the travelling and out of pocket expenses reasonably incurred by him in attending that place; or	—	—	—	—
	(b) if an agent is employed, for correspondence with the agent	1.00	2.00	3.00	4.00

Note.—Where in the opinion of the registrar, it would have been reasonable to employ a solicitor carrying on business nearer to the relevant place, he shall not allow under paragraph (a) more than he would have allowed to such a solicitor.

* These items are subject to increase under Order 47, Rule 21 (3).

APPENDIX C

COMPENSATION FOR LOSS OF TIME

Class of Person	Column 1 Sum to be paid or tendered at time of service of witness summons	Column 2 Maximum sum per day allowable on taxation (including any sum paid under Column 1)
		£
(a) Police officers	4.00	7.00
(b) All other persons	4.00	10.00

APPENDIX D

FIXED COSTS

PART I

ORDINARY, DEFAULT AND GARNISHEE SUMMONSES

Directions

1. The Tables in this Part of this Appendix show the amount to be entered on the summons in respect of solicitor's charges—
   (a) in an action for the recovery of a sum of money (other than a rent action), for the purpose only of Order 11, Rule 7, Order 47, Rule 5 (4), and Part II of this Appendix; or
   (b) in garnishee proceedings, for the purpose only of Order 27, Rule 7; or
   (c) in an action for the recovery of property, including land, with or without a claim for a sum of money, for the purpose of Part II of this Appendix or of fixing the amount which the plaintiff may receive in respect of solicitor's charges without taxation in the event of the defendant giving up possession and paying the amount claimed, if any, and costs; or
   (d) in a rent action, for for the purpose of Part II of this Appendix and of fixing the amount which the plaintiff may receive in respect of solicitors' charges without taxation in the event of the defendant paying the amount claimed in sufficient time to prevent the plaintiff's attendance at the hearing.

2. In addition to the amount entered in accordance with the relevant Table the appropriate court fees shall be entered on the summons.

3. In the Tables the expression "claim" means—
   (a) the sum of money claimed, or
   (b) in relation to an action for the recovery of land (with or without a claim for a sum of money), a sum exceeding £100, or
   (c) in relation to an action for the recovery of property other than money or land, the value of the property claimed or, in the case of goods supplied under a hire-purchase agreement, the unpaid balance of the hire-purchase price, or
   (d) in a rent action, for the purpose of Part II of this Appendix and of fixing the amount which the plaintiff may receive in respect of solicitors' charges without taxation in the event of the defendant paying the amount claimed in sufficient time to prevent the plaintiff's attendance at the hearing.

4. Where the solicitor has prepared a certificate for postal service of an ordinary summons, the amount of charges specified in paragraph (a) of the relevant Table shall be increased by 25p.

5. The Tables do not apply where the summons is to be served out of England and Wales or where substituted service is ordered.

TABLES OF FIXED COSTS

TABLE I

Where claim exceeds £5 but does not exceed £20

		Amount of Charges £
(a) Where service is not by solicitor	.. .. ..	1.50
(b) Where service is by solicitor	.. .. ..	2.00

TABLE II

Where claim exceeds £20 but does not exceed £100

		Amount of Charges £
(a) Where service is not by solicitor	.. .. ..	3.00
(b) Where service is by solicitor	.. .. ..	4.00

TABLE III

Where claim exceeds £100

		Amount of Charges £
(a) Where service is not by solicitor	.. .. ..	8.00
(b) Where service is by solicitor	.. .. ..	9.00

PART II

JUDGMENTS

Directions

Where an amount in respect of solicitor's charges has been entered on the summons under Part I of this Appendix and judgment is entered or given in the circumstances mentioned in one of the paragraphs in Column 1 of the following Table, the amount to be included in the judgment in respect of the plaintiff's solicitor's charges shall be the amount entered on the summons together with the amount shown in Column 2 of the Table under the sum of money by reference to which the amount entered on the summons was fixed.

Where judgment is entered or given for a sum less than the amount claimed or for the delivery of goods of which the value or the balance of the hire purchase price is a sum less than the amount claimed, the foregoing paragraph shall, unless the court otherwise directs, have effect as if the amount entered on the summons had been fixed by reference to that sum.

TABLE

Fixed Costs on Judgments

Column 1	Column 2 Sum of Money		
	A Exceeding £5 but not exceeding £20	B Exceeding £20 but not exceeding £100	C Exceeding £100
	£	£	£
(a) Where judgment is entered in a default action in default of defence ..	0.50	1.00	2.00
(b) Where judgment is entered on the defendant's admission and the plaintiff's acceptance of his proposal as to mode of payment			
(c) Where judgment is entered on an admission delivered by the defendant and the court's decision is given as to the date of payment or instalments by which payment is to be made ..			
(d) Where judgment is given in an ordinary action for— (i) recovery of a liquidated sum of money; or (ii) delivery of goods; or (iii) possession of land suspended on payment of arrears of rent, whether claimed or not, in addition to current rent, and the defendant has neither delivered a defence, admission or counterclaim, nor otherwise denied liability	1.00	2.00	5.00

PART III

JUDGMENT SUMMONSES AND APPLICATIONS ON LOWER SCALE

The following Table shows the amount to be allowed where costs awarded on the Lower Scale fall to be fixed and allowed without taxation under Order 25, Rule 66 (2) (b), or Order 47, Rule 37 (4).

Amount to be allowed

1. For each attendance on the hearing of a judgment summons   £1.00

2. For making or opposing an application in the course of or relating to the proceedings £1.00

3. For making or opposing an application for a new trial or to set aside a judgment £1.50

APPENDIX E

ASSESSMENT OF COSTS

Directions

1. This Table shows the amount which, pursuant to Order 47, Rule 37 (3), may be allowed where costs are to be assessed without taxation. The amount includes the fee for counsel where applicable.

2. In addition to the amount shown in the Table there may be allowed, where appropriate—

(i) court fees,
(ii) allowances to witnesses,
(iii) in a case on one of the Higher Scales, a charge on that scale in respect of service of process by the solicitor or substituted service or the preparation of a certificate resulting in postal service, and
(iv) in a case on the Lower Scale, a charge of 50p in respect of service of process by the solicitor.

	Column 1 Scale						*Column 2* Amount of Charges
Lower Scale ..	..	..	..	..	..	..	£3 to £8
Scale 1	..	..	..	..	..	..	£5 to £10
Scale 2	..	..	..	..	..	..	£10 to £15
Scale 3	..	..	..	..	..	..	£15 to £25
Scale 4	..	..	..	..	..	..	£15 to £55

COSTS IN MATRIMONIAL CAUSES

Costs in matrimonial causes proceeding in the County Court are regulated by the Matrimonial Causes (Costs) Rules 1971, as amended, as to which see p. 268, *post*.

SUMMARY OF COUNTY COURT FEES

See County Court Fees Order 1975 for further details

No. of Fee	Description of Proceeding	Amount of Fee
1	On entering a plaint—	
	(i) for the recovery of a sum of money—	
	not exceeding £10	£1
	exceeding £10 but not exceeding £15	£2.50
	,, £15 ,, ,, ,, £20	£3
	,, £20 ,, ,, ,, £30	£4
	,, £30 ,, ,, ,, £50	£5
	,, £50 ,, ,, ,, £80	£6
	,, £80 ,, ,, ,, £100	£7
	,, £100 ,, ,, ,, £200	£8
	,, £200 ,, ,, ,, £500	£10
	,, £500	£12
	(ii) for the approval of a settlement under O. 5, r. 19 (1)	£5
	(iii) for the recovery of land with or without a money claim	£5
	(iv) for the delivery of goods—	
	(a) under a hire-purchase agreement and/or against a guarantor	Fee No. 1 (i) on unpaid balance.
	(b) in any other case	Fee No. 1 (i) on value of goods.
	(v) for any other remedy or relief—	
	(a) under the Rent Acts	See Rent Rules.
	(b) in any other case	£5
2	On entering an originating application or petition—	
	(i) for an order under the Guardianship of Minors Act 1971 and 1973 or the Marriage Act 1949, or for an adoption order ..	£5
	(ii) for an order for the recovery of a sum of money awarded by a tribunal under O. 25, r. 7A	10p for every £2 or part thereof. Min. £1. Max. £5.
	(iii) for the taxation of costs awarded by a tribunal under O. 47, r. 41	For every £1 or part thereof allowed, 5p.
	(iv) for any other remedy or relief	£5
3	On entering an appeal to a county court.. ..	£5
4	On a request for service by bailiff—	
	(i) of an ordinary or default summons—	
	(a) where the amount claimed does not exceed £30	£1
	(b) where the amount exceeds £30 but does not exceed £100.. ..	£1.50
	(c) where the amount claimed exceeds £100 or any other relief is claimed ..	£2
	(ii) of any other document except an order in Form 179, an interpleader summons under an execution and an originating application for an adoption order	£1

No. of Fee	Description of Proceeding	Amount of Fee
5	On the delivery of a counterclaim	The amount (if any) whereby the fee payable on entering proceedings for the sum of money or other remedy or relief counter-claimed exceeds the fee paid by the plaintiff or applicant.
9	On the taxation of costs or expenses	For every £1 or part thereof allowed, 5p.
10	On an application to the judge to review a taxation	£2
12	(i) On an application for an attachment of earnings order to secure maintenance payments	£1
	(ii) On an application for an attachment of earnings order (other than a consolidated attachment order) to secure payment of a judgment which—	
	does not exceed £10	£1
	exceeds £10 but does not exceed £20	£2
	,, £20 ,, ,, ,, ,, £30	£3
	,, £30 ,, ,, ,, ,, £50	£4
	,, £50 ,, ,, ,, ,, £100	£5
	,, £100 ,, ,, ,, ,, £150	£6
	,, £150 ,, ,, ,, ,, £200	£7
	,, £200 ,, ,, ,, ,, £300	£8
	,, £300 ,, ,, ,, ,, £400	£9
	,, £400	£10
	(iii) On a consolidated attachment order under O. 25, r. 90	The same fee as would be payable if the order were an administration order.
14	Crown Proceedings Act 1947, s. 27 application..	For every £2 or part, 10p. Max. £10.
16	On any originating application under Landlord and Tenants Acts 1927 and 1954	£5
18	On an originating application under the Rent (County Court Proceedings) Rules 1970—	
	(i) for leave to distrain	£1
	(ii) for any other remedy or relief under the Rent Act 1968	£1
19	On an originating application for an order for the taxation of a solicitor's bill of costs	For every £1 or part thereof allowed, 5p.
	ENFORCEMENT OF JUDGMENTS	
21	On an application for an order for the attendance of a judgment debtor under O. 25, r. 2 or 3 ..	£2

No. of Fee	Description of Proceeding	Amount of Fee
22	On the issue of a warrant of execution against goods, except enforce payment of a court fee or an order for payment of a fine	For every £1 or part, 15p. Min. £1.05p. Max. £15.
29	On the issue of a warrant of possession whether or not for the recovery of money in addition..	£5
30	On the issue of a warrant of delivery	For every £1 or part of the value of the goods, 15p. Min. £1.05. Max. £15.
32	On the issue of a judgment summons ..	For every £2 or part, 20p. Max. £5.
33	On entering garnishee proceedings	For every £2 or part, 10p. Max. £10.
38	On payment into court under O. 38	£1 and in addition 5p for every £4.
42	For a photographic copy of all or part of any document, whether or not issued as an office copy, for each photographic sheet	25p
43	For a typewritten copy of any document, per page .. .. and for each page of any additional carbon copy bespoken, half of this fee.	50p
44	For examining a plain copy and marking the same as an office copy for each sheet ..	25p
48	(i) On a search by an applicant at the Registry	For every name, 50p.
	(ii) On a request to the Registrar (a) for a search	£1 plus £1 if the search is to extend for more than 5 years.
	(b) for a serial list of entries of a specified class	For every 50 entries, £10.
	(c) for a certified copy of an entry ..	£1
	(iii) On a request to cancel the registration of a satisfied judgment	50p

TIME TABLE IN THE COUNTY COURT

Enlargement or abridgment of time ..	..	.. .. O. 13, r. 5.
Service (normally on Sunday, Christmas Day and Good Friday)		O. 8, r. 3.
Computation of time		O. 48, r. 10.

MATTER	REFERENCE	TIME*
ADJOURNED ACTION—		
Struck out after 12 months	O. 13, r. 4 (4)	14 days' notice.
ADMISSION OF CLAIM—	O. 9, r. 1, O. 10, r. 4	14 days after service.
ADMISSION OF FACTS—		
Notice as to	O. 20, r. 9 (1)	Any time.
Admission	O. 20, r. 9 (2)	3 days after notice.
APPEAL		
Court of Appeal, to		
Notice of Appeal	R.S.C., O. 59, rr. 4 (1), 19 (3)	Within 14 days of judgment or order in interlocutory cases; 21 days in bankruptcy and winding-up and 6 weeks in other cases.
Setting down Appeal	R.S.C., O. 59, r. 5	Within 7 days from service of notice.
Respondent's notice	R.S.C., O. 59, r. 6	Within 21 days after notice of appeal.
Registrar, from		
Notice of Appeal	O. 37, r. 5 (2)	Within 6 days of judgment or order.
ARBITRATOR'S AWARD—		
Application to set aside	O. 37, r. 7 (1)	6 days from receipt.
ATTACHMENT OF EARNINGS—		
Application for, service of	O. 25, r. 81 (2)	21 c.d. before return day.
COSTS—		
Application after hearing, for increase	O. 47, r. 21 (4)	Within 14 days of order etc., for costs.
Security for, where defendant twenty miles from Court	O. 13, r. 7 (2)	14 days after service.
deposit by plaintiff	O. 13, r. 7 (4); Form 75.	Within 3 c.d. from notice.
Taxation of, notice	O. 47, r. 38 (1)	Within 14 days of order 3 c.d. notice.
Taxation, Review by Judge	O. 47, r. 42 (2)	Within 2 days of taxation 1 c.d. notice.
COUNTERCLAIM—		
Notice of	O. 9, r. 1, O. 10, r. 1	Within 14 days of service.
CROWN PROCEEDINGS—		
Leave to enter judgment	O. 46, r. 13 (12)	7 c.d.
DEFAULT SUMMONS—		
Acceptance of admission	O. 10, r. 4 (2)	8 days.
Entry of judgment on, when no notice or admission of defence	O. 10, r. 2	After 14 days from service of summons.
Return of, when served otherwise than by bailiff	O. 8, r. 2 (c)	Within 3 c.d. after service or within time allowed by registrar.

* The letters "b.r.d." mean "before return day"; the letters "c.d." mean "clear day."

MATTER	REFERENCE	TIME*
DEFENCE—		
Disputing liability	O. 9, r. 4 (1)	Within 14 days of service of summons.
Particulars required by Plaintiff	O. 9, r. 4 (7)	Within 5 c.d. of notice.
DIRECTIONS—		
Notice of application	O. 13, r. 1	1 c.d.
DOCUMENTS—		
Discovery	O. 14, r. 2 (1A)	3 days.
Notice to admit	O. 20, r. 10	5 c.d., b.r.d.
Notice to produce	O. 20, r. 11	Reasonable time.
EVIDENCE—		
Affidavit, notice of intention to use	O. 20, r. 5	5 c.d., b.r.d.
Objections	O. 20, r. 5	2 c.d., b.r.d.
EXECUTION—		
Claim to goods taken in, admitted; notice by registrar of application for protection order	O. 28, r. 4	1 c.d.
Notice by execution creditor of claim for damages against registrar	O. 28, r. 12	Within 8 days (of service of summons on claimant).
GARNISHEE—		
Acceptance by creditor	O. 27, r. 7 (3)	Within 7 days of notice.
Payment into court	O. 27, r. 7 (1)	Within 8 days of service.
INTERLOCUTORY APPLICATION	O. 13, r. 1	1 c.d.
INTERPLEADER—		
Notice by execution creditor of admission of title	O. 28, r. 3 (1)	Within 4 days after notice from registrar.
Request by execution creditor to registrar to withdraw	O. 28, r. 3 (1)	Within 4 days after notice from registrar.
JUDGMENT SUMMONS—		
Successive issue when judgment summons not served in time	O. 25, r. 41	Within 6 months of original summons.
Return of summons from foreign court.	O. 25, r. 40 (2)	6 c.d. before hearing.
JURISDICTION—		
Objection to, where claim exceeds £150 in contract and tort	O. 16, r. 18	Within 14 days of service.
LANDLORD AND TENANTS ACTS		
Answer to application	O. 40, r. 2 (2), r. 4 (2) and r. 8 (2)	Within 14 days of service.
Application for directions	O. 40, r. 18	8 days of receipt of notice otherwise to time of hearing.

* See note on page 134.

MATTER	REFERENCE	TIME*
NEW TRIAL— Application	O. 37, r. 1	Day of trial if both parties present, or first court after 12 c.d. or by leave of Judge at any subsequent Court.
Notice of application	O. 37, r. 1 (3)	6 c.d.
PARTICULARS, FURTHER— Delivery by Defendant Notice by Defendant	O. 9, r. 4 (6) O. 7, r. 9	Within 5 days of notice. Within 8 days of summons.
Delivery by Plaintiff	O. 7, r. 9	Within 5 days of notice.
PARTNER— Notice of application under s. 23 of 1890 Act	O. 25, r. 5 (1)	1 c.d.
PAYMENT INTO COURT Acceptance by plaintiff	O. 11, r. 7 O. 11, r. 7 (3)	Within 14 days of service. 7 days after notice, 2 days before return day.
	O. 11, r. 9	7 days after notice of payment in *or* if notice received less than 7 days before return day, before the hearing.
REQUEST FOR TAXATION	O. 11, r. 7 (3A)	7 days after notice, 2 days before return day.
REFERENCE TO ARBITRATION Request to refer application to judge where claim exceeds registrar's jurisdiction	O. 19, r. 1 (2A)	Any time before application is heard.
Application to rescind or vary reference made in absence of party	O. 19, r. 1 (8) (a) (b)	10 days after order.
REFERENCE FOR REPORT— Registrar's notice to adopt report Notice of party objecting	O. 19, r. 2 (h) (i) O. 19, r. 2 (h) (ii)	10 c.d. 5 days before hearing.
SERVICE— Affidavit of service effected otherwise than by bailiff	O. 8, r. 2 (c)	Within 3 c.d. after service.
Attachment of earnings, application for	O. 25, r. 81 (2)	21 c.d., b.r.d.
Short, order for, when defendant about to remove	O. 8, r. 8 (2)	Any time.
Summons ordinary	O. 8, r. 8 (4)	21 c.d., b.r.d.
Successive ordinary summons	O. 8, r. 32 (4)	21 c.d., b.r.d., on yearly extensions.
Judgment summons	O. 25, r. 40	10 c.d.
Successive judgment summons	O. 25, r. 41	Within 6 months of date of original summons.
SOLICITOR— Notice of change	O. 48, r. 11 (3)	48 hours.

* See note on page 134.

MATTER	REFERENCE	TIME*
TAXING OF COSTS—		
Notice	O. 47, r. 38	Within 14 days of order. 3 c.d. notice.
Solicitor and client—		
Notice of hearing	O. 47, r. 40 (3)	3 c.d.
Bill lodged	O. 47, r. 40 (2)	14 days after order.
Reconsideration by registrar or Review by Judge	O. 47, r. 42	Within 2 days of taxation; 1 c.d. notice.
THIRD PARTY—		
Notice	O. 12, r. 1 (2) (5)	Within 8 days of service on defendant; time for service as ordered, r. 1 (3).

* See note on page 134.

Criminal Law

ALLOWANCES TO WITNESSES IN CRIMINAL CASES

By the Costs in Criminal Cases (Allowances) Regulations, 1974 (S.I. 1974 No. 831) as amended by the Costs in Criminal Cases (Allowances) Amendment Regulations 1974 (S.I. 1974 No. 1580), and the Costs in Criminal Cases (Allowances) Amendment (No. 2) Regulations 1974 (S.I. 1974 No. 2179), the following sums are payable.

1. *Professional Witnesses*. Lawyers, Doctors, Dentists and Veterinary Surgeons may get a professional allowance of not exceeding £15.48 a day and a night allowance (if necessary), with the proviso that if they attend to give evidence in one case only and are not away from their residence or place of practice for more than 4 hours they may get not more than £7.74 except where necessary expense has been incurred in providing a *locum tenens*. An allowance may be made to a registered medical practitioner who makes a written report at the request of a court, and where travelling expenses are incurred in connection with his preparation of that report these may be at the rate of 7.7p per mile.

2. *Expert Witnesses*. These witnesses may be allowed an expert witness allowance of such amount as the court may consider reasonable having regard to the nature of the work, and a night allowance (where necessary).

3. *Ordinary Witnesses*. Persons who lose wages or other income by attendance at court may receive not more than £6.70 a day together with a subsistence allowance, varying according to the number of hours spent away from residence or employment, but not ordinarily more than £1.35 where absence from place of employment does not exceed 8 hours.

5. *Night Allowances*. A night allowance in any of the foregoing instances will only be allowed if the person is necessarily absent overnight from his place of residence, and in the case of professional or expert witnesses must not exceed £6.25 (£7.05 for London) and for an ordinary witness, £8.65 (£9.45 for London).

6. *Seamen*. A seaman detained on shore to give evidence and thereby missing his ship may be allowed not more than £6.70 a day for loss of wages (unless for special reasons the court decides to increase this sum) together with the sum actually and reasonably incurred for his maintenance.

7. *Travelling Allowances*. Railway fares, etc., may be refunded to the witness, with the proviso that unless

the court specially directs only second class fares shall be allowable. In a case of urgency or where no railway or other public conveyance is available an allowance may be paid for a person necessarily travelling by a hired vehicle of the sum actually paid.

Persons travelling in a private conveyance may receive between 7.1p and 7.7p a mile depending on the circumstances. Seriously ill persons and heavy exhibits may be allowed such sums as the court thinks have been reasonably incurred in excess of the sums previously mentioned.

8. *Interpreters.* Interpreters may be allowed such sums as the court considers reasonable (including night and travelling allowances).

9. *Persons attending otherwise than as witnesses.* Any prosecutor or other person who, in the court's opinion, necessarily attends for the prosecution otherwise than as a witness may receive the same allowances as an ordinary witness.

10. *Reports by Medical Practitioner.* A medical practitioner supplying a written report to a court may claim an allowance of not less than £4.45 and not more than £12.38, the actual amount to depend on the purpose for which the report is required and the professional status of the practitioner.

Travelling expenses incurred in connection with the preparation of the report may be allowed at 7.7 p per mile.

11. *Police and Prison Officers and Prisoners.* No sums are allowed.

CRIMINAL APPEAL

The Criminal Appeal Act 1968 consolidates the law relating to appeals to the criminal division of the Court of Appeal and thence to the House of Lords. The Criminal Appeal Rules 1968 (S.I. 1968 No. 1262) regulate procedure and prescribe forms.

Right of appeal.—There are enacted most comprehensive rights of appeal against a conviction for an offence on indictment or against a sentence passed on such a conviction or after conviction by a magistrates' court where sentence is imposed by the Crown Court after committal for sentence. An appeal against conviction lies without leave where it involves a question of law alone, but leave of the Court of Appeal or the trial judge is required where it involves a question of fact alone or of mixed law and fact. An appeal against sentence lies only with the leave of the Court of Appeal.

How and when to appeal.—Notice of appeal or of application for leave to appeal must be made within 28 days of the verdict or the sentence, as the case may be (s. 18). It must be signed by the appellant or on his behalf and sent to "The Registrar of the Court of Appeal, (Criminal Division), London." Sending by registered post or recorded delivery service suffices (r. 4).

Forms of appeal notices can be obtained from the Registrar and from governors of gaols, officers of courts, etc.

The time for appealing may be extended on application signed by the appellant and sent to the Registrar (s. 18(3)).

Time for appealing against a conviction runs from the giving of the verdict; time for appealing against sentence runs from the pronouncement of the sentence (s. 18(2)).

Getting leave.—Applications for leave to appeal are in practice first considered by one of the judges of the court who may exercise the powers of the court and from whom in the case of refusal to give leave, etc. there is an appeal to the full court (s. 31).

Refusals of applications are notified by the Registrar (r. 25).

A frivolous or vexatious appeal on grounds involving questions of law may be summarily rejected (s. 20).

Bail pending appeal may be granted by the Court of Appeal (s. 19; r. 4).

Obtaining legal aid.—The appellant may apply for legal aid on his notice of appeal, or if he does not, the Registrar may report that he thinks counsel and/or solicitor should be assigned to the appellant and the court may make such assignment (s. 47).

Preparation for hearing.—The Registrar is required to take all necessary steps to obtain the hearing of the appeal (s. 21). The Director of Public Prosecutions has a duty to appear for the Crown or the prosecutor when so directed by the court (Sch. 5, amending Prosecution of Offences Act 1879, s. 2). At any stage, too, the Director may be substituted for a private prosecutor.

The Registrar will get from the court of trial the particulars of the case and documents and other exhibits required for the appeal (s. 21; s. 22(1)).

Any interested party may obtain a copy of any document or other thing required for the purposes of the appeal from the Registrar (r. 8).

Exhibits used at the trial are to be produced if and when required by the court. A record of all exhibits put in at the trial is to be made, and the judges at the trial may order how such exhibits are to be kept (r. 7), but the Registrar may obtain them and allow access thereto (r. 8).

Copies of documents may be obtained from the Registrar on payment (r. 8(1)).

The Registrar enters the appeal and notifies the parties of the day for the hearing (r. 22(2)).

The Registrar may obtain a transcript of the shorthand note; an interested party may obtain a copy of it from the Registrar or from the shorthand writer (r. 19).

The hearing.—Appeals (which are listed) are heard before three or more judges.

An appellant is entitled to be present at the hearing of the appeal, except when the appeal is on a question of law only, in which case he must get leave to be present (s. 22).

An appellant in custody is brought to the court by prison officers; an appellant on bail must on attending the Appeal Court surrender into custody *pro tem.* and be searched (Form 7).

The court may have the witnesses at the trial examined again, and may order new witnesses to be examined, and new documents to be produced. New evidence may be taken before the court itself or by a commissioner (s. 23).

Result of Appeal.—Subject to the power of the court to substitute a verdict of guilty of some other offence, given by s. 3 of the Act, a successful appeal against a conviction normally amounts to an acquittal and the appellant is discharged forthwith, except when there is another indictment pending against him, when the court may remand him to custody to undergo his trial thereon, or where the appeal is allowed only by reason of fresh evidence when the court may order a new trial (s. 7).

When there has been no miscarriage of justice the court may dismiss the appeal although they are of opinion that the point raised on the appeal might be decided in favour of the appellants (s. 2 (1)). But where there is a real fear that there may have been a miscarriage of justice the appeal will be allowed and where there has been a substantial misdirection by the judge, at the trial on a question of law, or there has been misreception of evidence, the appeal will be allowed and an acquittal entered, unless the court come to the conclusion that on a right direction, or if the evidence had not been given, the jury would have found the same verdict.

An appeal against the severity of the sentence may be dealt with by changing the sentence to any other that the court below had power to pass subject to the rule that the appellant is not dealt with more severely (s. 11).

Costs.—Where an appeal is allowed the court may direct payment of the appellant's costs out of local funds. The expenses of counsel or solicitor assigned by the court to an appellant, and of witnesses ordered by the court and of bringing the appellant to the court are defrayed out of the central funds (Costs in Criminal Cases Act 1973, s. 7).

House of Lords.—Appeal lies to the House of Lords, at the instance of defendant or prosecutor, from a decision of the Court of Appeal, but only with the leave of the Court of Appeal or the House of Lords and where the Court of Appeal certifies that a point of law of general public importance is involved (s. 33).

POWER OF ARREST AND SEARCH

(See *Halsbury's Laws of England* (4th Edn.), vol. 11, *p.* 73 *et seq.*)

In ordinary cases, application should be made for a summons calling upon the offending party to answer the charge alleged against him, when, if he does not appear, the case may be heard and determined or a warrant may be issued.

Under the Criminal Law Act, 1967, s. 2, any person may arrest without warrant anyone who is, or whom he reasonably suspects to be, committing an arrestable offence, or where such an offence has been committed, anyone whom he reasonably suspects to be guilty of the offence. In addition, a constable may, where he reasonably suspects that such an offence has been committed, arrest without warrant any person he reasonably suspects to be guilty of it and may also arrest without warrant a person whom he reasonably suspects is about to commit such an offence. An arrestable offence is one for which the sentence is fixed by law (*i.e.* life imprisonment or imprisonment during Her Majesty's pleasure) or for which a person not previously convicted is liable to be sentenced to five years imprisonment for an attempt to commit such an offence. At common law any person may arrest when a breach of the peace has been committed or apprehended provided the arrest is made on view thereof or before the disorder is over or when there are reasonable grounds for apprehending its continuance or immediate renewal. In addition, there are numerous statutory powers of arrest conferred in the case of specific offences. Otherwise, in the case of non-arrestable offences, unattended with violence, there is no power to arrest without a warrant.

On a person being taken into custody without a warrant, the officer in charge of the police station may in any case and must where it is impracticable to present the offender at a Magistrates' Court within 24 hours (Sunday included) inquire into the case; and unless of opinion that the offence charged is a serious one, release the person charged upon recognizance with or without sureties (Magistrates' Courts Act, 1952, s. 38).

For the purpose of arresting a person under the powers conferred by the Criminal Law Act, 1967 (above) a constable may enter (if need be, by force) and search any place where that person is or where he reasonably suspects him to be. He may also enter by force where he hears an affray taking place in a house. And a constable may search a prisoner for weapons of offence should violence be threatened; and property found in an arrested person's possession or under his control, which may be material on a charge against either the person arrested or any other person, may be detained until the end of the trial.

Search Warrants. Where goods have been stolen, a search warrant can generally be had on oath as to reasonable cause; but a constable, if authorized in writing by a chief officer of police, may enter premises and search for property believed to have been stolen, provided (1) the premises are or within 12 months have been occupied by any person convicted of receiving stolen goods or harbouring thieves; or (2) if the premises are occupied by a person who has been convicted of an offence involving fraud or dishonesty and punishable with imprisonment; any person on whose premises such property is found may be summoned before a court of summary jurisdiction which will order as to the disposal of the goods (Theft Act, 1968, s. 26 (2)). Search Warrants may also be granted to discover bankrupts' property, in respect of explosives intended for unlawful purposes, implements of forgery, counterfeit coin, etc., dangerous drugs, gaming offences, and in the case of females detained for immoral purposes, children believed to be maltreated, etc.

PRACTICE AS TO INDICTMENTS

The Indictments Act, 1915 supplies rules as to indictments and forms of indictments. The rules are entitled Indictment Rules, 1971.

Technical terms are to be avoided. The description of any person named in the indictment must be reasonably sufficient without necessarily stating his correct name or his abode, style, etc.: thus, if the name is unknown, he may be described as "a person unknown." Documents referred to need not be exactly copied but may be described by characteristics or purport. Intent to defraud, etc. need not be charged unless part of the statutory offence. Previous convictions, etc., should be charged at the end by reference to time and place

without specifying particulars of the offence. Generally, references need only be reasonably sufficient. On the back of the indictment must be indorsed the name of every witness intended to be examined on behalf of the prosecution in support of the indictment.

The commencement of an indictment should be in this form:—

INDICTMENT

The Crown Court at Winchester

The Queen—v—Oliver Twist, David Copperfield and William Sikes who are charged as follows:—

Count one

Statement of Offence:	Burglary contrary to section 9 (1) b of the Theft Act 1968
Particulars of Offence:	Oliver Twist and David Copperfield on the 1st day of January 1972 at Winchester in the County of Hampshire having entered as trespassers a dwelling house known as 2 Acacia Gardens stole therein a gold watch the property of Samuel Weller

Count Two

Statement of Offence:	Handling stolen goods, contrary to section 22 (1) of the Theft Act 1968
Particulars of Offence:	William Sikes on the 2nd day of January 1972 at Winchester in the County of Hampshire dishonestly received a gold watch the property of Samuel Weller knowing or believing the same to be stolen.

Charges for any offences, may be joined in the same indictment if founded on the same facts or part of the same series of offences. Where several charges are "joined", all should be tried together; but in some instances it may be preferable to charge in separate indictments. A count charging more than one offence or offences in the alternative is bad for duplicity.

An indictment framed in accordance with the above rules will not be open to objection; at the same time, non-compliance with them so far as form is concerned will not of itself avoid an indictment. When before or during trial an indictment appears to be defective, the court may order amendment and also order as to the costs arising from such order. If necessary the trial may be postponed. A note of the order of the court will be indorsed. The court may also order separate trial of any count or counts.

Counts may be added without leave if founded on facts disclosed in the depositions (Administration of Justice (Miscellaneous Provisions) Act, 1933, s. 2 (2)).

A bill of indictment may be preferred by any person and if signed by the proper officer it thereupon becomes an indictment (*ibid.*, s. 2 (1)); but the bill may only be signed if the person charged has been committed for trial, or if the bill is preferred by the direction or consent of a judge, or by order under s. 9 of the Perjury Act, 1911 (*ibid.*, s. 2 (2)). As to applications for leave to prefer a bill *see* Indictments (Procedure) Rules, 1933.

It is the duty of the proper officer of the Court, after a bill has been signed, to supply to the accused person, on request, a copy of the indictment, free of charge, the costs to be treated as part of the costs of the prosecution.

Crown Court

The Courts Act 1971, which came into force on 1st January, 1972, abolished courts of assize and quarter sessions and replaced the criminal jurisdiction of assizes and the jurisdiction of quarter sessions by a single Crown Court established by s. 4 of the Act.

All proceedings on indictment are brought before the Crown Court (s. 6 (1)) and by s. 8 the appellate jurisdiction of quarter sessions has been transferred to the new court. This appellate jurisdiction included the jurisdiction of quarter sessions in matters such as licensing and juvenile appeals, as well as rights of appeal in civil or quasi-civil matters under numerous enactments. The Crown Court also hears proceedings on committal for sentence from magistrates' courts.

The jurisdiction and powers of the Crown Court are exercised by High Court judges, Circuit judges appointed under s. 16 of the Courts Act, part-time Recorders appointed under s. 21 of the Act and, when hearing appeals, committals for sentence and certain classes of indictable offences, by justices of the peace sitting with a High Court judge, a Circuit judge or Recorder. The classes of case suitable for allocation to a court comprising justices of the peace are determined in accordance with directions given by or on behalf of the Lord Chief Justice, with the concurrence of the Lord Chancellor, and these offences are broadly those which were previously triable at quarter sessions. Certain classes of serious offences are reserved for trial by High Court judges and other categories of offences may, depending on their difficulty or gravity, be tried by either a High Court or Circuit judge, or a Recorder.

Procedure in relation to indictable offences is unaltered except where modifications have been necessary because of the transfer of jurisdiction to the Crown Court (Courts Act, s. 6 (3)). The Crown Court Rules (S.I. 1971 No. 1292) have been made by a Rule Committee set up under s. 15 of the Act.

Appeals in indictable offences lies to the Criminal Division of the Court of Appeal. Appeals in matters other than trial on indictment go to the Divisional Court of the Queen's Bench Division, by way of case stated. Similarly the High Court has jurisdiction to make orders of mandamus, prohibition and certiorari in relation to the jurisdiction of the Crown Court except in matters relating to trial on indictment.

Under Part V of the Courts Act, the responsibility for summoning jurors for service in the Crown Court (as well as the High Court and county courts) is transferred to the Lord Chancellor and, in practice, the summoning officer is a designated official of the Crown Court at each centre where the court sits.

Section 4 (4) of the Courts Act provides that Crown Court business may be conducted in any place in England or Wales. By section 4 (6), the places at which the Crown Court sits and the days and times of its sitting will be determined in accordance with directions given by or on behalf of the Lord Chancellor. In practice, the work of the court is divided between first-tier centres, where both High Court and Circuit judges sit in the Crown Court (and the High Court also sits), second-tier centres where High Court and Circuit judges sit in the Crown Court (but the High Court does not sit) and third-tier centres which are visited by Circuit judges only for Crown Court business.

Employment

The statute law relating to employment is mainly contained in the Contracts of Employment Act 1972, the Trade Union and Labour Relations Act 1974, and the Employment Protection Act 1975. Other relevant statutes (not covered in this note) are the Redundancy Payments Act 1965, the Equal Pay Act 1970, certain provisions of the Health and Safety at Work Act 1974, and the Sex Discrimination Act 1975. (A Race Relations Bill replacing the Race Relations Act 1968 and in similar terms to the Sex

Discrimination Act is now before Parliament.)

Rights of employees under the Contracts of Employment Act.—Under this Act employees have the right to (i) written particulars of employment, and (ii) a minimum period of notice.

(i) *Written particulars of employment*

Every employee not in one of certain excluded categories is entitled to receive a written statement giving particulars of the major terms of his employment. The statement must be provided within 13 calendar weeks after the employee begins his employment (s. 4). When any change occurs in the particulars, the employer must give the employee a statement of the change not more than one month after it occurs. The following particulars must be given.

(a) *Basic particulars* (s. 4(1))

   —name of the employer;
   —name of the employee;
   —date when the employment began;
   —whether a previous employment is deemed continuous with the present employment, and if so giving the date on which the entire period of continuous employment began.

(b) *Terms of employment* (s. 4(1)(a)–(f))
Any terms relating to:

   —rates of pay, and frequency of payment;
   —hours of work;
   —holidays and holiday pay;
   —sickness or injury and sickness pay;
   —pensions and pension schemes (including, by the Social Security Pensions Act 1975, s. 30(5) whether a contracting-out certificate is in force), except in the case of some statutory pension schemes where the employee is given the information by the managers of the scheme instead (s. 4(1) proviso);
   —length of notice necessary on either side;
   —title of the employee's job.

If there are no terms relating to any of the above, the statement must say so (s. 1(3)). If the contract is for a fixed term, the note must also specify the date of expiry (s. 4(4)).

The items must be correct as at a date specified in the statement and that date must be not more than one week before the statement is given (s. 4(1)).

By s. 4(5), instead of including all the particulars in the statement, the employer may refer the employee to another document "which the employee has reasonable opportunity of reading in the course of his employment or which is made reasonably accessible to him in some other way."

(c) *Additional particulars* (s. 4(2))

The statement must include a note specifying any disciplinary rules applying to the employee or referring him to another document where he can find them (s. 4(2)(a), as substituted by the Employment Protection Act 1975). The note or document must also specify how and to whom he can complain if he is dissatisfied with any disciplinary decision relating to him and how and to whom he can take any other grievance (s. 4(2)(b) as substituted). It must also explain any further steps in the grievance procedure or refer the employee to a reasonably accessible document where he can find an explanation (s. 4(2)(c) as substituted). Rules and procedures under the Health and Safety at Work Act do *not* have to be included (s. 4(2A) as inserted by the Employment Protection Act).

Changes in particulars need not be notified individually—a collective notification will suffice (s.5(1)). The notification—whether given individually or collectively—may refer the employee to some other accessible document (s. 5(2)). The employer may, when referring to another document in the statement given under s. 4 or 5, indicate to the employee what future changes will be entered in the document. If he does so, he need not give a note of a change under s. 5(1) (s. 5(3)).

If the employee already has a written contract of employment ss. 4 and 5 do not apply (s. 6). This exemption is subject to the following conditions: the written contract must contain express terms dealing with each of the terms of employment listed above; the employee must be given, or there must be reasonably available to him: a copy of the contract and a note containing the additional particulars mentioned above.

If the employer fails to comply with s. 4 or 5, the employee may require a reference to be made to an industrial tribunal (s. 8).

(ii) *Minimum period of notice*

An employee who has completed four weeks' continuous employment is entitled to one week's notice for every year of continuous employment completed, subject to a minimum of one week and a maximum of 12 weeks' notice (s. 1(1) as amended by the Employment Protection Act). A "year of employment" is 52 weeks of employment (Sunday to Saturday) calculated to the date of expiry of the notice. The employee is entitled to minimum remuneration during the statutory period of notice laid down by s. 1 irrespective of the length of notice actually given (s. 2).

The remedy for failure to give the proper notice under s. 1 or for failure to pay the appropriate remuneration under s. 2 is by way of action for breach of contract in the county court or High Court (s. 3).

Rights of employees under the Trade Union and Labour Relations Act 1974

Every employee not in one of certain excluded categories has a right not to be unfairly dismissed (Sch. 1, para. 4). When amendments made by the EPA are fully implemented the excluded categories will be:

(a) any employment where the employer is the husband or wife of the employee (para. 9(1)(b));

(b) any employment as a registered dock worker (para. 9(1)(c));

(c) any employment as master or as member of the crew of a fishing vessel where the employer is remunerated by a share in the profits (para. 9(1) (d));

(d) any employment where the employee normally works outside Great Britain (para. 9(2));

(e) any employment where the employee has been continuously employed for less than 26 weeks (para. 15(a));

(f) an employee who has reached normal retiring age or who reaches the age of 65 for men or 60 for women (para. 10 (b));

(g) a fixed term contract of more than two years made before February 1972 where the dismissal consists solely of a failure to renew (para. 12 (a));

(h) a fixed term contract of more than two years made after February 1972 where the dismissal consists of a failure to renew, if, before that term has expired, the employee agrees in writing to exclude any claim in respect of his dismissal (para. 12 (b));

(i) any employment covered by a designated and approved dismissal procedure agreement (para. 13);

(j) employment for less than 16 hours per week (effect of para. 30(1) as read with Contracts of Employment Act 1972, Sch. 1, para. 3).

Exclusions (e) and (f) are not excluded if the reason for the dismissal is an inadmissible reason—*i.e.*, one relating to membership of an independent trade union.

To qualify for protection the employee must have been continuously employed for 26 weeks, except that there is no qualifying period in the case of dismissal due to membership of a trade union (TULRA, Sch. 1, para. 30; Contracts of Employment Act 1972, Sch. 1).

Dismissal may take place (a) where the contract of employment is terminated by the employer; (b) where a fixed term contract is not renewed; (c) where the employee himself terminates the contract but is entitled to resign without notice by reason of the employer's conduct.

A dismissal may be fair if the reason for it is:

(a) a reason relating to the capability or qualifications of the employee

(b) a reason which relates to the conduct of the employee

(c) redundancy

(d) that the continuance of the employment would have contravened a statutory provision (Sch. 1, para. 6(2));

(e) some other substantial reason (Sch. 1, para. 6(1) (b)).

Even if the employer can show that the reason for the dismissal fell within one of these categories, he must still show that in the circumstances, having regard to equity and the substantial merits of the case, he acted reasonably in treating that reason as a sufficient reason for the dismissal (Sch. 1, para. 6(8)).

Dismissal is also fair if it is the practice, in accordance with a union membership agreement for employees to belong to a specified independent trade union and the reason for the dismissal was that the employee was not a member of such union, and refused or proposed to refuse to join (Sch. 1, para. 6(5)). But dismissal is unfair if the employee genuinely objects on grounds of religious belief to being a member of any trade union whatsoever.

A dismissed employee may present a complaint to an industrial tribunal that he was unfairly dismissed (Sch. 1, para. 17). The complaint must be presented before the end of the period of 3 months beginning with the effective date of termination or within such further period as the tribunal consider reasonable where it is satisfied that it was not reasonably practicable for the complaint to be presented before the end of that period (Sch. 1, para. 21(4)).

A tribunal may *inter alia* make an award of compensation. This may consist of (a) a basic award (maximum 1½ weeks' pay for each of 20 years employment × £80), (b) a compensatory award (maximum £5,200), and where the employer ignores a tribunal order to re-instate or re-engage the employee an additional award (maximum 52 weeks × £80 per week). The total compensation could therefore reach £11,760.

Rights of employees under the Employment Protection Act 1975

Employers who are not within certain excluded categories (ss. 119 (2)–(16), 121) are given the following rights under the Act (i) a right to guarantee payments in certain circumstances, (ii) minimum pay during suspension from work on certain medical grounds, (iii) certain rights during pregnancy, (iv) a right not to be victimised in connection with trade union activities, (v) time off work in certain circumstances, (vi) rights in the event of the employer's insolvency, (vii) in the event of dismissal, a written statement of reasons, and (viii) an itemised pay statement.

(i) *Guarantee payments*

If the employee is given no work to do on a particular day he may be entitled to a minimum fall-back payment from his employer, called a guarantee payment (s. 22(1)). The employee must have completed four weeks' continuous employment ending with the last complete week before any day for which a guarantee payment is claimed (s. 22 (3)). The employee cannot claim if the interruption of normal working is caused by a trade union dispute involving any employee of the employer or within the group of companies (s. 23(1)), nor can he claim if he unreasonably refuses an offer of suitable alternative work for the day (s. 23(2) (a)) or if he does not comply with any reasonable requirements imposed by his employer with a view to ensuring that his services are available (s. 23(2) (b)). The method of calculating the payment is set out in s. 24, subject to the limits imposed by s. 25. If the employer fails to pay a guarantee payment, the employee may complain to an industrial tribunal. He must present his claim within 3 months of any day for which payment is claimed, unless it was not reasonably practicable to comply (s. 27).

(ii) *Minimum pay during suspension from work on certain medical grounds*

An employee suspended from work on certain medical grounds may be entitled to minimum pay during his suspension (s. 29). The right depends on the employee's completing four weeks' continuous employment ending with the last complete week before his suspension starts (s. 30(1)). The employee's right is to be paid by his employer at the statutory rate for a period of up to 26 weeks when, though capable of work, he is suspended by his employer on medical grounds in consequence of (a) any requirement imposed by or under any statute or statutory instrument, or (b) any recommendation in any provision of a code of practice issued or approved under s. 16 of the Health and Safety at Work etc. Act 1974. In either case t he relevant statutory provision must be listed in EPA, Sch. 2. The employee may lose his right if he unreasonably refuses an offer of suitable alternative work or if he refuses to comply with reasonable arrangements made by the employer to ensure his services are available (s. 30(3)). The amount of the payment is a week's pay as defined by Sch. 4 for every week of suspension (and *pro rata* for part of a week) up to a maximum of 26 weeks (s. 29(1)).

(iii) *Maternity*

A female employee who is pregnant has a right to compensation for unfair dismissal if she is dismissed on the grounds of her pregnancy (s. 34). She also has a right to maternity pay for up to six weeks if she is away from work because of pregnancy (ss. 35 and 36–50) and a right to return to work —*i.e.*, a right of up to 40 weeks (nine months) maternity leave (ss. 35 and 48–50).

To qualify for the right to maternity pay and the right to return to work, the employee must have completed 2 years' continuous employment by the beginning of the 11th week before the expected week of confinement (ss. 35(2) (*b*), 52). An exception is made in favour of an employee who is dismissed before the 11th week because she is physically or legally incapable of continuing her work (s. 35(3)).

As well as completing two years' continuous employment, the employee must inform her employer (in writing if he so requests), at least 3 weeks before her absence begins or as soon as reasonably practicable, that she will be (or is) absent from work wholly or partly because of pregnancy or confinement, and (in the case of the right to return) that she intends to return to work (s. 35(2) (*c*)). The employee must, if the employer asks for one, provide a medical certificate indicating the expected week of confinement (s. 35(4)).

The amount of the maternity pay is ascertained by taking nine-tenths of a week's pay as defined in Sch. 4 and deducting the standard flat rate maternity allowance payable under the Social Security legislation (s. 37(1)). If the employer fails to make the maternity payment, the employee may complain to an industrial tribunal (s. 38(1)). The complaint must be presented within 3 months' of the last day of the payment period, but the tribunal may extend the time limit if it was not reasonably practicable to present it in time (s. 38(2)).

The employee's right to return to work is a right to be reinstated after absence through pregnancy or confinement with her old employer (or his successor) in her old job or an equivalent one (s. 48(1) and (4)). The employee must normally return not more than 29 weeks after the birth of her baby.

Maternity leave will usually begin 11 weeks before the expected confinement (the period was chosen because that is the time when Social Security maternity allowance begins). To exercise her right of return, the employee must notify the employer at least one week before the day on which she proposes to return of her intention to return on that day (s. 49(1)). If the employer refuses to let her return on the notified day of return she is treated as dismissed within the meaning of the Trade Union and Labour Relations Act 1974 and the Redundancy Payments Act 1965, so that the employer will have to pay compensation for loss of her job by way of unfair dismissal or redundancy payment.

By ss. 39–47, the Act establishes a Maternity Pay Fund similar to the Redundancy Fund. Every employer pays into the Fund. Any employer who has to pay statutory maternity pay can claim the same amount from the Fund.

(iv) *Victimisation and union membership*

Every employee has the right not to have action short of dismissal taken against him by his employer for the purpose of (*a*) preventing or deterring him from being a member of an independent trade union, or penalising him for doing so, or (*b*) preventing or deterring him from taking part in the activities of an independent trade union at the appropriate time, or penalising him for doing so, or (*c*) compelling him to become a member of a trade union which is not independent.

There is no minimum period of continuous employment required to qualify for this right. An employee who is victimised may complain to an industrial tribunal (s. 54(1)). The claim must be presented within 3 months of the act or last act of alleged victimisation, unless it was not reasonably practicable to comply. The employer is not allowed to plead that he was threatened by or subjected to industrial action (s. 55(2)).

(v) *Time off work*

An employer must allow an employee to take time off work (*a*) to carry out union duties if he is an official of a recognised independent trade union (s. 57), (*b*) to take part in union activities (s. 58), (*c*) to perform his official duties if he is a J.P., a member of a local authority, statutory tribunal, health authority, water authority, or managing or governing body of an educational establishment maintained by a local education authority, (*d*) to look for other work or make arrangements for retraining if he is under notice of dismissal for redundancy (s. 61). If the employer refuses to allow time off, the employee's remedy is to complain to a tribunal for compensation—he may not simply take the time off. There is no minimum qualifying period for full-time exployees, except in relation to time-off in redundancy, where two years' continuous employment is necessay (s. 61(2)). In all cases the remedy lies in a complaint to a tribunal within nine months of the date when the failure occurred, unless it was not reasonably practicable to do so (ss. 60(1), 61(9)).

(vi) *Rights on insolvency*

If an employer becomes insolvent certain debts, including wages, are payable in preference to others. The EPA provides that the following debts shall also be paid in priority, *viz.* any guarantee payment, remuneration payable on suspension on medical grounds, payment for time off for trade union duties or to look for work or arrange for re-training on being made redundant, and remuneration payable under a protective award (s. 63). There is no qualifying period of continuous employment. Certain debts due to an employee on his employer's insolvency may be paid by the Secretary of State out of the Redundancy Fund (s. 64).

(vii) *Written Statement of Reasons for Dismissal*

A dismissed employee is entitled to be provided by his employer on request and within 14 days of that request, with a written statement giving particulars of the reasons for his dismissal (s. 70). The employee must have completed 26 weeks' continuous employment. The employee may complain to a tribunal that his employer has unreasonably refused to provide the statement, or that it is inadequate or untrue. If the complaint is well-founded the tribunal may make a declaration as to what it finds were the true reasons, and most make an award of two weeks' pay.

(viii) *Itemised Pay Statement*

An employee is entitled when he is paid his wages or salary to have a written statement giving a breakdown of the amount paid (s. 81). There is no qualifying period for full-time employees. Part-time employees need five years' continuous employment based on a normal working week of at least 8 hours. The particulars to be entered on the statement are: gross pay, deductions and net pay and where the net part is paid in different ways, the amount and method of payment of each part.

The pay statement must detail the amounts of each variable deduction and the purpose for which it is made. In the case of fixed deductions, the employer may do likewise or he may give a periodic "standing statement of fixed deductions" and then in each pay statement just list the aggregate total of fixed deductions for that pay period (s. 82 (1)). The employee may complain to an industrial tribunal that the employer has failed to give a pay statement.

European Communities

THE UNITED KINGDOM AND COMMUNITY LAW

Accession by the United Kingdom to the European Communities was achieved in the appropriate constitutional manner, that is, the Crown made and ratified the Treaty of Accession signed on 22nd January 1972, and Parliament subsequently legislated to give municipal effect to the Treaty provisions in the United Kingdom. Changes in the legal orders required by accession were made by and through the European Communities Act 1972 ("the Act").

The EEC Treaty provides, inter alia, for the elimination of customs duties and quantitative restrictions on imports and exports between Member States and other measures having equivalent effect (Articles 9–17); the establishment of a common customs tariff (Articles 18–29); the elimination of quantitative restrictions between Member States (article 30–37); the establishment of a common commercial policy with third countries (Articles 110–116); the abolition as between Member States of obstacles to free movement of persons, services and capital (Articles 48–73); the adoption of a common agricultural policy (Articles 38–47) and transport policy (Articles 74–84); the institution of a system to ensure that competition in the Common Market is not distorted (Articles 85–94); tax provisions (Articles 95–99); coordination of the economic policies of Member States (Articles 103–109), and the approximation of legislation in Member States to the extent required for the proper functioning of the Common Market (Articles 100–102). Reference should be made to the main Treaties (more particularly the Treaties relating to the ECSC, EEC, Euratom and Accession, but also those defined in Section 1(2) and Part 1 of Schedule 1 to the Act) and the secondary legislation adopted in implementation thereof in order to appreciate the scope of application of such Treaties. Unless otherwise stated, references to the 'Treaty' herein relate to the EEC Treaty, although the principles regarding the Community legal order are of general application.

With regard to Part 1 of the Act, the following features of Community law are particularly relevant:—

(a) the Treaty provides a framework within which the Community institutions are required to act in implementing the tasks assigned to them; in meeting these requirements, obligations are imposed by the Treaty on the Member States themselves, with which they are required to comply. In addition, in the case of Treaty provisions which have direct effect, rights and duties are available to and imposed upon individuals in the Member States, which are enforceable by those individuals before national courts. The European Court of Justice ('ECJ') has held that such effect must be respected by the national courts, since provisions with such effect create direct effect between the Member States and individuals subject to their legal orders (Case 26/62 Van Gend en Loos v. Nederlandse Administratie der Belastingen ([1963] ECR 1; 1963 CMLR 105). A Treaty provision has such direct effect if it is complete and legally perfect (Case 57/65 Lutticke v. Hauptzollamt Sarrelouis 1971 CMLR 674), as evidenced by the spirit and wording of the provision in question (Van Gend en Loos etc. supra), when clear, unconditional and leaving no room for the exercise of discretion on the part of the Member State concerned (Case 28/67 Molkerei Zentrale Westfalen Lippe v. Hauptzollamt Paderborn [1968] ECR 143; 1968 CMLR 187). Amongst the Treaty provisions in whole or in part which have been held by the ECJ to date to create such direct effects are included the following Articles: 9, 12, 16, 31, 32(1), 36 (last sentence), 48, 52 (first paragraph), 53, 59(1), 60 (third paragraph), 85, 86, 95 and 119.

(b) in carrying out the tasks assigned to them by the Treaty, the Council of Ministers and Commission may, under Article 189, adopt instruments of secondary legislation which themselves are directly applicable. A Regulation has general application, is binding in its entirety and is directly applicable in all Member States; it takes immediate legal effect throughout the Community, and requires no implementation by the national legislature in accordance with the traditional law making procedure. A Decision is likewise binding on those to whom it is addressed. In the case of a Directive, which is binding, as to the result to be achieved, upon each Member State to which it is addressed, but leaving to the national authorities of each Member State the choice of form and method of implementation (i.e. requiring legislative action in order to give effect to the obligations imposed by the Directive), the ECJ has held that a provision contained in such an instrument may likewise have direct effect on relations between a Member State and individuals where the nature, general scheme and wording of the provision is capable of having such effect, being subject to no exception, and requiring no intervention on the part of either the Community or a Member State (Case 41/74 *Van Duyn* v. *Home Office* [1974] ECR 1337; 1975 CMLR 1).

(c) the Treaty is silent as to the nature and form of Community law; but the ECJ has formulated fundamental principles as to its basic characteristics. Under Article 177 (which enables the ECJ to interpret, inter alia, the Treaty and acts of the Community institutions at the request of lower ranking national courts and tribunals (national courts and tribunals of the last instance being bound to make a referral on such matters)), the ECJ has no power to determine the validity of national law in relation to the Community legal order, or interpret national law. However, in interpreting the Treaty and secondary legislation, the ECJ has observed that the Community legal order and the domestic legislation of each Member State constitute independent legal systems. It has held that the Treaty is integrated into the legal systems of the Member States, with the result that no Member State may enforce a provision of national law which is adopted after the date on which the Treaty came into force and which conflicts with a Treaty obligation. The Treaty has created a legal order of its own which is integrated into the domestic law of the Member States and which is superior to their own jurisdiction;" ... the binding force of the Treaty and of measures taken in order to put it into effect cannot differ from state to state in consequence of domestic measures, if the operation of the Community system is not to be interfered with and the realisation of the purposes of the Treaty is not to be endangered ... conflicts between a Community rule and domestic legislation ... must be resolved by the application of the principle of primacy of Community law.' (Case 14/68 *Walt Wilhelm* v. *Bundeskartellamt* [1969] ECR 1; 1969 CMLR 100).

The Act seeks to recognise the principle of direct applicability of Community law in the United Kingdom, by Section 2(1) requiring that rights, powers, liabilities, obligations and restrictions from time to time created or arising by or under the Treaties, and all remedies and procedures thereby provided for "as in accordance with the Treaties are without further enactment to be given legal effect or used in the United Kingdom" are to be recognised and available in law, and be enforced, allowed and followed accordingly. Thus provisions in the Treaty which have direct effect, and instruments of secondary legislation which are directly applicable under Article 189, take direct effect in law in the United Kingdom without necessitating legislation from Parliament at Westminster. In order to give effect to provisions of Community law not in force at the date of the passing of the Act, Section 2(1) refers to rights etc. arising "from time to time", and, by Section 2(4), it is stipulated that any enactment "passed or to be passed ... shall be construed and have effect subject to the foregoing provisions of this section." By such means the legislature has sought to ensure that Community law takes precedence over any provision of the laws of the United Kingdom prevailing at any time and inconsistent with it, irrespective of the date on which such legislation is adopted.

In the case of the secondary legislation which requires implementation at the national level (i.e. Community law which is not directly applicable), the Government may, in addition to legislating by Act of Parliament, and subject to the exceptions contained in paragraph 1(1) of Schedule 2 to the Act, implement Community requirements by means of Order in Council or through regulations made by a Minister of the Crown or a Government department. (Section 2(2) of the Act.)

The fundamental role of the ECJ in evolving the concept of the Community legal order is apparent from preceding paragraphs; the Act seeks to ensure that Community law is observed and applied in the United Kingdom in accordance with the case law of the ECJ. Under Section 3(1), in legal proceedings any question as to the meaning or effect of any of the Treaties, or relating to the validity, meaning or effect of any Community instrument, must be treated as a question of law, and, if not referred to the ECJ for a preliminary ruling (see

(c) above), must be determined in accordance with the principles laid down by, and any relevant decision of, the ECJ. Since Community law is thus part of the law administered by the courts in the United Kingdom, a preliminary ruling of the ECJ given as a result of a request under Article 177 must be followed by a United Kingdom court and, subject to the rules of precedent, must be followed by any other court in the United Kingdom in the event that the same question requires adjudication.

Evidence

SEE ALSO UNDER HIGH COURT PROCEEDINGS, *p. 172, post*

AFFIDAVITS AND DEPOSITIONS

By O. 38, r. 2 (3), upon any motion, petition or summons, evidence may be given by affidavit unless, in relation to such proceedings, the R.S.C. provide otherwise, or the court otherwise directs; the court may, on the application of any party, order the person making the affidavit to attend for cross-examination and where, after such an order has been made, the person in question does not attend, his affidavit must not be used as evidence without the leave of the court. The rule applies only to affidavits as to facts which there is jurisdiction to consider (*Abrahams* v. *Dunlop Pneumatic Tyre Co.*, [1905] 1 K.B. 46); and in the preparation of affidavits care ought always to be taken to set out the real facts and such facts only as are within the knowledge of the witness. In interlocutory matters, it is frequently allowable to state matters of belief; but an omission to state the grounds of the belief may be punished by costs. A person will not be exempted from cross-examination merely by withdrawing his affidavit.

The general form is: 197.. No ... In the High Court of Justice, ... Division, (*if in Chancery*) Group A or B. In the matter of ——, Between A.B. plaintiff and C.D. defendant. I, E.F., of (*place and description*) make oath and say as follows: 1——; 2——, etc.

As to oaths and affirmations and form of jurat, see *post*. No affidavit is sufficient if sworn before the solicitor acting for the party on whose behalf it is to be used (O. 41, r. 8). As to affidavits in Commonwealth countries, *see* O. 41, r. 12. The fee in respect of each affidavit is 50p and for each exhibit marked, 20p. *See* the Commissioners for Oaths (Fees) Order, 1972. Affidavits sworn before issue of the writ may be used, but must be resworn and filed. The Commissioner's signature must be clearly legible or elucidated by means of a rubber stamp or otherwise in order that there may be no difficulty in identifying the person before whom the affidavit was sworn.

Affidavits should be written or typed or printed bookwise on judicature foolscap on both sides of the paper. Carbon duplicates of typewritten matter will not be accepted. An affidavit may be partly printed and partly written. Black ink should always be used. Dates and sums should be in figures and if this rule is infringed Chancery masters have authority to order the affidavit to be taken off the file and sworn correctly at the Solicitor's expense. The expression "and/or" must not be used. Alterations and interlineations should be authenticated by the initials of the Commissioner. Scandalous matter may be ordered to be struck out. In the case of an illiterate or blind deponent, the officer administering the oath should certify that the affidavit was read over and understood by such deponent.

When correspondence is copied and exhibited in a bundle the pages must be numbered consecutively and tied together with tape and the knot sealed. When original letters and copies of replies are exhibited as one document they must be tied together with tape and the knot sealed, a front leaf must be attached stating that the bundle consists of so many originals and so many copies. When documents other than correspondence are exhibited in one bundle a front leaf must be attached setting out a list of the documents, with dates, and the bundle must be tied together with tape and the knot sealed. The practice of putting in copies in order to save the originals from being marked as exhibits is wrong. An affidavit in a foreign language may be filed with a translation.

Before use, an affidavit must be stamped with the proper filing stamp; and when used, it must be left with the proper officer of court for filing. There should be indorsed a note showing on whose behalf it is filed. The general place of filing is the Central Office, but in appropriate cases this is done at the Admiralty and Probate Registries and in the Crown Office Department. When the original affidavit is filed, an office copy duly authenticated by the seal of the office may be used for all purposes. Where an affidavit is to be used in support of an application in Chancery Chambers, notice to the other parties must be given.

Affidavits for use in an action should not be sworn before the commencement of the action in which they are to be used, or they will have to be resworn (but see *Practice Direction*, [1969] 2 All E.R. 639, para. 2).

Depositions taken before an officer of the court or other person appointed to take the examination must be written by or in presence of the examiner. In form, they should be as it were the statement of the witness; but in special circumstances the form of question and answer may be used. If an objection is raised to any question, the examiner should state his opinion about the matter, and, without deciding upon the relevancy, etc., of the question he should note the objection in the deposition. When complete, the deposition should be read over to the witness and signed by him, all in the presence of the parties. Should the witness refuse to sign the examiner should do so.

The original deposition authenticated by the examiner should be filed in the Central Office (filing fee 25p).

Depositions are not allowed to be used in evidence at a trial without consent of the party against whom they are used unless the deponent is dead or unable from sickness, etc., to attend. One month's notice in writing of the intention to use must be given.

See further, Evidence taken by Examiners, p. 165, *post*.

OATHS AND AFFIRMATIONS

Since the Oaths Act, 1909, the oath is to be taken while the person sworn is holding the Testament in his uplifted [right] hand. The form of oath now taken by a witness in a cause is this: "I swear by Almighty God that the evidence I shall give shall be the truth, the whole truth, and nothing but the truth."

On an enquiry the witness's oath is: "I swear by Almighty God that I will true answer make to all such questions as shall be demanded of me."

The Children and Young Persons Act, 1963, s. 28, prescribed a new form of oath for use in juvenile courts and by children and young persons in other courts, the words "I promise before Almighty God" being substituted for "I swear by Almighty God".

Affirmation: "Every person upon objecting to being sworn, and stating, as the ground of such objection, either that he has no religious belief, or that the taking of an oath is contrary to his religious belief, shall be permitted to make his solemn affirmation instead of taking an oath in all places and for all purposes where an oath shall be required by law . . ." (Oaths Act, 1888, s. 1). The provisions of s. 1 of the 1888 Act also now apply to a person to whom it is not reasonably practicable to administer an oath in accordance with his religious belief (Oaths Act, 1961, s. 1 (1)). Such a person may also be required (as distinct from "permitted") to make a solemn affirmation (*ibid.*, s. 1 (2)). The form is: "I, A.B., do solemnly, sincerely, and truly declare and affirm that . . ."

Oaths and affirmations may be administered in Welsh in any court in Wales; *see* the Welsh Courts Act, 1942, s. 2, and for authorised translations of the prescribed forms, *see* the Welsh Courts (Oaths and Interpreters) Rules, 1943, S.R. & O. 1943 No. 683, as amended.

As to the administration of Oaths in this country in foreign civil proceedings see the Oaths and Evidence (Overseas Authorities and Countries) Act, 1963.

Affidavits: The Commissioner should ask the deponent his name and if the signature is his, and show him any exhibits and then request him, while holding the Testament in his uplifted hand, to repeat after him:—"I [John Denman Smith] do swear by Almighty God that this name [J. D. Smith] is my name and handwriting, that the contents of this my affidavit are true and that these are the exhibits therein referred to." Where there are two or more deponents to the affidavit the last part of the oath should be "and that the contents of this affidavit, so far as they are therein stated to be deposed to by me are true."

Forms of Jurat: "Sworn at in the county of   this   day of   , 19 Before me X.Y. a Commissioner for Oaths": or "Sworn by the deponent A.B. (or the deponents A.B. and C.D.) at," &c. [as before]. Where the deponent is blind or illiterate the Commissioner must read the affidavit over to him and explain the exhibits and ask if he understands, and the jurat then runs: "Sworn by the said A.B. at   , in the county of   , this   day of   , 19 . Before me, I having first truly, distinctly and audibly read over the contents of this affidavit [and explained the nature and effect of the exhibits therein referred to] to the deponent [who is blind], and he appeared perfectly to understand the same and made his mark, or signed his name] hereto in my presence, X.Y., a Commissioner for Oaths."

Where the deponent is deaf and dumb the Commissioner should first point to deponent's signature putting to him at the same time the following question in written form. "A.B. is that your name and signature?" On receiving gesticulation of assent Commissioner should then ask deponent in writing. "You do swear by Almighty God that the contents of this your affidavit are true?" to which deponent must indicate assent. Ordinary form of jurat can be used.

Executors and Administrators

SEE ADMINISTRATION OF ESTATES

High Court Proceedings

COMMENCING PROCEEDINGS IN THE HIGH COURT

(See generally The Supreme Court Practice 1976)

Proceedings in the High Court can be commenced by:—(*i*) writ of summons, (*ii*) originating summons, (*iii*) originating motion and (*iv*) petition. The mode of commencing proceedings is dealt with by O. 5. The four methods are dealt with in broad outline by a separate order for each method. O. 6 relates to writs of summons, O. 7 to originating summonses, O. 8 to originating motions and O. 9 to petitions. Motions in pending proceedings are also dealt with by O. 8.

PLACE OF ISSUE

Writs of summons and originating summonses in the Queen's Bench Division are issued out of the Central Office, Royal Courts of Justice, or the appropriate District Registry. In Chancery matters writs of summons are also issued in the Central Office or the District Registry, but originating summonses are issued only in the Central Office or in the Leeds, Liverpool, Manchester, Newcastle-upon-Tyne or Preston District Registeries. Applications under O. 88, r. 1 may be issued in the Liverpool and Manchester District Registries, or in any District Registry if the mortgaged property is within the district of that Registry. Applications under O. 97, r. 1 may be issued out of any district Registry for the district in which the premises to which the claim or application relates are situated.

Originating notices of motion by which proceedings assigned to the Queens Bench Division are begun in the Queens Bench Division, are issued out of the Central Office or in an Admiralty matter in the Admiralty Registry. Those in the Chancery Division are issued out of the Central Office or out of the Leeds, Liverpool, Manchester, Newcastle-upon-Tyne or Preston District Registries. Petitions in Chancery matters, a rare method of commencing proceedings now, except in patent matters, are presented in the Chancery Registrar's Office, Room 160, Royal Courts of Justice or in the Leeds, Liverpool, Manchester, Newcastle-upon-Tyne or Preston District Registries. This is excluding petitions in bankruptcy or company matters. Writs in Probate Actions are now issued out of the Central Office (O. 76, r. 2) and certain Admiralty Actions are now assigned to the Queen's Bench Division and taken by the Admiralty Court (O. 75, r. 2).

INDORSEMENT OF ADDRESS

The writ, if the plaintiff sues by a solicitor, must be indorsed with the address of the plaintiff and his solicitor's name or firm and place of business within the jurisdiction. If the solicitor is an agent the name and address of his principal should be given. If the plaintiff sues in person, the writ must be indorsed with his place of residence, and if it is not within the jurisdiction,

or if he has no place of residence, an address for service within the jurisdiction and his occupation (O. 6, r. 5).

INDORSEMENT OF CLAIM

Writs of summons must be indorsed before issue with a statement of the plaintiff's claim or a concise statement of the nature of the claim or relief required (O. 6, r. 2). If a concise statement only is given a separate statement of claim has to be served.

Where a party sues or is sued in a representative capacity the indorsement must show the capacity in which he sues or is sued (O. 6, r. 3); in probate actions the indorsement must state the nature of the interest of the plaintiff and defendant in the estate (O. 76, r. 2). Attention is drawn to O. 76 Rule 2(2) (b) and notes on "Leave to issue". In actions for libel the indorsement must state sufficient particulars to identify the publication (O. 82, r. 2).

For particulars to be given where the action is brought by a moneylender, see O. 83, rr. 2 and 3, and under hire purchase agreements (O. 84, r. 2).

For indorsement of claim in proceedings against the Crown, see O. 77, r. 3, and where the action is brought on behalf of a person resident outside the scheduled territories, see O. 6, r. 3 (2).

In the High Court the stamp fee on a Writ and Originating Summons (where no other fee is specially provided) is £15. On an Originating Summons for approval of an Infant Settlement it is £5 and on one for payment out of court of a sum not exceeding £500 it is £2. All other fees payable in the High Court and in Matrimonial Causes are set out in the new Supreme Court Fees Order 1975 (S.I. No. 1343/L15) and the Matrimonial Causes Fees Order 1975 (S.I. 1975 No. 1346) which both came into operation on the 1st October 1975.

ORIGINATING SUMMONSES

Originating summons must be served within 12 months of issue, except in the case of an application under s. 24 of the Landlord and Tenant Act, 1954, when the service limit is one month.

They may be taken out (A) where it is desired to get the declaration of the court as to the proper construction of a document or statute and as to the

rights of any party reference thereto, (B) where questions arise relating to Administrations and Trusts, (C) where questions arise relating to Mortgages, (D) where applications are made under a number of miscellaneous enactments including the Inheritance (Family Provision) Act, 1938, certain provisions of the Restrictive Trade Practice Act,

1956, the Charities Act, 1960 and the Landlord and Tenant Acts, 1927 and 1954. They are regulated (A) by O. 5, r. 4, (B) by O. 85, (C) by O. 88, r. 1, and (D) by various Orders, including, for the Acts mentioned above, O. 99, O. 105, O. 108 and O. 97.

The practice on issuing, serving, entering appearance, etc. is dealt with by O. 7, r. 5 (issuing), O. 10, r. 5 (serving); and O. 12, r. 9 (appearance).

For the practice after issue and service see O. 28.

For forms of originating summonses see the Supreme Court Practice, Vol. 2, Appendix A, Forms 8 to 11A.

See the 2nd Supplement to the Supreme Court Practice 1976 for alteration and addition to Form 10.

MORTGAGE ACTIONS

When all applications by mortgagees for possession of property or payment of principal or arrears of instalments or interest were transferred to the Chancery Division the Judges issued a special Practice Direction, which is contained in O. 88 and to a large extent has been embodied in the rules to this new Order:—

In every case the plaintiff's right to the order sought must be established. There is no right to an order merely because the defendant fails to appear.

This order also deals with foreclosure, sale in lieu thereof and redemption. No action with reference to a mortgage should be commenced without reference to this Order and the Notes thereto which have been considerably revised.

The Originating Summons may be issued in a District Registry.

Part IV of the Administration of Justice Act, 1970 which came into force on 1 February 1971 made alterations as to jurisdiction and procedure. By section 37 it gave the County Court exclusive jurisdiction in certain actions for possession. The Courts Act 1971 deleted the County Palatine of Lancaster from Section 37, and the limit imposed by Section 48 of the County Courts Act 1959 has been extended by the Administration of Justice Act 1973, Section 6 (1) and Schedule 2, Part I.

SERVICE OF WRIT

Service of writs is regulated by O. 10. A writ must be served personally. There are exceptions for which see the notes to O. 10, r. 1 two of these being (a). If a Solicitor endorses an acceptance of service on the writ and (b) an order for substituted service is made under O. 65, r. 4. If an appearance is not entered after acceptance of service a certificate of non-appearance can be obtained by production of the writ to the Central Office, containing the acceptance of service endorsed. Service is effected by handing to the defendant a true copy of the writ, and by producing to him the original if such production is requested by him. If requested a writ may be served at any time of the day or night, and on any day but Sunday, unless leave of the Court is obtained in the case of urgency (O. 65, r. 10). This rule does not apply in relation to the service of a writ *in rem* or the execution of a warrant of arrest in admiralty proceedings (O. 75, 11 (3)).

As to the service of documents on minors and patients, see O. 80, r. 16.

Partners, if named individually on the writ and not sued in the firm name, must be served individually, but if sued as a firm, the writ may be served upon any one or more of the partners or at the principal place of business of the partnership within the jurisdiction on any person having at the time of service control or management of the partnership business. Where partners are sued as a firm a notice in writing must also be handed to the individual served stating that he is served as a partner or as a person having control or management of the business, or in both characters (O. 81, r. 3). As to appearance after service on partner who denies he was partner or liable as such at material times, see O. 81, r. 4 (2)-(4).

Service on a body corporate is effected by serving the mayor, chairman or president of the body or the town clerk, clerk, secretary, treasurer or other similar officer thereof (O. 65 r. 3). It should be noted that clerk in this connection means the chief officer, such as the Clerk to an Urban District Council and not a clerk performing merely executive duties, such as a cashier.

As to service on an agent contracting for a principal out of the jurisdiction *see* O. 10, r. 2.

As to service of Legal Process in civil proceedings on members of H.M. Forces, the memorandum issued in December 1974 by The Lord Chancellor's Office, replaces that issued in April 1944 at page 1022 of the Supreme Court Practice 1973 Part I (65/2/7 to 65/2/16 inclusive). The new memorandum is set out on pages 1060–1063 of the *Supreme Court Practice* 1976 (Part I).

As to service on the Crown, *see* O. 77, r. 4.

In an action for possession of land, where the premises are vacant and service of writ cannot otherwise be effected, a copy of the writ may be affixed to some conspicuous part of the land and this will in a proper case be treated as good service. Judgment, however, cannot be obtained by default when service has been effected in this manner, unless leave has been previously given so to effect service, or unless an order is obtained that such service is to be deemed good and sufficient (O. 10, r. 4).

Unless within three days after personal service a person serving a writ indorses it with the day of the week and date on which it was served, where and upon whom it was served and in what capacity any person other than the defendant was served, the plaintiff is not entitled to enter final or interlocutory judgment against the defendant in default of appearance or defence (O. 10, r. 1 (4)). Failure to make the indorsement will not nullify any judgment entered in default but will be an irregularity which may be waived, or the Court may set aside the judgment, wholly or in part. There is power to extend the time beyond three days for indorsement.

SERVICE OUT OF THE JURISDICTION

Service out of the jurisdiction generally is regulated by O. 11 of the rules of the Supreme Court, but certain actions in Admiralty proceedings come within O. 75, r. 4.

Before service out of the jurisdiction of a writ can be allowed, the claim must fall within the provision of any one of the sub-rules of O. 11, r. 1.

If there is more than one defendant sued and some are within the jurisdiction, the writ is issued and marked "Not for service out of the jurisdiction.' Application is then made for leave to issue a concurrent writ for service out.

Unless the writ is to be served in Scotland, Northern Ireland, the Isle of Man or the Channel Islands application is for leave to issue the writ or a concurrent writ and serve notice of the writ or concurrent writ (O. 11, r. 3).

See also O. 11, r. 2 as to service out of the jurisdiction in certain actions of contract, rr. 5 and 6 as to service abroad, and r. 7 as to service on a High Contracting Party to the Conventions set out in Schedule 1 of the Carriage by Air Act 1961, and the Schedules to the Carriage by Air (Supplementary Provisions) Act 1962 and the Carriage of Goods by Road Act 1965.

The application for leave to effect service out of the jurisdiction is made *ex parte* in chambers supported by an affidavit showing the grounds upon which it is made. As to the details which such an affidavit should contain, see the practice notes in The Supreme Court Practice to O. 11, r. 4. As to the duty of a solicitor before applying for leave to examine with care the material put before him for the purpose of making the application, see *Bloomfield* v. *Serenyi*, [1945] 2 All E.R. 646, C.A.

Service of originating summonses, petitions, originating notices of motion and of some other proceedings, may also be allowed to be serviced out of the jurisdiction under O. 11, r. 9, which does not prejudice the practice by which notice may in proper cases be ordered to be given to persons out of the jurisdiction, of proceedings in the English courts which may affect their interests, without claiming or affecting to exercise jurisdiction over such persons.

O. 69 deals with service of foreign process in England and O. 11, r. 6,

with the service of English process abroad in those countries with which a convention has been concluded.

Order 11 applies in the case of proceedings by the Crown, but not in the case of proceedings against the Crown (O. 77, r. 4).

PLEADINGS

For general rules as to the contents and drafting of pleadings, *see* O. 18.

Service of Pleadings. Pleadings are to be served in accordance with the following rules before the issue of the summons for directions.

The Statement of Claim must be served with the Writ or within 14 days after the defendant appears unless the court gives leave to the contrary or a statement of claim is indorsed on the writ (O. 18, r. 1). In Probate actions the time is 6 weeks after entry of appearance or 8 days after the filing of an affidavit under O. 76, r. 5 whichever is the later (O. 76, r. 7).

The Defence must be served within 14 days from the time limited for appearance or from the service of the

statement of claim whichever is the later (O. 18, r. 2 (1)). These provisions do not apply (a) when a summons under O. 14, r. 1 is served on a defendant before he serves his defence, unless by the order made on the summons he is given leave to defend the action, in which case he must serve his defence within 14 days after the making of the order unless it specifies some other time (O. 18, r. 2 (2)); (b) when either party applies under O. 18, r. 21 for trial without further pleading.

Reply and Defence to Counterclaim are governed by O. 18, r. 3.

The Reply to a defence and a defence to a counterclaim must be served within 14 days (O. 18, r. 3 (4)).

No subsequent pleading is allowed without leave (O. 18, r. 4).

ORDER 14

PROCEDURE

The Application. The principal rules to be observed in obtaining summary judgment under O. 14 are as follows:—

Where a statement of claim has been served on a defendant and the defendant has entered an appearance the plaintiff may apply to the court for judgment on the ground that the defendant has no defence to a claim or part of a claim included in the writ, or no defence except as to the amount of damages. These provisions apply to all actions begun by writ in the Queen's Bench Division (including the Admiralty Court) or the Chancery Division except for actions which include a claim for libel, slander, malicious prosecution, false imprisonment or seduction, an action which includes a claim based on an allegation of fraud, and an Admiralty action in rem (O. 14, r. 1). O. 14 does not apply to actions to

which O. 86 (Specific Performance) applies.

Unless the court dismisses the application or the defendant satisfies the court that there should for any reason be a trial of the claim or part of a claim the court may give such judgment for the plaintiff as may be just having regard to the nature of the remedy or relief claimed (O. 14, r. 3).

The application by the plaintiff must be made by summons returnable not less than ten clear days after service accompanied by a copy of the affidavit and exhibits referred to therein (O. 14, r. 2).

A defendant may apply for summary judgment on a counterclaim (O. 14, r. 5).

An application under O. 14, r. 1 cannot be made in proceedings against the Crown and an application under O. 14, r. 5. cannot be made in proceedings by the Crown (O. 77, r. 7 (1)).

All allegations necessary to show a cause of action by the plaintiff against the defendant should be made on the writ, *e.g.* if the action is by indorsee against drawer of a bill of exchange, the drawing, acceptance, indorsements down to plaintiff and notice of dishonour to defendant (or the circumstances excusing such notice) should all be stated. So if plaintiff claims under an assignment, the assignor's right must be shown and the assignment stated.

Interest. On a specially indorsed writ interest is claimable but may not be awarded.

Delivery of Specific Chattel. See O. 14, r. 9.

LEAVE TO DEFEND

The defendant may show cause against the application by affidavit, or otherwise to the satisfaction of the Court (O. 14, r. 4 (1)).

"A defendant ought not to be shut out from defending unless it is very clear indeed that he has no case." (Lord Esher in *Shurmer* v. *Young* (1889), 33 Sol. Jo. 155). "By the very words of the order the plaintiff is not to be allowed to sign judgment merely because the defendant's affidavit does not show a complete defence" (Brett, L.J., in *Ray* v. *Barker* (1879), 4 Ex. D. 283). "Where there is a fair probability of a defence unconditional leave to defend ought to be given" (Wills, J., in *Ward* v. *Plumbley* (1890), 6 T.L.R. 198). But "when the judge is satisfied not only that there is no defence, but no fairly arguable point, it is his duty to give effect to [the rule] and to give judgment for the plaintiff (Jessel, M.R., in *Anglo-Italian Bank* v. *Davies* (1878), 38 L.T. 201).

Crown debts may now be recovered by this procedure; the affidavit in support need not be as full as required by O. 14, r. 2 when the Crown is suing (O. 77, r. 7).

Counterclaim. A counterclaim is not a defence, but if a good counterclaim be shown the defendant should as a rule be allowed to raise it in the action. But judgment may be given for the claim and a stay of execution ordered till the trial of the counterclaim (*Chirgwin* v. *Russell* (1910), 27 T.L.R. 21, C.A.).

Fraud. Where in an action on a bill by a holder in due course the defendant alleges fraud in the inception of the bill he is entitled to unconditional leave to defend (*Edwards* v. *Davis*, [1888] W.N. 59; *Jones* v. *Whitaker* (1888), 57 L.T. 216).

The Order. On the hearing of the application the master may allow the plaintiff to enter judgment where the claim is liquidated.

If leave to defend is given it may be given unconditionally, or subject to such terms as the master may think fit (O. 14, r. 4 (3)). There may be judgment for part of the Claim with leave to defend as to the residue (O. 14, r. 8). As to judgment against one of several defendants *see* O. 14, r. 8, and for entry of judgment against a defendant in default of appearance, in certain actions O. 13, rr. 1–6.

When judgment is given for assessment of damages and no method of assessment is therein specified they shall be assessed by a Master in Chambers, District Registrar or Admiralty Registrar (O. 37). The practice as to obtaining an appointment before the Chancery and Queen's Bench Masters is set out in 37/2/1 and 37/2/2 (page 564) of the *Supreme Court Practice*, 1976, Part I.

CONDITIONAL LEAVE TO DEFEND

The conditions of bringing money into court or giving security should not be applied where the defendant swears to facts which *may* be a defence even though their truth is doubtful (*Jacobs* v. *Booth's Distillery* (1902), 85 L.T. 262). "Even though the case for the plaintiff appeared to be supported by documents and letters yet it might be that there was a defence, and if there was a fair probability of a defence a defence ought to be allowed without imposing the condition of payment of money into court" (Wills, J., in *Ward* v. *Plumbley* (1890), 6 T.L.R. 198). When it seems clear that the plaintiff will succeed, but there are circumstances which make it reasonable that the defendant should test his right in court, conditional leave may be granted (*Parker* v. *Brand* (1891), 7 T.L.R. 462).

The affidavit proving the claim must be made by the plaintiff or someone who can speak positively to the facts.

SUBSEQUENT PROCEEDINGS

Where the court gives a plaintiff or defendant leave, whether conditional or unconditional, to defend an action or counterclaim with respect to a claim or part of a claim, or gives judgment but also orders a stay of execution pending trial of the action or counterclaim it shall give directions as to the further conduct of the action as if the application for judgment were a summons for directions under O. 25 (O. 14, r. 6). With the consent of the parties the action may be referred for trial to a Queen's Bench Master (O. 14, r. 6) in which case appeal lies to the Court of Appeal (O. 58, r. 2).

SUMMARY JUDGMENT FOR SPECIFIC PERFORMANCE

As to obtaining summary judgment in actions for specific performance, *see* O. 86.

APPLICATIONS FOR TRIAL WITHOUT PLEADINGS

This is governed by O. 18, r. 21, and application can be made by either plaintiff or defendant. The application is made by summons. There are exceptions to the type of actions to which this rule refers.

SUMMONS FOR DIRECTIONS UNDER ORDER 25

The intention of this Order is to enable all directions of an interlocutory nature to be given on one summons. In fact, in many cases it acts as a guide to the course an action takes.

The practice part of the Order may be summarised as follows:—

(1) *Rule 1 (1)*
The Plaintiff must take out a summons for directions within one month after close of pleadings. This summons is returnable in not less than 14 days.

(2) *Rule 1 (4)*
If the Plaintiff fails to take out the summons within one month, a Defendant may take out the summons or apply to dismiss the action.

(3) *Rule 2 (4)*
Subject to the provisions of r. 2 (5) and (6) and except where the parties agree to an order under O. 33, no Order as to place and mode of trial shall be made until all other directions asked for by the summons have been dealt with.

(4) *Rule 2 (7)*
On adjournment without a fixed day the summons may be restored for hearing by any party on two days' notice.

(5) *Rule 7 (1)*
Any party to whom the summons has been addressed may apply by notice in writing for such directions required if the directions required differ from those asked for in the summons. This notice is to be served on the other parties not less than 7 days before the hearing of the summons.

(6) *Rule 7 (2)*
This sub-rule allows any party to whom the summons is addressed to apply in a similar way for any directions different from those contained in the summons after the first hearing of the summons. The notice here is to be served at least 7 days before the hearing.

The notices referred to in r. 7 (1) and (2) are not issued in any office of the court and do not require a fee, but in each case a copy must be lodged in the appropriate summons room before the hearing.

(7) *Rule 7 (3)*
This sub-rule allows any party to issue a notice for further directions after the summons has been dealt with but must be issued before judgment. This is issued in the same way as the original summons. [NOTE.—It is issued at the risk of the party applying for costs (see Supreme Court Costs Rules, 1959, r. 7 (2)).]

(8) In the Chancery Division orders made on a summons for directions or on any notices thereunder are not drawn up unless requested by the solicitors.

(9) There are many exceptions to the actions to which Order 25 applies, as to which, *see* Rule 1 (2) thereof.

DISCOVERY AND INSPECTION OF DOCUMENTS

Discovery of Documents. O. 24, r. 2 provides for discovery to be given without an order. Each party must within 14 days after pleadings are deemed to be closed make and serve on the other party a list of documents relating to the action or matter except in actions relating to (a) accidents involving a vehicle; (b) for the recovery of any penalty recoverable by virtue of any enactment and (c) infringement of a Patent. Without prejudice to any directions under O. 16, r. 4; O. 24, r. 2 does not apply to third party proceedings. The list must be in form 26 of Appendix A and under O. 24, r. 9 be accompanied by a notice giving a time within 7 days after service and naming a place for inspection of the documents.

Again, by O. 24, r. 10, every party to an action is entitled at any time to serve a notice on any other party in whose pleadings or affidavits reference is made to any documents requiring him to produce such documents for inspection or to be copied. The party on whom such a notice is served must within 4 days serve on the party giving the notice a notice stating a time, within 7 days, and place at which the documents may be inspected and stating which, if any, he objects to produce and on what grounds.

Under O. 24, r. 7 power is given to order discovery of a particular document, documents, or class of documents. The application is supported by an affidavit stating the documents, and that the opposite party is believed to have or have had such documents in his possession, and that they are material to the action.

A new Rule 7a of Order 24 provides the machinery for dealing with disclosure of documents before commencement of proceedings and by a person not a party to proceedings already commenced (sections 31 and 32 of the Administration of Justice Act, 1970, respectively).

Rule 4 provides that any issue or question in the cause or matter may be determined before discovery. Where such an order is made O. 25, rr. 2 to 7, except with regard to service of a notice under r. 7 (1), apply as if the application upon which the order was made were a summons for directions under O. 25.

Generally, by O. 24, r. 16, if any party required to make discovery, etc., fails to comply with the rule or order in question he is liable to have his action dismissed or his defence struck out and to committal.

DISCOVERY BY INTERROGATORIES

Any party to an action may apply by summons or notice under O. 25, r. 7 for leave to deliver interrogatories relating to the matter in dispute (O. 26, r. 1). Other interrogatories are irrelevant, even though admissible on oral cross examination. In an action for libel or slander where the defendant pleads that the words or matters complained of are fair comment on a matter of public interest or were published on a privileged occasion, no interrogatories as to the defendant's sources of information or grounds of belief shall be allowed (O. 82, r. 6). The application for leave to deliver is to a Master in Chambers. There is a discretion as to allowing leave to interrogate. In the case of a corporation or company, application may be made for the interrogation of any officer or member:—such application should be served on

the body, and where the party proposed to be interrogated is not the secretary or other proper officer also on such party. In the case of proceedings by the Crown or to which the Crown is a party, *see* O. 77, r. 12. If documents are referred to in a statement of claim, a defendant is entitled to inspect other than privileged documents. The judge may order production at the trial (*Macalpine* v. *Calder*, [1893] 1 Q.B. 545).

Grounds for resisting Discovery. Discovery will not be ordered when and so far as the court or judge deems it unnecessary either for disposing fairly of the matter or to save costs. Further it may be resisted as of right: (1) as being incriminating (see *Blunt* v. *Park Lane Hotel, Ltd.*, [1942] 2 K.B. 253, C.A.); (2) on the ground of privilege;

(3) as disclosing the party's evidence; (4) as injunction to the public interest. Where a company is interrogated, the person answering need not disclose facts other than those acquired in the course of his employment. A restrictive stipulation, however, will not affect the right when litigation has arisen.

Form, etc. of Interrogatories. By O. 26, r. 1, a copy of the proposed interrogatories must be delivered with the summons or notice of application. In deciding, any offer of the party sought to be interrogated to deliver particulars or make admissions or produce documents is to be taken into account, and by r. 4 objection to answer any interrogatory on the ground of privilege may be taken in the affidavit in answer. It is permissible to interrogate as to facts which will inform as to evidence to be obtained or to gain admissions as to anything to be proved (*A.-G. v. Gaskill* (1882), 20 Ch. D. 519, C.A.). Accounts may sometimes be required. But discovery relating to the quantum of damages is irrelevant, although interrogations as to the amount of damages claimed are in some instances admissible; see the Supreme Court Practice.

The answer to interrogatories is by affidavit. Should an answer be insufficient, further answers can be ordered (O. 26, r. 5).

TRANSFER FROM HIGH COURT TO COUNTY COURT

GENERALLY

Ss. 45, 50, 54, 59, 63, 68 and 146 of the County Courts Act, 1959 deal with transfer from High Court to County Court. There is also provision in s. 67 for the transfer by agreement in certain cases.

The application to transfer is made to a Master by Summons supported by an Affidavit. It may be made at any stage though it should not be delayed.

Practice to effect Transfer after Order made.—See C.C.R., O. 16, Part II and s. 77. The order and the writ or copies thereof and other documents as the High Court may direct are to be lodged with the County Court Registrar and it is the duty of the party who does so to apply to the proper officer of the Supreme Court to send to the Registrar all pleadings etc. filed in the High Court. A statement as to names etc. of the several parties to the action is also to be lodged with the Registrar. The Registrar will then enter the action for trial. Upon being served with notice of trial the defendant will proceed as if the action had been brought in the County Court. If Plaintiff delays it is not necessary for the Defendant to apply to the High Court to have the action dismissed, as he can enter himself in the County Court. Until the Writ and Order are lodged in the County Court the action remains a High Court action and orders may be made in it by the High Court in the interval (*D'Errico v. Samuel,* [1896] 1 Q.B. 163).

After lodgment the action becomes a County Court action and the High Court ceases to have jurisdiction even to entertain an appeal from the order remitting (*Buckley v. Nat. Theatres,* [1913] K.B. 277 C.A.), but the County Court can amend, order discovery etc. (*Spring v. Fernandez,* [1912] 1 K.B. 294; *Mentors v. Evans,* [1912] 3 K.B. 174, C.A.)

S. 45. *Actions of Contract or Tort*
These actions may be transferred where the amount claimed or remaining in dispute does not exceed £1000. The fact that a Plaintiff has obtained an order entitling him to sue in the High Court in *forma pauperis* is immaterial (*Cook v. Imperial Tobacco Co.,* [1922] 2 K.B. 158, C.A.).

S. 50 *Actions for Recovery of Land*
S. 48 (1) gives the County Court jurisdiction to hear any such action. The limit of net annual value for rating of the land imposed by this section has now been extended to £1000 (Administration of Justice Act 1973 Section 6 (1) and Schedule 2 Part I).

S. 54. *Equity Proceedings*
This section applies to any action or matter assigned to the Chancery Division and is by virtue of any enactment for the time being in force within the jurisdiction of the County Court. Such jurisdiction is to be found in s. 52.

S. 59. *Admiralty actions*
S. 56 sets out the jurisdiction of the County Court.

S. 63. *Contentious Probate proceedings*
S. 62 sets out the jurisdiction of the County Court.

S. 68. *Interpleader proceedings*
Where the amount or the value

of the matter does not exceed £1000.

S. 146. *Applications to attach debts or levy execution against a member of a firm.*
This applies where the application is for the attachment of or leave to issue execution for a debt not exceeding £1000.

For costs in transferred cases see p. 97, *ante.*

TRANSFER TO HIGH COURT FROM COUNTY COURT

(1) GENERALLY

Under s. 115 of the County Courts Act, 1959, any proceedings commenced in a county court may, by order of the High Court or a judge thereof, be removed for trial in the High Court by certiorari (*see* O. 53, r. 7) or otherwise (*see e.g. Lee v. Hay's Wharf, Ltd. (Proprietors)*, [1940] 2 K.B. 306, C.A.: order for removal made by Master). Under s. 106 actions of replevin may be removed into the High Court by certiorari, if the defendant makes an application in that behalf and gives security to be approved by a master for such amount not exceeding £150 as he may think fit. As to how the application is made generally, see notes to O. 53, r. 7, in the Supreme Court Practice and as to the practice in the Chancery Division. After removal of the proceedings the defendant must enter an appearance in the High Court, and the proceedings thereafter are governed by the Rules of the Supreme Court.

Under s. 85 proceedings in a county court may be transferred to the High Court on an application made to the High Court for the issue of a commission, request or order to examine witnesses abroad for the purposes of such proceedings. The application is made to master in the Q.B.D. by summons under O. 107, r. 3.

For circumstances in which proceedings instituted against the Crown in a County Court may be removed and transferred into the High Court, and the procedure relating thereto, see Crown Proceedings Act, 1947, s. 20 and O. 78.

In addition to the above provisions the following proceedings may also be transferred from a country court to the High Court (A) by order of the county court under ss. 43, 44 and 66, and (B) by order of the High Court under ss. 49, 58 and 65.

(2) ACTIONS OF CONTRACT OR TORT

By s. 44 where there is commenced in a county court any action founded on contract or tort wherein the plaintiff claims a sum exceeding £150, the defendant may give notice that he objects to the action being tried in the court, and where such a notice is given the judge must order the action to be transferred to the High Court, if the defendant gives security approved by the registrar for such amount as the Registrar may determine and the judge certifies that in his opinion some important question of law or fact is likely to arise.

Application to Transfer.—The notice of objection is given under C.C.R., O. 16, r. 18.

Proceedings Transferred from the County Court.—O. 78 applies where an order has been made for the transfer of proceedings from a county court to the High Court under sections 43, 44, 49, 58, 65, 66 or 85 of the County Courts Act, 1959, or under s. 20 of the Crown Proceedings Act, 1947. When the documents have been sent to the proper officer under C.C.R. O. 16, r. 19 the documents are filed and an entry of the filing is made in the Clause Book and notice is sent to all parties that the Action is proceeding in the High Court in London or the District Registry and that the Defendant is required to enter an appearance within 7 days of receiving the notice. The defendant then enters an appearance and O. 78, r.

3 provides that O. 12, r. 1 to 4 shall apply as to such entry and O. 12 Rules 1, 2 and 4 shall apply as if the proceedings transferred were an Action begun by Writ, and as if the appropriate office for the purpose of those rules was either (a) The District Registry; (b) The Central Office or (c) The Admiralty Registry. If the defendant does not appear the plaintiff, after having entered an address for service in the cause book, may, with the leave of court, enter judgment with costs; and notwithstanding O. 65, r. 9 the summons must be served on the defendant at his address for service in the County Court (O. 78, r. 4); if the defendant appears the plaintiff within 7 days must cause the plaintiff's address for service to be entered in the cause book, and either serve a summons for directions on the defendant returnable in not less than 21 days or except where the defendant is the Crown, serve a summons for judgment under O. 14, r. 1 and where the plaintiff serves a summons for directions, O. 25, rr. 2–7, apply with any necessary modifications. If the plaintiff fails to do either within 7 days, the defendant may take out a summons for directions or apply for an order to dismiss the action. On an application by a defendant to dismiss the action the court may either dismiss the action or may deal with the application as if it were a summons for directions (O. 78, r. 5).

(3) PROCEEDINGS OUTSIDE JURISDICTION OF COUNTY COURT

By s. 66, where any proceedings are commenced in a county court in which a county court has no jurisdiction, the court must, unless it is given jurisdiction by an agreement made under ss. 42, 53 or 56 (5), order the proceedings to be transferred to the High Court; but, if on the application of any defendant, it appears to the court that the plaintiff or one of the plaintiffs knew or ought to have known that the court had no jurisdiction in the proceedings, the court may, instead of ordering the proceedings to be transferred order them to be struck out.

The Transfer, how effected.—See C.C.R., O. 16, r. 16.

Procedure on Transfer.—The procedure is the same as in actions transferred under s. 44; see *supra*.

(4) ACTIONS FOR RECOVERY OF LAND

By s. 49, where an action for the recovery of land is commenced in a county court, the defendant or his landlord may apply to a judge of the High Court at chambers for a summons to the plaintiff to show cause why the action should not be transferred to the High Court on the ground that the title to land having at the time when the action was commenced a net annual value for rating exceeding £1000 (Administration of Justice Act 1973 s. 6 (1) and Schedule 2, Part II would be affected by the decision in the action, and on the hearing of any such summons, the judge of the High Court may order the action to be transferred to the High Court.

Application to Transfer.—The application may be made to a master of the Queen's Bench Division; it must be made on notice within 8 days of the service of the summons on the defendant, inclusive of the day of service (C.C.R., O. 16, r. 17).

Procedure on Transfer.—The procedure is the same as in actions transferred under s. 44; see *supra*.

(5) COUNTERCLAIMS

By s. 65, where, in any action or matter commenced in a county court, any counterclaim or set off and counterclaim of any defendant involves matter beyond the jurisdiction of a county court, any party to the action or matter may apply to the High Court or a judge thereof for an order that the whole proceedings or the proceedings on the counterclaim or set off and counterclaim be transferred to the High Court. On any such application the High Court or judge may order either: (a) the whole proceedings to be transferred to the High Court; or (b) the whole proceedings to be heard and determined in the county court; or (c) the proceedings on the counterclaim or set off and counterclaim to be transferred to the High Court and the proceedings on the plaintiff's claim and the defence thereto other than the set off (if any) to be heard and determined in the county court; but where an order is made under para. (c) and judgment on the claim if given for the plaintiff, execution thereon, unless the High Court or a judge thereof at any time otherwise orders, must be stayed until the proceedings transferred to the High Court have been concluded.

Application to Transfer.—The application is made to a Master by originating summons under R.S.C., O. 107, r. 2; it must be made within 8 days of the receipt of the counterclaim by the plaintiff, or, if made by the Defendant within 8 days of the delivery of the counterclaim by him at the court office.

Procedure on Transfer.—See O. 78. The procedure thereafter is the same as in actions transferred under s. 44; see *supra.*

EVIDENCE TAKEN BY EXAMINERS

When witnesses cannot reasonably attend the trial, application by summons, supported by affidavit may be made to a master or Registrar that their evidence may be taken before an examiner or officer of the court, and if the affidavit is satisfactory an order will be made (O. 39, r. 1). The person to take the examination is either one named in the order, or "an examiner of the court" (r. 1). When it is the latter, the order is taken to Room 160 and the clerk there names the examiner. The order is then taken to the examiner for the examination who fixes time and place of the appointment. For the fees and expenses of Examiners of the Court see Rule 19. Notice of the appointment is given to the other side forthwith, and if necessary subpoenas are served on the witnesses requiring them to attend. Prior to the appointment the examiner must be furnished "with copies of such of the documents in the cause or matter as are necessary to inform the examiner of the questions at issue in the cause or matter" (r. 7).

As to taking the evidence of military witnesses liable to be sent abroad, see *Practice Note,* [1942] W.N. 87, C.A.

The public has no right to be present. The examiner writes the deposition in the first person and in narrative form, but whenever it is considered desirable question and answer are written down. Brief paper, written on one side, is generally used, and the first sheet is headed with the title of the cause and such words as these: "The deposition of A.B., a witness called on behalf of the [plaintiff] taken pursuant to the order of   herein dated before me, X.Y., an examiner of the court [or the examiner appointed by the said order]. A.B. of   , being sworn and examined by Mr.   , counsel for the [plaintiff] says:" When the cross-examination begins the examiner writes: "Cross-examined by Mr   , counsel for the [defendant]," and so for the re-examination.

The examiner has power to administer oaths and affirmations, and he may put any questions to the witness as to the meaning of any answer, or as to any matter arising in the course of the examination (r. 8 (2)).

Any question which may be objected to shall be set out in the depositions, together with the answers and the grounds for the objection. The validity of the objection must be decided by the court, not the examiner, but the examiner must state his opinion thereon to the parties and the statement of his opinion must be set out in the deposition or in a statement annexed thereto (r. 10).

In like manner the non-attendance of a witness or his refusal to be sworn or to answer is to be recorded and certified by the examiner (r. 5), and so apparently is his refusal to produce a document included in his subpoena. A witness duly subpoenaed is bound to attend, give evidence, and produce documents before an examiner just as he is before the court (rr. 4 and 5).

When the examination of a witness is completed, the examiner reads over the deposition to him, and if he desires to alter or qualify an answer, the alteration or qualification is written in the margin, prefaced by the words, "On reading over the deposition the witness said." The witness signs the deposition at the end, and it is better that he should sign each sheet. Alterations and interlineations are to be initialled by the examiner.

When the whole examination is concluded, the examiner writes at the foot of the depositions, "The above depositions, written on   sheets of paper, were taken by me at   on   and were read over by me to the witness; the examination began at   o'clock

and finished at   o'clock.   X.Y.,
examiner."

The examiner is not to hand the depositions to either of the parties, but is to send them in an envelope under seal, to "The Senior Master, Central Office, Royal Courts of Justice, London, WC2A 2LL" where the action is in the Chancery or Queen's Bench Division or to "The Senior Registrar Family Division, Somerset House, London WC2R 1LP" where the action is in that division. Where the proceedings are in Admiralty they are sent to the Admiralty Registrar, Royal Courts of Justice, or the examiner may himself file the depositions in the Admiralty Registry. For cases proceeding in the District Registry to the appropriate District Registrar. No postage need be paid unless posted abroad.

The examiner may make a special report to the court touching such examination, and the conduct or absence of any witness or other person thereat, and the court may direct such proceedings to be taken, or make such order upon the report as it thinks fit (r. 13).

The *examiner's fees* are fixed by r. 19. In addition to the £10.00 for the appointment (which is kept whether the matter goes further or not) he is entitled to £2.50 "for each hour or part thereof (after the first hour) occupied in an examination within 3 miles of the Royal Courts of Justice, or £17.00 for each day of 6 hours or part of a day occupied in an examination beyond 3 miles from the Royal Courts of Justice." His clerk gets 25p (payable on obtaining the appointment) and in addition 25p per day where the examination occupies more than 3 hours. The party prosecuting the order must also pay all reasonable travelling and other expenses, including charges for the room (other than the examiner's chambers) where the examination is taken.

MODE OF TRIAL: SETTING DOWN: NOTIFICATIONS

The place and mode of trial of an action begun by writ are determined by an order made on the summons for directions (O. 33, r. 4). There is absolute discretion over the order (*Hope v. G.W. Rly. Co.*, [1937] I All E.R. 625) except that (i) if a charge of fraud against a party or a claim in respect of libel, slander, malicious prosecution, false imprisonment, seduction or breach of promise of marriage is in issue in an action in the Queen's Bench Division, the action must be ordered to be tried with a jury unless trial requires prolonged examination of documents or accounts or some scientific or local investigation that cannot conveniently be made with a jury (see notes to O. 33, r. 5), and (ii) civil proceedings by or against the Crown must not be transferred from London unless the Crown consents (O. 77, r. 2). Actions in the Chancery Division or Queen's Bench Division other than a criminal proceeding by the Crown, may subject to any right to trial by jury, be ordered to be tried before an official referee (O. 36, r. 1). [N.B. City of London Special Jury abolished by Section 4 of Courts Act, 1971.] If it is desirable than an action in the Chancery Division should be tried with a jury, the action is usually transferred to the Queen's Bench Division.

Setting down: notification. An order made in an action begun by writ must, if the trial is before a judge, fix a period within which the plaintiff must set the action down for trial (O. 34, r. 2). In the Queen's Bench Division such an order (unless the action is placed in the commercial list or special paper or any corresponding list) must contain an estimate of the length of the trial and, if the action is to be tried in London, should, subject to directions, specify the list into which the action must be put. Requirements for the documents are to be lodged on setting down are in O. 34. R. 3, and O. 34. Rr. 4 & 5 deal with the lists of actions in the Queens Bench and Chancery Divisions set down for trial in and out of London. If an action is not set down for trial within the period fixed, the defendant may set the action down or may apply for it to be dismissed (*ibid.*, r. (2)).

A party who sets an action down for trial must notify the other parties within twenty-four hours that he has done so and must also notify them without delay of any official communication that he receives as to the date fixed for trial or the date before which the action will not be tried; but no notice of trial is necessary (*ibid.*, r. 8 (1)). All parties to an action entered in any list are under a duty to furnish without delay to the officer in charge of the list all available information as to the action being or being likely to be settled, or affecting the estimated length of the trial, and, if the action is settled or withdrawn, to notify that officer without delay and take such steps as are necessary to withdraw the record (*ibid.*, r. 8 (2); cf. *Williamson v. British Boxing Board of Control*, [1958] 2 All E.R. 228). There is also a new Rule 8 (3) regarding performance of the duty imposed by 8 (2) on a plaintiff who gives notice of acceptance of payment into Court pursuant to O. 22, r. 3 (1).

Admiralty actions. Distinct provision is made regarding the trial of admiralty actions, which, in the absence of special reason to the contrary, must be tried in London before a judge without a jury; the order must determine whether or not the trial is to be with assessors (O. 75, r. 25). The action must be set down within 7 days after the fixing of the date for trial (r. 26 (2)). All parties are under a duty, if an action set down for trial is settled or withdrawn, to notify the admiralty registry without delay and to take such steps as are necessary to vacate the date fixed for trial (*ibid.*, r. 26 (4)). The filing of an agreement of terms of settlement under O. 75, r. 35 will vacate the date fixed for trial unless the agreement expressly provides to the contrary.

Matrimonial Causes. See p. 263, *post.*

MISCELLANEOUS PRACTICE POINTS

Abandonment.—Should proceedings be abandoned, the defendant will be entitled to costs reasonably incurred before the abandonment. The costs of an abandoned motion should be asked for on next motion day. Where an appeal is abandoned, the respondent may obtain an order dismissing the appeal with costs; or the parties may consent to an order dismissing the appeal and directing taxation, etc. of respondent's costs. For the practice to be followed where an appellant does not desire to prosecute an appeal, see direction given on February 21st, 1938. (See 59/5/3, page 857 *Supreme Court Practice*, 1976, Part I.) Where a cause has been in abeyance for a year, a month's notice of intention to proceed must be given (O. 3, r. 6).

Abatement of Proceedings.—A cause or matter does not abate by reason of the death or bankruptcy of any of the parties if the cause of action survives (O. 15, r. 7 (1)). Where a party dies after the verdict or finding of issues of fact and before judgment is entered, judgement may be entered notwithstanding the death (O. 35, r. 9). And since, by the Law Reform (Miscellaneous Provisions) Act, 1934, the application of the maxim *actio personalis*

moritur cum persona is limited to cases of defamation, seduction, enticement of a spouse, and damages for adultery, there will not be many cases of abatement on the ground that the cause of action does not survive. Where at any stage of the proceedings the interest or liability of any party is assigned or transmitted to and devolves upon some other person the court may order that other person to be made a party in substitution for the first mentioned party (O. 15, r. 7 (2)). In both the Chancery and Queen's Bench Divisions application to continue an action by or against a new party is to the Master in Chambers *ex parte* on affidavit. In the case of a new plaintiff, his written consent is not essential (15/6/5). Where an appeal is pending to the House of Lords, leave to make the change is given by the Court of Appeal. After an order is obtained it is served and noted in the cause book O. 15, r. 7 (4).

Order for Early Trial.—Whenever an application is made before trial for an injunction or other order, the court may, without going into the whole merits of the application, make an order for early trial (O. 29, r. 5). The Court of Appeal will in a specially urgent case advance the hearing of an appeal.

Misjoinder and Joinder of Parties.—No cause or matter shall be defeated by the misjoinder or nonjoinder of any party, and the court may determine the issues or questions in dispute so far as they affect the rights and interests of the parties. At any stage in the proceedings the court may order an improper or unnecessary party to cease to be a party or order (*a*) any person who ought to have been joined as a party or whose presence is necessary, or (*b*) any person between whom and any party there is a question or issue arising out of or related to the cause or matter, which the Court considers can be determined between that person and the party, but no person may be added as a plaintiff without his consent signified in writing or in such other manner as may be authorised (O. 15, r. 6). In a representative action a person represented though not named in the writ will be added or substituted for a Plaintiff who falls out. If a plaintiff wishes to add a defendant, he will be allowed to do so where such defendant can properly be joined, on payment of the costs occasioned by the addition; the added defendant should not be served with the summons asking for leave to add him, but he must as a rule be duly served with the writ. A defendant can apply to add another party as a defendant. The jurisdiction of the court is entirely discretionary (*Gurtner* v. *Circuit*, [1968] 1 All E.R. 328; [1968] 2 W.L.R. 668). A person not a party may also apply to be added on showing that he has a legal, and not a commercial interest in the proceedings (*Re I. G. Farbenindustrie A. G. Agreement*, [1944] Ch. 41).

Amendments Generally.—For the purpose of determining the real question in controversy between the parties to any proceedings or for correcting any defect or error in any proceedings the court may at any stage order any document in the proceedings to be amended on such terms as to costs or otherwise as may be just. These provisions do not apply in relation to a judgment or order (O. 20, r. 8). As a general rule, any amendment will be made that is necessary "for the purpose of determining the real question in controversy between the parties" and the practice of allowing amendments in every case, even during the trial, has

been considered in *Hunt* v. *Rice & Son, Ltd.*, [1937] 3 All E.R. 715, and *Leavey & Co., Ltd.* v. *Hirst & Co., Ltd.*, [1944] K.B. 24. But if the party applying is acting *mala fide* or some irreparable injury to his opponent would result, amendment will be refused; so, the addition of a newly accrued cause of action or of a cause of action which has since the writ become barred by the Limitation Act will not be allowed leave to amend will usually involve the party amending in the costs occasioned by the application. A party may, without leave, amend any pleading of his once before the pleadings are deemed closed and, where he does so, he must serve the amended pleading on the opposite party. Where an amended statement of claim is served on a defendant he may amend his defence or counterclaim, which must be served within 14 days after the delivery of the amended statement of claim. Where an amended defence or counterclaim is served by a defendant the plaintiff may amend his reply or defence to counterclaim, which must be delivered within 14 days after the delivery of the amended defence or counterclaim (O. 20, r. 3).

Appearance.—O. 12, r. 1, allows a defendant other than a body corporate to enter an appearance either by a solicitor or in person. The memorandum of appearance (O. 12, r. 3) may be handed in or sent by post to the appropriate office (O. 12, r. 1 (3)).

Contempt of Court.—Disobedience to orders or process involves merely a punitive or disciplinary contempt, whereas obstruction of the administration of justice is of a criminal nature. Instead of ordering committal, the court may take the more lenient course of granting an injunction against repetition of the act or contempt. From 1st October, 1966, committal is the appropriate punishment for disobedience to an Order of the Court. No provision is now made for attachment. The application is by motion. If an application is heard in private under O. 52, r. 6 the court must publicly announce the name of any person committed and the nature of his contempt. There is a right of appeal to the Court of Appeal or (from certain inferior courts) to a Divisional Court. There is also a right of appeal from the

C.A. and the Div. Court to the House of Lords (Admin. of Justice Act, 1960, s. 13). A party in contempt will not as a general rule be allowed to make any application to the court, though it may appeal on the ground of want of jurisdiction from an order made after the contempt was committed.

Orders by ex parte Motion.—As a rule parties who will be affected by an order should have notice of the motion (O. 8, r. 2); but in case of emergency or to avoid mischievous delay, the court or a judge may make an order *ex parte* upon terms as to costs or subject to other undertaking as may seem just, in which case any party affected may move to set aside such order. Cases in which *ex parte* orders be made are: orders of course, applications for leave to apply for an order of *mandamus*, prohibition or *certiorari* injunction or a receiver, and proceedings under O. 54 for *habeas corpus*. Affidavits are generally required in support of motions other than of course. Where an *ex parte* application has been refused by the court below, a similar application may be made to the Court of Appeal *ex parte* within 7 days from such refusal or such enlarged time as either court may allow (O. 59, rr. 14 (3), 15).

Hours of Business.—The offices of the Supreme Court are open on every day of the year except

(a) Saturdays and Sundays
(b) Good Friday and the day after Easter Monday
(c) Christmas Eve or
   (i) if that day is a Saturday then 23rd December
   (ii) if that day is a Sunday or Tuesday then 27th December
(d) Christmas day and if that day is a Friday or Saturday then 28th December
(e) Bank holidays in England and Wales under the Banking and Financial Dealings Act 1971 and
(f) such other days as the Lord Chancellor with the concurrence of the Lord Chief Justice the Master of the Rolls and the President of the Family Division may direct

The hours of opening to the public are 10 a.m.–4·30 p.m. during term

sittings and all other days during the vacations except during the month of August when the hours are 10 a.m.–2·30 p.m. The Principal Probate Registry is open from 10 a.m.–4·30 p.m. during sittings and vacations

The District Registries are open on such days and during such hours as the Lord Chancellor may direct, and in the absence of any direction, shall be open on days and during the hours when the offices of the appropriate County Court are open (O. 64, r. 8).

Official Referees sit, and observe vacations as set out in O. 64, r. 1 but may sit during vacation if expedient to do so (O. 64, r. 6)

Moneylenders' Actions.—See O. 83.

Motions.—Any applications to a Divisional Court or to a judge in court are made by motion. In other cases application should be by summons. Two clear days' notice is invariably required except in cases of extreme urgency (O. 8, r. 2 (2)). The notice should state clearly the nature of the order sought; and in the case of motions to remit or set aside an award (O. 73, r. 5), or for committal (O. 52, r. 4) must state in general terms the grounds of the application; and a copy of any affidavit to be used should be served therewith. A notice of motion for judgment in the Chancery Division set down to be heard as a short cause must state the name of the judge sitting to hear motions on the day named in the notice of motion. In the Queen's Bench Division, motions for judgment are entered in the Crown Office (Room 478), fee £7.50 on the motion. In the Chancery Division, motions (other than Motions for Judgment) are not set down except in the long vacation, when they are set down in Room 136 but are heard on the ordinary motion days. A copy of the notice of motion must be supplied to the judge. Service will be under O. 65. Notice of motion to commit should be served personally upon the respondent. No formal appearance is necessary. Evidence may be given by affidavit (O. 38, r. 2 (3)), except in case of motion for judgment. Affidavits should correctly set out the facts (see *Rummens* v. *Cecil* (1910), 129 L.T.J. 263, *per* Eve, J.). Where an order has been made for the attendance for cross-examination of the person making an affidavit, if the person does not attend his affidavit shall not be used as evidence without the leave of the court (O. 38, r. 2 (3)). A motion may be saved by mentioning it any time before the court has risen on the day for which notice of the motion was given, and notwithstanding the court has finished the hearing of motions. But a motion entered by special notice, *e.g.* for judgment, new trial, an originating motion and the like, can only be saved by motion or by consent of the court. The hearing of any motion or application may be adjourned from time to time (O. 8, r. 5).

Office Copies.—All copies sealed with a seal of any office or department of the High Court and purporting to be copies of a document filed in that office or department are presumed to be office copies; and may be received in evidence; and no signed authentication or other formality is necessary (O. 38, r. 10). As to the examination of office copies, see *Coleman* v. *Coleman*, [1905] W.N. 160.

Payment into and out of Court.—In an action to recover a debt or damages, or in Admiralty proceedings, a sum may be paid into court by way of satisfaction at any time after appearance and in libel or slander actions this may be done with a defence denying liability. In London, payment in takes place at the Law Courts Branch of the Bank of England; in Liverpool and Manchester, at the respective branches of that Bank in these towns; and in District Registries, at the Registries. There must be presented to the Bank a request in prescribed form; and where the payment is on a notice or pleading, the latter must be produced and the Bank's receipt for the money will be given thereon; and where on an order, then the order or office copy thereof must similarly be produced. Payment out is on request to the Accountant-General (Forms 10 and 11 of the new forms in Appendix 1 to the Supreme Court Funds Rules 1975 which came into operation on the 15th December 1975), who will give a direction for payment unless the case falls within one of the exceptions mentioned in Supreme Court Funds Rules, 1975, r. 43. For payment out of the court money paid in

under the Exchange Control Act 1947, see O. 22, r. 9.

Order 22 allows a defendant, after appearance, to pay a sum of money into court in satisfaction of a claim for a debt or damages, and contains subsequent provisions for acceptance or non-acceptance by the plaintiff.

If the plaintiff accepts money paid into court in satisfaction of his claim, or if he accepts a sum or sums paid in respect of one or more of specified causes of action, and gives notice that he abandons the others, he may, after four days from payment-out and unless the court otherwise order, tax his costs incurred to the time of receipt of notice of payment into court, and forty-eight hours after taxation may sign judgment for his taxed costs (O. 62, r. 10 (2)).

If a party to an action who as third party or one of two or more tortfeasors in respect of the same damage, stands to be held liable to contribute towards any debt or damages received against another party, makes a written offer (at any time after appearance) to that party to contribute to a specified extent to the debt or damages, that offer shall not be brought to the attention of the judge until all the questions of liability and amount of debt or damages have been decided (O. 16, r. 10).

Where a party accepts money paid into court in satisfaction of a cause of action for libel or slander the plaintiff or defendant, as the case may be, may apply to a judge in chambers by summons for leave to make in open court a statement in terms approved by the judge (O. 82, r. 5 (1)) (see *Wolseley* v. *Associated Newspapers, Ltd.*, [1934] 1 K.B. 448, C.A.). For the practice, see *Practice Note*, [1943] W.N. 6.

Within 21 days of receipt of notice of payment into court the plaintiff may accept the money by giving notice in Form No. 24 in Appendix A to every defendant in the action (O. 22, r. 3 (1)), whereupon all further proceedings in the action or in respect of the specified cause or causes of action, as the case may be, shall be stayed (r. 3 (4)).

Counterclaim.—A plaintiff or other person made defendant to a counterclaim may pay money into court in accordance with O. 22, r. 1 with the necessary modifications (*ibid.*, r. 6).

Payment of hospital expenses.—Where in an action or counterclaim for bodily injury caused by a motor vehicle on a road or in a public place in which the claim for damages includes a sum for hospital expenses and the party against whom the claim is made pays the amount for which he is liable under s. 212 of the Road Traffic Act, 1960 for hospital treatment to the person making the claim, he must give notice of the payment to all other parties within 7 days (O. 22, r. 12).

Non-disclosure of payment into Court.—Except where a defence of tender before action is pleaded or proceedings are stayed by virtue of O. 22, r. 3(4) the fact that money has been paid into court under O. 22, rr. 1–6, must not be pleaded and no communication of that fact may be made to the court at the trial or hearing of the action or counterclaim or of any question or issue as to the debt or damages until all questions of liability and the amount of the debt or damages have been decided (O. 22, r. 7).

The judge, in exercising his discretion as to costs, will take into account both the fact that money has been paid into court and the amount of the payment (see O. 62, r. 5 (b)).

It was held that the former O. 22, r. 6, for which the present O. 22, r. 7 was substituted by the R.S.C. (Revision), 1962, was directory only, and not imperative, so that if by inadvertence or otherwise disclosure was made the whole proceedings were not vitiated, and the judge might exercise his discretion and allow the case to proceed; *Millensted* v. *Grosvenor House (Park Lane), Ltd.,* [1937] 1 All E.R. 736. The former r. 6 was held not to apply to a judge on an interlocutory application (*Williams* v. *Boag,* [1941] 1 K.B. 1, C.A.).

Printing of Documents.—Unless otherwise provided all documents for the use of the court must be written, printed or typed (O. 66, r. 2 (1)). Carbon copies will not suffice (*ibid.*). A document is deemed to be printed if produced by type lithography or stencil duplicating (*ibid.*, r. 2 (2)). A photographic copy is deemed to be produced by one of these methods (*ibid.*, r. 2 (4)). Any type used must not be smaller than 11 point type for printing or elite type for typewriting, stencil duplicat-ing or lithographic production (*ibid.,* r. 2 (3)).

On payment of the proper charges up to 10 copies of any printed document prepared by a party for use in the Supreme Court must be supplied by that party, on written request, to any other party entitled to a copy. Where the document in question is written or typewritten the party by whom it was prepared must have ready for delivery within 48 hours of the written request one copy of the document, and in the case of an affidavit of any document exhibited thereto, and must supply the copy thereafter on payment of the proper charges (O. 66, r. 3).

Unless the nature of the document renders it impracticable every document prepared for use in The Supreme Court must be of durable quality approximately 13 inches long by 8 inches wide with a margin of not less than $1\frac{1}{2}$ inches wide on the left side of the face of the paper and on the right hand of the reverse side, but paper approximately 10 inches by 8 inches may be used where these clauses take up only one side (O. 66, r. 1). International size paper A. 4 (297 mm long × 210 mm wide) will be accepted.

Shorthand Notes.—An official shorthand note is now taken of the evidence, summing up and judgment in all actions, summonses and motions tried or heard with witnesses in the Chancery Division and Queen's Bench Division, and in the Admiralty Court unless the judge otherwise directs, in pursuance of O. 68. Any reference in O. 68 to shorthand notes of proceedings now includes any record made by mechanical means (O. 68, r. 8). The fees for taking the notes are borne by public funds; the supply of, and payment for, transcripts for the use of the Court of Appeal of the official shorthand notes, and the supply of free transcripts for poor respondents, is regulated by O. 68 and the Authorised Notice of August, 1940, issued by the Lord Chancellor's Office; see also *Practice Direction,* [1943] W.N. 30. O. 68, r. 3 deals with exceptions to payments for transcripts out of Public funds in connection with Legal Aid. The official shorthand writers are provided in London by the Association of Official Shorthand Writers Ltd., whose office is Room 392.

Solicitor, where name indorsed on writ.—Where a solicitor, whose name is indorsed on any writ and who, on demand in writing made by or on behalf of any defendant, declares in writing that the writ was not issued by him or with his authority the court may, on the application of any defendant who has been served with or who has entered an appearance to the writ, stay all proceedings in the action begun by the writ (O. 6, r. 5 (4)).

Solicitor, Change of.—A solicitor acting in a matter may be changed without order for that purpose upon notice being filed in the Central Office or other appropriate office or in the district registry. A copy of the notice should be served on the other party or parties and on the former solicitor (O. 67, r. 1). When a solicitor of one party dies or becomes bankrupt or for any other reason ceases to practise and no notice of change of solicitor or notice of intention to act in person has been given, the other party may apply to the court by summons supported by affidavit for an order declaring that the solicitor has ceased to be the solicitor acting (O. 67, r. 5). When a solicitor has ceased to act for a party and the party has not given notice of change of solicitor under O. 67, r. 1 the solicitor may apply to the court for an order (see O. 67, r. 6).

As to costs in cases when a solicitor ceases to act see *Brendon* v. *Spiro*, [1937] 2 All E.R. 496, and *Warmingtons* v. *McMurray*, [1937] 1 All E.R. 562. As to the effect of a party becoming an enemy alien, see *Eichengruen* v. *Mond*, [1940] Ch. 785, C.A.: *Sovfracht (V/O)* v. *Van Udens Scheepvaart en Agentuur Maatschappij (N.V. Gebr.)*, [1943] A.C. 203.

Stay of Proceedings.—As to the general jurisdiction to stay, see Judicature Act, 1925, s. 41; the Arbitration Act, 1950, s. 4. As a general rule, pending proceedings cannot be restrained but a person may be restrained from instituting proceedings; and the court has always an inherent jurisdiction to stay proceedings which are in abuse of its process, *e.g.* where proceedings are *malâ fide*, or vexatious, etc., or where costs of a former action have not been paid, or pending the decision of a point of law, or pending payment of costs, or pending appeal. Stay of execution for

damages and costs pending an appeal will not be granted except on evidence that there is no reasonable likelihood of getting them back if the appeal succeeds. An injunction may be granted to restrain proceedings in inferior courts or before other tribunals in case of excess of jurisdiction or second action being brought in England claiming the same relief, etc. The procedure in the Queen's Bench Division is generally by summons before a Master in Chambers, and in the Chancery Division by summons or motion. In case of appeal, application may also be made either to the court appealed from at the trial after judgment, or to the Court of Appeal. Applications are frequently made on terms agreed upon between the parties. When this is done in the Chancery Division the terms, if all parties are *sui juris*, are embodied in a schedule to the order as a matter of record of the agreement between the parties, but the terms are not an order of the court. This is commonly known as a "Tomlin Order". The terms are enforced by a summons in Chambers for a 4-day order, or in some cases according to the terms by a specific performance action.

Vacation, Proceedings in.—Two judges are available during every vacation to act as vacation judges; they are normally the two last-appointed judges who have not already served as vacation judges and their term of vacation duty is one year (O. 64, r. 2 (2), (3)). All applications that require to be immediately or promptly heard must be heard in vacation by these judges. Any party may apply by summons to a judge during the long vacation for trial or hearing during that vacation and if the judge is satisfied as to the urgency of the case he may make an order accordingly (O. 64, r. 4 (2)). Applications for leave to make an application for an order of mandamus, prohibition or certiorari and the application, or an application for a writ of habeas corpus may be made in vacation to a Judge in Chambers (O. 53, rr. 1 (2), 3 (1), O. 54, r. 1 (1)).

Vexatious Proceedings.—The court has an inherent jurisdiction to dismiss any proceedings which are frivolous or vexatious or an abuse of its process. The abuse may either appear on the pleadings or be proved by affidavit or other evidence, though the court will not inquire whether the allegations in a claim or defence are true or false unless the defence is clearly inconsistent with admissions made by the party pleading it. Generally the jurisdiction will be exercised cautiously and in exceptional cases. Application should be by summons in chambers. For the purpose of appeal, the order made is an interlocutory order. Where an appeal is an abuse of process, security for costs may be ordered. A party who has made many frivolous and vexatious interlocutory applications may be precluded from doing so again without leave. And under the Judicature Act, 1925, s. 51, the Attorney General may obtain from the High Court an order prohibiting a persistent litigant from instituting proceedings without leave.

THE CONDUCT OF A TRIAL

Non-appearance of a Party.—If, when the trial of an action is called on, neither party appears, the action may be struck out of the list, or, if one party does not appear, the judge may proceed with the trial of the action or counter-claim in the absence of that party (O. 35, r. 1). Any judgment by default of this kind may be set aside on terms on application within seven days (r. 2).

As to the duty of a judge to grant an adjournment, where a party, or a witness, is prevented by illness from attending the hearing at which his evidence is material, see *Dick* v. *Piller*, [1943] 1 K.B. 497, C.A.

If both sides attend, he begins who in the absence of proof on either side would substantially fail in the action. The test is who will be entitled to judgment if no evidence is given? This being determined the other party begins. If on the case being called the defendant admits all the facts the plaintiff would have to prove, he begins; but if there are pleadings, he cannot claim the right to begin unless the admissions are on the pleadings. Where the plaintiff claims unliquidated damages this fact alone entitles him to begin, unless the defendant admits all facts as above and that the damages will be all the plaintiff claims, or unless it is clear that the damages must be an ascertained amount, or must be nominal (*Mercer* v. *Whall* (1845), 5 Q.B. 447).

Where the defence is pleaded affirmatively, the plaintiff may either adduce evidence to deal with it or wait till the defendant has endeavoured to prove his case and then call evidence in reply. If the point is simple the court will generally require the plaintiff to take the first course.

Burden of Proof.—While the burden of proof is as a rule on the person asserting a fact, it may be shifted where the truth of the allegation is peculiarly within the knowledge of one party, in which case the latter must disprove it, or where there is a presumption in favour of one party, when the opponent must rebut it.

Evidence in Libel Cases.—In actions for libel or slander, in which the defendant does not by his defence assert the truth of the statement complained of, the defendant shall not be entitled on the trial to give evidence in chief, with a view to mitigation of damages, as to the circumstances under which the libel or slander was published, or as to the character of the plaintiff, without the leave of the judge, unless seven days at least before the trial he furnishes particulars to the plaintiff of the matters as to which he intends to give evidence (O. 82, r. 7).

Miscellaneous.—It is in the judge's discretion whether he will allow a witness to be recalled.

A party will as a rule be bound by the way he has shaped and conducted his case at the trial, and will not get a new trial on points he has waived or overlooked.

On a point of law, two counsel a side will be heard.

Where there are several defendants defending separately, counsel for him who is named first in the record generally (but not necessarily) conducts the general defence: counsel for the others are not entitled to address the jury separately except in so far as the cases of their clients differ from the general defence.

The right to the general reply (the

"last word") belongs to him who does not adduce evidence or, failing this, to him who began (O. 35, r. 7): a plaintiff (assuming him to begin) may at the close of his case ask his opponent if he intends to adduce evidence and if told that he does not, the plaintiff proceeds to sum up, the defendant thus getting the last word. Summing up cannot be claimed as of right by either plaintiff or defendant in a County Court. When a defendant adduces evidence the plaintiff has a right to reply even in a County Court (*Clack* v. *Clack*, [1906] 1 K.B. 483).

Where a jury before hearing the defendant's evidence intimates its opinion for the plaintiff, this *per se* does not entitle the defendant to refuse to proceed (*Campbell* v. *Hackney Furn'g Co.* (1906), 22 T.L.R. 318).

If you want a certain question put to the jury, you must ask for it (*per* Lord Halsbury in *Neville* v. *Fine Arts Co.*, [1897] A.C. 76).

In *Ryland* v. *Jackson and Brodie* (1902), 18 T.L.R. 574, one defendant gave evidence which was material to the case of the other defendant who, however, called no witnesses. Bruce, J., after consulting with other judges, held that the proper order of speeches to the jury was, (1) the defendant who

called witnesses, (2) the plaintiff, (3) the defendant who did not call witnesses.

If in his summing up the judge incorrectly states the facts you may offer to correct him (*Payne* v. *Ibbitson* (1858), 7 L.J. Ex. 340), but you are not bound even in a County Court, to suggest to him at the time that he is wrongly directing the jury in point of law (*ibid.*, and *Handley* v. *London, Edinburgh & Glasgow Ass. Co.*, [1902] 1 K.B. 350).

When once a jury has returned a general verdict, the judge may not put any question to them (*Arnold* v. *Jeffreys*, [1914] 1 K.B. 512).

Counsel may bind his client by a compromise of the matter in dispute, but if he does so on terms different from those the client expressly stipulates for, the compromise is not binding (*Neale* v. *Gordon-Lennox*, [1902] A.C. 465). The rights of a person under disability, e.g., an infant or a mentally disordered person, cannot be compromised unless the court deems the compromise for his benefit (*Rhodes* v. *Swithinbank* (1889), 22 Q.B.D. 577, and O. 80, r. 10).

A certificate for a Special Jury must be obtained immediately after verdict (*Barker* v. *Lewis*, [1913] 3 K.B. 34). When the plaintiff gets no more than was paid into court, he usually puts all costs after the payment in.

RULES AS TO EVIDENCE

The *lex fori* governs as to what questions may or may not be asked, and as to what documents may be produced. The admissibility of any question is for the judge to decide, and he must discover what the issue is. Questions must be relevant to the issue to be tried, and will be so relevant if they inquire about *res gestae*, i.e., facts forming part of the transaction in dispute, as distinguished from *res inter alios actae*.

Primary evidence, *i.e.*, the best evidence procurable, should always be offered. The best evidence is that of persons who have directly observed facts or heard statements, original documents, etc. But where the best evidence is shown not to be procurable, secondary evidence will be allowed, *e.g.*, certified copies, counterparts, or oral evidence as to contents. The court will take judicial notice of certain

facts, *e.g.*, practice of the court, Acts of Parliament, the law of nations, and matters of general notoriety. Evidence may be rejected which cannot be adequately tested.

At common law, hearsay evidence was not generally admissible as evidence of the truth of the words spoken though it was admissible to prove in fact of the speaking when this was in issue. There were a certain number of well-defined exceptions to the "hearsay rule" both at common law and under the Evidence Act, 1938. Under Part 1 of the Civil Evidence Act, 1968, which came into force on 1st October 1969, both oral and documentary hearsay statements are in general admissible in civil proceedings subject to certain procedural safeguards.

For the detailed provisions as to different types of hearsay evidence, *e.g.* statements by persons to be called as witnesses in the proceedings (s. 2 (2)), witness's previous statements (s. 3), records compiled by person under a duty to make such records (s. 4) and statements produced by computers (s. 5), reference should be made to the 1968 Act. Under s. 9 there is a saving as to certain hearsay evidence formerly admissible at common law. In general such evidence continues to be admissible and the procedural safeguards of the Act do not apply.

Under s. 8 new rules of court have been made governing the procedure for the admission of hearsay evidence (see S.I. 1969 No. 1105 adding a new Part III to Order 38 (below)). In general a party wishing to introduce such evidence must give notice within 21 days of a cause being set down or adjourned into court (O. 38, r. 21). The notice must contain particulars required by rr. 22, 23 or 24 as appropriate. Within a further 21 days the other party may give a counternotice under r. 26 requiring the maker of the statement to be called as a witness. Otherwise the statement is admissible. Provision is made for determining the issue where it is alleged that the maker of the statement cannot be called (see rr. 25, 27).

Order 38, r. 1 provides that subject to O. 38, the Civil Evidence Act, 1968, and any other enactment relating to evidence, any fact required to be proved at the trial of any action commenced by writ of summons by the evidence of witnesses shall be proved by the examination of the witnesses orally and in open court. By r. 2 the court may, at or before the trial, order that all or any of the evidence therein shall be given by affidavit and the order may be made or given on such terms as to filing and giving of copies of the affidavits and as to production of the deponents for cross-examination as the court may think fit, but subject to any such terms and to any such subsequent order the deponents shall not be subject to cross-examination and need not attend the trial for the purpose. Rule 3 provides that at or before the trial the court may order that evidence of any particular fact may be given at the trial in such manner as may be specified by the order, (2) that this power extends in particular to ordering that evidence of any particular fact may be given at the trial

(a) by statement on oath of information or belief, or (b) by production of documents or entries in books, or (c) by copies of documents or entries in books, or (d) in the case of a fact which is or was a matter of common knowledge either generally or in a particular district, by the production of a specified newspaper which contains a statement of that fact. By r. 4, the number of medical or other expert witnesses to be called at the trial shall be limited as specified in the order. Rule 5 provides that, unless otherwise ordered, no plan, photograph or model shall be receivable in evidence at the trial unless at least 10 days before the trial the parties have been given an opportunity to inspect it and to agree to its admission without further proof. By the Rules of the Supreme Court (Amendment) 1974 (S.I. 1974 No. 295) Rule 6 has been deleted and the former Rule 7 becomes Rule 6. There is a new Rule 7 dealing with evidence of finding on foreign law. This was added by the same amendment. This amendment also introduced a new Rule 34 (Statements of Opinion) and a new Part IV of Order 38 (Expert Evidence) (Rules 35–44) and the old Rule 6 is substantially reproduced by the new Rule 40.

Privileged communications are such as contain secrets in the possession of public officials, communications between husband and wife (see *Shenton* v. *Tyler*, [1939] Ch. 620, C.A.) to or between counsel, solicitors, etc., information given with a view to the detection of crime and the like. Letters written without prejudice are privileged if *bona fide* written during a dispute or negotiation with a view to a settlement of differences; but such a letter containing a threat may be used to prove the threat, etc. A privileged letter will protect subsequent correspondence continuing the same subject.

Expert evidence is admissible where knowledge of a fact depends upon special training or experience; but not where the court is sitting with assessors or the jury can form an opinion. So medical evidence (see *Harrison* v. *Liverpool Corpn.*, [1943] 2 All E.R. 449, C.A.) is admissible to explain a disease, handwriting may be proved, a foreign language or law (see *Re Amand*, [1941] 2 K.B. 239; *Re Amand* (No. 2), [1942] 1 K.B. 445), may be interpreted; it is otherwise however, if the question is the probable cause of an accident, the construction of a document, etc.

By O. 40 an expert, to be called a "Court Expert", may be appointed by the court on the application of either party, to inquire and report on any question of fact or opinion not being one of law or construction of documents. This only applies to non-jury cases. O. 103, r. 27 provides for the appointment by the court of an independent scientific adviser in any proceedings under the Patents Acts, 1949–1961 or in proceedings for infringement of a patent and that the provisions of O. 40 (except rr. 1 and 5) shall apply to a scientific adviser as they apply to a "Court Expert". A scientific adviser appointed under O. 103, r. 27 may also be a Court Expert under O. 40 and may under O. 40, r. 2 make a formal report to the Court, but the informal advice given by a scientific adviser is not such a Report ([1972] R.P.C. 457 at p. 471) (*Valensi* v. *British Radio Corporation Ltd.*, [1973] R. P. C. 337 at p. 350).

Affidavits made in one proceeding are generally admissible in a subsequent proceeding against the party who made them. Banker's books are not generally producible without an order of court unless the bank is a party to the cause. Telegram forms can be produced by officials of the Post Office; and copies on proof of destruction of the originals.

Leading questions are questions which by their form suggest the answer desired.

Such questions are not permissible in examination in chief unless the evidence is of facts which are not disputed or unless the judge gives leave on the ground that your witness is hostile. Questions as to opinion and belief are not generally admissible.

A party producing a witness may not impeach his credit by general evidence of bad character, but if the judge is of the opinion that the witness is adverse he may contradict him by other evidence, or, by leave of the judge, prove that he has made at other times a statement inconsistent with his present testimony; in which latter case, the circumstances of the supposed statement, sufficient to designate the particular occasion, must be mentioned to the witness, and he must be asked whether or not he made such statement (Criminal Procedure Act, 1865, s. 3).

In cross-examination, leading questions may freely be asked so long as they do not wilfully mislead by misstatement or false assumption. Questions not confined to the subject matter may be asked in cross-examination if relevant to the matters in issue, or tending to impeach veracity, etc. Vexatious questions, however, must not be asked, nor questions not relevant to any matter proper to be inquired into in the case or matter. A witness may be cross-examined as to previous statements in writing made by him without the writing being shown to him, but before using the writing to contradict him, his attention must be called to the parts of the writing so intended to be used, and the judge may require the production to him of the writing for inspection.

In re-examination, questions may not be asked introducing wholly new matter.

Where a party is taken by surprise by a point made against him at the trial, the judge should allow him to produce rebutting evidence although he has "closed his case" (*Bigsby* v. *Dickinson* (1876), Ch. D. 24, C.A.). Evidence may be given to show that a witness is not impartial (*R.* v. *Yewin* (1811), 2 Camp. 638), or has been bribed (*R.* v. *Langhorn* (1679), 7 State Tr. 418), or has endeavoured to suborn others (*R.* v. *Strafford* (1640), 3 State Tr. 1381; *A.-G.* v. *Hitchcock* (1847), 1 Exch. 93).

JUDGMENT PROPER IN CERTAIN CASES

WHERE MONEY PAID INTO COURT.— Where the defendant pays into court, either with or without a denial of liability, and the verdict gives the plaintiff no more than the amount so paid in, the defendant is entitled to judgment. This is usually drawn up so that the plaintiff gets costs down to the paying in, and the defendant the costs afterwards (*Powell* v. *Vickers*, [1907] 1 K.B. 71, C.A.). The money paid in, up to the amount awarded by the jury, belongs to the plaintiff, and the onus is on the defendant to show why it should not be paid out to him (*Powell* v. *Vickers, supra*).

These principles are to be applied in the County Court (*Wood* v. *Leetham* (1892), 61 L.J.Q.B. 215; *Dunn* v. *S.E.R.*, [1903] 1 K.B. 358).

The question of costs is one for the discretion of the judge subject to the Supreme Court Costs Rules, 1959, r. 5.

MARRIED WOMEN.—Where the defendant was a married woman an ordinary judgment could not, before the Law Reform (Married Women and Tortfeasors) Act 1935, came into operation (August 2nd 1935), be given against her; it must be against her separate estate, in the form settled in *Scott* v. *Morley* (1887), 20 Q.B.D., 120, C.A. If a married woman began proceedings the court had power to deal with property which she was restrained from anticipating. Since the above Act a married woman can sue and be sued and judgment enforced against her as if she were a *feme sole* and the above special form of judgment is no longer applicable.

CLAIMS BY MINORS AND PERSONS UNDER DISABILITY.—O. 80, rr. 10 and 11 provide that in any cause or matter in which money is claimed by or on behalf of a person under disability, no settlement, compromise or payment and no acceptance of money paid into court whenever entered into or made shall, so far as it relates to that person's claim, be valid without the approval of the court, and where money paid into court is accepted by or on behalf of any such person or is recovered by or on behalf of or is adjudged, ordered or agreed to be paid to or for the benefit of any such person, it shall be dealt with in accordance with directions given by the court whether under s. 174 of the County Courts Act, 1959, or r. 12 of O. 80 or both and not otherwise; and the directions may provide that the money shall wholly or partly be paid into the High Court and invested or otherwise dealt with there and may include any general or special direction that the court or judge thinks fit to give as to how the money is to be applied or dealt with, etc. [NOTE.—As to the position regarding costs, see O. 62, r. 30.]

If a settlement is reached before action commenced the approval of the court or its directions can be obtained by issue of an Originating summons. It is no longer necessary to issue a Writ for this purpose (O. 80, r. 11).

PRACTICE AS TO INJUNCTIONS

An injunction is an order directing a party either to refrain from doing or to do some specified act or thing, being called in the former case a restrictive injunction and in the latter case a mandatory injunction. Again, a perpetual injunction finally determines the rights of the parties, whereas an interlocutory injunction merely operates until an action can be tried. An injunction is personal and does not run with the land (*A.-G.* v. *Dorking Union Guardians* (1882), 20 Ch. D. 595, C.A.). Injunctions, both perpetual and interlocutory, can be granted by the County Court (Judicature Act, 1926, s. 202).

Only a party who is able to show a sufficient interest will be entitled to this form of relief. If the public interest only is involved, the Attorney General must be joined. On the other hand, the party against whom relief is sought may be liable although as yet he has no active intention of doing the act complained of, if he as a matter of fact claims the right of doing the act. An injunction will not be made to extend to absent parties not directly interested who would be injuriously affected by it. Where relief is sought against a company, if the secretary has been joined as a defendant, the decree (with costs) may be made to include the latter.

A writ claiming an injunction should set out the nature of the relief claimed. Even though not claimed in the writ, an injunction may be granted at the hearing as a part of the remedy. A plaintiff or a defendant may make an application either *ex parte* or on notice. If, however, a defendant seeks relief in respect of a matter not connected with the plaintiff's claim, he cannot apply until he has delivered a counterclaim or commenced a cross action. And, in general, an application by a defendant for interim preservation may not be made before he enters an appearance (R.S.C., O. 29, r. 2 (6)). In the Queen's Bench Division injunctions are usually granted on summons in Chambers; but in the Chancery Division, if the courts are sitting, application should not be made in Chambers. In the Chancery Division, also motions are confined to particular days; and therefore, in a case of urgency, application should be made for an *ex parte* injunction over the next motion day. Unless special leave to the contrary has been obtained, two clear days must elapse between the service of the summons or the notice of motion and the day of hearing (O. 8, r. 2 (2)); in computing the two days, Saturday, Sunday or bank holiday, Christmas Day and Good Friday are not counted (O. 3, r. 2 (5)). In a proper case, leave to serve short notice of motion may be obtained; though only from the judge and not from a master (*Conacher* v. *Conacher*, [1881] 29 W.R. 230). Whenever special leave has been obtained, that fact must be stated on the face of the notice.

Upon a motion or summons, evidence will be by affidavit sworn by any one knowing the facts. An affidavit by the plaintiff is invariably necessary. Affidavits must be sworn after issue of the writ or Originating Summons unless the application is made under O. 29, r. 1 (3). All affidavits must be filed. The court may on the application of either party order the attendance for cross examination of the person swearing the affidavit.

An *ex parte* injunction may in urgent cases be granted for a very short period to protect the plaintiff's position until the application for an interim injunction can be heard after notice to the defendant. If after notice the defendant fails to attend, an interim injunction may be made on an affidavit of service of notice of the motion being filed. An interim injunction usually operates until judgment in the action or further order. Interlocutory injunctions are almost invariably made subject to the plaintiff's giving an undertaking in damages. As soon as the order is drawn up, it should be served personally; notice may also be given by telegram. For an appeal from an interlocutory order or judgment no leave is necessary; but no appeal shall be brought after the expiration of fourteen days, except with leave of the court or judge by whom the judgment or order appealed from was given or made, or of the Court of Appeal (O. 59, r. 4).

Costs may be given though not asked for in the notice of motion. As a rule, the court directs that the costs of the application be costs in the cause; but an application improperly made will be dismissed with costs. In the Chancery Division, an opposing party is not entitled to his costs as costs in the cause unless the party making the motion fails; but where a motion is not opposed, the costs of both parties are costs in the cause. So, although a defendant may be unsuccessful on the proceedings for an injunction, if he succeeds at the hearing of the action, his costs of opposing the motion for an injunction will be costs in the cause. Sometimes, as where a plaintiff has concealed material facts from the court, the applicant may be directed to bear the costs. If both parties have been at fault, no costs may be given on either side. And in a case of hardship, an injunction may be granted without costs. For special reasons, costs are sometimes ordered to be taxed on the higher scale.

In the County Court an injunction may be obtained wherever it is the appropriate remedy. But no cause or matter pending in the High Court or in the Court of Appeal may be restrained by injunction of the County Court. Application may be made at any time before or after judgment (C.C.R., O. 23, r. 13). If an immediate order is required, application may be filed and made to the judge in or out of court, on affidavits setting out the material facts (C.C.R., O. 13, r. 8). Obedience to the injunction granted may be enforced by committal.

APPEALS

From Master (Q.B.D.), The Admiralty Registrar or a Registrar of the Family Division.—By O. 58, r. 1, any person affected by any order or decision of such Master or Registrars may, except in the cases within O. 58, r. 2, appeal to a judge at chambers. Such appeal shall be by notice in writing within *five days* after the Order or decision complained of, or such further time as may be allowed.

By O. 32, r. 13 the judge in chambers may direct any summons, appeal or application of importance to be heard in court.

O. 58, r. 2, sets out the cases where an appeal from any Master of the Queen's Bench or Registrar of the Family Division is direct to the Court of Appeal.

FROM QUEEN'S BENCH JUDGE IN CHAMBERS.—The appeal from a judge in chambers except proceedings to which Order 53, r. 12, applies and subject to the conditions under the Judicature Act 1925 and the Administration of Justice Act, 1960 as mentioned in O. 58, r. 7 shall be to the Court of Appeal "in matters of practice and procedure every appeal from a judge shall be to the Court of Appeal" (Judicature Act, 1925, s. 31 (3)). "*No appeal* shall lie from an order of a judge giving unconditional leave to defend an action" (*ibid.*, s. 31 (1) (*c*)). "No appeal shall lie (*a*) from an order allowing an extension of time for appealing from a judgment or order (s. 31 (1) (b)), nor (*b*) without the leave of the judge or of the Court of Appeal from any interlocutory order or interlocutory judgment made or given by a judge, *except* in the following cases, namely: (i) where the liberty of the subject or the custody of minors is concerned; and (ii) cases of granting or refusing an injunction or appointing a receiver; (iii) any decision determining the claim of any creditor or the liability of any contributory or the liability of any director or other officer under the [Companies Act, 1948], in respect of misfeasance or otherwise; and (iv) any decree *nisi* in a matrimonial cause, and any judgment or order in an admiralty action determining liability; and (v) any order on a special case stated under s. 21 of the Arbitration Act, 1950; and (vi) such other cases to be prescribed by rules of court, as may in the opinion of the authority for making such rules be of the nature of final decisions." (Judicature Act, 1925, s. 13 (1) (i)). Application for leave to appeal may be made *ex parte*.

Interlocutory Orders.—The Court of Appeal determines what orders are final and what interlocutory. The question usually is: Does the judgment or order as made finally dispose of the rights of the parties? (Lord Alverstone, C.J., in *Bozon* v. *Altrincham U.D.C.*, [1903] 1 K.B. 547). What has to be looked at is the order under appeal. Unless the order is undoubtedly final the judge should be asked for leave to appeal if power to appeal be desired. An order upon an application under s. 14 of the Crown Proceedings Act, 1947, is interlocutory (O. 77, r. 8 (7)). An appeal by a company from an order for its compulsory winding up, although an appeal from a final order, should be treated as an interlocutory, and not a final, appeal and entered in the interlocutory appeals list (*Re Reliance Properties, Ltd.*, [1951] 2 All E.R. 327).

Time for Appealing. See "Appeals to Court of Appeal".

FROM QUEEN'S BENCH JUDGE IN COURT.—Appeal lies to Court of Appeal (see notes to O. 59, r. 2). See *post*, "Appeals to Court of Appeal".

FROM JUDGE AND JURY.—An Appeal, or rather a *Motion for a New Trial* lies to the Court of Appeal (Judicature Act, 1925, s. 30).

FROM DIVISIONAL COURT.—Appeal lies to the Court of Appeal, but by leave only if the Divisional Court heard the case by way of appeal from another court, for "in all cases where there is a right of appeal to the High Court from any court or person, the appeal shall be heard and determined by a Divisional Court" (Judicature Act, 1925, s. 63 (1), s. 31 (1) (f)).

FROM COURT OF APPEAL.—Appeal lies to the House of Lords in most, but not in all cases, and now in all appeals leave to appeal is needed. By statute, some decisions of the Court of Appeal are final, *e.g.* where the decision is as to costs only, where the Court acted as arbitrator merely, in bankruptcy appeals from the County Courts, in registration appeals, etc. In some other cases, leave of the Court of Appeal is a condition, but such leave will be refused if the question is merely one of fact; and there is no appeal from such refusal.

FROM PRIZE COURT.—Appeal from a Prize Court decision lies to the Privy

Council. Appeal from the Registrar of the Prize Court lies to a Judge of the Admiralty Court.

FROM OFFICIAL REFEREE.—Appeal now lies to the Court of Appeal under R.S.C., O. 58, r. 5.

FROM CHANCERY MASTER.—There is a new Practice Direction governing adjournments from Chancery masters to the judge. This is to be found in [1974] 1 W.L.R. 1659 or in the 2nd Cumulative Supplement to the Supreme Court Practice 1976 and amends the Practice Direction issued in 1965 on page 513 of the Practice (32/14/4).

FROM CHANCERY JUDGE IN CHAMBERS.—The appeal is direct to the Court of Appeal, by leave of the judge. The decision of the judge as to whether he does, or does not give leave to appeal should be noted in the order. It is unnecessary for the judge to give a certificate of no further argument.

FROM CHANCERY JUDGE IN COURT.—Appeal lies to Court of Appeal. See *infra*.

APPEALS TO HOUSE OF LORDS.—The procedure is by petition and by the Administration of Justice (Appeals) Act, 1934. leave to appeal (of either the Court of Appeal or the House of Lords) is necessary.

APPEALS TO COURT OF APPEAL

How and when to be brought.—1 A notice of appeal must first be served upon the opposite parties and then entered with the proper officer. This must be done, in the case of (a) an appeal from an Interlocutory Order or from a Judgment or Order given or made under O. 14 or O. 86, within 14 days; (b) an appeal from an order or decision in the matter of a winding up of a company or bankruptcy, 21 days and (c) in any other case 6 weeks from the date on which the judgment or order was signed, entered or otherwise perfected (O. 59, r. 4). There is power to extend the time (O. 3, r. 5).

On setting down an appeal to the Court of Appeal one copy of the notice of appeal should be endorsed with a certificate of the solicitors for the appellant (or the appellant himself if in person) stating the date or dates upon which notice of appeal was served on the party or parties named as respondent(s).

The officer receiving the notice of appeal satisfies himself that it was served in due time on the respondent(s) and must refuse to set the appeal down if it appears that the notice was served out of time.

The copy of the notice of appeal containing the certificate as to service shall be in the custody of the officer in attendance on the Court of Appeal when the appeal comes on to be heard.

Notices of appeal should contain after the signature by the solicitor for the appellant a statement as follows:—

"No notice as to the date on which this appeal will be in the list for hearing will be given: it is the duty of solicitors to keep themselves informed as to the state of the lists. A Respondent intending to appear in person should inform the Appeal Clerk, Room 136, Royal Courts of Justice W.C.2 of that fact and give his address; if he does so he will be notified by telegram to the address he has given of the date when the Appeal is expected to be heard."

The notice may be given in respect of the whole or a specified part of the judgment, specifying the grounds of appeal, setting out the precise form of order the Court of Appeal is required to make, and every notice must specify the list in which the appeal is to be set down (O. 59, r. 3 (2) (4)).

To enter the appeal the Judgment or Order appealed from or an office copy thereof must be produced and two copies of the notice of appeal, a copy of the judgment or order, and an office copy of any list of exhibits made under O. 35, r. 11 must be lodged with the proper officer. Thereupon the appeal will be set down and will come on for hearing before the Court of Appeal according to its place in the appropriate list of appeals (O. 59, r. 5 (1), (2)).

Within two days after the appeal has been set down, notice must be given to all parties on whom the notice of appeal was served, specifying the list in which the appeal has been set down (O. 59, r. 5 (4)).

In the case of an appeal from a County Court application must be made to the County Court Registrar for a signed copy of the judge's note, and lodged, if available, when setting down the appeal. If not received in time to enable this to be done, it must be lodged at Room 136 as soon as received. Two plain copies of the judge's note, and three copies of any other documents necessary to be read by the Court of Appeal must be lodged with the Lords Justices' Clerks (Room 135A), Royal Courts of Justice, as early as possible and not less than one week before the appeal comes into the list for hearing.

Cross Appeal.—The respondent to an appeal who contends that the judgment of the court below should be varied need not give notice of motion by way of cross-appeal, but must give notice of his intention to any party who may be affected by such contention. The notice must be served within (a) seven days if the appeal is against an interlocutory order, (b) 21 days in any other case, after service of the notice of appeal. Two copies of this notice must be lodged with the proper officer within two days after service (O. 59, r. 6).

Papers for the use of the Court of Appeal.—The necessary papers must be lodged with the court, Room 135A, at least one week before the appeal is likely to be in the list for hearing. Failure to lodge papers in due time may entail personal liability on the solicitor to pay costs thrown away.

Stay pending Appeal.—An appeal does not operate as a stay of execution or of proceedings under the decision appealed against, but the court has power so to order. An application should be made first in the court below. In cases of urgency application to stay may be made *ex parte* and in proper cases it will be granted over the next motion day (generally Monday) on condition that notice to the other side for that day is given in the meantime.

Security for Costs.—The court can in special circumstances order security for the costs of the appeal (O. 59, r. 10 (5)).

Amendments.—It can make all proper amendments (O. 59, r. 10 (1)).

Time.—It can extend or abridge any time provided for doing an act (O. 3, r. 5) unless fixed by statute (*Re Oliver & Scott* (1889), 43 Ch. D. 310); but generally when by lapse of time a party has obtained a vested right in a judgment it will not lightly deprive him of it (*Craig* v. *Phillips* (1876), 7 Ch. D. 249; *cf.* 24 T.L.R. 16).

Procedure.—It can order the notice of appeal to be served upon any person whether or not that person was a party to the proceedings (O. 59, r. 8).

Hearing of the Appeal.—The court is to re-hear (O. 59, r. 3) and in cases tried without a jury may reverse the decision on the facts even when it turns on the credibility of witnesses (*Coghlan* v. *Cumberland*, [1898] 1 Ch. 704; *Smith* v. *Chadwick* (1884), 9 A.C. 194 (Lord Blackburn); *Montgomerie* v. *Wallace*, [1904] A.C. 73). The court will not reverse the trial judge on a question of damages, unless he acted on some wrong principle of law, or unless the amount awarded was so extremely high or so very small, as to make it an entirely erroneous estimate (*Flint* v. *Lovell*, [1935] 1 K.B. 360, C.A.).

It has power to draw inferences of fact and to give any judgment and make any order as the case may require (O. 59, r. 10 (3)).

It can send the case for a new trial if one ought to be had (O. 59, r. 11; *Jones* v. *Hough* (1879), 5 Ex. D. 125).

Fresh Evidence.—It has full discretionary power to receive further evidence upon questions of fact, such evidence to be either by oral examination in court, by affidavit, or by deposition taken before an examiner. Upon appeals from a judgment after trial or hearing of any cause or matter upon the merits, such further evidence (other than evidence as to matters which have occurred after the date of the trial or hearing) shall be admitted on special grounds only (O. 59, r. 10 (2)). Notice of intention to ask leave to adduce further evidence must be given to the other side (*Hastie* v. *Hastie* (1876), 1 Ch.D. 562), and when it is desired to examine witnesses orally, a special application on notice must be made for leave (*Dicks* v. *Brooks* (1879), 13 Ch.D. 652). As a rule additional evidence on affidavit by witnesses examined at the trial will not be received (*Taylor* v. *Grange* (1880), 15 Ch.D. 165).

In admitting or refusing fresh evidence the circumstances of the particular case must be looked to. A strong case should be made out; and the court should always act with caution (*The Hawke* (1912), 28 T.L.R. 319, C.A.). Parties ought to present their case in full to the court below, and not take their chances there and then offer fresh evidence to the Court of Appeal (*Re Phoenix Bessemer Steel Co.* (1876), 4 Ch. D. 116). Fresh evidence is generally refused when the appellant might have adduced the evidence at the trial (*Re Copiapo Co.* (1809), 10 T.L.R. 180. See also *Nash* v. *Rochford R.D.C.*, [1917] 1 K.B. 384; *Re Buchanan-Wollaston's Conveyance*, [1939] Ch. 738). When there is an element of surprise the Court "might well be liberal in the exercise of discretion" (*Technograph Printed Circuits, Ltd.* v. *Mills & Rockley (Electronics), Ltd.*, [1969] R.P.C. 395).

Powers generally.—O. 59, r. 10 (4) provides that the powers of the Court of Appeal under that rule may be exercised by the court notwithstanding that no notice of appeal or respondents' notice has been given in respect of any particular part of the decision of the court below.

Two judges instead of three can act in interlocutory matters, and on appeals where the parties consent (Judicature Act, 1925, s. 68 (1) and (5)).

If evidence has been wrongly received below without objection the Court of Appeal on re-hearing is not to act on it (*Jacker* v. *International Cable Co.* (1889), 5 T.L.R. 13).

After its order has been passed and entered the court cannot re-hear the appeal, but it can correct a slip and make the order conform to the intention of the court (*Preston Banking Co.* v. *Allsup*, [1895] 1 Ch. 144); and it can, in proper cases, sometimes remedy matters by a supplementary order (*ibid.*, and *Re Scowby*, [1897] 1 Ch. 741).

The function of the court is to decide, not abstract questions of law, but questions of law arising between the parties as the result of a certain state of facts (*per* Warrington, L.J., in *Stephenson, Blake & Co.* v. *Grant, Legros & Cohen* (1916), 86 L.J. Ch. 439; *Tindall* v. *Wright* (1922), 127 L.T. 149; *Sutch* v. *Burns*, [1944] W.N. 106, C.A.).

Costs.—As to the Court of Appeal power to deal with the costs of the proceedings and the appeal, see O. 62, r. 4 (2). As a general rule the successful party gets the costs; but there are cases in which a successful appellant has been deprived of costs, as in *Hussey* v. *Horne Payne* (1879), 8 Ch.D. 679, where the appellant succeeded on a point not taken below; *Ex parte Hauxwell* (1883), 23 Ch.D. 643, and *Arnot's Case* (1887), 36 Ch.D. 710, where he succeeded on evidence not before the court below; *Child* v. *Stenning* (1879), 11 Ch.D. 87, and *Barrow's Case* (1880), 14 Ch.D. 445 where he was only partially successful. And there are cases where the successful respondent was deprived of costs, e.g. *Jones* v. *Merionethshire Bldng. Socy.*, [1892] 1 Ch. 187. The costs of an unsuccessful appeal, even by trustees, ought not as a rule to come out of the fund (*Re Earl of Radnor's Trusts* (1890), 45 Ch.D. 402).

It is not usual to require a solicitor to give any undertaking as to return of costs on an intended appeal to the House of Lords (*Schweppe* v. *Gibbens*, [1904] W.N. 208).

JURY CASES.—*New Trial.*—O. 59 regulates applications for a new trial.

Grounds for granting New Trial.— A new trial is not to be granted on the ground that the verdict is against the weight of the evidence unless the verdict was such as the jury viewing the whole of the evidence reasonably, could not properly find (*Phillips* v. *Martin*, (1890), 15 A.C. 194). Nor is the Court of Appeal bound to order a new trial on the ground of misdirection or improper admission or rejection of evidence, or because the verdict was not taken on a question which the judge was not asked to leave to the jury, unless the court is of opinion that substantial wrong or miscarriage of justice have arisen therefrom (O. 59, r. 11 (2); *Bray* v. *Ford*, [1896] A.C. 44).

For a refusal to grant a new trial in a libel action on the ground that a plea of justification was bound to succeed see *Holdsworth, Ltd.* v. *Associated Newspapers, Ltd.*, [1937] 3 All E.R. 872.

On a motion for a new trial, if satisfied that it has all proper evidence before it, and that on the facts the judgment must be one way, the court may enter such judgment instead of sending the case down again for trial *Allcock* v. *Hall*, [1891] 1 Q.B. 444).

If the court thinks the damages are excessive or inadequate it may in lieu

APPEALS

APPEALS

of ordering a new trial substitute a proper sum with the consent of all parties, or with the consent of the party entitled to receive or liable to pay reduce or increase the sum in respect of any head of damage erroneously included or excluded from the sum awarded (O. 59, r. 11 (4)); *Watt* v. *Watt*, [1905] A.C. 115).

"A new trial may be ordered on any question without interfering with the finding or decision on any other question" (O. 59, r. 11 (3)).

On a motion for a new trial the court has all the powers it has on an appeal (O. 59, r. 2).

Non-direction does not stand on the same footing as misdirection; a party generally cannot get a new trial for non-direction, if having an opportunity for asking for the direction at the trial he did not ask for it (*per* Lord Halsbury in *Nevill* v. *Fine Arts &c. Co.*, [1896] A.C. 76).

It is not a misdirection for a judge to tell the jury how he would decide a question of fact (*Smith* v. *Dart* (1884), 14 Q.B.D. 108).

Costs.—The costs of a motion for a new trial are generally ordered to be borne by the unsuccessful party to the motion (*Hamilton* v. *Seal*, [1904] 2 K.B. 262) but the costs of the first trial generally abide the event of the new trial where one is ordered (*ibid.*, and *Jones* v. *Richards* (1889), 15 T.L.R. 398).

Appeal from Official or other Referee. See *ante*, p. 180.

Appeal from County Court.—Under O. 59, r. 19 appeal lies to the Court of Appeal in all cases, including admiralty and probate appeals (Administration of Justice (Appeals) Act, 1934, s. 2 (1); County Courts Act, 1959, ss. 108, 110), but not including bankruptcy appeals, which lie to the Divisional Court (Bankruptcy Act, 1914, s. 108 (2)).

In relation to any proceedings in the Principal Registry of the Family Division which by virtue of the Matrimonial Causes Rules are treated as pending in a County Court paragraphs (1) to (5) of O. 59, r. 19 shall have effect with the necessary modifications as if the Principal Registry were a County Court.

Any party to any proceedings in a County Court who is dissatisfied with the judge's determination in point of law or upon the admission or rejection of evidence may appeal to the Court of Appeal, but there is no appeal without the leave of the judge, in any action founded on contract or tort where the debt or damage claimed does not exceed £20 (County Courts Act, 1959, s. 108, and see proviso (b) and (c) to that section). The notice of appeal must be served (a) in the case of a final order within 6 weeks and (b) in the case of an interlocutory order within 14 days from the date of the order or judgment, and must be set down within 7 days of such service. The Registrar of the County Court must be served with a copy.

APPEALS TO DIVISIONAL COURT

Generally.—Appeals to divisional courts are regulated by Orders 55 and 56.

O. 55 sets out the method of appealing from a court tribunal or person and O. 56 the method when the appeal is by case stated.

Mandamus, prohibition and *certiorari* are dealt with by O. 53, *habeas corpus* by O. 54.

O. 94, r. 5, deals with the jurisdiction of the Divisional Court over question arising under the Representation of the People Acts.

Appeals from inferior civil courts.—Certain appeals from inferior courts of civil jurisdiction, *e.g.* County Courts are direct to the Court of Appeal, others *e.g.* from magistrates under the Guardianship of Infants Acts direct to a nominated Judge of the Chancery Division. Unless prohibited by the rules or by any enactment which provides for appeal to a particular Division or to a single judge appeals are to a Divisional Court of the Queen's Bench Division.

APPEALS IN CRIMINAL CASES

Appeals lie to the Criminal Division of the Court of Appeal. *See* Judicature Act, 1925, s. 31 (1) (a). As to appeals under the Criminal Appeal Act, 1968, *see* p. 140, *ante*.

SECURITY FOR COSTS

By O. 23, r. 1, if, having regard to all the circumstances of the case, the court thinks it just to do so, it may order the plaintiff to give such security for the defendant's costs as it thinks just. It is to be noted that the principles are not the same for appeals as for proceedings in the first instance, also that in both cases the order for security is discretionary.

1.—ACTIONS, PRIOR TO JUDGMENT

(A) *Security for costs may be required:*

(1) Where the plaintiff is ordinarily resident out of the jurisdiction.

(2) Where he is a nominal and not a representative plaintiff who is suing for the benefit of some other person and there is reason to believe that he would not be able to pay the defendant's costs. But a defaulter on the Stock Exchange is not such a plaintiff (*Hind v. Haskew* (1885), 1 T.L.R. 94), nor is an insolvent trustee of a deed of separation suing to enforce a covenant in the deed (*White v. Butt*, [1909] 1 K.B. 50; and see below (under B)).

(3) Where his address is not stated, or is wrongly stated, in the writ or other originating process, unless he can satisfy the court that the failure or misstatement was innocent and without intention to deceive.

(4) Where he has changed his address during the course of the proceedings with a view to evading the consequences.

(5) Against a defendant who by counterclaiming puts himself in the position of a plaintiff.

(6) Against a petitioner where a plaintiff would be so ordered (*Re Norman* (1849), 11 Beav. 401).

(7) Against a party who is substantially a plaintiff, *e.g.*, a party defendant to an interpleader (*Tomlinson v. Land & Finance Corporation* (1885), 14 Q.B.D. 539), or other claimant (*Apollinaris Co. v. Wilson* (1886), 31 Ch. D. 632).

(8) Against a Limited Company plaintiff or counterclaimant as above, when it "appears by any credible testimony that there is reason to believe that if the defendant [or opposite party] be successful . . . the assets of the Company will be insufficient to pay his costs" (s. 447 of Companies Act, 1948).

(9) Against a married woman on satisfactory evidence as to means. The making of the order is always a matter of discretion.

(B) *Security for costs cannot be obtained against:*—

(1) A plaintiff or counterclaimant simply because he is poor, insolvent, or even bankrupt, if he is suing for his own benefit (*Andrews v. Marris* (1841), 1 Dowl. 712; *Cowell v. Taylor* (1886), 31 Ch. D. 34; *Rhodes v. Dawson* (1886), 16 Q.B.D. 548; *Cook v. Whellock* (1890), 24 Q.B.D. 658).

(2) A plaintiff suing as executor or administrator, though insolvent (*Sykes v. Sykes* (1869), L.R. 4 C.P. 645; *Greener v. Kahn* (1906), 22 T.L.R. 694, C.A.; *Rainbow v. Kittoe*, [1916] 1 Ch. 313).

(3) A plaintiff trustee in bankruptcy or liquidator, although insolvent (*Cowell v. Taylor* (1886), 31 Ch.D. 34; *Re Strand Wood Co.*, [1904] 2 Ch. 1). The Court may order a Plaintiff limited company in liquidation to give security (*John Bishop (Caterers), Ltd. v. National Union Bank, Ltd.*, [1973] 117 Sol. Jo. 36).

(4) A next friend to an infant, although without means (*Fellows v. Barrett* (1836), 1 Keen 119).

(5) An Englishman who is temporarily abroad on the public service (*Garwood v. Bradburn* (1841), 9 Dowl. 1031; *Chappell v. Watts* (1860), 29 L.J., Q.B. 167).

(6) A plaintiff ordinarily resident in Scotland or Ireland (*Re Queensland Agency* (1882), 61 L.J., Ch. 48).

(7) A foreign plaintiff who has a co-plaintiff ordinarily resident within the jurisdiction (*Sykes v. Sykes* (1869), L.R. 4 C.P. 645; *D'Hormusjee v. Grey* (1883), 10 Q.B.D. 13).

(8) A lunatic plaintiff simply because of the lunacy (*Steel v. Alan* (1801), 2 B. & P. 437).

(9) An unlimited company, even if in liquidation (*United Ports Insurance Co.* v. *Hill* (1870), 5 Q.B. 395).

(10) A defendant who simply defends or a person really in the position of a defendant though nominally plaintiff (*Belontem* v. *Aynard* (1879), 4 C.P.D. 352).

(11) A shareholder resident abroad who opposes a winding up (*Re Percy Mining Co.* (1876), 2 Ch. D. 531).

(12) A defendant who raises the issue of domicile as part of his defence even though he is made the plaintiff on the trial of a preliminary issue (*Visco* v. *Minter* [1969] 2 W.L.R. 70; [1969] 2 All E.R. 714).

As to security of costs where plaintiff becomes an enemy alien, see *Geiringer* v. *Swiss Bank Corpn.*, [1940] 1 All E.R. 406.

As to security for costs in Prize cases, see *The Zamora*, [1916] 2 A.C. 77; *The Stanton*, [1917] A.C. 380.

Security for costs of action is applied for by summons in chambers.

II.—SECURITY FOR COSTS OF APPEAL

This is regulated by O. 59, r. 10 (5). The Court of Appeal may in special circumstances order that such security shall be given for the costs of the appeal as may be just. Security for costs of an appeal is often ordered when security for costs of an action would be refused. Therefore, if the court is satisfied that an appellant will not be able to pay the respondent's costs of an unsuccessful appeal, he will be ordered to find security for the costs of the appeal (*Harlock* v. *Ashberry* (1882), 19 Ch. D. 84; *Hall* v. *Snowden*, [1899] 1 Q.B. 593). A motion for a new trial is on the same footing as an appeal (*Wightwick* v. *Pope*, [1902] 2 K.B. 99).

Security for costs may be ordered against a married woman appellant who has no free property (*Whitaker* v. *Kershaw* (1890), 44 Ch. D. 296) or where the appeal appears to be vexatious (*Weldon* v. *Maple* (1888), 20 Q.B.D. 331) or where the appellant is out of the jurisdiction and has no available property within it (*Re Indian Mining Co.* (1883), 22 Ch. D. 83).

As to security for the wife's costs in divorce appeals, see *King* v. *King*, [1943] 2 All E.R. 253, C.A.

When the liberty of the subject is involved *bona fide* security will not as a rule be ordered (*Hood Barrs* v. *Heriot*, [1896] 2 Q.B. 375); but see *Re Carroll*, [1931] 1 K.B. 104, 109, C.A.

Application for proper security should be requested by letter, and if it is not given application should be made by original motion on notice to the Court of Appeal supported by affidavit which must assert inability to pay. A refusal to pay is not sufficient (*Hills* v. *L.P.T.B.*, [1937] 4 All E.R. 230, C.A.).

INTERPLEADER IN THE HIGH COURT

By O. 17, r. 1, relief by way of interpleader may be granted:—

(*a*) to a person who is under a liability in respect of a debt or any money, goods or chattels for or in respect of which he is being or expects to be sued by two or more persons making adverse claims thereto;

(*b*) to a sheriff in respect of a claim made to any money, or to any goods or chattels (or the proceeds or value thereof) taken or intended to be taken by him in execution under any process, by a person other than the debtor.

"Chattels" includes choses in action. Both legal and equitable claims may be thus recognized; nor will it be a bar to interpleader proceedings that the applicant is estopped from denying the claim of one of the claimants (*Ex parte Mersey Docks and Harbour Board*, [1899] 1 Q.B. 546). That the claims are independent and of diverse origin also is not a bar. So the mere fact that a claimant is a foreigner out of the jurisdiction will not disentitle an applicant to relief. But the granting of this form of relief is discretionary and it may be refused where an applicant proves to be liable to both claimants. A claim for unliquidated damages only is outside the scope of interpleader and in the case of a wagering contract, parties will be left to their remedy on the contract unless one is not a party or privy to the contract. Interpleader will not issue on the application of a defendant in an action after judgment (*Stevenson (H.) & Son, Ltd.* v. *Brownell*,

[1912] 2 Ch. 344, C.A.). Similarly, interpleader is not allowed after garnishee order absolute because the garnishee is sufficiently protected by the terms of the order. If after receiving notice of adverse claims, the applicant has disposed of the goods or their proceeds in accordance with the directions of one of the parties he may be refused relief.

A summons under O. 17 must be supported by evidence that the applicant claims no interest in the subject matter in dispute other than for charges or costs; that he is not in collusion with any of the claimants; and that he is willing to pay or transfer the subject matter into court or to dispose of it as the court may direct. Where the applicant is a sheriff he need not provide such evidence unless so directed by the court (O. 17, r. 3). If an applicant can with safety pay to one of the claimants he is not entitled to relief.

As a rule, an affidavit by the applicant is sufficient evidence. An affidavit by his solicitor may be held insufficient unless for good cause, *e.g.* absence abroad of the applicant. Where a company is the applicant, the affidavit may be by the statutory officer of the company. In the case of a firm applicant, an affidavit by two out of four partners has been accepted (*Glover v. Reynolds* (1867), 16 L.T. 84). As a rule, a sheriff need not support his interpleader summons by affidavit, and as he will not be entitled to the costs of it, he will be best advised to wait until the master directs that an affidavit is required by the circumstances. The execution creditor also need not make an affidavit.

In a proper case one claimant may be substituted for another, etc. Where the amount or value of the matter in dispute does not exceed £1000, and it appears to the court or judge that it may be more conveniently tried in a County Court, the proceedings may be transferred to any County Court in which an action or proceeding might have been brought by any one or more of the parties to the interpleader against the others or other of them if there had been a trust to be executed concerning the matter in question (County Courts Act, 1959, s. 68) as amended by the County Courts Jurisdiction Order 1974 (S.I. 1974 No. 1273).

When sheriff can interplead.—It has been decided that a sheriff is not obliged to interplead, and that he may withdraw instead of doing so (*Scarlett v. Henson* (1883), 12 Q.B.D. 213, C.A.). But to enable the sheriff to resort to interpleader proceedings, the property in question must be actually claimed by some third party (*Bentley v. Hook* (1834), 2 C. & M. 426); the sheriff need not have actually seized, but must have had an intention of seizing (*Lea v. Rossi* (1855), 24 L.J. Ex. 280); so too he may interplead when he has seized goods claimed by A., and A. pays him out under protest (*Smith v. Critchfield*, (1885), 14 Q.B.D. 873, C.A.).

When sheriff may not interplead.— Where the execution creditor does not admit the claim and the sheriff withdraws and delivers over all or part of the goods to the claimant, he may disentitle himself to relief. The same applies where he is guilty of delay unless he can satisfactorily explain it. There is no fixed rule as to when a sheriff must apply, except that he must apply promptly and within such time as the court under the circumstances of the case thinks reasonable. Again, he cannot interplead where the goods belonging to the execution debtor are already in the possession of his landlord, to whom rent is due, under a distress for the rent unless fraud is alleged. *Semble,* in any case where the claim is by a landlord for rent alone interpleader proceedings cannot be resorted to. Where the sheriff seizes goods belonging to a person other than the tenant on the premises in respect of which rent is due, the landlord has a right to be paid the amount of the rent due out of the proceeds of the execution provided the seizure is rightful (*Hughes v. Smallwood* (1890), 25 Q.B.D. 306). Again, he cannot interplead where the difficulty arises from the sheriff's own wrongdoing, *e.g.* where he has knowingly seized goods wrongfully (*Tufton v. Harding* (1859), 6 Jur. (N.S.) 116).

Arbitration.—By s. 5 of the Arbitration Act, 1950, in cases in which the claims in question are matters to which an arbitration agreement to which the respective claimants are parties applies, the court has power to direct an issue between the claimants to be determined by arbitration in accordance with the agreements,

Form of Application.—An application for relief under O. 17 must be made by originating summons unless made in a pending action, in which case it must be made by summons in the action (O. 17, r. 3 (1)). No appearance need be made to an originating summons under r. 3 (r. 3 (3)). Personal service is necessary. An originating summons must be served not less than four and a summons in the action not less than two clear days before the hearing (O. 28, r. 3 (2); O. 32, r. 3). If the application is made by a defendant in an action, the court or a judge may stay all further proceedings in this action (O. 17, r. 7).

Particulars of Claim.—Claimants must state the nature and particulars of their claims on oath, and with such reasonable precision and certainly as will enable the execution creditor or competing claimant to decide upon his line of action. Where proceedings have been commenced, the affidavit should as a general rule be by the claimant himself. A claimant is not entitled to require the sheriff to deliver particulars of the goods seized in order to enable him to prepare his claim. Should a claimant desire to withdraw his claim, he must give notice in writing to the sheriff or his officer; and if such withdrawal is subsequent to the summons but before its return, the court may order as to costs, etc., as may appear reasonable. Upon receipt of a claim, the sheriff must forthwith give notice to the execution creditor who has four days within which to admit or dispute the claim. After notice in response by the execution creditor, or lapse of the said time, the sheriff may make his application for relief (O. 17, r. 2); and to save expense he should do so promptly, though there is no rule as to time. A claimant need not enter any formal appearance. If the claimants appear on the hearing of a summons the court may order (*a*) that any claimant be made a defendant in any action pending, in substitution for, or in addition to the applicant, or (*b*) that an issue between the claimants be stated and tried, and may direct which of the claimants is to be plaintiff and which defendant (O. 17, r. 5). Claimants should be prepared with affidavits in support. Discovery may be had (O. 17, r. 10) and Interrogatories served.

Orders on Interpleader Summons.—The order made will of course depend on the value of the subject matter, and the whole circumstances. Where a substantial grievance has been caused by the sheriff, proceedings against the sheriff will not be barred even though he may not have been guilty of any actual misconduct. Proceedings against the execution creditor may also be restrained. When a sale has been properly conducted under an interpleader order, neither sheriff nor execution creditor will be liable to a claimant for damages arising from such sale.

Relief to Stakeholder.—A stakeholder can issue an originating summons calling upon the claimants to state their claims but a stakeholder who has been sued may make his application immediately after service of the writ upon him, and in any case he should do so with due diligence. He may be mulcted in costs in case of undue delay. In ordinary cases, it is too late to apply after judgment in the action. There is no rule as to who shall be plaintiff and who defendant in interpleader proceedings by a stakeholder; the circumstances of each case must decide this matter. A new trial may be granted where a substantial injury has been done by the wrong party being made plaintiff.

Appeal.—Appeals in interpleader proceedings are dealt with by O. 58, r. 8.

An appeal from the summary decision of a master lies to the Court of Appeal under O. 58, r. 2 (*c*), by leave of the master or the Court of Appeal. Where interpleader proceedings have been transferred to the County Court under the County Courts Act, 1959, s. 68, an appeal lies to the Court of Appeal from the judgment of the County Court. Appeals in Interpleader proceedings are the same as appeals from interlocutory orders for the purpose of the time for giving notice, *i.e.* 14 days.

Costs.—By O. 17, r. 8, the court may, in or for the purposes of any interpleader proceedings, make all such orders as it thinks just. Wherever a stakeholder acts properly he will be allowed his costs out of the subject matter or fund as well as any other charges he is entitled to as warehouse-man, auctioneer, etc.; but it will be otherwise if costs have been incurred through misconduct. In sheriff's interpleader whichever party is successful is entitled to recover as costs from the other party the sheriff's charges subsequent to the interpleader order (*Goodman* v. *Blake* (1887), 19 Q.B.D. 77), and also the charges which the sheriff has deducted from the amount of the levy (*Blaker* v. *Seager* (1897), 76 L.T. 392), as well as his own costs of the proceedings.

ATTACHMENT OF DEBTS BY WAY OF GARNISHEE

It frequently happens that after having obtained judgment for payment of a sum of money the judgment creditor finds that he has difficulty in enforcing his order. Order 49, which deals with garnishee proceedings, enables a judgment creditor as one of his remedies to attach money due to the judgment debtor by way of garnishee proceedings. Any person who has obtained a judgment or order for the recovery of money may apply *ex parte* to a master, and upon affidavit by himself or his solicitor stating that judgment has been recovered, that it is still unsatisfied and to what amount, and that some other person is indebted to the debtor and is within the jurisdiction, an order may be made attaching the debt due from the third person (called the garnishee), and ordering the garnishee to appear before the master or a judge to show cause why he should not pay the amount he owes to the judgment debtor, or so much thereof as will satisfy the judgment debt and the costs of the application, to the judgment creditor. Such anorder is called a garnishee order nisi, and must be served on the garnishee, and unless the court otherwise directs on the judgment debtor, or his solicitor, seven days before the hearing to make absolute the order *nisi* (O. 49, r. 3).

Rule 3 (2) of O. 49 provides that service of a garnishee order nisi binds the debt referred to in such order in the hands of the garnishee. It therefore prevents the garnishee from paying his debt to the judgment debtor, and, if the order is made absolute, the judgment creditor may enforce payment from the garnishee, by execution if necessary. If the garnishee admits liability to the judgment debtor, he should appear on the day on which the summons is returnable and make such admission, in which case he will usually be allowed his costs, which he may deduct from the amount due to the judgment debtor. If he does not appear, and the order is made absolute, it must be served upon the garnishee, and execution will not as a rule be allowed to issue until this has been done. For the procedure where the judgment creditor is resident outside the scheduled territories, as defined by the Exchange Control Act, 1947, *see* O. 49, r. 7.

If the garnishee denies his liability to the judgment debtor, the usual practice is to direct an issue to be tried and such issues are commonly heard before a master. The garnishee should not on the first occasion make an affidavit denying his liability. If he appears and denies liability and the judgment creditor is not satisfied with such denial, an adjournment will be granted to enable the garnishee to put his denial of liability upon oath.

Rule 8 provides that payment made by, or execution levied upon a garnishee is a valid discharge to him as against the judgment debtor, up to the amount paid or levied, even though the order is subsequently set aside. This does not apply where payment is made to the judgment creditor immediately on service of the garnishee order nisi, since that is not an order upon him to pay, but merely an order attaching the money in his hands until the order nisi is made absolute.

It should be noted that where, as frequently happens, it is sought to garnishee an account standing to the credit of a judgment debtor at a bank, and the bank has both a head office and branch offices, the affidavit used on the application for a garnishee order nisi must show at which branch of the bank the judgment debtor's account is believed to be or that this information is not known to the deponent.

When a wife who was a judgment debtor had an account in her name opened for her by her husband with his moneys in circumstances impressing it with a resulting trust for the husband it was held that the judgment creditors could not garnishee the account (*Harrods, Ltd.* v. *Tester*, [1937] 2 All E.R. 236).

See also, as to a joint banking account of husband and wife, *Hirschhorn* v. *Evans*, [1938] 3 All E.R. 491.

Order 49 does not apply in respect of any money due or alleged to be due from the Crown (O. 77, r. 16). For the attachment of money payable by the Crown, *see* s. 27 of the Crown Proceedings Act, 1947.

COSTS IN THE SUPREME COURT OF JUDICATURE

(*See Butterworth's Costs, 4th Edn.*)

Costs in the High Court and Court of Appeal are regulated by R.S.C., O. 62. The substance of the Order is reproduced below, together with some of the more important case law relative thereto.

R.S.C. ORDER 62

RULE 1

This rule sets out the definitions of words used in the Order and in particular definitions of "costs".

RULE 2

Rule 2 (1) sets out the applications the Order has to all criminal proceedings in the Supreme Court.

Rule 2 (2) brings within the ambit of the rules proceedings before an Umpire, Arbitrator, or before a tribunal, etc. constituted under any Act.

Rule 2 (3) provides that the Order will have effect subject to ss. 47 and 60 of the County Courts Act, 1959. See pp. 193-4.

Rule 2 (4) vests the determination and award of costs in the discretion of the court.

[NOTE.—The following cases on the discretion of the court are relevant:

Powers of the court.—The court's discretion is to be exercised judicially, the general rule being that the successful party gets his costs. See *The Ophelia* (1886), 11 P. 46; *Donald Campbell & Co., Ltd.* v. *Pollak* (1927), 43 T.L.R. 787; *Baylis Baxter, Ltd.* v. *Sabath*, [1958] 2 All E.R. 209, and *Butterworths' Costs*, 4th Edn., pp. A 41 *et seq.*

Appeal from Order as to Costs.—Where the judge below has acted on wrong principles, an appeal is allowed (see *Civil Serv. Co-op.* v. *G.S.N. Co.*, [1903] 2 K.B. 756, C.A.) and also when discretion had never really been exercised, and without the materials on which discretion could be exercised (*Wagnan* v. *Vare Motors*,

Ltd., [1959] 3 All E.R. 326) otherwise the judge having rightly exercised his discretion the Court of Appeal will not intervene except in special circumstances (*Holtquist* v. *Universal Pattern and Precision Eng. Co., Ltd.*, [1960] 2 All E.R. 266).

A successful Plaintiff is prima facie entitled to Costs.—(*Cooper* v. *Whittingham* (1880), 15 Ch.D. 501).

A Successful Defendant cannot be deprived of costs without good cause (*Civil Service Co-operative Society* v. *General Steam Navigation Co.*, [1903] 2 K.B. 756, C.A. *King* v. *Gillard*, [1903] 2 Ch. 7 (in both of which cases the Court of Appeal held no good cause)); still less can he be made to *pay* the costs of an action which the plaintiff had no legal right to bring (*Dicks* v. *Yates* (1881), 18 Ch. D. 76, *Andrew* v. *Grove*, [1902] 1 K.B. 625) but he may be deprived of costs where he has been unreasonable (*Pélegrin* v. *Coutts*, [1915] 1 Ch. 696) or has by his improper conduct, brought the litigation on himself (*Sutcliffe* v. *Smith* (1885), 2 T.L.R. 881).

When it is doubtful which of two defendants are liable, A or B, and the plaintiff sues both and loses against A and wins against B, the judge may order that the plaintiff shall recover against B his costs, including the costs he has to pay to A (*Bullock* v. *London General Omnibus Co.*, [1907] 1 K.B. 264, C.A.; *Besterman* v. *British Motor Cab Co.*, [1914] 3 K.B. 181, C.A.); or order payment direct by B to A (*Sander-*

son v. *Blyth Theatre Co.*, [1903] 2 K.B. 523, C.A.).

Judgment for Plaintiff, but Plaintiff to pay Defendant's Costs.—This may be ordered whenever the action is unnecessary, *e.g.* where the plaintiff could without proceedings have got what he recovers (*Mentors* v. *Evans*, [1912] 3 K.B. 174, C.A.) or where he recovers but a trifle after maintaining extravagant and unreasonable demands (*Rouse* v. *Graveworks, Ltd.*, [1940] 1 K.B. 489, C.A.) or where the action was needless.

Arbitration. The Arbitration Act, 1950, s. 18 gives the Arbitrator discretion as to costs and when he makes an order for taxation in the High Court reference must be made to the High Court Scales unless otherwise directed. Sec. 47 of the County Courts Act 1959 is not applicable to any arbitration heard under a contract containing an arbitration clause. (*Perkins (H.G.) Ltd.* v. *Best-Shaw*, [1973] 2 All E.R. 924).

RULES 3 TO 11

These rules deal with entitlement to costs. By Rule 3 (2)-(11) (i) costs are normally to follow the event, (ii) costs of and occasioned by any amendment are to be borne by the party amending, unless otherwise ordered, (iii) costs of application to extend time are to be borne by the party applying, unless otherwise ordered, (iv) on the non-admission of facts, and the cost of proving shall be borne by the person on whom the notice is served, (v) in cases of non-admission of documents, or refusal or neglect to admit facts by a party to whom notice has been given the costs of proving them are to be paid by him, (vi) discontinuance of counterclaim and/or payment into court, (vii) a creditor seeking to prove his claim will be entitled to his costs if his claim succeeds and will have to pay costs if it fails. All such costs as the claimant may be entitled to under (vi), *supra*, are to be fixed by the court (unless taxation is directed) and the amount allowed is to be added to the claimant's debt and (viii) clarifies the rights and liabilities as to costs of claiming and non-creditor claimants.

Rule 4 provides for the stage of proceedings at which costs are to be dealt with.

Rule 5 provides that certain special matters are to be taken into account.

Rule 6 sets out certain restrictions.

Rule 7 imposes a penalty for costs arising from misconduct or neglect and the court may give a direction to the taxing officer to inquire into anything that is done or omission that is made improperly or unnecessarily by or on behalf of a party.

Rule 8 imposes a personal liability on the solicitor for costs where the costs are improperly incurred through undue delay, or other misconduct, imposes the one-sixth rule, and authorises the official solicitor to attend and take part in any proceedings under this rule, etc.

By rule 9, where the court orders any costs to be paid to a person, including a litigant in person, then that person is entitled to his taxed costs. The court is also empowered to order payment of a gross sum in lieu of taxed costs.

[NOTES.—As to division of costs and costs of issues, see *Butterworths' Costs*, 4th Edn., pp. A 51 *et seq.*

Claim and Counterclaim.—Where both action and counterclaim either succeed or fail the rule is that there should be no appointment of the general costs. A party who is to receive or pay the costs of the action is to receive or pay the whole o such costs of action as if there were no counterclaim, and the party who is to receive or pay the costs of the counterclaim is to receive or pay only the costs of the action so far as they have been increased by the counterclaim and would not have been incurred but for the counterclaim (*Medway Oil and Storage Co. Ltd.* v. *Continental Contractors, Ltd.*, [1929] A.C. 88; *Cinema Press, Ltd.* v. *Pictures and Pleasure, Ltd.*, [1945] K.B. 356; [1945] 1 All E.R. 44, C.A.; *Childs* v. *Blacker, Childs* v. *Gibson*, [1954] 2 All E.R. 243; *Hanak* v. *Green*, [1958] 2 All E.R. 141. The costs of the counterclaim are on the High Court scale even when the amount claimed or recovered comes within the County Court limits (see *post*).

Appeal and Cross Appeal.—The principle of no apportionment applies as in *Medway Oil* v. *Continental Contractors* (*supra*) and only those extra costs incurred by reason of the cross appeal will be allowed in the absence of a special order to the contrary (*The Stentor* (*No.* 2), [1934] P. 133, C.A.).]

Rule 10 provides for a plaintiff who accepts money paid into court in satisfaction of his claim to tax his costs four days after payment out and sign Judgment for his costs two days after taxation, without an Order. Where a plaintiff by notice in writing and without leave discontinues his action or withdraws part of it the defendant may likewise tax his costs of the action, or his costs occasioned by the matter withdrawn, and if not paid within four days of taxation sign judgment for them.

Rule 11 deals with matters where an order for taxation of costs is not required.

RULES 12 TO 20A

The powers of Taxing Officers are contained in rules 12 to 20.

Rule 12 deals with applications under s. 21 of the Administration of Justice Act, 1969 and ss. 31 and 32 of the Administration of Justice Act, 1870.

Rule 20A deals with the powers of Registrars under Part III of the Solicitors Act 1957. (Now Solicitors Act 1974.)

RULES 21 to 27

These rules outline the procedure on taxation. Rule 21 sets out the mode of beginning proceedings for taxation and refers the practitioner to Appendix 1 to the Order for the requisite document for commencing the proceedings for taxation in each division of the Supreme Court. Rule 22 deals with the notification of time appointed for taxation and in general a minimum of seven days' notice is required (except taxations which are short and urgent (see rule 24, *infra*)) and those in the Family Division where in cases to be taxed by a Principal clerk and where only the party entitled to costs is entitled to be heard the taxing officer may inform the party of the costs he proposes to allow. The party may within 14 days require an appointment to tax if he wishes to be heard in the proceedings. (In Admiralty Proceedings, however, it has always been the practice to give seven clear days'

notice.) No notice need be given to a party who has not entered an appearance. Rule 23 deals with delivery of bills, etc. Short and urgent taxations are dealt with in rule 24, the practical effect of which is to enable the party entitled to taxation to apply to the proper officer for an appointment to tax in the Sitting Masters' list.

[Note.—So far as the use of the word "short" in this rule is concerned, a monetary limit of £100 is imposed and the fact that a party is likely to lose the fruits of his judgment through delay in taxation would be considered a ground for "urgency".]

The party whose bill is to be taxed must, not less than two days before the day appointed for the taxation send a copy of his bill together with the time and date of the appointment to every other party entitled to be heard in the proceedings.

[NOTE.—Any bill that is short and urgent, either Chancery or Queen's Bench, may be dealt with under this rule, excepting those cases which require a certificate (not Allocatur) to be issued (*e.g.* taxations under the Legal Aid Act, 1974).]

Provisions as to the form bills of costs are to take are contained in rule 25 which requires separate columns for professional charges and disbursements, and in certain instances for V.A.T. and every column must be cast [in pencil] before being left for taxation. The bill must also be indorsed with the name or firm and business address of the solicitor and if the solicitor is an agent also with the name or firm and business address of the other solicitor.

By rule 26 the Taxing Officer may proceed with the taxation, if any party entitled to be heard does not attend within a reasonable time after the time appointed for the taxation (usually 15 minutes) provided he is satisfied that due notice has been given. He may also, where necessary, adjourn the proceedings from time to time.

Where the costs are to be paid out of a fund, rule 27 provides that the Taxing Officer may give directions as to the parties entitled to attend on the taxation, and disallow the costs of attendance of parties not entitled to appear whose attendance he thinks unnecessary. He may also, if he thinks fit, adjourn the taxation for a reasonable period and direct a solicitor whose bill is being taxed to send to any person having an interest in the fund a copy of the bill, or part thereof, free of charge with a letter to the effect that the bill (or part thereof) has been referred to a Taxing Officer, the Taxing Officer's name and address, the time appointed by the Taxing Officer at which the taxation will be continued, and such other information (if any) as the Taxing Officer may direct.

RULES 28 TO 32

These rules deal with assessment of costs.

Rule 28 deals with costs to be taxed *inter partes* or out of a fund and rule 28 (2) sets out the basis on which such costs are to be taxed "Subject to the following provisions of this rule, costs to which this rule applies shall be taxed on the party and party basis, and on a taxation on that basis there shall be allowed all such costs as were necessary or proper for the attainment of justice or for enforcing or defending the rights of the party whose costs are being taxed." Rule 28 (3), however, goes on to provide "the court in awarding costs to which this rule applies may in any case in which it thinks fit to do so order or direct that the costs shall be taxed on the common fund basis".

[NOTE.—The common fund basis compares with Class No. 2 mentioned in the taxing master's answers to objections in the case of *Giles* v. *Randall*, [1915] K.B. 290. It is however on a more generous basis than that of a party and party taxation and is applicable to the allowance of "all costs reasonably incurred".]

Rule 28A deals with costs of a litigant in person.

Rule 29 deals with the costs payable to a solicitor by his own client, except bills to be paid out of the legal aid fund under the Legal Aid Act, 1974, or bills in respect of non-contentious business, and on a taxation under this rule "all costs shall be allowed, except in so far as they are of an unreasonable amount or have been unreasonable incurred". All costs incurred with the express or implied approval of the client will be conclusively presumed to have been reasonably incurred, and where the amount thereof has been expressly or impliedly approved by the client then the amount will be deemed to be reasonable, but any costs of an unusual nature which would not be allowed on a party and party basis, will, unless the solicitor expressly informed his client before they were incurred that they might not be so allowed, be presumed, until the contrary is shown to have been unreasonably incurred.

Rule 30, as amended applies to any proceedings:

(a) in which money is claimed or recovered on behalf of an infant or person incapable by mental disorder of managing his property;

(b) under the Fatal Accidents Acts, 1846–1959 in which money is recovered on behalf of a widow of the person whose death gave rise to the proceedings or is accepted on her behalf if the proceedings were also for the benefit of an infant;

(c) in the Court of Appeal in connection with the aforementioned proceedings (see r. 30 (1)).

The Taxing Officer must tax the plaintiff's costs as between party and party and as between solicitor and own client (*i.e.* a four-column bill is necessary in addition to the columns for V.A.T.) unless the solicitor certifies he is prepared to waive any costs not recoverable against the other side. Normally the Taxing Officer will accept such a waiver but see *Butterworths' Costs*, 4th Edn., Vol. 1, pp. A 119 *et seq.* No costs other than those so certified shall be payable to the solicitor for any plaintiff in the cause or matter and any adult plaintiff joined is similarly affected. The paying party will on occasions only pay costs on a common fund basis, in which case, should the solicitor wish to have costs over and above those allowed on such a basis, he must still bring in for taxation a four-column bill; this applies to proceedings in the Chancery Division and in the Queen's Bench Division and also in the Court of Appeal. It should be noted that this rule applies to unsuccessful plaintiffs as well as to successful plaintiffs.

Rule 31 deals with costs payable to

a trustee out of a trust fund and confirms the previous practice as laid down in *Practice Direction*, [1953] 2 All E.R. 1159, and *Re Grimthorpe's (Baron) Will Trusts*, [1958] 1 All E.R. 765.

Rule 32 prescribes the scales of costs contained in Appendix 2 and details the charges for non-contentious work for sales, etc. are to be under the Solicitors' Remuneration Order 1972 (see *Butterworths' Costs*, 4th Edn., Vol. 2).

RULES 33 TO 35

These rules deal with review. Rule 33 limits the time for lodging objections to 14 days or such shorter period as the Taxing Officer may fix, and every applicant for review must deliver to the Taxing Officer objections in writing and a copy of such objections to each other party who attended the taxation, who may within 14 days of delivery of the objections or such shorter time as may be fixed by the Taxing Officer, deliver answers in writing to the objections.

Under rule 34 applications for the review of a decision of a principal clerk will be carried out by a registrar of the principal registry of the Family Division or by a Taxing Master, as the case may be, but otherwise any review will be carried out by the Taxing Officer to whom the taxation was originally assigned. The Taxing Officer on any review has power to award costs of and incidental to the proceedings before him and if requested so to do by any party to the proceedings before him, shall state in his certificate (or otherwise in writing) the reasons for his decision and any special circumstances relevant to it.

In the concluding rule 35, a party who is dissatisfied with the decision of a Taxing Officer on review may apply to the judge within 14 days after the signing of the Taxing Officer's certificate for an order to review the taxation as to any item or part of an item if one of the parties had requested that officer to state his reasons for his decision in respect of that item or part on the review, and the judge if he thinks fit may appoint not less than two assessors one of whom shall be a Taxing Officer. On the hearing of the application the judge may make such order as the circumstances require.

See *Butterworths' Costs*, 4th Edn., pp. A 130A *et seq.*, for practice directions as to practice on review.

APPENDICES 1 TO 3

It is regretted that space does not permit the inclusion of these Appendices. Their text will however be found set out in full in *Butterworths' Costs*, 4th Edn., pp. A 141 *et seq.*

ACTIONS WHICH COULD HAVE BEEN BROUGHT IN A COUNTY COURT.—

Section 47 of the County Courts Act, 1959 provides as follows:—

47.—(1) Where an action founded on contract or tort is commenced in the High Court which could have been commenced in the County Court then, subject to subsections (3) and (4) of this section, the plaintiff

    (a) if he recovers a sum less than £650, shall not be entitled to any more costs of the action than those to which he would have been entitled if the action had been brought in the County Court; and

    (b) if he recovers a sum less than £150 shall not be entitled to any costs of the action;

so, however, that this section shall not affect any question as to costs if it appears to the High Court or a judge thereof (or where the matter is tried before a referee or officer of the Supreme Court, to that referee or officer) that there was reasonable ground for supposing the amount recoverable in respect of the plaintiff's claim to be in excess of the amount recoverable in an action commenced in the County Court.

For the purposes of paragraphs (a) and (b) of this subsection, a plaintiff shall be treated as recovering the full amount recoverable in respect of his claim without regard to any deduction made in respect of contributory negligence on his part or otherwise in respect of matters not falling to be taken into account in determining whether the action could have been commenced in the County Court.

(1A)—In relation to an action brought to enforce a right to recover

For Table of FIXED COSTS, *see* p. 193 *et seq.*, *post.*

possession of goods, or to enforce such a right and to claim payment of a debt or other demand or damages, sub-section (1) of this section shall have effect as if—

(a) in paragraph (a) of that sub-section, for the words "he recovers a sum less than £650" there were substituted the words "the aggregate amount recovered by him in the action, including the value of any goods ordered in the action to be delivered to him, less than £650"; and

(b) in paragraph (b) of that sub-section, for the words "he recovers a sum less than £150" there were substituted the words "the aggregate amount recovered by him in the action, including the value of any goods ordered in the action to be delivered to him, is less than £150";

and as if, in the words so substituted, any reference to an order for the delivery of goods to the plaintiff included a reference to an order to deliver goods to the plaintiff or to pay their value to him.

(2) Where a plaintiff is entitled to costs on a County Court scale only, the taxing master shall have the same power of directing on what County Court scale costs are to be allowed, and of allowing any item of costs, as the judge would have had if the action had been brought in a County Court.

(3) In any such action as aforesaid, whether founded on contract or tort, the High Court or a judge thereof (or where the matter is tried before a referee or officer of the Supreme Court, that referee or officer), if satisfied—

(a) that there was sufficient reason for bringing the action in the High Court; or

(b) that the defendant or one of the defendants objected to the transfer of the action, to a County Court;

may make an order allowing the costs or any part of the costs thereof on the High Court scale or on such one of the County Court scales as he may direct.

[If the court refuses to exercise its discretion and make an order then it has no power to order payment of the costs of a particular witness (*Puro-*

shotham Das Kapur v. *Trentham*, [1939] 1 K.B. 253).]

(4) [*This subsection has ceased to have effect.*]

(5) This section applies only to the costs of the proceedings in the High Court, and shall have effect subject to the provisions of section sixty of this Act (which deals with Admiralty cases).

(6) This section shall not apply in the case of any proceedings by the Crown.

A plaintiff "recovers" the excess of his claim over reductions, payments, or set-off proved by the defendant, or admitted (*Turner* v. *Bray* (1870), 5 Ex. 858). He "recovers" parts of his claim paid after action (*Pearce* v. *Bolton*, [1902] 2 K.B. 111); but not what was tendered before action and is pleaded as a tender (*James* v. *Vane* (1860), 2 E. & E. 883).

Where an injunction is the main remedy obtained, in an action which remains in the High Court, the plaintiff gets costs though the damages be under £10 (*Keates* v. *Woodward*, [1902] 1 K.B. 532).

The following actions cannot be brought in a County Court (subject to those cases in which there may be jurisdiction by agreement or by abandonment of part of claim).

(a) *Actions in respect of claims* where the amount exceeds £1,000 and where, in the High Court, such claim would form the subject of an action founded on contract or tort in the Queen's Bench Division (defendant, when claim is for over £100 can give notice that he objects to trial in the County Court).

Action (before the County Courts Act, 1955) brought in County Court (limited to £200). Defendant applied under s. 44 to transfer to High Court. Judgment for plaintiff for £87. Held in *Turner* v. *Jacaranda Clubs, Ltd.*, [1953] 1 All E.R. 548, that as action had been commenced in County Court, s. 47 did not apply to disentitle the plaintiff to High Court scale.

(b) *Actions for Libel, Slander,* or *Seduction* (County Courts Act, 1959, s. 39).

(c) *Recovery of Land or in which title to hereditament in question* where the net annual value for rating of the land or hereditament in question exceeds £1,000.

(d) *Patent Cases. R. v. County Court J. of Halifax*, [1891] 2 Q.B. 263.

(e) *Equity Proceedings* where the estate, fund, loan or value of the property involved exceeds £5000 and which, in the High Court,

would form the subject of an action in the Chancery Division.

(f) *Admiralty Proceedings* where the amount claimed exceeds £1,000 or the value of the property salvaged exceeds £3,500.

(g) *Contentious Probate Proceedings* where the value of the estate is £1,000 or over.

TABLE OF FIXED COSTS AS FROM 1st OCTOBER 1975

QUEEN'S BENCH DIVISION

Note.—Country Cases are defined as:—

(a) In actions commenced in the Central Office, where the plaintiff's solicitor has no place of business within a radius of 5 miles of the Royal Courts of Justice, London, or where he has such a place of business but any defendant is served outside that radius.

(b) In actions commenced in a District Registry, where the plaintiff's solicitor has no place of business within a radius of 5 miles from the District Registry, or where he has such a place of business but any defendant is served outside that radius.

FOURTEEN-DAY COSTS

The amount of costs indorsed on a Writ of Summons under Order 6, rule 2 (1) (b):—

	Town Cases £p	Country Cases £p
When the amount claimed is not less than £150 but does not exceed £200	17.00	17.50
For each extra defendant	1.00	1.00
When the amount claimed exceeds £200 but does not exceed £500	19.00	19.50
For each extra defendant	1.00	1.00
When the amount claimed exceeds £500 but is less than £650	21.00	21.50
For each extra defendant	1.00	1.00
When the amount claimed is not less than £650	28.85	30.90
For each extra defendant	2.05	2.05

The above apply to all writs for service within the jurisdiction, indorsed with liquidated demand only, whether indorsed with a Statement of Claim or not.

In addition to the above the following may be added to provide for the contingency of substituted service:—

	£p	£p
When the claim is not less than £150 but less than £650	2.00	2.00
When the claim is not less than £650	7.20	7.20

Additional Allowance where Service out of the Jurisdiction Ordered

For service in Scotland, Northern Ireland, Isle of Man or Channel Islands:—

	£p
Where the amount claimed is less than £650	6.00
Where the amount claimed is not less than £650	10.60

For service in any other place out of the jurisdiction:—

	£p
Where the amount is less than £650	9.00
Where the amount is not less than £650	16.65

JUDGMENT IN DEFAULT OF APPEARANCE OR OF DEFENCE FOR A DEBT OR
LIQUIDATED AMOUNT ONLY OR FOR POSSESSION OF LAND
(The following sums apply whether the statement of claim is indorsed on the
writ or not)

		Town Cases £p	Country Cases £p
1.	Under £150 no costs unless allowed by Master under the County Courts Act, 1959. S. 47(3)		
2.	Where not less than £150 but not more than £200 is recovered	19.00	19.50
	For each extra service effected	1.00	1.00
3.	Where more than £200 but not more than £500 is recovered	21.00	21.50
	For each extra service effected	1.00	1.00
4.	Where more than £500 but less than £650 is recovered	23.00	23.50
	For each extra service effected	1.00	1.00
5.	Where not less than £650 is recovered	35.90	37.95
	For each extra service effected	2.05	2.05
6.	Possession of land		
	(a) Judgment for possession and a liquidated sum of not less than £150 but not more than £200	19.00	19.50
	For each extra service effected	1.00	1.00
	(b) Judgment for possession and a liquidated sum of more than £200 but not more than £500	21.00	21.50
	For each extra service effected	1.00	1.00
	(c) Judgment for possession and a liquidated sum of more than £500 but less than £650	23.00	23.50
	For each extra service effected	1.00	1.00
	(d) Judgment for possession and liquidated sum of not less than £650	35.90	37.95
	For each extra service effected	2.05	2.05

Additional allowances applicable to all the above cases unless taxation is ordered:—

	£p
(1) Where substituted service ordered and effected:—	
(a) Where not less than £150 but less than £650 is recovered	2.00
(b) Where not less than £650 is recovered	7.20
(2) Where the judgment is in default of defence and notice of appearance is not given on the day on which the appearance is entered and Plaintiff has made an affidavit of service for the purpose of judgment in default of appearance (including search)	
Where less than £650 is recovered	1.25
Where not less than £650 is recovered	3.50
(3) Where service ordered and effected out of the jurisdiction:—	
(a) In Scotland, Northern Ireland, the Isle of Man, or Channel Islands:—	
Where less than £650 is recovered	6.00
Where not less than £650 is recovered	10.60
(b) In any other place out of the jurisdiction:—	
Where less than £650 is recovered	9.00
Where not less than £650 is recovered	16.65

	Town Cases £p	Country Cases £p
(4) Moneylender's Cases—Application for leave to enter judgment under O. 83, Rule 4:—		
(a) When an affidavit of justification is not allowed:—		
Where less than £650 is recovered	1.50	
Where not less than £650 is recovered	2.70	
(b) When an affidavit of justification is allowed:		
Where less than £650 is recovered	2.50	
Where not less than £650 is recovered	4.80	
(c) Where more than one defendant:—		
For each additional defendant:—		
Where less than £650 is recovered	0.50	
Where not less than £650 is recovered	2.05	
(5) Hire Purchase Cases:—Application for leave to enter judgment under O. 84 Rule 3:—		
(a) Where less than £650 is recovered	2.50	
For each extra defendant	0.50	
(b) Where not less than £650 is recovered	3.35	
For each extra defendant	1.35	
(6) Mileage:—Where not less than £650 is recovered and there is no available solicitor carrying on business within 2 miles of the place where the defendant is served, a mileage allowance in respect of each mile after the first 2 miles between that place and the nearest place of business of an available solicitor	0.15	

JUDGMENT UNDER ORDER 14

	Town Cases £p	Country Cases £p
1. Under £150 (where less than £150 recovered)—no costs without Special Order under the County Courts Act, 1959. S. 47 (3)		
2. Where not less than £150 but not more than £200 is recovered	22.00	22.50
For each extra defendant served	1.00	1.00
3. Where more than £200 but not more than £500 is recovered	24.00	24.50
For each extra defendant served	1.00	1.00
4. Where more than £500 but less than £650 is recovered..	26.00	26.50
For each extra defendant served	1.00	1.00
5. Where not less than £650 is recovered	40.65	42.70
For each extra defendant served	2.05	2.05
6. Possession of land		
(a) Judgment for possession and a liquidated sum of not less than £150 but not more than £200	22.00	22.50
For each extra defendant served ..	1.00	1.00
(b) Judgment for possession and a liquidated sum of more than £200 but not more than £500	24.00	24.50
For each extra defendant served ..	1.00	1.00
(c) Judgment for possession and a liquidated sum of more than £500 but less than £650	26.00	26.50
For each extra defendant served ..	1.00	1.00
(d) Judgment for possession and liquidated sum of not less than £650	40.65	42.70
For each extra defendant served ..	2.05	2.05

Additional allowance applicable to all the above cases unless taxation is ordered:—

		£p
(1) Where an affidavit of service is required:—		
Where less than £650 is recovered	..	1.25
Where not less than £650 is recovered	..	3.85
(2) Where notice of appearance is not given on the day on which the appearance is entered, and plaintiff makes an affidavit of service for the purpose of judgment in default (including search):—		
Where less than £650 is recovered	..	1.25
Where not less than £650 is recovered	..	3.90
(3) Costs of adjournment of summons:—		
Where less than £650 is recovered	..	1.00
Where not less than £650 is recovered	..	2.05
(4) Where substituted service ordered and effected:—		
Where not less than £150 but less than £650 is recovered	..	2.00
Where not less than £650 is recovered	..	7.20
(5) Where service ordered and effected out of the jurisdiction:—		
(a) In Scotland, Northern Ireland, the Isle of Man or Channel Islands:—		
Where less than £650 is recovered..	..	6.00
Where not less than £650 is recovered	..	10.60
(b) In any other place out of the jurisdiction:—		
Where less than £650 is recovered..	..	9.00
Where not less than £650 is recovered	..	16.65

(6) Mileage:—see note above.

JUDGMENT ON DISCONTINUANCE OR ON ACCEPTANCE OF MONEY PAID INTO COURT
(Order 62, Rule 10)

						£p
Costs of Judgment	..	..	..	..	..	2.15

JUDGMENTS EXTENSION ACT, 1868

Where a Judgment is registered under the Judgments Extension Act, 1868, within 12 months of its date, without order.

Costs of Registration..	..	..	..	..	10.45

GARNISHEE PROCEEDINGS
(Order 49)
Judgment Creditor's Costs

Where the Judgment Creditor recovers from the Garnishee:—

					£p
(1) less than £5 ..	..	..	..	..	No Costs
(2) from £5 to £10 inclusive	..	..	..	..	2.00
(3) Over £10	..	..	..	..	8.45
(4) Where garnishee fails to attend hearing and an affidavit of service is required (*extra*)	..	..			3.70

Garnishee's Costs   £p

In town case (no affidavit)	2.05
In town case (with affidavit)	4.75
In country cases (no affidavit)	3.40
In country cases (with affidavit)	6.40

CHARGING ORDERS
(Order 50)

Costs allowed	11.30
Where an affidavit of service is required (*extra*) ..	3.70

WRIT OF POSSESSION
(Order 45, Rule 3)

Application for Writ of Possession:—

Costs added to Judgment:—

(1) Where no costs are allowed on the Judgment ..	Nil
(2) Where costs are allowed on the Judgment ..	3.70
(3) For each additional Person given notice of the proceedings (if allowed)	0.55

ISSUING EXECUTION

Costs allowed:—

Where less than £150	Nil
Where more than £150	8.40

SUMMARY OF HIGH COURT FEES

See Supreme Court Fees Order, 1975, for further details

SECTION 1.—FEES PAYABLE IN EVERY DIVISION OF THE HIGH COURT

Column 1	Column 2	Column 3
Item	Fee	Document to be Marked
Commencement of a cause or matter 1.—(i) On sealing—	£	
(a) a writ of summons,		The filed copy.
(b) an originating summons, where no other fee is specially provided,		The filed copy.
(c) an originating notice of motion, except a notice of appeal to the High Court, or		The notice of motion.
(d) on presenting an originating petition except where a fee under section 9 of this Schedule is payable:		
In each case	15.00	The petition.
(ii) On sealing an originating summons for approval of an infant settlement ..	5.00	The filed copy.

Section 1—*cont.*

Column 1	Column 2	Column 3
Item	Fee	Document to be Marked
2. On an originating ex parte application where no other fee is specifically prescribed: .. .. .. Provided that, where the applicant is directed to issue an originating summons, credit for the fee paid on the ex parte application is to be given against the fee payable on the summons.	2.00	The affidavit filed in support of the application.
Entry or setting down for trial in court 6. On setting down a cause on motion for judgment	7.50	The præcipe or notice of motion.
7. On entering or setting down a cause or matter in the Short Cause List or entering a Probate action as a short cause ..	7.50	The filed copy of pleadings.

8. On filing—
    (a) a notice of appeal to the High Court, or
    (b) a case stated or a special case for the opinion of the High Court pursuant to statute
    and setting the appeal or case down for hearing .. ..
	10.00	The notice or case.

9. On entering or setting down any other cause or matter, including a reference to an Official Referee, for trial, hearing or further consideration in court, except where—
    (a) it is otherwise provided in this Schedule, or
    (b) Fee No. 1 (c), 51, 52 or 53 has been paid, or
    (c) in the case of a reference to an Official Referee, this fee has already been paid in respect of the same cause or matter .. ..
	15.00	The præcipe or the filed copy of the pleadings.

Writs 10. On sealing a writ of subpœna ad testificandum or duces tecum, for each witness	1.00	The præcipe.
11. On sealing a writ of execution	3.00	The præcipe.

SECTION 2.—FEES PAYABLE IN THE CHANCERY DIVISION

Column 1	Column 2	Column 3
Item	Fee	Document to be Marked
	£	
14. On adjourning from chambers into court		The summons,
(a) an originating summons	7.50	notice or sealed
(b) any other summons or a notice under Order 25, Rule 7 (3) ..	7.50	copy thereof.
23.—(a) On referring a bill of costs to a Taxing Master from chambers without an order	1.00	The reference.
(b) on assessing costs for every £1 or fraction of £1 of the sum assessed	0.05	The bill.

Note.—Chancery Orders. Court fees are no longer payable on Orders, but certain Orders will still have to be stamped with Revenue duty.

The Controller of Stamps, Inland Revenue, has advised the Chancery Registrars' Office that the following statement represents the current practice with reference to the stamping of Judgments and Orders of the High Court:

1. A judgment or order for, or having the effect on an order for, foreclosure is chargeable with *ad valorem* duty as a Conveyance on sale by reference to the total amount owing for principal interests and costs on the mortgage foreclosed (together with the amount due on any prior incumbrance), provided that the *ad valorem* stamp duty upon any such judgment or order shall not exceed the duty on a sum equal to the value of the property which the judgment or order relates (section 6, Finance Act 1898).

A foreclosure decree or a conveyance to a mortgage by order of the Court, when made in favour of a second or subsequent mortgagee, is (subject to the above-noted limitation with reference to the value of the property) to be charged on the amount of the prior mortgages, as well as on the amount of the mortgage in respect of which the order of conveyance is made (section 57, Stamp Act 1891).

Where duty is paid on the value of the property, the judgment or order should be adjudicated. Where either (a) the sum due for principal, interest and costs (together with the amount due on any prior mortgage), or (b) the value of the property, does not exceed one or other of the statutory limits (see section 55, Finance Act 1963, as amended by section 125, Finance Act 1972) the corresponding certificate of value should be inserted in the judgment or order, so that it may be stamped at the appropriate lower rate of duty.

2. Order appointing new trustees: one stamp of 50p.

3. Order appointing new trustees and vesting in them the right to transfer stock (including shares and any annuity, security, etc. transferable in books kept by any company, etc.): one stamp of 50p.

4. Order appointing new trustees and vesting in them land or other property (except as below) capable of being so vested: two stamps of 50p.

5. Order appointing new trustees and vesting in them the right to sue for any chose in action: two stamps of 50p each, except if the chose in action is money secured by a mortgage, bond, debenture or covenant (other than a marketable security) or by any judgment, when only one stamp of 50p is required.

6. An order vesting in trustees (separately appointed) the right to transfer stock, etc. and also the right to receive dividends due and to become due: one stamp of 50p.

No stamp is required in respect of an order merely vesting the right to transfer, or to call for the transfer of any stock, etc. or in respect of any order appointing original trustees under the Settled Land Act 1925 or the Law of Property Act 1925.

SECTION 3—FEES PAYABLE IN THE QUEEN'S BENCH DIVISION

Column 1	Column 2	Column 3
Item	Fee	Document to be Marked
	£	
25. On inquiry, trial or assessment of damages before a Master or District Registrar, or on any summons, adjourned for the examination of witnesses ..	5.00	The order, summons, judgment or certificate.
26. On sealing a summons for bail	1.00	The summons.
27. On sealing a notice of appeal from a Master or District Registrar to a Judge in Chambers	5.00	The notice.
28. On taking a receiver's account	2.00	The account or certificate.

SECTION 5.—FEES PAYABLE IN THE COURT OF APPEAL

Column 1	Column 2	Column 3
Item	Fee	Document to be Marked
	£	
35. On filing a notice of appeal		
(a) from a county court		
(i) if the appeal is entered in an interlocutory list	6.00	
(ii) if the appeal is entered in any other list	10.00	
(b) in any other case		
(i) if the appeal is entered in an interlocutory list	7.50	The notice of appeal.
(ii) if the appeal is entered in any other list	15.00	
36. On filing a notice of cross-appeal or a respondent's notice under Order 59, Rule 6 (1)		
37. On filing a notice of motion	5.00	The notice.

SECTION 6.—FEES PAYABLE FOR COPIES OF DOCUMENTS

Column 1	Column 2	Column 3
Item	Fee	Document to be Marked
	£	
38. For a photographic copy or of part of any document, whether or not issued as an office copy, for each photographic sheet	0.25	The copy or fee sheet.
39. For a typewritten copy of any document, per page .. .. .. and for each page of any additional carbon copy bespoken, half of the fee above.	0.5	The fee sheet.
40. For examining a plain copy and marking the same as an office copy—for each sheet	0.25	The office copy.
41. For a copy in a foreign language and for a copy of a plan, map, section, drawing, photograph or diagram— the reasonable cost thereof as certified by the officer of the court		The præcipe or copy.

SECTION 7.—FEES PAYABLE IN THE SUPREME COURT PAY OFFICE

Column 1	Column 2	Column 3
Item	Fee	Document to be Marked
	£	
43. On a request for		
(a) a certificate of		
(i) the amount and description of any fund	0.25	
(ii) lodgment in court of any fund	0.25	
(iii) non-lodgment in court of any fund	0.50	
(iv) any transaction for which no other fee is prescribed ..	0.25	The request.
(b) the redating of a certificate of the amount and description of any fund	0.13	The certificate.
(c) a transcript of an account, for each opening	0.25	The transcript.
Provided that the fees prescribed in paragraphs (a) (i), (b) and (c) shall not be payable in respect of any matter in the Court of Protection		

Section 8.—Fees Payable on the Taxation of Costs

Column 1	Column 2	Column 3
Item	Fee	Document to be Marked
	£	
48. On taking a cash account between solicitor and own client under the Solicitors Act 1974 or otherwise— for every £100 or fraction of £100 of the amounts found to have been received and paid	0.10	The fee sheet.
49. On the taxation of a bill of costs— for every £1 or fraction of £1 of the amount allowed	0.05	The bill.
Provided that the taxing officer may in any case require the bill of costs to be stamped before taxation with the whole or part of the amount of fees which would be payable if the bill were allowed by him at the full amount thereof (including, in cases under the Solicitors Act 1974, the fee payable in respect of the cash account).		
50. On the withdrawal of a bill of costs which has been lodged for taxation, such fee (not exceeding the amount which would have been payable under Fee No. 49 if the bill had been allowed in full) as may be reasonable having regard to the amount of work done in the court office		The bill.
[Note.—For Table of fees worked out in detail see p. 205 post]		

Section 9.—Fees Payable in Companies Matters

Column 1	Column 2	Column 3
Item	Fee	Document to be Marked
	£	
51. On presenting a petition under one or more of the following:— (a) section 56, to confirm the reduction of a share premium account, (b) section 57, to sanction the issue of shares at a discount, (c) section 67, to confirm a reduction of a capital redemption reserve fund, (d) section 67, to confirm a reduction of capital, or (e) section 206, to sanction a compromise or scheme of arrangement	25.00	The petition.

Section 9—*cont.*

Column 1	Column 2	Column 3
Item	**Fee**	**Document to be Marked**
	£	
52. On presenting a petition under one or more of the following:—		
(a) section 5, to cancel an alteration of objects.		
(b) section 23, to cancel an alteration in conditions in a memorandum of association,		
(c) section 72, to cancel any variation of the rights attached to any class of shares,		
(d) section 353, to restore a name to the register of companies,		
(e) section 395, to cancel an alteration in the form of the constitution of a company or		
(f) section 448, for relief by officers of a company	12.00	The petition.
53. On presenting a petition for the winding-up of a company by or under the supervision of the court, or for an order under section 210	12.00	The petition.

SECTION 10.—MISCELLANEOUS FEES

Column 1	Column 2	Column 3
Item	**Fee**	**Document to be Marked**
Bill of Sale	£	
56. On filing—		
(a) any document under the Bills of Sale Act, other than a fiat of satisfaction	2.00	The document filed.
(b) a fiat of satisfaction	1.00	The fiat.
57. (a) For an official certificate of the result of a search in one name in any register or index under the custody of the Registrar of bills of sale	1.00	
for every additional name, if included in the same certificate	0.50	
(b) for a continuation search, if made within one calendar month of date of official certificate (the result to be endorsed on each certificate)	0.50	The requisition for search.

Section 10—*cont.*

Column 1	Column 2	Column 3
Item	Fee	Document to be Marked
	£	
Production of documents, etc.		
58. Upon an application for the production of records or documents to be given in evidence—		
(a) where the records or documents are sent by post—		
for the first document　..	1.00	The application.
for each additional document	0.25	The application.
(b) where an officer is required to produce the records or documents in court and, in addition		
(i) for every half-day or part thereof that he is necessarily absent from his office, and (ii) his reasonable expenses of attendance:	5.00	The application or fee sheet.
Provided that the Court may require—		
(1) a deposit of money on account of any further fees and a deposit of money on account of any further expenses which may probably become payable beyond the amount paid for fees and expenses on the application, receipt of which shall be marked on the application;		
(2) an undertaking in writing to pay any further fees and expenses which may become payable beyond the amounts so paid and deposited.		
Judge sitting as arbitrator		
60. On the appointment of a judge of the Commercial Court as an arbitrator or umpire under section 4 of the Administration of Justice Act, 1970 (a)　..	250.00	The arbitration agreement or other document produced to the judge as constituting the submission to arbitration.
61. For every two days or part thereof (after the first two days) of the hearing of the reference before a judge so appointed an arbitrator or umpire　..　..	250,00	The arbitration agreement or other document produced to the judge as constituting the submission to arbitration.

TABLE OF TAXING FEES UNDER FEE NO. 49

NOTE.—The fees are calculated on the amount of the Bill *as allowed* on taxation.

Bill not exceeding	Fee	Bill not exceeding	Fee	Bill not exceeding	Fee
£	£	£	£	£	£
5	0.25	47	2.35	89	4.45
6	0.30	48	2.40	90	4.50
7	0.35	49	2.45	91	4.55
8	0.40	50	2.50	92	4.60
9	0.45	51	2.55	93	4.65
10	0.50	52	2.60	94	4.70
11	0.55	53	2.65	95	4.75
12	0.60	54	2.70	96	4.80
13	0.65	55	2.75	97	4.85
14	0.70	56	2.80	98	4.90
15	0.75	57	2.85	99	4.95
16	0.80	58	2.90	100	5.00
17	0.85	59	2.95	150	7.50
18	0.90	60	3.00	200	10.00
19	0.95	61	3.05	250	12.50
20	1.00	62	3.10	300	15.00
21	1.05	63	3.15	350	17.50
22	1.10	64	3.20	400	20.00
23	1.15	65	3.25	450	22.50
24	1.20	66	3.30	500	25.00
25	1.25	67	3.35	550	27.50
26	1.30	68	3.40	600	30.00
27	1.35	69	3.45	650	32.50
28	1.40	70	3.50	700	35.00
29	1.45	71	3.55	750	37.50
30	1.50	72	3.60	800	40.00
31	1.55	73	3.65	850	42.50
32	1.60	74	3.70	900	45.00
33	1.65	75	3.75	950	47.50
34	1.70	76	3.80	1,000	50.00
35	1.75	77	3.85	2,000	100.00
36	1.80	78	3.90	3,000	150.00
37	1.85	79	3.95	4,000	200.00
38	1.90	80	4.00	5,000	250.00
39	1.95	81	4.05	6,000	300.00
40	2.00	82	4.10	7,000	350.00
41	2.05	83	4.15	8,000	400.00
42	2.10	84	4.20	9,000	450.00
43	2.15	85	4.25	10,000	500.00
44	2.20	86	4.30	15,000	750.00
45	2.25	87	4.35		
46	2.30	88	4.40		

TIME TABLE OF PROCEEDINGS IN SUPREME COURT

ADMISSIONS

Notice in writing of admission of facts may be given.	Not later than 21 days after action set down for trial.

AMENDMENT

Plaintiff or Defendant may amend his pleading without leave once	Before pleadings are deemed to be closed.
Application to disallow may be made	Within 14 days of service of amended document.
Where leave to amend granted amendment must be made	Within time limited by the order or if no time limited within 14 days from date of order.
Pleading to amended pleading	Within time limited for pleading or within 14 days from delivery of amendment whichever shall last expire.

APPEALS

From chambers.

From Queen's Bench Master in Chambers by notice to attend before Judge	Within 5 days of decision complained of.

To Court of Appeal.

I. *Service of Notice*

(a) From an interlocutory order (other than in Companies' winding-up or Bankruptcy)	14 days from the time the order was signed, entered or otherwise perfected.
(b) From order or decision in Companies winding-up or Bankruptcy	21 days from the time the order was signed, entered or otherwise perfected.
(c) From County Court	6 weeks from date of final judgment or order and 14 days from date of interlocutory judgment or order.
(d) Any other case	6 weeks from the time the order was signed, entered or otherwise perfected.

II. *Setting Down*

In all cases	Within 7 days of service of Notice or such further time as may be allowed.

III. *Notice of Setting Down*

To all parties on whom notice of appeal was served	Within 2 days of setting down.

IV. *Respondent's notice of intention to contend that decision should be varied in case of appeal from*

(a) an interlocutory order	Within 7 days of service of notice of appeal.
(b) in any other case	Within 21 days of service of notice of appeal.

To Divisional Court

From inferior courts of civil jurisdiction by notice of motion, O. 55, r. 4. Appeal does not operate as stay unless so ordered by inferior court.	Within 28 days, but see exceptions in Note to O. 55, r. 4 (55/4/1).

APPEARANCE

Time for entry by defendant	Within the time limited for appearance, *i.e.*, 14 days after service inclusive of day of service when writ or Originating Summons served within the jurisdiction; within time limited by order when writ or Originating Summons served out of the jurisdiction: or, in either case, at any time before judgment. Appearance can now be entered by post subject to certain conditions
By person other than defendant served with notice	Within same time as to writ of summons.
Where proceedings transferred from County Court	Within 7 days of receipt of notice from High Court that action proceeding in London.

ATTACHMENT OF DEBTS

Service of order nisi	At least 7 days before day of hearing.

COPIES OF DOCUMENTS

Time for supplying	Within 48 hours of receipt of written request.

DEFENCE AND COUNTERCLAIM

Where defendant has appeared	Within 14 days from time limited for appearance or from service of statement of claim, whichever is later, unless plaintiff in the meantime has served a summons for leave to sign judgment under O. 14. This exception would also appear to apply to applications under O. 86.
Where leave to defend given under O. 14	Within 14 days after the making of the order giving leave to defend or within the time specified in the order.
Reply to defence	With 14 days from service of the defence.
Defence to counterclaim	Within 14 days of service of counterclaim.

DISCONTINUANCE

Notice by plaintiff in writing may be given	Within 14 days after service of Defence.
Judgment by defendant for costs may be signed.	After 4 days from taxation.

DISCOVERY AND INSPECTION

List of documents to be served	Within 14 days after close of pleadings.
Notice that documents are available for inspection	To be served within 4 days from receipt of notice to produce.

EXECUTION

Duration in force if unexecuted	1 year from issue.
When may issue	Within six years from judgment or order without leave or afterwards by leave.

INTERPLEADER

Notice by execution creditor that he admits or disputes claim to goods to be given to sheriff.	Within 4 days after receiving notice of claim.

JUDGMENT

Default of appearance	After expiration of time limited for appearance. As to Moneylenders' Actions *see* O. 83, r. 4.
In District Registry action where defendant may appear in London	Not till after course of post from London on expiration of time limited for appearance.
O. 14. Return of summons for leave to sign judgment	10 clear days after service.
Motion for: where issues of fact ordered to be tried, motion for judgment may be set down by plaintiff and by defendant	As soon as issues determined. On expiration of 10 days from the determination or within 1 year afterwards.

NEW TRIAL

Motion for: (no return date necessary)	Within 6 weeks from the time the order was signed, entered or otherwise perfected.

ORIGINATING SUMMONSES (TO WHICH APPEARANCE REQUIRED)

Duration in force	12 months from date of issue inclusive of that day.
Must be renewed	Within that time.
Duration of renewal	Not more than 12 months at any one time.

PAYMENT INTO COURT

In satisfaction or denying liability	Any time after appearance.
Notice of acceptance by plaintiff to be given	Within 21 days of receipt of notice of payment into Court or within 21 days of the last payment when there is more than one payment, but before trial begins.
Taxation of costs by plaintiff where notice of acceptance given	At expiration of 4 days from payment out.
Judgment after taxation if costs not paid	At expiration of 48 hours after taxation.

STATEMENT OF CLAIM

Probate Actions (unless indorsed on the Writ)	Within 6 weeks of defendant's appearance, or within 8 days of filing an affidavit under O. 76, r. 5.
All other actions	With the Writ: after service of writ and before Appearance or within 14 days of appearance.

SUMMONS FOR DIRECTIONS

To be issued	
Under O. 25, r. 1	Within one month from the close of the pleadings.
Under O. 78, r. 5	Within 7 days after appearance.
Returnable	
Under O. 25, r. 1	In not less than 14 days.
Under O. 78, r. 5	In not less than 21 days.
Subsequent application made by notice	2 clear days' notice to be given to other party.
Applications by defendant to dismiss action if summons not taken out	
Under O. 25, r. 1	After expiration of one month from the close of the pleadings.
Under O. 78, r. 5	After 7 days has elapsed from appearance.

THIRD PARTY NOTICE

Appearance to	Within 14 days of service of notice.
Application for leave to issue	After delivery of defence.
Issued without leave	Before delivery of defence.
Service of	The provisions of Order 10 (except r. 1(4), and Order 11 (except r. 3) apply, (O. 16 r. 3 (4)).

TRIAL

Action to be set down:	
By plaintiff in actions to which O. 25, r. 1 applies and when directions have been given under O. 14	Within time fixed by order for directions.
By defendant	At expiration of time fixed by order for directions.
Notice of setting down to be given	Within 24 hours of setting down.
Trial out of London	See Practice Directions 34/4/3 and 34/4/4 Supreme Court Practice 1976, Part I.

WRIT

Duration in force	12 months from date of issue inclusive of the day.
Must be renewed	Within above time.
Duration of renewal	Not more than 12 months at any one time.
Indorsement of service of	Within three days from service.

Income Tax

SEE TAXATION, p. 341, *post*

Indictments

SEE CRIMINAL LAW
p. 137

Jury Service

The qualification for jury service is now set out in s. 25 of the Criminal Justice Act 1972, which in effect provides that a person is liable for jury service if:

(a) he is registered as a parliamentary or local government elector, and

(b) he is not less than eighteen years old, and not more than sixty-five, and

(c) he has been ordinarily resident in the United Kingdom for a period of at least five years since his thirteenth birthday, and

(d) he does not fall within the classes of persons who are ineligible or disqualified from jury service.

Those ineligible are set out in Part I of Section 2 of the Criminal Justice Act 1972 and comprise four main groups: *Group A—The Judiciary* (including holders of high judicial office, Circuit judges and Recorders, Metropolitan and stipendiary magistrates, Justices of the Peace); *Group B— Others concerned with the administration of justice* (including Barristers and solicitors, their clerks, legal executives, justices' clerks and assistants, probation officers, members of any police force); *Group C—The Clergy, etc.* (including a man in holy orders, a regular minister of any religious denomination, a vowed member of any religious order living in a religious community); *Group D—The Mentally Ill.*

Those disqualified are set out in Part II of Sched. 2 of the Criminal Justice Act 1972 and include a person who has been sentenced to imprisonment for life or for a term of five years or more or to be detained during Her Majesty's pleasure, and a person who, at any time in the last ten years has served any part of a sentence of imprisonment or detention of three months or more or has been detained in a borstal institution.

Part III lists those persons excusable as of right and this group comprises peers, members of the House of Commons, officers of the House of Commons and House of Lords, full-time serving members to any of Her Majesty's forces.

S. 34 (2) of the Courts Act 1971 provides that if any person summoned under the Act shows to the satisfaction of the appropriate officer that there is good reason why he should be excused from attending in pursuance of the summons, the appropriate officer may excuse that person from so attending. A right of appeal exists to the court before which the person is summoned to attend against any refusal of the appropriate officer to excuse him under s. 34 (2).

S. 37 of the Courts Act 1971 allows for exemption for previous jury service.

Grand Juries were abolished by the Administration of Justice (Miscellaneous Provisions) Act, 1933, s. 1, and the Criminal Justice Act, 1948, ss. 31, 83.

Special Juries have been totally abolished by the Courts Act 1971, s. 40.

Payments in respect of Jury Service are provided for by ss. 1–17 of the Juries Act, 1949 (as amended). By the Jurors' Allowances Regulations, 1974 (S.I. 1974 No. 1461), payments to which a juror is entitled under s. 1 of the Juries Act, 1954, are:—(i) Travelling allowance (if by railway or other public conveyance the actual fare, but only the second class fare is allowed for travel by railway; where a person travels by hired vehicle the allowance is the amount of fare and any reasonable gratuity paid but, if it is not a case of urgency and public services services are available, the amount of the fare by public service; where a private conveyance is used: 6p a mile for vehicles under 1000 cc, 7.1p between 1000 cc, and 1750 cc, 7.7p over 1750 cc. In any other case, a rate not exceeding 2.8p a mile is allowed; (ii) Subsistence allowance (for a period away from home or place of business of not more than 4 hours, 62p is allowed, for a period of more than 4 hours but not more than 8 hours, £1.35; for a period of over 8 hours but not more than 12 hours, £2.40; for a period of more than 12 hours but less than 16 hours, £3.40; for a period of more than 16 hours, £4.05; if the person is away overnight the allowance is £8.65 for each period

of 24 hours or fraction thereof); (iii) Compensation for loss of earnings and additional expense (other than travelling or subsistence) (for the amount of the loss or additional expense for a period of not more than 4 hours, £3.35 is allowed; for a period of over 4 hours, £6.70, but after 10 days' jury service this maximum is increased to £13.40).

As to Juries in County Courts, *see* County Courts Act, 1959, s. 94, (as amended).

JUROR'S OATH

In criminal proceedings, a new form of oath was recommended by Lord Goddard, C. J. ([1957] 1 All E.R. 290), as follows:—

"I swear by Almighty God that I will faithfully try the several issues joined between Our Sovereign Lady the Queen and the prisoner at the bar and give a true verdict according to the evidence."

Landlord and Tenant

(*See Hill and Redman's Law of Landlord and Tenant, 16th Edn.*)

PRELIMINARY NOTE

By s. 11(1) of the Housing Rents and Subsidies Act 1975 "An order may provide for restricting or preventing increases of rent for dwellings which would otherwise take place, or for restricting the amount of rent which would otherwise be payable on new

lettings of dwellings". Section 7 of and Schedule 2 to the Act provide for phasing of Rent Increases where the rent was previously subject to control under s. 11 of the Counter-Inflation Act 1973, which expired on 31st March 1976. At present there are no orders restricting rents in force under the Housing Rents and Subsidies Act 1975.

AGRICULTURAL HOLDINGS

(*See also Scammell's Law of Agricultural Holdings, 5th Edn.*)

[NOTE: At the time of going to press no changes had been made in the law so as to necessitate changes in this section. However, two Bills now going through Parliament will make sweeping changes in the law as stated below: Part II the Agriculture (Miscellaneous Provisions) Bill (which is to come into force when the Act receives the Royal Assent) would make new provision for succession on the death of a tenant; the Rent (Agriculture) Bill (which is likewise to come into force on the passing of the Act) would provide security of tenure for certain agricultural workers and ex-workers who are not protected by the Rent Acts because they occupy dwelling-houses, in consequence of their employment, under licences or tenancies at a low or nil rent. It would also place a duty on housing authorities to re-house ex-agricultural workers in certain circumstances.]

SECURITY OF TENURE

A notice to quit the whole or part of an agricultural holding is invalid if it

purports to end the tenancy in less than 12 months from the end of the current year of tenancy (Agricultural Holdings Act, 1948, s. 23 (1)). There are, however, five exceptions to this rule: (1) where a receiving order in bankruptcy is made against the tenant; (2) where the notice is given in pursuance of a provision in the contract of tenancy authorising resumption of possession of the holding or some part thereof for some specified purpose other than the use of the land for agriculture; (3) where the notice is given by a tenant to a sub-tenant; (4) where the tenancy is under an agreement made before 25 March 1947 and the notice is given by (a) the Admiralty Board, Army Board or Air Force Board, possession being required for naval, military or air force purposes, or (b) a corporation carrying on certain public undertakings or a government department or a local authority, possession being required for the purpose for which the land was acquired or appropriated by the corporation, department or authority; (5) where the tenancy is a "lease for life" or other uncertain interest which by virtue of the Law of Property Act 1925, s. 149 (6) is converted into a lease for 90 years (1948 Act, s. 23 (1) (a)–(e)).

Where notice to quit the whole or part of an agricultural holding is given to the tenant and he serves on the landlord within one month a written counter-notice requiring that s. 24 (1) of the 1948 Act shall apply to the notice to quit then, subject to the exceptions set out below, the notice to quit shall not have effect without the consent of the Agricultural Land Tribunal.

In the following cases the consent of the Tribunal is not required: (1) where the Tribunal has previously given its consent (s. 24 (2) (a)); (2) where the land is required for a use, other than for agriculture, for which town planning consents have been given, or for which such permission is not required (s. 24 (2) (b)); (3) where a bad husbandry certificate has been issued in pursuance of an application made to the Tribunal not more than 6 months before the date of the notice (s. 24 (2) (c)); (4) where the tenant has failed to comply with a previous notice served on him in writing by the landlord requiring him to pay arrears of rent within two months (s. 24 (2) (d)); (5) where the tenant has failed to remedy within such reasonable period as was specified in the notice any breach

that was capable of being remedied of a term or condition of the tenancy which was not inconsistent with the rules of good husbandry (*ibid.*); (6) where at the date of the notice the landlord's interest in the holding has been materially prejudiced by any breach by the tenant that was not capable of being remedied of a term or condition of the tenancy that was not inconsistent with the rules of good husbandry (s. 24 (2) (e)); (7) where the tenant has become bankrupt or compounded with his creditors (s. 24 (2) (f)); (8) where the tenant, or the survivor of joint tenants, has died within three months before the date of the notice (s. 24 (2) (g) and Agricultural (Miscellaneous Provisions) Act, 1954, s. 7); (9) where the tenant fails to give the requisite counter-notice within one month of receipt of the notice to quit, as required by s. 24 (1) of the 1948 Act; (10) in the case of a notice to quit by a tenant to a sub-tenant where the tenant has himself had notice to quit and states the fact in the notice to the sub-tenant (S.I. 1964 No. 706); (11) where a tenant of worked ironstone land has not complied with certain conditions under the Mineral Workings Act, 1951, s. 22.

The Agriculture (Notices to Remedy and Notices to Quit) Order 1964 Art 9. requires the reasons given in a Notice to quit under s. 24(2)(b) or (d) or (e) ((2), (4), (5) or (6) above) to be referred to arbitration.

Unless the tenant asks for a reference to arbitration within the month of service of the notice to quit he is without remedy and the court has no option but to enforce the notice to quit even though the reason stated is in fact false: *Magdalen College Oxford* v. *Heritage*, [1974] 1 All E.R. 1065.

Further restrictions have been placed on notices to quit by the Agriculture Miscellaneous Provisions Act, 1963, s. 19. Notices requiring a tenant to remedy a breach of the terms of the tenancy must be in the prescribed form and specify the period within which the breach is to be remedied. Such a notice requiring repairs to be done can be disregarded if a second similar notice is served within 12 months unless the tenant agreed in writing to the withdrawal of the earlier notice. A period of less than 6 months is unreasonable for the execution of any such work.

Any question arising under such a notice must be determined by arbitration. This includes the reasonableness of the time allowed for compliance; where that time is extended, fixing a new date for the termination of the tenancy; and for the recovery of the cost of any work which the arbitrator finds that the tenant was not required See S.I. 1964 Nos. 705, 706 (as amended by 1972 No. 1207), 707.

The Tribunal must not consent to the operation of a notice to quit unless it is satisfied (1) that the purpose for which the landlord wishes to end the tenancy is desirable in the interests of good husbandry, or (2) that such purpose is desirable in the interests of sound estate management of the estate of which the land to which the notice relates forms part or which that land constitutes, or (3) that such purpose is desirable for the purposes of agricultural research, education, experiment or demonstration or for the purposes of the enactments relating to small-holdings or allotments, or (4) that greater hardship would be caused by withholding than by giving consent, or (5) that the landlord proposes to use the land for a use, other than for agriculture, not falling within head (2) of the preceding paragraph. Notwithstanding that the Tribunal is satisfied on these matters it must withhold consent if a fair and reasonable landlord would not in all the circumstances insist on possession (1948 Act, s. 25, as substituted by the Agriculture Act 1958, s. 3 (2)).

COMPENSATION FOR DISTURBANCE

If a landlord gives notice to quit to a tenant and the tenant duly quits the holding, the landlord must, in general, pay him compensation for disturbance. Where, however, (a) the notice was given for any of the reasons set out in s. 24 (2) (c) to (g) of the 1948 Act (summarised in "Security of Tenure", *supra*) and the reason was specifically stated in the notice to quit, or (b) the notice was given under s. 22 of the Mineral Workings Act, 1951, following a certificate by the Minister of the tenant's failure to comply with the provision of that section, no compensation is payable.

The amount of the compensation has been increased by the Agriculture (Miscellaneous Provisions) Act, 1968. Before the Act, it was simply the loss or expense directly attributable to the quitting of the holding unavoidably incurred by the tenant in connection with the sale or removal of his household goods, implements of husbandry, fixtures, farm produce or farm stock on or used in connection with the holding and reasonable expenses of the preparation of the claim (not being costs of an arbitration). In this respect the tenant is entitled as a minimum to a sum equal to one year's rent without proof of loss, and is restricted to that sum unless the landlord is given an opportunity of valuing before sale such goods, implements, fixtures, produce or stock and unless notice of claim is given not less than one month before the termination of the tenancy. In no case is the tenant entitled under these provisions (but see below) to a sum greater than two years' rent. Where the tenant has sub-let and has to pay compensation to the sub-tenant, he is not barred from claiming compensation merely by the fact that on the termination of the tenancy he does not quit the holding (that is to say that in fact the sub-tenant and not the tenant quits the holding).

The Agriculture (Miscellaneous Provisions) Act, 1968, provides that where compensation has become payable under the provisions of the Act of 1948, such compensation shall be increased to include "a sum to assist in the reorganisation of the tenant's affairs" (s. 9 (1)). This sum will normally be four times the annual rent of the holding (s. 9 (2)). But there are several important cases in which the increased compensation is not obtainable (see s. 10 and Schedule 1) and in two of these the landlord must, if he is to claim exemption from paying it, include certain specific statements in his notice to quit.

BUSINESS AND PROFESSIONAL PREMISES

[In these notes references to Forms are to the forms prescribed in the Appendix to the Landlord and Tenant (Notices) Regulations, 1957, S.I. 1957, No. 1157 as amended by S.I. 1963, No. 795; by S.I. 1967, No. 1831; S.I. 1969, No. 1771 and by S.I. 1973 No. 792].

SECURITY OF TENURE

Nature of statutory protection under the Landlord and Tenant Act, 1954.—Part II of the Landlord and Tenant Act, 1954, which must be read with the relevant supplementary provisions of Part IV and the related Schedules, provides security of tenure for occupying tenants of business and professional premises, with certain exceptions. This is effected by making the tenancy only determinable as provided by Part II. Unless so determined, the tenancy continues but the tenant also has the right to apply to the court for a new lease which must be granted unless the landlord establishes the existence of one of certain grounds which entitle him to possession. If he does so the tenant is, in some cases, entitled to compensation on quitting.

References to Part II of the Landlord and Tenant Act 1954, are to it as amended by the Law of Property Act 1969 (set out at Sch. 1 to that Act with amendments).

Tenancies to which protection extends under the 1954 Act.—In general the protection of Part II applies to the tenancy of any premises occupied by the tenant for business purposes or for business and other purposes (s. 23 (1)). On the meaning of "occupied", see *Lee-Verhulst (Investments)* v. *Harwood Trust*, [1972] 3 All E.R. 619 and *Morrison Holdings, Ltd.* v. *Manders Property (Wolverhampton), Ltd.* [1976] 1 W.L.R. 533. The word "business" is defined as including a trade, business or profession and any activity carried on by an incorporated or unincorporated body (s. 23 (2)). Living accommodation occupied by the tenant's employee for the purposes of a business carried on by the tenant on the premises is deemed to be occupied by the tenant for the purposes of that business and the word "premises" has been held to apply not only to buildings but to such premises as training gallops for racehorses: *Bracey* v. *Read*, [1962] 3 All E.R. 472.

If a tenancy is held by joint tenants all of whom once carried on the business but some of whom have ceased to do so, those who still carry it on may be able to apply for a new tenancy: (s. 41A)

The principal exceptions are for:—

(1) A tenancy where the tenant is carrying on business in breach of a covenant which has not been waived (s. 23 (4)).

(2) A tenancy during the term whereof the parties have agreed for the grant of a new tenancy on its expiration (s. 28).

(3) Tenancies of agricultural holdings (s. 43 (1) (a)).

(4) Mining leases (s. 43 (1) (b)). As to what is a mining lease, see *O'Callaghan* v. *Elliott*, [1965] 3 All E.R. 111 (a lease of a quarry).

(5) Tenancies of on-licensed premises with certain exceptions (s. 43 (1) (d)).

(6) Tenancies *virtute officii* (s. 43 (2)).

(7) Tenancies without right of renewal or extension for not more than six months certain unless the tenant or his predecessor has been in occupation for twelve months at least (s. 43 (3)).

(8) Tenancies which have been extended under the provisions of the Leasehold Reform Act, 1967 (see s. 16 (1) of that Act).

(9) Tenancies excluded by s. 9 (3) of the Rent Act 1968 (s. 43 (1) (c)). These are "controlled" tenancies under the Rent Acts when there is both residential and business ("mixed") user—see *Levermore* v. *Jobey*, [1965] 2 All E.R. 362. But tenancies which would be "regulated" under the Rent Acts but which have mixed user are excluded from the Rent Acts by s. 9 (5) of the Rent Act 1968, and come within Part II. For "controlled" and "regulated" see *post* under heading "Residential Premises", Lettings within the Rent Acts.

(10) Tenancies at Will—see *Hagee* v. *A. B. Erikson and Larson,* [1975] 3 All E.R. 243.

S. 38 (1) and (2) avoid agreements purporting to restrict or exclude the tenants' right to claim a new lease or to claim compensation where he (or a predecessor) has carried on business in the premises for 5 years. But s. 38 (4) enables the Court, on the application of both parties, to authorize an agreement excluding the application of the Security of Tenure provisions (ss. 24–28) or providing for the future surrender of the tenancy. (See *Tottenham Hotspur* v. *Princegrove Publishers Ltd.* [1974] W.L.R. 113).

"Until terminated as provided for by the Act the existing tenancy continues after its contractual term date on the same terms (s. 24 (1)). For the effect of continuation on sub-tenancies see *William Skelton & Son* v. *Harrison and Pinder, Ltd.,* [1975] 1 All E.R. 182 and *Cornish* v. *Brook Green Laundry,* [1959] 1 All E.R. 373. For the liability of a guarantor of rent under the terms of the lease during continuation see *Junction Estates* v. *Cope,* [1974] 27 P. & C.R. 482.

Termination of tenancies.—A tenancy to which Part II applies only comes to an end:

(1) If the landlord gives notice (which normally must be in Form 7) to terminate the tenancy not earlier than the date when it would have determined or could have been brought to an end apart from the Act. In general the length of such notice must be not less than six or more than twelve months (s. 25). Minor departures from the prescribed form will not necessarily invalidate the notice; see *Sun Alliance and London Assurance Co., Ltd.* v. *Hayman,* [1975] 1 All E.R. 248, *Snook* v. *Schofield* (1975), 234 *Estates Gazette* 197, and *Bond* v. *Graham* (1975), 236 *Estates Gazette* 563. One notice may validly be served in respect of several properties if they are all in reality granted by the same lease; see *Dodson Bull Carpet Co., Ltd.* v. *City of London Corporation,* [1975] 2 All E.R. 497. A notice given under a break clause complying with the terms of the lease need not be in the form of a notice to terminate under s. 25 (Form 7)—*Re Bleacher's Association Ltd.'s leases,* [1957] 3 All E.R. 663. But by virtue of s. 24 (1) a lease so broken will continue until a valid s. 25 notice is served and has expired. Where the lease requires no particular form of notice to exercise a break clause, a s. 25 notice can exercise the break clause and terminate the tenancy under the Act, provided it expires not earlier than the date when the tenancy could be terminated under the break clause. (*Scholl Mfg. Co. Ltd.* v. *Clifton Slimline,* [1966] 1 All E.R. 993).

(2) If the tenant makes a request in Form 12 for a new tenancy. This may not be made if the landlord has already given notice to determine the tenancy or if the tenant has given notice to quit and may only be made by a tenant who holds for a term certain exceeding one year or for a term or years certain and thereafter from year to year (s. 26), see *Meah* v. *Sector Properties Ltd.* [1974] 1 W.L.R. 547 and *Winter* v. *Mobil Oil,* [1975] 7 C.L. 140; C.L.Y. 1878, or

(3) If the tenant under a tenancy for a fixed term gives notice in writing that he does not wish it to be continued after the due date unless the notice is given before the tenant has been in occupation for one month (s. 27), or

(4) If the tenant gives notice to quit, or the tenancy is ended by surrender or forfeiture or forfeiture of a superior tenancy unless the notice is given or The surrender executed before the tenant has been in occupation for one month), (s. 24 (2)), see *Watney* v. *Boardley,* [1975] 1 W.L.R. 857.

Interim rent.—Once the landlord has given notice to terminate the tenancy, or the tenant has requested a new one, the landlord may apply to the court to determine a reasonable interim rent which is to be paid until the new tenancy commences (s. 24A). See *Regis Property Co., Ltd.* v. *Lewis and Peat,*

Ltd., [1970] Ch. 195; [1970] 3 All E.R. 227, and *English Exporters (London), Ltd.* v. *Eldonwall, Ltd.*, [1973] 1 All E.R. 726; [1973] 3 W.L.R. 435.

Applications to court for new tenancies.—Where the landlord has given notice in Form 7 to determine the tenancy and the tenant has notified the landlord within 2 months that he is unwilling to give up possession or the tenant has had a request in Form 12 for a new tenancy, the tenant may apply to the Court for a new tenancy. Service of a valid counter notice in answer to a landlord's s. 25 notice is a condition procedent to the tenant's right to apply to the Court, *Chiswell* v. *Griffin Land and Estates, Ltd.*, [1975] 32 All E.R. 665. The application must be made not less than 2 nor more than 4 months thereafter (s. 29 (3)). This time limit can be "waived" by the landlord. See *Kammins Ballrooms Co. Ltd.* v. *Zenith Investments (Torquay) Ltd.*, [1971] 2 All E.R. 871. And where the last day for making application falls on a day when the Court office is closed, the application may be filed on the next day it is open. See *Hodgson* v. *Armstrong*, [1967] 2 Q.B. 299. Failure to send the correct fee, or making the wrong person respondent, does not stop the application being "made". See *Re No 55 and 57 Holmes Road, Kentish Town,*]1959] Ch. 298 and *Phillips* v. *Milne* (1962), 106 Sol. Jo. 731. For this purpose the court is the County Court where the rateable value of the premises does not exceed £5,000 and the High Court where it exceeds that sum (s. 63 (2) as amended by Administration of Justice Act 1973, s. 6), but provision is made for transfer of jurisdiction by agreement (s. 63 (3)). Disputes as to rateable value are referred to the Commissioners of Inland Revenue, for determination by a Valuation Officer, procedure being regulated by the Landlord and Tenant (Determination of Rateable Value Procedure) Rules 1954, S.I. 1954, No. 1255, and an appeal from the Valuation Officer going to the Lands Tribunal (ss. 37 (5), 56 (8)). In the County Court the application for a new tenancy is made by originating application (County Court form 335) which must be served within one month of issue unless extension is granted. The landlord must within

fourteen days from service of the application on him file an answer in County Court form 336 stating, *inter alia,* whether he opposes the grant of a new tenancy, and if he opposes it the grounds on which he does so (C.C.R. Order 40, r. 8 (2)).

In the High Court the application is made by originating summons in the Chancery Division. It must name the premises, give particulars of the current tenancy and the proposed terms of the new tenancy, and be verified by affidavit. Not less than 4 days before the hearing the landlord must file an affidavit stating whether and if so on what grounds he opposes a new tenancy. When he objects to any of the proposed terms of the new tenancy he must specify them and what he proposes instead. He must also state whether he is a tenant under a lease with less than 16 years to run, and if so, the name and address of his immediate landlord. There are provisions for persons affected by the summons to be joined as parties (R.S.C. O. 97).

Landlord's grounds of opposition.—On the hearing of the application the court must order the grant of a new tenancy (s. 29 (1)) unless the court dismisses the application (s. 31) on the ground that the landlord has established one or more of the following grounds set out in s. 30 (1):—

(a) Disrepair of the property due to tenant's failure to perform his obligations.

(b) Persistent unpunctuality in payment of rent.

(c) Substantial breaches of covenant, other than as to repairs, or misuse or mismanagement of the premises.

In considering grounds (a) (b) and (c) above the court may consider the tenant's conduct as a whole with regard to his obligations under the tenancy. It is not restricted to the specific breaches set out in the Landlord's notice of opposition. See *Eichner* v. *Midland Bank Executor and Trust Co.*, [1970] 2 All E.R. 598.

(d) Suitable alternative accommodation offered and available.

(e) Tenant's interest is a sub-tenancy of part of premises the letting or disposal whereof as a whole would be prejudiced by the existence of a sub-letting.

(f) Intended demolition or reconstruction. (For "intention" see *Betty's Cafes Ltd.* v. *Phillips Furnishing Stores*, [1956] 2 All E.R. 497). If the only erections on the site are a shed and wall, the intention to demolish them is sufficient to justify a refusal to grant a new tenancy; *Housleys Ltd.* v. *Bloomer-Holt, Ltd.*, [1966] 2 All E.R. 966. But the landlord will not succeed on this ground if either (i) the tenant agrees to give the landlord access and other facilities which would enable him to do the work without obtaining possession and without interfering substantially with the tenant's user, or (ii) the tenant is willing to accept a tenancy of part of the holding and either the position is as in (i) in regard to that part or possession of the remainder of the holding is sufficient by itself to enable the landlord to do the work—which means the work he actually intends to carry out (see *Decca Navigator Co.* v. *G.L.C.*, [1974] 1 W.L.R. 748): s. 31A. See also *Heath* v. *Drown*, [1972] 2 All E.R. 561; [1972] 2 W.L.R. 1306.

(g) Intended occupation wholly or partly for business purposes or as a residence by the landlord, or for business purposes by a company in which the landlord has a controlling interest (s. 30 (3)), (see *Re Crowhurst Park*, [1974] 1 W.L.R. 583 and *Manchester Garages, Ltd.* v. *Petrofina (U.K.) Ltd.*, [1974] 233 Estates Gazette 509) provided that the landlord's interest has not been purchased or created within the previous five years (s. 30 (2)).

As to the proviso in (g) above, see *Cornish* v. *Brook Green Laundry, Ltd.*, [1959] 1 All E.R. 373, *Artemiou* v. *Procopiou*, [1965] 3 All E.R. 539 and *Method Developments, Ltd.* v. *Jones*, [1971] 1 All E.R. 1027. Note also that transfers within a group of companies do not rank as purchases for the purposes of the proviso: s. 42 (3).

In certain cases the court may make a declaratory order that though the

relevant ground does not exist at the date of application it will exist within the ensuing years (s. 31 (2)).

Terms of new tenancy.—Where the court orders the grant of a new tenancy the property to be comprised therein is in default of agreement to be designated by the court having regard to the existing circumstances, see *G. Orlik* v. *Hastings and Thanet Building Society* (1974), 118 Sol. Jo. 811, but in some cases the landlord can require the inclusion of all the property subject to the current tenancy (s. 32) If the current tenancy includes rights enjoyed by the tenant in connection with the holding, they are to be included in the new tenancy (s. 32 (3)) unless the parties otherwise agree or the court otherwise determines (s. 32 (3)).

In default of agreement the term is to be fixed by the court, but a fixed term must not exceed fourteen years (s. 33), the rent is to be the current market rent, disregarding certain specified factors (s. 34), and disregarding also improvements made by the tenant or his predecessors during the period of 21 years before the application for renewal (s. 34 (1) (c), s. 34 (2)) and the other terms are to be fixed by the court (s. 35). The term may contain a "break clause" giving the landlord the option to determine: *McCombie* v. *Grand Junction Co. Ltd.*, [1962] 2 All E.R. 65. The court may now include in the new tenancy a term providing for a variable rent: s. 34 (3).

Carrying out of order for new tenancy. —When a new tenancy has been ordered and the terms settled by agreement or fixed by the court the landlord must grant and the tenant must accept a tenancy on those terms save that the tenant may apply to the Court for the order to be revoked within 14 days (s. 36).

Compensation where application for new tenancy refused.—Where the court does not order the grant of a new tenancy because the landlord has successfully opposed the application on any of grounds (e) (f) or (g) above, these being grounds personal to the landlord, and which the court must certify if the tenant so requires (or where the tenant does not make, or drops, his application for a new tenancy, such application not being opposed by the landlord on any ground other than those just mentioned: s. 37 (1) the landlord must pay compensation to the tenant. The amount of compensation is twice the rateable value of the holding or the rateable value of the holding according to whether the tenant or his predecessor has or has not carried on business on the holding for fourteen years (s. 37). Disputes as to rateable value are determined as mentioned above. "Business" means the business carried on by the particular tenant not his type of business: *Cramas Properties, Ltd.* v. *Connaught Fur Trimmings, Ltd.*, [1965] 2 All E.R. 382.

Where the court is induced to refuse an order for the grant of a new tenancy by misrepresentation or concealment of material facts the tenant may obtain compensation for the resulting loss (s. 55).

Special cases.—Part II of the Act contains special provisions designed to meet cases where either the landlord's interest or the tenant's interest is held upon trust (s. 41) or by a company which is a member of a group (s. 42), and where the immediate landlord is not the freeholder (s. 44, Sched. VI) or the immediate or any superior landlord is the incumbent of a benefice (s. 61).

Subject to certain modifications Part II applies where there is Crown interest in the property (s. 56, Sched. VIII).

A Government department, local authority, statutory undertaker, development corporation or one of certain hospital authorities may defeat the right of a tenant to a new lease if the appropriate Minister certifies that the premises are required for public purposes (s. 57). A Government department in some cases may obtain early possession, where the premises are required for national purposes (s. 58), but where the right to a new tenancy is so defeated compensation is generally payable (s. 59, Sched. IX, para. 5). The right to a new lease may be defeated without any right to compensation arising in certain cases where the premises were provided under the Distribution of Industry Acts, 1945 and 1950 (s. 60).

Exchange of information.—During the last two years of a term certain, or any period during which the tenancy could be determined within two years by notice to quit by the landlord, the tenant may be required by notice in Form 13 to inform the landlord whether he occupies the premises for business purposes and whether he has sub-let and the tenant may by notice in Form 14 or Form 15, as may be appropriate, obtain information as to the landlord's interest in the premises.

COMPENSATION FOR IMPROVEMENTS

Under the Landlord and Tenant Act, 1927 (amended in some respects by the Act of 1954) a tenant of premises used wholly or partly for carrying on any trade or business or regularly used for carrying on any profession may be entitled on quitting his holding to compensation for an improvement made on or after 25 March 1928 by him or his predecessor which adds to the letting value of the premises at the end of the tenancy.

Exceptions.—This right does not apply to premises:

(1) held under a mining lease (1927 Act, s. 17 (1); mining lease defined in s. 25 (1)).

(2) which are an agricultural holding (s. 17 (1)).

(3) let to the tenant *virtute officii*—for full details, see s. 17 (2).

(4) used for the business of subletting as residential flats with or without the provision of meals or services (s. 17 (3) (b)).

Mixed premises.—Where premises are used partly for trade, business or professional, and partly for other, purposes, compensation can be obtained only for improvements in relation to the trade, business or profession (s. 17 (4)).

Authorised improvements.—The right to compensation extends only to improvements which the tenant was authorised to make, and these are dealt with by s. 3 of the 1927 Act. To become authorised, the tenant must serve on the landlord a prior notice of intention with specification and plan. If the landlord objects, he may within 3 months serve notice of objection on the tenant. In that case the tenant may apply to the court (the County Court where the rateable value of the holding does not exceed £5,000, otherwise the High Court) which may, if satisfied on certain points (see **s. 3 (1)**), and after making such modifications as it thinks fit, certify the improvement to be a proper one. But if the landlord proves that he has offered to do the improvement himself in consideration of a reasonable increase in rent, or of such increase as the court may determine, the court may not give the certificate just mentioned unless it is subsequently shown that the landlord has failed to carry out his undertaking. If no objection has been made within 3 months to a proposed improvement, or the court has certified it to be a proper one, the tenant may carry it out despite anything in the lease.

Where an improvement has been authorised the tenant must, to preserve his right to compensation, comply with any conditions imposed by the court and complete it within such time as he may agree with the landlord or as is fixed by the court.

Where the tenant has executed the improvement, he may require the landlord to certify that he has done so properly; and if the landlord does not give a certificate within 1 month of the requisition the tenant may apply to the court which must itself give a certificate if satisfied that one is justified.

There are special provisions relating to an improvement begun after 1 October 1954 and made in pursuance of a statutory obligation (Act of 1954, s. 48 (1)).

The claim for compensation.—This is governed by **s. 1** of the 1927 Act as amended by **s. 47** of the 1954 Act. It must be made in the manner prescribed by CCR O. 40 and served:

(1) in the case of a tenancy terminated by notice to quit, within 3 months of the notice.
(2) in the case of a tenancy ended by effluxion of time, between 6 and 3 months before the ending of the tenancy.
(3) in the case of a tenancy ended by forfeiture or re-entry, within 3 months of the order for possession becoming effective or (if this

is later) the date when it ceases to be subject to appeal, or if the tenancy is terminated by re-entry without an order for possession then within 6 months of the re-entry.

There are special provisions for a case where the tenancy is terminated by a tenant's request under Part II of the 1954 Act for a new tenancy.

The amount of compensation.—S. 1 (1) of the Act of 1927 provides that "the sum to be paid as compensation for any improvement shall not exceed:

(a) the net addition to the value of the holding as a whole which may be determined to be the direct result of the improvement; or
(b) the reasonable cost of carrying out the improvement at the termination of the tenancy, subject to a deduction of an amount equal to the cost (if any) of putting the works constituting the improvement into a reasonable state of repair, except so far as such cost is covered by the liability of the tenant under any covenant or agreement as to the repair of the premises."

The section goes on to make further provisions in regard to compensation, including provision for the determination of its amount in the absence of agreement between the parties. In this event the question is to be referred to the court.

Ancillary provisions.—The Act of 1927 contains special provisions relating to:—

Deductions from and payment of compensation.
Rights of mesne and head landlords.
Increases in taxes, etc., payable by the landlord in consequence of an improvement carried out by the tenant: these can normally be passed on to the tenant.
Ecclesiastical and charity property.

RESIDENTIAL PREMISES

In this section are summarised the main provisions of the Rent Acts 1968–1975. These Acts cover security of tenure, rent, mortgages and premiums. References in what follows to section numbers are to those of the Rent Act 1968. Amendments made by the Rent Act 1974 are specifically mentioned.

I. Lettings within the Rent Acts
  (1) Regulated tenancies
  (2) Controlled tenancies
  (3) Statutory tenancies, and sub-tenancies
  (4) Grounds for possession

II. Premiums anf Mortgages
III. Part VI Contracts
IV. Miscellaneous

Other legislation
  Much recent legislation has attended the provisions of the Rent Act 1968: additionally, various changes have been made to the general law of landlord and tenant insofar as it relates to residential premises within the Rent Acts. Specific provisions are dealt with in the appropriate part of the text; the following is a general summary:—

Housing Finance Act 1972
  Part III provides for conversion of "controlled" tenancies (q.v.) provided with "standard amenities" (defined in Housing Act 1974, s. 58) and in good repair, into regulated tenancies.

  Part IV introduced *automatic* de-control of controlled tenancies in stages ss. 35, 36, ("creeping de-control"). This was stopped by s. 9 of the Housing Rents and Subsidies Act 1975. It also amended the law relating to registration and recovery of fair rents, and as to statutory succession.

  Part VIII applies the provisions of the Rent Act 1968, relating to the registration of rents, to tenancies of housing associations (except co-owner-ship associations), housing trusts and the Housing Corporation.

  Part IX (ss. 90, 91, as amended by Housing Act 1974, Sch. 12 and s. 124)

safeguards the tenants of flats against unreasonable or excessive service charges.

Counter Inflation Act 1973
  S. 14 raised the rateable value limits for protected tenancies.

Housing Act 1974
  S. 121 provides that the tenant is entitled to discover the landlords name and address from the rent collector or landlords agent, and if the landlord is a company, can further request the names and addresses of the directors and Secretary.
  S. 122 provides that an asignee of the landlords interest must give the tenant notice of the assignment and the name and address of the new landlord.
  S. 123 provides for notices to quit to be in writing, and to contain information to be prescribed by regulations.
  S. 124 contains important provisions entitling tenants to challenge service charges and ensure they represent value for money.
  S. 125 enables a tenant of a dwelling house to claim specific performance of a landlord's repairing covenant relating to any part of the premises in which the dwelling house is contained, whether or not the breach relates to the part let to the tenant.

Rent Act 1974
  The main object of this Act is to extend protection to furnished tenants, subject to an important exception when there is a "resident landlord".

Housing Rents and Subsidies Act 1975
  S. 11 (1) gives the minister power to restrict the rents of dwellings.
  S. 7 provides for phasing or rent increases from their "frozen" level. (See introduction.)
  S. 8 and Sch. 3 provide for certain assumptions to be made where assessing fair rents.
  S. 10 authorizes landlords of controlled tenants to increase the rent if they spend money on repairs.
  S. 12 extends rent allowances for almspeople, previously disqualified as being licencees of their accommodation.

I. LETTINGS WITHIN THE RENT ACTS

The Rent Acts affect both the rent and the security of tenure of tenants of certain premises "let as a separate dwelling" (s. 1 (1)) as to which see *Horford Investments, Ltd.* v. *Lambert*, [1974] 1 All E.R. 131. Such tenancies are termed "protected" tenancies.

The Rent Act 1965 introduced "regulated" tenancies and these are dealt with in a later part of this summary. "Controlled tenancies" on the other hand are tenancies subject to the pre-1965 rent control.

Decontrol in 1957. The Rent Act 1957, removed from the Rent Acts any tenancy coming into force on or after 6th July 1957, so that no tenancy beginning on or after this date can be a controlled tenancy. This release from control did not apply however, where immediately before the grant of a new tenancy the tenant was a statutory tenant, or a tenant protected by the Rent Acts, of the same premises, nor to the first tenancy created after a controlled tenancy of the premises had been determined by reason of overcrowding (see now Rent Act 1968, Schedule 2, para. 4).

A former licensee in requisitioned premises who had become a statutory tenant of the same premises was not affected by the 1957 Act and the 1965 Act converted his statutory tenancy into a regulated tenancy.

Some of these controlled tenancies were still in existence when the Act of 1965 (later replaced by the Rent Act 1968) was passed, and that Act preserves them for the time being. The Housing Finance Act 1972, however, provided for the phased conversion of all controlled tenancies to regulated tenancies from January 1973 to July 1975. The process was stopped as from 1st January 1974 (see below). Controlled tenancies are however of diminishing practical importance.

Certain premises are however outside the Acts even though they are let as a separate dwelling and would otherwise qualify as "protected":—

(i) certain licensed premises (s. 9 (2));

(ii) premises let at a rent inclusive of payments for board or attendance (s. 2 (1) (b));

(iii) premises which are comprised in an agricultural holding and occupied by the person responsible for its control or farming (s. 2 (1) (d));

(iv) tenancies where the rent is less then ⅔ rateable value (s. 2 (1) (a)). But controlled tenancies converted to regulated tenancies under Part III of the Housing Finance Act 1972 are within the Act notwithstanding that their rent is less than ⅔rds the rateable value (H.F.A. 1972, s. 37 (4));

(v) dwelling houses owned by the Crown (s. 4);

(vi) parsonages (*Gloucester* v. *Cunnington*, [1943] 1 All E.R. 61);

(vii) premises leased by local authorities, development corporations and housing associations and trusts, or comprised in a scheme or project under s. 75 of the Housing Finance Act 1972 or s. 29 of the Housing Act 1974 (s. 5);

(viii) student lettings (s. 2 (1) (bb) and S.I. 1974 No. 1366);

(ix) Holiday lettings (s. 2 (1) (*bbb*) see *Buchmann* v. *May* (1976), *Times*, May 6th; 120 Sol. Jo. 384;

(x) Lettings by Resident Landlords (see below under "Part VI Contracts");

(xi) Houses let with other land;

(xii) Premises used partly for business purposes (s.9 (5)) but where premises would otherwise be "controlled" they must be *wholly* used for business to be outside the Acts (*Phillips* v. *Hallohan*, [1925] 1 K.B. 756;

(xiii) Premises originally let for a period of more than 21 years, if they would otherwise be *controlled* tenancies. (Sch. 2, para. 1 (c) and s. 113 (1).) S. 80 of the Housing Act 1969 provides that in relation to long tenancies which would otherwise qualify as "regulated" all sums payable by the tenant in respect of rates, services, repairs, maintenance and insurance are to be disregarded in determining whether the tenancy is or ever was at a rent high enough for it to be protected, as being at a rent of more than ⅔rds the rateable value. So long tenancies which would be "regulated" only if such sums were treated as rent are outside the Act.

S. 102 provides that lettings where the tenant shares accommodation with persons other than his landlord, are to be protected (otherwise they would be excluded as not "let as a separate dwelling").

Premises part of which has been sub-let are not excluded from the application of the Rents Acts merely by the sharing of certain accommodation nor by the provision of board or attendance (s. 103).

(1) REGULATED TENANCIES

Regulated tenancies are tenancies of premises let as a separate dwelling, the rateable value of which on "the appropriate day" did not exceed certain limits, as follows (s. 1, as amended by s. 14, Counter-Inflation Act, 1973):—

(1) Where the appropriate day was before 22 March, 1973—

  (a) the rateable value on the appropriate day must have been in excess of £400 in Greater London and £200 elsewhere; and

  (b) the rateable value on March 22, 1973 must have been in excess of £600 in Greater London and £300 elswhere; and

  (c) the rateable value on April 1, 1973 must have been in excess of £1,500 in Greater London, to £750 elsewhere;

(2) where the appropriate day was on or after March 22, 1973 and before April 1, 1973, (b) above applies with the substitution of appropriate day for March 22, 1973, and (c) above also applies;

(3) where the appropriate day is on or after April 1, 1973, (c) of the foregoing applies with the substitution of the appropriate day for April 1, 1973.

The expression "the appropriate day" is dealt with by s. 6 (3). In the case of a dwelling-house which on 23rd March 1965 was or formed part of a hereditament for which a valuation was Shown on the valuation list then in force, or consisted or formed part of more than one such hereditament, it means that date. In other cases it means the date on which such a value was first shown on the valuation list.

(a) Rent

The rent under a regulated tenancy is a "fair" rent calculated in accordance with s. 46 and s. 8 of the Housing Rents and Subsidies Act 1975. Part IV of the Act provides for its determination by the rent officer or an approval by the rent assessment committee, and for the rent so fixed to be registered: it is then known as the "registered rent".

Rent regulation during contractual periods.—The expression "regulated tenancy" covers both contractual and statutory periods of the tenancy. The rent payable during any *contractual* period is limited to what is called "the contractual rent limit" (s. 20 (1)). The contractual rent limit is the registered rent if there is one. If none is registered the recoverable rent until the first rental period after 1st January 1973 is that of any previous regulated tenancy during the previous three years, in accordance with the provisions of ss. 20 (3) and 21 of the Rent Act 1968.

Section 42 of the Housing Finance Act 1972 repeals, from January 1st 1973, the provisions of ss. 20 (3) and 21 above. The rent under a subsisting regulated tenancy can now be increased by a "rent agreement with a tenant having security of tenure". This term includes both an agreement increasing the rent payable under a regulated tenancy and the grant of a new tenancy at a higher rent to the sitting tenant, or a person who might succeed him as a statutory tenant (1972 Act, s. 43 (1)). Such an agreement must be in writing signed by both parties, to be headed by a statement that the tenant's security under the Rent Act will not be affected if he refuses to enter into it and that it does not prevent either party from applying to the Rent Officer to register a rent.

S. 45 of the 1972 Act requires additional statements to be included where a grant has been given under Part I of the Housing Act 1969.

Rent regulation during statutory periods.—When the contractual period of tenancy ends, the tenant enjoys security of tenure similar to that of a controlled tenant (see above). The rent payable during periods of statutory tenancy is not normally to exceed rent limit for the last contractual period (s. 22). Also, see now s. 37, Housing Finance Act 1972. But where there is a registered rent, any excess over the registered rent is irrecoverable. And conversely, the landlord may by notice increase the rent up to the amount of the registered rent (s. 22 (2)). In regard to notices of increase, see s. 26.

If there is no registered rent:

(a) the rent recoverable may be increased if the rates payable by the landlord rise (though a notice of increase is necessary) and will drop if they drop (s. 23);

(b) it may be increased or decreased if the situation has changed since the contractual period in regard to the provision of services or the use of furniture (s. 24);

(c) it may be increased (again by notice of increase) if certain improvements are made (s. 25).

Sections 33–35 contain enforcement provisions, providing *inter alia* for the recovery from the landlord of sums paid in excess of recoverable rent, and for the giving by the landlord to the tenant of a statement of rent under a previous tenancy.

Registration of rents under regulated tenancies.—Application for the registration of a rent may be made to the rent officer for the area in question (appointed under the provisions of s. 40) by the landlord or by the tenant or by them both jointly. The procedure which then applies is set out in Schedule 6. The rent officer gives notice (in cases where the application is not joint) to the other party, and may require information from either party. If neither party objects to the proposed figure and the rent officer himself is satisfied that it is fair, he may register it without more ado. If there are representations against the proposed figure, or he himself is not satisfied, he may fix an appointment to consider it in consultation with the parties. He may then determine a fair rent and notify the parties. If a written objection is made within 28 days he must refer the matter to the rent assessment committee. If the objection is made after 28 days, he may either refer the matter to the committee or seek the committee's guidance whether to do so. See *R. v. Brent London Borough Rent Officer, Ex Parte, Ganatra*, [1976] 2 W.L.R. 330.

Section 46 deals with the basis on which the fair rent is to be determined, and it is important to note that the element of scarcity of accommodation is to be disregarded (s. 46 (2)). The section is amended by s. 83 of the Housing Act 1969 and s. 8 of the Housing Rents and subsidies Act 1975. See *Metropolitan Property Holdings* v. *Finegold*, [1975] 1 W.L.R. 349.

Section 39 of the Housing Finance Act 1972 inserts a new section in the Rent Act, 1968, s. 44A, empowering a local authority to refer to the rent officer the rent of a dwelling let on a regulated tenancy.

Where the rent for property has been registered, no further application by one party alone will be entertained before the expiry of three years except on the ground that there has been a change in the condition of the property, the terms of the tenancy or any other circumstances taken into consideration when the rent was registered (s. 44 (3)). But s. 44 3A (added by Rent Act 1974, s. 4 (1)) allows an application to be made by the landlord alone within the last 3 months of the 3 year period.

Section 41 of the Housing Finance Act 1972 inserts a new section in the Rent Act, 1968, s. 48A, providing for the cancellation of rent registrations if the rent officer is satisfied that the rent proposed jointly by landlord and tenant does not exceed the fair rent.

S. 102 A (added by Rent Act 1974, Sch. 2, part 2) provides that where a tenancy which is precluded from being protected because there is a resident landlord becomes protected, any rent registered under Part VI becomes the registered rent under Part IV. Where the landlord paid the rates, this is to be noted under s. 47 (2), if it was noted under s. 74 (2A) (added by Rent Act 1974, s. 7 (3)).

Certificates of fair rent.—Certain landlords may apply in advance for a certificate of fair rent. This right exists where the landlord intends:

(a) to provide a dwelling-house by the erection or conversion of any premises or to make any improvements in a dwelling-house, or

(b) to let on a regulated tenancy a dwelling-house which is not for the time being subject to such a tenancy and in respect of which there is no registered rent or only a rent registered not less than 3 years ago.

In such cases the landlord may apply to the rent officer for a certificate specifying a rent which in the opinion of the officer would be a fair rent for the dwelling-house or for the dwelling-house after erection, conversion or improvement. The procedure applicable to certificates of fair rent is set out in Schedule 7.

(2) CONTROLLED TENANCIES

Controlled tenancies are tenancies of premises the rateable value of which on 7th November 1956 did not exceed:

(a) in London, £40, or
(b) in Scotland, £40, or
(c) elsewhere, £30;

Housing Finance Act 1972—Conversion of controlled tenancies.

General conversion. Part IV of this Act provided for the general conversion of all tenancies which remained controlled into regulated tenancies by stages (s. 35). Dwellings with a higher rateable value were to be decontrolled first but according to the Act (and the Secretary of State had power to alter the time-table) all were to be decontrolled by 1 July 1975. But this progressive conversion was suspended during the rent freeze and was finally abolished by s. 4 of the Housing Rents and Subsidies Act 1975. The last conversions were on 1st January 1974 and related to premises with rateable values on 31st March 1972 of £70 and over in Greater London and £35 and over elsewhere. To be decontrolled under these provisions the dwelling in question did not need be in such a condition as to merit a qualification certificate under Part III (see below), but it was not decontrolled if it was classified as unfit for human habitation. Application could be made for registration of a fair rent prior to actual decontrol. When decontrol took place a new rent might be agreed subject to the completion of a prescribed form which then had to be lodged with the local authority. But rent increases resulting from decontrol were phased.

Conversion by qualification certificate procedure. Conversion of controlled to regulated tenancies may take place in advance of the appropriate date specified by Part IV (see above) by the issue of a qualification certificate by the local authority under Part III of the Act.

(a) premises qualify for a qualification certificate if they satisfy the "qualifying conditions"; namely, if the dwelling is provided with all the standard amenities (as defined in s. 58 Housing Act 1974) for the exclusive use of its occupants, is in good repair (having regard to its age, character, and locality and disregarding internal decorative repair) and is in all other respects fit for human habitation.

(b) an application for a qualification certificate is made to the appropriate district council.

(i) where no standard amenity is lacking, if the local authority are satisfied that the premises comply with the qualifying conditions, they must issue a qualification certificate. If they are not satisfied, they must give notice of refusal of the application giving reasons therefor in writing: s. 28 (5) and (6).

(ii) where one or more standard amenities are lacking at the date of the application, the local authority must consider whether, if the work specified in the application is completed, the premises will satisfy the qualifying conditions. If they will, the local authority must issue a certificate of provisional approval to the landlord, sending a copy to the tenant (s. 29 (3)). Once the works specified in the application which led to the issue of a certificate of provisional approval have been completed, and the local authority are satisfied that the premises are in the state to be expected after completion of such works, they must issue the qualification certificate (s. 29 (5)).

(c) There is a right of appeal to the County Court by the landlord against the authority's refusal of a certificate, and by the tenant against the issue of a certificate (s. 32). The tenant's appeal may be on the grounds that the certificate ought not to be issued and/or that it is invalid by reason of a failure to comply with a statutory requirement, or for some informality, defect, or error.

(d) A landlord applying for a qualification certificate, and intending to carry out works to add standard amenities to the premises to make them comply with the qualifying conditions, may apply in advance for a certificate of fair rent (s. 30).

(e) The County Court has power to grant to the landlord of a statutory tenancy an order enabling him to enter and carry out improvement works required to satisfy the qualifying conditions even though the tenant is unwilling to consent to them (s. 33).

In all cases of conversion under Parts III and IV of the 1972 Act, increases towards a registered rent are phased under s. 38 and Schedule 6.

Jurisdiction. Jurisdiction to determine questions as to the applicability of the Rent Acts is vested in the County Court (s. 105).

Long Tenancies. Until the passing of the Leasehold Reform Act, 1967 (see s. 39 thereof) tenancies exceeding 21 years were outside the Rent Acts (though the rights of sub-tenants were expressly saved), and the only statutory protection given to these tenancies was that in the Landlord and Tenant Act, 1954, Part I. Now, however, they are (if not at a low rent) capable of being regulated tenancies (see below) and Part I of the 1954 Act now applies primarily to long tenancies at a low rent.

(a) *Rent*

The annual rent of controlled premises is not to exceed the 1956 gross value multiplied by the "appropriate factor", *plus* (1) the rates paid by the landlord; (2) a reasonable charge (fixed by the parties or the County Court for services or the use of furniture (s. 52 and see *Regis Property Co., Ltd.* v. *Dudley*, [1958] 1 All E.R. 511); (3) 12½% per annum of the cost of repairs effected by the landlord, completed on or after 6th April 1973 (Housing Rents & Subsidies Act 1975, s. 10). If the tenant is responsible for all repairs, the appropriate factor is 4/3; if he is responsible for none, then it is 2; and if he is responsible for some but not all, then it is some fraction between

2 and 4/3 (fixed by the parties or the County Court (s. 52 and Schedule 9, Part I)). "Repairs" does not include internal decorative repairs: if the landlord is responsible for the latter, or assumes such responsibility under the Act, the appropriate factor is 7/3 (instead of 2) or 5/3 (instead of 4/3) (Schedule 9, Part I).

The rent limit is subject to adjustment (see ss. 53–61) and reduction in case of failure to repair (s. 52 (3) and Schedule 9, Part II). For the enforcement of the landlord's duty to repair see Schedule 9, paras. 3–6. For the reduction of rent pending the remedying of defects, see Schedule 9, paras. 7–9.

If on 6th July 1957 the recoverable rent of controlled premises exceeded the rent limit mentioned above such rent is the rent limit but may be adjusted under ss. 53–61, or reduced under Schedule 9, Part I (s. 52 (4)). The recoverable rent of any controlled premises on 6th July 1957 remains the rent recoverable in future rental periods except as varied in the way outlined above.

Any money paid as rent in excess of the rent limit is recoverable by the tenant from the landlord (by deduction from rent or otherwise) but only within two years of the date of payment (s. 62).

Rates paid by Landlord. If the amount of rates (ascertained according to Schedule 4) borne by the landlord should vary, the rent limit will vary accordingly (s. 54). Where the rent is increased in consequence of such variation the date specified by the notice must not be earlier than 6 weeks before service of the notice. Where the operative date is prior to service, any rent underpaid is due on the day after service (s. 54 (2)). Such increase of rent is disregarded for the purpose of s. 53 (2) (b), (s. 54 (3)).

Payment for Services, etc. Where it becomes reasonable to vary the rent payable for services or use of furniture, the rent limit may be varied by an appropriate amount agreed between parties or determined by the County Court: notwithstanding s. 53, an increase may be made without service of notice (s. 55).

Increase for Improvements. If an improvement to controlled premises has been completed after 5th July 1957, s. 56 provides that the rent limit is increased by "the appropriate percentage" per annum of the amount expended. If the improvement was completed before 24th November 1961, the appropriate percentage is 8%. If it was completed on or after that date, it is generally 12½%. The amount expended is, by s. 57, taken to be reduced by any improvement grant (including a "standard grant"; see House Purchase and Housing Act, 1959, s. 27) or repayment under the Clean Air Act, 1956 received in respect of such improvement. In a notice of increase under s. 56, the operative date may be any date after the service of notice: such increase is disregarded for the purposes of s. 53 (2) (s. 56 (4)).

A tenant on whom notice under s. 56 has been served may apply to the County Court for cancellation or reduction of the increase on the grounds that more was spent on the improvement than was necessary or that the improvement was unnecessary. This latter ground of application is not available to him if an improvement grant has been made or he consented in writing to the improvement (s. 59).

It may be noted that these increases will still be available in the case of regulated tenancies but the procedure differs from the above both before and after registration of the rent. Before registration the increase is to be agreed between the landlord and tenant subject to appeal to the court and after registration the amount is subject to the satisfaction of the rent officer or the rent assessment committee.

Contractual Tenancies. No increase of rent can be made which is inconsistent with the terms of a contractual tenancy (s. 60 (1)). Where a notice of increase is served in respect of a tenancy which could be brought to an end by a notice to quit served at the same time which would be effective before the date specified in the notice of increase, the tenancy will become a statutory tenancy (s. 60 (2)).

If the rent for a contractual tenancy includes an increase under the Housing Repairs and Rents Act, 1954, s. 40 in respect of services not provided for by the contract and such services are discontinued, the recoverable rent is reduced accordingly (s. 60 (3)); any

question whether or by what amount the recoverable rent is reduced being settled according to s. 60 (4).

Apart from the provision last mentioned, the Rent Acts do not affect any contractual tenancy in so far as it provides for a reduction of rent (s. 60 (5)).

Rents of Subsidised Houses. The conditions referred to in the H. (F.P.) Act, 1924, s. 2; H. (R.W.) Act, 1926, s. 3; H. (F.P.) Act, 1938, s. 3; H. Act, 1949, s. 23 and H. Act, 1957, ss. 104, 105, in so far as they relate to rent, take effect as if they limited such rent to the rent limit unless they were imposed before 6th July 1957 and limited a rent in excess of the rent limit ascertained in accordance with s. 52 (1) and (2) (in which case such rent is the rent limit although subject to s. 52 (3) and Schedule 9, para. 7 (2) (s. 110)).

A tenancy (other than a controlled tenancy, which does not include a regulated tenancy), the rent of which is limited by conditions referred to in the above-mentioned Acts, is now subject to the Housing Act, 1964, s. 56 and the limit is to be fixed with reference to the 1963 gross value. Special provisions apply where the landlord is a housing association or trust (Schedule 13).

As to application to local authority to fix higher rent on improvements being made, see the amendment made by Schedule 15 to s. 46 (1) of the Housing (Financial Provisions) Act, 1958.

On this subject, see also Part III of the Housing Finance Act 1972, *ante.*

Jurisdiction. Jurisdiction is vested in the County Court either in pending proceedings relating to dwellings or on *ad hoc* applications to determine questions as to the rent limit and as to the rent actually recoverable (s. 105). Any apportionment of rates, gross value or rateable value made by the County Court under s. 58 (private street works to count as improvements) shall be final and conclusive (s. 58 (5)).

Rateable Value. As to the ascertainment and adjustment of the rateable value for the purposes of the 1957 Act, see Schedule 8. An agreement as to the rateable value between a landlord (who is himself a tenant with not more than 7 years to run) and a tenant is ineffective without the concurrence of the superior landlord (Schedule 8, para. 7).

1956 Gross Value. Subject to Schedule 8, this is the gross value of a dwelling as shown in the valuation list on 7th November, 1956 or such proportion of the gross value of a hereditament (where the dwelling only forms part of the hereditament) as may be fixed by the parties or the County Court (Schedule 8, para. 1).

(3) STATUTORY TENANCIES AND SUB-TENANCIES

(i) *Statutory tenants.*—A statutory tenant, *i.e.* a tenant whose original tenancy has expired, and who remains in possession only by virtue of the Rent Act, cannot assign his tenancy (*Keeves* v. *Dean*, [1924] 1 K.B. 685) except in accordance with s. 14, though he may sub-let part of it unless prohibited by the terms of the original tenancy (*Roe* v. *Russell*, [1928] 2 K.B. 117). Moreover, he may not hold the tenancy in trust for another person (*Wilkins* v. *Carlton Shoe Co.* (1930), 94 J.P. 207). A statutory tenant who has let for business purposes cannot be "the landlord" for the purposes of the Landlord and Tenant Act, 1954, Part II. (*Piper* v. *Muggleton*, [1956] 2 All E.R. 249 C.A.). The position of a statutory tenant is dealt with by s. 12, which provides that so long as he retains possession, he shall observe and be entitled to the benefit of all the terms and conditions of the original contractual tenancy, so far as they are consistent with the provisions of the Act. He has a duty to afford access to the landlord and facilities for repairs. He is entitled to give up possession if, and only if, he gives such notice as would have been required under the contractual tenancy or, if no notice would have been required, not less than 3 months' notice. Despite anything in the contractual tenancy, a landlord who obtains an order for possession is not required to give the statutory tenant any notice to quit.

A statutory tenant cannot leave his interest in the tenancy by will (*Lovibond (John) & Sons* v. *Vincent* (1929), 45 T.L.R. 383). But on his death the statutory tenancy enures for the benefit of certain members of his family (s. 3 (1) (b) and Schedule 1), the word

"family" here being used in the colloquial sense (*Brock* v. *Wollans*, [1949] 1 All E.R. 715, C.A.; *Jones* v. *Whitehill* [1950] 1 All E.R. 71 C.A.; *Langdon* v. *Horton*, [1951] 1 All E.R. 60, C.A.). The Rent Act 1965 extended this provision to a second transmission on the death of the first successor—see now paras. 5, 6 and 7 of Schedule 1. Paragraph 10 of Schedule 1 (inserted by s. 47, Housing Finance Act 1972) provides that where the tenant is a statutory successor, a new tenancy granted to him does not create any new succession rights. On his bankruptcy it does not vest in the trustee, and the tenant can remain in possession (*Sutton* v. *Dorf*, [1932] 2 K.B. 304). But where the tenant goes bankrupt during the contractual term his tenancy rests in his trustee; therefore when it ends the tenant does not become a statutory tenant. *Smalley* v. *Quarrier*, [1975] 1 W.L.R. 938. A statutory tenant who gives up possession of the premises loses the protection of the Act. For this purpose possession requires not only "*animus possidendi*" but "*corpus possessionis*" as well (*Brown* v. *Brash*, [1948] 1 All E.R. 922), but continuous residence is not necessary (*Langford Property Co. Ltd.* v. *Athanassoglou*, [1948] 2 All E.R. 722, C.A.), though there must be more than occasional visits (*Beck* v. *Scholtz*, [1953] 1 All E.R. 814, C.A.), but see *Tickner* v. *Hearn*, [1961] 1 All E.R. 65, C.A. where the tenant had been absent in a mental hospital for six years. A statutory tenant may remain in possession through his wife and furniture (*Old Gate Estates Ltd.* v. *Alexander*, [1949] 2 All E.R. 872, C.A.) but not through his deserted mistress (*Colin Smith Music Ltd.* v. *Ridge*, [1975] 1 W.L.R. 463) and *Bevington* v. *Crawford*, 232 E.G. 191. But see *Dyson Holdings, Ltd.* v. *Fox*. [1975] 3 W.L.R. 744. A person who does not occupy any part of the premises as a dwelling when his contractual tenancy comes to an end never becomes a statutory tenant (*Brown (John M.) Ltd.* v. *Bestwick*, [1950] 2 All E.R. 338, C.A.). Where by sub-letting the tenant has created more than one dwelling-house possession will be ordered of those in which he does not reside (*Crowhurst* v. *Maidment*, [1952] 2 All E.R. 808, C.A.).

Section 13 (1) provides that a statutory tenant who, as a condition of giving up possession, asks or receives the payment of any sum, or the giving of any other consideration, by any person other than the landlord, shall be guilty of an offence. Also, s. 13 (2) provides that where he requires that furniture or other articles shall be purchased as a condition of his giving up possession, the price demanded shall, at the request of the person from whom the demand is made, be stated in writing, and if it exceeds the reasonable price of the articles the excess shall be treated as a payment within the ambit of s. 13 (1). S. 13 (3) prescribes the penalty (not exceeding £100), and s. 13 (4) gives the court certain powers to order repayment.

It should be noted that these provisions do not apply as between a contractual tenant and his landlord.

(ii) *Sub-tenants.*—By s. 18 (2), where the interest of a tenant of a dwelling-house to which the Act applies is determined, either as the result of an order for possession, or for any other reason, any sub-tenant to whom the premises or any part thereof have been lawfully sub-let shall, subject to the provisions of the Act, be deemed to become the tenant of the landlord on the same terms as he would have held from the tenant if the tenancy had continued.

To entitle a sub-tenant to the protection of the Act as against his superior landlord, the sub-letting to him must have been lawful. Subject to this, a sub-tenant is entitled to the benefit of the Act (s. 18 (1)), but where the sub-tenant formerly shared accommodation with the tenant, he will not be protected, by virtue of s. 101. *Stanley* v. *Compton*, [1951] 1 All E.R. 859.

S. 18 (3) gives this protection to sub-tenants even in certain cases where the tenancy out of which their sub-tenancy is derived is not within the protection of the Act because it was a long tenancy at a low rent, provided that a notice to terminate it has not been served under Part I of the Landlord and Tenant Act 1954, and that it is not being continued by virtue of that Act (s. 18 (4)).

By s. 18 (5) the protection extends to cases where the dwelling-house forms part of premises let as a whole and the tenants interest was not protected, provided that the sub-let

dwelling is within the Act. (See *Legge* v. *Matthews* [1960] 1 All E.R. 595.) But see *Hobhouse* v. *Wall*, [1963] 1 All E.R. 701, where this was held not to apply where part of a farm, composing a cottage and 10 acres, was sub-let.

Particulars of any sub-letting must be given to the landlord by the tenant (s. 104).

Certain sub-tenancies which were formerly outside the Acts were brought under control by s. 9 of the Landlord and Tenant (Rent Control) Act, 1949: see now s. 103 of the 1968 Act.

An initially unlawful sub-letting can be made lawful if the landlord waives the breach, e.g. by accepting rent with knowledge of the breach. *Muspratt* v. *Johnson*, [1963] 2 All E.R. 339.

For the position of a furnished sub-tenant following the determination of an unlawful tenancy, see Rent Act 1974, s. 13.

(4) GROUNDS FOR POSSESSION

(i) *The landlord's right to possession where premises are protected.*—The provisions restricting a landlord's right to possession under the Rent Acts apply in general to regulated tenancies and controlled tenancies alike.

It is provided by s. 10 (1) that no order for possession of any dwelling-house let on a protected or statutory tenancy shall be made unless the court considers it reasonable to make such an order, *and* either:—

(a) the court is satisfied that suitable alternative accommodation is available for the tenant or will be available for him when the order in question takes effect, *or*

(b) the circumstances are as specified in any of the Cases in Part I of Schedule 3.

As to the matters to be considered in determining whether it is "reasonable" to make an order, see *e.g.* *Cresswell* v. *Hodgson* [1951], 1 All E.R. 710, C.A.

Sch. 3, Part IV, defines suitable alternative accommodation. A certificate of the housing authority is conclusive evidence that suitable alternative accommodation will be available (Schedule 3, Part IV, para. 1). In the absence of such a certificate accommodation is deemed to be suitable, if it consists of (a) a protected house, or

(b) premises with reasonable equivalent security of tenure. It must also conform to the other conditions in Schedule 3, Part IV. By para. 3 (2) of that part of Schedule 3 a certificate of the housing authority on certain points relative to this question is also conclusive.

Alternative accommodation must not produce overcrowding (Schedule 3, Part IV, para. 4).

Part of the accommodation already occupied by the tenant can constitute suitable alternative accommodation: *Thompson* v. *Rolls*, [1926] 2 K.B. 426.

In considering whether alternative accommodation is suitable such matters as the absence of a garage are irrelevant: *Briddon* v. *George*, [1946] 1 All E.R. 609. (See also *Mykolyshyn* v. *Noah*, [1971] 1 All E.R. 48).

Reference was made above to the Cases in Part I of Schedule 3. These are the cases in which the court may (if satisfied that it is reasonable) make an order for possession without proof of suitable alternative accommodation being available. These Cases are as follows:

Case 1.—Where any rent lawfully due from the tenant has not been paid, or any obligation arising under the Act or (if the contractual tenancy still continues) any other obligation of that tenancy which is consistent with Part II of the Act or (if the contractual tenancy has ended) any other obligation of the previous contractual tenancy which is applicable to the statutory tenancy has been broken or not performed.

Case 2.—Where the tenant or any person residing or lodging with him or any sub-tenant of his has been guilty of conduct which is a nuisance or annoyance to adjoining occupiers, or has been convicted of using the dwelling-house or allowing it to be used for immoral or illegal purposes.

Case 3.—Where the condition of the dwelling-house has, in the opinion of the court, deteriorated owing to acts of waste by, or the neglect or default of, the tenant or any person residing or lodging with him or any sub-tenant of his and, in the case of acts or neglects by a lodger or sub-tenant, where the court is satisfied that the tenant has not, before the making of the order,

taken such steps as he ought reasonably have taken for his removal.

Case 3A.—Where the condition of any furniture provided for use under the tenancy has, in the opinion of the court, deteriorated owing to ill-treatment by the tenant or any person residing or lodging with him and or any subtenant of his and, in the case of any ill-treatment by a person lodging with the tenant or a sub-tenant of his, where the court is satisfied that the tenant has not, before the making of the order, taken such steps as he ought reasonably to have taken for his removal.

Case 4.—Where the tenant has given notice to quit and as a result the landlord has contracted to sell or let the dwelling-house or taken any other steps as the result of which he would, in the opinion of the court, be seriously prejudiced if he could not obtain possession.

Case 5.—Where the tenant has without the landlord's consent at any time after 1st September 1939 in the case of a controlled tenancy, or 8th December 1965 in the case of a regulated tenancy, or 14th August 1974 in the case of a regulated furnished tenancy assigned or sub-let the whole of the dwelling-house, or sub-let part of it, the remainder being already sub-let. (Note that where sub-letting of the whole is alleged, it is enough to prove arrangements (such as division into flatlets) and intention to sub-let the whole: *Finkle* v. *Strzelczyk*, [1961] 3 All E.R. 409).

Case 6.—Where in the case of a controlled tenancy the dwelling-house consists of or includes premises licensed for the sale of intoxicating liquor for consumption off the premises only, and

(a) the tenant has committed an offence as holder of the licence, or
(b) the tenant has not conducted the business to the satisfaction of the licensing justices or the police authority, or
(c) the tenant has carried on the business in a manner detrimental to the public interest, or
(d) the renewal of the licence has for any reason been refused.

Case 7.—Where the dwelling-house is reasonably required by the landlord for occupation as a residence for some person engaged in his whole-time employment, or in the whole-time employment of some tenant from him or with whom, conditional on housing being provided, a contract for such employment has been entered into, and the tenant was in the employment of the landlord or a former landlord, and the dwelling-house was let to him in consequence of that employment and he has ceased to be in that employment. (Note that if the contract was a contract of service and not of tenancy, and the servant occupies a house as one of the terms of his employment, he is not protected by the Act at all.)

Case 8.—Where the dwelling-house is reasonably required by the landlord for occupation as a residence for

    (a) himself, or
    (b) any son or daughter of his over 18 years of age, or
    (c) his father or mother, or
    (d) in the case of a regulated tenancy, the father or mother of his spouse,

and the landlord did not become landlord by purchasing the dwelling-house or any interest therein after 7th November 1956 in the case of a controlled tenancy, or 8th December 1965 in the case of a regulated tenancy, or 14th August 1974 in the case of a regulated furnished tenancy. (But note that by virtue of para. 1 of Part III of Schedule 3 the court must not make an order on this ground if satisfied that, having regard to all the circumstances of the case, including the question whether other accommodation is available for the landlord or the tenant, greater hardship would be caused by making it than by refusing it. See *Kelley* v. *Goodwin*, [1947] 1 All E.R. 810.)

Case 9.—Where the court is satisfied that the rent charged by the tenant for any sub-let part of the dwelling-house is or was in excess of the maximum rent for the time being recoverable for that part, having regard to the provisions of Part III or, as the case may be, Part V of the Act.

Case 10 covers a situation where a person who formerly occupied the dwelling-house as his residence lets it on a regulated tenancy giving the prescribed notice to the tenant that possession might be required under this Case. In such circumstances the owner-occupier can regain possession if he needs it for himself or certain members of his family.

The court has power to waive compliance with the rules relating to Notices. See proviso added by s. 3 (3) Rent Act 1974.

There are new cases 10A, 10B, and 10C (added by Rent Act 1974, ss. 2 and 3).

Case 10A applies where an owner originally purchased a dwelling for his retirement and has given the prescribed notice to the tenant that possession could be recovered under this case, and requires the premises for his retirement, or (if the owner has died) the premises are required for a member of his family residing with him at his death.

Case 10B covers the case of a holiday letting, where the tenancy is for a fixed term of not more than 8 months, the landlord has given the prescribed notice, and the premises were occupied at some time within the 12 months prior to the commencement of the tenancy under a right to occupy for a holiday.

Case 10C deals with lettings for fixed terms of not more than 12 months by specified educational institutions (see Rent Act 1974, s. 2), provided the letting is to a student and the prescribed notice has been given.

Case 11. This applies to premises held for the purpose of being available for occupation by a minister of religion. Its provisions are rather similar to those of Case 10.

Case 12. This applies to a situation where the dwelling-house was at any time occupied by a person under the terms of his employment as a person employed in agriculture, and is now let to someone who is not and never was so employed by the landlord and is not the widow of a person who was so employed. If the court is satisfied that the dwelling-house is required for occupation by a person employed or to be employed by the landlord in agriculture, the landlord can recover possession. But he must have given notice to the tenant at the commencement of the tenancy or, if it commenced before 8th

December 1965, within 6 months after that date. (It is to be noted that this Case applies to dwelling-houses occupied by an agricultural employee *at any time*: such occupation need not have been in the recent past or under the present landlord.)

Case 13. This applies where proposals for amalgamation, approved for the purposes of a scheme under s. 26 of the Agriculture Act 1967, have been carried out and, at the time when the proposals were submitted, the dwelling-house was occupied by a person responsible for the control or farming of any part of the land comprised in the amalgamation. In such a situation, the landlord can in certain circumstances gain possession of the dwelling-house from the present tenant to make it available to an agricultural employee.

Case 14 is added by s. 100 of the Agriculture Act 1970. This contains provisions for the recovery—on the conditions set out in the section—of certain redundant farm houses. S. 99 of the Act may also be noted.

In any case the court may adjourn any application for possession or suspend execution or postpone the date for possession on such terms as it may think fit. Such orders are commonly made on proper terms in cases in which possession is applied for on the ground of non-payment of rent (s. 11).

An order for possession once it has been made devolves on the landlord's personal representatives or beneficiaries (*Goldthorpe* v. *Bain*, [1952] 2 All E.R. 23).

By s. 19 of the Act where the landlord has obtained possession by misrepresentation, etc., he may be ordered to pay compensation to the tenant.

II. PREMIUMS AND MORTGAGES

(1) Premiums

S. 85 of the Rent Act 1968 provides that any person who, as a condition of the grant, renewal or continuance of a protected tenancy, requires, in addition to the rent, the payment of any premium or the making of any loan (secured or unsecured) shall be guilty of an offence and liable to a fine not exceeding £100. This also applies to a person who, though he does not *require* a premium, nonetheless *receives* one. See *Zimmerman* v. *Grossman*, [1971] 1 All E.R. 363; [1971] 2 W.L.R. 199. The court may order repayment.

S. 86 contains similar provisions relating to the payment of premiums on the *assignment* of protected tenancies. But certain payments can be demanded on assignment without these provisions being infringed: these are set out in detail in the section (see also Counter-inflation Act 1973, Sch. 5). The court has power to sever from a contract to assign a protected tenancy a requirement that the assignee pays an illegal premium and to order specific performance of the contract excluding such requirement—*Ailion* v. *Spiekermann*, [1976] 1 All E.R. 497.

S. 87 contains provisions relating to the payment of premiums on the grant or assignment of furnished lettings, though here again there are saving provisions.

S. 88 provides that where an excessive price has been demanded for furniture, required to be bought as a condition of the grant, renewal, continuance or assignment of a protected tenancy or certain furnished lettings, the excess ranks as a premium.

S. 89 provides for the punishment of attempts to obtain from prospective tenants excessive prices for furniture, and s. 90 provides for the recovery of premiums and loans unlawfully required or received. See *Farrell* v. *Alexander*, [1975] 3 W.L.R. 642.

Certain requirements for payment of rent in advance are made void by s. 91.

Housing Act 1969, s. 81.—This deals with tenancies which are both protected tenancies within the meaning of the Rent Act 1968 and long tenancies within the meaning of Part I of the Landlord and Tenant Act 1954. These are divided into two groups: (a) those in respect of which certain conditions (see below) are satisfied, and (b) those in respect of which any of those conditions is not satisfied. As to group (a), it is provided that nothing in Part VII of the Rent Act 1968 (which relates to premiums, etc.) or the enactments replaced by it applies, or ever did apply. As to group (b), it is provided that Schedule 7 of the Act shall apply and if the tenancy was granted before the passing of the Act, be deemed always to have applied. Schedule 7 gives a qualified right to charge a premium on assignment in certain circumstances.

The conditions mentioned above are: (i) that the tenancy is not, and cannot become, terminable by notice to the tenant within 20 years of its grant, (ii) that unless the tenancy was granted before the passing of the Act or in pursuance of Part I of the Leasehold Reform Act 1967, the sums payable by the tenant otherwise than in respect of rates, services, repairs, maintenance or insurance are not varied or liable to be varied within 20 years of the grant (though there is an exception here in the case of certain sub-tenancies: see sub-s. (3)) nor, thereafter, more than once in any 21 years, and (iii) that assignment or underletting of the whole premises is not precluded by the tenancy and, if it is subject to any consent, there is neither a term excluding s. 144 of the Law of Property Act 1925 (no payment in the nature of a fine) nor a term requiring an offer to surrender the tenancy.

(2) MORTGAGES

Mortgages created after 8th December 1965 are not subject to Rent Acts control except where Sch. 5, para. 8 of the Counter Inflation Act 1973 applies. Apart from these the only mortgages now controlled, are those which were controlled by the pre-1965 Acts. The Act of 1965 (in provisions now reproduced in the Rent Act, 1968) introduced two new provisions of importance in connection with mortgages:

(a) In certain cases involving hardship to the lender, the court may mitigate the restrictions imposed on his rights by the pre-1965 control (s. 96).

(b) As regards mortgages created before 8th December 1965 which are not themselves subject to pre-1965 control but which comprise premises let on a *regulated tenancy* which is binding on the lender, the court may in certain circumstances limit the rate of interest, extend the time for repayment, or otherwise vary the terms of the mortgage, if satisfied that the borrower would otherwise suffer severe financial hardship (s. 95).

It is appropriate now to turn to mortgages which *do* remain subject to pre-1965 control and to outline the provisions of this control. S. 93 of the Act provides that "a mortgage is a controlled mortgage at any time when, had this Act not been passed, it would have been a mortgage to which the Increase of Rent and Mortgage Interest (Restrictions) Act, 1920, would have applied (whether by virtue of the modifications of that Act effected by Schedule 1 to the Rent and Mortgage Interest Restrictions Act, 1939, or otherwise)." Mortgages within this definition are all mortgages comprising one or more dwelling-houses to which the pre-1965 Acts apply except:

(a) any mortgage comprising one or more dwelling-houses to which the Acts apply and other land, if the rateable value of the dwelling-houses is less than one-tenth of the rateable value of the whole of the land comprised in the mortgage;

(b) an equitable charge by deposit of title deeds or otherwise.

In regard to (a) it should be noted that if the rateable value of the dwelling-houses is more than one-tenth of the rateable value of the whole, the lender may by notice apportion the mortgage money between the houses and the land and upon such apportionment becoming binding the Acts shall cease to apply to the apportioned part of the mortgage relating to the land (s. 97, and see *Coutts & Co.* v. *Duntroon Investment Corporation Ltd.*, [1958] 1 All E.R. 51).

A second, third or subsequent mortgage appears to be within the Acts.

If the mortgage was created before 2nd July 1920, it will be subject to "old control". Otherwise it will be subject to "new control".

(a) *Interest*

The provisions as to interest are now to be found in Part I of Schedule 12 to the Rent Act, 1968.

Para. 1 deals with old control. The rate of interest must not be increased by more than 6¼% per annum or 1% above the "standard rate of interest", whichever is the less. The standard rate of interest means (a) in the case of a mortgage in force on 3rd August 1914, the rate of interest payable on that date, and (b) in the case of other mortgages, the original rate of interest.

Para. 2 deals with new control. Here the interest must not be increased beyond (a) in the case of a mortgage in force on 1st September 1939, the rate of interest payable on that date, and (b) in the case of other mortgage, the original rate of interest.

S. 98 contains provisions as to the recovery by the borrower of excessive interest paid.

(b) *Enforcement of security*

The provisions restricting the lender's right to enforce his security are now to be found in Part II of Schedule 12.

Para. 5 provides that a lender shall not be entitled to take any steps for enforcing his security or recovering the principal money if and so long as:

(a) interest at the permitted rate is paid and not more than 21 days in arrear;

(b) the borrower's convenants (other than covenants as to repayment of principal money) are observed;

(c) the borrower keeps the property repaired; and

(d) the borrower pays all interest and instalments of principal recoverable under any prior incumbrance.

But this provision does not apply (a) where the principal money is repayable by instalments over not less than 10 years from the creation of the mortgage (para. 6 (1)), (b) where the borrower consents to the lender exercising his powers (para. 6 (2)), or (c) in the case of "old control", where the lender was in possession on 25th March 1920 or, in the case of "new control", where the lender was in possession on 1st September 1939 or whatever other date is relevant (see para. 5 (2)).

Para. 7 gives the court power to allow a lender to call in a mortgage of leasehold property if he shows that his security is seriously diminishing in value or otherwise in jeopardy.

By Sch. 5, para. 8 of the Counter-Inflation Act 1973, where a tenancy of a dwelling-house became regulated as a result of s. 14 of that Act (which raised the rateable value limits), then in relation to that dwelling-house Sections 94 and 95 are to have effect as if for the reference to 8th December 1965 there were substituted a reference to 22nd March 1973, and the

"appropriate day" in s. 94 becomes 7th March 1973. S. 95 (1) (b) (which relates to the requirement that the court cannot exercise its powers under s. 95 unless a rent, lower than that prior to registration, has been registered) is not to apply to such premises.

III. PART VI CONTRACTS

Some lettings though not protected may enjoy the modified protection of Part VI of the Act.

Prior to the Rent Act 1974 the most important category of these was furnished lettings, but s. 1 (1) of that Act provides that:—

"a tenancy of a dwelling-house shall no longer be prevented from being a protected tenancy by reason only that under the tenancy the dwelling-house is bona fide let at a rent which includes payments in respect of the use of furniture."

The main applications of Part VI are thus now where:—

(a) accommodation is shared between landlord and tenant (s. 101);

(b) where the rent includes payment for attendance or less than substantial (see s. 70 (3) (b)) board.

(c) where the landlord is a "resident landlord" (s. 5A, added by Rent Act 1974, Sch. 2, and s. 102A, added by Rent Act 1974, Sch. 2, para. 4)

To qualify under (c) the following conditions must be satisfied:—

(1) The letting must have been after 14th August 1974, or, if before, must have been furnished—Rent Act 1974, Sch. 3. Thus the distinction between furnished and unfurnished tenancies (as to which see *Woodward v. Docherty*, [1974] 1 W.L.R. 966) is still important *and*

(2) The dwelling must form part only of a building not a purpose-built block of flats, S. 5A (6), *and*

(3) The tenancy was granted by a person occupying another dwelling in the same building as his residence *and*

(4) Since the grant the landlord has always been a person qualified under (3) above. S. 5A contains provisions to prevent the benefit of the exemption being lost e.g.

on the death of the landlord (sub-ss. 2–4).

(5) The tenancy must not be for a fixed term if granted to a tenant who was previously a tenant of that or another dwelling in the same building on terms which meant he was not protected by virtue of s. 5A—s. 5A (5) (b). Part VI also applies to furnished tenants and student lettings with fixtures or services.

Rateable Value Limits

(A) Where the appropriate day (s. 6 (1)) is before 1st April 1973, these are £400 (Greater London) £200 (elsewhere), or £1,500/£750 on 1st April 1973.

(B) Where the appropriate day is after 1st April 1973 the limits are £1,500/£750.—Rent Act 1974, s. 6. The minister can vary those limits by order.

(a) *Rent*

Tribunals, known as "Rent Tribunals" (see s. 69 and Schedule 10), are established to deal with rent and other questions arising under the statutory provisions in regard to furnished lettings. Either landlord or tenant may refer a letting which is subject to protection to the Rent Tribunal, and the local authority also has power to do so (s. 72). The procedure in regard to the determination of a fair rent for the property is not unlike that applicable in the case of a regulated tenancy (see above). The tribunal can elicit information and may either (a) approve the rent payable under the letting contract, (b) reduce it, (c) dismiss the reference, or (d) increase the rent (s. 73, as amended by Rent Act 1974, s. 7 (1)).

By s. 74 the local authority is under the duty of preparing and keeping up to date a register which will contain particulars of contracts of lettings, descriptions of the premises to which the contracts relate, and the rent approved by the tribunal. Except in cases of sharing with the landlord the tribunal has no jurisdiction in the absence of a *contractual* obligation to provide services (*R. v. Hampstead and St. Pancras Rent Tribunal, Ex parte Ascot Lodge Ltd.*, [1947] 2 All E.R. 12; *R. v. Paddington and St. Marylebone Rent Tribunal, Ex parte Bedrock Investment Ltd.*, [1947] 2 All E.R. 15).

The tribunal has power to determine the preliminary question whether premises come within its jurisdiction before considering the question of reduction of rent (*R. v. City of London, etc., Rent Tribunal, Ex parte Honig*, [1951] 1 All E.R. 195). It has no power to reduce rent merely because the landlord is not providing what he contracted to provide (*R. Hampstead and St. Pancras Rent Tribunal, supra, R. v. Paddington and St. Marylebone Rent Tribunal, Ex parte Bell London and Provincial Properties Ltd.*, [1949] 1 All E.R. 720), or to reduce it below the standard rent (*R. v. Paddington and St. Marylebone Rent Tribunal, Ex parte Bedrock Investments Ltd.*, [1948] 2 All E.R. 528 C.A. *R. v. Fulham, Hammersmith and Kensington Rent Tribunal, Ex parte Marks*, [1951] 2 All E.R. 465). The Rent Tribunal has under s. 81 jurisdiction to deal with any premises, provided that it appears that had an apportionment been made it would have had jurisdiction, and the landlord does not bring apportionment proceedings in the County Court. Subject thereto rent must be fixed *rebus sic stantibus* in each case and regard paid to any non-contractual services in fact supplied and also to any non-contractual services formerly but no longer supplied (*R. v. Paddington and St. Marylebone Rent Tribunal, Ex parte Bell London and Provincial Properties Ltd.* [1949], 1 All E.R. 720).

The rent fixed attaches *in rem* and no application to re-consider it will be entertained in the absence of changed circumstances (*R. v. Fulham, Hammersmith and Kensington Rent Tribunal, Ex parte Gormly* [1951] 2 All E.R. 1030; *R. v. Fulham, Hammersmith and Kensington Rent Tribunal, Ex parte Hierowski* [1953], 2 All E.R. 4).

By s. 7 (2) Rent Act 1974 a tribunal need not entertain a reference to review the rent unless *either* it is made formally by landlord and tenant *or* more than 3 years have elapsed since the registration.

S. 76 makes the requiring of rent in excess of registered rent illegal and the requiring of premiums is also illegal (see above).

(b) *Security*

S. 77 provides that if, after a contract has been referred to a tribunal by a tenant or by the local authority, a notice to quit the premises to which the contract relates is served by the landlord on the tenant at any time before the decision of the tribunal is given, or within six months thereafter, the notice shall not take effect before the expiration of the said six months unless the tribunal directs that a shorter period shall be substituted for the said six months (and see *Alexander v. Springate*, [1951] 1 All E.R. 351).

S. 78 gives the tribunal power in certain circumstances to extend the period of a notice to quit served by the landlord, whether or not the letting has, at the time the notice is served, been referred to the tribunal. The six month period under this section of s. 77 can be extended for further periods of not more than 6 months each (and see *R. v. Folkestone and Area Rent Tribunal, Ex parte Sharkey*, [1951] 2 All E.R. 921; *R. v. Preston and Area Rent Tribunal v. Pickavance*, [1953] 2 All E.R. 438 H.L.). *R. v. Paddington South Rent Tribunal, Ex parte Millard*, [1955] 1 All E.R. 691.

Ss. 77 and 78 do not apply to cases of owner-occupiers who let premises, giving notice to the tenant that they may want to regain possession, and do in fact want possession for themselves or certain members of their families (s. 79). And s. 80 gives the tribunal power to reduce an extension period given under s. 77 or s. 78 in certain circumstances.

Rent tribunals are subject to the control of the Court through the prerogative writs for breach of the rules of natural justice or excess of jurisdiction. A tribunal has jurisdiction even if the tenancy is surrendered after the reference has been made, *Ex parte Napper*, [1965] 3 All E.R. 734.

IV. MISCELLANEOUS

Notices may be duly served upon the landlord's agent named as such in the rent book, or on the person who receives the rent. The agent can be compelled to disclose the name and address of the landlord (s. 109).

In general, weekly tenants must be provided by the landlord with a rent book (Landlord and Tenant Act, 1962, s. 1), and the landlord is guilty of an offence if he fails to do so (s. 4). In certain circumstances, the court may order the rectification of rent books (Rent Act, 1968, s. 35 (as to regulated tenancies) and s. 64 (as to controlled ones)). The Rent Book must contain certain notices to the tenant, by virtue of s. 2 (1) of the Landlord & Tenant Act 1962 as amended by s. 117 (2) and Sch. 15. See now S.I. 1976 No. 378.

No distress for rent due under a protected tenancy shall be levied without the leave of the County Court (Rent Act, 1968, s. 111).

Restrictions are imposed on re-entry and on eviction without a court order being first obtained (Rent Act, 1965, ss. 32 and 33).

Unlawful eviction and harassment of tenants is made an offence by Rent Act, 1965, s. 30.

Notice to Quit. A notice to quit a dwelling is invalid unless (a) it is in writing; (b) it contains such information as may be prescribed (by statutory instrument); see S.I. 1975 No. 2196. For a precedent see *New Law Journal* 26/2/76; (c) unless at least 4 clear weeks elapse before it takes effect (Rent Act 1957, s. 16, as amended by Housing Act 1974, s. 123). See *Thompson v. Stimpson*, [1960] 3 All E.R. 500. The day on which notice is given is included and the day on which it is to take effect is excluded in calculating the four weeks: *Schnabel* v. *Allard*, [1966] 3 All E.R. 816.

S. 6 of the Housing Act 1957 provides that on the letting of a house for human habitation at a rent not exceeding £40 p.a. in London, £26 in other urban areas and £16 elsewhere there is an implied condition that the house is at the commencement of the tenancy and will be kept during the tenancy by the landlord fit for human habitation.

S. 32 of the Housing Act 1961 implies a covenant on the part of the lessor of a house for a term of less than 7 years to keep the structure exterior and installations of the house in good repair and proper working order. See *Liverpool City Council* v. *Irwin*, [1976] 2 W.L.R. 562.

Leasehold Enfranchisement

The Leasehold Reform Act, 1967 (as amended by S. 118, Housing Act 1974) allows certain tenants holding under long leases at low rents, and occupying their houses as residences, either to purchase the freehold or to extend their leases for a further period of 50 years. This summary outlines its main provisions.

Tenants entitled.—To qualify under the Act, the tenant must satisfy the following conditions:
Rateable Value. This must not exceed:—

(a) If the appropriate day was before 1st August 1973 £400 (in Greater London) or £200 elsewhere. But when the Rateable Value exceeds this limit, if the tenancy was created on or before 18th February 1966, the limits are £1,500/£750; Housing Act 1974, s. 118 (1).
(b) Appropriate day after 1st April 1973. If the tenancy was created on or before 18th February 1966, £1,500 (in Greater London) or £750 (elsewhere). If it was created after that date, the limits are £1,000/£500.
The appropriate day means 23rd March 1965 (if the premises were or formed part of a hereditament whose rateable value appeared in the valuation list in force on that date) or the date when the premises first appeared in the valuation list (if not) (s. 1 (4)).
(b) He must hold under a long tenancy (s. 1 (1) (a)), which is defined, broadly as a tenancy granted for a term of years certain exceeding 21 (s. 3, which also contains provisions applicable to special cases). (See *Roberts* v. *Church Commissioners*, [1972] 1 Q.B. 278, and *Austin* v. *Dick Richards Properties, Ltd.*, [1975] 1 W.L.R. 1033.)
(c) His tenancy must be at a low rent (s. 1 (1) (a)), which means a rent of less than ⅔ the rateable value of the property on "the appropriate day" or, if later, on the first day of the term (s. 4). The appropriate day means the same as in (a) above (s. 4 (1) (a)).
(d) When he gives notice under the Act the tenant must have been occupying the premises as his only or main residence (s. 1 (2)) for the last 5 years,

or for periods, amounting to 5 out of the last ten years (s. 1 (1) (b)). (See *Harris* v. *Swick Securities Ltd.*, [1969] 3 All E.R. 1131; [1969] 1 W.L.R. 1604, C.A., and *Fowell* v. *Radford* (1969) 114 Sol. Jo. 34, C.A.).
(e) The premises in question must be a house, or a house and premises. By s. 2 a house is defined as including any building designed or adapted for living in and reasonably so called (See *Lake* v. *Bennett*, [1970] 1 Q.B. 663; [1970] 1 All E.R. 457, C.A., and *Peck* v. *Anicar Properties Ltd.*, [1971] 1 All E.R 517, C.A.). If a house is divided *horizontally* into flats, the individual flats will not qualify, but the house as a whole may qualify. If it is divided *vertically* into flats, the house as a whole will not qualify, but the individual flats may. (See *Parsons* v. *Trustees of Henry Smith's Charity*, [1974] 1 All E.R. 1162.) *Gaidowski* v. *Gonville and Caius College, Cambridge*, [1975] 1 W.L.R. 1066. S. 2 contains a number of ancillary provisions.
(f) The premises must not be part of an agricultural holding or let to and occupied by the tenant with other land or premises to which they are ancillary (s. 1 (3)).

Notices.—Notices by tenants under the Act must be in the prescribed form (set out in the Leasehold Reform (Notices) Regulations, 1967 (S.I. No. 1768, as amended by the Leasehold Reform (Notices) Regulations 1969 (S.I. No. 1481)). (See *Byrnlea Property Investments Ltd.* v. *Ramsay*, [1969] 2 All E.R. 311. Once notice is served the parties' rights and obligations are the same as if a contract for sale or a lease (as the case may be) had been freely entered into between them (s. 5 (1)). The tenant can assign his rights and obligations with the tenancy if he wishes (s. 5 (2)).
S. 5 (5) provides that an existing lease does not become registrable under the Land Charges Act 1925, and is not deemed to be an estate contract, by reason of the rights given to the tenant by the Act. If the tenant actually serves notice of his desire for the freehold or an extended lease, the rights arising from this notice do not con-

stitute an overriding interest under the Land Registration Act 1925, but the notice may be registered under the Land Charges Act 1925 or be the subject of a caution under the Land Registration Act 1925.

Having received the tenant's notice, the landlord has two months in which to give a notice in reply. The tenant cannot take court proceedings to enforce his rights until the notice in reply is given or until two months elapse without it being given. The landlord's notice may admit the tenant's claim. If it does, the landlord is taken to have admitted that the tenant holds on a long tenancy at a low rent, that the house is within the rateable value limits, and that the tenant has occupied it for the requisite period or periods. If the landlord refuses to admit the tenant's claim, he must state his grounds. The tenant can then institute proceedings to determine his rights. As to these points, see generally Sched. 3, Part II.

Sub-tenants.—S. 5 (4) brings into effect the provisions of Schedule 1, which deal with a situation where the tenant giving the notice is a sub-tenant. In such a case there will be one or more superior landlords in ascending scale, at the top of which will be the freeholder. One of these persons is to act for all the others, and one finds him by looking up the scale until one first comes to a superior landlord who "has a tenancy of the house carrying an expectation of possession of 30 years or more." If one reaches the top of the scale without finding anyone who fits this description, then the appropriate person is the freeholder himself.

Trusts and trustees.—S. 6 provides:

(a) That a tenant who now occupies a house as a direct tenant and used to occupy it as a tenant for life under a Settled Land Act settlement or under a trust for sale may treat periods of occupation in the earlier capacity as qualifying periods under the Act.

(b) That one who is currently a tenant for life under a S.L.A. settlement shall have the same rights in respect of his occupation as if the tenancy belonged to him absolutely.

(c) That where a house is vested in trustees (e.g., under a trust for sale) and a person beneficially interested

under the trust is permitted by reason of his interest to occupy the house, the *trustees* shall have the same rights as the occupant himself would have had if he were occupying in right of the tenancy.

Ancillary powers are also given.

Death and the family.—Section 7 provides that for the purposes of the Act certain members of the family of a deceased tenant may, if on his death they become entitled to the tenancy, treat any periods when they were living with him in the house as periods of qualifying occupation.

Enfranchisement.—Sections 8 to 13 deal in detail with the tenant's acquisition of the freehold. Briefly:

(a) Once the tenant has served his notice then, except as provided in the Act, the landlord shall be bound to make, and the tenant to accept, a grant of the premises in fee simple, subject to the tenancy and to the tenant's incumbrances, but otherwise free from incumbrances, at the price provided in the Act (s. 8 (1)).

(b) Unless the parties agree otherwise, the contract arising between them as a result of the service of the tenant's notice incorporates the provisions set out in Part I of the Schedule to the Leasehold Reform (Enfranchisement and Extension) Regulations 1967 (S.I. No. 1879).

(c) The price is to be the amount which the premises would fetch in the open market on certain assumption (s. 9 (1)). One of these assumptions is that the tenancy was to be extended (if it had not in fact been extended) under the Act—i.e., for another 50 years at a ground rent (s. 9 (1) (a)). It is clear from this that the value of the landlord's reversion under the Act may be much smaller than it was before the Act was passed. But the price may include any value attributable to the landlord's right, on paying compensation, to determine the (notionally) extended lease for development purposes (see s. 17 and Schedule 2, para. 5). If the parties cannot agree on a price, it is to be determined by the Lands Tribunal (s. 31 (1)). The Housing Act 1969, provides (s. 82) that the tenant and members of his family who reside in the house shall be assumed not to be in the market.

S. 118 (4) of the Housing Act 1974 sets out the assumptions when the house has a rateable value of more than £1,000 (Greater London) or £500 (elsewhere).

(d) After the price has been ascertained, the tenant has one month within which he can withdraw from the intended purchase. If he does, he cannot make another claim to buy the freehold within 5 years, though his right to an extended lease is not affected (s. 9 (3)).

(e) Easements, restrictive covenants, and the other contents of the conveyance to the tenant are dealt with by s. 10, and rent charges by s. 11.

(f) If the landlord's reversion is mortgaged, the tenant takes free of the mortgage provided that he pays the enfranchisement price in or towards redemption of the mortgage (s. 12) or, in cases of difficulty, etc., into court (s. 13).

Extension.—Ss. 14–16 deal with the tenant's right to an extended lease.

Under s. 17, the landlord may get possession in order to redevelop the property if he applies to the court at any time during the 50 year extension or within 12 months before it begins. He will have to pay compensation to the tenant under Schedule 2.

Management powers.—S. 19 as amended by Housing Act 1974, s. 118 (2), a long and complicated section, provides, in the case of comprehensively managed estates fulfilling certain conditions that the landlord may retain management powers by means of schemes to be approved by the High Court. (See also *Re Sherwood Close (Barnes) Management Co., Ltd.,* [1971] 3 All E.R. 1293; [1971] 3 W.L.R. 902, and *Re Abbots Park Estate,* [1972] 2 All E.R. 177). The court cannot consider a scheme, however, unless the landlord (or a representative body of tenants) has, on an application made before 1st January 1970, obtained a certificate from the Minister of Housing and Local Government that in his opinion the area fulfils the necessary conditions.

Jurisdiction.—Section 20 deals with the jurisdiction of the County Court and s. 21 with that of the Lands Tribunal.

Notices.—Section 22 and Schedule 3 deal with the validity of tenant's notices and the effect of the Act on the Landlord and Tenant Act 1954 and on notices to quit generally.

Contracting out.—By s. 23, any agreement relating to a tenancy is made void in so far as it purports to exclude or modify any right to acquire the freehold or an extended lease, or to compensation, under the Act, or provides for the termination or surrender of the tenancy, or for the imposition of any penalty or disability on the tenant, in the event of his acquiring or claiming such a right. The section continues with detailed ancillary provisions.

Application of the price.—Section 24 deals with the way in which the landlord must deal with any sum received under the Act as proceeds of sale or compensation, and with betterment levy. (As to the latter, a conveyance to the tenant of the freehold is a Case A disposition and must be notified to the Land Commission in the normal way but little, if any, levy is likely in fact to be payable.)

Mortgage in possession.—Section 25 deals with the position where a mortgagee of the landlord's reversion is in possession of the property (which will seldom be the case) or where a receiver has been appointed (which is probably of more importance).

Sections 26 and 27 deal with the situation where the landlord is a custodian trustee or under disability, or cannot be found.

Sections 28–33 deal with land held for public purposes, ecclesiastical land, etc.

Transitional provisions.—Sections 34–36 contain transitional provisions. The most important of these is that certain tenants whose tenancies terminated (at or after the term date) after 8th December 1964, but who are still in occupation, could claim the benefit of the Act—but only if they gave notice of their desire to have the freehold or an extended lease within 3 months from 27th October 1967 (the date of the passing of the Act).

Legal Aid

A. Legal Advice and Assistance

The "statutory advice scheme" (under Section 7 of the Legal Aid and Advice Scheme 1949) and The Law Society's "voluntary scheme" ceased to have effect on 2nd April, 1973 when the new advice and assistance provisions (known as the "green form scheme") came into force. The new provisions are now contained in the Legal Aid Act 1974 and the Legal Advice and Assistance Regulations 1973. A solicitor on the "Legal Advice panel" may do any work (whether of a civil or criminal nature) that is normally considered within the scope of a solicitor's practice, subject to an initial £25 limit (see below). He may thus give advice, write letters, enter negotiations, prepare documents (including wills), do conveyancing, obtain counsel's opinions and in particular obtain evidence in order to assist his client in obtaining a legal aid certificate or legal aid order. He may not however take steps in proceedings before a court or tribunal.

When first seeing the client, the solicitor should enter his financial details on the "green form" (LA/REP/6) and obtain his signature to it. A "key card" may be obtained from the Area Secretary which will be useful in working out the client's eligibility and checking whether a contribution is payable.

The client's eligibility is broadly the same as that for legal aid for civil proceedings (see B below) as far as income is concerned, but the capital limit (£250) is much lower. The contribution, where payable, will be retained by the solicitor in respect of his costs but any surplus must be returned to the client after the matter has been completed.

If the costs of the work done (including disbursements and counsel's fees) will exceed £25, authority to incur costs beyond this sum must be obtained from the Area Committee, by letter addressed to the Area Secretary.

If money is recovered or preserved for the client, and the costs are more than the contribution (if any) payable, then there is a charge in favour of the solicitor, although it may not apply in certain cases (e.g. maintenance orders)

and, in addition, a solicitor may obtain authority from the Area Committee not to enforce it where grave hardship or distress would be caused or it could only be enforced with unreasonable difficulty. Similarly the charge applies to property, other than money, that is recovered or preserved: Reg. 6.

The payment of costs (if they are not covered by the client's contribution or the charge) is made from the Legal Aid Fund. The solicitor should use the same green form that his client has signed and insert the details of his claim. The form must then be submitted to the Area Secretary accompanied by a consolidated claim form LA/ACC/8A.

It should be noted that under Section 2 (4) of the 1974 Act a magistrates' court or county court may request a solicitor who is present in the precincts of the court to act for the litigant under the green form scheme.

B. Legal Aid for Civil Proceedings

(See Matthews & Oulton on Legal Aid)

Legal Aid is available under the Legal Aid Act 1974. The main regulations are the Legal Aid (General) Regulations 1971.

Legal Aid is available for most civil courts, with the following main restrictions:—

(i) it is not available in the Privy Council, in a Coroner's Court nor in a Tribunal, with the exceptions of the Employment Appeal Tribunal, the Lands Tribunal and of proceedings before the Commons Commissioners.

(ii) it is only available in a magistrates' court or the Crown Court for:—

(a) proceedings for or relating to an affiliation order within the meaning of the Affiliation Proceedings Act 1957 or an order under the Matrimonial Proceedings (Magistrates' Courts) Act 1960.

(b) proceedings under the Guardianship of Minors Acts 1971 and 1973.

(c) the Education Act 1944, s. 40.

(d) the Children Act 1948, ss. 2 and 4.

(e) National Assistance Act 1948, s. 43.

(f) Maintenance Orders Act 1950, s. 22.

(g) Maintenance Orders Act 1958, s. 4.

(h) Children and Young Persons Act 1963, s. 3.

(i) Supplementary Benefits Act 1976, s. 18.

(j) Adoption Act 1958, s. 5 (being proceedings where a parent or guardian opposes the making of an adoption order and the court is asked to dispense with his consent).

(k) Maintenance Orders (Reciprocal Enforcement) Act 1972, Part I.

(iii) it is not available for proceedings wholly or partly in respect of defamation, except that the making of a counterclaim for defamation in proceedings for which legal aid may be given shall not of itself affect any right of the defendant to the counterclaim to legal aid to defend such counterclaim.

A person is not financially eligible for legal aid unless:—

(i) his disposable income (i.e. income after making due allowances for certain prescribed deductions etc.) does not exceed £1,790 per annum and

(ii) his disposable capital does not exceed £1,200 (unless it appears that he cannot afford to proceed without legal aid).

The applicant may be required to pay a contribution:—

(i) of an amount equal to one-third of the amount by which the disposable income exceeds £570, and

(ii) of an amount by which the disposable capital exceeds £250.

The applicant's financial eligibility is determined by the Supplementary Benefits Commission, but a table was published in the 18th June 1975 issue of The Law Society's Gazette which is a useful guide for checking whether a person's gross income is likely to make him eligible for legal aid, and, if so, whether he is likely to be required to pay a contribution.

There are various forms of application for legal aid (available from the Area Secretary) and solicitors normally assist applicants in completing them. The completed forms should contain sufficient information, together with accompanying documents, to enable

(i) the financial eligibility to be checked and

(ii) the certifying committee to decide whether reasonable grounds are shown for taking, defending or being a party to proceedings and whether it appears reasonable in the particular circumstances of the case that legal aid should be granted.

In urgent cases emergency certificates may be obtained without delay.

Application forms are sent to the Local Secretary (except where they relate to appellate proceedings, when they should go to the Area Secretary).

As soon as possible after receiving instructions, the solicitor should apply for a legal aid certificate, in order to keep down the pre-legal aid costs, which are payable by the client. However, a certain amount of work, usually the obtaining of evidence, is often necessary before the application will be likely to be granted. The solicitor may be able to do this work under a "green form" (see Section A above). If the application is refused, the copy notice of refusal which is sent to the solicitor will indicate whether there is a right of appeal.

Once a legal aid certificate has been issued, the solicitor is responsible for notifying the other parties to the proceedings. A copy of the certificate must accompany any papers sent to counsel. The certificate must be filed in court if proceedings have begun, or otherwise upon their commencement.

The conduct of the case will, in general, be the responsibility of the solicitor and will not differ from that of a fee-paying client's case, but it should be noted that there may be limitations or conditions on the legal aid certificate. Various authorities may be obtained from the Area Committee to safeguard the solicitor on taxation. Where the prospects of success or of enforcing judgment become doubtful or the client no longer has reasonable grounds for continuing to be a party to the proceedings, acts unreasonably so as to incur unjustifiable expense or it becomes unreasonable in the particular circumstances for him to continue to be legally aided, then the matter should be reported to the Area Committee for their decision whether or not the legal aid certificate should be discharged. The statutory charge may apply to money or property recovered or preserved in the proceedings and the position should be explained to the client where this occurs. The solicitor should ensure that the client appreciates the effect of the charge before agreeing to any settlement to which it will apply. The solicitor must report to the Area Committee the receipt of money or property that has been recovered and is obliged to pay all such money into the Legal Aid Fund: Reg. 18.

The solicitor's bill must usually be taxed, subject to the following main exceptions:—

(a) magistrates' court proceedings
(b) where the proceedings were not commenced, and
(c) where the costs are less than £75.

If the costs are agreed between the parties, an abbreviated form of taxation is usually necessary—see Regulation 22(7). Where the bill is not to be taxed it must be sent, with a form of report on case and all the supporting documents, to the Area Secretary for assessment by the Area Committee. The solicitor or counsel may appeal to the Council of The Law Society against the assessment.

Where the solicitor or counsel is not satisfied with the amount allowed on taxation, he may obtain permission from the Area Committee to lodge objections. If he wishes to have the taxation reviewed or to apply against a review, he must obtain permission from the Council. Regulation 22 covers all these points and should be consulted before any steps of this nature are taken.

Where a certificate has been issued, neither the solicitor nor the counsel is permitted to accept payment for work done, except from the Legal Aid Fund.

S. 13 of the Legal Aid Act 1974 con-fers power on the various courts in which legal aid is available to award costs to successful unassisted parties. The court has to be satisfied that it is just and equitable in all the circumstances that provision should be made out of public funds for the costs and apart from this prime consideration costs incurred in a court of first instance can only be awarded:—

(a) where the proceedings were instituted by the party receiving legal aid and
(b) the court is satisfied that the unassisted party would suffer severe financial hardship unless the order for costs is made.

The practice of applying for costs under section 13 is set out in the Legal Aid (Costs of Successful Unassisted Parties) Regulations, 1964.

C. LEGAL AID FOR CRIMINAL PROCEEDINGS

Part II of the Legal Aid Act 1974, restates (with amendments) the law on legal aid in criminal proceedings which was previously contained in a number of statutes. Since 1967 there has been a liability on the part of a legally assisted person to contribute towards or repay the costs incurred if his finances warrant.

The Legal Aid in Criminal Proceedings (General) Regulations 1968 set out, *inter alia*, the procedure to be followed in applying for legal aid in the various courts and provide the necessary forms.

In the magistrates' court application should be made to the justices' clerk in Form 1 in the Schedule to the Regulations or orally to the court. The power of the court to determine an application for legal aid may be exercised by the clerk or by a justice to whom the clerk has referred the application and an oral application may be referred to the clerk. Before an order for legal aid is made the court, the clerk or a justice of the peace must consider a statement of means (Form 4 or Form 5 where the applicant is an infant). The justices' clerk must (a) make an order for legal aid, (b) refuse to make an order unless the applicant first makes a payment on account of his contribution towards the costs or (c) refer the application to the court or a justice.

In the Crown Court application is made to the appropriate officer of the court in Form 2 or orally to the court, or to the magistrates' court at the conclusion of the proceedings in that court. On retrial the application can be made to the appropriate officer of the Crown Court or orally to the Court of Appeal or House of Lords immediately after that court's decision. In all other respects similar provisions to those mentioned above regarding magistrates' courts apply.

On appeal to the Court of Appeal or the House of Lords application is made to the Registrar of the Court in Form 3 (Court of Appeal) or 3A (House of Lords) or orally to the Court of Appeal, a judge of the court or the Registrar. In all other respects provisions similar to those mentioned above regarding magistrates' courts apply.

The General Regulations also contain provisions covering the assignment of a solicitor and or counsel, the payment of contributions towards legal aid costs, references at the request of the legally assisted person for the Supplementary Benefits Commission to enquire into his means, the refund of payments made on account, and the enforcement of orders for payment of costs.

The Legal Aid in Criminal Proceedings (Fees and Expenses) Regulations 1968 make provision as to the fees and expenses payable to solicitors and counsel assigned to legally assisted persons in the magistrates' court, Crown Court and in the Court of Appeal. All such fees and expenses must now be taxed. There is a right of review before the taxing authority (i.e. the appropriate officer of the Crown Court or the Registrar of the Court of Appeal) and for a further review by a taxing master appointed by the Chief Taxing Master in the Supreme Court and an appeal from the taxing master lies to a single judge of the Queen's Bench Division. In the case of proceedings in a magistrates' court the Area Committee is the taxing authority and there is a right of review to the Council of The Law Society. See Practice Directions (Crime: Legal Aid Taxation) [1969] 1 W.L.R. 370 for the directions of the Lord Chief Justice in regard to review by the Chief Taxing Master and for review of the nominated Judge under regulation 10 of the Legal Aid in Criminal Proceedings (Fees and Expenses) Regulations, 1968.

Licensing Law

(*See Halsbury's Laws of England*, (3rd Edn.) vol. 22, p. 511 et seq., and *Paterson's Licensing Acts*.)

Note.—The present law relating to the licensing of premises for the sale of intoxicating liquor is contained in the Licensing Act, 1964, a consolidating measure reproducing earlier enactments with minor amendments. The 1964 Act has itself been amended by later Acts, in particular by the Finance Act 1967 and the Local Government Act 1972.

New Licences. Justices' licences are granted at the general annual licensing meeting held within the first 14 days of February in every licensing district or at the transfer sessions mentioned later. When the licensing justices have appointed the time and place for holding any such licensing sessions their clerk must advertise this in a newspaper circulating in the district and send notice of it to members of the licensing committee, holders of justices' licences, applicants for such licences and the chief officer of police.

Notice of application for a licence must be in writing and set forth the applicant's name and address and previous occupation and a description of the licence required and of the situation of the premises; the name of the owner of the premises must be stated on making application, and may conveniently be included in the notice. The notice must be served 21 days at least before the session at which the application is to be made on the chief officer of police, on the proper local authority, and on the clerk to the justices, and the applicant must display notice of the application for 7 days beginning not more than 28 days before the day of the licensing sessions in a place where it can be conveniently read by the public on or near the premises to be licensed and he must advertise notice of the application in a newspaper circulating in the place where the premises are (not necessarily a local paper) at least two and not more than four weeks before the application is made and on such other days (if any) as may be fixed by the justices. Service on the "proper local authority" referred to above is effected in respect of premises outside Greater London, by service on an officer of the district council appointed for the purpose by the council; if the premises are in a parish, the notice, in addition to service on the district council, must also be served on the officer so appointed by the parish council, on the chairman of the parish meeting and, if the premises are in a community where there is a community council, it must be served on the officer so appointed by that council. Service on any "proper officer" of a council should be effected by addressing it to the council and leaving it at, or sending it by post to the principal office of the council. In London the notice has to be served on the London borough council concerned, or on the Common Council of the City, according to the situation of the premises. Notice must also be given to the fire authority. In computing times the day on which application is made and the day on which notice is given are excluded.

A member of the public may appear and oppose a grant without previous notice.

In the case of an on-licence or the provisional grant of an off-licence, plans must be deposited with the justices' clerk with the notice of application.

Evidence generally can be required to be on oath at the discretion of the justices. In the case of a firm, the licence is normally granted to the several partners (although it is sometimes taken in the name of one partner). In the case of a company, the justices will normally require the grant to be to a director or other official of the company and not to the company in its own name. Where, however, the actual day-to-day management of the premises is in the hands of a subordinate employee either of a company or of a partnership, the justices may require him to hold the licence, either by himself or jointly with a director or, as the case may be, a partner. In the case of a club (*i.e.* where the grant is to the club itself, and not to a club proprietor in his own name) it must be in the name of a duly nominated officer. There is an appeal to the Crown Court against the grant or the refusal to grant a new licence or against conditions imposed on such a grant.

Restaurants, guest houses, etc. Application for an on-licence subject to conditions prescribed in relation to restaurant, residential, or residential and restaurant licences may not be refused except on specified grounds.

Conditions. Besides the conditions appropriate to restaurant, etc. licences referred to above other conditions may be attached to on-licences for various purposes, *e.g.* to create six-day, early-closing or seasonal licences, to restrict sales to limited classes of persons such as the members of a club, to limit the use of a separate off-licence department to off-sales so as to enable advantage to be taken of the longer hours of sale enjoyed by the holders of off-licences, and so on. Some conditions must be imposed at the request of the applicant; others are discretionary. Some may be removed or varied during the currency of the licence; others can be avoided only by abandoning the licence and obtaining another free from conditions. Conditions may not be attached to off-licences, but the effect of certain conditions has in the past been achieved as the result of undertakings given by the licence-holders. Recent decisions of the High Court that certain undertakings relating to the descriptions of liquor which might be sold were *ultra vires* have, however, cast doubt upon the propriety of the whole practice of granting licences subject to undertakings. In so far as any undertaking may be lawfully required, unlike a condition, which attaches to the licence itself, it affects only the person who gave it, and lapses on transfer of the licence unless the transferee in turn gives a similar undertaking.

Provisional grants. Where premises are in course of construction or about to be constructed application for a licence (whether on or off) may be made by any person interested in the premises. Plans of the proposed premises (or a site plan and description) must be submitted. A "site" grant will lapse unless "affirmed" within 12 months. Affirmation requires further notices and the deposit of plans of the proposed premises. A provisional grant will not be valid until declared final by order of the licensing justices on their being satisfied that the plans (or plans modified with their agreement) have been carried out and that there is nothing against the character of the holder. The same notices are required (for affirmation as well as for an originating application) as for new licences granted otherwise than provisionally.

Renewals. These are granted at the general annual licensing meeting. The person entitled to apply is the holder of the licence. No formal notice is required; and personal attendance is unnecessary unless the application is opposed, but applicants should always attend or send an authorised representative or make arrangements for postal application. No objection is entertained or evidence taken unless notice in writing, stating grounds of objection, has been served on the holder of the licence 7 days before the meeting; but on objection taken without such notice at the meeting consideration of the renewal may be adjourned. A renewal cannot include any part of premises not in the old licence but by consent of all interested part of the premises covered may be dropped out. Structural alterations may be directed and deposit of plans may be required. An appeal lies to the Crown Court against refusal of renewal. No application can be made after the end of the annual meeting unless the justices are satisfied there was good reason for not then applying when the application will be considered at a transfer session or at the annual meeting in the following year, but not in any circumstances later than that meeting. In the case of application at transfer sessions 21 days notice must be given by the applicant to the clerk, the chief officer of police and the proper local authority.

Transfers and removals. Transfer sessions are held at more or less regular intervals during the year as appointed by the justices. The number of such sessions is not less than 4 nor more than 8 in the year. Transfers are granted on death, incapacity, bankruptcy, giving up occupation, wilful omission to apply for renewal when about to quit the premises, and where on the forfeiture of a licence the owner of the premises has obtained a protection order; (for other cases in which transfers may be granted, *see* the Licensing Act, 1964, ss. 138 and 145). Notice with a view to a transfer must be signed by the applicant or his agent and must set out the name and address and occupation of the transferee; 21 days' notice must be given to the clerk of the justices, the chief officer of police, the proper local authority and the holder of the licence (if any). In any case in which transfer could be granted temporary authority to carry on the business until the next available transfer session may be granted to the proposed transferee by any magistrates' court for the area concerned. Such authority is called a "protection order". Seven days' notice of application for a protection order has to be given to the chief officer of police.

Application for an ordinary removal order must be made at licensing sessions (*i.e.* the general annual licensing meeting or transfer sessions) by the person desiring to hold the licence when removed. The removal can be from any premises, not merely from premises in the same licensing district. Notices are as for a new licence; but in addition notice must be served on the registered owner of the premises from which the licence is to be removed and on the holder of the licence unless he is also the applicant. Justices will not make an order unless satisfied that no objection is made by the owner of the premises to which the licence is attached, or by the holder of the licence, or other person entitled to object to the removal. An appeal to the Crown Court lies against any grant or refusal of an ordinary removal order.

In cases where an old on-licence (but no other description of licence) is attached to premises that are to be pulled down for public purposes or that have been rendered unfit by fire or other calamity, a special removal to other premises in the same licensing district may be granted. As to old on-licences see below under "Compensation authority".

Duration of licences. All licences, whether granted as new licences or by way of renewal, transfer or removal expire on April 5 next following the grant, unless the grant was made between January 5 and April 4, in which case the licence will endure until April 5 in the following year. A grant by way of renewal, transfer or removal supersedes the existing licence. This means in relation to a licence renewed from year to year that its effective duration is from February to February, but that it would endure as above mentioned in the event of non-renewal.

Upgrading. An existing on-licence may be extended to additional types of liquor, either on renewal or transfer, or on *ad hoc* application at any licensing sessions.

Alterations to premises. No alterations increasing the facilities for drinking in a public or common part of the premises, concealing such a part from observation, or affecting communication between such a part and the remainder of the premises or a street or other public way may be made without the consent of the justices. Consent may be given to an alteration involving an extension of the licensed premises by incorporation of adjoining premises, provided that such alteration will not destroy the identity of the premises as already existing and will bring the altered premises within the ambit of the licence (*R. V. Weston-super-Mare Licensing Justices,* [1939] 1 K.B. 700, C.A.). On complaint to a magistrates' court that alterations have been made without consent of the licensing justices, the licence may be declared forfeited or the premises ordered to be restored to their former condition. In case of forfeiture, the owner may apply to a magistrates' court for a protection order authorising him to carry on business until next sessions. The justices when asked to renew an on-licence may order structural alterations; such an order will be subject to appeal to the Crown Court as also will refusal to consent to proposed alterations.

Fees. The following fees are payable. On a grant or transfer or removal or renewal of any justices licence, £2;

affirming provisional grant or declaring provisional grant final .50p; insertion, variation or revocation of specified conditions, 50p; extending existing on-licence to additional types of liquor, £1; consent to alterations, £1; grant of protection order 50p.

Compensation authority. The renewal authority may refer the question of renewal, transfer or special removal of an old on-licence (*i.e.* one in force on August 15, 1904, other than for wine alone) or of an old beerhouse licence (*ante* 1869 licence) to the compensation authority where the grounds of objection are other than the character of the licence holder or the conduct of the premises or (except in the case of an old beerhouse licence) structural defects. The most usual ground for such a reference is that the premises are no longer required for the needs of the neighbourhood. Notice of objection must have been given to the licensed person and evidence on oath must have been heard. Licences so referred are renewed provisionally by the referring authority. Outside the City of London, there is a compensation committee for every county. There is a separate committee for the City of London. Committees may hold three meetings, any of which may be adjourned for the conclusion of their business. The preliminary meeting must be held before the last day of May, except where no reports are to hand before April 30 from the renewal authorities. The latter authorities are entitled to 7 days' notice. At this meeting the reports received are considered generally and it may be decided in the case of any licence not to proceed further. The principal meeting is held after 14 days' notice to the general public, to the renewal authorities, the licensee and the registered owner. Owners should be registered so as to be sure of getting notice. Copies of reports may be had on payment of a fee by persons interested from the clerk of the compensation authority. All persons interested are entitled to be heard. Notice of the decision arrived at will be sent to the renewal authorities, the licensee, and the registered owner. The public have access to this meeting. Finally, a supplemental meeting is held after 7 days' notice to ascertain the persons entitled to compensation and to settle the distribution thereof. At this meeting, the licensee and the owner and any other claimant are entitled to be heard.

Meetings need not be held if no licences are referred by renewal authorities in the committee's area.

Life Assurance

(See Houseman's Law of Life Assurance 8th Edn.)

TYPES OF CONTRACT

A large part of the business transacted by Life Offices falls within the following classes of policy:—

Whole Life Policy. A policy securing a capital sum at death whenever that may occur.

Endowment Assurance Policy. A policy securing a capital sum on survival to a fixed date or at earlier death.

Temporary Assurance Policy. A policy securing a capital sum only if death occurs within a specified term and not otherwise.

Family Income Policy. A policy providing that if the life fails within a specified term (normally 20 years) a monthly or quarterly instalment of capital is payable throughout the balance of the specified term. These instalments may or may not be preceded by, and are sometimes followed by, a substantial capital sum.

Child's Deferred Assurance Policy. A policy providing a life assurance for a child at majority or some age over majority up to age 25. The title to such policies requires careful attention (see *Barclays Bank Ltd.* v. *Webb*, [1941] 1 Ch. 225; *Re Foster's Policy*, [1966] 1 All E.R. 432 and the criticism in *Beswick* v. *Beswick*, [1967] 2 All E.R. 1197 of *Re Engelbach's Estate*, [1924] 2 Ch. 348 and *Re Sinclair's Life Policy*, 1938] Ch 799).

Such a policy can take the form of an assurance on the life of the parent during the deferred period, and if the policy is so arranged that no further premiums will be payable during the deferred period in the event of the death of the parent, the policy would qualify for relief of income tax on the premium if it fulfils the necessary conditions (*see* p. 249, *post*). Vesting of the policy in the child on attainment of the age stated could give rise to a charge to capital transfer tax and so, in future, to avoid this possible liability Child's policies should be written under an appropriate trust.

Last Survivor Assurance A policy securing a sum payable at the death of the last survivor of two or more lives. This type of policy is a means of providing funds for payment of capital transfer tax on the second to die of husband and wife.

INSURABLE INTEREST

Under the Life Assurance Act, 1774, a life policy is unenforceable unless the assured has an interest in the life of the person assured. Husband and wife each have an insurable interest to any amount in the life of the other.

A life policy is not a contract of indemnity, and if an insurable interest is present when the policy is effected, its subsequent cesser will not affect the validity of the policy.

CONDITIONS OF POLICY

Suicide. This risk is sometimes specifically excluded from the cover provided during a fixed period from the issue of the policy, sometimes as short a time as 6 months or as long as 2 years, subject to a reservation in favour of assignees or encumbrancers for value.

Renewal Premium. Normally 30 days of grace are allowed for payment of the renewal premium but the standing of the policy during the days of grace and subsequently must be ascertained from the particular conditions in the policy in question.

Residence. In the ordinary way policies are issued without restriction as to residence, travel or occupation except in cases where the proposer is known to be likely to be exposed to exceptional hazard.

ASSIGNMENTS

The Policies of Assurance Act, 1867, provides for service on the life office of notice of the date and purport of any assignment.

The policy must bear upon it the address for service of such notice. The life office may charge a fee not exceeding 25p for acknowledgment, though in some cases acknowledgments are given without any charge where notices are served in duplicate.

On service of notice enquiry should always be made of the life office for information as to previous dealings so that the assignee may obtain possession of or acknowledgment for production of deeds which are necessary to perfect his title.

LOST OR DESTROYED POLICIES

The title to a life policy is not the subject of registration with the life office in manner similar to that adopted for registration of stocks and shares. Where therefore a life policy is lost or destroyed, the life office cannot issue a *duplicate* copy. It may, however, upon request, issue a copy of the lost or destroyed policy; and it is well to report the loss or destruction of a policy so that such evidence of the loss or destruction as may be available can be produced and recorded.

SETTLEMENTS

Many marriage settlements contain express clauses as to dealing with reversionary bonus. Such clauses are strictly construed.

An appointment or retirement of trustees by deed will vest a life policy under an implied vesting declaration (*see* Trustee Act, 1925, s. 40). No assignment is necessary.

Where a policy is reassigned to the settlor or is transferred to a beneficiary, the deed should contain an acknowledgment of the right of the assignee to production of the settlement.

BANKRUPTCY

Discharge in bankruptcy will not suffice to revest in the debtor a policy on his life effected by him before adjudication or acquired by him before discharge even though such a policy had on the bankruptcy little or no value, either owing to its recent issue or because of encumbrances upon it.

An assignment from the trustee in bankruptcy should always be obtained.

MARRIED WOMEN'S PROPERTY ACT 1882. SECTION 11

A policy effected by a man on his own life and expressed to be for the benefit of his wife or children or any of them will create a trust. The identity of the beneficiaries and the nature of their interests must be ascertained by reference to the policy (*Cousins v. Sun Life Assurance*, [1933] 1 Ch. 126). Similarly a woman may effect a policy on her life for the benefit of her husband or children or any of them. "Children" is deemed to include adopted children and illegitimate children. (*See* Adoption Act, 1958, s. 14 (3) and Family Law Reform Act 1969, s. 19 (1)).

The assured may appoint trustees of the policy and in default of appointment the policy vests in the assured or his legal personal representatives as trustees. The protection of the policy moneys against the creditors of the assured is more complete than that which can be obtained in any other way.

EXCHANGE CONTROL

Except with the permission of the Treasury no person resident in the United Kingdom may transfer a policy or annuity to a person resident outside the scheduled territories or to a nominee for him (Exchange Control Act, 1947, s. 28).

Applications for permission to remit moneys payable on death or maturity, and other payments under policies, to or for the credit of persons resident outside the scheduled territories will normally be made by the life office through its bankers.

INCOME TAX

Allowance in respect of life premiums. Relief from income tax is given in respect of premiums on assurances made by a man on his own life or the life of his wife. The total amount of premiums available for relief must not exceed one-sixth of the total income of the taxpayer.

In respect of assurances made after 22 June, 1916, the relief is calculated at one half the basic rate of tax on the whole of the premium. At the basic rate of tax of 35% the relief is thus $17\frac{1}{2}$% of the premiums. Where premiums do not exceed £20, relief is allowed at basic rate on the lower of the premiums paid or £10.

Reliefs depend on *payment* of premium and are independent of questions of title.

In the case of policies effected after 19th March 1968, s. 19 (4) and Part I of Sch. 1 of ICTA 1970 limit the relief from income tax described above to "qualifying policies" within the meaning of that Act.

Most ordinary life assurance policies are "qualifying policies". The conditions for qualification are set out in the Schedule separately for whole life and term assurances and endowment assurances, and there are provisions dealing with special types of policies and variations of policies.

A number of changes and additions to the conditions for qualification were introduced by s. 10 and Part II of Sch. 2, F.A. 1975, in respect of policies issued on or after 1st April 1976. In addition, the Act provides (Part I, Sch. 2) that as from that date the certification of life policies as qualifying policies will be taken over from the life offices by the Revenue.

Claw-back. Where a qualifying policy is surrendered or made paid-up within four years of commencement then, by s. 7, F.A. 1975, the life office is required to retain out of the proceeds and pay over to the Revenue a sum ("claw-back") representing the whole or a part of the total tax relief which will normally have been allowable on the premium from the commencement of the policy. The claw-back calculation varies according to the number of years which have elapsed from commencement to the event giving rise to the claw-back, but is subject to a "ceiling" to ensure that the claw-back does not exceed the amount by which the policyholder's profit can be regarded as having been made out of the tax relief. A similar principle, with appropriate modifications, applies where policies are made partly paid-up or partially surrendered.

Further, s. 8 of the Act provides, in respect of qualifying policies that where, in the fifth or later years from commencement, money is taken out of the policy by way of total or partial surrender the life office is required to retain out of the proceeds and pay to the Revenue a proportion of that year's premium equal to one-half the basic rate of tax in force for that year. This provision does not apply where the surrender etc. in question (even a total surrender) is the *first* since the commencement of the policy.

The surrender of a bonus and the taking of a loan on a policy will be treated as equivalent to a partial surrender under the above provisions unless, in the case of a loan, interest at a Commercial rate is payable on the sum lent.

These provisions apply to policies issued after 26th March 1974 and to increases in rights under earlier policies where premiums are increased by more than 25%.

TAX LIABILITY ON GAINS

In the case of a policy issued (or in some cases varied) after 19th March 1968 which does not qualify for income tax relief, there will be a charge to income tax on the happening of a "chargeable event" viz. death, maturity, surrender, part surrender or sale, which gives rise to a gain. Generally, such gains are subject to higher rates of income tax and investment income surcharge but not basic rate tax. Gains arising on qualifying policies may also be subject to this charge to tax if they are surrendered, made paid-up or sold within a certain period from commencement (normally 10 years). The method for computing the chargeable gain is set out in Ch. III, Part XIV, I.C.T.A. 1970 (Ss. 393–402) and is, normally, the excess of the proceeds over the premiums paid. However, F.A. 1975 (Part IV of Sch. 2) contains lengthy and detailed provisions amending the previous method of computing the tax and in general these provisions apply to any event happening in a policy year (i.e. the year beginning with the date of effecting the policy or its anniversary) which falls wholly after the passing of the Act. The rate of tax to be applied is determined by "top-slicing", i.e. by reference to the number of years that have elapsed since the policy was effected or, in some cases, back to the previous chargeable event.

CAPITAL TRANSFER TAX

Capital transfer tax (F.A. 1975) may affect life assurance policies on a number of quite separate occasions.

Premiums paid by the policyholder towards an own-life own-benefit policy or a life-of-another policy will not be chargeable to capital transfer tax as there is no transfer of value. Where a policy is written in trust for (or kept up for the benefit of) another, however, each premium payment is a chargeable transfer unless one or more of the available exemptions applies. Payment of a premium, to the extent that it is not exempt, will constitute a net transfer which must be grossed up for the purposes of calculating the tax, unless the donee (i.e. the beneficiary under the policy) pays the tax on it. The principal exemptions which may apply to free premiums from the tax are the spouse, £1,000 p.a. (proposed increase to £2,000 p.a. in Finance Bill 1976) and normal expenditure exemptions (Sch. 6, paras 1, 2 and 5). The capital element of a purchased life annuity purchased after 12th November 1974 will not be regarded as income in applying the normal expenditure exemption.

The death of the life assured under a trust policy will not be a chargeable transfer unless the beneficiaries have predeceased him and he has acquired an interest in possession through the will or intestacy of the last of them to die. However, if the life assured under a trust policy effected prior to 27th March 1974 dies before March 1981 then, as a result of s. 22(5) F.A. 1975, there could be a charge to tax on part of the policy proceeds calculated in accordance with the old gifts of rights basis (F.A. 1959, s. 34) unless, as in most cases, the proceeds would have been free from estate duty as e.g. the premiums were part of the life assured's normal expenditure.

On the death of the life assured under an own-life own-benefit policy, the value of the policy will form part of his estate for the charge to tax on the deemed transfer on death, unless the spouse exemption applies. The value for this purpose will be the proceeds payable on death (Sch. 10, para. 9).

The death of the policyholder of a life-of-another policy and the death of a beneficiary with an interest in possession in a settled policy will constitute transfers and give rise to a charge to tax unless the spouse exemption applies. The value of the transfer in these circumstances will be taken as the greater of (i) the market value of the policy (generally the surrender value) and (ii) the total of the premiums paid to the date of transfer, less any sum paid out by way of partial surrender (Sch. 10, para. 11). This rule of valuation does not apply to unit-linked policies and most temporary life assurance policies when, broadly, the market value will be taken as the value of the transfer (para. 11(3) and (4)).

The assignment of an interest in a policy, other than for full consideration is a transfer giving rise to a charge to tax unless any exemptions apply. The value of the transfer will be calculated in accordance with the principles in the preceding paragraph.

There is a special rule relating to combinations of a life policy, effected after 26th March 1974, and annuity where these are regarded as "associated operations". The person who purchased the annuity is treated as having made a transfer at the time the policy became vested in the beneficiary, the value of the transfer being the lesser of (i) the consideration paid for the annuity plus any premiums paid under the policy before the transfer and (ii) the proceeds of the policy (F.A. 1975, s. 42). The purchase of an annuity and the effecting of a life policy will not be treated as associated operations if it is shown that the policy was issued after full medical evidence of health had been obtained and that it would have been issued on the same terms had the annuity not been purchased.

Section 22(7) continues under the capital transfer tax the principle of non-aggregation which formerly applied under estate duty for policies effected prior to 20th March 1968 in which the deceased never had an interest and where the total sum related to the death does not exceed £25,000. Where the £25,000 maximum is exceeded the balance is included with the rest of the deceased's estate.

PERSONS WHO DIE DOMICILED OUTSIDE THE UNITED KINGDOM

Where a policy has been effected by a person who dies domiciled outside the United Kingdom, an English grant of representation is not necessary to collect the policy money (Revenue Act, 1884, s. 11 as amended by Revenue Act 1889, s. 19).

ANNUITIES AND PENSIONS

ICTA ss. 226–231, as amended by F.A. 1971 contains provisions for relief in the taxation of the cost of pensions and death benefits for the self-employed and their dependants and those in non-pensionable employment and of purchased annuities as follows:—

1.—Where a person not in pensionable employment effects a Pension Policy the premium ranks as an expense and so affords complete relief from income tax (including higher rate tax) provided that

(a) the amount of the premium does not exceed 15% of the assessable earned income, with a maximum premium of £1,500 (although a provision, increasing by 50% to £2,250 to maximum premium allowable, is included in the Finance Bill for 1976 for the year 1976/77 and subsequent years of assessment). In the case of an entrant born in or before 1915 the maxima are:—

Year of Birth	Sum	%
1914 or 1915	£1,600	16
1912 or 1913	£1,700	17
1910 or 1911	£1,800	18
1908 or 1909	£1,900	19
1907 or earlier	£2,000	20

(again, the Finance Bill 1976 provides for a corresponding increase of 50% in these allowable maxima).

(b) the pension, which may be guaranteed for any period not exceeding 10 years (whether the pensioner lives or not), is to commence not earlier than age 60 or later than age 70 (an amendment increasing this to age 75 is provided in the Finance Bill 1976), though an earlier age for commencement (but not before age 50) can be allowed for an occupation where earlier retirement is customary; and in any event early retirement is allowed in cases of incapacity.

(c) the policy is in a form approved by the Commissioners of Inland Revenue; the policy should confer no benefit other than a non-assignable non-commutable pension, though the policy can provide that on the death of the pensioner before retirement the life office may return to his executors the full premiums paid together with interest, or may alternatively pay a pension to the widow or other dependant.

Note. By virtue of F.A. 1971, s. 20 (3) contracts may be approved which carry the right to commute part of the pension for a lump sum. Existing contracts may be endorsed to this effect if the insurance company agrees.

The pension when enjoyed ranks as earned income.

ICTA 1970, s. 226A allows an approved contract which provides either mainly an annuity for the taxpayer's spouse or dependants, or only a lump sum payable to the taxpayer's personal representatives on his death before 70 (age 75—Finance Bill 1976). The maximum premium allowable for approved contracts is £500 (£750—Finance Bill 1976) or 5% of net relevant earnings, but the overall amount paid for retirement annuities and approved contracts must not, subject to date of birth, exceed £1,500 (£2,250—Finance Bill 1976) or 15% of earnings. Spouses' or dependants annuities are commutable at the Board's discretion.

2.—Where a person whether or not in pensionable employment enjoys a "purchased" annuity he is *not* taxed on the whole annuity as income but only on the part left after deduction of the capital element, which is to be ascertained in any particular case by dividing the cost of the annuity by the number of years of expectation of life at the date when it commences. An annuity is *not* a "purchased" annuity if:—

(a) it arises under a Pension Policy, or a pension scheme, or

(b) it is provided by an employer for his employee, or

(c) it arises under a will or settlement (as to which see ICTA, s. 230 (7) (c)).

ANNUITIES

As a matter of convenience the balance of the annuity (after deduction of the capital element) can in certain circumstances be paid by the life office without deduction of income tax. Limits of income for this purpose are as follows:—

	Single Person	Married Person
Under age 65 ..	£735	£1,085
Over age 65 ..	£1,010	£1,555

Similar arrangements apply for Pensions Annuities except that where assured pension schemes received Inland Revenue approval under s. 208 of the I.C.T.A. 1970, annuities are paid to a Trust in full and the Trustees pay the pensioners under P.A.Y.E. This arrangement is extended by Schd. 5 of F.A. 1970 to all schemes approved under the revised provisions introduced by that Act.

PURCHASED ANNUITIES

The following table shows approximate amounts of annuities which can be purchased for each £100 of purchase money at the time of going to press, and the years of expectation of life to ascertain the capital element.

Age	Male Life	Years of Expectation	Female Life	Years of Expectation
	£		£	
50	14.50	26	14.00	30
55	15.50	22	14.50	26
60	16.50	18	15.50	21
65	18.00	14	16.50	17
70	20.00	11	18.00	14
75	23.00	8	20.00	11
80	27.50	6	23.50	8

Limitation of Actions

The relevant statutes are, the codifying statute: the Limitation Act 1939, the Law Reform (Limitation of Actions, etc.) Act 1954, the Limitation Act 1963, and the Limitation Act 1975. These Acts may be cited together as the Limitation Acts 1939 to 1975.

Periods of Limitation for different classes of action. The following are the periods of limitation prescribed by the Act in relation to the most common forms of action:—

Account (action for), 6 years (s. 2 (2)).

Action for damages for negligence, nuisance or breach of duty. Where the damages claimed by a plaintiff for negligence, nuisance or breach of duty (whether the duty exists by virtue of a contract, or of a statutory provision, or independently of any contract or statutory provision), consist of or include damages in respect of personal injuries to any person, 3 years (s. 2 (1), as amended by Law Reform (Limitation of Actions, etc.) Act, 1954, s. 2 (1)). This time limit is extended for certain actions by s. 1 of the Limitation Act 1963, as amended by the Law Reform (Miscellaneous Provisions) Act 1971, s. 1 (1). The law has been further extended in respect of personal injuries and actions under Fatal Accidents Acts by the Limitation Act 1975.

Award (action to enforce), where submission not by an instrument under seal, 6 years (s. 2 (1)).

Advowson (action to enforce), 60 years or 3 successive incumbencies whichever is the longer, but not in any case more than 100 years (s. 14).

Breach of trust (action for), if fraudulent no limitation (s. 19 (1)), if non-fraudulent 6 years (s. 19 (2)).

Conversion (action for), 6 years (s. 2 (1)). Where there have been successive conversions, 6 years from the original conversion (s. 3 (1)). Where trust property converted by trustee to own use, no limitation (s. 19 (1)).

Detinue (action for), 6 years (s. 2 (1)). Where there have been successive wrongful detentions, 6 years from original wrongful detention (s. 3 (1)).

Dower (action to recover arrears of), 6 years (s. 17).

Foreclosure action, 12 years (s. 18 (2)). This applies to mortgaged personal property only. Foreclosure actions in respect of mortgaged land follow the provisions relating to recovery of land (s. 18 (4)). See *Land, infra*.

Forfeiture (action to recover), 2 years (s. 2 (5)).

Fraud (action for, against trustee), no period of limitation (s. 19 (1)). As to other actions based on fraud see *infra*.

Judgment (action on), 12 years from date when judgment became enforceable (s. 2 (4)).

Judgment debt (action to recover arrears of interest on), 6 years from date when interest became due (s. 2 (4)).

Land (action for recovery of), (a) if brought by Crown 30 years (60 years in case of foreshore) (s. 4 (1)); (b) if brought by spiritual or eleemosynary corporation sole 30 years (s. 4 (2)); (c) if brought by any other person 12 years (s. 4 (3)). Where the person entitled to a particular estate was not in possession when that estate determined, 6 years from the determination of the particular estate or 12 years from

the date when the right of action first accrued to the person entitled to the particular estate (s. 6). Actions to recover equitable interests in land are subject to the same periods of limitation as actions in respect of legal estates (s. 7).

Legacy (action to enforce payment of), 12 years (s. 20), action to recover interest on, 6 years (*ibid.*).

Mortgage or charge on real or personal estate (action to recover money secured by), 12 years (s. 18 (1)).

Mortgage interest (action to recover), 6 years (s. 18 (5)).

Penalty (action to recover), 2 years (s. 2 (5)) (does not apply to fines).

Personal estate of deceased person (action to recover share or interest in), 12 years (s. 20).

Personal injuries (action for damages for negligence, nuisance or breach of duty), 3 years (s. 2A).

Proceeds of sale of land (action to recover), 12 years (s. 18 (1)).

Recognisance (action to enforce), 6 years (s. 2 (1)).

Redemption action in respect of land, 12 years (s. 12).

Rent (action to recover), 6 years (s. 17).

Simple contract (action founded on), 6 years (s. 2 (1)). But see *Action for damages for negligence, nuisance or breach of duty, supra.*

Specialty (action founded on), 12 years (s. 2 (3)).

Tort (action for), 6 years (s. 2 (1)). But see *Action for damages for negligence, nuisance or breach of duty, supra.*

Trust property (action to recover where no other period prescribed), 6 years (s. 19(2)).

When time begins to run. In ordinary cases the limitation period runs from the time when an action could first be brought, *e.g.*, from the expiration of the credit, when goods are sold on credit; from the time when a promise ought to be performed, in the case of an executory contract; etc. Where damage is the gist of the action it runs from the first accruing of the damage, not from the act causing it; in cases of indemnity, from the time when the indemnity could be sued for at common law. In trover, in the absence of concealed fraud, the statute runs from the conversion even though the plaintiff is ignorant of it; in malicious prosecution, from the time of putting the law in motion; in false imprisonment; from each day of the imprisonment, and so in other cases of continuing tort.

In the case of present interests in land, time generally runs from the dispossession of the claimant or person through whom he claims (s. 5 (1)). Where the claim is based on the will or intestacy of a person who was in possession at his death time runs from the death (s. 5 (2)). Where the claim is based on an assurance *inter vivos* time runs from the date of the assurance. In the case of an action by a remainderman time runs from the date when the remainder fell into possession (s. 6 (1)). A right of action to recover land by virtue of forfeiture or breach of condition runs from the date when the forfeiture was incurred or condition broken (s. 8). The right of action of a person entitled to land subject to a tenancy at will accrues at the end of one year from the commencement of the tenancy, and that of a person entitled subject to a tenancy from year to year or other period without a lease in writing at the expiration of the first year or other period or at the date of the last receipt of rent, whichever is the later (s. 9). No right of action for the recovery of land accrues or continues in the absence of adverse possession (s. 10).

Extension of limitation period in case of disability. (See s. 22, as amended by the Law Reform (Limitation of Actions, etc.) Act, 1954, s. 2 (2), and by the Limitation Act, 1963, s. 4 (3)).

Acknowledged and part payment (see ss. 23–25).

Concealed fraud and mistake. In the case of any action for which a period of limitation is prescribed by the Act based on fraud or for relief from the consequences of mistake or where the cause of action is concealed by the defendant's fraud the limitation period does not begin until the plaintiff has or might with reasonable diligence have discovered the fraud or mistake. This provision does not, however, enable any action to be brought to recover, or enforce any charge against, or set aside any transaction affecting property which has been purchased for value by a person who was not party to the fraud or the transaction in which the mistake was made, and did not know and had no reason to know of the fraud or mistake (s. 26). *See also* the Limitation Act, 1963, s. 4 (3).

Proceedings against the Crown. Actions in respect of damage or loss caused to or by any of Her Majesty's ships are limited by the provisions of s. 8 of the Maritime Conventions Act, 1911. Subject to this, the Crown is in the same position as a public authority (Crown Proceedings Act, 1947, s. 30, as amended by the Law Reform (Limitation of Actions, etc., Act, 1954, s. 5 (2)). No proceedings lie against the Crown in respect of loss of, or damage to, registered inland postal packets under the Crown Proceedings Act, 1947, s. 9 (2), unless such proceedings are begun within 12 months, beginning with the date on which the packet in question was posted (Law Reform (Limitation of Actions, etc.) Act, 1954, s. 5 (3)).

Proceedings under the Fatal Accidents Acts. Actions must be commenced within 3 years after the death of the deceased person (Fatal Accidents Act, 1846, s. 3, as amended by the Law Reform (Limitation of Actions, etc.) Act, 1954, s. 3). This time limit is extended in certain cases by the Limitation Act 1963, ss. 3, 3A, 3B, as substituted by the Law Reform (Miscellaneous Provisions) Act 1971, s. 2 (1) and Sched. 1, Part I.

Magistrates

(*See Stone's Justices' Manual*)

MAGISTRATES' COURTS

Proceedings are regulated by the Magistrates' Courts Act, 1952 and the Rules made thereunder. Jurisdiction falls into five main classes: (1) Summary offences; (2) Indictable offences triable summarily; (3) Indictable offences triable only on indictment; (4) Offences triable either summarily or on indictment; (5) Civil debts.

I. SUMMARY OFFENCES

Proceedings before the Hearing. Proceedings are commenced either by information or complaint upon which a summons or warrant is granted. An information is laid in cases where an offence has been committed, and a complaint is made when an order for the payment of money (*see Civil Debts, post*) or for other matters is asked for. In all cases in which a warrant is granted, it is essential that the information should be taken either upon oath or affirmation. As a general rule the person aggrieved attends at the court or at the Office of the Clerk to the Justices and lays an information or makes a complaint. An information may be laid or a complaint made by the prosecutor or complainant in person or by his counsel or solicitor or other person authorised by him to do so: But an information laid on oath or affirmation must be by the informant in person. The summons is usually (though not always) served by the police, and warrants are almost invariably executed by them.

If the court refuses to grant process, application may be made to the High Court for a *mandamus*, if it can be shown that judicial discretion has not been exercised.

Witness Summons. Either of the parties is able to seek a witness summons in the event of a witness being unwilling to attend voluntarily. A witness summons may require a witness to produce documents or things likely to be of material evidence.

Where documents, etc., are in the possession of the other side, a notice to produce should be served, otherwise such documents cannot be proved by means of secondary evidence.

Juvenile Courts. The ordinary procedure for the hearing of charges and applications is simplified and adapted, *see* Magistrates' Courts (Children and Young Persons) Rules, 1970.

The Hearing. All cases against adults must be heard in open court. The charge is read to the defendant. If he is liable to a term of imprisonment exceeding three months for an offence which is not an assault or an offence against a male person or soliciting for immoral purposes or of trading on prostitution, he must be informed before he pleads to the charge (if he is present) of his right to be tried by a jury at a Crown Court. If there is to be a summary trial he is then asked by the Clerk of the Court whether he pleads guilty or not guilty. If he pleads guilty it is not necessary to call evidence, although it is often desirable to do so. If he pleads not guilty, or does not appear, counsel or solicitor (if any) for the prosecution opens his case. Witnesses for the prosecution are then called and examined, cross-examined and re-examined. When the witnesses for the prosecution have been called and the case for the prosecution closed, counsel or solicitor for the defence (if any) opens the case for the defence. He may address the court either at the conclusion of the prosecution's case or at the conclusion of the evidence for the defence. Where oral evidence is given by witnesses for the defence in addition to the evidence of the defendant, the court may allow the defendant or his advocate to address the court both at the conclusion of the prosecution's case and at the conclusion of the evidence, but in that case the prosecutor may also address the court immediately before the accused does so for the second time.

Any party may be represented by counsel or solicitor and an absent party so represented is deemed not to be absent, unless the case is one which some enactment or a condition of a recognizance expressly requires the party's presence; for instance, a "means inquiry" relating to an unpaid fine, or proceedings for enforcement of an order for periodical payments, must take place in the presence of the defendant in person.

Adults

The Judgment of the Court. After hearing all the evidence the justices either convict or discharge the defendant, or in the case of a complaint make an order or dismiss the case. Offenders may be dealt with in the following ways:—

(a) The Court may defer passing sentence to a specified date not more than six months from the date of conviction so as to have regard for the accused's conduct after conviction. Sentence may only be *deferred* once but the case can be further *adjourned* in appropriate circumstances.

(b) Fine or imprisonment or both. A Magistrates' Court shall not impose imprisonment on a person under 17 years of age; and not on a person under 21 years of age unless, after considering information of his character and physical and mental condition the court is of the opinion that no other punishment is appropriate. Similarly, a sentence of imprisonment may not be imposed on a person who has not already served a term of imprisonment, unless the court is of opinion that no other method of dealing with him is appropriate and he is either represented at the time of sentence being passed or, having been informed of his right to be represented and of applying for legal aid has not exercised these rights.

A sentence of imprisonment may be imposed as a suspended sentence, *i.e.*, a sentence that will not take effect unless, during a specified period of not exceeding two years, the offender commits another offence punishable with imprisonment.

Where a fine is imposed, there may be an order that the defendant shall be under the supervision of some person (usually the probation officer) until it is paid. Where the offender is under 21 years of age, such an order *must* be made (unless the court considers it undesirable or impracticable) before he may be committed to prison for non-payment.

A fine is recoverable by distress and/or imprisonment, or detention in police custody. Where money is found on the prisoner on his apprehension, or upon being searched by order of the court, or found on him when taken to prison, such money may be applied towards payment of a sum adjudged in pursuance of a conviction, and where a distress

warrant is issued it may authorise the taking of the defendant's money as well as his goods. Verbal applications should be made either to the court or the Clerk to the Justices to issue a distress warrant.

Where time is allowed for payment of a fine, the defendant shall not be committed to prison in default of payment until an inquiry as to his means has been made by the court in his presence. This inquiry is not necessary where the defendant is in prison for some other matter.

(c) In certain cases, if the offence is punishable by imprisonment, the accused can be ordered to perform unpaid work under a Community Service Order for a specified number of hours being not less than 40 nor more than 240 in the aggregate. The work is to be completed within 12 months of the date of the order.

(d) Absolute or conditional discharge after conviction.

(e) Probation order, requiring the offender to be under the supervision of a probation officer for one to three years, with or without requirements as to residence, etc.

(f) Detention in detention centre (where offender is under 21 years).

(g) Detention in police station, or at court.

(h) Attendance at attendance centre (where under 21 years of age).

(i) In addition to any of the above,

(i) the accused may be ordered to pay damages for injury or compensation for loss not exceeding £400 for each offence charged.

(ii) In cases in which the maximum penalty is not less than two years imprisonment, an order may be made depriving the defendant of property used in the course of committing the offence.

(j) Order to enter into recognizances, with or without sureties, to keep the peace and/or to be of good behaviour.

Young Persons and Children

(a) Deferrment of sentence (see as for adults).

(b) Absolute or conditional discharge after finding of guilt.

(c) Supervision order.

(d) Order on parent or guardian to give security for offender's good behaviour.

(e) Committal of offender to care of a local authority.

(f) Fine, damages or compensation and costs—which may be ordered to be paid by the offender, or parent or guardian.

(g) Attendance at attendance centre (where offender 10 years or over).

(h) Detention in detention centre (where offender 14 years or over).

Where a fine is imposed, it is recoverable by distress and/or imprisonment, when ordered to be paid by the parent or guardian, and, nominally, by distress when ordered to be paid by a young person or child.

2. INDICTABLE OFFENCES TRIABLE SUMMARILY

Children and Young Persons. All indictable offences (other than homicide) are triable summarily, usually in a Juvenile Court.

Adults. Where an adult is charged with any of the offences specified in Sch. I to the Magistrates' Courts Act, 1952, the court may if it thinks expedient deal with the case summarily with the consent of the accused.

The number of offences so triable has been greatly increased and is too long to set out here in sufficient detail to make it useful. See *Stone*, 1976 Edn., for detailed information.

Procedure. Prior to the hearing an information is laid and summons issued or warrant granted. When a warrant is granted in the first instance the information must be in writing and on oath or affirmation. Accused persons are however, frequently arrested without warrant for "arrestable" offences.

Witness summonses may be granted in respect of witnesses who reside within England or Wales. They may be ordered to produce documents, etc.

Before deciding whether to deal summarily with an indictable offence, the court must have regard to (i) any representation made in the presence of the prosecutor; (ii) the nature of the offence; (iii) the absence of circumstances which would render the offence one of a grave or serious character; (iv) all the other circumstances of the case (including the adequacy of the punishment which a Magistrates' Court has power to inflict). A decision to try the offence summarily is not binding on the court; at any time before the conclusion of the evidence for the prosecution summary trial may be discontinued, and inquiry as examining justices resumed.

Since the power of a Magistrates' Court to try summarily an indictable offence is dependent on the consent of the accused, given in person, the case cannot proceed in his absence, even though counsel or solicitor is present on his behalf.

At the hearing counsel or solicitor (if any) opens the case for the prosecution, stating the facts. If the accused has pleaded "not guilty" witnesses are then called and examined in the presence and hearing of the accused.

After all the evidence for the prosecution has been called, counsel or solicitor for the defence then opens his case and calls evidence in the same way as in a summary offence (*vide ante*).

Methods of dealing with Children and Young Persons. All the methods enumerated under the heading Summary Offences (see *ante*, p. 254).

Methods of dealing with Adults. As specified under Summary Offences, *ante*, except that in respect of each offence dealt with the accused may be committed to prison for six months (a maximum of 12 months in aggregate), fined a sum not exceeding £400, or both, and damages for injury or compensation for loss can be awarded up to £400.

After conviction for an indictable offence tried summarily the court will receive information of the character and antecedents of the offender. If it then appears that he deserves greater punishment than the court had power to inflict he may be committed in custody to the Crown Court for sentence. The Crown Court may sentence as if the accused had just been convicted on indictment.

"MATTERS COMMON TO BOTH PRECEDING CLASSES OF CASE"

Costs

Costs may be ordered to be paid in addition to a fine.

Where costs in addition to a fine are to be paid by a child or young person himself they must not exceed the amount of the fine.

Payment of Fines

It is obligatory on all Magistrates' Courts to allow time for the payment of fines unless either (1) it appears to the court that the offender has sufficient means to pay the sum forthwith, (2) the offender fails to satisfy the court that he has a fixed abode, or (3) the offender, for the same or another offence, is sentenced to or is at the time serving, imprisonment or detention in a detention centre.

Further time may be allowed for which applications may be made in writing.

Enforcing payment of Fines, etc.

A sum adjudged to be paid on a conviction, or an order of a Magistrates' Court (other than a civil debt) may in default of payment be recovered by distress or, if it appears to the court to be more expedient to commit the offender to prison, the court may adopt that course, but only after the court has held an inquiry as to his means in his presence. Where a commitment is issued, and the amount of the sum or sums of money adjudged to be paid:—

	The Period shall not exceed
Does not exceed £2	7 days
Exceeds £2 but does not exceed £5	14 days
Exceeds £5 but does not exceed £20	30 days
Exceeds £20 but does not exceed £50	60 days
Exceeds £50	90 days

An appropriate reduction must be made where part of the fine has been paid. Imprisonment shall not be imposed for less than five days but for small fines the court may order detention in Police cells for periods less than five days.

Formal convictions and orders are not to be drawn up, unless they are required for an appeal or some other legal purpose. The Clerk is obliged to notify convicted persons of fine imposed and time (if any) allowed for payment. The records of proceedings are entered in the Court Register. For the purpose of proving a previous conviction an extract certified by the Clerk to the Justices is admissible.

3. INDICTABLE OFFENCES TRIABLE UPON INDICTMENT

In indictable offences which cannot be dealt with summarily, or in those cases where the accused elects to be tried by a jury proceedings before examining justices are in open court, but the law prohibits publication of the detailed evidence except where the accused positively asks for it. The Criminal Justice Act 1967, s. 1, prescribes a procedure for committal for trial without consideration of the evidence where that evidence takes the form of written statements and the accused, being legally represented, does not submit that the evidence is insufficient to put him on trial. The Act (s. 2) also prescribes a procedure whereby the evidence of some or all of the witnesses may be tendered in the form of written statements and, subject to prescribed safeguards, these statements may be considered in substitution for the depositions of witnesses taken in accordance with the Magistrates' Courts Act, 1952. This Act requires that each witness for the prosecution shall be normally examined in the presence and hearing of the accused and the evidence written down in deposition form. Each witness's deposition is read over to him and signed by him as soon as may be after he has given evidence.

If then a *prima facie* case is made out the charge is reduced into writing, and read to the accused, who if not represented by solicitor or counsel is to be cautioned that he need not say anything unless he wishes to do so, but that whatever he says will be taken down in writing, and may be given in evidence upon his trial, and that he has nothing to hope from any promise, and nothing to fear from any threat, which may have been held out to induce him to make any admission or confession of guilt; and anything the accused says is to be taken down in writing and read over to him and signed by the justice. After the accused has been duly cautioned as above, counsel or solicitor addresses the court on behalf of the accused, who may give evidence either in addition to, or in substitution for, a statement, and may call witnesses. The justices may either commit the accused for trial, or discharge him. If the justices decide to commit for trial, the witnesses should be ordered to appear at the proper Crown Court. Examining justices are required to inform the accused that the law requires him to give advance notice to the prosecution, with particulars, of his intention to plead an alibi in his trial before a jury.

After the case has been committed for trial copies of depositions may be obtained from the Clerk to the Justices, if still in his possession. The charge to the prosecution is at the rate of 2p per folio, for the defence at 1p per folio. If, before application for a copy the Clerk to the Justices has transmitted them to the clerk of the court to which the accused has been committed for trial, a copy can be obtained from the clerk of such court. The brief is usually drawn from the copy depositions. Where witnesses have not been ordered by examining justices to appear, application should be made to the High Court or to the Crown Court for witness summonses requiring them to appear at the court of trial.

4. Offences Triable Summarily or on Indictment

These are offences where statute provides different maximum punishments according to mode of trial. There is a special procedure where the person charged is over 17 years of age. Prosecution may ask for case to be tried summarily; otherwise trial must be on indictment. Except in case where Director of Public Prosecutions is appearing and does not consent, justices may assume summary jurisdiction (after beginning as for an indictable offence) after representations from prosecution or defence; in such a case witnesses who have given evidence must be recalled for cross-examination. Before conclusion of case for prosecu-

tion, justices may change from summary to indictable procedure.

5. Civil Debts

Where under any Act a sum of money claimed to be due is recoverable on complaint to a Magistrates' Court, and not on information, such sum shall be deemed to be a civil debt, and the court may make an order for the payment thereof. No warrant of apprehension may be granted. Enforcement is by distress and in default or in first instance by committal. Before a person can be committed to prison for non-payment of a civil debt, it is necessary to issue a judgment summons, and it must be proved that the person ordered to pay any sum of money (including costs) either has, or has had since the date of the order the means to pay. In default of payment the defaulter may be committed to prison for not exceeding six weeks. Evidence of means may be given in such manner as the court thinks just, and the defaulter and any witness may be summoned and examined on oath. The cases which most frequently come before the courts are those of non-payment of income tax and disputes as to wages under the Employers and Workmen's Act, 1875.

6. Bail

Bail may be granted either on adjournment of the hearing of any case or after the accused has been committed for trial. Bail may be granted either with or without sureties. As to the amount of bail, regard should be had to the gravity of the offence, and also to the means of the accused. If bail is not allowed, the accused must be informed of his right to apply to a judge of the High Court or after committal for trial to a Judge or the Crown Court. At the time of going to press the Bail Bill is being considered by Parliament.

7. Legal Aid in Criminal Proceedings

See the Legal Aid Act 1974, ss. 28–40.

8. Appeals

To the Crown Court.—Any person convicted by Magistrates' Court who did not plead guilty may appeal against his conviction and sentence. If he pleaded guilty he may appeal against sentence only.

The following is the Procedure:—
Within twenty-one days after the decision give notice in writing to the other party and the Clerk to the Justices The Crown Court has power to direct that notice not given within 21 days shall be treated as if given within that period.

The appellant may be released from custody at the discretion of a magistrates' court or the Crown Court. Legal aid may be granted to appellant and/or the other party to the appeal. (*See* 6 *supra*).

Case stated

A party in proceedings before a magistrates' court or a person aggrieved by a conviction, order, determination or other proceeding, may question the proceeding on the ground that it is wrong in law or in excess or jurisdiction. This appeal is by way of case stated to the Q.B.D. The following course *must* be followed within the times named, and it is to be noted that Sundays count as days: 1. Within 14 days of the

decision apply *in writing* to the court to state a case (do this even though the court stated that it would grant one), serve the application on the justices clerk either personally or by post; 2. Before the case is stated the appellant must enter into a recognizance to prosecute the appeal without delay, and to pay any costs awarded by the court; 3. The case shall be stated within three calendar months after the date of the application, and after the recognizance shall have been entered into; 4. Within 14 days after receiving the case the appellant must serve upon the respondent himself notice in writing of the appeal and a copy of the case; and there shall be at least 8 clear days between service of the notice and the day named therein for the hearing; 5. Within 10 days of the receipt of the case it must be at the Crown Office, Royal Courts of Justice; and at the same time £1.50 paid for filing and hearing fees. Notices may be served by registered letter, but they are deemed served when received, not when posted. The magistrates may refuse to state a case if they think the application frivolous, but the Q.B.D. may, on motion by the party aggrieved by such refusal, by *mandamus* order a case to be stated.

AFFILIATION

Application by mother of child.—A single woman who has given birth to an illegitimate child, or who is expecting to do so, may apply to a justice for the petty sessions area in which she resides for a summons against the alleged father of the child. The term "single woman" includes a widow, or a divorced woman, or a married woman living apart from her husband under a separation order or in other circumstances in which *consortium* has ceased to exist.

If the application be made after the birth of the child it may be made either (i) within 3 years of the birth, or (ii) at any time upon proof that the alleged father has within 3 years of the birth paid money for the child's maintenance, or (iii) if the alleged father has left the country before the birth of the child or within 3 years thereafter, then at any time within 12 months after his return. It is convenient and usual

for this application to be made in writing. If the application be made before the birth of the child it must be in writing and upon oath or affirmation.

Summons to alleged father.—The justice to whom application is made (or if he has died or been removed or otherwise has ceased to hold office or is unable to act any other justice for the same area) may issue a summons to the putative father to appear before a magistrates' court for the area on a date to be named. The date must be after the birth of the child.

The Hearing.—For special procedure see title "Domestic Proceedings", below. At the appointed date the court may proceed to the hearing, either upon appearance by the defendant or upon proof of service of the summons upon him or that the summons was left at his last-known place of abode a reasonable time before the hearing. Evidence of paternity must be given by the mother of the child; and this evidence must be corroborated in some material particular by testimony which must tend to show not merely a possibility of the defendant being the father but also a probability that he is. The defendant may be called and examined as a witness for the complainant.

The Order.—If justices be satisfied they may adjudge the man to be the putative father of the child; and may then make an order upon him to pay a weekly sum of money for the maintenance and education of the child for such period as the justices may deem proper not exceeding the age of sixteen years. If the application has been made before the birth of the child or within two months thereafter, the weekly payments may be ordered to be calculated from the birth of the child. The order may also require the putative father to pay the expenses incidental to the birth of the child; and if the child has died, the funeral expenses; and to pay also costs incurred in obtaining the order. Payments may be ordered to be made direct to the mother of the child, but in the absence of special reason to the contrary the payments should be ordered to be made through the Clerk to the Justices as collecting officer of the court. The order may also require the putative father to give notice of any change of address to a person specified.

Variation, etc., of Order.—The periodical payments due under any order may be revoked or revived or varied by a Magistrates' Court, either as regards amount or as to the person to whom the amounts are to be made payable, or as to the period of payment.

Appeals.—There is a right of appeal to the Crown Court either against the making or the refusal of an Order; or against any revocation, revival or variation of such an Order.

Enforcement of Order.—Application for enforcement of any sums due under an order may be made after the expiration of fourteen clear days from the making of the order. Justices have power to enforce by distress and/or imprisonment for not exceeding six weeks; but a commitment must not be issued until after justices have made inquiry in defendant's presence as to whether failure to pay has been due to his wilful refusal or culpable neglect and unless the failure is due to one of those causes a commitment must not be issued. Justices have power to remit all or part of the amount due; after having considered representations made by the persons entitled to receive the payments; but further application may be made in respect of any amount not so remitted and in respect of which a commitment has not been issued, if the defendant's circumstances have changed (Magistrates' Courts Act, 1952, ss. 74, 76).

There is also power whereby compliance with an order for maintenance may be secured by an attachment of earnings order directed to a defaulter's employer.

DOMESTIC PROCEEDINGS

See Pugh's Matrimonial Proceedings in Magistrates' Courts, 3rd Edn.

"Domestic proceedings" are proceedings for matrimonial orders under the Matrimonial Proceedings (Magistrates' Courts) Act, 1960, orders for the custody and guardianship of infants under the Guardianship of Minors Act, 1971, applications by infants for consent to marry under the Marriage Act, 1949, applications for orders under the Family Allowances Act, 1945, and proceedings for an affiliation order. No person shall be present in court during the hearing of these matters, except (a) officers of the court; (b) parties to the case, witnesses and other persons directly concerned with the case, and other persons whom either party desires to be present; (c) counsel and solicitors; (d) newspaper representatives; (e) other persons by permission of the court.

Restrictions are placed on the particulars which may be published by any newspaper.

Husband and Wife.—The law relating to the granting of matrimonial orders by Magistrates' Courts, and proceedings for variation, etc. of such orders is contained in the Matrimonial Proceedings (Magistrates' Courts) Act, 1960. The grounds on which such an order may be made are: (1) *Where either husband or wife is the complainant*, that the defendant (a) has deserted the complainant; (b) has been guilty of persistent cruelty to the complainant or an infant child of the complainant or of the family; (c) has been found guilty of an offence involving an assault on the complainant or of a sexual offence against an infant child of the complainant or of the family; (d) has committed adultery; (e) while knowingly suffering from a venereal disease has insisted on or permitted sexual intercourse; (f) is an habitual drunkard or drug addict; (2) *Where the wife is the complainant*, (a) that the husband has compelled the wife to submit herself to prostitution; (b) that the husband has wilfully neglected to provide reasonable maintenance for her or for a child of the family; (3) *Where the husband is the complainant*, that the wife has wilfully neglected to provide or to make proper contribution towards reasonable maintenance for him or for a child of the family, in a case where by reason of the impairment of the husband's earning capacity through age, illness, or a disability of mind or body, it is reasonable that the wife should provide or contribute.

A matrimonial order may include provisions (a) for non-cohabitation; (b) for the payment of a weekly sum for maintenance; (c) for the legal custody of any child of the family who is under sixteen years to be given to either party, or to a third party, or in exceptional circumstances to the local authority; (d) for access to a child by a parent who is not given custody of that child; (e) for a payment of money for maintenance of any child of the family, to be paid by the complainant or the defendant, or by both of them where custody is given to a third party or a local authority; (f) for costs.

Subject to an exception in the case of an order made on the ground that the defendant is an habitual drunkard or a drug addict, no provision may be included requiring payment to be made by the complainant for the maintenance of the defendant in the proceedings.

Provision is made for extending the period of the order for maintenance of a child up to the age of twenty-one where the child is undergoing a course of education or training. An interim order for maintenance may be made pending the final disposal of a case where there is an adjournment for more than one week or where an order is refused on the ground that the case would be more conveniently dealt with by the High Court.

Where a matrimonial or an interim order is made while the parties are cohabiting it is not enforceable and no liability accrues under it until they cease to cohabit, and in any case it will lapse if the parties continue to cohabit for three months after the date of the order.

The court has the widest powers to revoke, revive or vary any order that has been made, and provision is made whereby this may be done by the Magistrates' Court for the district in which the complainant or defendant is resident notwithstanding that this court did not make the original order. The order ceases to be in force on a resumption of cohabitation.

The order is enforced as an affiliation order: see p. 259, *ante*.

Guardianship of Infants.—Either mother or father may apply to a Magistrates' Court for an order for custody of an infant child and, where the application is by the mother, for an order against the father for payment of a weekly sum for maintenance. In making such an order, the court shall regard the welfare of the infant as the first and paramount consideration. The order may be made while the parents are residing together; but no liability accrues while they continue to reside together and the order lapses if they do so for three months after the order was made. There may be included in an order a provision giving a right of access to the child by the parent deprived of custody. A Magistrates' Court may refuse to assume jurisdiction where it considers that an application would more conveniently be dealt with by the High Court. After the order has been made, it may be varied or discharged on the application of either party. The order is enforced as an affiliation order. See, generally, the Guardianship of Minors Act, 1973.

Consent to Marriage.—A Magistrates' Court may consent to the marriage of an infant of 16 or 17 years of age not being a widower or widow, where the marriage is intended to be solemnized on a certificate by a superintendent registrar, or on a licence by an ecclesiastical authority. The person whose consent is ordinarily required is set out in the 2nd Schedule to the Marriage Act, 1949, and it is where that person refuses consent that application to the court is appropriate: the consent of the court has the same effect as if it had been given by the person who has refused consent.

Affiliation Order.—See title "Affiliation", p. 259, *ante.*

Matrimonial Causes

(See Rayden on Divorce: Jackson on Matrimonial Finance and Taxation)

The law relating to matrimonial causes is to be found mostly in statute law.

STATUTE LAW

The statute law relating to matrimonial causes and matrimonial property and financial relief is to be found mainly in the Married Women's Property Act 1882, the Matrimonial Causes Act 1967 (as amended by the Family Provision Act 1965, the Maintenance Orders Act 1968, the Civil Evidence Act 1968 and the Matrimonial Causes Act 1973), the Law Reform (Miscellaneous Provisions) Act 1970 (as amended by the Act of 1973), the Matrimonial Proceedings and Property Act 1970 (as amended by the Act of 1973), the Recognition of Divorces and Legal Separations Act 1971, the Matrimonial Proceedings (Polygamous Marriages) Act 1972 (as amended by the Act of 1973), the Maintenance Orders (Facilities for Enforcement) Act 1972, the Civil Evidence Act 1972, the Matrimonial Causes Act 1973 and the Inheritance (Provision for Family and Dependants) Act 1975; *see also* Guardianship of Minors Act 1971 (as amended by the Act of 1973); the Children Act 1975. The jurisdiction of the court in cases of divorce, nullity, judicial separation and certain other matrimonial causes is now governed by the Domicil and Matrimonial Proceedings Act 1973, which introduces the basis of habitual residence for one year prior to the date when proceedings are begun, in addition to domicil: this statute also enables a wife to have a domicil independent of her husband's, and makes rules as to a minor's domicil: it also enacts provisions as to stays when there are competing proceedings abroad.

Divorce

Section 1 (1) of the Matrimonial Causes Act, 1973, provides that the sole ground on which a petition for divorce may be presented to the court by either party to a marriage shall be that the marriage has broken down irretrievably. Section 1 (2) of the Act provides that the court hearing a petition for divorce shall not hold the marriage to have broken down irretrievably unless the petitioner satisfies the court of one or more of the following facts, that is to say—

(a) that the respondent has committed adultery and the petitioner finds it intolerable to live with the respondent;

(b) that the respondent has behaved in such a way that the petitioner cannot reasonably be expected to live with the respondent;

(c) that the respondent has deserted the petitioner for a continuous period of at least two years immediately preceding the presentation of the petition;

(d) that the parties to the marriage have lived apart for a continuous period of at least two years immediately preceding the presentation of the petition and the respondent consents to a decree being granted;

(e) that the parties to the marriage have lived apart for a continuous period of at least five years immediately preceding the presentation of the petition.

Except in cases of exceptional hardship suffered by the petitioner or exceptional depravity on the part of the respondent a petition for divorce may not be presented in the first three years of the marriage (s. 3).

A petition for divorce may be brought on the same facts as those on which a decree of judicial separation or an order under the Matrimonial Proceedings (Magistrates' Courts) Act, 1960, has already been granted and the court may accept the decree or order as evidence of the facts, though it must receive evidence from the petitioner (s. 4).

Bars to divorce

The traditional bars to divorce, absolute or discretionary are abolished, and discretion statements likewise have gone. But the respondent to a petition for divorce in which the petitioner alleges any such fact as is mentioned in section 1 (2) (e) of the Matrimonial Causes Act, 1973, may oppose the grant of a decree nisi on the ground that the dissolution of the marriage will result in grave financial or other hardship to him and that it would in all the circumstances be wrong to dissolve the marriage (s. 5). Where the grant of a decree nisi is opposed by virtue of this section, then, (a) if the court finds that the petitioner is entitled to rely in support of his petition on the fact of five years' separation and makes no such finding as to any other fact mentioned in s. 1 (2), and (b) if apart from this section it would grant a decree on the petition, the court must consider all the circumstances, including the conduct of the parties to the marriage and the interests of those parties and of any children or other persons concerned, and if the court is of opinion that the dissolution of the marriage will result in grave financial or other hardship to the respondent and that it would in all the circumstances be wrong to dissolve the marriage it must dismiss the petition. "Hardship" includes the loss of the chance of acquiring any benefit which the respondent might acquire if the marriage were not dissolved. Where the court is satisfied that a respondent giving consent on the fact of two years' separation was misled by the petitioner (intentionally or unin-

tentionally) the court may rescind a decree nisi (s. 10). There is further financial protection where a petition is brought by reason of two years' or five years' separation (s. 10 (2), (3), (4)).

Nullity of Marriage

1. A marriage celebrated after 31st July 1971 is void where:

    (a) the marriage is not valid under the provisions of the Marriage Acts, 1949 to 1970;

    (b) either party was already lawfully married at the time of the marriage;

    (c) the parties are not respectively male and female; or

    (d) in the case of a polygamous marriage entered into outside England and Wales, that either party was at the time of the marriage domiciled in England and Wales (s. 11).

2. A marriage celebrated after 31st July 1971 is voidable where:

    (a) the marriage has not been consummated owing to the incapacity of either party to consummate it;

    (b) the marriage has not been consummated owing to the wilful refusal of the respondent to consummate it;

    (c) absence of valid consent;

    (d) at the time of marriage either party was suffering from mental disorder so as to be unfitted for marriage;

    (e) venereal disease in a communicable form at the time of marriage;

    (f) pregnancy by a person other than the petitioner at time of marriage (s. 12).

Approbation, ratification and lack of sincerity as bars to relief are replaced by s. 13 (1) which provides that the court must not grant a decree if the respondent satisfies the court that the petitioner led the respondent reasonably to believe that he would not have the marriage avoided and it would be unjust to the respondent to grant a decree.

Proceedings on grounds (c)–(f) must be instituted within 3 years of the marriage (s. 13 (2)). A decree can be granted on grounds (e) or (f) only if the petitioner was ignorant of the facts at the time of marriage (s. 13 (3)).

Judicial separation

A judicial separation may be obtained on the ground that any such fact as is mentioned in s. 1 (2) of the Matrimonial Causes Act, 1973 (s. 17).

Restitution of conjugal rights

Restitution of conjugal rights was abolished as a remedy by the Matrimonial Proceedings & Property Act, 1970 (s. 20).

Presumption of death

A married person who has reason to suppose that the other party to the marriage is dead may petition the court for a decree of presumption of death and dissolution of the marriage. Absence for seven years, where the petitioner has no reason to believe that the other party has been living within that time is evidence of death (Matrimonial Causes Act, 1973, s. 19).

A petition under this section may be granted only if the petitioner is domiciled in England and Wales or, in the case of a wife, if she has been resident in England for three years immediately preceding the commencement of the proceedings (s. 19 (2)).

Ancillary relief

The court has on a petition for divorce, nullity or judicial separation, to award maintenance pending suit (Matrimonial Cause Act, 1973, s. 22). On granting a decree of divorce, nullity or, judicial separation, it can (as "financial provision") award joint lives periodical payments, secured provision for the life of the recipient, lump sum or sums, including a lump sum for liabilities and expenses already incurred (s. 23). It has like powers to make financial provision for children of the family. It has powers (as "property adjustment") to order transfer and settlements of property and to vary settlements (s. 24). It must have regard, when exercising its powers under ss. 23 and 24, to all the circumstances of the case and so exercise those powers as to place the parties, so far as it is practicable and, having regard to their conduct in which they would have been if the marriage had not broken down and each had properly discharged his or her financial obligations and responsibilities towards the other (s. 25).

Where one party has been guilty of wilful neglect to maintain the other party or children the court may make an order for periodical payments, secured provision and a lump sum, as well as interim orders where there is immediate need of financial assistance but in the case of a husband applicant, he has to show impairment of earning if capacity by reason of age, illness or disability of mind or body (s. 27). On the death of a former spouse maintenance may in certain circumstances be awarded from the estate (s. 26 of Matrimonial Causes Act, 1965, as amended).

Sections 35 and 36 of the Matrimonial Causes Act, 1973, make provisions as to the validity of maintenance agreements and their alteration because of changed circumstances, inadequate provision, or the death of one of the parties.

Protection of children

The court may not, in general, make absolute a decree of divorce or nullity or make a decree of judicial separation unless it is satisfied either that satisfactory arrangements for the care and upbringing of the children of the family have been made, or that it is impracticable for the party or parties appearing before the court to make such arrangements. An exception may be made, however, if it is desirable for any reason that a decree should be made absolute without delay or if the court has obtained a satisfactory undertaking from either or both of the parties to bring the question of the arrangements before the court within a specified time (Matrimonial Causes Act, 1973, s. 41).

The court may make orders for the custody, maintenance and education of any relevant child of the family and has power, when necessary, to commit children to the care of the local authority or to provide for their supervision by a welfare officer or the local authority (ss. 43, 44).

Damages

These claims are abolished (Law Reform (Miscellaneous Provisions) Act, 1970, s. 4).

Evidence

A husband or wife may give evidence to prove that marital intercourse did or did not take place between them, and in civil cases they can now be compelled to give such evidence; Matrimonial Causes Act, 1973, s. 48 (1); Civil Evidence Act, 1968, s. 16 (4).

A witness in any proceedings instituted in consequence of adultery can now be compelled to answer any question tending to show that he or she has been guilty of adultery whether or not he or she has already given evidence in the same proceedings in disproof of the alleged adultery: Civil Evidence Act, 1968, s. 16 (5).

In any nullity proceedings evidence as to sexual capacity should be heard in camera unless the judge is satisfied that in the interests of justice any such evidence ought to be heard in open court: Matrimonial Causes Act, 1973, s. 48 (2).

CASES

The following cases should be noted:—

Adultery.—As to what amounts to adultery, see *Sapsford* v. *Sapsford*, [1954] 2 All E.R. 373; and *Dennis* v. *Dennis (Spillet and Others cited)*, [1955]. As to "intolerable" adultery, see *Goodrich* v. *Goodrich*, [1971] 2 All E.R. 1340; *Cleary* v. *Cleary*, [1974] 1 All E.R. 498, C.A.; *Carr* v. *Carr*, [1974] 1 All E.R. 1193, C.A.

Desertion. The two year period must immediately precede the presentation of the petition, but not a supplemental petition, *Spawforth* v. *Spawforth*, [1946] 1 All E.R. 379, and be a continuous period, but see Matrimonial Causes Act, 1973, s. 2 (4). Where there is a desertion charge in an answer the period of 2 years is to be calculated up to the date of the answer and not to that of the petition, *Faulkner* v. *Faulkner*, [1941] 2 All E.R. 748. Whether this period is interrupted by the filing of a previous petition is fully discussed in *W.* v. *W.* (*No. 2*), [1954] 2 All E.R. 829, C.A. in which previous decisions are referred to. No account shall be taken of any one period (not exceeding six months) or of any two or more periods (not exceeding six months in all) during which the parties lived with each other in the same household (Act of 1973, s. 2 (6)).

Where the wife having deserted the husband wished to resume cohabitation and the husband refused her an interview to discuss the matter, it was held that there was no desertion after such refusal: *Pratt* v. *Pratt*, [1939] 3 All E.R. 437 (H.L.), but see *Ware* v. *Ware*, [1942] P. 49.

The fact that payments under a deed of separation have ceased is not sufficient evidence of repudiation of the deed. If, however, all the facts show a repudiation of the deed there can be desertion notwithstanding the deed: *Ratcliffe* v. *Ratcliffe*, [1938] 3 All E.R. 41. See also *Starkey* v. *Starkey*, [1938] 3 All E.R. 773; *Pardy* v. *Pardy*, [1939] All E.R. 779 (C.A.); *Tate* v. *Tate* [1938] 4 All E.R. 264; *Eaves* v. *Eaves*, [1939] 2 All E.R. 789; cf. *Clark* v. *Clark*, [1939] 2 All E.R. 392 (payments stopped but no repudiation); *Tickler* v. *Tickler*, [1943] 1 All E.R. 57 (C.A.), and *Crabtree* v. *Crabtree*, [1953] 2 All E.R. 56, C.A.

Desertion does not necessarily terminate because the spouse who has been deserted has himself or herself, committed adultery, after the desertion complained of: *Richards* v. *Richards*, [1952] 1 All E.R. 1384, C.A.; see *Parrock* v. *Parrock*, [1956] 1 All E.R. 556; *Herod* v. *Herod*, [1938] 3 All E.R. 722.

There may be desertion even though parties are living in the same house; see *Walker* v. *Walker*, [1952] 2 All E.R. 138, C.A. and *Bull* v. *Bull*, [1953] 2 All E.R. 601, C.A.

For effect of sexual intercourse between the spouses during period of alleged desertion, see *Perry* v. *Perry*, [1951] 1 All E.R. 1076, C.A.

As to drunkenness, see *Hall* v. *Hall*, [1962] 2 All E.R. 129, *Pratt* v. *Pratt*, [1962], 106 Sol. Jo. 433.

Unreasonable behaviour. See *Thurlow* v. *Thurlow*, [1975] 2 All E.R. 979; *Ash* v. *Ash*, [1972] 1 All E.R. 582; *Pheasant* v. *Pheasant*, [1972] 1 All E.R. 587; *Katz* v. *Katz*, [1972] 3 All E.R. 219; *Livingstone-Stallard* v. *Livingstone-Stallard*, [1974] 2 All E.R. 766.

Living apart. See *Santos* v. *Santos*, [1972] 2 All E.R. 246.

Refusal of Intercourse. See *Weatherley* v. *Weatherley*, [1947] 1 All E.R. 563 (H.L.). Invincible repugnance to sexual act, see *Beevor* v. *Beevor*, [1945] 2 All E.R. 200. Birth control, see *Baxter* v. *Baxter*, [1947] 2 All E.R. 886 (H.L.). Coitus interruptus, see *Cackett* (*otherwise True*) v. *Cackett*, [1950] 1 All E.R. 677; and cf. *R.* v. *R.*, [1952] 1 All E.R. 1194.

Wilful neglect to maintain. A deed of separation is no bar to an application, even though the husband may have kept up the payments under the deed. The deed is of high evidential value but not binding. *Tulip* v. *Tulip*, [1951] I All E.R. 91, C.A. and *Morton* v. *Morton*, [1954] 2 All E.R. 248, C.A.; but where there has been a consensual separation without any formal agreement regarding the maintenance of the wife, it is a good answer to an allegation of wilful neglect to maintain; *Stringer* v. *Stringer*, [1952] I All E.R. 373; *Pinnick* v. *Pinnick* [1957] I All E.R. 813. See *Woodward* v. *Woodward*, [1952] P. 299, as to the jurisdiction of the court to entertain the application. The maintenance can be ordered as from the date of the filing of the application and not merely from the finding of wilful neglect: *McLellan* v. *McLellan*, [1954] I All E.R. 1.

Privilege—communications without prejudice. Negotiation for reconciliation are usually "without prejudice", but if such communications are made through a probation officer, the privilege is that of the spouses, and not of the probation officer, *McTaggart* v. *McTaggart*, [1949] P. 94; [1948] 2 All E.R. 754 (C.A.); *Mole* v. *Mole*, [1950] 2 All E.R. 328 (C.A.); *Bostock* v. *Bostock*, [1950] I All E.R. 25.

Exceptional hardship or depravity. See *A proposed petition, Bowman* v. *Bowman*, [1949] 2 All E.R. 127 (C.A.). *Hillier* v. *Hillier*, [1958] 2 All E.R. 261 (C.A.) and *Brewer* v. *Brewer*, [1964] I All E.R. 539, C.A., for examples of what acts might come within the scope of these words.

Maintenance. For the current approach of the courts to financial provision and property adjustment orders, see *Wachtel* v. *Wachtel*, [1973] I All E.R. 113, C.A. *Harnett* v. *Harnett*, [1974] I All E.R. 764, C.A.; *Griffiths* v. *Griffiths*, [1974] I All E.R. 932, C.A. As to effect of remarriage, see *H.* v. *H. (Family Provision: Remarriage)*, [1975] I All E.R. 367. A deed by which a wife may agree not to involve her rights under the statute to apply for maintenance for herself or the children of the marriage is invalid; *Bennett* v. *Bennett*, [1952] I All E.R. 413, C.A. See now ss. 35–36 of the Matrimonial Causes Act 1973, which give the court power

to vary written agreements containing financial arrangements made for the purposes of the parties living separately (s. 1): see *Ewart* v. *Ewart*, [1958] 3 All E.R. 561; *K.* v. *K.*, [1961] 2 All E.R. 266. In certain circumstances the court may vary payments even after the death of one of the parties. Where husband dies before execution of deed securing sum in respect of maintenance the husband's executors were ordered to complete the deed; *Mosey* v. *Mosey & Barker*, [1955] 2 All E.R. 391. The court has power to make provision for a former wife out of the estate of her deceased former husband; see Matrimonial Causes Act 1965, ss. 26–28; *Askew* v. *Askew*, [1961] 2 All E.R. 60; *Eyre* v. *Eyre*, [1968] I All E.R. 968. The Divorce Court has power to refuse to permit enforcement of arrears of maintenance: Matrimonial Causes Act 1973, s. 32; see *W.* v. *W. (No. 4)*, [1962] P. 131.

Matrimonial Home. See the Matrimonial Homes Act, 1967, and *Tarr* v. *Tarr*, [1973] A.C. 254, H.L.

Marriage. The court will in certain cases presume the existence of a valid marriage without formal proof thereof: see *Merker* v. *Merker*, [1962] 3 All E.R. 928, where the doctrine of the "common law" marriage is reviewed: *Mahadervan* v. *Mahadervan*, [1962] 3 All E.R. 1108 (*omnia praesumuntur pro matrimonio*).

Declaratory decrees. The court has power, in certain circumstances, to make declaratory decrees as to the validity or otherwise of foreign divorces or marriages: see *Garthwaite* v. *Garthwaite* [1964] 2 All E.R. 233, C.A.; *Aldrich* v. *A.-G.* [1968] P. 281.

PROCEDURE

Whereas previously all matrimonial causes were heard in the High Court, the Act of 1967, which came into force on April 11, 1968, conferred jurisdiction on county courts to hear and determine undefended causes. Procedure in both the county courts and the High Court is governed by the Matrimonial Causes Rules, 1973 (S.I. 1973 No. 2016, supplemented where appropriate by the County Court Rules and R.S.C. (see r. 3 of the 1973 Rules).

Under the 1973 Rules matrimonial

causes must be begun in a county court designated by the Lord Chancellor as a divorce county court (s. 1 (3) of the 1967 Act) and a petition may be filed in any court so designated without any limit on territorial jurisdiction (see r. 12 (1)). However a cause may only be tried in such of those courts as are designated as courts of trial. The Divorce Registry is to be regarded as a county court for the purpose of undefended proceedings (r. 4).

Provision is made for the transfer to the High Court of causes that become defended (see r. 18 (4) and (5)) and for the retransfer to the county court of causes that become undefended (see r. 27). An "undefended cause" in general means one to which no answer has been filed or where the answer has been struck out and includes a petition based on mental disorder to which an answer has been filed simply to put the petitioner to strict proof of the facts alleged (r. 2). The court, *i.e.* the registrar or a judge may order an undefended cause to be transferred to the High Court in view of the difficulty or importance of the issues raised (r. 32). In cases where the main suit is undefended and thus remains within the jurisdiction of a county court, applications for ancillary relief may nevertheless be transferred to the High Court for hearing; the registrar, before beginning the hearing of an application for ancillary relief in a county court case must first consider whether to transfer it to the High Court. Criteria by which such a decision may be decided are laid down in the rules (see r. 80).

Causes pending in the High Court will be tried at the Royal Courts of Justice or at one of the divorce towns (r. 43 (2), as amended).

There is a "special" procedure list whereby, in certain cases where there are no children to whom s. 41 of the Act of 1973 applies, the court may pronounce a decree without hearing oral evidence.

Costs

Proceedings in the High Court are taxed on the High Court scale of costs (see *Rayden on Divorce* Appendix VI) Costs for proceedings in the county courts are governed by the Matrimonial Causes (Costs) Rules, 1971 (S.I. 1971 No. 987) as amended. Where proceedings are transferred from the county court to the High Court or *vice versa* bills have to be prepared in parts for taxation according to the scales applicable to each Court. Furthermore, where appropriate the bill must be split into parts applicable respectively to costs incurred before the imposition of V.A.T. charges and costs incurred thereafter (with V.A.T. percentages shown as appropriate). V.A.T. was imposed on 1st April 1973.

A party entitled to require taxation of costs must begin proceedings within 3 months of the final decree or order or, where an application for ancillary relief is brought within 3 months of the final decree or order, within 3 months of the order on the application (r. 3).

In relation to the county court proceedings the applicant must lodge his bill of costs, with vouchers and papers, and sufficient copies of the bill to be served on all parties liable to pay costs. The registrar will send a copy of the bill to the parties who must inform him within 14 days if they wish to be heard. If they do, the registrar will fix an appointment for taxation giving 7 days' notice to the applicant and party concerned. Otherwise the registrar will send to the applicant a notice specifying the amount he proposes to allow and requiring the applicant to inform him within 14 days if he wishes to be heard. This procedure applies with modifications to the taxation of a bill to be paid out of the legal aid fund (r. 4 (6)). Costs must be paid within 7 days of the making of the order for payment unless otherwise directed (r. 8 (1)). In practice in Divorce Registry cases the order requires payment within the period of 14 days, which period will allow time for the order to be served before the expiration of the time for payment.

The Rules provide a scale of taxed costs (see p. 269, *post*) based upon Scale 4 of the County Court Scales of costs and known as the divorce scale. Except where the judge otherwise directs, the registrar may, if he thinks fit, allow a sum exceeding the maximum charge in relation to items 1–3, 6–9, 19, 21, 26, 27, 30 and 31 (r. 6 (1)).

As an alternative to taxed costs a solicitor may elect to have costs fixed in accordance with rule 7 in undefended cases for divorce or judicial separation including legal aid cases. A petitioner's solicitor who so elects must give notice to the registrar, stating the sums claimed to be allowed, lodging all necessary papers and vouchers (r. 7 (5)). Fixed costs must be paid within 7 days of the making of the order for payment unless otherwise directed (r. 8 (2)).

The fixed costs are provided for by paras. (3), (4) and (6) of r. 7 as set out below. "The principal rules" means the Matrimonial Causes Rules 1973.

"(3) Where costs are fixed there shall be allowed as between party and, party such of the following items as are applicable:—

(a) in respect of solicitors' charges—

(i) if counsel was briefed at the hearing, £67,

(ii) if counsel was not briefed at the hearing, £77,

(iii) if the cause was dealt with in the special procedure list, £55,
[for the special procedure which enables decrees to be made in certain circumstances on the certificate of a registrar where there are no children concerning whom the court needs to be satisfied so far as arrangements for them are concerned, see r. 48].

(iv) where an order has been made for substituted service or to dispense with service, £8.50;

(v) for any statement as to the arrangements for the children filed under rule 8 (2) of the principal rules, £2;

(vi) where an affidavit of means has been filed under rule 8 (3) of the principal rules, £3.

(b) in respect of counsel's fees—

(i) for settling the petition, £4.50,

(ii) for settling an affidavit of means filed under rule 8 (3) of the principal rules, £3,

(iii) for giving written advice on evidence, £3.50,

(iv) with brief on hearing, £10 and, where there is no local Bar in the court town or

within 25 miles thereof, a further sum of £4, and

(v) on conference, £2.50;

(c) in respect of other disbursements—

(i) the court fees paid on the petitioner's behalf,

(ii) such sums in respect of witnesses' allowances, medical reports and the other disbursements mentioned in items 32, 33 and 34 of the divorce scale as would have been allowed if the costs had been taxed, not exceeding, in the case of inquiry agents' fees, the sum of £25.

(iii) such sums in respect of travelling to court or to inspect documents or, alternatively, in respect of agency correspondence in the circumstances mentioned in items 36, 37 and 39 of the divorce scale as would have been allowed if the costs had been taxed, not exceeding, in the case of travelling expenses, £3.

(4) If a petitioner whose costs are to be fixed is an assisted person, then, notwithstanding that the costs have been ordered to be taxed for the purposes of the Third Schedule to the [Legal Aid and Advice] Act of 1949 [since replaced by Schedule 2 and the Legal Aid Act 1974]

(a) the sums payable under section 6 (5) of that Act [see now section 10 of Act of 1974] to the solicitor acting for him shall be such of the fixed amounts specified in paragraph (3) (a) and (c) as are applicable, together with a further sum of £7;

(b) the sums payable under the said section 6 (5) to counsel acting for the assisted person shall be such of the fixed amounts specified in paragraph (3) (b) as are applicable.

(6) Where an ancillary application is granted with costs, whether as between party and party or not, in the circumstances mentioned in any of the following items, then, unless the registrar otherwise directs, the costs shall,

if the applicant's solicitor so elects, be fixed at the sum mentioned in that item instead of being taxed:—

(a) in respect of solicitor's charges—

    (i) where a consent order for ancillary relief has been made, £10;

    (ii) where any other consent order has been made and no affidavit has been filed by either party, £10;

    (iii) where an order has been made after a hearing at which the respondent has not appeared, £15;

    (iv) where an order has been made after a hearing at which the respondent has appeared, £25, or, if counsel is allowed, £22;

(b) in respect of counsel's fees where counsel is allowed—

    (i) in the circumstances mentioned in item (a) (ii) or (iii), £10;

    (ii) in the circumstances mentioned in item (a) (iv), £10 with brief and, in addition, £2.50 for any conference;

(c) in respect of other disbursements—

    (i) such of the items mentioned in paragraph (3) (c) as are appropriate;

    (ii) such amount as the Law Society certifies to be reasonable for conveying or transferring property pursuant to the order made on the application.

In addition to the amount of costs allowed as above in respect of the supply of goods or services on which value added tax is chargeable there may be allowed as a disbursement a sum equivalent to value added tax at the appropriate rate on that amount (r. 7A).

R.S.C. Ord. 62, r. 8 applies with modifications in relation to the personal liability of solicitors in matrimonial proceedings (r. 9).

(2) On taxation, whether as between party and party or on the common fund basis, of the costs of a cause for divorce or judicial separation which has proceeded throughout in a divorce county court, the amount to be allowed in respect of any item of costs opposite which a sum appears in brackets in the divorce scale shall not be more or less than that sum unless the registrar, taking into consideration the factors mentioned in C.C.R. Order 47, rule 16, is satisfied that, in the circumstances of the particular case, a higher or, as the case may be, a lower figure than the average for that item in a cause under the same provision of the Act of 1973 is justified.''

Divorce Scale

Item No.		£

Taking instructions

| 1 | (i) To file or oppose originating application or petition or application for re-hearing; (ii) to prepare any document to which item 3 (b) applies or to make or oppose any application to which item 7 (ii) or 9 applies, where in the opinion of the registrar the instructions were necessary; (iii) to appeal or oppose an appeal to the judge from a decision of the registrar; | (2.00) 1.00 to 2.00 (1.00) |

Preparation of petition, etc.

		£
2	Preparing originating application, petition, answer or supplemental pleading	1.50 to 8.00 (6.00)

Note 1.—This item includes copy for service on opposite spouse but not copy for service on any other party and it

is only to be allowed where the document is signed by the solicitor or his clerk duly authorised in that behalf.

Note 2.—Where the document is settled by counsel, items 3 (*a*) and 4 are allowable and not this item.

Preparation of documents

		£
3	(*a*) Preparing instructions to counsel to settle any pleading or other document or to advise on evidence or to advise on merits where counsel's fee is allowed under item 31	1.00 to 3.00 (2.00)

(*b*) Preparing any necessary document not otherwise provided for and all necessary copies thereof 0.50
and per folio beyond five 0.10

Note.—Item 3 (*b*) is not to be allowed for preparing a praecipe.

Copies

4 For copies of documents (including brief) not otherwise provided for which the registrar considers necessary—

(*a*) for photographic copies, the actual and reasonable cost;

(*b*) for carbon copies, per two folios 0.05

(*c*) in any other case, per folio 0.05

Perusing

5 Any document not otherwise provided for which the registrar is satisfied justifies a charge for perusal ..   0.25
and per folio beyond five 0.05

Preparing for trial

6 (*a*) Preparing for trial of cause of matter .. ..   Such sum as is fair and reasonable in all the circumstances not exceeding £45.00. Special procedure cases (£36.00) other cases (£42.00)

(*b*) Preparing for hearing of ancillary application, such sum as is fair and reasonable.

Note 1.—These items are intended to cover the work of preparing for trial or hearing not otherwise provided for, including considering facts, evidence and law, preparation of notes of facts or argument, interviewing witnesses and taking proofs of their evidence, preparing and serving notices to produce and admit documents, and to admit facts, perusing such notices and correspondence, making

*Item
No.*

£

necessary searches, negotiating any settlement and, where counsel is instructed, instructions for and drawing brief, and attending counsel therewith.

Note 2.—Item 6 (*a*) may only be allowed once in the same cause or matter, but item 6 (*b*) may be allowed in respect of each ancillary application.

Attendances

7   (i) At court on trial of cause or matter, for each day or part of a day—

(*a*) without counsel	}	3.00 to 20.00 (12.00)
(*b*) with counsel	}	2.00 to 4.00 (4.00)

(ii) At court or in chambers on hearing of ancillary application, for each day or part of a day—

(*a*) without counsel	}	1.00 to 20.00
(*b*) with counsel	}	2.00 to 4.00

8   (i) At court where trial of cause or matter is adjourned for want of time or upon payment of the costs of the day—

(*a*) without counsel	}	2.00 to 5.00
(*b*) with counsel	}	1.00 to 3.00

(ii) At court or in chambers where hearing of ancillary application is adjourned for want of time or upon payment of the costs of the day—

(*a*) without counsel	}	1.00 to 5.00
(*b*) with counsel	}	1.00 to 3.00

9   At court or in chambers on any other application to judge or registrar in the course of or relating to the proceedings, including notice and service, and brief where counsel is instructed—

(*a*) without counsel	}	1.00 to 9.00
(*b*) with counsel	}	1.00 to 4.50

10   [*Omitted*].

Item No.		£
11	On examination of witness under C.C.R. Order 14, Rule 1 (10), Order 20, Rule 18 (1), or Order 25, Rule 2, for each hour	1.00
12	Where in consequence of anything done by the opposite party during the proceedings, attendance on the client is necessary to advise or receive instructions, for each attendance not otherwise provided for	0.50 to 1.00
13	(a) To obtain or give any necessary and proper consent or admission	1.00
	(b) Upon the opposite party, for each attendance not otherwise provided for	1.00
	(c) To arrange for attendance of a witness without subpoena	0.50
	(d) On counsel in conference where counsel's fee allowed under item 29 (to include appointing conference), for the first hour or part thereof	2.00
	and for each subsequent hour or part thereof	1.50

Note to items 12 *and* 13 (*a*) *and* (*b*).—If the attendance is by telephone, half of the charge is to be allowed.

Note to item 13 (*c*).—Only one charge is to be allowed where only one attendance is necessary to arrange for more than one witness.

14	At court to hear a deferred judgment—	
	(a) without counsel	1.00 to 5.00
	(b) with counsel	1.00 to 2.00
15	At court, on hearing of judgment summons if costs allowed by judge and for each attendance where the hearing is not concluded on the day on which it is commenced—	
	(a) without counsel	2.00
	(b) with counsel	1.00

Note.—This item includes attending to enter and service (unless allowed under C.C.R. Order 25, Rule 66 (2)).

16	On deponent being sworn to an affidavit, including an affidavit of service	0.50

Note.—This charge may be allowed where the solicitor or his clerk is the deponent.

17	To deliver any documents pursuant to any County Court Rule or Matrimonial Causes Rule	0.50
18	Any attendance at the court office not otherwise provided for which the registrar is satisfied justified a charge ..	0.50

Service

19	Of any document required to be served personally, other than a judgment summons (unless allowed under C.C.R. Order 25, Rule 66 (2)), including copy	0.50 to 1.00

		£

Item No.

20 Of any document authorised to be served by post, including copy 0.25

Notes to items 19 and 20—

Note 1.—Where any two or more documents to be served on the same party have been or could have been served together, one charge only for service is to be allowed.

Note 2.—Where two or more parties have been or could have been served together, one charge only for service is to be allowed.

Note 3.—These items are not to be allowed where item 21 or 33 (*d*) is applicable.

21 Drawing any document, attending on any application and doing any other work necessary to obtain, and to carry out the terms of, an order for substituted service of any document.   2.00 to 10.00 (8.50)

22 Of process out of England and Wales, to include drawing, copying, attending to swear and file all affidavits and to obtain order, and the fees paid for oaths, such sum as the registrar thinks reasonable.

Letters, etc.

23 [*Omitted*].

24 Letters in lieu of attendances which could properly be allowed under items 12, 13, 17 and 18 .. .. ..   0.50

25 Circular letters 0.25

Taxation of costs

26 (*a*) For taxation of the costs of the cause or matter   2.00 to 6.00

(*b*) For taxation of the costs of any ancillary application   2.00 to 6.00

(*c*) For any other taxation   1.00 to 2.00

Note 1.—These items include preparing bill and all necessary copies, correspondence and attendances.

Note 2.—Items 26 (*b*) and (*c*) are not to be allowed where the costs to which they relate have been or could have been included in the bill of costs of the cause or matter.

Disbursements
Fees to Counsel

27 (*a*) With brief on trial of cause or matter   7.50 to 28.00 (10.00)

(*b*) With brief on hearing of ancillary application   5.50 to 30.00

Item
No.   £

28   Where there is no local Bar in the court town or within
      25 miles thereof, if in the opinion of the registrar the
      maximum fee allowable with the brief is insufficient, a
      further fee may be allowed, not exceeding for each day
      on which the trial or hearing takes place 4.00

      Note 1.—For the purpose of this item there shall be
      deemed to be a local Bar only in such places as may from
      time to time be specified in a certificate of the General
      Council of the Bar published in their Annual Statement.
      Note 2.—This item is not to be allowed in any court with-
      in 25 miles of Charing Cross.

29   On conference in chambers or elsewhere, if tne fee was
      marked on the brief when delivered, or in the opinion of
      the registrar the conference was necessary, for each half
      hour or part thereof 2.50
      and for leading counsel if case certified fit for more coun-
      sel than one 3.50

30   (*a*) Where trial of a cause or matter or hearing of an⎫   3.00
      ancillary application is not concluded on day on which⎪   to
      it is commenced or is adjourned for want of time or on⎬   15.00
      payment of the costs of the day, for each day or part of⎪
      day on which it is continued   ⎭

      (*b*) With brief to hear a deferred judgment; with brief⎫   3.00
      on application in the course of or relating to proceedings⎪ to
      (other than an ancillary application); with brief on an ⎬   8.00
      examination of witnesses under C.C.R. Order 14, rule 1 ⎪
      (10), Order 20, rule 18 (1), or Order 25, rule 2; with brief⎪
      on hearing of judgment summons   ⎭

                                                                  3.00
31   (*a*) For settling any document which in the opinion of the⎫ to
      registrar is proper to be settled by counsel   ⎬   8.00
                                                              ⎭ settling
                                                                petition (4.50)

      (*b*) For advising in writing on any question in the pro-⎫ 3.00
      ceedings on which in the opinion of the registrar it was⎪   to
      proper to obtain counsel's advice, including advising on⎬   8.00
      evidence and advising on merits before proceedings   ⎪
      brought or answer filed   ⎭ (3.50)

      Note to items 27 *to* 31
      Fees to counsel are not to be allowed unless the payment
      of them is vouched by the signature of counsel

                        Plans, Photographs, etc.

32   For plans, drawings, charts, photographs or models for
      use at the trial, which in the opinion of the registrar it was
      reasonable to obtain, the sum actually and reasonably
      paid.

                           Miscellaneous

33   (*a*) For obtaining any documentary evidence (including
      translations) or police reports or statements from the
      police which in the opinion of the registrar it was reason-
      ably necessary to obtain for the purpose of the proceed-
      ings,

(*b*) for an advertisement in pursuance of an order for substituted service by advertisement,

(*c*) for making any search in the companies register, the business names register or any other public register which in the opinion of the registrar it was reasonably necessary to make for the purpose of the proceedings,

(*d*) for employing an inquiry agent to effect personal service of any document or to make inquiries or to obtain evidence which in the opinion of the registrar were or was reasonably necessary for the purpose of the proceedings,

(*e*) for obtaining any professional advice or assistance which in the opinion of the registrar it was reasonably necessary to obtain for the purpose of the proceedings, and

(*f*) for an examination and report by a medical inspector appointed in proceedings for nullity,

the sum actually and reasonably paid.

Note.—Item 33 (*e*) is intended to cover the advice and assistance of such persons as accountants and foreign lawyers.

34   For oaths, the sum paid, unless included in another item.

35   (*a*) For postage, carriage and transmission of documents, a sum not exceeding   ..   ..(2.00) } 5.00

(*b*) For telegrams and telephone calls, the sum actually and reasonably paid.   (1.00)

36   Where solicitor does not reside or carry on business within 2 miles of the court at which the trial takes place,

     (*a*) the sum actually and reasonably paid for travelling to attend the trial or,

     (*b*) if an agent was reasonably employed, for correspondence with the agent   } 1.00 to 3.00

37   Where solicitor does not reside or carry on business within 2 miles of the place of inspection of documents—

     (*a*) the sum actually and reasonably paid for travelling to inspect the documents; or

     (*b*) if agent employed, for correspondence with agent   1.00

38   In addition to item 26 (taxation) where solicitor does not reside or carry on business within 2 miles of the court office—

     (*a*) the sum actually and reasonably paid for travelling to attend the taxation; or

     (*b*) if agent reasonably employed, for correspondence with agent 1.00

Item
No.

£

39   Where solicitor does not reside or carry on business within
      2 miles of the court or court office at which the hearing of
      an ancillary application takes place—

> (*a*) the sum actually and reasonably paid for travel-
>   ling to attend the hearing, or

> (*b*) if agent employed, for correspondence with agent   } 1.00 to 3.00

Note to items 36 (*a*), 37 (*a*), *and* 39 (*a*)—

Where in the opinion of the registrar it would have been
reasonable to employ a solicitor residing or carrying on
business nearer to the court, the place of inspection of
documents or the court office, as the case may be, he shall
not allow more than he would have allowed to such a
solicitor.

Fees

Fees in both the High Court and
county courts are prescribed by the
Matrimonial Causes Fees Order 1975
(S.I. 1973, No. 1346). Any fee prescribed
by the Order must be taken in cash
(para. 5). Impressed judicature fee
stamps are no longer used in the Divorce Registry. Questions arising with
regard to the amount of fees may be
reported by the registrar to the Lord
Chancellor for direction (para. 6) and

in cases of undue hardship the Lord
Chancellor may reduce or remit the fee
(para. 7).

The fees to be taken in all matrimonial proceedings are set out in the
Table below (see para. 3 and Schedule
1). In addition Schedule 2 specifies certain fees in the County Court Fees
Order 1971 and the Supreme Court Fees
Order 1970 which are to be taken in
matrimonial proceedings as indicated
in that Schedule (para. 4).

Schedule 1

Fees to be Taken in all Matrimonial Proceedings

Fee	Amount
	£
1. On filing an originating application or on sealing an originating summons	
(a) under rule 5 or rule 128	5.00
(b) in any other case	10.00
2. On presenting a petition except in a case to which rule 12 (4) applies	16.00
3. On presenting a petition in a case to which rule 12 (4) applies	8.00
4. On filing a notice in Form 11 or 13 [of the Matrimonial Causes Rules 1973] except where the terms of any agreement as to the order which the court is to be asked to make are set out in the notice	10.00
5. On making a search in the index of decrees absolute kept under rule 67 (3)	0.25
6. On request for a photographic or office copy of a decree or of a certificate that a decree has been made absolute ..	0.25
7. On the issue of a notice under rule 54	2.00

National Insurance

THE SOCIAL SECURITY ACT 1975

CONTRIBUTIONS

On 6 April 1975 the provisions of the Social Security Act 1975 replaced those of the National Insurance Act 1965 and introduced a new national insurance scheme based on earnings-related contributions. Under this new scheme there are four classes of contribution, viz.:—

CLASS 1 CONTRIBUTIONS

These are payable by employers and employed earners aged 16 or over and not retired, on earnings up to a prescribed limit. (For 1976/77 this is £95 per week or £411.67 per month.) Contributions are collected along with Schedule E income tax under the PAYE procedure. They are not payable if weekly earnings are less than £13 (or £56.33 a month).

An employed earner (employee) means a person gainfully employed in Great Britain under a contract of service or in an office (including elective office) with remuneration assessable under Schedule E for income tax purposes.

Class 1 contributions consist of:—

(i) *Primary.*—payable by employers over the age of 16 and not retired. These are set at two rates: standard rate of 5.75% of earnings up to the prescribed limit, and reduced rate of 2% payable by certain married women and widows.†

(ii) *Secondary.*—payable by employers at 8.75% of earnings irrespective of the rate of primary contribution.

Married women and most widows are liable to pay contributions at the reduced rate only for any period after the end of the tax year which includes their 59th birthday whatever their earlier choice about paying contributions may have been.

Employees in the following groups are not liable to pay any contributions:—

(a) Men over 65 and women over 60 who have retired for national insurance purposes;

(b) Men over 65 and women over age 60 who have not retired for national insurance purposes and, at age 65 (60) did not qualify for retirement pension on their own contributions;

(c) all men over age 70 and women over age 65.

CLASS 2 CONTRIBUTIONS

These are flat-rate contributions payable weekly by self-employed earners, either by stamping a card or by direct debit

From 6 April 1976 a flat rate Class 2 contribution (self employed) is £2.41 for a man and £2.20 for a woman. The voluntary Class 3 contribution is at one rate, £2.10.

† The Social Security Pensions Act 1975 abolishes the right of married women and certain widows to choose reduced contribution liability. In general, the 1977–78 tax year will be the last year for which women will be able to make a fresh choice of reduced contribution liability. This means that a woman who wishes to make such a choice must be entitled to make an election from 6 April 1977 and must register her choice no later than 11 May 1977. Special provisions apply, however, to women who are widowed during the 1977/78 tax year which enable them to have automatically reduced liability from the date of widowhood. When the husband dies on or after 6 April 1978, a woman can only be entitled to reduced liability for contributions if an election of reduced liability as a married woman is already in effect. Women will however continue to be allowed to have reduced liability after the end of the 1977/78 tax year if, on 5 April 1978, they are married women or widows who already have elections of reduced liability in force, provided that they do not have a break of two consecutive tax years away from employment in which contributions are payable, or from self-employment.

Small Earnings Exception. A self employed person may apply to be excepted from liability to pay Class 2 contributions if in a particular year his earnings from self-employment are expected to be low (for the tax year beginning on 6 April 1976 exception may be claimed if earnings from self-employment are expected to be less than £775). A self-employed person granted exception on these grounds can pay Class 2 or Class 3 contributions voluntarily.

CLASS 3 CONTRIBUTIONS

These are payable voluntarily by persons not in employment and others (e.g., earners with insufficient Class 1 and 2 contributions) to help them qualify for a limited range of benefits, the most important of which is retirement pension.

CLASS 4 CONTRIBUTIONS

These are payable on profits or gains chargeable to income tax under cases I and II of Schedule D. Cases I and II refer to profit or gains from a trade, profession or vocation. The rate for 1976/1977 is 8 per cent of such profits or gains between £1,600 and £4,900. Men who are 65 or women who are 60 at the beginning of a year of assessment and have either retired from regular employment or do not satisfy the contribution conditions for a retirement pension may apply to the DHSS for exception from Class 4 contributions. Men over age 70 and women over age 65 at the beginning of a year of assessment are automatically exempt from Class 4 contribution.

BENEFITS

The flat rate benefits payable (from the appropriate day in the week commencing 15 November 1976) under the Act provided that the relevant contribution conditions are satisfied) are:—

(i) *Unemployment benefit.*—This is normally £11.10 (£12.90)* per week plus allowances for dependants. Benefit may be drawn for a maximum of 312 days.

(ii) *Sickness benefit.*—This is also normally £12.90 per week plus allowances for dependants.

(iii) *Invalidity benefit.*—Normally replaces sickness benefit after 168 days. Consists of invalidity pension of £15.30 weekly and invalidity allowance payable to those where incapacity began more than 5 years before pension age. The allowance is payable at 3 rates: £3.20 if incapacity began before the age of 35; £2.00 if it began between 35–44 and £1.00 if it began between 45 and 54 for women and 45 and 59 for men. Allowances are also payable for dependants at rates preferential to the sickness benefit increases.

(iv) *Maternity benefits.*—There are two types of maternity benefits:—

   (a) maternity grant, a lump sum payment of £25 to assist with the general expense of having a child and which may be claimed between fourteen weeks before the expected weeks of confinement and no later than three months after the child's birth;

   (b) maternity allowance, normally paid at the rate of £12.90 per week and increase in certain cases for dependants. It is paid to expectant mothers to enable them to give up work and is awarded normally for 18 weeks.

(v) *Widow's benefits.*—Widow's benefits are of three kinds:—

   (a) widow's allowance payable for the first 26 weeks after the death of her husband. This is at the rate of £18.60 (£21.40) per week plus £6.50 (£7.45) per week where there is one qualifying child, £5.00 (£5.95) and for each subsequent child.

   (b) widowed mother's allowance which, where there is one qualifying child is payable at the rate of £13.30 (£15.30) per week plus £6.50 (£7.45) per week where there is one qualifying child, and £5.00

* Figures in brackets subject to Parliamentary approval (November 1976).

(£5.95)* for each subsequent child; and

(c) widow's pension: woman over 50 at date of husband's death or when entitlement to widowed mother's allowance ends: £13.30 (£15.30). If a widow is between 40 and 50 at either of these times she can qualify for a widow's pension ranging from 93% of the full rate (i.e. £12.37 (£14.23)) for the widow who was then 49, to 30% of the full rate, i.e. £3.99 (£4.59) for the widow who was then 40.

(vi) *Family Allowances.*—Payments (to families with more than one child) of £1.50 where there are two children with a further £1.50 for each additional child. A child is under the age limits up to the minimum school-leaving age, 16, and during any further period before his 19th birthday while he is receiving full-time instruction at a school, college or university or is an apprentice with low earnings.

(vii) *Guardian's allowance.*—A guardian's allowance is paid to a person who has taken into his family an orphan child one of whose parents satisfied a nationality or residence condition. It is normally a condition that both parents of the child are dead but the allowance can sometimes be paid on the death of only one parent, e.g. where the surviving parent is undergoing a long term of imprisonment. Guardian's allowance is at the rate of £6.50 (£7.45) per week for each such child.

(viii) *Child's special allowance.*—This is payable when a woman's marriage has been dissolved or annulled on the death of her former husband, and is at the rate of £6.50 (£7.45) per week for the first child, and £5.00 (£5.95) per week for each subsequent child.

(ix) *Flat rate retirement pension.*—This is normally £13.30 (£15.30) per week plus allowances for dependants, payable to men retiring at 65 years of age and women retiring at 60, or at 70 and 65 respectively if they do not retire earlier. A married woman who has not maintained her own insurance may claim a pension of £7.90 (£9.20) a week on her husband's contributions.

(x) *Graduated pension.*—The amounts payable are added to the normal flat rate pension in accordance with the amount of graduated contributions paid by the employee up to 5th April 1975. A man earns a "unit" or 2½p a week pension for each £7.50 paid in contributions and a woman earns 2½p for each £9 paid, because she retires earlier than a man. From 5th April 1975 the graduated pension scheme was wound up but any graduated pension earned up to that date will be paid with basic retirement pension when a person retires.

Provision has been made in the Social Security Pensions Act 1975, which comes into force in April 1978, for graduated pensions already in payment, and the pension rights earned by people who are still working age, to be protected against price increases from the start of the new scheme.

(xi) Full death grant is available only for men over 18 years born since 5th July, 1893 and women over 18 born since 5th July, 1898. In such instances a lump sum of £30 is payable normally to the deceased's executors or administrators or to the person paying the funeral expenses. Reduced amounts are payable for younger persons and for men born between 1883 and 1893 and women born between 1888 and 1898.

Provision was made in the 1969 National Insurance Act for payment of Death Grant on the insurance record of a close relative of an insured person, where the deceased was a handicapped person who had always been incapacitated for regular employment.

* Figures in brackets subject to Parliamentary approval (November 1976)

Earnings related supplement.—An addition to sickness or unemployment benefit or maternity allowance and widow's allowance payable for a maximum of 6 months and based on the amount of earnings on which class I contributions have been paid in the relevant income tax year in excess of fifty times the lower earnings limit for that year.

Maximum weekly payment £12.18 where 1975/6 tax year is relevant.

Future Developments.—Under the provisions of the Social Security Pensions Act 1975, the benefits of which are due to start on 6 April 1979 (i.e. one year after the start of the scheme on 6 April 1978), pensions for retirement, widowhood and invalidity will be in two parts—a basic pension and, where a person is not a member of a contracted-out occupational pension scheme, an additional earnings-related pension.

The basic pension will be equivalent to and calculated in the same way as the present flat-rate pension. The additional pension will build up year by year over a 20 year period at the rate of 1¼% per year of a person's earnings above the qualifying level for the basic pension and when the scheme has been running for more than 20 years it will be based on a person's 20 best years of revalued earnings.

Once in payment the basic pension will be uprated in line with the movement of earnings or prices (whichever is the more favourable) and the additional pension will be uprated in line with prices.

The Act enables employees who are members of occupational pension schemes that fulfill specified requirements to be contracted-out of the additional part of retirement pension and half the additional widows pension by their employers. The main conditions to be satisfied if a scheme is to be contracted-out are that it must provide

(a) a personal pension which is

 (i) not less than 1¼% of final salary (or average salary revalued in line with the growth of earnings generally) for each year of contracted-out service, and

 (ii) not less than the additional part of retirement pension the employee would have earned in the State scheme had his employment not been contracted-out (referred to as the "guaranteed minimum pension"), and

(b) a widow's pension of at least half the husband's pension entitlement.

The contributions of contracted-out employees to the State scheme on earnings up to a lower earnings limit will be 6½%, the same as for other employees; and their employers will pay 10% up to that level. On earnings between that lower limit and the upper earnings limit for contributions, employees will pay 4% (a reduction of 2½%) and their employers 5½% (a reduction of 4½%).

The decision on whether or not an occupational pension scheme satisfies the contracting-out condition is for the Occupational Pensions Board, an independent statutory body, who will also have a general responsibility for supervising contracting-out.

Patents and Designs

The Statute law relating to Patents is mainly contained in the Patents Act, 1949 (and certain enactments not wholly repealed as in the 2nd Schedule thereto set out), the Patents Act, 1957, the Defence Contracts Act, 1958, the Patents & Designs (Renewals Extentions of Fees) Act, 1961, the Courts Act, 1971, s. 46, the Patents Rules 1968, the Patents (Amendment) Rules 1975 No. 371, and 1021, the Patents Appeal Tribunal Rules, 1972, No. 1940, L. 28, Patents Appeal Tribunal Rules (Fees) Order, 1973, No. 164, L. 1, Practice Directions re Appeals dates 20/11/1972, 30/11/1972, 21/2/1973.

Insofar as certain transitional provisions of the Patents Act, 1949 are concerned it is still necessary to refer to the Patent Rules 1939, the Patents (Amendment) Rules, 1942, and the Patents (Amendment) Rules 1946, See also the Enemy Property Act, 1953, and the Aircraft (Exemption from Seizure on Patent Claims Order 1961, No. 332). The law relating to Designs is contained in the Registered Designs Act, 1949, the Designs Rules, 1949, the Designs (Amendment) Rules, 1955, the Defence Contracts Act, 1958, the Patents and Designs (Renewals, Extensions and Fees) Act, 1961, the Designs (Amendment) Rules, 1959, S.I. No. 1924, the Designs (Amendment) Rules 1962, S.I. 1962, No. 2729, the Designs (Amendment) Rules, 1964, No. 229, the Designs (Amendment) Rules, 1965, No. 1551, the Designs Amendment Rules, 1967, S.I. 1967, No. 393 and the Designs (Amendment) Rules, 1969, 1971, S.I. 1971, No. 262, the Designs (Amendment) Rules, 1975 No. 372, Registered Designs, Appeal Tribunal Rules, 1950, the Registered Designs Appeal Tribunal (Amendment) Rules, 1970, No. 1075, L. 23, the Registered Designs Tribunal (Fees) Order, 1973, No. 165. Further provisions are also contained in the Patents, Designs, Copyright and Trade Marks (Emergency) Act, 1939 and the Patents, Designs, Copyright and Trade Marks (Emergency) Rules, 1939, and (Emergency) Amendment Rules 1940. Provisions affecting Designs also appear in ss. 10 and 44 of the Copyright Act, 1956 as amended by the Design Copyright Act, 1968, in the Copyright (Industrial Designs) Rules 1957 and the Registered Designs Appeal Tribunal Rules, 1950, No. 430 and 1970. No. 1075. As to patents and designs see 24 Halsbury's Statutes, 3rd Edn., 544 *et seq.*

PATENTS. An application for a Patent may be made by any person who claims to be the true and first inventor of an invention either alone, or jointly, with any person, or by the applicant for an invention in a Convention country (see below) or by the assignee of the true and first inventor or of such applicant. The personal representative of any such person may also apply (s. 1). An invention means any manner of new manufacture the subject of letters patent and grant of privilege within section 6 of the Statute of Monopolies and any new method or process of testing applicable to the improvement or control of manufacture and includes an alleged invention. The expression true and first inventor includes a person to whom the invention has been first communicated in this country.

APPLICATION FOR A PATENT. An application other than a Convention application may be accompanied either by a provisional specification or by a complete specification (s. 3 (1)). Where a provisional specification is filed a complete specification must be filed within 12 months of the filing of the provisional specification or on payment of extra fees within 15 months (s. 3 (2)). A complete specification must particularly describe the nature of the invention and the manner in which the same is to be performed and the best method known to the inventor of performing it (s. 4 (3)). The complete specification ends with claims, which define the scope of the invention and, where necessary, is accompanied by drawings, which may be called for by the Comptroller of Patents.

When a complete specification is filed it is allotted to an Examiner, who examines the application and any specification or specifications to ascertain if they are prepared in the prescribed manner. A search is made through specifications for any anticipation of the invention published prior to the date of filing of the complete specification and any specifications so found are notified to the applicant who has an opportunity to amend his specification (s. 7). The Examiner may cite any publication of the invention of which he is aware in the United Kingdom in any document, other than an United Kingdom specification or a specification describing the invention for the purposes of an application for protection made in any country outside the United Kingdom more than fifty years next before that date, or any abridgement of or extract from, any such specification published under the authority of the Comptroller or of the Government of any country outside the United Kingdom (s. 50).

If the invention is wholly anticipated by any publication so found or if the complete specification is not amended to the satisfaction of the Examiner, the

Comptroller may refuse the application. Otherwise the specification is accepted. An appeal from a decision of the Comptroller lies to the Patents Appeal Tribunal which consists of a single Judge of the High Court.

In addition to the examination above referred to, an investigation is also made to ascertain whether the invention has been wholly or in part claimed in any specification published on or after the date which the patent applied for would bear if granted and deposited pursuant to an application made for a patent which if granted would bear a date prior to the date which the patent applied for would bear if granted (s. 8). Any such patent is cited and the applicant has an opportunity of amending. In the event of his failing to do so the Comptroller decides what reference should be made to the cited specification and his decision is subject to appeal to the Patents Appeal Tribunal.

The priority of any claim in a patent dates *prima facie* from the date of the filing of the complete specification unless it can be regarded as fairly based on the provisional specification or on the Convention application on which it is based, in which case priority rates from the provisional specification or Convention document (s. 5). The effect of this provision is that new matter can be introduced into a complete specification which is not in the provisional or Convention application and it is an answer to any publication cited by the Examiner that the contents of the publication are in the provisional specification or Convention application if these are prior in date to the publication.

In considering whether a provisional specification or a complete specification should be filed with the application, it should be borne in mind that the fees payable on a provisional specification are considerably less than those payable on a complete specification. The application thus has twelve months within which to develop or dispose of his invention before incurring the increased expense of filing the complete specification. On the other hand, the combined cost of filing a provisional specification followed by a complete specification exceeds that of a complete specification in first instance. The fees and forms appear in the Schedule of Fees and Forms hereunder.

It is possible to deal with patent applications by post, the address being The Comptroller, The Patent Office, 25 Southampton Buildings, Chancery Lane, London, W.C.2. The forms appear in the Schedules to the Patents (Amendment) Rules 1955, and stamped forms may be obtained on personal application to the Patent Office or by post on prepayment by banker's draft, money order or postal order from the Comptroller of Stamps, Bush House, South-West Wing, Strand, London, W.C.2. They may also be obtained at one week's notice and on prepayment of the value of the stamp from any Money Order Office in Great Britain and Northern Ireland.

POST DATING.—An application may be post-dated up to six months or in the case of a Convention application up to the last date for claiming priority (s. 6 (3)).

CONVENTION APPLICATIONS.—These applications are entitled to priority of the date of first application in any Convention country [that is to say a country in the case of which there is an Order in Council in force to the effect that it is a Convention country]. Such countries have agreed under International and Inter-Imperial arrangements to give the patents of other Convention countries priority of date as aforesaid provided the application is made within 12 months of the date of first application in a Convention Country. Most of the important foreign states and colonies are within the arrangements (ss. 68–72).

ACCEPTANCE.—An application should be in order for acceptance within a prescribed period from the date of filing the complete specification, but 3 months' extension of time may be obtained on payment of fees. Extension is also allowed where an appeal is pending or possible (s. 12) as amended by Patents Act, 1957, s. 1. The prescribed period is 3½ years (Patents (Amendment) Rules, 1957). When an application is accepted the applicant has all the right of a patentee except that he cannot institute proceedings for infringement until the patent is sealed (s. 13 (4)).

OPPOSITION.—When a patent has been accepted the acceptance is advertised in the Official Patents Journal (s.

13) and the specification becomes open to public inspection. At any time within three months from such publication any person may oppose the grant of a patent. The grounds, which are set out in detail in s. 14, are briefly as follows:—

1. That the applicant obtained the invention or part thereof from the opponent or from a person whose legal representative he is; or

2. That the invention has been published in a specification or other document (with certain exceptions) within the last 50 years; or

3. That the invention has been claimed in the complete specification of a patent which will be of prior date when granted; or

4. That the invention claimed in any claim of the complete specification was used in the United Kingdom before the priority date in that claim; or

5. That the invention is obvious and does not involve any inventive step having regard to prior publication or user; or

6. That the subject of any claim is not an invention within the meaning of the Act; or

7. That the complete specification does not sufficiently and fairly describe the invention or the method by which it is to be performed; or

8. That, in the case of a Convention application, the application was not made within 12 months from the date of the first application for protection for the invention made in a convention country by the applicant or a person from whom he derives title.

The procedure in opposition proceedings is set out in Rules 40 to 48 of the Patents Rules, 1958, and the hearing is before the Comptroller with appeal to the Patents Appeal Tribunal. The opponent must show an interest to enable him to oppose.

GRANT OF PATENT.—A patent is normally to be sealed within 4 months from the date of publication, except where extension of time has been obtained (s. 19).

TERM OF PATENT.—A patent bears the date of filing of the complete specification and extends for a period of 16 years. In the case of patents granted before 1st August, 1938, this period runs from the date of application. The date of a Convention patent is the date of filing of the complete specification except in the case of applications filed before 1st January, 1950, where it is the date of application, *i.e.* the priority date. Renewal fees are payable annually in advance, for the 5th to 16th year of a patent, the first of £6 being payable before the expiration of the fourth year from the date of the patent. The fees increase from year to year.

REVOCATION OF PATENT.—At any time within twelve months of the date of sealing of a patent application for revocation thereof may be made to the Comptroller on any of the grounds upon which the same might have been opposed (s. 33).

By section 32 revocation of a patent may be applied for by petition to the Court on any of the following grounds:—

(a) That the invention was the subject of a valid prior grant;

(b) That the patent was granted on the application of a person not entitled to apply therefor;

(c) That the patent was obtained in contravention of the rights of the petitioner or any person under or through whom he claims;

(d) That the subject of any claim is not an invention within the Act;

(e) that the invention is not new;

(f) that the invention is obvious;

(g) that the invention is not useful;

(h) that the complete specification does not sufficiently and fairly describe the invention and the method by which it is to be performed or does not disclose the best method of performance of the invention known to the applicant;

(i) that the patent was obtained on a false suggestion or representation;

(j) that the invention is contrary to law;

(k) that the invention was secretly used in the United Kingdom before the priority date (except as in the section provided).

A patent may also be revoked on the petition of a Government department if the Court is satisfied that the patentee has without reasonable cause failed to comply with a request of the department to make use or exercise the patented invention for the service of the Crown on reasonable terms.

S. 50 sets out certain matters which shall not be deemed to be prior publication and includes a provision that a patent granted on the application of the true and first inventor shall not be deemed to have been anticipated by reason of an application in contravention of his rights or by any publication thereof without his consent.

S. 51 provides that communication of an invention to a Government department shall not invalidate a patent and further that exhibition of an invention at certain exhibitions or the communication thereof in a paper to a learned society shall not do so if application is made for a patent within 6 months.

ASSIGNMENT OF PATENTS.—A patent may be assigned in whole or in part and an assignment of the legal estate must be by deed. An assignment must be registered (s. 74). Provision is made by s. 17 whereby an agreement to assign a patent application may be registered, so that the patent when granted, shall issue to the assignee and the assignee may be substituted as applicant.

LICENCES.—Licences may be exclusive or non-exclusive and may be granted by parole, in writing or by deed. They may be for any period within the life of the patent or for any territory. They must be registered (s. 74). A patentee may at any time request the Comptroller that a patent may be indorsed "Licences of Right". The effect of this is that anyone can request a licence under the patent on terms to be agreed or, failing agreement, to be settled by the Comptroller. The renewal fees payable on the patent are reduced by one half (s. 35). In certain cases compulsory licences may be granted (see *infra*). Since the accession of the United Kingdom to the Treaty of Rome certain provisions of licences have to be considered in relation to Art. 85 and the regulations made by the European Economic Community.

COMPULSORY LICENCES.—Any person interested may at any time after 3 years from the date of sealing of a patent apply to the Comptroller for a compulsory licence or for the patent to be indorsed "Licences of Right" on any of the following grounds (s. 37):

(a) That the patent is not being

worked commercially in the United Kingdom or is not being worked to the fullest extent that is reasonably practicable;

(b) That a demand for the patented article in the United Kingdom is not being met on reasonable terms or is being met to a substantial extent by importation;

(c) That the commercial working of the invention in the United Kingdom is being prevented or hindered by importation;

(d) If by reason of a refusal of the patentee to grant licences on reasonable terms:
  (i) An export market is not being supplied; or
  (ii) Working of any other patented invention which makes a substantial contribution to the art is being prevented or hindered; or
  (iii) The establishment or development of commercial or industrial activities in the United Kingdom is unfairly prejudiced;

(e) That by reason of conditions imposed by the patentee, the manufacture, use or sale of materials not protected by the patent or the establishment or development of commercial or industrial activities in the United Kingdom is unfairly prejudiced.

Reference should be made to the exact wording of the section. Where an order has been made and two years have since elapsed the Comptroller may in certain circumstances revoke the patent (s. 42).

By s. 40 any Government Department may make on application on any of the grounds of s. 37 and a competent authority has power to make certain applications where a report has been made under the Monopolies and Restrictive Practices (Inquiry and Control) Act, 1948. By s. 41, the Comptroller has power to grant licences in respect of patents relating to food or medicine or surgical or curative devices.

RESTORATION OF PATENT.—Where a patent has lapsed due to non-payment of a renewal fee and the omission was unintentional and there is no undue delay in making application, the Comptroller may restore the patent upon application made within 3 years (s. 27). For the terms of the usual order, see Rule 84, Patents Rules, 1949.

EXTENSION OF TERM OF PATENT.—By s. 23 of the Act any patentee may apply for an extension of the term of his patent to the Court on the ground that he has been inadequately remunerated. Application must be made between 12 and 6 months before the expiration of the patent. The term of extension which may be granted shall not exceed 10 years. In addition application may be made either to the Comptroller or to the Court where the patentee has suffered loss or damage due to hostilities. Applications on the ground of loss due to hostilities may be made after the expiration of the patent, where the patentee has been prevented from applying by reason of his having been on active service or by other circumstances arising by reason of the hostilities. More than one such application may be made, but the total extensions granted shall not exceed 10 years (s. 24). A licensee may apply under s. 24 (s. 25).

PATENTS AND THE CROWN.—By s. 46, as extended by the Defence Contracts Act, 1958, s. 1, any Government department and any person authorised in writing by a Government department may make, use and exercise any patented invention for the service of the Crown as therein provided. The terms of any agreement or licence concluded between the patentee and any person other than a Government Dept. are inoperative so far as concerns the making, use or exercise of the invention for the service of the Crown (s. 47). Any dispute as to the exercise of the powers of a Government department or a person authorised by it or as to terms of payment is to be referred to the Court (s. 48).

S. 18 provides for certain patents relating to defence to be kept secret.

By s. 2 of the Defence (Contracts) Act, 1958, provision is made for the use for defence purposes of technical information by the Crown notwithstanding anything to the contrary in any licence or agreement. For the necessary procedure see s. 3. Payments for such use are regulated by s. 4. Technical information is defined as including any specification or design in articles and any process in their production and also includes the use of drawings, models, plans, etc. (s. 2 (7)).

PATENTEES' RIGHTS.—A patentee may enforce his rights by an action for infringement of his patent in the Chancery Division, the claim being for damages, or an account of profits; an injunction and delivery up or destruction of infringing articles. The defence may include a counterclaim for revocation on any of the grounds set out above. For procedure see Rules of the Supreme Court, particularly O. 95. The Comptroller has certain powers to deal with questions of infringement by agreement between the parties (s. 67). An exclusive licensee may sue for infringement (s. 63). A declaration may be sought from the Court as to whether any manufacture is an infringement of a patent (s. 66).

By s. 59 a patentee cannot recover damages from a defendant who proves that he was not aware and had no reasonable means of making himself aware of the existence of the patent, and the marking of the article "patent" or "patented" or any word or words expressing or implying that a patent has been obtained applied to the article is not to be such notice unless it is accompanied by the number of the patent. Any party who is subjected to groundless threats of proceedings for infringement may proceed against the person threatening him and obtain damages and an injunction against their continuance (s. 65).

The Patents Act, 1949 contains provisions for the mention of the inventor as such in the patent (s. 16), for settling disputes between joint applicants (s. 17) or joint patenters (s. 55), between employer and employee (s. 56), for the grant of Patents of Addition (s. 26), for amendment of the specification (ss. 29 to 31) and for the avoidance of certain conditions when attached to the sale or licence of patented articles (s. 57).

The Patents and Designs Act, 1946, s. 4 deprives German and Japanese inventions made during the war period of the right to protection.

TRANSITIONAL PROVISIONS.—Important transitional provisions are scheduled to the Act.

Proceedings before the Comptroller of Patents and the Patents Appeal Tribunal may now be heard and decisions given in public (S.I.s 1959 Nos. 278 and 524).

SCHEDULE OF FORMS AND FEES

Forms No.	———	Fee
1	Application for Patent	£1
1 CON	Application for Patent under International and Inter-Imperial arrangements, for each priority claimed ..	£1
2	Provisional Specification	—
3	Complete Specification	£48
6	Request for Post-dating	£10.00
12	Notice of Opposition to Grant of Patent	£10.00 by each party
13	Notice that hearing will be attended	£6.00
18	Claim under Section 17 to proceed as applicant or co-applicant for grant of Patent	£13.00
20	Request to have Patent Sealed	£20.00
24	Payment of Renewal Fee:—	
	Before the expiration of the 4th year from date of Patent and in respect of the 5th year	£40
	,, ,, 5th ,, ,, 6th ,,	£42
	,, ,, 6th ,, ,, 7th ,,	£46
	,, ,, 7th ,, ,, 8th ,,	£50
	,, ,, 8th ,, ,, 9th ,,	£56
	,, ,, 9th ,, ,, 10th ,,	£62
	,, ,, 10th ,, ,, 11th ,,	£68
	,, ,, 11th ,, ,, 12th ,,	£76
	,, ,, 12th ,, ,, 13th ,,	£84
	,, ,, 13th ,, ,, 14th ,,	£92
	,, ,, 14th ,, ,, 15th ,,	£100
	,, ,, 15th ,, ,, remainder of the term of the patent	£108
	One moiety only of the above fees payable on Patents indorsed "Licences of Right."	
59	Application for entry of name of proprietor or part proprietor in Register:—	
	If made within 6 months from date of acquisition of proprietorship:—	
	In respect of one patent	£4.00*
	For each additional patent devolving under the same title..	£1.00
60	Application for entry of notice of Mortgage or Licence in Register:—	
	If made within 6 months from date of acquisition of interest or sealing of patent (whichever is the later):—	
	In respect of one patent	£4.00*
	For each additional patent devolving under the same title..	£1.00
61	Application for entry of notification Document in Register of Patents, if made within 6 months from date of document or sealing of patent (whichever is the later). In respect of one patent	£4.00*
	For each additional patent	£0.50

* If the application is made after the expiration of six months but within twelve months from the date of acquisition of proprietorship of the patent or interest therein or the date of the document, or the sealing of the patent, as the case may be, the fee is £10.00 and if made after twelve months from such date £15.00.

DESIGNS.—A design means only the features of shape, configuration, pattern or ornament applied to any article by any industrial process or means, being features which in the finished article appear and to and are judged solely by the eye, but does not include a method or principle of construction, or features of shape or configuration which are dictated solely by the function which the article to be made in that shape or configuration has to perform (s. 1 (3)). Certain articles which are primarily literary or artistic in character are excluded (s. 1 (4) and Rule 26, Designs Rules, 1949).

The proprietor of a new or original design is the person for whom a design is executed for good consideration and where the design is acquired by any person, the person by whom it is acquired. In any other case the proprietor is the author of the design or his successor in title (s. 2).

APPLICATION FOR REGISTRATION OF DESIGNS.—Prior to the 1st January, 1950, designs had to be registered according to the material of which they were made in accordance with a classification set out in the third schedule to the Designs Rules, 1932. They are now registered in respect of the article or set of articles specified in the application (s. 1 (1)). The procedure is set out in the Designs Rules, 1949. The application form must be accompanied by 3 representations of the design and prior designs are cited against the application. There is an appeal to the Patents Appeal Tribunal from a refusal of the Comptroller to register a design.

By s. 4 where a design has been registered for one article its registration for another article is not prevented by such registration. Also registration of a modification of a design already registered is not prevented by reason of the prior registration for a different article or user pursuant thereto. The copyright in the modified design, however, does not extend beyond the copyright in the original registration.

TERM OF REGISTRATION.—Registration is for 5 years from the date of application and may be extended on payment of fees for two further periods of 5 years (s. 8).

MARKING.—The provisions as to marking articles with the number of a registered design are the same as those for patents (*supra*) (s. 9).

DISCLOSURE.—Disclosure or publication of a design in breach of good faith will not invalidate a design registration, nor will the acceptance of a first and confidential order for textile goods bearing a new or original design, provided in each case registration is subsequently obtained (s. 6).

Designs are not published in the same way as patents, but are in general open to inspection after registration on payment of fees (s. 22 and Rule 45, Designs Rules, 1949). Provision is made for applications for cancellation to be made to the Comptroller (s. 11), and for applications for compulsory licences (s. 10). Convention applications may be made within 6 months of the first application in a Convention Country (ss. 13, 14, 15). The provisions as to user by the Crown are in the First Schedule to the Act. See also Defence (Contracts) Act, 1958. Publication of a design at certain Exhibitions will not invalidate a subsequent registration if certain conditions are complied with (s. 6 (2)).

INFRINGEMENT OF DESIGN.—S. 7 provides that registration gives the proprietor the exclusive right to make or import for sale or for use for the purposes of any trade or business, or to sell, hire or offer for sale any article in respect of which the design is registered and to which it is applied, and to make anything for enabling any such article to be made.

ASSIGNMENTS AND LICENCES.—The remarks under these headings as to patents apply, except that there is no provision for endorsement "Licences of Right."

Stamped forms may be obtained as in the case of patents.

Proceedings before the Comptroller and the Appeal Tribunal may now be heard and decisions given in public (S.I. 1959 Nos. 278 and 1924).

SCHEDULE OF FORMS AND FEES

Number of Form	Title of Form	Fee £
Designs No. 1	Authorisation of Agent	—
Designs No. 2 or 3	Application for registration of a design (except textile articles)	21.00 (lace, 5.00)
Designs No. 4 or 5	Application for registration of a design to be applied to a set (except textile articles) ..	42.00 (lace, 10.00)
Designs No. 1 (Manchester)	Application for registration of a design for textile article other than checks or stripes ..	21.00
Designs No. 2 (Manchester)	Application for registration of a textile design consisting of checks or stripes..	10.00
Designs No. 9	Application for extension of copyright for second period of five years	52.00
Designs No. 10	Application for extension of copyright for third period of five years	74.00
Designs Nos. 12 and 13	Application for entry of notification of document (*e.g.* assignment, mortgage, licence) in the Register:—	
	In respect of one design	6.00†
	For each additional design, the devolution of title being the same as for the first design	1.00

† If the application be made after the expiration of six months but within twelve months from the date of acquisition of proprietorship, etc., of the design the fee is £10.00, and if made after twelve months from such date £15.00.

Persons Suffering from Mental Disorder

1. RECEPTION AND DETENTION

Mental Health Act, 1959.—The Mental Health Act, 1959, which came into operation fully on November 1, 1960, introduced a complete new code and system for the care, treatment and detention of persons suffering from mental disorder. "Mental disorder" is now a statutory term (defined by s. 4) embracing all forms of unsoundness of mind, previously dealt with under the Lunacy and Mental Treatment Acts, 1890 to 1930, and mental deficiency, to which the Mental Deficiency Acts, 1913 to 1938 applied.

The previous central authority, the Board of Control, has been dissolved (s. 2), its duties and functions, in a greater or lesser degree, being now performed by the Department of Health and Social Security, the local health authorities and the Mental Health Review Tribunals.

N.B.—The Act has been varied by the National Health Service Reorganisation Act 1973 with regard to the functions of local health authorities.

Meaning of Mental Disorder.— "Mental disorder" means mental illness, arrested or incomplete development of mind, psychopathic disorder, and any other disorder or disability of mind; and "mentally disordered" is to be construed accordingly (s. 4 (1)).

"Severe subnormality" means a state of arrested or incomplete development of mind which includes subnormality of intelligence and is of such a nature or degree that the patient is incapable of living an independent life, or will be so incapable when of an age to do so (s. 4 (2)).

"Subnormality" means a state of arrested or incomplete development of mind (not amounting to severe subnormality) which includes subnormality of intelligence and is of a nature or degree which requires or is susceptible to medical treatment or other special care or training of the patient (s. 4 (3)).

"Psychopathic disorder" means a persistent disorder of personality (whether or not accompanied by subnormality of intelligence) which results in abnormally aggressive or seriously irresponsible conduct on the part of the patient, and requires or is susceptible to medical treatment (s. 4 (4)).

Informal Admission.—Wherever possible patients are now admitted voluntarily with absence of formality in the same way as any other person requiring medical treatment (s. 5).

Compulsory Admission.—A magistrate's order is no longer necessary to secure the admission and detention of a patient against his will. This is secured by an application, duly supported by medical evidence, to the managers of the hospital concerned, including certain mental nursing homes (see ss. 14 and 15), the application being the authority for detention (see ss. 26, 28 and 31).

A patient suffering from any of the forms of mental disorder mentioned in s. 4 may be admitted for observation and detained for 28 days under s. 25 and in case of urgent necessity an emergency application for admission for observation can be made under s. 29. The normal way to secure admission and detention is by way of an application under s. 26, but in this case it is to be noted that "subnormality" or "psychopathic disorder" is not a ground unless the patient is under 21.

An application for admission for observation or treatment may be made either by the nearest relative or by a mental welfare officer but when admission is for treatment, the mental welfare officer must, where practicable, consult with the person appearing to be the nearest relative and may not proceed if he objects (s. 27). An emergency application may be made by any relative or a mental welfare officer (s. 29).

Two medical recommendations are required (s. 28) but in the case of emergency one is sufficient in the first instance (s. 29 (3)).

Generally, see The Mental Health (Hospital and Guardianship) Regulations, 1960.

Guardianship.—Under s. 33 a patient may be placed under the guardianship of a local health authority or some other person, provided that if it is a case of "subnormality" or "psychopathic disorder" the patient must not be over 21. What is said above as to who may make an application for admission for treatment and as to medical evidence applies to a guardianship application.

A guardian has such powers as would be exercisable by him in relation to the patient if he were the father of the patient and the patient were under 14 (s. 34).

Duration of Detention or Guardianship.—This lasts for 1 year and then may be renewed for a further year and then for successive periods of 2 years (s. 43). As regards psychopathic or subnormal patients guardianship ceases completely on attaining the age of 25 (no renewal) and so will any authority for his detention in hospital unless specially renewed under the provisions of s. 44.

Discharge—Wide powers of discharge are conferred upon the various hospital, medical and health authorities and it is to be noted that the nearest relative of the patient has a power to order his discharge (s. 47). Such power of the nearest relative cannot be executed, however, where the responsible medical officer certifies that the patient, if discharged, would be likely to act in a manner dangerous to other persons or to himself (s. 48).

Transfer of the Functions of the Nearest Relative.—As to who are, or are deemed to be "relatives" and "nearest relatives" for the purposes of the Act, *see* ss. 49–51.

In view of the functions of a "nearest relative", *e.g.* to make an application for admission for treatment and to order discharge, the County Court has jurisdiction to make orders transferring these functions to another person and to make other consequential orders (ss. 52 and 53).

Mental Health Review Tribunals.—A Mental Health Review Tribunal is constituted for every region for which a Regional Health Authority is established under the National Health Service Reorganisation Act 1973 (s. 3), whose function it is to provide the patient, and, in some instances relatives, with an independent body to whom they can apply to review any case in which it is contended that the patient should not be liable to be detained or subject to guardianship. The constitution of these Tribunals is governed by the First Schedule to the Act. They comprise legal, medical and lay members, the chairman being a lawyer.

The legality of detention, as distinct from the question of the necessity therefor, is a matter for the courts and not the Tribunals.

See The Mental Health Review Tribunal Rules, 1960.

Orders in Criminal Proceedings.— Part V contains wide powers for the courts to make orders for offenders who are suffering from mental disorder to be detained in hospital or placed under guardianship. There is no requirement that in a case of "subnormality" or "psychopathic disorder" the patient must be under 21. Not only may such a hospital order or guardianship order be made but under s. 65 the Crown Court may make an order restricting discharge under which the power of discharge can only be exercised with the consent of the Home Secretary.

2. THE COURT OF PROTECTION

Management of Patients' Property and Affairs.—The Court of Protection is situate at 25, Store Street, London, WC1E 7BP (Tel.: 01-636 6877). The function of the Court is to protect and administer the property and affairs of persons who are incapable by reason of mental disorder of managing and administering their own property and affairs, whether or not compulsorily detained or under guardianship under the provisions of the Mental Health Act, 1959, and whether residing in their own homes or elsewhere.

Any such patient is not in a position to give a power of attorney or other authority to any person to manage his property and any such authority given prior to his illness becomes inoperative by reason of that incapacity. Any person continuing to act under authori-

ty so given, or a bank or company in which the patient has money or other property, who permits any dealings with the same with knowledge of the patient's incapacity, incurs considerable risk. In such circumstances it is nearly always necessary to apply for the appointment of a receiver.

Part VIII of the Act deals with the Court of Protection matters, and in particular s. 100 prescribes the judicial authorities of the Court. The judges of the Chancery Division are nominated under subs. (1) to act for the purpose of Court of Protection matters. In addition there are the Master and Deputy Master and Assistant Masters nominated under subs. (3).

A wide and plenary jurisdiction, no longer based on the Royal Prerogative or requiring recourse to any inherent jurisdiction, is conferred by s. 102 (1) which provides that:—

The judge may, with respect to the property and affairs of a patient, do or secure the doing of all such things as appear necessary or expedient—

> (a) for the maintenance or other benefit of the patient,
> (b) for the maintenance or other benefit of members of the patient's family,
> (c) for making provision for other persons or purposes for whom or which the patient might be expected to provide if he were not mentally disordered, or
> (d) otherwise for administering the patient's affairs.

See Re D.M.L., [1965] 2 All E.R. 129, *Re L.* (*W.J.G.*), [1966] 2 W.L.R. 233, *Re T.B.*, [1967] 2 W.L.R. 15 and *Re C.L.*, [1968] 2 W.L.R. 1275, *Re W.* (*E.E.M.*), [1971] 1 Ch. 123, as to scope of (b) and (c) *supra*.

The Rules are the Court of Protection Rules, 1960.

Appointment of a Receiver.—Under s. 105 (1) a receiver may be appointed for a "patient"—*i.e.* a person with regard to whom the Court is satisfied, after considering medical evidence, that he is incapable, by reason of mental disorder (as defined by s. 4) of managing and administering his property and affairs (s. 101). No longer is a person automatically disenfranchised from dealing with his own affairs upon becoming lawfully detained. Each case requires an objective test of mental capacity.

The powers of a receiver are limited and specified in the order appointing him and the further directions of the Court are required for matters outside the scope of the order. In some cases, *e.g.* where a small sum of money is payable under a policy or an estate, it is not always necessary to appoint a receiver and an order can be made limited to the property in question. The Court has wide powers to deal with a case in an emergency (s. 104).

It is usual for a near relative to apply to be appointed receiver. If a spouse is not the applicant his or her consent should be filed if possible. In any event relatives of a nearer degree than the applicant to the patient should be notified.

Procedure is by way of originating application returnable not less than 7 clear days from the date of issue and normally notice of such application must be served on the patient personally. Printed forms are obtainable in sets from the Court, free of charge. In applying for forms it is essential for the solicitors to say whether or not they are required for a "Certificate" case (see below).

The following documents and evidence are required.

  (i) Originating Application in duplicate (C.P. 1);
 (ii) Notice of Originating Proceedings (C.P. 6);
(iii) Combined form of Affidavit or Certificate of Service (C.P. 7);
 (iv) Certificate of Kindred and Fortune (C.P. 5), unless the income exceeds £300 a year *and* the capital value exceeds £3,000 in which case an affidavit (Form C.P. 4) is required.
  (v) Medical Certificate (C.P. 3).

No fees are payable upon the issue of the application. Attendance of solicitors is usually excused. The order is drafted in Chambers and sent to the Solicitors by post. Where security is directed (usual method, fidelity guarantee bond) the order will not issue until it has been completed. Normally a fee of £4 is payable on the order.

The practice of the Court is to disturb the property as little as is consis-

tent with the patient's paramount interests and in all things to endeavour to do what the patient would have done if sane and properly advised.

An order appointing a Receiver will give certain formal directions as to receipt of income, maintenance and duty to account and in addition will give directions as to such matters as lodgment in Court of cash, carrying on the patient's business and any other matters which the circumstances of the case require.

Personal Application Branch.—Applications in simple cases, not involving questions of title to property, sale of land, the preparation of deeds or other legal documents, etc., may be made through the Personal Application Branch of the Court, the matter being dealt with either through the post or by personal attendance. The fees are:— (i) on originating applications, where the annual income does not exceed £40, 10%, minimum 50p, and where such annual income exceeds £40, 4%, minimum £4 and maximum £50; (ii) on applications on recovery of patient, 50p. and (iii) on other applications, £1.

In extremely simple cases, *e.g.* where the estate consists of a sum of cash of say not exceeding £1,000, it may sometimes be possible to dispense with the appointment of a Receiver by providing for the lodgment of the funds in Court or suitable investment out of Court and for payments of the income or other periodical sums direct to the hospital, residential home or institution in which the patient is residing for the purpose of providing the patient with extra comforts under what is known as "Short Procedure" order.

Death of Patient.—The Court's jurisdiction ceases on the death of the patient (s. 105 (2); *Re Wheater*, [1928] 1 Ch. 223) and the Receiver's powers are thereby terminated though his liability to account to the Master remains. When representation to the estate has been obtained the personal representatives must apply for a final order where there is a fund in Court exceeding £1,500 in value or, if there is no such fund, for final directions, without a summons. Where otherwise the net estate does not exceed £1,500 in value, the estate may be transferred to those entitled without a grant (Rule 83 (2)).

Recovery of the Patient.—Discharge from detention does not of itself determine the Receivership (*Re B.A.S.*, [1898] 2 Ch. 392). To determine the proceedings and restore the patient to the management of his own affairs an order of the Court is necessary (s. 105 (2)). Application for such an order requires to be supported by medical evidence as to recovery.

Accounts.—A Receiver is usually required to account annually. The printed form of account (C.P. 28)—with a rent statement (C.P. 28A), if required—may be obtained from the Court, free of charge. The account must be accompanied by vouchers and (if any) agents' rent accounts, trustees' income accounts, business accounts, bank statements. Percentage is levied at the rate of 5% on the clear income of the patient's disposal. When, however, the annual income appears to be not more than £100 a fixed percentage of £1.50 is taken for each completed year and where such income appears to be between £100 and £150 the rate is 4% (Rule 87).

Sales, Leases, Conveyancing, etc.—Under s. 103 (1) (b), an order may be made for (*inter alia*) a sale, etc., of the patient's property. The Order may either be an order adopting a conditional agreement entered into by the Receiver on behalf of the patient or may be open "general" order. In the latter case also any agreement entered into pursuant to the order will be a conditional agreement to which the approval of the Court will have to be obtained. Conveyances, leases, etc., on behalf of a patient will be made by the Receiver, "in the name and on behalf of the patient". The draft is settled by the Court and the engrossment is sealed with the seal of the Court as evidence of such approval (rr. 84 and 85). Section 107 avoids conversion and otherwise preserves the interests of persons expectant on the death of the patient in any property dealt with under an order of the Court, and s. 51 (2), Administration of Estates Act, 1925, protects the rights of the heir-at-law in the case of a patient under disability on the 1st January, 1926.

Testamentary Capacity.—A person under mental disability may make a valid will provided at the time of making the will he is of testamentary capacity, *i.e.* capacity to understand the nature of the document being executed, the extent of the property to be disposed of, and the claims of those to be benefited or excluded from the will (see *Banks* v. *Goodfellow*, L.R. 5, Q.B. 549). Before taking instructions from a mental patient, the solicitor should first bring the matter to the notice of the Court otherwise his costs may not be allowed. The Court may sometimes request one of the Lord Chancellor's Visitors to visit the patient and report as to whether he is of testamentary capacity. It is advisable for one of the attesting witnesses to be a doctor. Any hospital doctor asked to report as to testamentary capacity should be of consultant status.

Statutory Will for Patient.—Under Part VIII of the Mental Health Act 1959, as amended by Part III of the Administration of Justice Act 1969, the Court has jurisdiction to provide for the making of a will (generally referred to as a 'statutory will') for a patient. Such jurisdiction is not exercisable where the patient is an infant (minor) and is not exercisable unless the Court has reason to believe that the patient does not possess testamentary capacity (Mental Health Act 1959, ss. 103 (1) (*dd*) and (2), as amended).

A statutory will has to be:—

(a) signed by the person authorised by the Court in that behalf with the patient's name and his own name in the presence of two or more witnesses present at the same time and

(b) attested and subscribed by those witnesses in the presence of the authorised person and

(c) sealed with the official seal of the Court of Protection (*ibid.*, s. 103A).

Such a will, save as to certain reservations as to property and matters outside England and Wales, has generally the same effect as a normal will.

Settlements.—Under s. 103 (1) (d) of the new Act, replacing s. 171 of the Law of Property Act, 1925, the Court may direct a settlement to be made of the property of a patient on such trusts, etc., as it may deem expedient. (See *Re Freeman*, [1927] 1 Ch. 479; *Re Greene*, [1928] Ch. 528; *Re C.W.M.*, [1951] 2

All E.R. 707; *Re C.*, [1960] 1 All E.R. 393; *Re R.H.C.*, [1963] 1 All E.R. 524; *Re C.E.F.D.*, [1963] 1 W.L.R. 329; *Re D.M.L.*, [1965] 2 All E.R. 129; *Re L. (W.J.G.)*, [1966] 2 W.L.R. 233); *Re T.B.*, [1967] Ch. 247.

Appointment of New Trustees.—A power of appointing new trustees (express or statutory) vested in a patient may be exercised by the Receiver under an order under s. 103 (1) (j), with (if necessary) a consequential vesting order under s. 103 (2). Procedure is by summons.

Under s. 54, Trustee Act, 1925, the Court of Protection has concurrent jurisdiction with the Chancery Division to make an order appointing new trustees in place of a patient (and vesting) in certain instances, the principal case being where the patient has some beneficial interest in the trust property. Procedure is by summons.

It should also be remembered that where a patient being a trustee is entitled in possession to some beneficial interest in trust property, no appointment of a new trustee in his place may be made by the continuing (or retiring) trustee, under s. 36, Trustee Act, 1925, unless leave has been given by the Court of Protection (s. 36 (9), *ibid.*). Procedure is by summons though sometimes this is dispensed with.

Appeal.—Appeal from the Master, the Deputy Master or an Assistant Master lies to the Judge upon notice of appeal within 8 days. Appeal from Judge lies to Court of Appeal (s. 111 and Rules 62 and 63), in accordance with R.S.C., and thence to House of Lords.

Probate

SEE ADMINISTRATION OF ESTATES

Real Property

SEE ALSO LANDLORD AND TENANT

COSTS IN CONVEYANCING AND OTHER NON-CONTENTIOUS BUSINESS

Commencing the 1st January 1973, the Solicitors Remuneration Order 1972 revoked scale charges for both registered and unregistered conveyancing (but the Law Society's agreed scales with Building Societies and Local Authorities still remain—see *post*).

The 1972 Order provides as follows:—

A solicitor's remuneration for non-contentious business (including business under the Land Registration Act 1925) shall be such sum as may be fair and reasonable, having regard to all the circumstances of the case and in particular to

(1) the complexity of the matter or the difficulty or novelty of the questions raised;

(2) the skill, labour, specialised knowledge and responsibility involved;

(3) the time spent on the business;

(4) the number and importance of the documents prepared or perused, without regard to length;

(5) the place where and the circumstances in which the business or any part thereof is transacted;

(6) the amount or value of any money or property involved;

(7) whether any land involved is registered land within the meaning of the Land Registration Act 1925; and

(8) the importance of the matter to the client:

The 1972 Order then provides:

(a) With prejudice to the provisions of sections 69, 70 and 71 of the Solicitors' Act 1957, (which relate to taxation of costs) the client may require the solicitor to obtain a certificate from The Law Society stating whether in their opinion the sum charged is fair and reasonable, or, as the case may be, what other sum would be fair and reasonable, and in the absence of taxation the sum stated in the certificate, if less than that charged, shall be the sum payable by the client.

(b) Before the solicitor brings proceedings to recover costs on a bill for non-contentious business he must, unless the costs have been taxed, have informed the client in writing—

    (i) of his right under paragraph (a) to require the solicitor to obtain a certificate from The Law Society, and

    (ii) of the provisions of the Solicitors' Act 1957 relating to taxation of costs;

(c) The client shall not be entitled to require the solicitor to obtain a certificate from The Law Society under paragraph (a) after one month from the date on which he was given the information in paragraph (b), after the bill has been paid or after taxation has been ordered;

(d) On the taxation of any bill delivered under the Order it shall be the duty of the solicitor to satisfy the taxing officer as to the fairness and reasonableness of the sum charged;

(e) If the taxing officer allows less than one half of the sum charged, he shall bring the facts of the case to the attention of The Law Society.

NOTE.—For the practice on an application to The Law Society for a certificate under paragraph (a) above, see *Law Society's Gazette*, March 1956, which also contains a copy of the application form and questionnaire.

The 1972 Order provides for the solicitor to charge interest on unpaid bills and to take security for payment, as follows:

After the expiry of one month from the delivery of any bill for non-contentious business a solicitor may charge interest at a rate not exceeding the rate for the time being payable in judgment debts on the amount of the bill (including any disbursements) so, however, that before interest may be charged the client must have been given the information required under (b) above. If the client applies for the bill to be taxed or requires the solicitor to obtain a certificate from The Law Society interest shall be calculated by reference to the amount finally ascertained.

A solicitor may take from his client security for the payment of any remuneration including the amount of any interest to which the solicitor may become entitled.

BUILDING SOCIETIES—MORTGAGE CHARGES

The following (which is reproduced from *The Law Society's Gazette* by kind permission of The Law Society) is the revised scale of mortgage charges agreed between the Council of The Law Society and the Building Societies Association.

1. Where there are contemporaneous transactions of purchase and mortgage, the following scale of mortgagee's solicitor's charges will apply, subject, however, to the charge made (hereinafter called "Scale 1") not exceeding in any instance as appropriate scale charge under the Solicitors' Remuneration Orders and Solicitors' Remuneration (Registered Land) Orders (see note (vii) (a) and (b) below)—

Advance

	Mortgage Charge £
Under £100	4.72
£100 or over and not exceeding £200	6.00
Exceeding £200 " " " £300	7.00
" £300 " " " £400	7.50
" £400 " " " £500	7.50
" £500 " " " £600	7.86
" £600 " " " £700	8.62
" £700 " " " £800	9.36
" £800 " " " £900	10.00
" £900 " " " £1,000	10.00
" £1,000 " " " £1,100	10.00
" £1,100 " " " £1,200	10.00
" £1,200 " " " £1,300	10.50
" £1,300 " " " £1,400	11.00
" £1,400 " " " £1,500	11.50

Plus 50p per £100 above £1,500 up to £7,000.

2. Where the mortgage is not contemporaneous with a purchase, Scale 1 above is increased throughout by 50 per cent (the resultant scale being hereinafter called "Scale 2"), subject to the charge not exceeding in any instance the scale charge under the Remuneration Orders (such excess occurs only in relation to registered land—see Note (vii) (c) and (d) below).

3. Scale 1 and Scale 2 do not apply to further advances or similar transactions, the fees for which are to be fixed by further arrangement between the solicitor and the building society.

4. Where an advance is payable by instalments, there shall be payable to the solicitor an extra £1.05 for each instalment after the first (the first instalment being regarded as covered by the fee under paragraph 1 or 2 above, as the case may be), subject to a maximum of £3.15 for each transaction and to all the following conditions being fulfilled:—

(a) the property the subject of the advance is a new house in course of construction, and

(b) the mortgagor is an individual who is buying the house for his own occupation and who is under an obligation to make stage payments, and

(c) the solicitor acts as the intermediary between the builder and the building society (e.g. by informing the society that the stage has been reached at which an interim valuation report is necessary) and receives the society's instalment cheques.

5. The following additional fee is payable where a life policy is charged to a building society by way of additional security whether or not the mortgage is an endowment one:—

(a) where the dealing with the life policy is contemporaneous with the mortgage transaction, whether the charge over the life policy is effected by the principal deed charging the property or by a separate deed—£3;

(b) where the dealing with the life policy is not contemporaneous with the mortgage transaction—£5.

These fees will be payable in all cases where instructions are received by the solicitor from the building society on or after 1st November, 1970.

6. Except where provision is made herein for payment of a specific fee, an additional charge may be made, as hitherto, under Schedule II in respect of any work not covered by the scale charge under the Solicitors' Remuneration Orders or the Solicitors' Remuneration (Registered Land) Orders, as the case may be.

NOTES ON THE SCALE

(i) In determining whether Scale 1 or Scale 2 applies, it is emphasised that the test is whether the mortgage is or is not contemporaneous with the purchase of the property, and *not* whether the same solicitor acts for the mortgagor and the building society or whether they are separately represented.

(ii) It is also emphasised that these scales only apply to the charges of the solicitor acting for the building society as mortgagee and *not* to the mortgagor's solicitor's charges.

(iii) Where more than £7,000 is advanced in one sum the fee is to be fixed by arrangement between the solicitor and the building society.

(iv) The scales apply to mortgages both of freehold and of leasehold property and it is immaterial for this purpose whether the mortgage is made on the grant of a new lease or on the assignment of an existing lease. If the mortgage is contemporaneous either with the granting of a new lease or with the assignment of an existing one, Scale 1 is applicable.

(v) Where the same solicitor acts for a purchaser-mortgagor and for a building society, he is not entitled to charge more than the building societies' scale of charges in respect of the mortgage, i.e., he may not make an additional charge to the mortgagor in respect of mortgagor's solicitor's costs (see Rule 6 of the Rules applicable to Schedule 1, Part 1, to the Solicitors' Remuneration Order, 1883, as amended, and paragraph 1 (L) of the Solicitors' Remuneration (Registered Land) Order, 1925, as amended).

(vi) Scale 1 and Scale 2 are intended to be adopted as mortgagee's solicitor's charges in place of the statutory scales under the Solicitors' Remuneration Orders and the Solicitors' Remuneration (Registered Land) Orders (subject to the qualifications mentioned in paragraphs 1 and 2 above, as explained further in Note (vii) below).

(vii) Scale 1 and Scale 2 are less than the statutory scales under the Solicitors' Remuneration Orders and the Solicitors' (Registered Land) Orders, except in the circumstances mentioned below, when the solicitor must ensure

that his charges as mortgagee's solicitor do not exceed the appropriate statutory scale charge:—

As to Unregistered Land:

(a) Where a solicitor acts for a building society and for a purchaser-mortgagor—Note that Scale 1 exceeds above £6,500 the "half-scale", etc., fees allowed by Rule 6 of the Rules applicable to Schedule I, Part 1, to the Solicitors' Remuneration Order, 1883, as amended. To calculate the "quarter scale" on the excess above £5,000 mentioned in Rule 6 *see* Opinion No. 1269 in Volume 1 of *The Law Society's Digest*.

As to Registered Land:

(b) Where a solicitor acts for a building society and for a purchaser-mortgagor—Note that Scale 1 above £2,400 exceeds the "half scale", etc., fees allowed by paragraph 1 (L) of the Solicitors' Remuneration (Registered Land) Order 1925, as amended. To calculate the "quarter scale" on the excess above £5,000 mentioned in paragraph 1 (L), *see* Opinion No. 1629 in Volume 1 of *The Law Society's Digest*.

(c) Where a solicitor acts for a building society alone and there is no contemporaneous purchase—Note that Scale 2, above £5,000, exceeds the full scale fees allowed by the Solicitors' Remuneration (Registered Land) Orders.

(d) Where a solicitor acts for a building society and a mortgagor, and there is no contemporaneous purchase—Note that Scale 2, above £5,000, exceeds the full scale fees allowed by the Solicitor's Remuneration (Registered Land) Orders.

FEES FOR REPORTS ON TITLE TO BANKS

The fees previously specified are abolished and the basis for work done with effect from 1st January 1973 is the Solicitors' Remuneration Order, 1972. See Butterworth Costs Fourth Edition, noter-up M8.

SALES TO LOCAL AUTHORITIES

Costs Payable by Local Authorities to Vendors' Solicitors

(1) *Unregistered Title*

The following (which is reproduced from *The Law Society's Gazette* by kind permission of The Law Society) is the scale of costs agreed between the Council of the Law Society and the Local Authority Associations.

Where the vendor's solicitor negotiates the compensation for the acquisition of the property, whether the title be registered or unregistered without the employment of a valuer, the acquiring authority will pay (in addition to the appropriate fee for deducing title) a negotiating fee on the total compensation (calculated in accordance with Note 8 below) equal to three-quarters of the special scale where the total compensation does not exceed £5,000, or two-thirds of it in every other case.

	Purchase Price			Special Scale* £
Under	£100 ..	..	..	20.00
at	£100 ..	..	..	20.00
Over	£100 not exceeding	£150	..	20.00
,,	£150 ,,	,,	£200	20 00
,,	£200 ,,	,,	£250	20 00
,.	£250 ,,	,,	£300	20.00
,,	£300 ,,	,,	£350	20.00
Over	£350 ,,	,,	£400	20.00
,,	£400 ,,	,,	£450	20.00
,,	£450 ,,	,,	£500	20.00
,,	£500 ,,	,,	£550	25.00
,,	£550 under	£600	..	25.00
at	£600 ..	..	..	25.00
Over	£600 not exceeding	£700	..	25.00
,,	£700 ,,	,,	£1,000	30.00
,,	£1,000 ,,	,,	£1,500	35.00
,,	£1,500 ,,	,,	£2,000	40.00
,,	£2,000 ,,	,,	£2,500	45.00
,,	£2,500 ,,	,,	£3,000	50.00
,,	£3,000 ,,	,,	£3,500	54.00
,,	£3,500 ,,	,,	£4,000	58.00
,,	£4,000 ,,	,,	£5,000	64.00
,,	£5,000 ,,	,,	£6,000	70.00
,,	£6,000 ,,	,,	£10,000	75.00
Over	£10,000 not exceeding	£15,000	..	100.00
,,	£15,000 ,,	,,	£20,000	125.00
,,	£20,000 ,,	,,	£30,000	150.00
,,	£30,000 ,,	,,	£40,000	180.00
,,	£40,000 ,,	,,	£50,000	215.00
,,	£50,000 ,,	,.	£60,000	250.00
,,	£60,000 ,,	,,	£70,000	285.00
,,	£70,000 ,,	,,	£80,000	320.00
,,	£80,000 ,,	,,	£90,000	355.00
,,	£90,000 ,,	,,	£100,000	390.00
,,	£100,000 ,,	,,	£125,000	400.00
,,	£125,000 ,,	,,	£150,000	450.00
,,	£150,000 ,,	,,	£175,000	500.00
,,	£175,000 ,,	,,	£200,000	550.00
,,	£200,000 without ceiling—by negotiation but not less than £550.			

(2) *Registered title*

After 1st January 1973 the Solicitors Remuneration Order 1972 will apply.

NOTES ON THE SCALE

1. The special scale is to apply to all sales of property with unregistered title, whether compulsory or by agreement, which are completed on or after January 1st, 1972, provided that the sale is one to which are applicable the provisions of the Lands Clauses Consolidation Act 1945, the Compulsory Purchase Act 1965, or any other public or private Act which provides that the vendor's solicitor's charges are payable wholly or in part by the purchaser. The revised Notes are intended to apply as from the same date and not to be retrospective (where they differ from the notes previously published), except in cases where questions have been left in abeyance pending further discussion between The Law Society and the Local Authority Associations.

2. The special scale is limited to the local authority's liability for the vendor's solicitor's costs; it does not preclude the vendor's solicitor from making a Schedule II charge against his own client in respect of any work for which the local authority is not legally liable.

3. Under Section 82 of the Lands Clauses Consolidation Act 1845 or section 23 of the Compulsory Purchase Act 1965, coupled with Rule 11 of the Rules applicable to Schedule I, Part I, to the Solicitor's Remuneration Order 1883 (as amended), the purchasing authority's legal liability extends only to the vendor's solicitor's Schedule II charges for work from the preparation of the abstract of title onwards (see *Re Hampstead Junction Rail Co., ex parte Buck* (1883), 1 H. and M. 519); in the case of those local authorities who have in the past paid a small fee for the vendor's solicitor's preliminary work before the abstract, that work, unless otherwise agreed, is intended also to be covered by the scale.

Where instructions are accepted on or after 1st January 1973 instead of the previous basis under the Registered Land Sale the basis under the 1972 Remuneration Order will apply.

4. In the absence of any special agreement to the contrary, the local authority will pay to the vendor's solicitor, in addition to the special scale (except where (b) below applies):—

(a) Where a vendor's mortgage is redeemed or released—

(i) in respect of mortgagee's solicitor's costs—

(A) where it is necessary for the mortgagee to join in a conveyance (e.g., because only part of the property is being purchased)—the sum of £7.00.

(B) In all other cases—the sum of £4.00.

(ii) in respect of vendor's solicitor's costs, whether the mortgagee joins in the conveyance or whether there is a separate reconveyance or receipt—the sum of £4.00. Provided that, where the same solicitor acts for the vendor and the vendor's mortgagee the sum of £5.00 will be paid when (i) (A) above instead of £7.00, and the sum of £3.00 under (i)(B) and (ii) above instead of £4.00.

(b) where the local authority is satisfied that in order to deduce title the vendor's solicitor is obliged to pay a fee to some other solicitor for an abstract of title—either two-thirds of the scale fee plus the costs of such abstract or the scale fee without any addition, whichever is the greater.

(c) Where the local authority requires some step to be taken to perfect title (e.g. the appointment of new trustees or the obtaining of a grant of representation), which (i) time would render unnecessary and which would be unlikely to be taken but for the local authority's purchase, and (ii) will not be of benefit to the vendor in respect of his other property—the Schedule II costs and disbursements incurred in taking such step including those of any third party.

(d) Where the local authority requires the vendor to obtain the consent of some third party to the sale or to ascertain that such consent is not necessary—the Schedule II costs and disbursements of the vendor's solicitor and of the third party.

(e) Reasonable fees paid by the vendor's solicitor to third parties for the production of documents (including documents in the possession of the vendor's mortgagee or trustee).

(f) Where the vendor's solicitor peruses a draft on behalf of several parties (other than mortgagees) having distinct interests, joining in the conveyance, and proper to be separately represented—the sum of £3 for each such party after the first.

(g) Where a party, other than the vendor's mortgagee, joins in a conveyance and is represented by a separate solicitor—the Schedule II charges of such separate solicitor.

(h) An amount to be arrived at by agreement between the vendor's solicitor and the local authority for the extra work involved in respect of any rent-charges or overriding rent-charges subject to which the property is sold.

5. In the absence of any special agreement to the contrary, the local authority will not make any payment in respect of:—

(a) Costs incurred by the vendor in connection with a dispute as to title, e.g. an adverse claim to the property.

(b) Any statutory declaration reasonably required to constitute the vendor's title.

(c) Additional costs incurred by one of joint vendors availing himself of his right of separate representation.

(d) Any disbursements in respect of letters, messengers, telephone, postages or other similar petty disbursements.

6. Where the local authority is acquiring more than one property from the same vendor at the same time:—

(a) It will pay separate scale fees (based on the consideration apportioned to each property):—

(i) If there are substantially separate titles, whether the properties are included in one or more conveyances to the local authority, or

(ii) If there is one title, but the local authority requires more than one conveyance.

(b) If there is a common title and only one conveyance is taken, only one special scale fee will be paid, even if the properties are not contiguous.

7. Where title is deduced and a conveyance taken, but there is no monetary or other consideration, the local authority will pay to the vendor's solicitor the sum of £20.00.

8. Where, in addition to the purchase price, a payment is made for injurious affection, severance or disturbance, or under Part II of the Second Schedule to the Housing Act, 1957, or any Act or statutory provision amending or replacing the same, the scale fee is to be calculated on the total of the purchase price and such payments, provided that such payments are made to the vendor by the local authority at the time of completion of the purchase of the property. The cost of accommodation works is not to be included.

9. Where the property is dealt with by a dedication agreement the following payments (in addition to the negotiating fee, if applicable) will be made:—

(a) Where title is shown and there is a money payment—the special scale fee.

(b) Where title is shown and there is no money payment—the sum of £20.00.

(c) Where no title is shown and whether or not there is a money payment—the sum of £10.00.

(d) Where the local authority requires only the conveyance to the vendor or a copy thereof to be produced—the sum of £12.00.

(e) Where the local authority requires a report on title in lieu of deducing title—the fee as under (a) or (b) above, as appropriate.

(f) Where any of the circumstances mentioned in Notes 4, 5, 6, 8, 10 and 11 apply in relation to a dedication agreement instead of a conveyance—the same sums as are provided in such Notes, reference therein to fees under the special scale to be construed as meaning the fees provided by this Note.

10. Where the title to the property is in part unregistered and in part registered, the local authority will pay the

special scale fee in respect of the consideration for the unregistered land and the scale fee under the Solicitor's Remuneration (Registered Land) Orders in respect of the consideration for the registered land calculated on the value of each part as apportioned for the purpose of assessing Land Registry fees.

11. Where the purchase is not completed, the local authority will pay the vendor's solicitor's costs under Schedule II (but not exceeding the amount of the scale fee) in the following circumstances only and provided that the vendor or his solicitor has previously agreed with the local authority that this Note shall apply:—

(a) Where the local authority has in the first instance approached the vendor with a view to the sale of the property by agreement, and

(b) the local authority decides not to proceed with the purchase because:—

　　(i) it no longer wishes to acquire the property, or

　　(ii) it is not prepared to pay the price assessed by the District Valuer.

Provided that no such payment of vendor's solicitor's costs will be made where:—

(a) the vendor has indicated an intention to sell by a public announcement, or

(b) the local authority breaks off negotiations through a failure to agree terms.

12. The scale is not applicable to:—

(a) transactions carried out in accordance with the provisions of s. 30 of the Town and Country Planning Act 1968 (general vesting declaration procedure) or to transactions where a similar expedited procedure has been used under any other statute.

(b) exchanges of land.

In such cases the charges must be made under Schedule II.

SALES TO GOVERNMENT DEPARTMENTS

NOTE. REGISTERED LAND

As from the 1st January 1973 the basis for work done is the Solicitor's Remuneration Order 1972. See Butterworths Costs Fourth Edition.

The Local Authorities Scale has been agreed by the Treasury Solicitor to apply to the payment of vendor's solicitor's charges on acquisitions of property with unregistered title and to property with registered title in respect of negotiating fees to the extent as hereinafter mentioned in respect of the following Government Departments where transactions are completed on or after January 1st, 1972:—

　(1) Department of the Environment;
　(2) Department of Trade and Industry;
　(3) Home Office;

(4) Welsh Office (limited to sales for motorways and trunk road purposes).

The local Authorities Scale is expressly subject to the following points:—

(1) the negotiating fee (see para. 5) will not be payable where the vendor requires the Government Department to purchase land in excess of that sought to be acquired.

(2) The scale will not apply to transactions where the "shortened procedure" is used for the acquisition of land for motorways or trunk roads.

It should be understood that the scale has been adopted by both the Government Departments and the Law Society on trial only and may be determined at any time.

TABLE

REGISTERED LAND

FEES PAYABLE UNDER SCALE No. 1 (first Registration)

Note: *When a charge by the applicant for first registration is delivered either with the application or before the application is completed no fee is payable on the charge.*

Value not exceeding £	Fee £ p	Value £	Fee £ p	Value £	Fee £ p	Value £	Fee £ p
500	0.80	13,000	18.15	25,500	33.90	38,000	49.65
1,000	1.60	13,500	18.80	26,000	34.55	38,500	50.30
1,500	2.40	14,000	19.40	26,500	35.15	39,000	50.90
2,000	3.20	14,500	20.05	27,000	35.80	39,500	51.55
2,500	4.05	15,000	20.70	27,500	36.45	40,000	52.20
3,000	4.85	15,500	21.30	28,000	37.05	40,500	52.80
3,500	5.65	16,000	21.95	28,500	37.70	41,000	53.45
4,000	6.45	16,500	22.55	29,000	38.30	41,500	54.05
4,500	7.25	17,000	23.20	29,500	38.95	42,000	54.70
5,000	8.10	17,500	23.85	30,000	39.60	42,500	55.35
5,500	8.70	18,000	24.45	30,500	40.20	43,000	55.95
6,000	9.35	18,500	25.10	31,000	40.85	43,500	56.60
6,500	9.95	19,000	25.70	31,500	41.45	44,000	57.20
7,000	10.60	19,500	26.35	32,000	42.10	44,500	57.85
7,500	11.25	20,000	27.00	32,500	42.75	45,000	58.50
8,000	11.85	20,500	27.60	33,000	43.35	45,500	59.10
8,500	12.50	21,000	28.25	33,500	44.00	46,000	59.25
9,000	13.10	21,500	28.85	34,000	44.60	46,500	60.35
9,500	13.75	22,000	29.50	34,500	45.25	47,000	61.00
10,000	14.40	22,500	30.15	35,000	45.90	47,500	61.68
10,500	15.00	23,000	30.75	35,500	46.50	48,000	62.25
11,000	15.65	23,500	31.40	36,000	47.15	48,500	62.90
11,500	16.25	24,000	32.00	36,500	47.75	49,000	63.50
12,000	16.90	24,500	32.65	37,000	48.40	49,500	64.15
12,500	17.55	25,000	33.30	37,500	49.05	50,000	64.80

Note: Above £50,000, the fee calculated under scale 1 of the 1970 Fee Order should be reduced by 10% until the maximum fee of £217.80 is reached.

V.A.T. and Land Registry Fees—Subject only to the minor exceptions detailed below, all services provided by H.M. Land Registry for which fees are payable under the Land Registration Fee Order 1970, the Land Charges Fees Order 1974 and the Agricultural Credits Fees Order 1970 have been deemed to fall wholly outside the scope of Value Added Tax.

The exceptions referred to relate to the following services provided under section 9 of the Agricultural Credits Act 1928:—

(1) Personal search in the register or of a memorandum filed thereunder;

(2) Official search of the register;

(3) Expedition of an official search;

(4) Telegraphing or telephoning the result of an official search;

(5) Certified copy of any field memorandum.

TABLE II
REGISTERED LAND
FEES PAYABLE UNDER SCALE No. 2

Annual rent not exceeding £	Fee £ p	Annual rent £	Fee £ p	Annual rent £	Fee £ p	Annual rent £	Fee £ p
50	0.90	300	3.15	550	5.40	800	7.65
100	1.35	350	3.60	600	5.85	850	8.10
150	1.80	400	4.05	650	6.30	900	8.55
200	2.25	450	4.50	700	6.75	950	9.00
250	2.70	500	4.95	750	7.20	1000	9.45

Note: (a) Above £1,000, fees calculated under Scale 2 of the 1970 Fee Order will be reduced by 10%.

(b) Any capital money payment is chargeable in addition, with a fee under Scale No. 1 (p. 300, *ante*) provided that a combined maximum fee of £217.80 on the rent and money payment is not exceeded.

(c) Scale No. 2 applies to applications for first registration on the grant of a lease, other than a mining lease, and on the grant of freehold land in consideration of a rent.

TABLE III
REGISTERED LAND
FEES PAYABLE UNDER SCALE 4 (dealings)

Value not exceeding £	Fee £ p	Value £	Fee £ p	Value £	Fee £ p	Value £	Fee £ p
500	1.15	13,000	27.50	25,500	52.25	38,000	77.00
1,000	2.30	13,500	28.50	26,000	53.25	38,500	78.00
1,500	3.50	14,000	29.50	26,500	54.25	39,000	79.00
2,000	4.65	14,500	30.50	27,000	55.25	39,500	80.00
2,500	5.85	15,000	31.50	27,500	56.25	40,000	81.00
3,000	7.00	15,500	32.45	28,000	57.20	40,500	81.95
3,500	8.15	16,000	33.45	28,500	58.20	41,000	82.95
4,000	9.35	16,500	34.45	29,000	59.20	41,500	83.95
4,500	10.50	17,000	35.45	29,500	60.20	42,000	84.95
5,000	11.70	17,500	36.45	30,000	61.20	42,500	85.95
5,500	12.65	18,000	37.40	30,500	62.15	43,000	86.90
6,000	13.65	18,500	38.40	31,000	63.15	43,500	87.90
6,500	14.65	19,000	39.40	31,500	64.15	44,000	88.90
7,000	15.65	19,500	40.40	32,000	65.15	44,500	89.90
7,500	16.65	20,000	41.40	32,500	66.15	45,000	90.90
8,000	17.60	20,500	42.35	33,000	67.10	45,500	91.85
8,500	18.60	21,000	43.35	33,500	68.10	46,000	92.85
9,000	19.60	21,500	44.35	34,000	69.10	46,500	93.85
9,500	20.60	22,000	45.35	34,500	70.10	47,000	94.85
10,000	21.60	22,500	46.35	35,000	71.10	47,500	95.85
10,500	22.55	23,000	47.30	35,500	72.05	48,000	96.80
11,000	23.55	23,500	48.30	36,000	73.05	48,500	97.80
11,500	24.55	24,000	49.30	36,500	74.05	49,000	98.80
12,000	25.55	24,500	50.30	37,000	75.05	49,500	99.80
12,500	26.55	25,000	51.30	37,500	76.05	50,000	100.80

Note: Above £50,000, the fee calculated under scale 4 of the 1970 Fee Order should be reduced by 10% until the maximum fee of £379.80 is reached.

ENROLMENT OF DEEDS

Any document *may* be enrolled. The necessity for enrolling disentailing deeds executed after 1925 was abolished by the Law of Property Act, 1925, s. 133, but any document *may* still be enrolled other than a deed poll evidencing change of name by an alien. The procedure to be followed on the enrolment of a deed poll evidencing the change of name of a British subject is prescribed by the Enrolment of Deeds (Change of Name) Regulations, 1949, S.I. 1949 No. 316/L.3, and Enrolment of Deeds (Change of Name) (Amendment) Regulations, 1951, S.I. 1951 No. 377/L.1.

Enrolment is effected by lodging the document with the grantor's signature duly attested and duly stamped, at the Filing Department (Room 81), at the Central Office, within 6 months from the date of execution. The enrolled copy may be typewritten. The number of folios should be marked on the back of the document together with the cost of making a copy of any plan appearing on the document, which cost is ascertainable at the office. A receipt showing the total amount payable for enrolling is issued for the document. The *fees* are in the case of a deed enrolled under statute, £1; or if out of date upon affidavit, £1.50; and in the case of any other deed, £2; and in addition for each folio of 72 words, 5p. For making an office copy, the fee is 3½p per folio, or for examining a copy and marking it as an office copy, 1p per folio. For searches the fee is 12½p per folio. Fees for making and examining photographic copies of enrolled deeds are prescribed by the Enrolment of Deeds (Fees) (Amendment) Regulations 1951, S.I. 1951 No. 1937/L.9.

REGISTRATION AT THE YORKSHIRE DEEDS REGISTRIES

(1) The Deeds Registries for all three Ridings of the former County of Yorkshire have now closed and searches are no longer possible. The records have been transferred to the District Archivists and these may still be inspected on application. Custody of the records is the responsibility of the County Councils concerned, in accordance with the provisions of section 18 of the Law of Property Act 1969.

(2) All applications for the registration, re-registration, modification or cancellation of land charges must now be made to the land charges department of H.M. Land Registry. Such applications should be addressed as follows: The Superintendent, Land Charges Department, Burrington Way, Plymouth, Devon, PL5 3LP.

REGISTRATION OF TITLE

See Halsbury's Laws of England, 3rd Edn., vol. 23, pp. 141 et seq., Halsbury's Statutes (3rd Edn.), vol. 27, pp. 787 et seq., and Encyclopædia of Forms and Precedents (3rd. Edn.), Vol. 13, pp. 235 et seq. For contentious matters, see the Encyclopædia of Court Forms (2nd Edn.), Vol. 23, pp. 403 et seq.

Registration of Title is compulsory on sale throughout Greater London and the counties of Berkshire, Cleveland, Greater Manchester, Kent, Merseyside, South Glamorgan, South Yorkshire, Surrey, Tyne and Wear, West Glamorgan, West Midlands, West Yorkshire and elsewhere in the whole of 68 districts, all of which together contain about 65 per cent of the population of England and Wales. These districts are too numerous and the description of them too complex to be set out here. However, Explanatory Leaflet No. 9 (which may be obtained free of charge on request from any of the district land registries of H.M. Land Registry: see p. 305, *post*) contains a list in alphabetical order of all the compulsory areas and indicates the district land registry currently serving each of them.

Within these areas, failure to register a conveyance on sale of freeholds, or a grant, or assignment on sale of lease-holds having 40 or more years to run, will (unless the Registrar orders otherwise) result in such conveyance, grant or assignment becoming void as regards the legal estate after two months. Elsewhere in England and Wales voluntary applications for registration have been suspended under the Land Registration Act, 1966, the principal exception being developing building estates. For details, see Practice Leaflet for Solicitors No. 12, which may be obtained free of charge from any of the offices of the Registry set out on p. 305, *post*. A lease originally granted for 21 years or less is incapable of registration. After registration, dealing with the land may only be effected in accordance with the Land Registration Acts 1925 to 1971, and the Land Registration Rules of 1925 and 1967. Fees are payable under the Land Registration Fee Order 1970 (as amended by the Land Registration Fee Orders 1971, 1973 and 1975), in cash or by cheque, money order, or postal order, etc., payable to "H.M. Land Registry". Solicitor's charges are governed by the Solicitors' Remuneration Order 1972.

First Registration

Prior to registration:—

(a) An interested person may be entitled to lodge a caution so as to enable him to oppose first registration (*see* s. 53 of the Act of 1925 and rr. 64–70).

(b) A person entitled to apply for first registration may reserve priority for his application (r. 71).

Applications for first registration (*see* rr. 19–21), are made by posting to the proper office of H.M. Land Registry, at the appropriate address given below *sub nom.* "Lodgment of Applications":—

(i) A written application in the appropriate one of the undermentioned forms:—

Freehold	Leasehold	Rentcharge	Application
1A	2A	1K	By owner in person.
1B	2F	1F	By solicitor for purchaser or grantee (absolute title).
—	2B	—	The like (good leasehold title).
1C	2C	1G	By solicitor—where no recent purchase.
1C (Co.)	2C (Co.)	1G (Co.)	By solicitor for corporation—where no recent purchase.
1E	2F (Co.)	1H	By solicitor for corporate purchaser, etc. (absolute title).
—	2E	—	The like (good leasehold title).
—	3A	—	By original lessee in person (good leasehold title).
—	3B	—	By solicitor for original lessee (good leasehold title).
—	3E	—	By solicitor for original corporate lessee (good leasehold title).
—	3F	—	By solicitor for original lessee (absolute title).
—	3F (Co.)	—	By solicitor for original corporate lessee (absolute title).

(ii) All original deeds and documents of title in the applicant's possession or control, including counsel's opinions, abstracts, contracts for sale, searches, and requisitions and replies.

(iii) A certified copy of the deed inducing registration.

(iv) Sufficient particulars, by plan or otherwise, to enable the land to be identified on the Ordnance Map or Land Registry General Map.

(v) A list of documents in triplicate.

(vi) The appropriate fee.

The title is then examined by the Registrar, who may approve a good holding title in spite of its being open to objection. After entry on the register of existing incumbrances, adverse easements and the like (rr. 40, 41), and after disposal of any objection, the registration will be completed as of the date of original application, and the land certificate (or charge certificate) will be delivered to the applicant (or his chargee). Normally, absolute title is granted in respect of freeholds (*i.e.* the registered proprietor has vested in him the fee simple absolute in possession together with all appurtenant rights, etc., whether or not they are mentioned, but subject to matters appearing on the register and to "overriding interests" as described in s. 70 of the 1925 Act), and either absolute leasehold title or good leasehold title is granted in respect of leaseholds. In the case of a good leasehold title the proprietor has a term of years absolute in possession, subject similarly, but without guarantee as to the lessor's title to grant the lease.

DEALINGS WITH REGISTERED LAND

Provided he is not restrained by restriction, caution or inhibition (*see* ss. 54–58 of the 1925 Act), the registered proprietor may transfer the whole or part of his land with or without the minerals, either for, or without consideration, grant leases, and grant or reserve rentcharges, easements and rights (ss. 18 and 21), impose, release or vary restrictive covenants (s. 40), and enter into contracts (s. 107). He may create a settlement or trust for sale (*see* ss. 86–95). Besides creating a lien on his certificate (s. 66), he may charge his land (s. 25) and the chargee will possess all the powers of a legal mortgagee (s. 34) and may transfer (r. 153) or subcharge (r. 163) his security. Until completed by registra-

tion, all dispositions merely take effect in equity.

Apart from mortgages and leases (which, broadly speaking, may be in any form), dealings with registered land may only be effected by use of the official forms set out in the Schedule to the 1925 Rules, where these are applicable or adaptable, subject to such alterations or additions as the Registrar may allow (r. 74). Prints of many of the commoner forms (none of which is obtainable at the Registry) may be purchased at H.M. Stationery Office or through a law stationer. The Registrar may refuse to accept improper forms (r. 78) but in cases of difficulty draft documents (which should be accompanied by a carbon copy and fee of £1.50 if a plan is included) may be submitted for approval as to form (£1.50 if a plan is included). In the Encyclopædia of Forms and Precedents, 4th Edn., vol. 17, pp. 111 *et seq.*, will be found the precedents necessary for carrying out all the more usual and some less common transactions.

Normally, the land certificate must be produced on a dealing with the land, (*see* s. 64). On registration of a charge the land certificate is retained in the Registry and the chargee is given a charge certificate (s. 65); this must be produced on any dealing with the charge. The principal exceptions to the requirement as to production concern registration of a caution and notice of deposit of a certificate.

Some of the Land Registration Rules, 1925, that may be met with in practice are:—

Subject Matter	*Rules relating thereto*
Bankruptcy and liquidation	173–185.
Charges, subcharges and disposition thereof	139–167, 92, 93, 114.
Charities	60–62 (first regn.) 122–124, 128–130, 132, 260 (dealings).
Corporations	80, 121, 123, 145, 185, 259.
Death, transmission on, etc. ..	168–172.
Exchange	136, 137.
Incorporeal hereditaments, mines, etc. ..	50–55 (first regn.).
Leaseholds, registration of ..	44–47.
Leaseholds, transfer of	115–117, 79, 91.
Leases, determination of	200–203, 205–209.
Lien by deposit of certificate ..	239–246.
Rentcharges	50, 52, 55 (first regn.), 107–109, 113 (dealings).

Subject Matter				Rules relating thereto
Restrictions ..	..	..	..	.. 39, 213, 214, 235–237.
Settled Land..	..	..	..	.. 30, 50–59 (first regn.), 99–106, 133, 144, 156, 170, 171 (dealings).
Transfers generally ..	..	..		.. 98, 110–115, 135, 136, 167, 79.
Trustees for sale	..	..		.. 213, 214, 134, 172.

For class F land charges which affect registered land, see the Land Registration (Matrimonial Homes) Rules 1967; for the proof of powers of attorney, see the Land Registration (Powers of Attorney) Rules, 1971; for souvenir land, see the Land Registration (Souvenir Land) Rules 1972; for entries relating to liability for capital transfer tax, see the Land Registration (Capital Transfer Tax) Rules 1975.

LODGMENT OF APPLICATIONS

All applications should be lodged by post. It is a convenience if printed application form A.4 is used for the lodgment of all dealings with the whole of the land in one or more titles and printed form A.5 for all dealings with part of the land in a title.

It is essential that applications of all kinds (whether for first registration, dealings with registered land, office copies or official searches) should be sent to the proper office of the Registry, according to the location of the land, because they are not otherwise deemed to have been effectively delivered. (See the Land Registration (District Registries) Order 1974.) The addresses to which applications should be sent are set out below. In view of the details involved, as well as the changes that occur from time to time, it is not practicable to set out particulars of the areas allocated to each District Registry.

However, if a request is made to any of the addresses below, the latest edition of Explanatory Leaflet No. 9 containing full particulars of these matters will be supplied free of charge.

The addresses are:—

The Chief Land Registrar, The Tunbridge Wells District Land Registry, Tunbridge Wells, Kent, TN2 5AQ.

The Chief Land Registrar, The Lytham District Land Registry, Lytham St. Annes, Lancs., FY8 5AB.

The Chief Land Registrar, The Nottingham District Land Registry, Chalfont Drive, Nottingham, NG8, 3RN.

The Chief Land Registrar, The Harrow District Land Registry, Lyon House, Lyon Road, Harrow, Middx., HA1 2EU.

The Chief Land Registrar, The Gloucester District Land Registry, Bruton Way, Gloucester, GL1 1DQ.

The Chief Land Registrar, The Stevenage District Land Registry, Brickdale House, Danestrete, Stevanage, Herts, SG1 1XG.

The Chief Land Registrar, The Durham District Land Registry, Aykley Heads,Durham, DH1 5TR.

The Chief Land Registrar, The Croydon District Land Registry, Sunley House, Bedford Park, Croydon, CR9 3LE.

The Chief Land Registrar, The Plymouth District Land Registry, Railway Offices, North Road, Plymouth, Devon, PL4 6AD.

The Chief Land Registrar, The Swansea District Land Registry, 37 The Kingsway, Swansea, West Glamorgan, SA1 5LF.

PRACTICE NOTE

Reference should be made to the Acts of 1925 to 1971 (*see* Halsbury's Statutes of England (3rd Edn.), Vol. 27, pp. 778 *et seq.*) and to the rules made thereunder for details of procedure in a particular case, but the following points deserve attention because, not only do they arise frequently in practice, but also failure to observe any one of them would involve the raising of requisitions by the Registrar:—

(1) Where a transfer imposes restrictive covenants a certified copy thereof must be lodged (r. 135).

(2) A certified copy is required of any mortgage or charge lodged for registration (r. 92 or r. 139).

(3) Certification should be by a solicitor in the firm name.

(4) A transfer to joint proprietors should be accompanied by a certificate, signed, by the applicant's solicitor, stating whether or not the survivor can give a valid receipt for capital moneys.

(5) When a limited company is to be registered as proprietor of land or a charge, certified copies of its memorandum and articles should be lodged. Normally, the secretary or solicitor must certify that any charge to be registered does not contravene the provisions thereof.

(6) As to merger of a lease, see Practice Leaflet for Solicitors No. 1.

(7) If conversion under s. 77 (3) (b) of the Act is desired, a certificate that the applicant is in actual occupation or in receipt of rents and profits, should be lodged.

(8) A proprietor's registered address is his address for service (r. 315), may be altered without fee, and should be kept up to date.

(9) Delays will be avoided if all business is done by post. It is essential to quote all title numbers correctly.

(10) The Registry does not stamp documents with Inland Revenue duty nor does it sell any forms.

SEARCHES

Anyone may personally inspect, or, by using printed form 96, bespeak an official search of the Public Index Map in order to learn whether land is registered (rr. 12 and 286). Registers of title may be inspected under the written authority of the proprietor (r. 287). A person having such authority may obtain office copies of the register and filed plan and of all documents referred to on the register on payment of the prescribed fees. For details, see Practice Leaflet for Solicitors, No. 13.* Official searches of the register may be bespoken free of charge in Form 94A* (dealing with whole of title) or 94B* (dealing with part of title), under the Land Registration (Official Searches) Rules 1969, whereby a prospective purchaser, chargee or lessee is enabled to complete with the assurance that no entry adverse to his title will be made if his disposition is lodged for registration within 15 working days. The same Rules provide for an extension of the priority period, and for searches by teleprinter and other matters. For details, see Practice Leaflet for Solicitors, No. 2.*

CAUTIONS AGAINST DEALINGS

An interested third party may lodge a caution in Form 63* supported by a declaration in Form 14* (fee £1) entitling him to notice of proposed dealings with power to object thereto. This procedure is hostile and should not be resorted to lightly as the cautioner may become liable in damages (see ss. 54–56 and rr. 215–222).

For notices and cautions under the Matrimonial Homes Act 1967, see Practice Leaflet for Solicitors No. 10.*

LOST CERTIFICATES

These may be replaced under r. 271 and special facilities exist for the replacement of certificates destroyed by enemy action. See Practice Leaflet for Solicitors No. 3* for details.

*Obtainable from H.M. Stationery Office.

SEARCHES AND ENQUIRIES

Having regard to the increased importance of registration under the present law of property and the number of land charges which include puisne mortgages, equitable charges, death duties, restrictive covenants, equitable easements, etc., official searches under the Land Charges Act, 1925, are advisable in every transaction. The Land Charges Rules 1974 (S.I. 1974 No. 1286) apply.

Conclusive effect of search.—If there is any ambiguity or doubt in the description of the land in the application for search, then the certificate of search will not be conclusive: *Du Sautoy* v. *Symes*, [1967] 1 All E.R. 25. Errors relating to the name of the person against whom an estate contract was registered were considered in *Oak Co-operative Building Society* v. *Blackburn*, [1968] 2 All E.R. 117, C.A.

SEARCHES.—The usual searches made by a purchaser or mortgagee are now:—

1.—*For pending actions, annuities, writs and orders affecting land, deeds of arrangement affecting land, and land charges of the various classes mentioned in the Land Charges Act, 1925,* s. 10. The registers (including an alphabetical index) are kept at the Land Charges Dept., Burrington Way, Plymouth PL5 3LP and either may be searched personally (Fee 80p per name), or an official certificate of search may be obtained on application on the prescribed form (Fee 50p per name). Searches may also be made by teleprinter (70p), telephone (80p) and visual display (35p). The Land Charges Fees Order 1975 (S.I. 1975 No. 1315) applies.

In favour of a purchaser, such certificate is conclusive (*see* s. 17). By notice dated May 17, 1944, the Chief Land Registrar reminded solicitors of the protection given by s. 4 (2) of the Law of Property (Amendment) Act, 1926 as varied by r. 1 (2) of the Land Charges Rules 1940 where an official certificate of search is granted within 14 days before completion of a purchase, and recommended that in all cases application for a certificate be made not less than 7 days before the date fixed for completion. The 14 days are working days and non-working days are not included in reckoning the 14 days. (*Note.* The Law of Property Act, 1969 provides that charges created by companies on unregistered land (other than floating charges) must, with certain exceptions, be registered in this register).

2.—*For Bankruptcies.* Petitions and Receiving Orders are now registrable in the registers of pending actions and writs and orders affecting land. A separate search for Bankruptcies in the records of the Bankruptcy Courts is, therefore, seldom necessary.

N.B.—In the case of registered land the above searches are not necessary since these matters would properly appear on the Register, and if they are not noted or otherwise referred to on the Register, a purchaser takes free from them and notice of such land charges does not affect him in any way; *Hodges* v. *Jones*, [1935] Ch. 657 at pp. 670, 671; nor will the fact that unregistered property has been conveyed to a purchaser subject to a land charge which is not registered in the Land Charges Register: *Hollington Bros., Ltd.* v. *Rhodes*, [1951] 2 All E.R. 578.

3.—*For Local Land Charges.* These include private street and improvements expenses, building lines, housing restrictions, compulsory purchase orders, declaratory orders and lists of buildings of special architectural and historic interset under the Town and Country Planning Acts, 1944, 1947, and the consolidating Act of 1962 (from April 1, 1963) and the Town and Country Planning Act, 1968, compulsory purchase orders and designation orders under the New Towns Act, 1946, orders under the Civil Aviation Act, 1949 (and see the Civil Aviation Act, 1968, ss. 21, 22), works schemes under the Coast Protection Act, 1949, agreements for the use of land for cattle-grids byepasses under the Highways Act, 1959, ss. 87–97, conditions imposed by local authorities on dwellings sold by them or applied to cottages by regulations under the Hill Farming and Livestock Rearing Acts, 1946 to 1956, notices under s. 112 of the Town and Country Planning Act, 1962, recoverable expenses under the Clean Air Act, 1956 (see also the Clean Air Act, 1968), matters required to be registered under the Highways Act, 1959, s. 197, and wayleave orders, etc. made registrable under the Land Powers (Defence) Act, 1958. Compulsory rights orders and compulsory purchase orders under the Opencast Coal Act, 1959; notices under the Rights of Light Act, 1959, and drainage schemes under the Land Drainage Act, 1961. The registers are kept by Local Authorities under s. 15 of the Land Charges Act, 1925. Searches should be made at the offices of each Local Authority having jurisdiction over the area in which the land is situate, *i.e.* the County Council and the Borough or District Council. Official Certificates of search can be obtained. *See, generally,* the Local Land Charges Rules, 1966, S.I. 1966 No. 579, as amended by S.I. 1968 No. 1212, and the Register of Local Land Charges (Right of Light), etc., Rules, 1959, S.I. 1959 No. 1733.

N.B.—In the case of registered land, the searches in para. 3 are necessary since these will not appear on the Register.

4. For dealings with Registered Land: the searches should be made in the appropriate District Registry on the official form. There is no fee (Note: the Yorkshire Deeds Registries have closed and the records have been transferred to the District Archivists).

5.—*Court Rolls.*—In cases where land formerly of copyhold tenure is being dealt with, the Court Rolls should be searched when the title prior to 1926 is being investigated. The usual method is by enquiring of the Steward having the custody thereof and obtaining a letter from him as to the result of the search. The fee is generally in the discretion of the Steward, and is regulated by the time occupied in the actual search.

6.—*For disentailing deeds.*—When the title depends on an estate tail—prior to 1926—at the Enrolment Department—Room 81—of the Central Office.

N.B.—The title before 1926 will now seldom have to be investigated since the 15 years' title which under the Law of Property Act, 1969 must be shown on an open contract will only go back to 1954.

7.—*Company's file*, at The Companies Registration Offices, particularly the register of mortgages, when an incorporated company is the vendor. (Search fee, 5p). Note: From April 1976 to June 1977 the Companies Registration offices will be transferred in stages from London to Crown Way, Maindy, Cardiff CS4 3UR.

ENQUIRIES.—The following enquiries should be made generally:—

1.—*Of each tenant* as to his landlord, rental and terms of tenancy and of the *local authority* or rent officer whether any rent has been registered. The authorities concerned are county councils and borough councils.

When *life and reversionary* interests are being dealt with, then:—

2.—Of *all the trustees* as to what notice of incumbrances or dealings have been received.

3.—The *trust documents* and securities should also be inspected, and when the trust funds comprise stocks or shares enquiry should be made of the companies for distrigases and stop orders. One trustee may sign a valid authority to a company to answer an enquiry.

4.—When a *life or endowment policy* is being dealt with enquiry should be made of the Assurance Company as to what notices of incumbrances, affecting the policy, have been received.

As to searches generally and Precedents *see* Encyclopædia of Forms, 4th edition, Vol. 18, pp. 253 *et seq.* and Service.

Reference should also be made to forms Con. 29A-E which have been agreed between the Law Society and Local Authority Associations and which set out lists of enquiries which can be addressed to Local Authorities in addition to the normal searches of the registers maintained by them. The forms list a wealth of queries which can be addressed to Local Authorities as to Town and Country Planning provisions, etc. These searches should be made in the case of registered land as well as unregistered land. Printed copies of the forms are readily available at any Law Stationers. Where a house is in multiple occupation, the local authority should be asked whether a control order under the Housing Act, 1964, is in force.

Registered Land

SEE REAL PROPERTY

Registration of Births, Marriages and Deaths

(*See Halsbury's Laws of England* (3rd Edn.), *vol.* 32)

The general supervision of the registration of births, marriages and deaths in England and Wales is in the hands of the Registrar General; and he appoints the days on which registrars must make their returns. The country is divided for the purpose of registration into districts and sub-districts, there being in each district a superintendent registrar and registrars of marriages and in each sub-district one or more registrars of births and deaths. The superintendent registrar and registrars are appointed by the non-Metropolitan County or Metropolitan District Council or in London by the Common Council of the City of London or the Councils of the London Boroughs (Registration Service Act, 1953, s. 6). As to changes *see generally* Registration Service Act, 1953. Registrars of marriages are appointed by the Registrar General, or by a superintendent registrar subject to the approval of the Registrar General or all or any of the functions of a registrar of marriages may be conferred or imposed on a registrar of births and deaths by the Council appointing that officer. Generally as to registration of a Birth or Death *see* the Births and Deaths Registration Act, 1953 and Regulations made thereunder.

Registration of Births

The following particulars of a birth are required: (1) the date and place of birth; (2) the name and surname and sex of child; (3) the name and surname, place of birth and occupation of the father; (4) the name and surname, maiden surname, surname at marriage if different from maiden surname and place of birth of the mother; (5) mother's usual address if different from the child's place of birth; (6) the name and surname, qualification, usual address and signature of informant; (7) date of registration and (8) signature of registrar.

Registration of a birth must take place within forty-two days, the required particulars being furnished by the father or mother, and in default of the father or mother the occupier of the house in which to his knowledge the birth occurred; a person present at the birth or the person having charge of the child. Where a living new-born child is found exposed, particulars must be registered within forty-two days from the date on which the child was found, the duty of giving information to the registrar being placed by Statute on "the person finding the child, and of any person in whose charge such child may be placed." No fee is payable.

The particulars relating to the father of an illegitimate child can only be entered in the birth register if the father either attends the register office with the mother to sign the register with her, or makes a statutory declaration of acknowledgement of paternity, before a Magistrate a Justice of the Peace a Solicitor or a Commissioner for Oaths, which the mother can produce to the registrar when she gives information for the registration of the birth alone. When the latter course is followed the mother must make a declaration before the registrar stating that the said person is the father of the child.

A person required by the Registration Act to give information concerning a birth may, however, give the information by making and signing in the presence of a prescribed officer other than the registrar for the sub-district in which the birth occurred, a declaration in writing of the particulars required to be registered concerning the birth. After three months a birth must be registered in the presence of the superintendent registrar, and after twelve months the authorisation of the Registrar General must be obtained. Under the National Health Service Reorganisation Act 1973, births must (under a penalty) be notified to the Area Medical Officer of the Area Health Authority within thirty-six hours, in addition to the above provisions being observed. *See also* generally the Births and Deaths Registration Act, 1953 and the Registration Service Act 1953.

Still-born children. Under the provisions of the Births and Deaths Registration Act, 1953, the births of still-born children must be registered.

Adopted Children. Adoption Orders granted by the Courts under the Adoption Act, 1958, contain a direction to the Registrar General to make in the Adopted Children Register an entry recording the adoption. The adoption is registered accordingly in the prescribed form and when the entry contains a record of the date of birth or the country of birth of the adopted child, a certified copy of any such entry is evidence of that date or that country in all respects as if the copy were a certified copy of an entry in the Register of Births. Under the Adoption Act, 1968, a child born in this country but adopted in some countries overseas may have that adoption registered in the Adopted Children's Register for England and Wales and a certified copy may be issued from an entry in that register.

Legitimated persons. The parents of a legitimated person have a duty to furnish the Registrar General with information with a view to the re-registration of the birth of that person. If satisfactory evidence is produced the Registrar General may thereupon authorise the re-registration, and on receipt of his written authority the registrar of the sub-district in which the birth took place must enter the birth in the register in the prescribed manner. The entry must be made in the presence of the informant unless he has removed from the sub-district, in which case he may be permitted to make a declaration in writing of the particulars to be entered. *See* Births and Deaths Registration Act, 1953, s. 14.

Registration of Deaths

The following particulars of a death are required; (1) the date and place of death; (2) the name, surname and sex (and the maiden surname if the deceased was a woman who had married); (3) the date and place of birth of the deceased; (4) the occupation (and the name and occupation of her husband if the deceased was a married woman or widow) and the usual address; (5) the cause of death; (6) the name and surname, qualification, usual address and signature of informant; (7) date of registration; (8) signature of registrar and (9) in the case of a death at sea, the nationality and last place of abode of the deceased.

Registration of a death must take place within five days or within 14 days if the registrar has been notified in writing of the death. Where a person dies in a house the required particulars must be furnished by the nearest relative of the deceased present at the death or in attendance during the last illness and in default of such relative any other relative residing or being in the sub-district where the death occurred and in default of such relative any person present at the death, or the occupier of the house in which to his knowledge the death took place, or any inmate of the house, or the person causing the disposal of the body.

Where a person dies in a place which is not a house or a dead body is found elsewhere than in a house any relative having knowledge of any of the particulars required to be registered concerning the death, and in default of such relative any person present at the death, or any person who found the body or any person taking charge of the body, or the person causing the disposal of the body, must give to the registrar such information of the particulars required to be registered as the informant possesses.

If the deceased person was attended during his last illness by a registered medical practitioner, a medical certificate of the cause of death must be signed and delivered forthwith by that practitioner to the registrar and the registered medical practitioner on signing such certificate shall give in the prescribed form a notice of the signing of the certificate to the person required to register the death, and such person shall, except in the case of an inquest, deliver that notice to the registrar.

Where an inquest has been held, the coroner's certificate after inquest is sent to the registrar and the death is registered from such certificate without the attendance of an informant. No fee is payable.

After twelve months a death can be registered only by the Registrar General's express authorisation.

With regard to funerals, the Act of 1926 provides that the body of a deceased person may not be disposed of before a certificate of the registrar or an order of the coroner authorising the disposal has been delivered to the person effecting the disposal. Where, however, the person effecting the disposal by burial of the body of any deceased person is satisfied by a written declaration in the prescribed form by the person procuring the disposal that a certificate of the registrar or order of the coroner has been issued, he may proceed with the burial notwithstanding that the certificate or order has not been previously delivered to him.

Any person intending to remove out of England the body of a deceased person must give notice of such intention to the coroner within whose jurisdiction the body is lying, and the body must not be removed before the expiration of four clear days after the day on which the notice is received by the coroner. Where, however, the coroner in acknowledging the receipt of notice states that he is satisfied that no further enquiries by him are necessary, the body may be removed at any time after he so states although the period of four days has not expired.

Where it is intended to dispose of the body of a deceased person by cremation the further requirements made by the Secretary of State under the Cremation Act, 1902, and the Births and Deaths Registrations Act, 1926, must be fulfilled. The person effecting the disposal of the body of any deceased person is required, with 96 hours of the disposal, to deliver to the registrar, in the prescribed manner, a notification as to the date, place and means of disposal of the body.

Births and Deaths at sea, in the air and abroad. Births and deaths at sea are recorded in the log book of the ship by the master, and by him reported to the Registrar General of Shipping and Seamen who sends returns of them to the Registrar General, St. Catherines House, 10 Kingsway, London, WC2 B6JP. Births and Deaths in British civil aircraft are notified to the Civil Aviation Authority where registration is effected and returns sent to the Registrar General. Births and deaths outside the United Kingdom occurring among members of the armed forces and their families are registered by the service authorities, and returns are sent to the Registrar General, St. Catherines House. Consular officers abroad and High Commissioners for the United Kingdom in certain Commonwealth countries are registration authorities for the purposes of recording births and deaths of British subjects within their districts and send returns to the Registrar General, St. Catherines House.

Population (Statistics) Acts, 1938 and 1960. These Acts require the informant in the case of the registration of a birth, stillbirth or death to provide certain additional information, which is not entered in the register, being treated as confidential and used only for the preparation of statistics by the Registrar General.

Registration of Marriage

The following particulars of a marriage are required: (1) the date thereof; (2) name and surname, of the parties; and (3) the name, condition, rank or profession and residence of each of the parties and surname and rank or profession of the male parent. In the case of a marriage in the Church of England, there must further be stated the church and the parish and county or metropolitan district in which it is situated, and whether the marriage was by common licence, after banns or by superintendent registrar's certificate; in all other cases it is required that the building in which the marriage took place shall be stated, and whether the marriage was by licence or certificate.

In the case of a marriage in the Church of England, registration is by the clergyman solemnizing the marriage; in the case of a nonconformist marriage solemnized in the presence of an authorized person appointed under the Marriage Act, 1898, or the Marriage Act, 1949, without the presence of a registrar, registration is by the authorised person, and in the case of any other nonconformist marriage, by the registrar; in other cases—it is by the registering officer of the Society of Friends in the case of a marriage according to the usages of that Society; the secretary of the synagogue to which the husband belongs in the case of a Jewish marriage; or the registrar in the case of a marriage in the superintendent registrar's office. It is usual to pay £1.00 to the clergyman and 25p to the clerk in the case of a marriage at a church.

Fees on Marriage

Church of England Weddings. Following the making of the Parochial Fees Order, 1972, a revised table of fees issued by the Church Commissioners came into operation on the 1st June, 1972. These revised fees are applicable in all parishes in the provinces of Canterbury and York and extracts from them are set out below together with other relevant fees:

	Total Fee £
Marriage after Banns	
At Church in which marriage celebrated	5.05
At any other Church where banns read	1.75
Marriage by Common Licence	
At Church where marriage celebrated	4.00
For the licence	8.50

	Total Fee
Marriage on authority of Superintendent Registrar's Certificate	£
At the Church	4.00
Fee for certificate in each relevant Registration district	2.50

There are extra fees for a church wedding. The fees payable at the Faculty Office for a special licence are £25. Information as to special and ordinary ecclesiastical licences can be obtained in London at the Faculty Office, 1 The Sanctuary, Westminster, S.W.1, and elsewhere at the offices of the Bishop's registrars.

Other weddings. In regard to marriages other than those according to the rites of the Church of England the total fees payable for a marriage by superintendent registrar's certificate are £5 if both parties live in the same registration district, and £7 if they live in different districts. For a marriage by superintendent registrar's licence the fee is £13. These fees include, when required by law, the attendance of the registrar of marriages but not the fee for a certificate of the marriage, which, at the time of registration is £1.25. In the case of a marriage in a registered building, however, further fees may be found to be payable to the Minister or authorised person.

Under the Marriage (Registrar General's Licence) Act 1970, the Registrar General can issue a licence to enable a marriage to take place, otherwise than according to the rites of the Church of England or the Church in Wales, in circumstances where one of the parties is seriously ill and not expected to recover and cannot be moved to a place at which the marriage could be solemnized under the provisions of the Marriage Act 1949. The fee for the Registrar General's licence is £15.

Marriages Abroad

Returns are required to be made to the Registrar General, St Catherines House, of marriage outside the United Kingdom solemnized among, or among the families of, members of the armed forces and registered by the service authorities, and of marriages of British subjects in foreign countries registered by British Consular officers.

Bilingual Registration

The Registration of Births, Still-births and Deaths (Welsh Language) Regulations 1969, the Registration of Marriages (Welsh Language) Regulations 1971 and the Registration of Births, Still-births and Deaths (Welsh language) and the Registration of Marriages (Welsh Language) (Amendment) Regulations 1974 provide for the bilingual registration of births, still-births, deaths and marriages in Wales. Registration may be effected in English or English and Welsh but not in Welsh alone.

Searches and Certificates

Searches of the various registers in the custody of a registrar of births and deaths and of marriages, a clergyman of the Church of England, an authorised person under the Marriage Act, 1949, a registering officer, or a secretary of a synagogue are allowed. Searches may also be made of the indexes maintained by a superintendent registrar or at St Catherines House, 10 Kingsway, London, WC2B 6JP. The fee for a general search during up to six consecutive hours in the indexes kept by a superintendent registrar is £6; no fee is payable for other searches. Certified copies of any entries may be obtained, the fee for each copy being £1.25 when application is made to the registrar by whom the register containing the entry is kept or, in the case of marriage entries, at the time of registration, and £2.50 in all other cases. If application is made by post to St Catherines House, the fee is £4.50 for each copy. A reduced fee of 75p is payable for certified copies issued for the purposes of the following Acts:—Savings Bank Act, 1887, Young Persons (Employment) Act, 1938, Education Act, 1944, Shops Act, 1950, Factories Act, 1961, Child Benefit Act, 1975, Industrial Injuries and Diseases (Old Cases) Act, 1975, Social Security Act, 1975, and the Friendly Societies Acts. Such certified copies at reduced fees can be obtained only from the superintendent registrar, registrar or other person having the legal custody of the register containing the original entry.

The Births and Deaths Registration Act, 1953, provides for an additional type of birth certificate. Under the Act any person shall, on furnishing the prescribed particulars, be entitled to obtain from the Registrar General, a superintendent registrar, or a registrar, a certificate in the prescribed form of the birth of any person compiled from the records and registers in the custody of the Registrar General or from the registers in the custody of that superintendent registrar or registrar as the case may be. The certificates issued under the Act will contain such particulars as may be prescribed, not being particulars relating to parentage or adoption. One such certificate is issued free of charge at the time of registration and a fee of £1.25 is payable for subsequent certificates where application is made to a superintendent registrar or registrar, or £4 where application is made by post to St Catherine's House.

Revenue

SEE TAXATION

Road Traffic

(*For authoritative works of reference on Motor Vehicles and the Road Traffic Act, see Bingham's Motor Claims Cases and Mahaffy and Dodson on Road Traffic*).

NOTE.—The financial penalties shown as are amended by the Road Traffic Act 1974.

1. *Introduction.*—Below are set out offences under the Road Traffic Act 1972 for which disqualification and endorsement may be ordered (see the Road Traffic Act 1972, ss. 93, 101, 177, 179, 180, 181, 183 and Sch. 4), and also offences under certain other Acts. For further details of these offences, see the works referred to at the head of this note.

2. *Causing death by reckless or dangerous driving* (s. 1).—This is triable only on indictment and is punishable by imprisonment not exceeding 5 years. Disqualification and endorsement are obligatory.

3. *Reckless and dangerous driving* (s. 2).—This is triable summarily or on indictment. On summary conviction it is punishable by imprisonment not exceeding 4 months or a fine not exceeding £400. On conviction on indictment it is punishable by imprisonment not exceeding 2 years and/or a fine. When committed within 3 years of a conviction under s. 1 or s. 2, disqualification and endorsement are obligatory: if not committed within 3 years of such a conviction, disqualification is discretionary but endorsement is obligatory.

4. *Careless and inconsiderate driving* (s. 3).—This is triable summarily and is punishable by a fine not exceeding £200, Disqualification is discretionary but endorsement is obligatory.

5. *Driving or attempting to drive when unfit through drink or drugs* (s. 5(1)).— This is triable summarily or on indictment. On summary conviction it is punishable by imprisonment not exceeding 4 months or a fine not exceeding £400. On conviction on indictment it is punishable by imprisonment not exceeding 2 years and/or a fine. Disqualification and endorsement are obligatory.

6. *Being in charge of a motor vehicle when unfit to drive through drink or drugs* (s. 5(2)).—This is triable summarily or on indictment. On summary conviction

it is punishable by a fine not exceeding £200. On conviction on indictment it is punishable by imprisonment not exceeding 12 months and/or a fine. Disqualification is discretionary but endorsement is obligatory.

7. *Driving or attempting to drive with blood-alcohol concentration above prescribed limit* (s. 6(1)).—This is triable summarily or on indictment. On summary conviction it is punishable by imprisonment not exceeding 4 months or a fine not exceeding £400. On conviction on indictment it is punishable by imprisonment not exceeding 2 years and/or a fine. Disqualification and endorsement are obligatory.

8. *Being in charge of a motor vehicle with blood-alcohol concentration above prescribed limit* (s. 6(2)).—This is triable summarily or on indictment. On summary conviction it is punishable by a fine not exceeding £200. On conviction on indictment it is punishable by imprisonment not exceeding 12 months and/or a fine. Disqualification is discretionary but endorsement is obligatory.

9. *Failing to provide a specimen of breath for a breath test* (s. 8(3)).—This is triable summarily and is punishable by a fine not exceeding £50.

10. *Failing to provide specimen of blood or urine for laboratory test* (s. 9(3)).—This is triable summarily or on indictment. On summary conviction it is punishable: (i) where it is shown that at the relevant time the offender was driving or attempting to drive a motor vehicle on a road or other public place by a fine not exceeding £400; (ii) where in any other case it is shown that at the relevant time the offender was in charge of a motor vehicle on a road or other public place, by a fine not exceeding £200. On conviction on indictment it is punishable by imprisonment not exceeding 2 years and/or a fine where it is shown as mentioned in (i) above, or by imprisonment not exceeding 12 months and/or a fine where it is shown as mentioned in (ii) above. Disqualification is obligatory if it is shown as in (i) above, but discretionary if it is not so shown; endorsement is obligatory.

11. *Motor racing and speed trials on highways* (s. 14).—This is triable summarily and is punishable by a fine not exceeding £200. Disqualification and endorsement are obligatory.

12. *Unlawful carriage of passenger on motor-cycle* (s. 16).—This is triable summarily and is punishable by a fine not exceeding £50. Disqualification is discretionary but endorsement is obligatory.

13. *Failing to comply with traffic directions* (s. 22).—This is triable summarily and is punishable by a fine not exceeding £50. Disqualification is discretionary if the offence is committed in respect of a motor vehicle by a failure to comply with a direction of a constable or specified road signs, but endorsement is obligatory in respect of those offences.

14. *Leaving vehicle in dangerous position* (s. 24).—This is triable summarily and is punishable by a fine not exceeding £100. Disqualification is discretionary if committed in respect of a motor vehicle but endorsement is obligatory if committed in respect of a motor vehicle.

15. *Failing to stop after accident and give particulars or report accident* (s. 25 (4)).—This is triable summarily and is punishable by a fine not exceeding £100. Disqualification is discretionary but endorsement is obligatory.

16. *Contravention of construction and use regulations* (s. 40(5)).—This is triable summarily and is punishable by a fine not exceeding £400 in the case of an offence of using, or causing or permitting the use of, a goods vehicle (a) so as to cause, or to be likely to cause, danger by the condition of the vehicle or its parts or accessories, the number of passengers carried by it, or the weight distribution, packing or adjustment of its load; or (b) in breach of a construction or use requirement as to brakes, steering-gear, tyres or any description of weight; or (c) for any purpose for which it is so unsuitable as to cause or to be likely to cause danger; £400 in the case of an offence of carrying on a goods vehicle a load which, by reason of its insecurity or position, is likely to cause danger and by a fine not exceed-

ing £100 in any other case. Disqualification is discretionary but endorsement is obligatory if committed by using, or causing or permitting the use of, any motor vehicle or trailer (i) as described in (a) or (c) above, or (ii) in breach of a construction or use requirement as to brakes, steering-gear or tyres, except where the offender proves that he did not know and had no reasonable cause to suspect that the facts of the case were such that the offence would be committed; but discretionary if committed by carrying on a motor vehicle or trailer a load which, by reason of its insecurity or position, is likely to cause danger, but subject to the exception above.

17. *Driving without a licence* (s. 84 (1)).—This is triable summarily and is punishable by a fine not exceeding £100. Disqualification is discretionary if the offence is committed by driving a motor vehicle in a case where either no licence authorising the driving of that vehicle could have been granted to the offender or, if a provisional (but no other) licence to drive it could have been granted to him, the driving would not have complied with the conditions thereof. Endorsement is obligatory if committed as described above.

18. *Failing to comply with provisional licence conditions* (s. 88(b)).—This is triable summarily and is punishable by a fine not exceeding £100. Disqualification is discretionary but endorsement is obligatory.

19. *Driving with uncorrected defective eyesight* (s. 91(1)).—This is triable summarily and is punishable by a fine not exceeding £100. Disqualification is discretionary but endorsement is obligatory.

20. *Refusing to submit to test of eyesight* (s. 91(2)).—This is triable summarily and is punishable by a fine not exceeding £100. Disqualification is discretionary but endorsement is obligatory.

21. *Driving whilst disqualified* (s. 99(b)).—This is triable summarily or on indictment. On summary conviction it is punishable by imprisonment not exceeding 3 months and/or a fine not exceeding £400. On conviction on indictment it is punishable by imprisonment not exceeding 12 months and/or a fine. Disqualification is dis-

cretionary but endorsement is obligatory.

22. *Using motor vehicle while uninsured or unsecured against third-party risks* (s. 143).—This is triable summarily and is punishable by a fine not exceeding £200. Disqualification is discretionary but endorsement is obligatory.

23. *Manslaughter.*—This is triable only at Crown Courts and is punishable by life imprisonment. By Sch. 4, Part II, disqualification and endorsement are obligatory.

24. *Stealing or attempting to steal a motor vehicle.*—By Sch. 4, Part III, conviction of these offences involves discretionary disqualification but obligatory endorsement.

25. *Contravention of motorways regulations* (R.T.R. Act 1967, s. 13(4), *and* R.T. Act 1972, Sch. 4, *Part III*).—This is triable summarily. When committed in respect of motor vehicles (otherwise than by unlawfully stopping, etc.) it is punishable by a fine not exceeding £100. Disqualification in such cases is discretionary but endorsement is obligatory.

26. *Pedestrian crossing regulations offences* (R.T.R. Act 1967, s. 23(5), *and* R.T. Act 1972, Sch. 4, *Part III*).—When committed in respect of a motor vehicle this is triable summarily and is punishable by a fine not exceeding £100. Disqualification is discretionary but endorsement is obligatory.

27. *Failure to obey school crossing patrol* (R.T.R. Act 1967, s. 25(2), *and* R.T. Act 1972, Sch. 4, *Part III*).—When committed in respect of a motor vehicle this is triable summarily and is punishable by a fine not exceeding £100. Disqualification is discretionary but endorsement is obligatory.

28. *Contravention of street playground order* (R.T.R. Act 1967, s. 26(6) *or* 26A(5), *and* R.T. Act 1972, Sch. 4, *Part III*).—When committed in respect of a motor vehicle this is triable summarily and is punishable by a fine not exceeding £100. Disqualification is discretionary but endorsement is obligatory.

29. *Speeding offence* (R.T.R. Act 1967, s. 78A(1), *and* R.T. Act 1972, Sch. 4, *Part III*).—This is triable sum-

marily and is punishable by a fine not exceeding £100. Disqualification is discretionary but endorsement is obligatory.

30. *Taking or attempting to take a motor vehicle without authority (Theft Act 1968, s. 12, and R.T. Act 1972, Sch. 4, Part III).*—This is triable on indictment, and is punishable by imprisonment not exceeding 3 years. Disqualification is discretionary but endorsement is obligatory.

31. *Going equipped for stealing, etc. (Theft Act 1968, s. 25, and R.T. Act 1972, Sch. 4, Part III).*—When committed with reference to the theft or taking of motor vehicles it is triable on indictment and is punishable by imprisonment not exceeding 3 years. Disqualification is discretionary but endorsement is obligatory.

32. *Disqualification (R.T. Act 1972, s. 93).*—Where it is stated above that disqualification is obligatory, a court must disqualify for at least 12 months unless it decides for special reasons not to disqualify or to disqualify for a shorter period. In the case of offences under ss. 5(1), 6(1) or 9(3) (or the latter where obligatory disqualification is involved), if during the preceding 3 years the driver has been convicted of any such offence, the period of disqualification must be for at least 3 years. Where it is stated above that disqualification is discretionary a court may disqualify for such period as it thinks fit. In respect of all the above offences the cumulative convictions procedure (totting up) applies.

33. *Endorsement (R.T. Act 1972, s. 101).*—Where disqualification is ordered, it must be endorsed on the driver's licence. Where disqualification is not ordered, a court need not order particulars of the conviction to be endorsed on the driver's licence if for special reasons it thinks fit not so to do

Sale of Land

SEE REAL PROPERTY

Searches and Enquiries

SEE REAL PROPERTY

Solicitors

(See Cordery on Solicitors, 6th Edn.)

SOLICITORS' ACCOUNTS

GENERAL NOTE

The Solicitors Act 1933 endeavoured to regularize the position with regard to solicitors' accounts. In particular rules were issued in 1935 with the principal object of securing the separation by solicitors of their own moneys from those held by them for their clients (see now the Solicitors' Accounts Rules 1975).

In 1941 further provisions were made which provided that with a few exceptions, every solicitor should produce for each 12 months' accounting period a certificate by an accountant stating whether he is satisfied from inspection of the books and documents that the solicitor's accounts have been properly kept.

The statute law relating to solicitors has been consolidated in the Solicitors Act 1974 and the relevant sections of that Act (ss. 32 to 34) relating to Solicitors' Accounts are set out below.

32. *Accounts rules and trust accounts rules.*—(1) The Council shall make rules, with the concurrence of the Master of the Rolls—

   (a) as to the opening and keeping by solicitors of accounts at banks for clients' money; and

(b) as to the keeping by solicitors of accounts containing particulars and information as to money received or held or paid by them for or on account of their clients; and

(c) empowering the Council to take such action as may be necessary to enable them to ascertain whether or not the rules are being complied with;

and the rules may specify the location of the banks' branches at which the accounts are to be kept.

(2) The Council shall also make rules, with the concurrence of the Master of the Rolls—

(a) as to the opening and keeping by solicitors of accounts at banks for money comprised in controlled trusts;

(b) as to the keeping by solicitors of accounts containing particulars and information as to money received or held or paid by them for or on account of any such trust; and

(c) empowering the Council to take such action as may be necessary to enable them to ascertain whether or not the rules are being complied with;

and the rules may specify the location of the banks' branches at which the accounts are to be kept.

(3) If any solicitor fails to comply with rules made under this section, any person may make a complaint in respect of that failure to the Tribunal.

(4) The Council shall be at liberty to disclose a report on or information about a solicitor's accounts obtained in the exercise of powers conferred by rules made under subsection (1) or (2) to the Director of Public Prosecutions for use in investigating the possible commission of an offence by the solicitor and, if the Director thinks fit, for use in connection with any prosecution of the solicitor consequent on the investigation.

(5) Rules under this section may specify circumstances in which solicitors or any class of solicitors are exempt from the rules by virtue of their office or employment.

33. *Interest on clients' money.*—(1) Rules made under section 32 shall make provision for requiring a solicitor, in such cases as may be prescribed by the rules, either—

(a) to keep on deposit in a separate account at a bank for the benefit of the client money received for or on account of a client; or

(b) to make good to the client out of the solicitor's own money a sum equivalent to the interest which would have accrued if the money so received had been so kept on deposit.

(2) The cases in which a solicitor may be required by the rules to act as mentioned in subsection (1) may be defined, among other things, by reference to the amount of any sum received or the period for which it is or is likely to be retained or both; and the rules may include provision for enabling a client (without prejudice to any other remedy) to require that any question arising under the rules in relation to the client's money be referred to and determined by the Society.

(3) Except as provided by the rules, a solicitor shall not be liable by virtue of the relation between solicitor and client to account to any client for interest received by the solicitor on money deposited at a bank being money received or held for or on account of his clients generally.

(4) Nothing in this section or in the rules shall—

(a) affect any arrangement in writing, whenever made, between a solicitor and his client as to the application of the client's money or interest on it; or

(b) apply to money received by a solicitor being money subject to a trust of which the solicitor is a trustee.

34. *Accountants' reports.*—(1) Every solicitor shall once in each period of twelve months ending with 31st October, unless the Council are satisfied that it is unnecessary for him to do so, deliver to the Society, whether by post or otherwise a report signed by an accountant, (in this section referred to as an "accountant's report") and containing such information as may be prescribed by rules made by the Council under this section.

(2) An accountant's report shall be delivered to the Society not more than six months (or such other period as may be prescribed by rules made under this section) after the end of the accounting period specified in that report.

(3) Subject to any rules made under this section, the accounting period for the purposes of an accountant's report—

(a) shall begin at the expiry of the last preceding accounting period for which an accountant's report has been delivered;

(b) shall cover not less than twelve months; and

(c) where possible, consistently with the preceding provisions of this section, shall correspond to a period or consecutive periods for which the accounts of the solicitor or his firm are ordinarily made up.

(4) The Council shall make rules to give effect to the provisions of this section, and those rules shall prescribe—

(a) the qualification to be held by an accountant by whom an accountant's report is given;

(b) the information to be contained in an accountant's report;

(c) the nature and extent of the examination to be made by an accountant of the books and accounts of a solicitor or his firm and of any other relevant documents with a view to the signing of an accountant's report;

(d) the form of an accountant's report; and

(e) the evidence, if any, which shall satisfy the Council that the delivery of an accountant's report is unnecessary and the cases in which such evidence is or is not required.

(5) Rules under this section may include provision—

(a) permitting in such special circumstances as may be defined by the rules a different accounting period from that specified in subsection (3); and

(b) regulating any matters of procedure or matters incidental, ancillary or supplemental to the provisions of this section.

(6) If any solicitor fails to comply with the provisions of this section or of any rules made under it, a complaint in respect of that failure may be made to the Tribunal by or on behalf of the Society.

(7) A certificate under the hand of the Secretary of the Society shall, until the contrary is proved, be evidence that a solicitor has or, as the case may be, has not delivered to the Society an accountant's report or supplied any evidence required under this section or any rules made under it.

(8) Where a solicitor is exempt from rules under section 32—

(a) nothing in this section shall apply to him unless he takes out a practising certificate;

(b) an accountant's report shall in no case deal with books, accounts or documents kept by him in the course of employment by virtue of which he is exempt from those rules; and

(c) no examination shall be made of any such books, accounts and documents under any rules made under this section.

RULES

The Solicitors' Accounts Rules
(Made under s. 32 of the Solicitors Act, 1974.)

1. These Rules may be cited as the Solicitors' Accounts Rules, 1975, and shall come into operation on the 1st day of May, 1975, whereupon the Solicitors' Accounts Rules, 1967, shall cease to have effect.

2.—(1) In these Rules, unless the context otherwise requires—

"Solicitor" shall mean a solicitor of the Supreme Court and shall include a firm of solicitors;

"Client's Money" shall mean money held or received by a solicitor on account of a person for whom he is acting in relation to the holding or receipt of such money either as a solicitor or, in connection with his practice as a solicitor, as agent, bailee, stakeholder or in any other capacity; provided that the expression "client's money" shall not include—

(a) money held or received on account of the trustees of a trust of which the solicitor is a solicitor-trustee; or

(b) money to which the only person entitled is the solicitor himself or, in the case of a firm of solicitors, one or more of the partners in the firm;

"Client" shall mean any person on whose account a solicitor holds or receives client's money;

"Trust Money" shall mean money held or received by a solicitor which is not client's money and which is subject to a trust of which the solicitor is a trustee whether or not he is a solicitor-trustee of such trust;

"Client Account" shall mean a current, or deposit account in the name of the solicitor at a bank in the title of which account the word "client" appears;

"Bank" shall mean the branch, situated in England or Wales, of a Bank as defined by section 87(1) of the Solicitors Act 1974;

"Solicitor-Trustee" shall mean a solicitor who is a sole trustee or co-trustee only with one or more of his partners or employees;

"Public Officer" shall mean an officer whose remuneration is defrayed out of moneys provided by Parliament, the revenues of the Duchy of Cornwall or the Duchy of Lancaster, the general fund of the Church Commissioners, the Forestry Fund or the Development Fund;

"Statutory undertakers" shall mean any person authorised by or under an Act of Parliament, to construct, work, or carry on any railway, canal, inland navigation, dock, harbour, tramway, gas, electricity, water or other public undertaking;

"Local Authority" shall have the same meaning as is given to this expression by the Local Government Act, 1972.

(2) Other expressions in these Rules shall except where otherwise stated have the meanings assigned to them by the Solicitors Act, 1974.

(3) The Interpretation Act, 1889, shall apply to these Rules in the same manner as it applies to an Act of Parliament, and for the purposes of section 38 of the said Act the Solicitors' Accounts Rules, 1967, shall be deemed to be an enactment repealed by these Rules.

3. Subject to the provisions of Rule 9 hereof, every solicitor who holds or receives client's money, or money which under Rule 4 hereof is permitted and elects to pay into a client's account, shall without delay pay such money into a client account. Any solicitor may keep one client account or as many such accounts as he thinks fit.

4. There may be paid into a client account—

(a) trust money;

(b) such money belonging to the solicitor as may be necessary for the purpose of opening or maintaining the account;

(c) money to replace any sum which for any reason may have been drawn from the account in contravention of paragraph (2) of Rule 8 of these Rules; and

(d) a cheque or draft received by the solicitor which under paragraph (b) of Rule 5 of these Rules he is entitled to split but which he does not split.

5. Where a solicitor holds or receives a cheque or draft which includes client's money or trust money of one or more trusts—

(a) he may where practicable split such cheque or draft and, if he does so, he shall deal with each part thereof as if he had received a separate cheque or draft in respect of that part; or

(b) if he does not split the cheque or draft he shall, if any part thereof consists of clients' money, and may, in any other case, pay the cheque or draft into a client account.

6. No money other than money which under the foregoing Rules a solicitor is required or permitted to pay into a client account shall be paid into

a client account, and it shall be the duty of a solicitor into whose client account any money has been paid in contravention of this Rule to withdraw the same without delay on discovery.

7. There may be drawn from a client account—

(a) in the case of a client's money—

    (i) money properly required for a payment to or on behalf of the client;

    (ii) money properly required for or towards payment of a debt due to the solicitor from the client or in reimbursement of money expended by the solicitor on behalf of the client;

    (iii) money drawn on the client's authority;

    (iv) money properly required for or towards payment of the solicitor's costs where there has been delivered to the client a bill of costs or other written intimation of the amount of the costs incurred and it has thereby or otherwise in writing been made clear to the client that money held for him is being or will be applied towards or in satisfaction of such costs; and

    (v) money which is transferred into another client account;

(b) in the case of trust money—

    (i) money properly required for a payment in the execution of the particular trust, and

    (ii) money to be transferred to a separate bank account kept solely for the money of the particular trust;

(c) such money, not being money to which either paragraph (a) or paragraph (b) of this Rule applies, as may have been paid into the account under paragraph (b) of Rule 4 or paragraph (b) of Rule 5 of these Rules; and

(d) money which for any reason may have been paid into the account in contravention of Rule 6 of these Rules;

provided that in any case under paragraph (a) or paragraph (b) of this Rule the money so drawn shall not exceed the total of the money held for the time being in such account on account of such client or trust.

8.—(1) No money drawn from a client account under sub-paragraph (ii) or sub-paragraph (iv) of paragraph (a) or under paragraph (c) or paragraph (d) of Rule 7 of these Rules shall be drawn except by—

(a) a cheque drawn in favour of the solicitor, or

(b) a transfer to a bank account in the name of the solicitor not being a client account.

(2) No money other than money permitted by Rule 7 to be drawn from a client account shall be so drawn unless the Council upon an application made to them by the solicitor specifically authorise in writing its withdrawal.

9.—(1) Notwithstanding the provisions of these Rules a solicitor shall not be under obligation to pay into a client account client's money held or received by him—

(a) which is received by him in the form of cash and is without delay paid in cash in the ordinary course of business to the client or on his behalf to a third party; or

(b) which is received by him in the form of a cheque or draft which is endorsed over in the ordinary course of business to the client or on his behalf to a third party and is not passed by the solicitor through a bank account; or

(c) which he pays into a separate bank account opened or to be opened in the name of the client or of some person designated by the client in writing or acknowledged by the solicitor to the client in writing.

(2) Notwithstanding the provisions of these Rules a solicitor shall not pay into a client account money held or received by him—

(a) which the client for his own convenience requests the solicitor to withhold from such account, such request being either in writing from the client or acknowledged by the solicitor to the client in writing; or

(b) which is received by him for or towards payment of a debt the solicitor from the client or in reimbursement of money expended by the solicitor on behalf of the client; or

(c) which is expressly paid to him either—

   (i) on account of costs incurred in respect of which a bill of costs or other written intimation of the amount of the costs incurred has been delivered for payment; or

   (ii) as an agreed fee (or on account of an agreed fee) for business undertaken or to be undertaken.

(3) Where a cheque or draft includes client's money as well as money of the nature described in paragraph (2) of this Rule such cheque or draft shall be dealt with in accordance with Rule 5 of these Rules.

(4) Notwithstanding the provisions of these Rules the Council may upon application made to them by a solicitor specifically authorise him in writing to withhold any client's money from a client account.

10. No sum shall be transferred from the ledger account of one client to that of another except in circumstances in which it would have been permissible under these Rules to have withdrawn from client account the sum transferred from the first client and to have paid into client account the sum so transferred to the second client.

11.—(1) Every solicitor shall at all times keep properly written up such accounts as may be necessary—

(a) to show all his dealings with—

   (i) client's money received, held or paid by him; and

   (ii) any other money dealt with by him through a client account; and

(b) (i) to show separately in respect of each client all money of the categories specified in sub-paragraph (a) of this paragraph which is received, held or paid by him on account of that client; and

   (ii) to distinguish all money of the said categories received, held, or paid by him, from any other money received, held or paid by him.

(2) (a) All dealings referred to in sub-paragraph (a) of paragraph (1) of this Rule shall be recorded as may be appropriate—

   (i) either in a client's cash book, or a clients' column of a cash book, or

   (ii) in a record of sums transferred from the ledger account of one client to that of another, and in addition—

   (iii) in a clients' ledger or a clients' column of a ledger, and no other dealings shall be recorded in such clients' cash book and ledger or, as the case may be, in such clients' columns, and

(b) all dealings of the solicitor relating to his practice as a solicitor other than those referred to in sub-paragraph (a) of paragraph (1) of this Rule shall (subject to compliance with the Solicitors' Trust Accounts Rules, 1975) be recorded in such other cash book and ledger or such other columns of a cash book and ledger as the solicitor may maintain.

(3) In addition to the books, ledgers and records referred to in paragraph (2) of this Rule, every solicitor shall keep a record of all bills of costs (distinguishing between profit costs and disbursements) and of all written intimations under Rule 7(a)(iv) and under Rule 9(2)(c) of these Rules delivered or made by the solicitor to his clients, which record shall be contained in a bills delivered book or a file of copies of such bills and intimations.

(4) Every solicitor shall within three months of the coming into force of this sub-rule or of his commencing practice on his own account (either alone or in partnership) whichever shall be later and thereafter not less than once in every succeeding period of three months cause the balance of his clients' cash book (or clients' column of his cash book) to be agreed with his client bank statements and shall keep in the cash book or other appropriate place a reconciliation statement showing this agreement.

(5) In this Rule the expressions accounts", "books", "ledgers" and "records" shall be deemed to include looseleaf books and such cards or other permanent documents or records as are necessary for the operation of any system of book-keeping, mechanical or otherwise.

(6) Every solicitor shall preserve for at least six years from the date of the last entry therein all accounts, books, ledgers and records kept by him under this Rule.

(7) No money may be withdrawn from a bank account, being or forming part of a client account, otherwise than under the signature of one at least of the following (either alone or in conjunction with other persons) namely:

(a) a solicitor who holds a current practising certificate, or
(b) an employee of such a solicitor being either a solicitor or a Fellow of the Institute of Legal Executives who is confirmed by the Institute as being of good standing and who shall have been admitted a Fellow for not less than five years.

12.—(1) In order to ascertain whether these Rules have been complied with the Council acting either—

(a) on their own motion; or
(b) on a written statement and request transmitted to them by or on behalf of the Governing Body of a Local Law Society or a Committee thereof; or
(c) on a written complaint lodged with them by a third party,

may require any solicitor to produce at a time and place to be fixed by the Council, his books of account, bank pass books, loose-leaf bank statements, statements of account, vouchers and any other necessary documents for the inspection of any person appointed by the Council and to supply to such person any necessary information and explanations and such person shall be directed to prepare for the information of the Council a report on the result of such inspection. Such report may be used as a basis for proceedings under the Solicitors Act, 1974.

(2) Upon being required so to do a solicitor shall produce such books of account, bank pass books, loose-leaf bank statements, statements of accounts, vouchers and documents at the time and place fixed.

(3) In any case in which the Governing Body of a Local Law Society or a Committee thereof are of opinion that an inspection should be made under this Rule of the books of account, bank pass books, loose-leaf bank statements, statements of account, vouchers and any other necessary documents of a solicitor, it shall be the duty of such Governing Body or Committee to transmit to the Council a statement containing all relevant information in their possession and a request that such an inspection be made.

(4) Before instituting an inspection on a written complaint lodged with them by a third party, the Council shall require prima facie evidence that a ground of complaint exists, and may require the payment by such party to the Council of a reasonable sum to be fixed by them to cover the costs of the inspection and the costs of the solicitor against whom the complaint is made. The Council may deal with any sum so paid in such manner as they think fit.

13. Every requirement to be made by the Council of a solicitor under these Rules shall be made in writing under the hand of the Secretary of the Society as defined in section 87 of the Solicitors Act, 1974, and sent by registered post or the recorded delivery service to the last address of the solicitor appearing in the Roll or in the Register kept by the Society under section 9 of the Solicitors Act, 1974, and, when so made and sent, shall be deemed to have been received by the solicitor within forty-eight hours (excluding Saturdays, Sundays and Bank Holidays) of the time of posting.

14. Nothing in these Rules shall deprive a solicitor of any recourse or right, whether by way of lien, set off, counterclaim, charge or otherwise, against moneys standing to the credit of a client account.

15. These Rules shall not apply to a solicitor acting in the course of his employment as (a) a public officer, or (b) an officer of statutory undertakers, or (c) an officer of a local authority.

The Accountant's Report Rules, 1975

(Made under s. 34 of the Solicitors Act, 1974.)

The Rules lay down the qualifications which an auditor must possess in order to give an accountant's report on behalf of a solicitor (r. 3). The extent of the work carried out by an accountant for the purpose of giving a report is more clearly defined in r. 4.

R. 5 makes clear the solicitor's right to withhold files on the grounds of privilege between solicitor and client. Solicitors who need not deliver an accountant's report are specified in r. 7, and the accounting period is defined in rr. 8 and 9. A form of report appears in the Schedule to the Rules.

The Solicitors' Trust Accounts Rules, 1975

(Made under s. 32 of the Solicitors Act, 1975.)

1. These Rules may be cited as the Solicitors' Trust Accounts Rules, 1975, and shall come into operation on the 1st day of May, 1975, whereupon the Solicitors' Trust Accounts Rules, 1967, shall cease to have effect.

2.—(1) In these Rules unless the context otherwise requires—

"Client account" shall mean a current or deposit account at a bank, in the title of which the word "client" appears, kept and operated in accordance with the provision of the Solicitors' Accounts Rules, 1975;

"Solicitor-trustee" shall mean a solicitor who is a sole trustee or co-trustee only with one or more of his partners or employees;

"Trust Bank account" shall mean a current or deposit account in the title of which the word "trustee" or "executor" appears, or which is otherwise clearly designated as a trust bank account, kept at a bank and kept solely for money subject to a particular trust of which the solicitor is a solicitor-trustee;

"Bank" shall have the meaning assigned to it by the Solicitors' Accounts Rules, 1975;

"Public officer" shall mean an officer whose remuneration is defrayed out of moneys provided by Parliament, the revenues of the Duchy of Cornwall or the Duchy of Lancaster, the general fund of the Church Commissioners, the Forestry Fund or the Development Fund;

"Statutory undertakers" shall mean any person authorised by or under an Act of Parliament, or an order having the force of an Act of Parliament, to construct, work, or carry on any railway, canal, inland navigation, dock, harbour, tramway, gas, electricity, water or other public undertaking;

"Local authority" shall have the same meaning as is given to this expression by the Local Government Act, 1972.

(2) Other expressions in these Rules shall except where otherwise stated have the meanings assigned to them by the Solicitors Act, 1974.

(3) The Interpretation Act, 1889, shall apply to these Rules in the same manner as it applies to an Act of Parliament and for the purposes of section 38 of the said Act, the Solicitors' Trust Accounts Rules, 1967, shall be deemed to be an enactment repealed by these Rules.

3. Subject to the provisions of Rule 9 of these Rules every solicitor trustee who holds or receives money subject to a trust of which he is a solicitor trustee, other than money which is paid into a client account as permitted by the Solicitors' Accounts Rules 1975, shall without delay pay such money into the trust bank account of the particular trust.

4. There may be paid into a trust bank account—

(a) money subject to the particular trust;

(b) such money belonging to the solicitor-trustee or to a co-trustee as may be necessary for the purpose of opening or maintaining the account; or

(c) money to replace any sum which for any reason may have been drawn from the account in contravention of Rule 8 of these Rules.

5. Where a solicitor holds or receives a cheque or draft which includes

money subject to a trust or trusts of which the solicitor is solicitor-trustee—

(a) he shall where practicable split such cheque or draft and, if he does so, shall deal with each part thereof as if he had received a separate cheque or draft in respect of that part; or

(b) if he does not split the cheque or draft, he may pay it into a client account as permitted by the Solicitors' Accounts Rules, 1975.

6. No money, other than money which under the foregoing Rules a solicitor is required or permitted to pay into a trust bank account, shall be paid into a trust bank account, and it shall be the duty of a solicitor into whose trust bank account any money has been paid in contravention of this Rule to withdraw the same without delay on discovery.

7. There may be drawn from a trust bank account—

(a) money properly required for a payment in the execution of the particular trust;

(b) money to be transferred to a client account;

(c) such money, not being money subject to the particular trust. as may have been paid into the account under paragraph (b) of Rule 4 of these Rules; or

(d) money which may for any reason have been paid into the account in contravention of Rule 6 of these Rules.

8. No money other than money permitted by Rule 7 of these Rules to be drawn from a trust bank account shall be so drawn unless the Council upon an application made to them by the solicitor expressly authorise its withdrawal.

9. Notwithstanding the provisions of these Rules a solicitor shall not be under obligation to pay into a trust bank account money held or received by him which is subject to a trust of which he is solicitor-trustee—

(a) if the money is received by him in the form of cash and is without delay paid in cash in the execution of the trust to a third party; or

(b) if the money is received by him in the form of a cheque or draft which is without delay endorsed over in the execution of the trust to a third party and is not passed by the solicitor through a bank account.

10.—(1) Every solicitor trustee shall at all times keep properly written up such accounts as may be necessary—

(a) to show separately in respect of each trust of which he is solicitor-trustee all his dealings with money received, held or paid by him on account of that trust; and

(b) to distinguish the same from money received held or paid by him on any other account.

(2) Every solicitor-trustee shall preserve for at least six years from the date of the last entry therein all accounts kept by him under this Rule.

11.—(1) In order to ascertain whether these Rules have been complied with the Council acting either—

(a) on their own motion; or

(b) on a written statement and request transmitted to them by or on behalf of the Governing Body of a Local Law Society or a Committee thereof; or

(c) on a written complaint lodged with them by a third party.

may require any solicitor trustee to produce at a time, and place to be fixed by the Council all books of account, bank pass books, loose leaf bank statements, statements of account, vouchers and documents relating to all or any of the trusts of which he is solicitor-trustee for the inspection of any person appointed by the Council, and to supply to such person any necessary information and explanations and such person shall be directed to prepare for the information of the Council a report on the result of such inspection. Such report may be used as a basis for proceedings under the Solicitors Act, 1974.

(2) Upon being required so to do a solicitor-trustee shall produce such books of account, bank pass books, loose leaf bank statements, statements of account, vouchers and documents at the time and place fixed.

(3) In any case in which the Governing Body of a Local Law Society or a Committee thereof are of opinion that an inspection should be made under this Rule of books of account, bank pass books, loose-leaf bank statements, statements of account, vouchers and documents relating to all or any of the trusts of which a solicitor is solicitor-trustee it shall be the duty of such Governing Body or Committee to transmit to the Council a statement containing all relevant information in their possession and a request that such an inspection be made.

(4) Before instituting an inspection on a written complaint lodged with them by a third party, the Council shall require prima facie evidence that a ground of complaint exists, and may require the payment by such party to the Council of a reasonable sum to be fixed by them to cover the costs of the inspection, and the costs of the solicitor-trustee against whom the complaint is made. The Council may deal with any sum so paid in such manner as they think fit.

12. Every requirement to be made by the Council of a solicitor-trustee under these Rules shall be made in writing under the hand of the Secretary of the Society as defined in section 87 of the Solicitors Act, 1974, and sent by recorded or registered delivery service to the last address of the solicitor-trustee appearing in the Roll or in the Register kept by the Society under section 9 of the Solicitors Act, 1974, and, when so made and sent, shall be deemed to have been received by the solicitor-trustee within forty-eight hours (excluding Saturdays, Sundays and Bank Holidays) of the time of posting.

13. Nothing in these Rules shall deprive a solicitor of any recourse or right whether by way of lien, set off, counterclaim, charge or otherwise, against moneys standing to the credit of a trust bank account.

14. These Rules shall not apply to a solicitor acting in the course of his employment as (a) a public officer, or (b) an officer of statutory undertakers, or (c) an officer of a local authority.

Solicitors' Accounts (Deposit Interest) Rules, 1975

(Made under ss. 32 and 33 of the Solicitors Act, 1974.)

1. These Rules may be cited as the Solicitors' Accounts (Deposit Interest) Rules, 1975, and shall come into operation on the 1st day of May, 1975, whereupon the Solicitors' Accounts (Deposit Interest) Rules, 1965, shall cease to have effect.

2.—(1) Subject to Rule 5 of these Rules, when a solicitor holds or receives for or on account of a client money on which, having regard to all the circumstances (including the amount and the length of time for which the money is likely to be held), interest ought in fairness to the client to be earned for him, the solicitor shall either—

    (a) deposit such money in a separate designated account and account to the client for any interest earned thereon; or

    (b) pay to the client out of his own money a sum equivalent to the interest which would have accrued for the benefit of the client if the money had been deposited in a separate designated account under this Rule.

(2) In this Rule the expression "a separate designated account" shall mean a deposit account at a bank in the name of the solicitor or his firm in the title of which the word "client" appears and which is designated by reference to the identity of the client or matter concerned; the expression "bank" shall have the meaning assigned to it by the Solicitors' Accounts Rules, 1975.

(3) The Interpretation Act, 1889, shall apply to these Rules in the same manner as it applies to an Act of Parliament, and for the purposes of the said Act the Solicitors' Accounts (Deposit Interest) Rules, 1965, shall be deemed to be an enactment repealed by these Rules.

3. Without prejudice to the generality of Rule 2 of these Rules, it shall be deemed that interest ought in fairness to a client to be earned for him where a sum of money is received

for or on account of the client which exceeds £500 and at the time of its receipt is unlikely within two months thereafter to be either wholly disbursed or reduced by payments to a sum less than £500.

4. Without prejudice to any other remedy which may be available to him, any client who feels aggrieved that interest or a sum equivalent thereto has not been paid to him under these Rules shall be entitled to require the solicitor to obtain a certificate from The Law Society as to whether or not interest ought to have been earned for him and, if so, the amount of such

interest and upon the issue of such a certificate the sum certified to be due shall be payable by the solicitor to the client.

5. Nothing in these Rules shall—

(a) affect any arrangement in writing, whenever made, between a solicitor and his client as to the application of the client's money or interest thereon; or

(b) apply to money received by a solicitor being money subject to a trust of which the solicitor is a trustee.

SOLICITORS' PRACTICE RULES

Solicitors' Practice Rules, 1936-1975

Rules dated 22nd July 1936 (save as regards r. 1 (dated 2nd April 1971), r. 2 dated 6th October 1972), rr. 3 and 4 (dated 28th July 1972), made by the Council of the Law Society as approved by the Master of the Rolls under s. 31 of the Solicitors Act, 1974.

RULE 1

A solicitor shall not obtain or attempt to obtain professional business by:

(a) directly or indirectly without reasonable justification inviting instructions for such business, or

(b) doing or permitting to be done without reasonable justification, anything which by its manner, frequency or otherwise advertises his practice as a solicitor, or

(c) doing or permitting to be done anything which may reasonably be regarded as touting.

Examples forming no part of the Rule.

"indirectly", e.g., where a solicitor or his clerk has an arrangement with an estate agent for prospective purchasers to be recommended to retain such solicitor, or with insurance brokers for claims in respect of uninsured losses of their clients to be referred to such solicitor.

"without reasonable justification", e.g., there would be reasonable justification where a solicitor

writes to a Building Society asking to be included on its panel but not for a solicitor instructed by clients affected by a planning proposal or Compulsory Purchase Order to write on the strength of those instructions to other persons similarly affected inviting their instructions.

"inviting instructions", e.g., directly (viz. by himself or his staff) or indirectly (viz. through an estate agent, employer or other intermediary) giving clients or prospective clients estimates for future work which are or may reasonably be regarded as a device to encourage the giving or procuring of instructions for the solicitor.

"manner or frequency", e.g., it would be objectionable for a solicitor to announce a change of practising address in the Press in such a way as to constitute an advertisement for his practice, as opposed to a bare announcement of the change of address. Similarly, it would be objectionable for a solicitor to write frequent letters to the Press advertising his professional qualifications, which would give rise to the inference that he had the intention of advertising his practice for ulterior motives.

"touting", e.g., the offer of free conveyancing to prospective purchasers when acting for a vendor, or the imposition of a condition by or with the knowledge of the solicitor that the lender's solicitor must be instructed either in connection with the loan and/or a contemporaneous purchase.

RULE 2

(1) A solicitor or two or more solicitors practising in partnership or association shall not act for both vendor and purchaser on a transfer of land for value at arm's length or for both lessor and lessee on the grant of a lease for value at arm's length.

(2) Provided no conflict of interest appears and the vendor or lessor is not builder or developer selling or leasing as such this rule shall not apply if:—

(a) the parties are associated companies; or

(b) the parties are related by blood, adoption or marriage; or

(c) both parties are established clients (which expression shall include persons related by blood, adoption or marriage to established clients); or

(d) on a transfer of land the consideration is less than £1,000; or

(e) there are no other solicitors in the vicinity whom the client can reasonably be expected to consult; or

(f) two associated firms or two offices of the same firm are respectively acting for the parties, provided that:—

    (i) the respective firms or offices are in different localities, and

    (ii) neither party was referred to the firm or office acting for him from an associated firm or from another office of the same firm and

    (iii) the transaction is dealt with or supervised by a different solicitor in full-time attendance at each firm or office.

RULE 3

A solicitor shall not share or agree to share his professional fees with any person except:

(a) another solicitor; or

(b) a person who is entitled to practise as a lawyer in any country

other than England and Wales and has his principal office in such country.

Explanatory notes forming no part of the Rule.

(1) This rule prevents a solicitor (as a matter of conduct) from sharing or agreeing to share his professional fees with an unqualified person (see, however, the general waiver as to bonus schemes granted by the Council on 28th July, 1972). The rule and section 34 of the Solicitors Act, 1957 (now section 39 of the Solicitors Act, 1974) find their origin in section 32 of the Solicitors Act, 1843 and the purpose which they have in common is to safeguard the solicitor's independence. Section 34 (section 39) provides that a solicitor shall be struck off the roll if he be proved to have permitted the use of his name for the profit of an unqualified person.

(2) As to provision for a retired partner or his dependents, see *Aubin* v. *Holt* (1855), 25 L.H. Ch. 36 and in *re Flavell* (1883), 25 Ch. D. 89 (see also the waiver concerning this provision granted by the Council on 28th July, 1972).

(3) It was decided in *Galloway* v. *Corporation of London* (1867), L.R. 4 Eq. 90; 36 L.J. Ch. 978, that where a solicitor agrees in consideration of a salary to act for his employer (being an unqualified person), but for no other client, he may also (without any breach of the Act) agree with his employer that the legal costs received by his employer from opponents or third parties should be paid to the employer to the extent of the solicitor's salary, notional rent and reasonable office expenses, and there would therefore be no breach of the rule in those circumstances. If, however, that solicitor agrees to act not only for his employer but also for other clients (e.g. fellow employees) he must retain all the costs he receives from those clients. If he pays any part of those costs to his employer he is in breach of the rule, and probably of section 34 (now section 39) also (but see the waiver concerning compulsory moves granted by the Council in November, 1971).

RULE 4

(1) In this Rule the following words shall have the following meanings respectively, that is to say—

"accident claim" means any claim arising as a result of death or personal injury;

"claims assessor" means any organisation or person (not being a solicitor) whose business or any part of whose business is to make, support or prosecute (whether by action or otherwise, and whether by a solicitor or agent or otherwise) accident claims in such circumstances that such organisation or person solicits or receives any payment, gift, or benefit in respect of such claims;

"contingency fee" means any sum (whether fixed, or calculated either as a percentage of the proceeds or otherwise howsoever) payable only in the event of success in the prosecution of any action, suit or other contentious proceeding.

(2) A solicitor shall not act either in association with a claims assessor or in respect of any accident claim for any client introduced (whether directly or indirectly) by a claims assessor acting as such for that client and it shall be the duty of a solicitor, before accepting instructions in respect of an accident claim, to make reasonable enquiry to find out whether acceptance would contravene the provisions of this paragraph.

(3) A solicitor who is retained or employed to prosecute any action, suit or other contentious proceeding shall not enter into any agreement or arrangement to receive a contingency fee in respect of that action, suit or other contentious proceeding.

Explanatory notes forming no part of the Rule.

(i) For a detailed analysis of rule 4 in its previous form see Scott, L.J.'s, judgment in *Re a Solicitor* (1945) 1 All E.R. at pp. 446-7.

(ii) Criminal and civil liability for maintenance and champerty have been abolished by the Criminal Law Act, 1967 but section 14 (2) provides that the Act shall not affect any rule of law relating to cases in which a contract is to be treated as contrary to public policy or otherwise illegal (see Law Commission Report dated 25th October, 1966).

(iii) Paragraph 3 of the rule reflects, as a matter of professional conduct, section 65 (1) (b) of the Solicitors Act, 1957 (now section 59 (2) (b) of the Solicitors Act 1974), which in effect declares that nothing in that Act is to be treated as giving validity to any agreement by which a solicitor stipulates for a contingency fee.

RULE 5

The Council of The Law Society shall have power to waive in writing any of the provisions of these Rules in any particular case or cases.

RULE 6

In these Rules, unless the context otherwise requires, expressions shall have the meanings assigned to them by section 87 of the Solicitors Act, 1974.

Words importing the masculine gender shall include females and words in the singular shall include the plural and words in the plural shall include the singular.

Solicitors' Practice Rules, 1967

Rules under s. 28 of the Solicitors' Act, 1957, dated 24th January, 1967, made by the Council of The Law Society and approved by the Master of the Rolls.

RULE 1

These Rules may be cited as the Solicitors' Practice Rules, 1967, and

shall come into operation on the 1st day of March, 1967.

RULE 2

A solicitor shall not permit to appear on his nameplate or to be printed on his professional stationery the name of any person other than a solicitor who holds a current practising certificate: provided always that this rule shall not preclude

(a) the appearance in the style or name of a solicitors' practice of the name of a predecessor or former partner in that practice or

(b) the use of a style or firm name in use at the date of the coming into operation of these Rules or approved in writing by the Council.

RULE 3

In these Rules, unless the context otherwise requires, expressions shall have the meanings assigned to them by Section 86 of the Solicitors Act, 1957. (see now section 87 of the Solicitors Act, 1974).

Solicitors Practice Rules 1975

Rules under s. 31 Solicitors Act 1974 made by the Council of The Law Society with the concurrence of the Master of the Rolls on the 9th day of May 1975. Notes forming no part of the Rules are not printed here.

The Rules

1. These Rules may be cited as the Solicitors Practice Rules 1975 and shall come into operation on the 1st day of January 1976.

2. A solicitor shall ensure that every office where he or his firm practise is and can reasonably be seen to be properly supervised in accordance with the following minimum standards:

(a) Every office shall be managed by either a solicitor holding a Practising Certificate or by a Fellow of the Institute of Legal Executives, confirmed by the Institute as being of good standing and having been admitted a Fellow for not less than five years. Such solicitor or Fellow shall normally be in attendance at that office during all the hours when it is open to the public.

(b) Every such office shall be attended on each day when it is open to the public by a solicitor who holds a Practising Certificate and has been admitted for at least three years, being either a principal or a solicitor employed by the firm, and who shall spend sufficient time at such office to ensure adequate control of the staff employed there and afford requisite facilities for consultation with clients.

3. At the date of the making of these Rules:

(a) A solicitor who has been admitted for less than three years

and practises as a sole principal, or two or more solicitors of like seniority who practise in partnership, shall be entitled to exercise the duty of daily attendance under Rule 2(b).

(b) A solicitor's employee who would otherwise be disqualified but who is 50 years of age or more and has been continuously employed in connection with the practice of that solicitor for not less than 20 years shall, provided he already does so, be entitled to exercise the duty of management under Rule 2(a) until retirement or attaining the age of 70 years, whichever first happens.

(c) A solicitor's employee who would otherwise be disqualified but who is 35 years of age or more and has been continuously employed in connection with the practice of that solicitor for not less than 10 years shall, provided he already does so, be entitled to exercise the duty of management under Rule 2(a), for a period not exceeding 3 years from the date these Rules come into force and provided his employer notifies The Society of the employee's appointment, and identifies the office which he manages within six months of that date.

4. The Council of The Law Society shall have power to waive in writing any of the provisions of these Rules, and to revoke any such waiver, in any particular case or cases.

5. In these Rules, unless the context otherwise requires, expressions shall have the meaning assigned to them by s. 87 of the Solicitors Act 1974.

SOLICITOR'S LIEN

A solicitor is entitled to three kinds of lien to protect his right to recover his costs from his client, namely:—(1) a passive or retaining lien; (2) a common law lien on property recovered or preserved by his efforts; (3) a statutory lien enforceable by a charging order.

(1) Under the retaining lien the solicitor may hold all deeds, papers or other personal chattels coming into his possession in the course of his professional employment, in respect of taxable costs and expenses incurred by him as solicitor for his client. The lien is not available against third parties in cases where the client would be bound to produce the documents. It is discharged by the costs being paid, by the solicitor parting with the documents, by waiver, where the act in a manner inconsistent with his retention of the lien, or by proving in bankruptcy for the amount of the costs.

(2) Under the common law lien a solicitor may hold property (but not real property) of his client preserved or recovered by his exertions in litigation, though not in mere negotiation. It is a particular lien as opposed to (1) which is general. By virtue of this common law lien, the solicitor has a right to ask for the intervention of the court if there is danger of the client depriving him of his costs.

(3) By s. 73 of the Solicitors Act, 1974, the Court may make a charging order in connection with any property which is not inalienable in the hands of the solicitor and recovered or preserved through his instrumentality for his client in an action or proceedings, for the payment to the solicitor of his taxed costs thereof.

A London agent has a general lien over moneys and documents in his hands in any particular transaction for any costs and disbursements in any transaction, against the country solicitor. He has, however, no lien for the general balance of his account against the country solicitor, and a lien is only available against the client in so far as the country solicitor himself remains unpaid.

Stamps

STAMP DUTIES

(See Sergeant on Stamp Duties (including Capital Duty) 6th Edn. and 2nd Cumulative Supplement) and Sims on Capital Duty)

NOTE.—Where reference is made to a section of an Act, the Act referred to is the Stamp Act, 1891 unless otherwise indicated.

Documents may be stamped at the head office of the Controller of Stamps, Bush House (South-West Wing), London, W.C.2B 4QN or at the branch offices of the Controller situated in the principal cities throughout the country. Documents may also be stamped through principal post offices.

ACKNOWLEDGMENT OF RIGHT TO PRODUCTION OF DEEDS

if contained in separate document:

under hand	..	nil
under seal	..	50p

ADJUDICATION

The Commissioners of Inland Revenue may be required by any person to express their opinion as to whether an executed instrument is chargeable with any duty and if so the amount of duty (Stamp Act 1891, s. 12). Certain instruments are required to bear the adjudication stamp before they can be regarded as duly stamped. They include:

(a) Voluntary dispositions *inter vivos* (F.A. (1909–10) 1910 s. 74).

(b) Conveyances and transfers on sale in connection with schemes for the reconstruction or amalgamation of companies relieved from duty under F.A. 1927, s. 55.

(c) Returns or statements made in

connection with company re-structuring operations relieved from Capital Duty under F.A. 1973, s. 47 (6) and paras. 9 and 10, Sch. 19.

(d) Conveyances and transfers on sale between closely associated bodies corporate relieved from duty under F.A. 1930, s. 42.

(e) Conveyances or transfers of property in contemplation of a sale (F.A. 1965, s. 90).

(f) Conveyances to charities (F. A. 1974, s. 49).

In practice the Court requires an undertaking that Orders made under the Variation of Trusts Act 1958 or Orders under Section 208, Companies Act 1948 vesting property be presented for adjudication.

Executed instruments for adjudication may be sent by post (the applicant paying the postal charges) to:—

The Controller of Stamps
Adjudication Section
Inland Revenue (D)
West Block
Barrington Road
Worthing, Sussex BN12 4SF.

Alternatively they may be handed in at any of the branch offices of the Controller of Stamps.

AGREEMENT

1. Made or entered into pursuant to Highways Acts, relating to making, maintenance or repair of highways, if under seal, 5p.

2. For lease or any letting. See LEASE OR TACK.

3. Under hand only, accompanied with a deposit of stock, shares or marketable securities, exempt (s. 23 as amended by F.A. 1970 Sched. 7, para. 1 (3) (a)).

4. For option for purchase or sale of any stock, etc. see under CONTRACT NOTE.

5. For sale of property. See CONVEYANCE OR TRANSFER (see also s. 59).

AGREEMENT OR ANY MEMORANDUM OF AN AGREEMENT

Under hand ..   nil
Under seal   ..   5op

ANNUITY

1. Conveyance in consideration of. See CONVEYANCE OR TRANSFER.

2. Purchase of. See CONVEYANCE OR TRANSFER.

3. Superannuation annuity and purchased life annuity. See BOND, COVENANT, ETC.

APPOINTMENT

1. Of a new trustee, 5op.

2. In execution of a power over any property, or of any use, share, or interest in any property, by any instrument not being a will, 5op.

3. Receiver, under power contained in a debenture, 5op.

[NOTE: if an appointment of new trustee contains also a conveyance of trust property, or an express Vesting Declaration under the Trustee Act, 1925, s. 40, an additional 5op is charged; but a mere direction for conveyance (by separate deed), or the usual implied declaration, does not attract further duty.

A Minute of acceptance of office, although indorsed on settlement and signed, is not liable to duty.]

ARRANGEMENT, DEED OF

1. Assignment for benefit of creditors, 5op.

2. Re-assignment by a trustee to a debtor, 5op.

ARTICLES OF PARTNERSHIP

Under seal, 5op.

[NOTE: if a premium is paid by incoming partner ad valorem conveyance on sale duty is payable on the amount of the premium.]

ASSENT

To a devise of freeholds or a bequest of leaseholds:—
under hand, nil.
under seal, 5op.

ASSIGNMENT

1. Upon sale. See CONVEYANCE OR TRANSFER.

2. Upon gift. See CONVEYANCE OR TRANSFER.

ATTORNEY

Letter or power of. *See* LETTER OR POWER OF ATTORNEY.

BEARER INSTRUMENT

1. Inland bearer instrument (other than deposit certificate for overseas stock), three times the transfer duty on the market value.

2. Overseas bearer instrument (other than deposit certificate for overseas stock or bearer instrument by usage), twice the transfer duty on the market value.

3. Instrument excepted from para. 1 or 2, 10p for every £50 or part of £50 of the market value.

4. Inland or overseas bearer instrument given in substitution for a like instrument duly stamped *ad valorem* (whether under this heading or not), 10p.

[NOTE: Exempted from this heading are bearer instruments relating to shares in Government or Parliamentary stocks, allotment letters, letters of rights, scrip, etc., required to be surrendered or renounceable not later than six months after issue, and instruments relating to stock expressed in currencies of territories outside the scheduled territories.]

As regards relief on shares purchased by certain overseas residents, *see* F.A. 1974, Sched. 11, Pt. III.

BILL OF EXCHANGE OR PROMISSORY NOTE

Nil (duty abolished as from 1.2.1971, F.A. 1970 Sched. 7, para. 2 (2) (a)).

BILL OF SALE

1. Absolute. *See* CONVEYANCE OR TRANSFER.

2. By way of gift. *See* CONVEYANCE OR TRANSFER.

BOND, COVENANT OR INSTRUMENT

1. Instrument increasing the rent reserved by another instrument. *See* s. 77(5), and Finance Act 1971, s. 64.

2. Bond in relation to any annuity upon the original creation and sale thereof. *See* CONVEYANCE OR TRANSFER.

3. Bond, covenant or instrument of any Bond whatsoever, being a grant or contract for payment of a superannuation annuity, that is to say a deferred life annuity granted or secured to any person in consideration of annual premiums payable until he attains a specified age, and so to commence on his attaining that age—

For every £10, and also for any fractional part of £10 of the annuity, 5p.

4. Bond, covenant or instrument of any kind whatsoever, being a grant or contract for payment of a purchased life annuity, whether or not the annuity is a superannuation annuity as defined in paragraph (3) above—

For every £10, and also for any fractional part of £10 of the annuity, 5p.

BUILDING LEASE. *See* LEASE.

CAPITAL DUTY

CAPITAL DUTY, per £100 or part of £100 of the amount of the assets contributed to the share capital of a capital company . . . £1.

The duty is payable on the returns or statements required in connection with share capital actually issued by a capital company and does not apply to an increase in authorised capital.

A "capital company" includes a company incorporated with limited liability, limited partnerships, and companies limited by guarantee whether or not with share capital, but not an unlimited company.

The main chargeable transactions are the formation of a capital company and the subsequent increase in the issued capital of such a company by the contribution of assets of any kind. Where shares are issued for cash, duty is chargeable on the higher of the nominal value of the shares issued and the cash consideration paid to the company. Where consideration is other than cash, duty is assessed on the higher of the nominal value of the shares issued and the net value of the assets contributed. An issue of bonus shares, not being a contribution of assets, is not subject to the duty.

An overseas company may be liable if it ranks as a "capital company" and is controlled in or in certain circumstances has its registered office in Great Britain.

Company restructuring operations which satisfy certain conditions are exempt from the duty.

CHARITIES

For reduced rates see note to table of *ad valorem* stamp duties, *post.*

CHEQUE, Nil

CONTRACT NOTE

1. For or relating to the sale or purchase of any stock or marketable security—

Where the value of the stock or marketable security exceeds £100 and does not exceed £500, 10p; exceeds £500 and does not exceed £1,500, 30p; exceeds £1,500, 60p. [*Appropriated adhesive stamp or impressed stamp may be used.*]

[NOTE: See F.A. 1946, s. 54 (6) as to when managers of a unit trust scheme are treated as persons dealing as a principal in stock.]

2. Contract for an option for the sale or purchase of any stock or marketable security at a future time at a certain price—

One-half of the duty chargeable under paragraph 1.

[NOTE: Duty on Contract Notes may now be paid in advance by way of composition—F.A. 1966, s. 46.]

CONVEYANCE OR TRANSFER

1. Conveyance or transfer on sale, or by way of voluntary disposition *inter vivos* of any property (unless exempt from stamp duty).

[NOTES: Certificates of value are not applicable to conveyances or transfers of stock or marketable securities—F.A. 1963, s. 55 (2).

Conveyances on sale of government securities and of ships are exempt from duty–Stamp Act Sched. 1, General Exemptions.

Transfer of stock or marketable securities on sale to a stockbroker or jobber to be held pending resale in the course of their business, provided

transfer is impressed with a "supplementary stamp" are charged with a maximum of 50p—F.A. 1920, s. 42. This exemption also applies where a dealer borrows stock to sell and subsequently pays it back, both the transfer and the retransfer being charged a maximum duty of 50p.—F.A. 1961, s. 34.

Transfers of shares in Building Societies are exempt—Building Societies Act, 1962, s. 117.

Transfers of stock guaranteed by the Treasury are exempt—F.A. 1947, s. 57.

Conveyances, agreements, etc., for carrying out nationalisation schemes are exempt—F.A. 1948, s. 74.

Certain transfers between associated companies are exempt (F.A. 1930, s. 42; and F.A. 1967, s. 27). Similarly transfers on the amalgamation and reconstruction of companies are relieved from duty when certain conditions are complied with (F.A. 1927, s. 55; F.A. 1928, s. 31.

Transfers of stock or other security for money lent issued by a local authority are exempt (F.A. 1967, s. 29 (2)).

Transfer of certain loan capital are exempt (F.A. 1976, s. 106. See under Loan Capital, *post.*

As to relief for conveyances, transfers, and lettings to, Charities, under F.A. 1974, s. 49 (1). *See also* Charities.

As to relief for purchases of stocks and shares by certain overseas residents, *see* F.A. 1974, Sched. 11, Pt. III.

As to other exemptions and special rates, *see* F.A. 1951, s. 42; F.A. 1952, s. 74; F.A. 1953, s. 31 (1); F.A. 1958, s. 35; F.A. 1963, ss. 62, 65.

Instruments conveying property in contemplation of a sale (i.e. conferring an option) are treated as conveyances at the value of the property (F.A. 1965, s. 90).

2. Conveyance or transfer of any kind not hereinbefore described, 50p (unless exempt from stamp duty).

COUNTERPART. See DUPLICATE.

COVENANT (*and see* BOND, COVENANT, ETC.)

1. In relation to any annuity upon the original creation and sale thereof. *See* CONVEYANCE OR TRANSFER, and s. 60.

2. In relation to any instrument increasing the rent reserved by another instrument. *See* BOND, COVENANT, ETC.

3. Any separate deed of covenant (not being an instrument chargeable with *ad valorem* duty as a conveyance on sale) made on the sale of any property, and relating solely to the conveyance or enjoyment of, or the title to, the property sold or to the production of the muniments of title relating thereto, or to all or any of the matters aforesaid—

Where the *ad valorem* duty in respect of the consideration does not exceed 50p, a duty equal to the amount of such *ad valorem* duty.

4. In any other case, 50p.

DEBENTURE

for securing the payment or repayment of money or the transfer or retransfer of stock. *See* CONVEYANCE OR TRANSFER, *ante*, and LOAN CAPITAL, *post*.

DECLARATION

of any use or trust of or concerning any property by any writing, not being a will, or an instrument chargeable with *ad valorem* duty as a Unit Trust instrument or as a voluntary disposition *inter vivos*, 50p.

DEED

1. Deed of arrangement. *See* ARRANGEMENT, DEED OF.

2. Deed of Gift. *See* CONVEYANCE OR TRANSFER.

3. Deed of partnership. *See* ARTICLES OF PARTNERSHIP.

4. Deed of any kind whatever not otherwise described, 50p.

DUPLICATE OR COUNTERPART

of any instrument chargeable with any duty.

Where duty on the original does not amount to 50p, the same duty as the original instrument.

In any other case, 50p.

EXCHANGE

Where consideration exceeding £100 is paid for equality of exchange, conveyance duty thereon is payable. In any other case, 50p.

FORECLOSURE ORDER

As a conveyance on full value of the property, Finance Act, 1898, s. 6.

GIFT

GIFT *inter vivos*. *See* CONVEYANCE.

HIRE-PURCHASE AGREEMENT

Any agreement for or relating to the supply of goods on hire, whereby the goods in consideration of periodical payments will or may become the property of the person to whom they are supplied:

under hand	..	nil
under seal	..	50p.

LEASE OR TACK

1. For any definite term less than a year:

(*a*) Of any furnished dwelling-house or apartments where the rent for such term exceeds £250, £1.

(*b*) Of any lands, tenements, or heritable subjects otherwise than as aforesaid, the same duty as a lease for a year at the rent reserved for the definite term. ["From week to week" &c. is indefinite.]

2. For any other definite term or for any indefinite term of any lands, tenements or heritable subjects:

(*a*) Where the consideration, or any part of the consideration, moving either to the lessor or to any other person, consists of any money, stock, or security:

In respect of such consideration, the same duty as a conveyance on a sale for the same consideration.

(*b*) Where the consideration or any part of the consideration is rent:

In respect of such consideration, if the rent, whether reserved as a yearly rent or otherwise, is at the rates in the Table on p. 338.

3. Of any other kind whatsoever not hereinbefore described, £2.

[NOTE: Where the agreement for lease is full stamped *ad val.*, the lease itself requires 5p only, but the denoting stamp is necessary.]

4. Building lease: *ad val.* on the rent.

5. Charities, leases to, relief. (*See* F.A. 1974, s. 49 (2)).

LETTER OR POWER OF ATTORNEY,

or other instrument in the nature thereof:

1. By any petty officer, seaman, marine, or soldier serving as a marine, or his representatives, for receiving prize money or wages, 5p.

2. For the receipt of the dividends or interest of any stock:

Where made for the receipt of one payment only, 5p.

In any other case, 25p.

3. For the receipt of any sum of money, or any bill of exchange or promissory note for any sum of money, not exceeding £20, or any periodical payments not exceeding the annual sum of £10 (not being hereinbefore charged), 25p.

4. Of any kind whatsoever not hereinbefore described and not specially exempted, 50p.

Exemptions:

(1) Letter or power of attorney for the receipt of dividends of any definite and certain share of the Government or Parliamentary stocks or funds producing a yearly dividend less than £3.

(2) Letter or power of attorney or proxy filed in the Probate Division of the High Court of Justice in England or Ireland, or in any ecclesiastical court.

(3) Order, request, or direction under hand only from the proprietor of any stock to any company or to any officer of any company or to any banker to pay the dividends or interest arising from the stock to any person therein named.

(4) Letter or power of attorney for the sale, transfer or acceptance of any of the Government or Parliamentary stocks or funds.

(5) A power of attorney given exclusively for the purpose of authorising the receipt of money payable or the redemption of Government stock.

(6) Letter or power of attorney for the sole purpose of appointing or authorising a proxy to vote at any one meeting at which votes may be given by proxy, whether the number of persons named in such instrument be one or more.

[NOTE: A power of attorney is not to be charged with duty more than once by reason only that more persons than one are named in the instrument or that the powers conferred relate to more than one matter (Finance Act, 1927, s. 56).]

LOAN CAPITAL

No duty of any kind on issue of loan capital Transfers of certain loan capital (as defined) are exempt from duty if certain requirements are satisfied (F.A. 1976, s. 126).

For this purpose "loan capital" means—

(a) any debenture stock, corporation stock or funded debt (by whatever name known) issued by any body corporate or other body of persons formed or established in the United Kingdom or any capital raised by any such body, being capital which is borrowed, or has the character of borrowed money, whether it is in the form of stock or any other form; and

(b) stock or marketable securities issued by the government of any country or territory within the Commonwealth outside the United Kingdom.

Loan capital having any of the features mentioned below is outside the exemption and is still subject to *ad valorem* duty on transfer. The disqualifying features are—

(i) the existence *at the time of the transfer* of any unexpired conversion, subscription etc. rights even if they are only exercisable at some time in the future. Rights of that nature which attached to the loan capital in the past will not offend this condition if they have been wholly exercised or have wholly expired at the time of the transfer; *or*

(ii) a right *at any time* to an interest return which is unusually high by reasonable commercial standards or which is geared to business results or property values; *or*

(iii) the existence *at any time* of a right to a premium or redemption which is unusual by comparison with similar Officially Listed loan capital.

As to duty on share capital, *see* CAPITAL DUTY, *ante.*)

MARKETABLE SECURITY

Transfer, assignment, disposition or assignation of a marketable security of any description:

Upon a sale thereof—*see* CONVEYANCE. In any other case (except by way of gift), 50p.

As to exemption from duty on transfers of certain loan capital, see under LOAN CAPITAL, *ante*.

MORTGAGE, BOND, DEBENTURE, COVENANT

Nil. (Duty abolished as from 1st August, 1971 by the Finance Act 1971, s. 64 (1) (*c*)).

PARTITION OR DIVISION

Instrument effecting:—

1. If the consideration for equality does not exceed £100, 50p.

2. If the consideration for equality exceeds £100, *ad valorem* conveyance on sale duty on the amount of such consideration only.

POLICY OF INSURANCE OTHER THAN LIFE INSURANCE

Exempt (as from 1.8.70, F.A. 1970, Sched. 7, para. 1 (2) (*b*)).

POLICY OF LIFE INSURANCE

If the period does not exceed two years, 5p. Where the period exceeds two years and the sum insured exceeds £50 but does not exceed £1,000, 5p for every £100 or part of £100; exceeds £1,000, 50p for every £1,000 or part of £1,000.

A policy made solely in connection with re-insurance of a risk in which a policy duly stamped relates is chargeable only if it is under seal and the duty then chargeable is not to exceed 50p, (F.A. 1970, Sched. 7, para. 17 (3)).

POWER OF ATTORNEY. *See* LETTER OR POWER OF ATTORNEY.

PRODUCED STAMP

On the occasion of any transfer on sale of the fee simple of land or grant of a lease for seven or more years, or a transfer on sale of any such lease, the instrument must be produced to the Inland Revenue with prescribed particulars on Form Stamps L(A) 451.

PROMISSORY NOTE

Nil (Duty abolished as from 1.2.71, F.A. 1970, Sched. 7, para. 2 (2) (a)).

RECEIPT

Nil (Duty abolished as from 1.2.71, F.A. 1970, Sched. 7, para. 2 (2) (b)).

RELEASE OR RENUNCIATION of any property, or of any right or interest in any property—

1. Upon a sale. See CONVEYANCE OR TRANSFER.

2. In any other case, 50p.

REVOCATION

of any use or trust of any property by any writing, not being a will, 50p.

SHARE CAPITAL, issue of: *See* CAPITAL DUTY.

SURRENDER

of any kind whatsoever not chargeable with duty as a conveyance on sale or by way of voluntary disposition *inter vivos*, 50p.

TRANSFER. *See* CONVEYANCE.

UNIT TRUSTS

1. Any trust instrument of a unit trust scheme within the meaning of Part VII of the F.A., 1946—

For every £100, and also for any fractional part of £100, of the amount or value of the property subject to the trusts created or recorded by the instrument, 25p.

NOTE: As to returns to be made to the Commissioners and additional duty payable in respect of property added to the trust, *see* F.A. 1946, s. 53 and as to credits in respect of property represented by extinguished units see F.A. 1962, s. 25.

2. Transfers of units:

(a) Registered Units—the same duty as registered stock, *see* CONVEYANCE.

(b) Unit certificates to bearer—the same duty as a bearer instrument according to whether the unit trust scheme is governed by the law of any part of the United Kingdom or not, *see* BEARER INSTRUMENT.

VOLUNTARY DISPOSITION *inter vivos. See* CONVEYANCE.

GENERAL EXEMPTIONS FROM ALL STAMP DUTIES

1. Under the Stamp Act, 1891 Sched. 1:

(1) Transfers of shares in the Government or Parliamentary stocks or funds.

(2) Instruments for the sale, transfer, or other disposition either absolutely or otherwise, of any ship or vessel, or any party, interest, share, or property of or in any ship or vessel.

(3) [*Repealed, Finance Act 1971, Sched. 13, Part VI.*]

(4) Testaments and testamentary instruments.

(5) [*Repealed, Finance Act 1971, Sched. 13, Part VI.*]

2. Under F.A. 1949, Sched. 8.

(1) Instruments of apprenticeship.

(2) Articles of clerkship to a solicitor.

(3) Bonds given pursuant to any Act, or of the Commissioners of Customs and Excise, or any of their officers, for or in respect of any of the duties of excise or customs or purchase tax, or for preventing fraud or evasion thereof, or for any other matter or thing relating thereto.

(4) Bonds on obtaining letters of administration.

(5) Charter Parties.

3. Under the F.A. 1948, s. 74:

Where the Treasury so directs, transfers of stock of nationalized industries.

4. Under the F.A. 1953, s. 31:

Certain receipts in connection with National Savings made or executed for purposes of any Savings Committee, Savings Group, etc.

5. Under the F.A. 1963, s. 65 (3):

Applications, etc., for Legal Aid.

6. Under the F.A. 1964, s. 23:

Contracts of service in any office or employment, including a memorandum thereof, and any contract varying or terminating such a contract.

7. Under the F.A. 1976, s. 106:

Transfers of certain loan capital. See under LOAN CAPITAL, *ante.*

TABLES OF AD VALOREM STAMP DUTIES

CONSIDERATION for a Conveyance or Transfer on Sale, or PREMIUM for a Lease

1 Consideration or premium		2 Instrument certified at £15,000*	3 Instrument certified at £20,000*	4 Instrument certified at £25,000*	5 Instrument certified at £30,000*	6 Instrument not certified*
Exceeds £	does not exceed £		£ p	£ p	£ p	£ p
	5	Nil	5	5	10	10
5	10	Nil	5	10	15	20
10	20	Nil	10	20	30	40
20	30	Nil	15	30	45	60
30	40	Nil	20	40	60	80
40	50	Nil	25	50	75	1 00
50	60	Nil	30	60	90	1 20
60	70	Nil	35	70	1 05	1 40
70	80	Nil	40	80	1 20	1 60
80	90	Nil	45	90	1 35	1 80
90	100	Nil	50	1 00	1 50	2 00
100	120	Nil	60	1 20	1 80	2 40
120	140	Nil	70	1 40	2 10	2 80
140	160	Nil	80	1 60	2 40	3 20
160	180	Nil	90	1 80	2 70	3 60
180	200	Nil	1 00	2 00	3 00	4 00
200	220	Nil	1 10	2 20	3 30	4 40
220	240	Nil	1 20	2 40	3 60	4 80
240	260	Nil	1 30	2 60	3 90	5 20
260	280	Nil	1 40	2 80	4 20	5 60
280	300	Nil	1 50	3 00	4 50	6 00
300	15,000	Nil	25	50	75	1 00 per £50 or part of £50
15,000	20,000	—	25	50	75	1 00 per £50 or part of £50
20,000	25,000	—	—	50	75	1 00 per £50 or part of £50
25,000	30,000	—	—	—	75	1 00 per £50 or part of £50
30,000			—	—	—	1 00 per £50 or part of £50

* An instrument which is "certified" at a particular amount is one which contains a statement certifying that the transaction effected by the instrument does not form part of a larger transaction or series of transactions in respect of which the amount or value, or aggregate amount or value, of the consideration exceeds that amount. For the purpose of determining the amount at which an instrument is to be certified the consideration for any sale or contract or agreement for the sale of goods, wares or merchandise should be disregarded (except where the instrument is itself an actual conveyance or transfer of the goods, wares or merchandise, with or without other property).

NOTES.—(1). There is no provision for the certification of Transfers of stock (including units under unit trust schemes) and marketable securities, or of Leases at a yearly rate of rent exceeding £150, and all such instruments are chargeable with the duty shown in Column 6.

(2). *Non-resident purchasers.*—Transfers of Shares or securities purchased for the beneficial ownership of any person who is resident outside the scheduled territories are relieved from the increases in stamp duty made by F.A. 1974, i.e. such transfers if appropriately certified are liable to duty at one half only of the rates shown in the table.

(3). *Charities.* A conveyance, transfer or letting to a charity may be stamped with duty at one half the rates shown in the table of *ad valorem* stamp duties, but the instrument is required to be adjudicated. (F.A. 1974, s. 49 (2).)

(4). *Loan Capital.* Transfers of certain loan capital are exempt from duty if certain conditions are satisfied. See under LOAN CAPITAL, *ante*.

LEASE—Annual Rent (for premium see Columns 1-6)

7 Annual rent		8 Term not exceeding 7 years or indefinite	9 Term exceeding 7 years but not exceeding 35 years	10 Term exceeding 35 years but not exceeding 100 years	11 Term exceeding 100 years
Exceeds	does not exceed				
£	£		£ p	£ p	£ p
	5	Nil	10	60	1 20
5	10	Nil	20	1 20	2 40
10	15	Nil	30	1 80	3 60
15	20	Nil	40	2 40	4 80
20	25	Nil	50	3 00	6 00
25	50	Nil	1 00	6 00	12 00
50	75	Nil	1 50	9 00	18 00
75	100	Nil	2 00	12 00	24 00
100	150	Nil	3 00	18 00	36 00
See NOTE above 150	200	Nil	4 00	24 00	48 00
See NOTE above 200	250	Nil	5 00	30 00	60 00
		50p per £50 or part of £50	£1 per £50 or part of £50	£6 per £50 or part of £50	£12 per £50 or part of £50

FURNISHED LETTINGS.—A letting agreement for any definite term less than a year of any furnished dwelling house or apartment ... for the term exceed £50 attracts a fixed duty of £1.

Taxation

(See Simon's Taxes, 3rd Edn. and De Voil: Value Added Tax)

Taxation is covered under the following headings in the order shown:

Income Tax
Capital Allowances
Capital Gains Tax
Corporation Tax
Close Companies
Interest on Unpaid Tax
Value Added Tax

Statutory references are:—Income and Corporation Taxes Act 1970, "I.C.T.A."; Taxes Management Act 1970, "T.M.A."; Capital Allowances Act 1968, "C.A.A."; Finance Act, "F.A."

Taxation of Capital and Wealth
Capital transfer tax. See p. 85.
Wealth tax. An annual wealth tax will be introduced and a Green Paper (Cmnd. 5704) was introduced in August 1974.

INCOME TAX

Unified tax. From 1973 a broad band of income whether earned or unearned is taxed at basic rate. Higher rates of tax apply to higher incomes. Thus income tax is charged on part of an individual's total income at basic rate and on the remainder at higher rates: F.A. 1971, s. 32 (1).

Investment income surcharge. Investment income exceeding a certain amount is charged at additional rate(s): F.A. 1971, s. 32 (1).

Investment income is income which is not earned income and income chargeable as investment income is income chargeable at the additional rate(s): F.A. 1971, s. 32 (2).

Personal reliefs. Personal reliefs are deducted from total income except life assurance relief which is given by deduction of tax at (generally) one half of the basic rate: F.A. 1971, s. 33 (2), (3).

The reduction of personal reliefs for family allowances applies at both the basic and higher rates: F.A. 1971, s. 33 (4).

Effect of deductions from total income.

Subject to any express provision deductions in computing or to be made from total income reduce income of different descriptions so as to maximise reduction in tax liability: F.A. 1971, s. 34.

To determine investment income subject to the surcharge personal reliefs are set off first against non-investment income, then against the slice of investment income exempt from surcharge, then against the rest: F.A. 1971, s. 34 (4).

Construction of references. References in the Acts and in instruments and wills after 3 September 1939 to deduction of income tax are construed as deduction at basic rate, references to standard rate are construed as to basic rate: F.A. 1971, s. 36 and Sch. 7 paras. 2–4.

Year of Assessment. Every assessment to income tax is for a year commencing on April 6 and ending the following April 5.

Scheme of the Income Tax. Income tax is charged under Schedules and Cases:

Schedule/Case	Income Charged	Basis of Assessment	Date/Method of Payment
Schedule A	Rents, profits from land, premiums treated as rent.	Current year	1 January
Schedule B	Occupation of commercial woodlands	Current year on $\frac{1}{3}$ annual value	1 January

Schedule/Case	Income Charged	Basis of Assessment	Date/Method of Payment
Schedule C	Interest or dividends from Government and similar securities	Current year	Deduction at source
Schedule D			
Cases I & II	Profits of trade, profession or vocation	Preceding accounting year. Special rules for opening and closing years	Earned: 1 January, 1 July; Unearned: 1 January
Case III	Interest not within Schedule C, War Loan, bank interest, annuities and other annual payments not taxed at source, small maintenance payments	Preceding year. Special rules for opening and closing years.	1 January
Cases IV & V	Dividends and interest from securities outside U.K.; income from other property abroad	Preceding year. Special rules for opening and closing years	1 January
Case VI	Residual; also specific items, *e.g.* furnished lettings, post-cessation receipts, income of settlors; *see also* conveyancing transactions, p. 331	Current year	1 January
Case VII	Short-term gains	Abolished for 1971–72 onwards	
Case VIII	Rents, etc.	*See* now Schedule A	
Tax deducted	Annuities and other annual payments	Current years	Deduction at source
Schedule E			
Case I	Emoluments of a person resident and ordinarily resident but where any duties are performed wholly outside the United Kingdom or are foreign emoluments, tax is reduced.	Current year	P.A.Y.E.

Schedule/Case	Income Charged	Basis of Assessment	Date/Method of Payment
Case II	Emoluments of a non-resident and of a resident not ordinarily resident, for duties in U.K. but foreign emoluments bear reduced tax	Current year	P.A.Y.E.
Case III	Emoluments of a resident, remitted from abroad, relative to any year of residence	Amounts actually remitted to U.K. for year of assessment	Direct assessment
General charge	Pensions and some National Insurance benefits	Current year	P.A.Y.E., or direct assessment
Schedule F	Dividends and distributions from U.K. companies	Current year	Tax credit

Rates for 1976–77

Basic Rate	35%

Investment Income Surcharge

general	10% on £1,000 to £2,000; 15% on excess
over 65's	10% on £1,500 to £2,000; 15% on excess

Basic and Higher Rates

Band of taxable income		Rate per cent of tax	Tax on full band	Cumulative tax on top of each band
Exceeding £	Not exceeding £	£	£	£
	5,000	35	1,750	1,750
5,000	5,500	40	200	1,950
5,500	6,500	45	450	2,400
6,500	7,500	50	500	2,900
7,500	8,500	55	550	3,450
8,500	10,000	60	900	4,350
10,000	12,000	65	1,300	5,650
12,000	15,000	70	2,100	7,750
15,000	20,000	75	3,750	11,500
	Over £20,000	83		

Reliefs

Personal Relief	Single	£735
	Married	£1,085
	In year of marriage, reduced by £29⅙ for each complete month from April 6 to date of marriage	
Wife's Earned Income Relief	Maximum relief..	£735
†Child Relief	Born 7.4.65 to 5.4.77	£300
	,, 7.4.60 to 6.4.65	£335
	,, 6.4.60 or earlier and receiving education	£365
	Relief reduced by excess of child's income in own right over £115	

Age Allowance	Single: income up to £1010	
	Married: income up to £1555	
	Excess over personal relief withdrawn by £2 for every £3 income over £3250.	
Housekeeper Relief Widow(er)s, etc. Additional Relief	(including charge of brother or sister)	£100
	Child, but no housekeeper	£350
Dependent Relative Relief	Single women, etc.	£145
	Others	£100
	Relief reduced by excess of dependant's income over basic retirement pension.	
Daughter's Services Relief	.. ..	£55
Blind Person's Relief	Each person	£180
	Reduced by any disability payments received; no relief if £100 or more	
Life Assurance Relief	On post-22.6.16 policies:	
	Premiums not over £10 Premiums @ 35%	
	Premiums exceed £10, but not £20 .. £10 @ 35%	
	Premiums exceed £20 .. .. Premiums @ 17½%	
†Reduction of Total Reliefs	For each family allowance received ..	(£52)

Exemptions. Charities, except on trade etc. profits under Schedule D, Cases I and II; even these are exempt if applied solely for the charity and either

(i) the trade is conducted as a primary purpose of the charity; or
(ii) the work in the trade is mainly carried on by the beneficiaries of the charity; I.C.T.A., s. 360 (1) (2), (3).

Unemployment, sickness and maternity benefits and invalidity benefit attendance allowances under the National Insurance Acts, including the death grant: I.C.T.A., s. 219 (1).

Disabled persons' vehicle maintenance grant: F.A. 1972, s. 70.

Family income supplements: F.A. 1971, s. 18 (1).

Redundancy payments: I.C.T.A., s. 412, but such payments are taken into account in connection with "golden handshake" provisions.

Accumulated interest on savings certificates: I.C.T.A., s. 95.

The first £40 of interest on ordinary deposits with the National Savings Bank or a trustee savings bank is exempted from income tax at all rates: I.C.T.A., s. 414.

Allowances made to Crown servants in compensation for the extra cost of living outside the U.K.: I.C.T.A., s. 369.

Ambassadors and High Commissioners or Agents-General, and certain members of their staffs: I.C.T.A., s. 372.

Consular staff in respect of their remuneration and income from abroad: I.C.T.A., ss. 367, 373.

Members of visiting forces of designated countries: I.C.T.A., s. 367.

Re-engagement bounties and gratuities payable to members of the Armed Forces and Women's Services and allowances in lieu of food or for mess expenses: I.C.T.A., s. 366.

Wounds and disability pensions: I.C.T.A., s. 365.

Annuities and additional pensions to holders of the V.C., G.C., Albert Medal and Edward Medal: I.C.T.A., s. 368.

Compensation for Nazi persecution: I.C.T.A., s. 377.

Housing grants: I.C.T.A., s. 376.

Life Assurance. An allowance may be claimed in respect of premiums paid by the claimant (or his wife) on policies on the claimant's own life (or on the spouse's life): where separate taxation of wife's earnings is claimed, the words in brackets do not apply; (*see* Life Assurance, *ante*). Insurances made after 19th March 1968 must qualify within I.C.T.A., Sched. 1.

As to rates of relief on policies *post-22.6.16*, see above; as to policies *pre-22.6.16* see I.C.T.A., s. 20.

Total allowable premiums cannot exceed one-sixth of total income

A system of "claim back" of tax relief applies to certain transactions in the early years of the policy: F.A. 1975, ss. 7, 8.

Sums borrowed against life policies are treated as income in certain cases: I.C.T.A., s. 405.

A liability to tax, but not at the basic rate, may rise on the termination of a qualifying policy issued in respect of an insurance made after 19 March 1968 if termination takes place within ten years of the making of the insurance; in the case of a non-qualifying policy there is no time limit: I.C.T.A., ss. 393, 399.

Partnerships. The assessment is made on the firm and the return must be made by the precedent acting partner. Failing payment any partner may be sued. On a change there is a cessation unless all partners, before and after, give notice within 24 months to retain a continuing basis: I.C.T.A., s. 154.

Schedule D, Case I and II expenses. No deduction is allowed for expenses not wholly and exclusively laid out for the trade etc., domestic or private expenditure, rent of house except part used for trade, improvements as opposed to repairs, losses unconnected with the trade, capital withdrawn, sums covered by insurance, patent royalties and annual payments other than interest: I.C.T.A., s. 130. Business entertainment except of overseas customers is not deductible.

Losses. Losses made in trades and professions can be carried forward against the profits of the same trade made in subsequent years. Moreover, such losses can be set against other income of the same or the succeeding year; and then the balance can be carried forward, I.C.T.A., ss. 168, 171. Restriction in this regard is imposed, in relation to hobbies, by I.C.T.A., s. 170 and, in relation to farming and market gardening, by I.C.T.A., s. 180.

A loss made in the last 12 months of trading can be carried back for up to 3 years of assessment: I.C.T.A., s. 174.

Copyrights. Where copyrights are sold for a lump sum relief may be obtained under I.C.T.A., ss. 389(6), 390. Similar relief for painters, sculptors and artists is available under I.C.T.A., s. 392.

Patents. The capital consideration for the sale of patent rights is liable to tax under Schedule D, Case VI, but the receipts may be spread by residents over six tax years: I.C.T.A., s. 380.

Schedule A expenses. Deductions are allowed for maintenance, repairs, insurance, management; other services not separately paid for; rates actually paid; superior rents, rent-charges, ground-rents, feu-duties and annual payments out of the land: I.C.T.A., ss. 72, 73, 7*, 75 and 83.

Schedule E. Expenses must be incurred in the performance of the duties of the employment and must be wholly, exclusively and necessarily incurred in the performance of the duties. Expenses of travelling to work are not deductible. Nor are business entertainment expenses except those incurred on overseas customers: I.C.T.A., s. 411, T.M.A., s. 98.

Fees and subscriptions paid to certain professional organisations are deductible: I.C.T.A., ss. 192, 195 (1).

Schedule E—benefits in kind. From 1977–78 onwards the amount of benefit taxable in respect of a car will normally be according to a scale which varies according to the type of car provided and private use will no longer be taken into account. The limit on expenditure on cars for normal writing-down allowances will at the same time be increased to £5,000. The rules about taxing benefits will apply to all directors and to those employees earning £5,000 a year and not merely to those employed by trading concerns. Tangible assets other than cars will be taxed at 10 per cent. per annum of value on first use. The provision for employees of certain loans at less than commercial rates of interest and of certain other facilities in connection with share incentive schemes will become taxable as benefits. Services provided (such as reduced rate air travel) will also be taxed as benefits.

Husband and Wife. The income of a woman during a year or part of a year during which she is a married woman living with her husband is his income for tax purposes except in the year of marriage: I.C.T.A., s. 37. They are regarded as living together unless separated formally or in circumstances likely to be permanent; regarded as separated if one is and the other is not resident for a year of assessment or both are resident and one is and the other is not absent from U.K. throughout the year: I.C.T.A., s. 42.

In the year of marriage the whole of the wife's income is treated as hers and she gets reliefs as a single person.

Separate assessment may be claimed; this does not affect the total tax payable: I.C.T.A., s. 38 (1).

Tax on deceased wife's income may be collected from her estate: I.C.T.A., s. 40, and the husband may disclaim liability within two months of her probate etc.: I.C.T.A., s. 41.

A husband and wife may jointly elect for separate taxation of wife's earnings; such earnings are then assessed on her as if they were single. Husband's income still includes wife's investment income, but he receives single persons' reliefs: F.A. 1971, s. 23.

Widows. From date of husband's death a widow is taxed as a feme sole and receives personal reliefs as such. By concession if she carries on her husband's business there is no discontinuance unless claimed. But no losses or unrelieved capital allowances can be carried forward.

Building Societies. Arrangements exist whereby interest and dividends to depositors and shareholders are treated as the grossed amount less tax at basic rate, but tax is never repayable: I.C.T.A., s. 343.

Housing Associations. Co-operative housing associations are exempt from tax on rents paid by members; and the interest they pay is treated as payable by the members: I.C.T.A., s. 341.

Post-War Credits. Credits not repaid should be claimed without delay: the Treasury may by order fix a terminal date for claims: F.A. 1972, s. 131.

Persons resident abroad. No personal reliefs are granted to non-residents unless British subjects or employed in the service of the Crown or that of a protected native state, or by some missionary society, or resident abroad for reasons of health or resident in the Channel Isles or the Isle of Man, or a widow of a person in Crown service. In these cases the personal allowances can be claimed, but scaled down in the proportion of the United Kingdom income to the aggregate income. Income eligible for D.T.R. is treated specially: I.C.T.A., s. 27 (3), (4).

Double Taxation Relief. Relief is given from double taxation as respects many countries by agreements and conventions under I.C.T.A., s. 497; unilateral relief is given in other cases by I.C.T.A., s. 498.

Deduction of Tax. Much of the income tax is collected by deduction at the source. Annuities and interest paid by companies, are examples.

I.C.T.A., s. 52 permits deduction of income tax from annuities and other annual payments (other than interest) payable wholly out of profits chargeable to income tax. Payer retains tax but is not allowed to deduct payments in computing trading income; s. 52 does not apply to companies as they are not liable to income tax. I.C.T.A., s. 53 requires deduction of income tax from annuities and other annual payments (other than interest) where payment is not wholly made out of profits chargeable to income tax; tax deducted must be handed over to Revenue. I.C.T.A., s. 54 requires deduction of income tax from yearly interest paid by companies or to persons outside the U.K. Persons deducting tax under ss. 52–54 must, if requested, furnish deduction certificate I.C.T.A., ss. 55 and 232 (4).

The capital element in a purchased life annuity is ignored in ascertaining the amount of the annual payment: s. 232.

Tax-free payments (including remuneration and pensions), which are made pursuant to pre-war liabilities which have not been varied, are reduced in such a way as to require the payer to find tax at only 27.5% in the £. This is done by reducing the stated amount which is free of tax to the appropriate fraction of its original amount; and the payer deducts tax at the basic rate on the reduced sum. The appropriate fraction for any given year is $\dfrac{100-A}{72.5}$

where A is the basic rate of income tax for the year: I.C.T.A., s. 422.

The Crown can deduct tax: I.C.T.A., s. 524.

Disallowance of non-business interest. The 1974 rules apply to interest paid by individuals, executors and trustees. Relief applies to yearly interest applied for a qualifying purpose but never to an overdraft (except a business overdraft). Money borrowed to purchase or improve land, a caravan or a houseboat is eligible for relief only for ones' main residence (up to £25,000) or for a property which is to let. Special rules apply for bridging loans. The 1974 rules apply to loans taken out after 26 March 1974 but where the interest obligation was incurred before 26 March 1974 relief continues up to 6 April 1980 except for overdrafts only up to 6 April 1975. Qualifying purposes include business expenditure, purchase of shares in or capitalisation of a partnership, purchase of shares in non-investment close companies, the purchase of plant or machinery by an employee, the payment of estate duty, the purchase or improvement of property and the purchase of a life annuity.

Maintenance Orders. Payments under maintenance orders are normally made subject to tax. Payments under orders not exceeding £12 per week or £52 per month are payable in full, are assessed on the recipient and the payer can deduct the payment in computing his income: I.C.T.A., s. 65, as amended.

Anti-Evasion. As from 1936–37 there is no time limit for the making of additional assessments, etc. in cases where income has escaped assessment by reason of the assessee's fraud or wilful default: T.M.A., s. 36 and Sched. 4, para. 3. The production of statements, etc. made by him to the Revenue on the understanding that the Revenue would accept a pecuniary settlement in satisfaction of his defaults is permitted as evidence in criminal proceedings against a taxpayer accused of fraud or wilful default: I.C.T.A., Sched. 14, para. 27 (4). The inspector may demand inspection of a taxpayer's books; and may in certain circumstances call for the papers of a tax accountant and may with a warrant enter premises to obtain documents: T.M.A., ss. 20, 20A, 20B, 20C, 20D.

Anti-Avoidance. Principal provisions are:—

I.C.T.A., ss. 460–468: cancellation of tax advantages from certain transactions in securities.

I.C.T.A., ss. 469–477: bond-washing transactions.

I.C.T.A., ss. 478–481 counteract the avoidance of tax arising from transfers of assets abroad by persons ordinarily resident in the U.K.

I.C.T.A., s. 482 prohibits certain overseas transactions by companies unless the prior consent of the Treasury is obtained.

I.C.T.A., ss. 483 and 484 restrict relief for trading loss where there has been a change in the ownership of a company.

I.C.T.A., s. 485: transactions between associated companies which are not at arm's length.

I.C.T.A., s. 486: transactions between dealing companies and associated companies.

I.C.T.A., s. 487 counteracts the tax advantage previously obtained by actors, etc., from the sale of the income derived from their personal activities in return for a capital sum.

I.C.T.A., s. 488 charges to tax certain gains arising from artificial and other sales of land which are not already subject to tax.

I.C.T.A., ss. 491–495; F.A. 1972, s. 80: sale and lease-back transactions.

I.C.T.A., s. 496 deals with transactions associated with loans or credit which circumvent the provision for disallowance of interest.

I.C.T.A., ss. 434–459 deal with income arising from settlements. See *Provisions applicable to higher rates only, post.*

F.A. 1972, s. 76: dated securities bought with borrowed money.

Post-cessation receipts. Post-cessation receipts accruing after discontinuance are chargeable under I.C.T.A., s. 145; those accruing before but not included in profits (cash basis) are chargeable when received, with relief for those born before 6 April, 1917: I.C.T.A., ss. 144–5, 150.

Conveyancing transactions. Assignments of leases at under values and sales of land with right of reconveyance may give rise to a charge under

Schedule D, Case VI: I.C.T.A., ss. 81 and 82. Certain capital gains, arising after 17 December 1973 from the disposal of land and buildings with development value or potential, are taxed as income: F.A. 1974, s. 38. The first letting following material development of a building for other than residential purposes will be an occasion of capital gains tax: F.A. 1974, s. 45.

Retirement Benefits. The sum annually paid by an employer to provide retirement benefits for an employee is a part of the latter's taxable income; and if the employer undertakes to provide the benefit himself, the sum representing the annual worth of the benefit is similarly treated. Payments made to (*a*) statutory superannuation funds; (*b*) superannuation funds approved by the Inland Revenue under I.C.T.A., s. 208 excepted provident funds or staff assurance schemes or similar schemes; (*c*) schemes based on life or endowment assurance, or life annuity contracts, in force before 6 April, 1947, are exempt; as are also schemes having as their main benefits the provision of a life pension or annuity to the employee, if the scheme was in operation before that day, or it is approved by the Inland Revenue under I.C.T.A., s. 222.

F.A. 1971, s. 21 and Sched. 3 contain new provisions relating to occupational schemes; provisions operate after 5.4.73 for new schemes and after 5.4.80 for existing schemes.

Relief from tax is given on premiums paid for a life annuity in old age, and on contributions for the same purpose under an approved Trust Scheme or for an annuity for dependants or life insurance, I.C.T.A., ss. 226–8 and F.A. 1971, s. 20. The allowable amount of the premium or contribution cannot exceed £2,250 or 15 per cent. of net relevant earnings but with higher limits for persons born before 1916.

Short-term gains: Schedule D, Case VII. Case VII losses unutilised at 5.4.71 may be set against gains chargeable under the capital gains tax rules.

Provisions applicable to higher rates only. Building society interest is "grossed" up: I.C.T.A., s. 343.

Income tax, other than at the basic rate, is payable on sums received for restrictive covenants in connection with Schedule E employment: I.C.T.A., s. 34.

Income from most settlements on the settlor's children is treated as the settlor's income: I.C.T.A., ss. 437–44. This treatment is applied to any settlement in which the settlor retains any interest (I.C.T.A., ss. 445–54); and it is applied to settlements which are diminishable or in which there is a discretionary power for the settlor's benefit: ss. 445–51. Payments under settlements on individuals, and all income not derivable from property of which the settlor has divested himself absolutely, or which is caught by other provisions, cannot be deducted for higher rate tax by the payer: I.C.T.A., ss. 457–9. Allowance is made for annual payments under a partnership agreement to a former member or his dependants, or by an individual to an individual or former partner (or his dependants) in connection with the acquisition of a business, or under divorce, nullity and separation arrangements: s. 457.

Gains from qualifying life policies realised within 10 years and all non-qualifying policies are chargeable to income tax other than at the basic rate: I.C.T.A., ss. 393, 399.

Income from a deceased person's estate during the administration period is subject to special provisions in ss. 426–33. Relief is given in respect of estate duty payable on the residuary income of the estate: s. 430.

CAPITAL ALLOWANCES

The Capital Allowances Act 1968 consolidated as at 6 April 1968 most capital allowances legislation. It applies both for income tax and corporation tax.

Major alterations regarding capital allowances on plant and machinery contained in F.A. 1971, ss. 40–50.

Capital allowances are usually made in taxing a trade, employment, etc. (*see* C.A.A., ss. 70 and 73); in a few cases capital allowances are made by way of discharge or repayment of tax available primarily against a specified class of income, e.g. to a lessor or on agricultural land and buildings (*see* I.C.T.A., s. 385).

Grants, etc., received, other than Regional Development Grants, are deducted in arriving at the qualifying expenditure.

The main reliefs for capital expenditure are:

1. Industrial buildings and structures (defined in C.A.A., ss. 7 and 10)
   On cost of construction
   Initial allowance   50%
   Writing-down allowance
   on cost (straight line)   4%
   (2% on expenditure before 6.11.62)

2. Machinery and plant (purchased after 26.10.70)
   On cost to purchaser
   First year allowance:
   Development areas or Northern Ireland (industrial only pre-20.7.71)   100%
   Ships   100%
   Others to 19 July 1971   60%
     after 20 July 1971,   80%
     after 21 March 1972,   100%
   Fire precaution expenditure
     after 1 June 1972   100%
   Thermal insulation
     after 12 November 1974   100%
   Writing down allowances   25%
   Ships bought new after 5.4.65 get free depreciation (C.A.A., s. 31);
   Private type motor cars attract no initial or first year allowance and a maximum of £1,250 writing-down allowance (C.A.A., ss. 18(3), Sch. 2 and F.A. 1971, Sch. 7).

   Machinery and plant (purchased before 27.10.70)
   Initial allowance   30%
   Writing-down allowance:
     On reducing balance method (C.A.A., s. 20)

Years life	%
18 or more	15 (min.)
14 to 17	20
less than 14	25 or more

On the alternative straight line or cost method, these percentages are 6¼, 8½ and 11¼ (C.A.A., s. 21);

Subject to exceptions the system of capital allowances for plant and machinery acquired before 27 October, 1970 is largely to be merged with the new system by F.A. 1976.

3. Mines, oil wells, etc.
   (a) for qualifying expenditure as defined in C.A.A., ss. 51–54.
   Initial allowance   40%
   Initial allowances on mining works:
     In development areas and Northern Ireland   100%
     Other and all prior to 27.10.70   40%
   Writing-down allowance on reducing balance method   5% (min.)
   or according to
   output in period (A)
   $\dfrac{\text{A + potential output}}{}$
   (b) for mineral depletion in the U.K.
   Writing-down allowance:
   C.A.A., s. 60.
   (c) for contributions to public services abroad
   Writing-down allowance on cost   10%
   C.A.A., s. 61.

4. Dredging (C.A.A., s. 67)
   On capital expenditure
   Initial allowance   15%
   Writing-down allowance on cost   4%
   (2% on expenditure before 6.11.62).

5. Agricultural buildings (C.A.A., s. 68)
   On cost of construction
   Writing-down allowance on cost   10%

Scientific research. All revenue expenditure can be deducted; and capital expenditure can be deducted in the first year: C.A.A., ss. 90–95.

Maintenance expenses on agricultural property which exceed the rents received are treated as allowances: I.C.T.A., s. 79 (1).

Expenditure on patent rights qualifies for writing-down allowances over 17 years or their life if shorter, but the recipient is chargeable under Sched. D, Case VI: I.C.T.A., ss. 378–88.

Know-how, i.e. industrial information and techniques: C.A.A., ss. 4 (11), 36, 40 (3), 55, 92 (4), 93 (3).

Writing-down allowance 16⅔% on cost.

Sale proceeds taxed as trading receipt.

Capital allowances can in certain circumstances be set against general income: I.C.T.A., s. 169. This is subject to I.C.T.A., s. 170. Investment allowances were abolished in 1966 for expenditure on or after 17 January, 1966. Investment grants in operation from 17.1.66 to 27.10.70; deductible from allowable cost and expenditure not eligible for initial allowance.

Other deductions. Capital expenditure on the provision of land can be written off against the profits of a trade which consists of or includes the carrying on of a cemetery or a crematorium (including the maintenance of memorial garden plots): I.C.T.A., s. 141.

CAPITAL GAINS TAX

The capital gains tax was introduced by F.A. 1965, Part III; it was originally designed as a tax on gains realised on the disposal of assets held for more than one year. As a result of the 1971 abolition of the short-term gains tax (Sched. D, Case VII) all capital gains fall within the capital gains tax legislation. Persons, other than companies, resident or ordinarily resident in the U.K. are liable to capital gains tax; and non-residents who make gains from business assets here are also taxable, unless a double taxation agreement is applicable.

Capital gains tax is chargeable on a person's total chargeable gains in any year of assessment after deducting allowable losses for the year and any unrelieved losses brought forward from previous years from 1965–66 onwards. The rate of tax is 30 per cent; but by s. 21 the capital gains tax for an individual is, if less, measured as the amount of additional income tax which he would have to pay if one-half of the gains were unearned income and added to his total income.

Small disposals:

Capital gains tax is not chargeable where an individual's total disposals in a year of assessment do not exceed £1,000. Marginal relief is available where proceeds exceed £1,000.

Losses:

Losses are computed in the same way as gains: F.A. 1965, s. 23. A loss may be claimed when an asset becomes of negligible value: F.A. 1965, s. 23. There are restrictions on use of losses accruing on disposals to connected persons: F.A. 1965, Sched. 7, para. 17.

Companies:

Chargeable gains of companies are charged to corporation tax (*see post*).

Chargeable assets:

All forms of property are chargeable assets including options, debts and incorporeal property generally. Capital sums of compensation for damage to assets, or received under an insurance policy on assets, or for forfeiture or surrender on non-exercise of rights, or for use or exploitation of assets are regarded as disposal proceeds. As a rule the gain (or loss) is the difference between the acquisition price and the disposal price, but where there is no such price, the market value is taken.

Non-domiciled persons:

Gains accruing to non-domiciled persons on disposal of overseas assets are only liable to the extent remitted to the U.K. No relief for losses on overseas assets.

Exemptions include:

  (i) private type motor vehicles,
 (ii) total gifts worth £100 or less,
(iii) savings certificates,
 (iv) non-marketable securities within the National Loans Act 1939,
  (v) currency for personal use abroad,
 (vi) betting (including pool betting) winnings,
(vii) compensation for personal or professional wrong or injury,
(viii) rights or policy money in or from life assurance policies,
 (ix) the private residence of the taxpayer,
  (x) chattels sold for £1,000 or less,
 (xi) gifts to a charity or for the preservation of the national heritage: F.A. 1965, s. 32; F.A. 1972, s. 119,
(xii) objects of national etc. interest (as for capital transfer tax),
(xiii) gains made by charities,

(xiv) gains of approved pension funds,

(xv) gains made by persons entitled to diplomatic privileges,

(xvi) decorations awarded for valour;

(xvii) business or shares disposed of by individual of 60 or over: F.A. 1965, s. 34,

(xviii) wasting assets disposed of after 19 March 1968,

(xix) gilt edged securities disposed of after 15 April 1969.

Reliefs include:

(i) certain business assets replaced: F.A. 1965, s. 33,

(ii) delayed remittances: F.A. 1965, s. 40,

(iii) business or shares disposed of by individual aged 60 or over: F.A. 1965, s. 34,

(iv) overseas tax suffered on gain: F.A. 1965, s. 39,

(v) certain guaranteed stocks where gain falls with exempt price range: F.A. 1965, s. 27 (3),

(vi) reorganisations of company's share capital, e.g. bonus issues, conversion of shares and share for share takeovers: F.A. 1965, Sched. 7, paras. 4–7.

(vii) On disposals after 5 April 1972 of units in unit trust schemes and shares in approved investment trusts the total net gains are no longer apportioned and treated as expenditure under F.A. 1965, s. 37; instead a credit of 17½ per cent. of the gain on the disposal is allowed against the tax on the gain: F.A. 1972, s. 112.

Assets held on 6 April 1965:

1. *Quoted securities.* The gain is computed by reference to notional acquisition at the value on 6 April 1965 unless the actual gain is less. The restriction to the actual gain does not apply to disposals after 19 March 1968 if election has been made under F.A. 1968, s. 32 and Sched. 11 for pooling, ignoring cost.

2. *Land with development value.* Acquisition on 6 April 1965 is assumed unless the actual gain is less.

3. *Other assets.* The gain is assumed to accrue evenly over the period of ownership, and only the part falling after 6 April 1965 is chargeable; and in such instances the taxpayer can elect to be treated as if he had acquired the asset at its market value on 6 April, 1965. An election is irrevocable.

Settlements. A gift in settlement is treated as a disposal of all the settled assets. When a person becomes entitled absolutely to a settled asset otherwise than as the result of a death, it is deemed to have been disposed of by the trustee, and immediately acquired by him, at its market value. The trustee is thus liable for the tax; but if the tax is not paid within 6 months, the beneficiary can be assessed within two years from the due date. The tax becomes payable on the termination of a life interest otherwise than as the result of a death (or of an annuity from an appropriated fund) as if the whole of the settled property had been disposed of at market value.

Overseas companies and trusts. Gains realised by a non-resident company which would be a close company if resident and which are not distributed may be apportioned to U.K. shareholders: F.A. 1965, s. 41. Similar provisions apply to non-resident trusts: F.A. 1965, s. 42.

Development gains and first lettings, see *ante.*

CORPORATION TAX

General:

A company is liable to corporation tax on its profits, *i.e.* its income, other than franked investment income, plus its chargeable gains: F.A. 1972, s. 93. The rate is fixed for each financial year which begins on 1 April: I.C.T.A., s. 527. The rate for the financial years 1964, 1965 and 1966 was 40%; for 1967, 42½%; for 1968, 45%; for 1969, 42½%; for 1970–1972, 40%; for 1973, 52%; for 1974, 52%; for 1975, 52%.

There is a special lower rate of corporation tax for companies whose annual profits do not exceed £30,000 with tapering provisions for companies with profits up to £50,000. For the financial year 1975 the lower rate is

42%. Capital gains accruing to companies are charged at an effective rate of 30% for 1973–74 onwards.

Payment is due nine months after the end of an accounting period or within one month of assessment, whichever is later. But companies trading before April 1965 and which continue to trade may pay at the same interval after the end of the accounting period as they used to pay income tax Schedule D, Case I: I.C.T.A., s. 244.

Corporation tax applies to all the profits of a company wherever arising, but a non-resident company is liable only if it carries on a trade in the U.K. through a branch or agency.

The tax is assessed and charged on the profits of each accounting period of not more than 12 months and if necessary the assessment is divided between the financial years in which the accounting period falls.

In general a company's income is computed under the same Schedules and Cases as for income tax, but always on an "actual basis": I.C.T.A., ss. 250, 251.

Franked investment income (F.I.I.) consists of distributions (including dividends) received by one U.K. company from another such company with the benefit of a tax credit. The tax credit is available for set-off against any A.C.T. which the recipient of F.I.I. must account for on dividends paid. If a surplus of F.I.I. arises special rules govern its application.

Unfranked investment income is received subject to deduction of income tax but is also subject to corporation tax. The income tax suffered may be set-off against income tax on charges paid, then against corporation tax and subject thereto a repayment may be claimed. Building society interest must be grossed up in the computation of profits.

Charges on income (i.e. yearly interest, annuities or other annual payments (but not rents and other Sched. A sums) patent royalties, bank, stock exchange and discount interest) are deductible from the total profits including any chargeable gains, provided

the payment is not charged to capital, is borne by the company and was made for valuable and sufficient consideration or was a covenanted donation to charity: I.C.T.A., s. 248.

Capital allowances and balancing charges are treated as a trading expense (or receipt) or deducted from (or added to) income of the class to which they relate (C.A.A., ss. 73, 74 and I.C.T.A., s. 385 (3)). Investment companies can deduct their expenses of management, in so far as the items are not deductible under Schedule A: I.C.T.A., s. 304. Overseas trading income attracts an "overspill" relief up to 1976–77.

Loss relief, as for income tax, applies: the amount of a trading loss goes to reduce the trading income of the company, period by period, until the loss is exhausted. The company can set a trading loss against all profits of the same and an immediately preceding period. Twelve months terminal trade loss can be set against the profits of accounting periods falling (wholly or partly) within the three preceding years. A Case VI loss can be set against Case VI income. Losses can also be set against "franked investment income", i.e. distributions received from another U.K. company. I.C.T.A., ss. 177–9, 254.

Groups of companies may obtain group relief whereby one company can surrender certain trading losses, capital allowances, management expenses or charges on income in favour of another company, under I.C.T.A., ss. 258–64.

Distributions, including dividends of companies, are not allowed as deductions for corporation tax but are charged to income tax on the recipient under Schedule F.

Income tax is not deducted from company distributions. Companies making qualifying distributions are liable to pay advance corporation tax (A.C.T.) on the distribution; such distribution carries an equivalent tax credit in the hands of United Kingdom resident and certain non-resident shareholders. The rate of A.C.T. is 35/65 from 6 April 1976 to 5 April 1977: F. A. 1976.

CLOSE COMPANIES

A close company is one under the control of five or fewer participators or under the control of any number of

participator directors. A company of which not less than 35% of the voting power is held by the public is not a close company, if those shares are quoted and dealt in on a recognised stock exchange, unless the principal members hold over 85%: I.C.T.A., s. 283 (1), (8). A participator is a person having share capital or voting rights in the company, a loan creditor, a person entitled to receive distributions and anyone able to secure that income or assets will be applied for his benefit.

On an apportionment the members are liable to income tax at rates in excess of the basic rate on the excess of the relevant income over the distributions made for an accounting period. For a trading company or a member of a trading group the relevant income is so much of the distributable income as can be distributed without prejudice to business requirements. For a close investment company the relevant income is so much of the estate or trading income as can be distributed without prejudice to business requirements so far as concerned with producing that income plus the whole of the remainder of the distributable income. In general the relevant income cannot exceed the distributable investment income plus 50% of the estate or trading income.

A trading company whose estate or trading income is not more than £5,000 does not have to bring in any such income in computing its maximum relevant income. For such a company with such income between £5,000 and £15,000 there is a tapering abatement of one half of the difference between the actual amount and £15,000; only 50% of this reduced amount comes into the maximum relevant income. If there is an associated company the rules are modified.

The amount assessable to income tax is the individual's share of the apportioned amount plus the corresponding amount of A.C.T., but income tax at the basic rate is treated as having been paid though it is not repayable or available to cover charges on income.

Income tax is leviable on any loan or advance (grossed up) made by a close company to any participator or associate. On recovery thereof, the tax is repaid. These rules do not apply to a case within I.C.T.A., s. 451 (capital sums paid to settlors). Nor to loans under staff housing schemes.

A payment for a restrictive covenant in connexion with employment is assessed to income tax on the company if surtax is payable by the recipient under I.C.T.A., s. 34.

Interest paid to a director or one of his associates is regarded as a distribution and not allowed as a deduction in computing profits in so far as it exceeds certain limits: I.C.T.A., s. 285.

INTEREST ON UNPAID TAX

Tax on assessments under Schedule A, C, D or E, at rates other than basic rate, capital gains tax and corporation tax (other than A.C.T.) generally carries interest from the reckonable date which is the due date for payment unless there has been an application under T.M.A. 1970, s. 55 to postpone payment of tax on an assessment under appeal and the application results in a deferral of the due date. In such cases the reckonable date will be the later of the original due date or the date specified in T.M.A. 1970, s. 86 (4). This latter date is the earlier of (a) the date on which the tax actually becomes due and (b) the date given in the Table to T.M.A. 1970, s. 86 (4). Interest is payable without deduction of tax. T.M.A., ss. 86–92.

From 1 July 1974, whether or not interest runs from before that date, the rate of interest is 9 per cent per annum (previously 6 per cent per annum since 19 April 1969).

Advance corporation tax and income tax or company payments which are not distributions carry interest similarly. T.M.A., ss. 87 (1), 109 (4).

If tax is repaid, a corresponding refund of interest has to be made. The amount repayable can be set against any other tax for the same tax year or period, but not against (a) an assessment made after the relief from tax was given or (b) more than one assessment so as to reduce, but not to extinguish the tax thereon: T.M.A., s. 19.

Interest may be remitted where tax is in arrear by reason of exchange restrictions: T.M.A., s. 92.

By concession, where a taxpayer dies before tax falls due, interest will not run until the executors or administrators obtain probate or letters of administration enabling them to pay the tax.

VALUE ADDED TAX

(See De Voil: VALUE ADDED TAX)

Introduction of V.A.T.—This applies to the supply of goods and services in the United Kingdom in the course of business and on imports of goods.

Rate.—From 1 April 1973, 10 per cent., From 29 July 1974, 8 per cent. From 12 April 1976, 12½ per cent. on petrol and on a large range of luxury and semi-luxury goods.

Zero-rating.—Items zero-rated include goods exported, food (except "meals out"), water, books, newspapers (including newspaper advertising) and journals, fuel and power but not petrol and road fuels, the construction of buildings, services to overseas traders or for overseas purposes, fares for public transport, drugs and medicines supplied on prescription, certain imports, exports, etc., charity shops and exports, children's clothing and footwear, essential aids to the disabled and protective clothing.

Exemption.—Exemption applies to grants of interests in land, insurance, postal services, betting, gaming and lotteries (which are subject to excise duty), finance, education, health and burial and cremation services.

Exemption of small traders.—Broadly traders whose business turnover in taxable supplies of goods and services (including zero-rated supplies) does not exceed £5,000 p.a. are not required to register.

Car Tax.—With effect from 1 April 1973 tax is imposed on both new and imported cars at the rate of 10 per cent of the wholesale value.

Title, Registration of

SEE REAL PROPERTY

Trade Marks

The Statute Law relating to Trade Marks is mainly contained in the Trade Marks Act, 1938, hereinafter called "the Act," and the Trade Marks Rules 1938 made thereunder, (S.R. & O. 1938 No. 661), the Trade Marks (Amendment) Rules 1955 (S.I. 1955 No. 461), 1956 (S.I. 1956 No. 1844), 1959 (S.I. 1950 No. 1925), 1961 (S.I. 1961 No. 127), 1963 No. 263, 1964 No. 227, 1971 No. 261 and The Trade Marks (Amendment) Rules 1975 No. 229 and The Trade Marks (Amendment No. 2) Rules 1975 No. 576. This Act, which consolidated the existing law and introduced important amendments, came into force on the 27th July, 1938. There are also provisions contained in the Patents, Designs, Copyright and Trade Marks (Emergency) Act 1939, and the Rules made thereunder (S.R. & O. 1939 No. 1375). The definition of a Trade Mark is given in s. 68 of the Act which also provides that references in the Act to the use of a Trade Mark in relation to goods shall be construed as references to the use thereof upon or in physical or other relation to the goods.

Trade Marks are of two kinds: (*a*) Common Law or Unregistered Trade Marks; (*b*) Registered Trade Marks.

(*a*) A *Common Law Trade Mark* is any mark which has been so extensively used on or in connection with a certain class or classes of goods that the public recognise goods bearing such a mark as emanating from the owner of the mark. In an action upon a Common Law Trade Mark, such distinctiveness must in every case be proved. The appropriate remedy is a "Passing Off" action.

(*b*) *Registered Trade Marks.* The Register is divided into two parts, Part A and Part B. For the rights given by registration in Parts A and B, see ss. 4 and 5 of the Act respectively.

Marks which may be registered in Part A. By s. 9 of the Trade Marks Act, 1938, a Trade Mark to be registrable must contain or consist of at least one of the following essential particulars: (1) The name of a Company, individual or firm represented in a special or particular manner. (2) The signature of the applicant for registration or of some predecessor in business. (3) An invented word or words. (4) A word or words having no direct reference to the character or quality of the goods and not being according to its ordinary significance a geographical name or surname. (5) Any other distinctive mark, but a name, signature word or words other than such as fall within the descriptions in paras. 1–4 *supra* are not to be deemed distinctive except upon evidence of distinctiveness.

For the purposes of this section "distinctive" means adapted in relation to the goods in respect of which a Trade Mark is registered or proposed to be registered, to distinguish goods with which the proprietor of the Trade Mark is or may be connected in the course of trade from goods in the case of which no such connection subsists either generally, or, where the trade mark is registered subject to limitations, in relation to use within the extent of the registration.

In determining whether a Trade Mark is adapted to distinguish as aforesaid, the tribunal may have regard to the extent to which—(a) the Trade Mark is inherently adapted to distinguish as aforesaid; and (b) by reason of the use of the Trade Mark or of any other circumstances, the Trade Mark is in fact adapted to distinguish as aforesaid.

Registration in Part A of the Register gives to the proprietor the exclusive right to the use of the Trade Mark, s. 4.

Marks which may be registered in Part B. By s. 10 a mark may be registered in Part B of the Register if it can be shown that it is capable of distinguishing the goods in question either generally or, if subject to limitations, within the extent of the registration. It is to be noted that a period of two years user is no longer necessary. The rights given by registration in Part B are the same as those given by registration in Part A but in proceedings for infringement of a mark in Part B, no relief shall (with

certain exceptions) be granted to the Plaintiff if the defendant establishes that the use complained of is not likely to deceive or cause confusion or be taken as indicating a connection in the course of trade between the goods and the proprietor or a registered user, s. 5.

No mark can be registered in either part which would be likely to deceive or cause confusion, or be otherwise disentitled to protection in a Court of Justice, or be contrary to law or morality or any scandalous design, s. 11. A mark cannot be registered if it conflicts with a mark already on the register. Provision is made for registration of identical or resembling marks in cases of honest concurrent user, s. 12.

A Trade Mark must be registered in respect of particular goods or classes of goods and a new classification is embodied in Sch. IV of the Rules. An Alphabetical Index to the new classification and a List of Goods in each of the new classes are on sale at the Patent Office. Provision is made for the reclassification of the goods of old registrations on application by the Registered Proprietor. Rule 6.

Date of Registration. A Trade Mark, when accepted, dates from the date of application to register.

Procedure. Any person claiming to be the proprietor of a registrable Trade Mark and desiring to register the same in Part A or Part B must apply to the Registrar of Trade Marks upon Form TM 2 or Form Textile No. 2, with 4 additional representations of the Mark upon Form TM 4 or 6 representations in the case of a Textile Mark. A *prima facie* opinion as to the distinctiveness of the mark may first be obtained from the Registrar by filing Form TM 29, and an official search for prior conflicting marks may be obtained by filing Form TM 28.

Upon receipt of the application, the Registrar may accept the Mark absolutely, or subject to conditions which he may think fit to impose, or he may refuse to register the Mark. The applicant is entitled to be heard before refusal. Conflicting Marks on the Register are cited against an application.

In case of refusal the Registrar gives notice of his refusal. A request for statement of grounds of decision may be made on Form TM 5.

The Registrar's decision is subject to appeal to the Board of Trade or to the Court at the option of the applicant.

Notice of appeal must be given within one month of the Registrar's decision; if to the B.O.T. upon Form TM 30; if to the Court, by notice of motion.

In case of acceptance whether subject to conditions or not, the Registrar as soon as possible thereafter, causes the application as accepted, to be advertised in the Trade Marks Journal. The Registrar may advertise the mark before acceptance (s. 18 (1)).

Opposition. Upon advertisement, any person aggrieved by such registration may within one month of advertisement or such longer time as the Registrar may in his discretion allow, give notice of opposition, to the Registrar upon Form TM 7, stating his grounds for such opposition.

Procedure in Opposition. A copy of the notice of opposition is sent by the Registrar to the applicant. If the applicant wishes to contest the opposition, he must within one month of receipt of such notice file a Counter-statement in duplicate, on Form TM 8, giving the grounds upon which he relies in support of his application. A copy of the Counter-statement is forwarded by the Registrar to the opponent who may within one month file by way of statutory declarations, such evidence as he thinks fit. Copies must be delivered to the applicant. If the opponent files no evidence, he is deemed to have abandoned the opposition.

Within one month of the receipt of the opponent's evidence, the applicant must deliver to the Registrar and to the opponent such evidence by way of statutory declarations as he desires to adduce in support of his application. The opponent may leave evidence in reply within 14 days.

Upon completion of the evidence, the Registrar fixes a day for the hearing and gives notice to both parties. Within seven days of receipt of such notice, each party must file Form TM 9 stating that he intends to appear. He may appear in person, by his patent, agent, or by solicitor or counsel, s. 18, rules 46–58.

Appeal. The decision of the Registrar is subject to appeal to the Court by motion within one month of the date of the decision. Fresh evidence may be filed with the permission of the Court, and notice served on any declarant to present himself for cross-examination. No fresh grounds of opposition may be taken without leave of the Court. The costs of appeal and of the hearing before the Registrar are in the discretion of the Court, but usually follow the event. Costs may be given against the Registrar, s. 48.

Rectification of the Register. After a Trade Mark has been registered, application may be made at the discretion of the applicant to the Registrar or to the Court to rectify the register upon the following grounds:—(1) That there was no *bona fide* intention to use the mark by the proprietor and that there has in fact been no *bona fide* user of the mark up to one month preceding the application. (2) That the mark has not been used for a continuous period of five years up to one month before the application to rectify. (3) That the Registered proprietor is not the person entitled to the use of the mark. (4) That the mark was wrongly registered or wrongly remains on the register. (5) That there has been fraud in the registration, assignment or transmission of the mark. (6) That there is an error or defect in the registration. (7) A mark may be expunged for a breach of condition entered on the register in relation thereto.

After the expiration of seven years from the date of registration, a Trade Mark in Part A is deemed to be valid in all respects unless it has been obtained by fraud, is calculated to deceive or otherwise disentitled to protection, is contrary to law or morality or is of a scandalous nature.

If any action is pending having reference to the Trade Mark sought to be expunged or rectified, application may only be made to the Court by motion. In any application to the Court by motion, notice must be served upon the Registrar and upon the registered proprietor of the mark. Costs are in the discretion of the Court but usually follow the event.

Application to rectify the register, if made to the Registrar must be upon Form TM 26 accompanied by a statement in duplicate fully setting out the applicant's interest and the facts upon which he bases his application. Thereafter the procedure is the same as in an opposition (see *supra*).

Assignment. A Trade Mark may now be validly assigned without the goodwill of the business in the goods for which it is registered. This provision is retrospective and it also applies to an unregistered Trade Mark if it is used in the same business as, and is transmitted with, and to the same person as, a registered Trade Mark. Such assignments are not effective unless they are advertised in a manner to be directed by the Registrar on application made to him. Such an application is not necessary where the goodwill accompanies the Trade Mark. The full provisions relating to assignments are set out in s. 22 and include provision for application to be made to the Registrar for a certificate of validity of certain assignments where it is proposed that more than one person shall be entitled to use the same or similar marks for the same goods or goods of the same description, or where user of the same mark is proposed to be divided territorially between two or more persons. Upon a person becoming entitled to a registered Trade Mark by assignment, transmission or other operation of law, application must be made on Form TM 15 or 16 that he may be registered as the owner.

Renewal of Registration. Registration is now for a period of 7 years in the first instance renewable for periods of 14 years. Marks registered as of dates before 27th July 1938, extend for an initial period of 14 years. Notice is given to the registered owner that the period is about to expire. Application for renewal must be made upon Form TM 11 or 12. Application may be made for restoration after the renewal period has expired on Form TM 13.

Defensive Trade Marks. Where a mark which consists of an invented word or words has become identified with the proprietor to such an extent that the use of the mark on goods other than those for which the mark is registered will create the impression that there is a connection between those goods and the proprietor of the mark, the proprietor may register the mark in respect of such other goods as a defensive trade mark, s. 27.

Registered Users. S. 28 enables the registered proprietor to allow anyone to become a registered user of a Trade Mark so that such person can make use of the mark absolutely or subject to restrictions. Application must first be made to the Registrar for his approval.

Company about to be formed. Provision is made for registration of a Trade Mark in favour of a Company about to be formed and also in favour of a Registered User, s. 29.

Use of Mark as name of Article. The registration of a Trade Mark shall not become invalid by reason only of its use as the name or description of an article or substance unless:—(1) There is a well-known and established descriptive use of the word in the trade concerned, or (2) the article was patented and it appears after two years or more have elapsed from the expiry of the Patent that it is the only practicable name for it, s. 15.

Textile Marks. These may now be registered in London as well as at Manchester and their scope has been enlarged to include articles of clothing, see s. 39.

Sheffield Marks. Special provisions apply to Sheffield marks for Cutlery and metal goods, s. 58, and Schedule II.

Parts of Marks and Series Marks. The registration of parts of marks and of certain marks as a series is provided for by s. 21.

Certification Trade Marks. Subject to the provisions of s. 37 a mark adapted in relation to any goods to distinguish in the course of trade goods certified by any person in respect of origin, material, mode of manufacture, quality, accuracy, or other characteristic, from goods not so certified shall be registrable as a certification trade mark in Part A in the name of such person as proprietor. The mark shall not be registrable, in the name of a person who carries on a trade in goods of the kind certified. Application for such a mark must be made to the Registrar upon Form TM 6 in duplicate accompanied by four copies of the proposed mark. The Registrar first examines the mark and reports thereon to the Board of Trade who consider whether the applicant is competent to certify, as to whether the draft regulations are satisfactory and as to whether the registration will be to the public advantage and may accept or refuse the application. There is no appeal from the decision of the Board of Trade. See also Schedule I.

Proceedings before the Registrar may now be heard in public (S.I. 1959 No. 1925).

Marking. It is an offence to mark a Trade Mark as Registered if this is not the case. See also Trade Descriptions Act, 1972.

SCHEDULE OF FEES

		£
TM 2 TM Textile No. 2 } Application to Register		20.00
TM 5	Application for statement of grounds of refusal	9.00
TM 6	Application for certification mark	17.00
TM 7	Notice of opposition	9.00
TM 8	Counter-statement	6.00
TM 9	Hearing of opposition—each party	9.00
TM 10	On registration of Trade Mark in one class or of first of a series of marks, or of a certification mark	30.00
	Addition where mark is associated or for every other mark in a series	1.00
TM 10	Reg. of a defensive mark in one class	34.00
TM 11	Renewal of registration	73.00
TM 15 or 16	Application to register assignment made within 6 months	6.00
	After 6 months but within 12 months	13.00
	After 12 months	22.00
	Each additional mark under same title	1.00
TM 26	Application to rectify register or remove mark	11.00
TM 30	Appeal to B.O.T.	9.00
TM 32	Application to register a defensive trade mark	30.00

Trusts and Trustees

See Underhill's Law of Trusts and Trustees (12th Edn.)

THE PUBLIC TRUSTEE

The Hutton Committee Report (*The Public Trustee Office,* Cmnd. 4913), which recommended the running-down of the Public Trustee Office, is not to be implemented, and the Public Trustee is accordingly accepting new business as before. The address of the office is Sardinia Street, Kingsway, London WC2B 6JX.

TRUSTEE INVESTMENTS

If trustees' powers of investment are not dealt with expressly in the will or settlement (or if the will or settlement merely gives them the statutory powers of investment) their powers are regulated by the Trustee Investments Act 1961. Those parts of the Trustee Act 1925, Part I, which are left unrepealed by that Act will also be relevant.

The will or settlement may confer wider powers than those contained in the 1961 Act: if it does, the powers conferred will not be controlled by the provisions of the Act which require the division of the trust fund or the obtaining of advice and valuation, though the trustee's normal duty to act prudently will still apply and so will s. 6 (1) of the

Act (see below). The will or settlement may also, if it is made after the passing of the Act, restrict the powers which the Act confers (and those powers will be exercisable only in so far as a contrary intention is not expressed); but no such restriction shall be imposed by any provision made before the passing of the Act (unless it is contained in an enactment or an instrument made under an enactment).

The court has jurisdiction, particularly under the Variation of Trusts Act 1958, to confer extended powers of investment upon trustees, but the court will not, except in special circumstances, confer powers wider than those contained in the Act of 1961 (*Re Cooper's Settlement, Cooper* v. *Cooper*, [1961] 3 All E.R. 636).

The decision in *Re Wellsted's Will Trusts, Wellsted* v. *Hanson*, [1949], All E.R. 577, C.A., makes it clear that trustees who have held land on trust for sale may invest the proceeds (so long as they are identifiable as such) in the purchase of land.

TRUSTEE INVESTMENTS ACT, 1961

The Act replaces the former list of trustee investments with a new list. The main division of this is into two parts: narrower-range investments and wider-range investments. The first part consists mainly of gilt-edged and other fixed interest securities, the second mainly of industrial equities (see s. 1 and Sched. 1).

Additions may be made to both parts of the list by Order in Council (s. 12). At present not more than one half of the fund may be invested in wider-range securities, but this proportion may be increased up to (and not exceeding) three-quarters by Treasury order (s. 13).

S. 2 provides that before a trustee makes any investment in wider-range securities he must divide the fund into two parts which must (no Treasury order having been made) be of equal value. One part must be invested in narrower-range securities. The other half may be invested in wider-range (or, if desired, in wider-range and narrower-range) securities.

The same section contains machinery for "compensating transfers" between the two parts of the trust fund, accruals to the trust fund and withdrawals from the fund. Save that property "generated" by one part of the fund (*e.g.* shares received on a bonus issue) is to belong to that part, each part is to be increased in value to the same amount (or, if a Treasury order has been made, in the proportion specified thereby: s. 13 (3) (a)) when any property accrues to the fund, this being effected by apportionment of the accruing property or by transfer from one part of the fund to the other. The acquisition of securities on a "rights" issue is for this purpose to be treated as investment and not as the accrual of property. Withdrawals from the fund in the exercise of any powers and duties of the trustees are to be made at the unfettered discretion of the trustees.

S. 3 and Scheds. 2 and 3 govern the relationship between the Act and other powers of investment. In particular, property, including wider-range but not including narrower-range investments, which a trustee is authorised to hold apart from s. 1 of the Act or of any provisions of Part I of the Trustee Act, 1925 or of any power to invest in investments authorised by law for the investment of trust funds and any securities acquired on an amalgamation, reconstruction or rights issue by virtue of ownership of any such property is called "special range property" and forms a separate fund which becomes subject to the provisions of Sched. 2. But where the powers of a trustee to invest in or postpone conversion of what would otherwise be "special-range property" have been conferred or varied by order of the court within ten years of the passing of the Act or by any enactment, or instrument having effect under an enactment, specifically relating to the trusts in question made or passed within that period or by an enactment contained in a local Act of the session 9 and 10 Eliz. 2, the position is governed, not by Sched. 2, but by Sched. 3.

S. 4 provides that, for the purposes of the Act, "property" includes real or personal property of every kind, defines the property that is to be deemed to constitute a single trust fund, and provides alternative ways in which property taken out of a trust fund by way of appropriation to form a separate fund is itself to be divided into narrower-range and wider-range parts if the trustee desires to take advantage of the provisions of the Act in relation to the separate fund.

S. 5 gives protection to a trustee who for the purposes of s. 2 or s. 4 acts on the valuation of a qualified valuer.

S. 6 lays down the general duty of trustees in making investments to have regard to the diversity and suitability of investments.

Narrower-range investments are subdivided into "narrower-range investments not requiring advice" (which consist of certain "small savings" investments) and "narrower-range investments requiring advice" (see Sched. 1), and s. 6 goes on to provide that before exercising any power (arising under the Act or being a power conferred before the Act to invest in trustee securities) to invest in narrower-range securities requiring advice or in wider-range securities, a trustee is to obtain and consider proper written advice (not necessarily from a stockbroker) as to the need for, and suitability of, any such proposed investments. So long as he retains any investment made under such a power he must periodically obtain and consider advice as to whether it should be retained, the responsibility for deciding how often a particular investment should be reviewed being placed upon the trustee, and being no small addition to his burdens. So far as mortgages are concerned the section dovetails in with s. 8 of the Trustee Act, 1925, so as to avoid duplication.

S. 9 makes a useful amendment to s. 10 of the Trustee Act 1925 by authorising trustees to concur in an amalgamation by exchange of shares, and s. 15 contains a saving for the pre-existing powers of the court.

The remaining sections of the Act deal with its application to particular cases. S. 7 provides that persons other than trustees (*e.g.*, local authorities) whose investment powers are limited to the trustee list shall have their investment powers extended as if they were in fact trustees, but leaves investment powers in respect of funds for the redemption of debt largely untouched. S. 8 applies to the person for the time being authorised to invest funds of the Duchy of Lancaster, and may be applied by statutory instrument to other persons (whether trustees or not) whose investment powers are derived from special enactments.

S. 11 provides machinery whereby schemes may be put forward for a number of local authorities to combine their investments in a common fund.

. . . . .

Sched. I dealing with the manner of investment is set out below, with the additions made by Orders in Council and with the few minor amendments made by subsequent legislation:

"*Part I—Narrower-range Investments not Requiring Advice.* 1. In Defence Bonds, National Savings Certificates, Ulster Savings Certificates, Ulster Development Bonds, National Development Bonds and British Savings Bonds.

2. In deposits in the National Savings Bank, ordinary deposits in a trustee savings bank [and the power to invest in these is to be construed as a power to invest in a savings deposit account in such a bank: Trustee Savings Bank Act 1964, s. 12] and deposits in a bank or department thereof certified under subsection (3) of section nine of the Finance Act 1956 [now s. 414 (3) and (5) of the Income and Corporation Taxes Act 1970]."

Part II.—Narrower-Range Investments Requiring Advice. 1. In securities issued by Her Majesty's Government in the United Kingdom, the Government of Northern Ireland or the Government of the Isle of Man, not being securities falling within Part I of this Schedule and being fixed-interest securities registered in the United Kingdom or the Isle of Man, Treasury Bills or Tax Reserve Certificates.

2. In any securities the payment of interest on which is guaranteed by Her Majesty's Government in the United Kingdom or the Government of Northern Ireland.

3. In fixed-interest securities issued in the United Kingdom by any public authority or nationalised industry or undertaking in the United Kingdom.

4. In fixed-interest securities issued in the United Kingdom by the government of any overseas territory within the Commonwealth or by any public or local authority within such a territory

being securities registered in the United Kingdom.

References in this paragraph to an overseas territory or to the government of such a territory shall be construed as if they occurred in the Overseas Service Act, 1958.

5. In fixed-interest securities issued in the United Kingdom by the International Bank for Reconstruction and Development, being securities registered in the United Kingdom, and in fixed interest securities issued by the Inter-American Development Bank. [In fixed interest securities issued in the United Kingdom by the European Investment Bank or by the European Coal and Steel Community, being securities registered in the United Kingdom: added by Trustee Investments (Additional Powers) Order 1972.]

6. In debentures issued in the United Kingdom by a company incorporated in the United Kingdom being debentures registered in the United Kingdom.

7. In stock of the Bank of Ireland.

8. In debentures issued by the Agricultural Mortgage Corporation Limited or the Scottish Agricultural Securities Corporation Limited.

9. In loans to any authority to which this paragraph applies charged on all or any of the revenues of the authority or on a fund into which all or any of those revenues are payable, in any fixed-interest securities issued in the United Kingdom by any such authority for the purpose of borrowing money so charged, and in deposits with any such authority by way of temporary loan made on the giving of a receipt for the loan by the treasurer or other similar officer of the authority and on the giving of an undertaking by the authority that, if requested to charge the loan as aforesaid, it will either comply with the request or repay the loan.

This paragraph applies to the following authorities, that is to say—

(a) any local authority in the United Kingdom;

(b) any authority all the members of which are appointed or elected by one or more local authorities in the United Kingdom;

(c) any authority the majority of the members of which are appointed or elected by one or more local authorities in the United Kingdom, being an authority which by virtue of any enactment has power to issue a precept to a local authority in England and Wales, or a requisition to a local authority in Scotland, or to the expenses of which, by virtue of any enactment, a local authority in the United Kingdom is or can be required to contribute;

(d) the Receiver for the Metropolitan Police District or a combined police authority (within the meaning of the Police Act, 1946);

(e) the Belfast City and District Water Commissioners.

(f) the Great Ouse Water Authority.

[(g) any district Council in Northern Ireland: added by Trustee Investments (Additional Powers) Order 1973.]

[And any river authority which would not otherwise be included among the authorities to which this paragraph applies is so included: Water Resources Act 1963, s. 6(6) and Sch. 4, para. 33.]

10. In debentures or in the guaranteed or preference stock of any incorporated company, being statutory water undertakers within the meaning of the Water Act, 1945, or any corresponding enactment in force in Northern Ireland, and having during each of the ten years immediately preceding the calendar year in which the investment was made paid a dividend of not less than five per cent on its ordinary shares [3½ per cent in relation to dividends paid during any year after 1972: Trustee Investments (Water Companies) Order 1973].

11. In deposits by way of special investment in a trustee savings bank or in a department (not being a department certified under subsection (3) or section nine of the Finance Act 1965 [now s. 414(3) and (5) of the Income and Corporation Taxes Act 1970]) of a bank any other department of which is so certified, and in Bank of Ireland 7 per cent. Loan Stock 1986/91.

12. In deposits in a building society designated under section one of the

House Purchase and Housing Act, 1959.

13. In mortgages of freehold property in England and Wales or Northern Ireland and of leasehold property in those countries of which the unexpired term at the time of investment is not less than sixty years, and in loans on heritable security in Scotland.

14. In perpetual rent-charges charged on land in England and Wales or Northern Ireland and fee-farm rents (not being rent-charges) issuing out of such land, and in feu-duties or ground annuals in Scotland.

15. In Certificates of Tax Deposit."

"Part III—Wider-Range Investments 1. In any securities issued in the United Kingdom by a company incorporated in the United Kingdom, being securities registered in the United Kingdom and not being securities falling within Part II of this Schedule.

2. In shares in any building society designated under section one of the House Purchase and Housing Act, 1959.

3. In any units, or other shares of the investments subject to the trusts, of a unit trust scheme in the case of which there is in force at the time of investment an order of the Board of Trade under section seventeen of the Prevention of Fraud (Investments) Act, 1958, or of the Ministry of Commerce for Northern Ireland under section sixteen of the Prevention of Fraud (Investments) Act (Northern Ireland), 1940."

"Part IV—Supplemental. 1. The securities mentioned in Parts I to III of this Schedule do not include any securities where the holder can be required to accept repayment of the principal, or the payment of any interest, otherwise than in sterling.

2. The securities mentioned in paragraphs 1 to 8 of Part II, other than Treasury Bills or Tax Reserve Certificates, securities issued before the passing of this Act by the Government of the Isle of Man, securities falling within paragraph 4 of the said Part II issued before the passing of this Act or securities falling within paragraph 9 of that Part, and the securities mentioned in paragraph 1 of Part III of this Schedule do not include—

(a) securities the price of which is not quoted on a recognised stock exchange within the meaning of the Prevention of Fraud (Investments) Act, 1958, or the Belfast stock exchange;

(b) shares or debenture stock not fully paid up (except shares or debenture stock which by the terms of issue are required to be fully paid up within nine months of the date of issue).

3. The securities mentioned in paragraph 6 of Part II and paragraph 1 of Part III of this Schedule do not include—

(a) shares or debentures of an incorporated company of which the total issued and paid up share capital is less than one million pounds;

(b) shares or debentures of an incorporated company which has not in each of the five years immediately preceding the calendar year in which the investment is made paid a dividend on all the shares issued by the company, excluding any shares issued after the dividend was declared and any shares which by their terms o issue did not rank for the divi dend for that year.

For the purposes of sub-paragraph (b) of this paragraph a company formed—

(i) to take over the business of another company or other companies, or

(ii) to acquire the securities of, or control of, another company or other companies,

or for either of those purposes and for other purposes shall be deemed to have paid a dividend as mentioned in that sub-paragraph in any year in which such a dividend has been paid by the other company or all the other companies, as the case may be.

4. In this Schedule, unless the context otherwise requires, the following expressions have the meanings hereby respectively assigned to them, that is to say—

"debenture" includes debenture stock and bonds whether constituting a charge on assets or not, and loan stock or notes;

"enactment" includes an enactment

of the Parliament of Northern Ireland;

"fixed-interest securities" means securities which under their terms of issue bear a fixed rate of interest;

"local authority" in relation to the United Kingdom, means any of the following authorities—

    (a) in England and Wales, the council of a county, [a borough, an urban or rural district or parish, the Common Council of the City of London, the Greater London Council and the Council of the Isles of Scilly: definition as amended by London Government Act 1963, ss. 83(1), 93(1), Sch. 17, para. 25 and Sch. 8, Part II and by local Government Act 1972, s. 272 (1) and Sch. 30];

    (b) in Scotland, a local authority within the meaning of the Local Government (Scotland) Act, 1947;

    (c) in Northern Ireland, the council of a county, a county or other borough, or an urban or rural district;

"ordinary deposits" and "special investment" have the same meanings respectively as in the Trustee Savings Banks Act, 1954;

"securities" includes shares, debentures, Treasury Bills, and Tax Reserve Certificates;

"share" includes stock;

"Treasury Bills" includes bills issued by Her Majesty's Government in the United Kingdom and Northern Ireland Treasury Bills. [This definition is printed as amended by National Loans Act 1968, s. 24(2) and Sch. 6, Part I (see also the saving at the end of Part I of the Schedule).]

5. It is hereby declared that in this Schedule "mortgage", in relation to freehold or leasehold property in Northern Ireland, includes a registered charge which, by virtue of subsection (4) of section forty of the Local Registration of Title (Ireland) Act, 1891, or any other enactment, operates as a mortgage by deed.

6. References in this Schedule to an incorporated company are references to a company incorporated by or under any enactment and include references to a body of persons established for the purpose of trading for profit and incorporated by Royal Charter.

7. The references in paragraph 12 of Part II and paragraph 2 of Part III of this Schedule to a building society designated under section one of the House Purchase and Housing Act, 1959, include references to a permanent society incorporated under the Building Societies Acts (Northern Ireland) 1874 to 1940 for the time being designated by the Registrar for Northern Ireland under subsection (2) of that section (which enables such a society to be so designated for the purpose of trustees' powers of investment specified in paragraph (a) of subsection (1) of that section)."

UNREPEALED PROVISIONS OF TRUSTEE ACT 1925, PART I

Those investment provisions of the Trustee Act 1925 which are not repealed by the Act of 1961 are briefly as follows.

Sect. 2 (1) (as amended by the 1961 Act): a trustee may invest in any of the securities authorised by s. 1 of the Act of 1961 even if they are redeemable and the price exceeds the redemption value. Sub-sect. (2) adds that a trustee may retain redeemable stock until redemption.

Sect. 3 (as so amended): powers of investment conferred by the 1961 Act shall be exercised according to the trustee's direction but subject to any consent or discretion required by the instrument creating the trust or by Statute.

Sect. 4: a trustee will not be liable for breach of trust merely because he has continued to hold an investment which has ceased to be authorised by the trust instrument or by the general law.

Sect. 5: a trustee with power to invest in real securities has power to invest on any charge, or on mortgage of any charge, made under the Improvement of Land Act, 1864; a trustee with such power may accept the security in the form of a charge by way of legal mortgage and may convert an existing mortgage into such a charge; and a trustee with power to invest in the mortgages or bonds of any railway or other company may invest in the company's debenture stock.

Sect. 6: a trustee who has power to invest in the purchase, or on mortgage, of land, may (unless the trust provides otherwise) exercise his power in respect of land charged with a rent under the provisions of the Public Money Drainage Acts 1846 to 1856 or the Landed Property Improvement (Ireland) Act 1847 or the Improvement of Land Act 1864.

Sect. 7 gives a trustee power, unless prohibited by the trust instrument and subject to certain conditions, to invest in securities payable to bearer which would, if not so payable, be authorised investments.

Sect. 8 provides that in certain situations involving the loan of trust money and the purchase of property, the trustee is not chargeable with breach of trust. Thus:

(a) When he lends money on the security of property on which he can properly lend, he is not chargeable merely by reason of the proportion borne by the amount of the loan to the value of the property at the time of the loan, if (i) when he made the loan he acted on the report of a person whom he reasonably believed to be an able practical surveyor or valuer instructed and employed independently of the owner of the property, and (ii) the amount of the loan does not exceed two-thirds of the value of the property given in the report, and (iii) the loan was made on advice given in the report.

(b) When he lends money on the security of leasehold property he is not chargeable merely because he dispensed wholly or partly with the production or investigation of the lessor's title.

(c) When he buys, or lends money on the security of, property he is not chargeable merely because he has accepted a title shorter than that to which he would be entitled under an open contract if the title is one which a person acting with prudence and caution would have accepted.

[Note.—In connection with this section see Re Dive, [1909] 1 Ch. 328; Salisbury (Marquis) v. Keymer, [1909] W.N. 31; Shaw v. Cates, [1909] 1 Ch. 389; Palmer v. Emerson, [1911] 1 Ch. 758 and Re Solomon, [1912] 1 Ch. 261. Trustees investing on mortgage must now obtain (in addition to the valuation required by this section) the advice of a financial expert under s. 6 of the Trustee Investments Act, 1961, but see sub-s. (7) of that section].

Sect. 9: if a trustee lends money on property which would at the time of the loan have been a proper investment for a smaller sum, the security is deemed an authorised investment for the smaller sum and the trustee will be liable only to make good the difference, with interest.

Sect. 10 gives trustees certain powers supplementary to their powers of investment. Thus:

(a) Sub-sect. (1) gives them limited powers to agree not to call in a mortgage loan for a period not exceeding 7 years.

(b) Sub-sect. (2) gives them limited powers, on a sale of trust property, to allow part of the price (not exceeding two-thirds) to remain on mortgage of the property.

(c) Sub-sect. (3) gives power to trustees who hold securities of a company to concur in certain schemes or arrangements affecting the company. The schemes and arrangements in question are set out in the sub-section and another one is added by s. 9 (1) of the 1961 Act. Trustees are relieved from liability for acts done in this connection in good faith.

(d) Sub-sect. (4) gives them certain powers in the event of any conditional or preferential right being offered them to subscribe for securities in a company, and s. 9 (2) of the 1961 Act augments these powers slightly.

(e) Sub-sects. (5) and (6) provide that the powers given by the section are exercisable subject to the consent of any person whose consent is required, by law or by the trust instrument, to a charge of investment; and provide that where the loan mentioned in para. (a) above, or the sale mentioned in para. (b), is made under a court order, the powers referred to in those paragraphs apply only if and so far as the court directs.

Sect. 11: pending the negotiation and preparation of any mortgage or charge, and during any other period when an investment is being sought, trustees may pay any trust money into a bank (to a deposit or other account) and any interest thus earned ranks as trust income. Trustees may apply trust capital in the payment of calls on shares subject to the trust.

Vendor and Purchaser

SEE TABLES UNDER REAL PROPERTY

Wills

EXECUTING A WILL

(See Williams on Wills (4th Edn.), pp. 64 et seq.)

The provisions as to the signing and attesting of wills are to be found in s. 9 of the Wills Act 1837, as amplified by s. 1 of the Wills Act Amendment Act 1852. A witness should not be a beneficiary, or the spouse of a beneficiary, under the will for if he is the benefit will be lost (Wills Act, 1837, s. 15) unless there were at least two other witnesses who were not beneficiaries or spouses of beneficiaries (Wills Act, 1968 s. 1). Only persons aged 18 years or over can make a will, s. 7 Wills Act 1837, as amended by s. 3 (1) (a) of the Family Law Reform Act, 1969.

A will must be signed "at the foot or end thereof" by the testator or by some other person in his presence and by his direction, who must sign in the presence of two or more witnesses. The witnesses must sign in his presence, whether or not in the presence of each other. It is advisable that each sheet should be signed by the testator and witnesses. Corrections should be initialled by all three, or recorded in the attestation clause.

No form of attestation is necessary by law, but every will should contain an attestation clause in order to avoid the risk of future difficulty and expense when the will has to be proved.

The shortest form of attestation clause which happens to have received judicial approval (in *Re Selby-Bigge*, [1950] 1 All E.R. 1009) is:

Signed by the testator[rix] in our presence and attested by us in the presence of him [her] and of each other.

But even this is longer than it need be and the following form can safely be used:

Signed by the testator[rix] in our presence and then by us in his [hers]

The Principal Probate Registry (now the Principal Registry of the Family Division) have confirmed that this form is accepted by all the Registries and is indeed welcomed because, by confining itself to essentials, it enables the Registry officials to see at a glance that all the statutory requirements have been satisfied.

Where the testator cannot sign the will but can make his mark, the following form may be used:

Signed by the testator[rix] with his [her] mark in our presence and then signed by us in his [her] presence (the will above having first been read over to him [her] and he [she] having appeared truly to understand and approve it).

If the circumstances are such that another person has to sign the will on behalf of the testator, then this form may be employed:

Signed by [name of signatory] of [address] with the name of the testator[rix] in his [her] presence and by his [her] direction and in our presence and then signed by us in the presence of the testator[rix] (the will above having first been read over to him [her] and he [she] having appeared truly to understand and approve it).

In the last-mentioned case the will should be signed, "A.B. [the testator] per C.D. [the signatory]."

Under Part III of the Administration of Justice Act 1969, the Court of Protection has power to direct or authorise the execution of a will or codicil on behalf of a person who is mentally disordered.

Notes

Notes

Notes

DIARY

for

1976–7

Mon. NOVEMBER 1

Tues. 2

Wed. 3

NOVEMBER

Thur. 4

Fri. 5

Sat. 6

Sun. 7   Twenty-first Sunday after Trinity

Mon. 8

Tues. 9

Wed. 10

Thur. 11

Fri. 12

Sat. 13   Lord Mayor's Day

Sun. 14   Twenty-second Sunday after Trinity
Remembrance Sunday

Mon. 15

Tues. 16

Wed. 17

Thur. 18

Fri. 19

Sat. 20

Sun. 21   Last Sunday after Trinity

Mon. 22

Tues. 23

Wed. 24

Thur. 25

Fri. 26

Sat. 27

Sun. 28   First Sunday in Advent

DECEMBER 1976

Mon. 29

Tues. 30   St. Andrew's Day

Wed. DECEMBER 1

DECEMBER

Thur. 2

Fri. 3

Sat. 4

Sun. 5   Second Sunday in Advent

Mon. 6

Tues. 7

Wed. 8

DECEMBER

Thur. 9

Fri. 10

Sat. 11

Sun. 12   Third Sunday in Advent

Mon. 13

Tues. 14

Wed. 15

Thur. 16

Fri. 17

Sat. 18

Sun. 19   Fourth Sunday in Advent

Mon. 20

Tues. 21   Shortest Day

Wed. 22

DECEMBER

Thur. 23

Fri. 24

Sat. 25   Christmas Day

Sun. 26

Mon. 27   Bank Holiday

Tues. 28   Bank Holiday

Wed. 29

Thur. 30

Fri. 31   Last Day for renewing Solicitors' Certificates

Sat. JANUARY 1   New Year's Day

Sun. 2

Mon. 3 Bank Holiday

Tues. 4

Wed. 5

Thur. 6

Fri. 7

Sat. 8

Sun. 9   First Sunday after Epiphany

Mon. 10

Tues. 11

Wed. 12

JANUARY

Thur. 13

Fri. 14

Sat. 15

Sun. 16   Second Sunday after Epiphany

Mon. 17

Tues. 18

Wed. 19

JANUARY

Thur. 20.

Fri. 21

Sat. 22

Sun. 23 Third Sunday after Epiphany

Mon. 24

Tues. 25

Wed. 26

JANUARY

Thur. 27

Fri. 28

Sat. 29

Sun. 30 Fourth Sunday after Epiphany

JANUARY—FEBRUARY 1977

Mon. 31

Tues. FEBRUARY 1

Wed. 2

FEBRUARY

Thur. 3

Fri. 4

Sat. 5

Sun. 6 Septuagesima
          Accession of Queen Elizabeth II, 1952

Mon. 7

Tues. 8

Wed. 9

FEBRUARY

Thur. 10

Fri. 11

Sat. 12

Sun. 13   Sexagesima

Mon. 14   St. Valentine

Tues. 15

Wed. 16

Thur. 17

Fri. 18

Sat. 19

Sun. 20   Quinquagesima

Mon. 21

Tues. 22   **Shrove Tuesday**

Wed. 23   **Ash Wednesday**

Thur. 24

Fri. 25

Sat. 26

Sun. 27   First Sunday in Lent

Mon. 28

Tues. MARCH 1

Wed. 2

Thur. 3

Fri. 4

Sat. 5

Sun. 6 Second Sunday in Lent

Mon. 7

Tues. 8

Wed. 9

MARCH

Thur. 10

Fri. 11

Sat. 12

Sun. 13   Third Sunday in Lent

Mon. 14

Tues. 15

Wed. 16

MARCH

Thur. 17   St. Patrick's Day
                 Bank Holiday in Northern Ireland

Fri. 18

Sat. 19

Sun. 20   Fourth Sunday in Lent
                Summer Time begins

Mon. 21

Tues. 22

Wed. 23

Thur. 24

Fri. 25

Sat. 26

Sun. 27   Fifth Sunday in Lent

Mon. 28

Tues. 29

Wed. 30

Thur. 31   Financial Year (1976–7) ends

Fri. APRIL 1

Sat. 2

Sun. 3   Palm Sunday

Mon. 4

Tues. 5   Income Tax Year (1976–7) ends

Wed. 6

Thur. 7   Maundy Thursday

Fri. 8   Good Friday
Bank Holiday in Scotland

Sat. 9

Sun. 10   Easter Sunday

Mon. 11   Easter Monday
              Bank Holiday

Tues. 12

Wed. 13

Thur. 14

Fri. 15

Sat. 16

Sun. 17   Low Sunday

Mon. 18

Tues. 19

Wed. 20

APRIL

Thur. 21 H.M. Queen Elizabeth II born, 1926

Fri. 22

Sat. 23 St. George's Day

Sun. 24 Second Sunday after Easter

Mon. 25

Tues. 26

Wed. 27

Thur. 28

Fri. 29

Sat. 30

Sun. MAY 1   Third Sunday after Easter

Mon. 2   Bank Holiday in Scotland

Tues. 3

Wed. 4

Thur. 5

Fri. 6

Sat. 7

Sun. 8   Fourth Sunday after Easter

Mon. 9

Tues. 10

Wed. 11

Thur. 12

Fri. 13

Sat. 14

Sun. 15   Rogation Sunday

Mon. 16

Tues. 17

Wed. 18

Thur. 19   Ascension

Fri. 20

Sat. 21

Sun. 22   Sunday after Ascension

Mon. 23

Tues. 24

Wed. 25

Thur. 26

Fri. 27

Sat. 28

Sun. 29   Whit Sunday

Mon. 30

Tues. 31

Wed. JUNE 1

JUNE

Thur. 2 Coronation Day 1953

Fri. 3

Sat. 4

Sun. 5   Trinity Sunday

Mon. 6 | Spring Bank Holiday

Tues. 7   Bank Holiday to mark the 25th anniversary of H.M. the Queen's accession

Wed. 8

Thur. 9

Fri. 10

Sat. 11

Sun. 12   First Sunday after Trinity

Mon. 13

Tues. 14

Wed. 15

Thur. 16

Fri. 17

Sat. 18

Sun. 19   Second Sunday after Trinity

Mon. 20

Tues. 21   Longest Day

Wed. 22

JUNE

Thur. 23

Fri. 24

Sat. 25

Sun. 26   Third Sunday after Trinity

Mon. 27

Tues. 28

Wed. 29

Thur. 30

Fri. JULY 1

Sat. 2

Sun. 3   Fourth Sunday after Trinity

JULY 1977

Mon. 4   Independence Day, U.S.A.

Tues. 5

Wed. 6

JULY

Thur. 7

Fri. 8

Sat. 9

Sun. 10   Fifth Sunday after Trinity

Mon. 11   Bank Holiday in Northern Ireland

Tues. 12

Wed. 13

Thur. 14

Fri. 15   St. Swithin's Day

Sat. 16

Sun. 17   Sixth Sunday after Trinity

Mon. 18

Tues. 19

Wed. 20

Thur. 21

Fri. 22

Sat. 23

Sun. 24   Seventh Sunday after Trinity

Mon. 25

Tues. 26

Wed. 27

JULY

Thur. 28

Fri. 29

Sat. 30

Sun. 31   Eighth Sunday after Trinity

AUGUST 1977

Mon. AUGUST 1   Bank Holiday in Scotland

Tues. 2

Wed. 3

AUGUST

Thur. 4

Fri. 5

Sat. 6

Sun. 7   Ninth Sunday after Trinity

Mon. 8

Tues. 9

Wed. 10

AUGUST

Thur. 11

Fri. 12

Sat. 13

Sun. 14   Tenth Sunday after Trinity

Mon. 15

Tues. 16

Wed. 17

Thur. 18

Fri. 19

Sat. 20

Sun. 21   Eleventh Sunday after Trinity

Mon. 22

Tues. 23

Wed. 24

Thur. 25

Fri. 26

Sat. 27

Sun. 28   Twelfth Sunday after Trinity

Mon. 29   Summer Bank Holiday

Tues. 30

Wed. 31

Thur. SEPTEMBER 1

Fri. 2

Sat. 3

Sun. 4 Thirteenth Sunday after Trinity

Mon. 5

Tues. 6

Wed. 7

Thur. 8

Fri. 9

Sat. 10

Sun. 11   Fourteenth Sunday after Trinity

Mon. 12

Tues. 13

Wed. 14

Thur. 15

Fri. 16

Sat. 17

Sun. 18   Fifteenth Sunday after Trinity

SEPTEMBER 1977

Mon. 19

Tues. 20

Wed. 21

SEPTEMBER

Thur. 22

Fri. 23

Sat. 24

Sun. 25   Sixteenth Sunday after Trinity

SEPTEMBER 1977

Mon. 26

Tues. 27

Wed. 28

ORDER FORM

To BUTTERWORTH & CO. (PUBLISHERS) LTD.
BOROUGH GREEN, SEVENOAKS, KENT TN15 8PH

(Showroom: Bell Yard, Temple Bar, WC2)

Please send me.......*cop*......*of* **"The Lawyer's Remembrancer"**
for 19 , *and continue annually until countermanded.*

Name...

Address...

Account No.............. ....

Date...............19

Thur. 29

Fri. 30

Sat. OCTOBER 1

Sun. 2   Seventeenth Sunday after Trinity

Mon. 3

Tues. 4

Wed. 5

Thur. 6

Fri. 7

Sat. 8

Sun. 9   Eighteenth Sunday after Trinity

OCTOBER 1977

Mon. 10

Tues. 11

Wed. 12

OCTOBER

Thur. 6

Fri. 7

Sat. 8

Sun. 9 Eighteenth Sunday after Trinity

Mon. 10

Tues. 11

Wed. 12

Thur. 13

Fri. 14

Sat. 15

Sun. 16   Nineteenth Sunday after Trinity

OCTOBER 1977

Mon. 17

Tues. 18

Wed. 19

Thur. 20

Fri. 21

Sat. 22

Sun. 23   Twentieth Sunday after Trinity
Summer Time ends

Mon. 24

Tues. 25

Wed. 26

Thur. 27

Fri. 28

Sat. 29

Sun. 30   Twenty-first Sunday after Trinity

OCTOBER—NOVEMBER 1977

Mon. 31   Solicitors' Certificates expire

Tues. NOVEMBER 1

Wed. 2

Thur. 3

Fri. 4

Sat. 5

Sun. 6   Twenty-second Sunday after Trinity

Mon. 7

Tues. 8

Wed. 9

Thur. 10

Fri. 11

Sat. 12   Lord Mayor's Day

Sun. 13   Twenty-third Sunday after Trinity
Remembrance Sunday

Mon. 14

Tues. 15

Wed. 16

Thur. 17

Fri. 18

Sat. 19

Sun. 20   Last Sunday after Trinity

Mon. 21

Tues. 22

Wed. 23

Thur. 24

Fri. 25

Sat. 26

Sun. 27 First Sunday in Advent

Mon. 28

Tues. 29

Wed. 30   **St. Andrew's Day**

DECEMBER

Thur. DECEMBER 1

Fri. 2

Sat. 3

Sun. 4   Second Sunday in Advent

Mon. 5

Tues. 6

Wed. 7

DECEMBER

Thur. 8

Fri. 9

Sat. 10

Sun. 11   Third Sunday in Advent

Mon. 12

Tues. 13

Wed. 14

DECEMBER

Thur. 15

Fri. 16

Sat. 17

Sun. 18 Fourth Sunday in Advent

Mon. 19

Tues. 20

Wed. 21   Shortest Day

DECEMBER

Thur. 22

Fri. 23

Sat. 24

Sun. 25   Christmas Day

DECEMBER 1977

Mon. 26   Bank Holiday

Tues. 27   Bank Holiday

Wed. 28

Thur. 29

Fri. 30

Sat. 31 Last Day for renewing Solicitors' Certificates

Sun. JANUARY 1 New Year's Day

TELEPHONE NOS. & TELEGRAPHIC ADDRESSES

NAME	NUMBER	ADDRESS
A	....	....
....	....	....
....	....	....
....	....	....
....	....	....
B BUTTERWORTH & Co. (Publishers) LTD. 88 Kingsway, WC2B 6AB	01-405 6900	Butterwort, London
Showroom, Bell Yard, WC2A 2LG	01-405 6900	
....	....	....
....	....	....
....	....	....
....	....	....
C	....	....
....	....	....
....	....	....
....	....	....
....	....	....
....	....	....
D	....	....
....	....	....
....	....	....
....	....	....
....	....	....
E	....	....
....	....	....
....	....	....
....	....	....
....	....	....
F	....	....
....	....	....
....	....	....
....	....	....
....	....	....
....	....	....

TELEPHONE NOS. & TELEGRAPHIC ADDRESSES

NAME	NUMBER	ADDRESS
G		
H		
IJ		
K		
L		

TELEPHONE NOS. & TELEGRAPHIC ADDRESSES

NAME	NUMBER	ADDRESS
M		
N		
O		
PQ		
R		

TELEPHONE NOS. & TELEGRAPHIC ADDRESSES

NAME	NUMBER	ADDRESS
S SHAW & SONS, LTD. Shaway House, Bellgreen Lane, Lower Sydenham, SE 26 5AE	01-778 5131	Shawsons, London, S.E.26.
T		
UV		
W		
Y		

Memoranda

ISBN 0 406 26909 2

Made and printed in Great Britain by
William Clowes & Sons, Limited
London, Beccles and Colchester